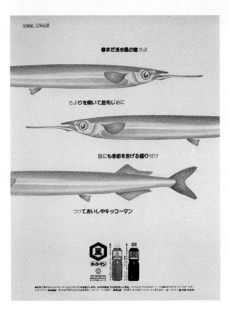

# ESSENTIALS OF ADVERTISING

Prepared by Doyle Dane Bernbach Inc. for Miles Laboratories.
© 1978 Miles Laboratories

**Here's a fine how-do-you-do.**

# You have our word on it.

**YOU CAN'T SQUEEZE BLOOD FROM A TURNIP.**

# ESSENTIALS OF ADVERTISING

## LOUIS KAUFMAN

HOFSTRA UNIVERSITY

HARCOURT BRACE JOVANOVICH, INC.

NEW YORK    SAN DIEGO    CHICAGO    SAN FRANCISCO    ATLANTA    LONDON    SYDNEY    TORONTO

Cover: Courtesy, Graphic Arts Technical Foundation

Technical illustrations by Fred Haynes

ISBN: 0-15-524100-1

Library of Congress Catalog Card Number: 79-91221

Printed in the United States of America

# on advertising: a foreword

Advertising is so close to the bone of America's free enterprise system that to carve it away would be to weaken and, ultimately, collapse the system.

There will be a pause while the reader groans and wonders whether this commercial message for advertising is being sponsored by the advertising business.

Dispel the notion and consider: in terms of American business, advertising is relatively small potatoes. It is, at this writing, still below $50 billion in terms of annual volume. And the largest ad agencies in the country—the so-called super-shops— must pull off spectacular acquisitions of such intricacy as to challenge the skills and patience of teams of lawyers and CPAs if they are to soar past the $1 billion or $2 billion billings' level.

Within this relatively small advertising business, most ad agencies are small companies. What they have in common is a reliance on people. People must come up with the ideas for advertising and execute them, even as technology and hardware intrude on business more and more.

It often comes as a revelation to "civilians" to learn that *one* U.S. corporation, General Motors, is bigger than the *entire* advertising business. GM's 1978 sales amounted to $63 billion. That's more than the entire advertising business puts directly into circulation, with its thousands of agencies, client company ad personnel, media sales organizations, and people who are engaged in collateral advertising.

Yet, advertising gets the play, aided by the "glamor" treatments in literature, television, motion pictures, and general media. It is a business that is more top-of-mind, say, than GM.

Advertising also spawns audience participation as no other business does. The saying is, "Everyone's an expert when it comes to advertising." Most people would hesitate to tell a GM executive which front disc brake works best with new transverse engines, or whatever, but just about every red-blooded American man, woman, or child will unhesitatingly tell an advertising man or woman how a new ad campaign ought to be handled, how the copy should read, and who should appear in the commercial.

But this is as it should be. A business that relies on people for its dynamics must accept feedback from the people it addresses.

If advertising is at center stage, under a spotlight, it's because that is where its media investments require it to be. It would be a cause for alarm if, after all the planning that went into a marketing program, after the advertising was carefully developed to advance the advertiser toward specific marketing goals, and after all the care that went into the media buys, if after all that, the campaign ran its course and nothing happened. Fortunately, this doesn't happen too often. When it does, it means that serious mistakes, or miscalculations, were made in the communication process and changes are called for. A new agency? That might be the first consideration. A new creative approach? A reformulation of the product? It all takes place publicly, for those who care to notice. So the top-of-mind status that advertising arouses—dare we say enjoys?—as opposed to, say, everyday chit-chat about an electrical ignition system, is no accident. It has been bought and paid for—by the advertiser and by the consumer. It's a by-product of its incessant call for public attention.

If the role of advertising is vital to our well-being, and if the theory behind it is understood and accepted, all too often it's the execution that can lead to trouble. Yes, there are misleading ads. And yes, ads will promote an unworthy proposition by misrepresentation because people are free to exercise their First Amendment rights. Yes, advertising attracts its share of con artists. In a free country, where no license is needed to enter advertising, the business is open to all who choose to enter.

The struggle against advertising abuses is continuous and no doubt could use more support, more legislative weaponry, more monitoring both within and outside the business. But the point that must be kept in mind is that good advertising—properly developed for useful goods or services—performs a vital function for the common good.

Is advertising, by definition, inflationary? Doesn't it add to the cost of a product? The customer pays for advertising—and also for the other overhead costs that a company must include in its pricing structure: rent, taxes, salaries and wages, employe benefits, supplies. To single out advertising as *the* lone culprit in pricing practices hardly seems fair.

Think of this: for General Motors to sell 2,200,000 Chevrolets in one year required the expenditure of $156,400,000 to advertise the Chevrolet line. That's about $71 worth of advertising behind each car sold. Would the customer save $71 on the car if GM eliminated the advertising expense? It's not quite that simple. Deprive GM of advertising, and when it comes time to tell prospective car customers about the Chevrolet, GM will have to hire people to spread the word, by knocking on doors or ringing doorbells, perhaps, and leaving behind lovely four-color brochures (if such items aren't considered advertising).

While waiting for this army of salespeople to visit prospects across the country, the GM factory workers would be on "furlough" and the steel company workers, and other automotive industry suppliers, would also stand by to await the first trickle of orders from Chevrolet. The newspapers, magazines, radio and tv stations that would be affected by GM's withdrawal from advertising? They'd just have to figure out another way to generate revenue. Charge the reader/subscriber more money? That's one possibility.

If this process took too much time and proved too costly, GM could always close down one of its other divisions, manufacture fewer cars, and employ fewer people. Would that bring down the cost of a car by $71?

The reality is that a growth-oriented economic system, one that is pressed to find new jobs for a growing work force, needs advertising in order to generate marketplace activity.

Advertising works. That is, it works if it is de-signed to do a job worth doing. Ads fail when they try to impart a quality that is not to be found in the advertised product or service. Suppose that a manufacturer hires the most creative ad agency in the world to develop a campaign for a new product called Greydent, "The toothpaste that tones down your smile." It's unlikely that the product would stand a chance, despite heavy and clever advertising support. Would the failure be blamed on advertising?

Good advertising works best when it is meshed with a good product.

It fails when it tries to push the consumer into the outer limits of credibility.

One might market a silk purse made from a sow's ear—once. Repeat sales would be a problem. But if an ad campaign honestly reflected the fact that what was being offered was an unusual, genuine-looking sow's ear, not a silk purse? Or if the manufacturer found a way to produce silk purses from sow's ears, given a technological breakthrough? Then the advertising would stand a chance.

This textbook plays an important part in the learning process as it joins reality with the stimulation that is inherent in so much of advertising's practices. *Essentials of Advertising* examines in detail every stage of the *business* of advertising, from initial concept to execution. Its extensive use of illustrations amplifies concepts where words alone cannot. Indeed, Lou Kaufman is uniquely qualified to prepare this book, for he has spent his whole life *practicing* the profession of advertising and *teaching* its practice. As a witness to the ways advertising performs services, helps to create businesses, enables companies to expand production facilities and employ more people, I salute those who are about to study the advertising business. I salute Professor Kaufman for *Essentials of Advertising:* it makes the study of the topic as exciting and challenging as the practice.

FRED DANZIG
Executive Editor
*Advertising Age*

# preface

It has long been my conviction that the art and business of persuasive communication—advertising, for short—is essential to the welfare of the business community itself and to the nation as a whole. This conviction has kept me in the business—as practitioner and teacher—for all my working life. I hope to transmit to all students some of the excitement that I continue to find in the field. I also hope to make use of my years in the business and the classroom to convey the liveliness, the flavor, and the challenge of my profession, both to students interested in a career in advertising and to those taking the course as an elective simply to learn a little about the field.

I have tried to make *Essentials of Advertising* a practical book, organized in a realistic way—to make its sequence of chapters correspond to the decisions and activities of the real world. Thus, media choice precedes creative strategy; budget decisions precede media choice.

The text moves from the pragmatic considerations that underlie the finished ad—marketing intelligence and research (increasingly important today) and the budget (whose constraints affect media choice as well as ad design)—through media, to the final campaign. The media chapters include a full range—from 60-second television commercials to embossed paperweights. There is a chapter on business and farm publications—a rapidly growing segment of the advertising industry that has been relatively neglected—as well as one on outdoor and transit media and another on trade and industrial advertising.

The four chapters that follow are devoted to the creative side of advertising—developing strategies, writing copy, creating art, and choosing appropriate printing processes. In this section, however, the emphasis is not so much on the technical "how to" as on the "why": on deciding and managing and on selecting the best artistic means to achieve the objectives of a particular advertising campaign.

The coordination of all the elements of advertising—budgeting, research, media selection, and creative strategy—is shown in the succeeding chapters on consumer advertising campaigns, retail advertising campaigns, business (trade and industrial) campaigns, and international and service campaigns.

Brief case histories, among them the marketing of Folger's Coffee, the Mr. Goodwrench campaign, and the Kent's Golden Lights campaign, are sprinkled throughout the text. These are designed to show what kinds of decisions and subsequent courses of action are needed to accomplish the marketing objectives that underlie all advertising.

Since advertising is really a "people business," dependent entirely on the creativity and verve of men and women, there are also twenty-one profiles of distinguished figures in the advertising business—Raymond Rubicam, David Ogilvy, George Gallup, Lois Wyse, and Jerry Della Femina are some of those included. I hope the profiles will enrich the students' appreciation of these personalities and even provide insights into career opportunities.

At the beginning of each chapter there is a *working vocabulary*, a list of real-world terms used every day in the field, that can serve as a framework for class discussion.

I would particularly like to draw your attention to the stunning illustration program in this text. Above all, it is truly functional. For every chapter, illustrations have been assembled to enhance the students' understanding of the principles in the text. Moreover, the captions are lengthy and elaborate: they are designed to teach, not merely identify. They tell the student what to look for, and what point is being demonstrated.

Of course, along the way I have dealt with some of the social aspects and issues of advertising, but as a practitioner, I have made no secret of my sympathies. How, why, and by whom advertising is policed is the subject of Chapter 21.

Although responsibility for this book is entirely

my own, a number of colleagues have made valuable suggestions. Those who provided detailed reviews and recommendations are Professor Garven F. Williams, Jr., Bucks County Community College; Professor Kenneth Shanley, Sinclair Community College; and Professor Robert Brooks, Pace University. I am grateful for their assistance. I also want to acknowledge the help of many people at many advertising agencies, publications, and trade associations: in particular, George Holtane, Creative Director of the New York Market, Foster & Kleiser (a division of Metromedia); Stefan Meyer, Creative Director, Institute of Outdoor Advertising; Doris Willens, Vice President and Director of Public Relations, Doyle Dane Bernbach, Inc.; Terry Munger, Manager of Information Services, J. Walter Thompson; Joyce Harrington, Manager of Public Relations, Foote, Cone & Belding; and Billie Brown, Vice President/Director of Corporate Communications, Cunningham & Walsh, Inc. If I do not acknowledge all the many contributors, it is only from lack of space. I am especially grateful for access to the library and files of *Advertising Age* in New York, and for the cooperation of Sharon Rennhack and Zvia Greenbaum.

My wife, Gloria, typed and retyped the drafts with great skill. Her support was essential.

Most thanks must go to the dedicated people at Harcourt Brace Jovanovich. Like good advertising itself, this book is the result of hard-working, self-effacing people. I must acknowledge the patient and painstaking work of the editors who watch for every detail, every misspelling, and every quotation—Bill Leitner and Robert Henry. A very special thanks is due Jerry Lighter for his exceptionally attractive design and, as a former advertising person himself, for his expert advice as the book was in progress; and to Yvonne Steiner for the superb selection and arrangement of the illustrations: she and Richard Lewis expended much energy and spent long hours in getting the right illustration for the right page. Their loving care and concern are responsible for the sheer aesthetics of the book. The coordination of text, illustrations, and four-color spreads was no accident but the result of careful planning. Kenzi Sugihara supervised the overall production and scheduling of the book. He kept all of us on our toes.

One final note of thanks must go to Dr. Karen Gillespie of New York University, who exhibited great patience while I worked through many drafts of my Ph.D. dissertation. She taught me the discipline of writing clearly and concisely for students; she introduced me to Alice Gallagher, who made me write this book.

You must forgive me, but I consider this book a work of art; you must realize, however, that I am prejudiced. It is my hope that every student who uses *Essentials of Advertising* will not only learn those essentials, but will enjoy learning them.

LOUIS KAUFMAN

# contents

on advertising—a foreword (by Fred Danzig)    v

preface    vii


## PART 1
## SURVEY OF ADVERTISING    1

**1  the story of advertising**    3

Advertising defined    3

Advertising through the ages    6

The ancient marketplace    6
Trade and craft guilds    6
The printed word    7
The explosive growth of the
    newspaper media    7
Sandwich men and space brokers    9
Magazines accept advertising    10
Dawn of the modern age    11
A new medium—radio    12
The Great Depression    13
How advertising won the war    13

PROFILE:
Raymond Rubicam    14


**2  the marketing foundations
   of advertising**    21

Marketing defined    22

Elements of the marketing mix    22

The product    22
The price    25
Channels of distribution    26
Promotional considerations    27

What is a market?    27

Segmenting the target market    27

Conditions that affect marketing success    28

The dynamics of consumer tastes    30
Changes in social and cultural influences    31
Changing demographics    31
Economic conditions    32
Legal and political climate    32
Changes in technology    32
Competitive actions    34

PROFILE:
Albert D. Lasker    36

CASE HISTORY:
Tempest in a coffee pot (Folger's)    37


**√3  the promotional mix**    43

The marketing plan and advertising    44

Marketing objectives    44
Factors influencing the promotional mix    45

Advertising as the main thrust    48

The decision to advertise    48
Factors influencing the decision
    to advertise    48
Advertising objectives    49
Advertising redefined    50

PROFILE:
Fairfax M. Cone    58


**√4  the advertising business**    63

The advertiser    63

Responsibilities of the advertising manager    65
The advertising department    65

The advertising agency 66

  The development of the agency 66
  Agency organization 66
  What does an agency do? 72
  Innovations in the agency business 72
  Agency compensation 77
  Agency recognition 79
  Serving competing advertisers 80

Advertising media 80

Ancillary advertising services 83

PROFILE:
David Ogilvy                                          78


                    PART 2

ADVERTISING  DECISIONS              87


5   marketing intelligence:
    statistics behind sales            89

The role of marketing intelligence 90

  Objectives for marketing intelligence 90
  Taking aim at sales potential 90

Intelligence sources 92

  Secondary data 92
  Primary data 96
  Collecting primary data 96
  Sampling 100

Motivation research 104

  Psychographics 105
  Copy testing 109
  Media research 109

PROFILE:
Ernest Dichter                                     106

CASE HISTORY:
The Mr. Goodwrench story
(General Motors Parts Division)           107


6   the advertising budget:
    investment or expense?             115

What is the advertising budget? 116

How management philosophy affects
  the advertising budget 116
The upper hand on the bottom line 117
The advertising-sales relationship 118

Methods of setting the advertising
budget 119

  Influence of the product on the
    appropriation 119
  The objective, or task, method 121
  Matching competitors—the
    share-of-the-market method 122
  Percentage-of-sales method 122
  An empirical method 127
  Take your choice 128

Time to set the budget 129

  Budget periods and flexibility 129

What belongs in the advertising budget? 130

PROFILE:
William Bernbach                                  127


7   advertising media:
    an overview                        135

Looking at the media 135

  Media strategy 136

Media selection factors 136

  Cost 138
  Matching media and market 138
  Geographical selectivity 140
  Medium and product 142
  Program objectives 143
  Other factors that influence
    media selection 143

Measuring the medium's audience 144

  Circulation and coverage 144
  Refining circulation data 144

The media mix 147

  Reasons for a mix 147
  Duplication 149
  Gross audience 149

The role of the media planner 149

  Cumulative audience 150
  Seasonal concentration 150

x

Scheduling   152
The use of computers in media selection   152
Media buying procedures   152

People in media   154

The media rep   154

PROFILE:
John Philip Cunningham   141

CASE HISTORY:
Herbal teas brew a marketing success
(Magic Mountain Tea)   153

Buying power   192
The audience for business publications   192
General business publications   194
Industrial publications   196
Trade publications   201
Institutional publications   201
Professional publications   201
Rates and spaces   204
Media decisions for business advertisers   204

Farm publications   206

National farm publications   208
State and regional publications   210
Specialized farm publications   210

PROFILE:
William A. Marsteller   199

CASE HISTORY:
Marketing a repair method for hospital
linens (Thermopatch Corporation)   207

# PART 3
# GUIDE TO ADVERTISING MEDIA   161

**8**   print media: newspapers and
consumer magazines   163

Newspapers: advertising workhorse   163

Advantages of newspapers as an
advertising medium   163
Limitations of newspapers   165
Tear sheets and checking copies   166
Newspapers by type   167
Buying newspaper space   170
Newspaper rates   171
Special newspapers   174

Consumer magazines   175

Types of consumer magazines   176
Advantages of magazines   176
Magazine circulations   180
Magazine space and rates   180
Demographic editions   184
Comparing magazines   184

PROFILE:
Leo Burnett   186


**9**   print media: business and
farm publications   191

Selling the decision makers   191

**10**   the broadcast media   215

Radio   215

Where it all came from   216
AM and FM radio   216
Radio as an advertising medium   217
Spot radio   218
Network radio   221
Radio audiences   221
Buying radio time   223

Television   225

UHF, VHF, and cable   225
The television audience   226
Network television   228
Spot television   228
Buying time   230
Audience ratings   233

PROFILE:
Lois Wyse   235

MEDIA PROFILE:
WIND 56 Chicago   237


**11**   outdoor, transit, and
directories   241

The story of outdoor advertising   241

Outdoor compared with other media  242
Billboards—an old friend  242
Who uses outdoor?  243
Advantages of outdoor  243
Limitations of outdoor  243
Types of outdoor  244
Measuring the audience  248
Buying outdoor  248

Transit advertising  252

Transit media  252
Advantages of transit  252
There are limitations  252
The transit advertising business  253
Buying transit: forms and rates  254

Directories  255

Yellow Pages  259

Miscellany media  259

PROFILE:
Karl Eller  253

CASE HISTORY:
How outdoor brought Miles Laboratories
fast relief (Alka-Seltzer)  261

**12**  nonmedia advertising  265

Direct advertising  265

Direct-mail advertising  266
Advantages of direct mail  266
Limitations  268
Circulation  268
Mailing lists  270
Forms of direct mail  273
Postal regulations  274
Advertising specialties  274
Premiums  276
External house organs  276

Point-of-purchase promotion (POP)  276

Forms of POP  278
Attributes of POP  278
Who benefits from POP?  279
Distribution of POP  279
Last word on POP  279

Trade shows  281

The advantages  281
But is it worth the cost?  281

PROFILE:
John Caples  280

**PART 4**
CREATIVE ASPECTS  285

**13**  product identification:
branding and packaging  287

Trademarks and brand names  287

Identifying the product  287
Trade names  288
Identifying the brand  288
Legalities  291
Objectives in trademarks  293
Choosing a trademark or brand name  293
Attributes of a trademark or brand  294
Family names  295
What's in a name  295
Trade characters  296
Other advertising marks  297

Packaging  298

Essentials of package design  298
Dealer requirements  302
Packaging is advertising  304

Slogans  308

CASE HISTORY:
A new corporate image starts
with a new name (Quanex)  303

PROFILE:
Roger Ferriter  306

**14**  creative strategies  311

Developing the appeal  311

The purchasing decision  312

What does the product offer?  313

How the product's life cycle affects
creative strategy  315
Uncovering the product's subjective
appeal  315

Consumer perceptions  318

Reference groups  318
The diffusion process  320
Attitudes, customs, and habits  322
Application of psychographics
   to advertising  323

Positioning the product  326

Media considerations  328

Brainstorming  330

PROFILE:
Jerry Della Femina                                327


**15**   copy for advertising                       335

The function of copy  336

   Fact finding  336
   Style  338
   Writing rules  340

Ideas for individual media  340

   Writing for magazines  340
   Writing the newspaper advertisement  344
   Copy for radio  347
   Writing for television  348
   Writing copy for direct mail  350
   Writing copy for outdoor  353
   The last word  353

PROFILE:
John O'Toole                                      352


**16**   advertising art                            357

The illustration  357

Layout  358

   Creating the layout  358
   Principles of design  359
   Constraints  363
   Getting attention  363
   Make the message easy to read  363
   Color  366
   Small space ads  366

Subjects for illustration  366

   Kinds of art work  369

The television commercial  371

   How a television commercial is produced  376

Filmed, videotaped, and live commercials  380
Restrictions  382
Terms used in radio and television
   commercial production  382

PROFILE:
Henry Wolf                                        381


**17**   reproduction processes                     387

Typography  390

   Measuring type  390
   Typefaces  391
   Selecting the typeface  393
   Specifying type  395
   Typesetting methods  398

Printing processes  399

   Letterpress  400
   Lithography  400
   Gravure  400
   Screen  402
   Halftones  402
   Plates, engravings, and duplicates  404
   Color reproduction  404

Paper  410

CASE HISTORY:
The making of an advertisement              388


PART 5
ADVERTISING WORLDS                            413

**18**   the advertising campaign                   415

Planning the campaign  416

   Campaign objectives  419
   Tactical objectives  419
   The influence of the product life cycle  420
   Duration of the campaign  420
   The importance of repetition  422

Types of campaigns  423

   Regional  423
   Product promotion  424
   Corporate, or institutional, advertising  424
   Horizontal cooperative advertising  424

Coordination with other
promotional efforts   426

Personal selling   426
Sales promotion   426
Publicity   428

Media selection   428

Measuring results   431

Have consumers changed their behavior?   431
Methods of evaluation   431

CASE HISTORY:
Winning the low-tar race (Kent
Golden Lights)                                          429

PROFILE:
George Gallup                                          434

**19**   retail advertising                            443

Planning retail advertising   445

Retail advertising objectives   446
Marketing information for retailers   447
Budgeting methods   449
Factors that influence the budget decision   450

Media for retailers   451

Advertising schedules   456
Building the schedule   456
Retail copy   459
The retail advertising department   459
Vertical cooperative advertising   460

PROFILE:
Jane Trahey                                            453

**20**   industrial and trade
advertising                                            467

Industrial advertising   468

Classifications of industrial goods   468
The industrial-buying process   471
The importance of advertising   475
Setting advertising objectives   476
Industrial copy appeals   478
Schedules and campaigns   480

Trade advertising   481

Why advertise to dealers?   482

Retailers buy for resale   485
Trade campaigns   490
One more look at co-op   490

PROFILE:
Harrison King McCann                                   487

CASE HISTORY:
Reaching hidden buying-influences
for industrial packaging (Tri-Wall
Containers)                                            489

**21**   advertising and society                       495

Criticisms of advertising   495

Advertising adds to the cost of goods   495
Advertising makes people buy things
   they don't need   498
Advertising reduces competition   500
Advertising is information   501

Policing advertising   503

The government regulates advertising   504
Advertising polices itself   508
Policing by the media   509

PROFILE:
Adrienne Hall                                          502

**22**   advertising in the future                     517

International advertising   517

The problems of advertising overseas   518
The need for continuity   523
The advertising climate in other lands   525
The challenge   527

The service economy   529

Characteristics of services   529
Advertising services   532
Government advertises services too   534

Changing media   536

PROFILE:
Hideharu Tamaru                                        537

glossary   541

index   557

# ESSENTIALS OF
# ADVERTISING

# SURVEY OF ADVERTISING

**1**
The story of advertising

**2**
The marketing foundations of advertising

**3**
The promotional mix

**4**
The advertising business

Direct magnification with a Polaroid Land camera reveals the brush strokes in a painting by Monet. This illustration was taken from the 1977 Annual Report of Polaroid Corporation, who used the photograph to demonstrate the versatility of their camera and their new film.

*Cap d'Antibes: Mistral*, by Claude Monet (1888).
Bequest of Arthur Tracy Cabot, 42.542, Museum of Fine Arts, Boston.

# THE STORY OF ADVERTISING

**Advertising defined**

**Advertising through the ages**

The ancient marketplace
Trade and craft guilds
The printed word
The explosive growth of the
    newspaper media
Sandwich men and space brokers

Magazines accept advertising
Dawn of the modern age
A new medium—radio
The Great Depression
How advertising won the war

CHAPTER **1**

# the story of advertising

*The old trader and his shop were known in the neighbour-hood. The talk of the countryside was their sufficient public-ity. But the new trader may be at the other side of the moun-tains or the other side of the world. As he cannot show his face, he must show a placard.*

H. G. WELLS
*The Work, Wealth and Happiness of Mankind*

BEFORE WE START with a description of what advertising is, we had better be certain we know what it is not and what it can not do. Advertising is *not* a science such as chemistry, with laws and rules that, if followed with reasonable precision, will lead to predictable results every time. Advertising is *not* a panacea that can restore a poor product or rejuvenate a declining market; it is *not* a substitute for sound business judgment. Nor is advertising merely the words and pictures that appear in newspapers and in magazines, on billboards and on television screens. These are the means, or the *media,* that advertising uses to communicate its information about products, services, and ideas to people: information designed to per-

suade them to make buying or action decisions. Advertising *is* the art and business of *persuasive* communication.

## Advertising defined

The most widely accepted definition of advertising is based on the definition developed by the American Marketing Association:

> Advertising is any form of nonpersonal presentation of goods, services or ideas for action, openly paid for, by an identified sponsor.[1]

Quite often, when a person is asked to define advertising, he or she will be confused as to the dif-

[1] *Journal of Marketing,* 12, no. 2 (October 1948), p. 202.

Mobil Oil Corporation sponsors advertising that provides information and *ideas*, not merely about its particular products but of value to all motorists. Of course, as the openly identified sponsor, Mobil promotes its corporate image in the second paragraph by telling us how the company conserves energy at its refineries. And, in the fourth paragraph, Mobil gives us a very "soft sell" for Mobil Super Unleaded gasoline.

ferences between advertising and personal selling and between advertising and publicity. If we take the above definition of advertising apart, however, these differences will become clear.

*Any form:* This phrase means exactly that—any form of presentation—a sign, an advertisement in a magazine or newspaper, a commercial on radio or television, circulars distributed through the mail or handed out on a streetcorner, skywriting, billboards, posters, and matchbooks—the possibilities are limited only by the imagination of the advertiser and the conditions of the definition.

*Nonpersonal:* This phrase excludes personal selling, which is usually done on a person-to-person or, in some cases such as a Tupperware party, on a people-to-people basis. If it's personal, it's not advertising.

*Goods, services, ideas for action:* Most definitions describe the application of advertising to goods and services, but often neglect the use of advertising by businesses to promote their *ideas.* Mobil Oil Corporation, for instance, sponsors advertisements like the one shown in the left column in order to present its thoughts on a variety of issues before the public. Moreover, the United States government, which was the 24th largest advertiser in the nation in 1977, advertises to recruit men and women for the Army, the Navy, the Air Force, and the Marines. It also uses advertising to try to persuade its citizens to pay their income taxes early and to use ZIP codes. The Red Cross advertises; local hospitals and museums advertise to attract financial contributors. And, political candidates advertise so that we will vote for them. In fact, political candidates employ advertising agencies or special-

These attractive, informative articles are just a sample of the helpful publicity material that manufacturers make available without cost to newspapers and magazines.

Because the manufacturer does not pay the media to print these articles, and because the sponsor is not openly identified, they are considered publicity, not advertising.

ists to help "sell" them to the public, like soap or toothpaste.

*Openly paid for by an identified sponsor:* This means that sponsors of the message must be clearly identified and must acknowledge that they have paid for the use of the media in which it appears. Otherwise, the message is considered to be

publicity. Publicity is not openly paid for, and the sponsor is not usually identified. The publicity organization that prepares the material is paid by the sponsor of the item—but the newspaper, magazine, or radio station that carries it does so free of charge. There is no implication of anything underhanded or manipulative about publicity. It is simply not advertising.

Eighteenth-century business cards. Notice how these three businessmen used illustration—not to identify their products, but their locations.

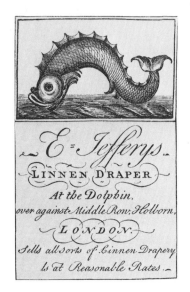

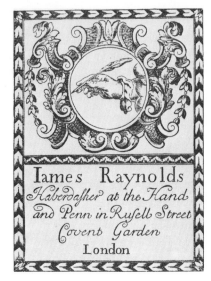

## Advertising through the ages

### The ancient marketplace

Although modern advertising as we perceive it today is less than a hundred years old, its roots go back a long time in history. The technological developments of the past fifty years have made advertising more extensive and more effective, but the idea behind it—the transmission of information—can be traced back to ancient Greece and Rome.

Over three thousand years ago criers were used to carry information from the king, or ruler, to the populace. Curiously, the crier's function was then thought to have derived from Hermes, the messenger of the gods and himself god of commerce and theft (an interesting combination?). Later, the criers of Rome performed a variety of services for both the state and private enterprise. An ancient Roman described the job of criers as that of drawing crowds to merchants with goods to sell.

During this era signs were also used to mark the location of mercantile establishments. An inn in ancient Greece was marked by a pine cone, which stemmed from the practice in those days of coating jugs of wine with pine resin to seal them. The pine cone was also one of the symbols of Dionysius, the god of wine. To this day the Greeks still drink resinated wine—retsina.

Among the signs still legible in the old Roman city of Pompeii (dating from A.D. 79) is that of a cloth merchant, depicting various methods of dyeing cloth. Bookshops fastened announcements of new books to the columns of temples. Perhaps our use of the word *columnist* is derived from the ancient practice of providing information in that fashion?

### Trade and craft guilds

After the fall of the Roman Empire in the fifth century A.D., advertising practices, whatever they might have been, are lost in obscurity. By the Middle Ages, however, advertising was primarily confined to signs. Frequently, one street of a town would be devoted to a particular trade, and it was the custom to have signs at both ends of the street that depicted that trade. In fact, the names of many streets in Europe and in the United States, such as Baker, Mercer, Haymarket, and Smithfield, are derived from the trade that had once been practiced there.

With time, the emblems of the signs could be seen on the banners carried during a guild procession and on the badges or medallions worn by the members of the guild. By the fourteenth century, signs painted on wood were widespread, suspended from the overhang of houses, swinging from long wrought-iron brackets. They were mostly

Iohn Wildbloodᵈ at the Rainbow ⅋
3 pidgons in Sᵗ Clements Lane
In Lombard Street London who
Marriedᵈ the Widdow Harrinton
Silk Dyer

It is not difficult to determine what was
sold in this shop with its wooden sign hanging
in front from a wrought iron support.

pictorial, because the population was largely illiterate. Some merchants, envious of the coats of arms of the nobility, tried to incorporate heraldic symbols into their signs whenever possible, but generally the sign was a symbol—a boot, a glove, a bush (for an inn)[2]—easily recognized.

In the thirteenth century, town criers were paid directly by the merchants whose goods they advertised. By the seventeenth century the streets were filled with criers who demonstrated their talent in singsong or even rhyme—"Fuller's earth, Fuller's earth![3] Freshly dug to clean your wool, come and buy, my sacks are full." Many of these cries can still be heard in small European towns where fish, produce, or baked goods are sold from wagons in the streets. And how about the American news vendor's cry: "Read all about it"?

## The printed word

But it was the invention of printing that really revolutionized the possibilities of advertising. Thirty years after Gutenberg issued the first book printed with movable type, the Catholic Church was using

[2] There still exists an old saying, "Fine wine needs no bush."
[3] Fuller's earth: an absorbent clay used for removing grease from wool that is being shrunk and thickened by a process known as "fulling."

printed circulars to advertise the "Grand Pardon de Notre Dame de Reims." By the year 1500 Frankfurt had become the headquarters for book publishers, and Albrecht de Menninger brought out the first book catalog. Albrecht's catalog contained over 200 titles. It is to William Caxton of London that we owe the first book to be printed in the English language. Caxton was a mercer, or cloth merchant, who in his later years turned from the cloth business to the newly discovered art of printing. To advertise his books, he issued handbills. Subsequently, these handbills (only 3 inches × 5 inches) became large posters, which were often pasted to the columns of St. Paul's Cathedral. We are still reminded of this nuisance by the admonition lettered on blank walls: *Post No Bills.*

## The explosive growth of the newspaper media

The seventeenth century marked the development of the newspaper. From the first, these newspapers were simply filled with advertisements. They were issued irregularly, their growth impeded by a scarcity of printers, the lack of an organized postal service, and the social and political climate of that era. The first publication similar to our modern newspaper appeared in Florence in 1597, when the grand duke gave a Florentine printer permission to

Mastheads of some early newspapers. With the exception of the London *Times*, they appear to be weekly papers. Until recently, the London *Times* published advertisements on its front page. The publishers assumed that readers interested in the news would open the paper to the inside pages.

publish weekly commercial bulletins. By the early 1600s there were gazettes[4] in Basle, Vienna, Frankfurt, Hamburg, Berlin, Amsterdam, and London.

At the end of the seventeenth century, a great number of commercial newspapers were being printed in England, all of them filled with quotations for imported goods and other commercial information. One of the most popular subjects of early advertisements was books, since only those few people who could read books could read the advertisements. Later, there appeared offers of marriage, advertisements for travel, and advertisements for the new beverage just becoming popular, imported from China and called *Tcha*. By 1710 there even existed a *frequency rate*—a reduced rate of charge for advertisements run a certain number of times within a given period without change.

Meanwhile, the government of King George, ever alert to fund-raising opportunities, levied a heavy tax on "news-papers." Advertising thereby became the *main* source of revenue for the newspapers, and they were filled with announcements of lotteries, rewards for stolen property, and many "indelicate" advertisements regarding lovers' meetings and "help for ladies finding themselves in difficult situations."[5] Of course, critics of that time attacked advertising as so much "puffery."

In the English colonies of North America, the growth of the newspaper industry followed a pattern similar to that of England's press. The first American newspaper, *The Boston Weekly News-Letter*, carried advertisements of sailings from Boston, imported goods, runaway slaves, and sales of slaves. By 1765 there were twenty-five newspapers in existence when the English imposed a stamp tax that aroused strong opposition among independent-minded colonists. In 1784 the first daily newspaper was issued—*The Pennsylvania Packet and Daily Advertiser*. The paper actually resembled today's pennysaver—that is, it contained far more advertisements than news.[6] The coffeehouses of that period were very instrumental in the development of the newspapers, because they served as clubs for intellectuals and businessmen. Some coffeehouse proprietors sought to build patronage by publishing their own news sheet.

## Sandwich men and space brokers

Newspaper advertising was not the only form of advertising that was growing. So many people were reluctant to spend a penny or two to purchase a newspaper that posters were utilized extensively. Bill posters were everywhere. When Dickens described the streets of nineteenth-century London, he included people handing out circulars and carrying signs, particularly the men with signs front and back, whom he dubbed "sandwich men." In fact, by the end of the nineteenth century, people were complaining about the number of advertisements that were to be found in railroad stations, along highways, and in other areas that were accustomed to much traffic. The major impetus for the growth of the advertising business during this

---

[4] Gazette: from the old Venetian word *gazeta*, a coin that was the price of the paper. *Gazeta* is a diminutive of the Italian word *gaza*, a magpie.

[5] Philippe Schumer, *History of Advertising* (London: Leisure Arts Ltd., 1966), p. 46.

[6] Today's *pennysaver* is usually an 8 to 24 page booklet, consisting almost entirely of advertising by local retailers or services. The penny that is "saved" refers to the cost of a newspaper many years ago. The reader received this little publication free and hence saved a penny. It is a highly localized advertising tool that is often distributed by hanging it in a plastic bag on the doorknob of a house or by mailing it to the house's "resident."

## THE QUADRUPLE ALLIANCE.

The Sun affords us light by day
The Moon and Stars by night,
While ASPINALL'S ENAMEL makes,
Our Homes refined and bright.

The artwork in this old advertisement appears to be a wood engraving, probably hand carved by an artist of the period. Mr. Aspinall enlisted the aid of the Sun, Moon, and Stars to form a quadruple alliance with his paint.

period was the Industrial Revolution. Local manufacturers discovered that their ability to produce goods far exceeded the ability of their local markets to absorb them. The need to find and exploit new markets was aided by the rapid development of rail transportation and the extension of public education.

By 1860, there were several advertising agencies in New York City. These were not advertising agencies as we know them today, but really only firms that served as brokers for advertising space. The distinction of being the first advertising agent in the United States goes to Volney B. Palmer, who established his business in 1841. In those days newspapers did not publish rates or circulation figures, and advertising rates were negotiated. It was not until 1912 that the Audit Bureau of Circulation was established as a joint effort by advertisers and newspapers to develop reliable figures on circulation.

During the Civil War one of the first nationwide advertising campaigns was launched. The financier Jay Cooke was charged with managing the government's fund-raising efforts, and he, in turn, enlisted the services of L. F. Shattuck, an advertising agent, to help sell United States war bonds. By advertising the bonds in over 5,000 publications, Shattuck was able to sell $2 billion worth. The bond issue owed its success to advertising.

### Magazines accept advertising

The years between the end of the Civil War and the beginning of the twentieth century were marked by the growth of drug and patent medicine advertising. For the most part, these advertisements appeared in newspapers, because the magazines of that day were not accepting advertising. A man named James W. Thompson, the founder of the J. Walter Thompson agency, was responsible for per-

Many of the early posters reflect the absence of the "marketing concept" that is so apparent in today's advertising. Mr. Suchard apparently expected that his name alone would induce people to buy his brand of chocolate.

suading American magazines to accept advertising. He then bought up all the space that these magazines made available and resold it, not only to advertisers, but to other advertising agents as well. As late as 1898, Thompson still controlled all the advertising space in most American magazines. Successful publications of this era included such currently popular magazines as *Cosmopolitan* and the *Ladies' Home Journal*.

## Dawn of the modern age

In 1900, the total volume of advertising in the United States was estimated at $542 million—an 11-fold increase since 1865. The space brokerage days were drawing to a close, and the new advertising agencies were beginning to offer their clients essentially the same services that they perform today—the planning, creation, and implementation of complete advertising campaigns. The American Newspaper Publishers Association, founded in 1887, agreed that general agents should be entitled to a commission, which was to be withheld from advertisers who placed their business directly with a newspaper. In 1901, Curtis Publishing Company would not allow the agent's commission to advertisers who placed ads directly with its magazines.

Meanwhile, advertising theory and practice were growing up. Agencies began to hire established writers and journalists—men who had a flair for expression—to write advertising copy. People in other professions were also becoming involved. Professors of psychology began to publish articles on the psychological aspects of advertising. Dr. Walter Dill Scott, who went on to become president of Northwestern University, published a series of articles on "Psychology in Advertising" in *Atlantic Monthly* in 1908.

The new approach to advertising that developed in the first two decades of the twentieth century brought sex, science, and romance to reinforce advertising appeals. Testimonials were extremely popular. Dr. Allen Pusey, professor of dermatology at the University of Illinois, helped to create advertisements for Pond's cold creams that were based on scientific facts and backed by testimonials from top stage and screen stars and from socialites. Fleischmann's Yeast promoted its product as an aid to health and adolescent skin care, with an impressive battery of bearded European medical men supplying the scientific background. One of these ads, for example, contained the headline: "'Yeast builds resistance,' says Prof. Doctor Paul Reyher, famous lecturer at the University of Berlin."

The first list of advertising agencies was published in 1917 by the National Register Publishing Company. It contained 1,400 agencies, some of which are still in business, while others have

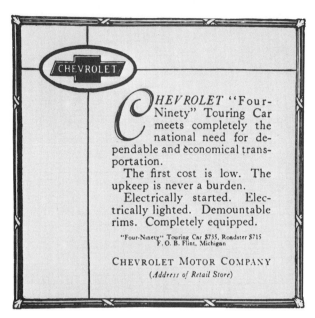

The Chevrolet Motor Company's first advertisement appeared in May, 1919. The Chevrolet trademark was prominently featured. Compare this advertisement to others for the same product that appear below and on the facing page.

The advertisement below is for the 1927 "coach model" Chevrolet. In contrast to the Chevrolet ad of 1919, this advertisement features a prominent illustration of the product.

merged with, or have been transformed into, some of today's well-known giant agencies. N. W. Ayer, the largest agency in 1917, is still alive and well and close to the top, as is J. Walter Thompson. The story goes that the designation J. Walter Thompson was made by James Walter Thompson, the magazine man, when he learned that there were numerous J. W. Thompsons, but no other J. Walter Thompson.[7] George Batten Co. went on to become Batten, Barton, Durstine & Osborn (BBD&O). H. K. McCann Co. and Erickson Co. ultimately merged to become McCann—Erickson. And so it went; as advertising volume grew, so did the agencies.

### A new medium—radio

By 1929, radio was well on its way to becoming the most important entertainment medium.[8] An agency in Chicago—Blackett, Sample, Hummert— was the leader in daytime radio. This agency subsequently became Dancer—Fitzgerald—Sample. The concept of the soap opera was launched in 1932, and these programs poured out of radio for the next twenty years, sponsored by advertisers such as General Mills, Sterling Drug, American Home Products, and Procter & Gamble. Daytime radio became an endless succession of fifteen-minute problems, Monday through Friday, with enormous emotional appeal for millions of Americans. Not until the homey voice of a former Washington taxi driver named Arthur Godfrey announced that it was "Arthur Godfrey Time" did a serious challenge to the "soapers" arise. Although the 1929 figures looked good, the $18 million of network radio bill-

---

[7] *Advertising Age* (December 7, 1964), p. 3.
[8] National Carbon Co. sponsored the first regular series of radio entertainments in 1923 with its "Ever-ready Hour."

**THE STORY OF ADVERTISING**

The 1949 Chevrolet was advertised as "The most Beautiful BUY of all." The Chevrolet trademark is still featured, as well as the slogan "Quality at Low Cost," which appeared in the 1927 advertisement.

ing then looked pretty small compared with the $81 million of 1942.

## The Great Depression

When the Great Depression hit, advertising volume dropped from the 1929 high of 3.4 billion to a low in 1933 of 1.3 billion, which was where it had been in 1914. The depression had a more pronounced effect on advertising than just a drop in volume, however. Gimmicks were needed to coax money from empty pockets. Contests, premiums, prizes, and "double-your-money-back" offers were extensively promoted.

As advertisers looked for ways to make their ads more effective, they came upon the Townsend brothers who had a secret checklist of twenty-seven points against which to appraise all advertising copy for effectiveness. It was not the quality of the Townsend formula that was important, but the growing interest among advertisers in making their advertising more productive. The Townsends were the forerunners of the great names in advertising and marketing research, men such as George Gallup, Claude Robinson, Daniel Starch, and A. C. Nielsen. Gallup joined Young & Rubicam in 1932 as its first director of research. After a successful career at that famous agency, Gallup went on to public opinion polling. Later he joined with Claude Robinson to develop the "impact" method of evaluating advertising. Daniel Starch left his job as a professor of psychology to become a director of research at the American Association of Advertising Agencies in 1924. There he developed techniques to study a reader's interest in the editorial and advertising material in a magazine. He left the four As in 1932 to found Daniel Starch & Staff, now Starch INRA Hooper, Inc.

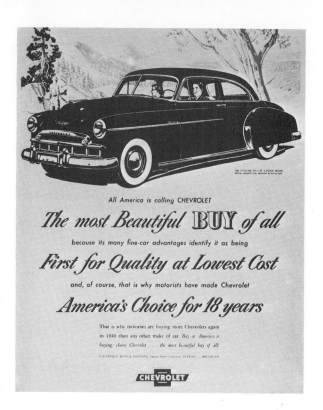

All America is calling CHEVROLET

*The most Beautiful* BUY *of all*

because its many fine-car advantages identify it as being

*First for Quality at Lowest Cost*

and, of course, that is why motorists have made Chevrolet

*America's Choice for 18 years*

That is why motorists are buying more Chevrolets again in 1949 than any other make of car. Buy as America is buying: choose Chevrolet . . . the most beautiful buy of all!

CHEVROLET MOTOR DIVISION, General Motors Corporation, DETROIT 2, MICHIGAN

CHEVROLET

The depression years also prompted the development of the well-known A. C. Nielsen Co. During this time, Nielsen started compiling the now widely used indexes of food and drug sales by checking drugstores. His idea was to form a permanent sample of stores and to audit the flow of selected merchandise through those stores to secure information on the market shares obtained by various advertisers.

## How advertising won the war

After the attack on Pearl Harbor in 1941, the talents of advertising people turned to helping the war effort. Advertising men set up the War Advertising Council, underwritten by the American Association of Advertising Agencies, the Association of National Advertisers, and four media associations representing newspapers, magazines, radio, and outdoor. Working primarily through the Office of War Information, the council helped promote war bonds. In fact, 85,000,000 people bought small denomination bonds, and $45 billion worth of bonds were in the hands of the public by the end of the war. It was the largest, most extensive advertising campaign ever conducted for anything anywhere.[9] The Advertising Council is still operating, supplying advertising and promotion for public service programs on forest fire prevention and aid to

[9] *Advertising Age* (December 7, 1964), p. 10.

higher education, as well as for such organizations as Radio Free Europe, Care, and the Peace Corps.

The radio industry experienced tremendous growth during the Second World War. Listener interest was at peak; wages and earnings were up. There was also a severe shortage of paper that limited magazine production. By 1945, radio billings were up to $125 million and peaked at $134 million

## RAYMOND RUBICAM

In 1944, at the age of 52, Raymond Rubicam retired as president of the agency that still bears his name—Young & Rubicam International, Inc. It was the pinnacle of a career that spanned thirty years in advertising.

Raymond Rubicam was born in 1892 in Brooklyn, New York. After a brief stint as a reporter for the *Philadelphia Inquirer* in 1916, he joined a small advertising agency in Philadelphia as a copywriter. Three years later, he was hired as a copywriter by N. W. Ayer & Son, Inc., then the largest advertising agency in the United States. While he was at Ayer, he wrote many successful advertisements, including well-known slogans for Steinway pianos ("The instrument of the immortals") and for E. R. Squibb & Sons ("The priceless ingredient of every product is the honor and integrity of its maker"). It was a Steinway executive who gave him the idea of starting his own agency. He teamed up with John Orr Young, then an account man at Ayer, to found Young & Rubicam in 1923.

Under Raymond Rubicam's direction the new agency became known for its work in a new medium—radio. He developed humorous, conversational commercials that other advertisers said would fail and which, in fact, proved to be very popular. He hired such popular radio stars as Jack Benny and Arthur Godfrey to be the spokesmen for Jell-O and Lipton Tea, and he also hired a recent graduate of the University of Iowa to run Young & Rubicam's research department—Dr. George Gallup.

On his retirement, he was the principal stockholder of the agency. He sold his stock to the agency's employees, however, because he wanted the company to belong to men and women who were still active in the advertising business. In 1974 he was elected to the American Advertising Federation's Advertising Hall of Fame, and, in the next year, to the Copywriter's Hall of Fame.

Every August, *Advertising Age*, the leading newspaper in the advertising field, publishes a list of the nation's leading advertisers. Most of the company names should be familiar to you, but the list reveals some interesting facts. First, the United States government was the 24th largest advertiser—ahead of such well-known corporations as International Telephone and Telegraph, Coca-Cola, and General Electric. Second, note that the top two advertisers alone in 1977 spent $772 million on advertising, over $200 million more than the *total* estimated advertising volume in the United States in 1900.

## 100 LEADING NATIONAL ADVERTISERS

(Ad dollars in millions: 1977)

| | | | | | |
|---|---|---|---|---|---|
| 1. Procter & Gamble | $460.0 | 34. Goodyear Tire & Rubber Co. | $ 93.9 | 67. Greyhound Corp. | $ 50.8 |
| 2. General Motors Corp. | 312.0 | 35. Johnson & Johnson | 91.8 | 68. Toyota Motor Sales U.S.A. | 49.2 |
| 3. General Foods Corp. | 300.0 | 36. B.A.T. Industries | 91.3 | 69. S. C. Johnson & Son | 48.9 |
| 4. Sears, Roebuck & Co. | 290.0 | 37. Gillette Co. | 90.0 | 70. Clorox Co. | 47.9 |
| 5. K mart | 210.0 | 38. Coca-Cola Co. | 89.0 | 71. Miles Laboratories | 46.5 |
| 6. Bristol-Myers Co. | 203.0 | 39. Pillsbury Co. | 85.8 | 72. Union Carbide Corp. | 46.1 |
| 7. Warner-Lambert Co. | 201.0 | 40. Eastman Kodak Co. | 85.5 | 73. American Express Co. | 46.0 |
| 8. Ford Motor Co. | 184.0 | 41. American Brands | 84.0 | 74. Time Inc. | 45.9 |
| 8. Philip Morris Inc. | 184.0 | 42. Ralston Purina Co. | 80.7 | 75. North American Philips Co. | 44.0 |
| 10. American Home Products Corp. | 171.0 | 43. Revlon Inc. | 80.0 | 76. Polaroid Corp. | 38.9 |
| 11. R.J. Reynolds Industries | 164.7 | 44. Seagram Co. | 78.0 | 77. A. H. Robins Co. | 38.8 |
| 12. General Mills | 160.5 | 45. Anheuser-Busch | 75.4 | 78. Mattel Inc. | 38.5 |
| 13. Richardson-Merrell | 148.8 | 46. Sterling Drug | 72.0 | 79. Pfizer Inc. | 37.5 |
| 14. Unilever | 145.0 | 47. Nestle Enterprises | 71.3 | 80. Squibb Corp. | 37.1 |
| 15. Mobil Corp. | 142.8 | 48. Kellogg Co. | 69.8 | 81. Morton-Norwich | 36.1 |
| 16. American Tel. & Tel. Co. | 132.0 | 49. Liggett Group | 68.4 | 82. Exxon Corp. | 35.3 |
| 17. Norton Simon Inc. | 127.1 | 50. Chesebrough-Pond's | 67.3 | 83. Noxell Corp. | 33.3 |
| 17. Chrysler Corp. | 127.1 | 51. Loews Corp. | 66.1 | 84. Eastern Airlines | 32.5 |
| 19. PepsiCo Inc. | 124.0 | 52. H. J. Heinz Co. | 65.8 | 85. Carnation Co. | 31.9 |
| 19. RCA Corp. | 124.0 | 53. Esmark Inc. | 65.0 | 86. American Motors Corp. | 31.5 |
| 21. Beatrice Foods Co. | 123.0 | 54. Schering-Plough | 63.0 | 87. Kimberly-Clark Corp. | 31.1 |
| 22. McDonald's Corp. | 122.2 | 55. Quaker Oats Co. | 60.8 | 88. Wm. Wrigley Jr. Co. | 31.0 |
| 23. Colgate-Palmolive Co. | 120.0 | 56. Hanes Corp. | 60.3 | 88. Block Drug Co. | 31.0 |
| 24. U.S. Government | 116.2 | 57. Campbell Soup Co. | 60.0 | 90. Beecham Group | 30.8 |
| 25. General Electric Co. | 112.2 | 58. Borden Inc. | 59.3 | 91. UAL Inc. | 30.3 |
| 26. Heublein Inc. | 106.5 | 59. Jos. Schlitz Brewing Co. | 59.1 | 92. American Airlines | 28.9 |
| 27. Int'l. Tel. & Tel. Corp. | 104.7 | 60. SmithKline Corp. | 57.6 | 93. ABC Inc. | 26.8 |
| 28. Gulf & Western Industries | 100.6 | 61. Nissan Motor Co. | 57.0 | 93. Shell Oil Co. | 26.8 |
| 29. J. C. Penney Co. | 100.0 | 62. Avon Products | 55.0 | 95. Trans World Airlines | 26.5 |
| 30. Kraft Inc. | 99.0 | 63. Volkswagen of America | 52.7 | 96. Consolidated Foods Corp. | 25.9 |
| 31. Nabisco Inc. | 96.4 | 64. CPC International | 51.0 | 97. Delta Air Lines | 25.7 |
| 32. CBS Inc. | 96.3 | 64. Mars Inc. | 51.0 | 98. Scott Paper Co. | 25.5 |
| 33. American Cyanamid | 96.0 | 64. Standard Brands | 51.0 | 99. Honda Motor Co. | 23.6 |
| | | | | 100. E. & J. Gallo Winery | 22.0 |

Reprinted with permission from the August 28, 1978 issue of *Advertising Age*. Copyright by Crain Communications, Inc.

In the 93 years of advertising history spanned by these advertisements for Chesebrough-Pond's Inc., both advertisers and consumers grew more sophisticated. From all-purpose panaceas, advertising appeals after 1912 shifted to scientific, reason-why copy. The 1920s saw the development of the *testimonial*—an endorsement of the product by a famous person. Though still in style, testimonials today are more likely to be given by athletes than by royalty. In the 1940s, advertising began to take a psychological approach, offering consumers not only the product but the implicit promise of a benefit—beauty, romance, success—to be obtained from using the product.

1886

1905

1912

1917

1926

1942

1948

1964

1979

in 1948. Thereafter, radio billings declined as television became more important.

When the war ended in 1945, total advertising volume in the United States was $2.87 billion, still below the 1929 record level. By 1948, however, advertising volume had surpassed the 1929 level by more than $1 billion, and advertisers were moving cautiously into a new medium—television. From 190,000 sets in use in 1948, the number zoomed to 15,800,000 by the end of 1952. By 1955, television had established itself as the most important national advertising medium.

## Summary

The American Marketing Association defines advertising as the "nonpersonal presentation of goods, services or ideas for action, openly paid for by an identified sponsor." Although the term *advertising*, as we understand its meaning today, was not used until about 200 years ago, the practice of using advertising for the transmission of information goes back to ancient Greece and Rome. Criers and signs were used to advertise goods and services long before the development of printing. During the Middle Ages, when most people could not read, advertising signs generally consisted of a very explicit illustration of, or a symbol for, what was being advertised. But, as printing techniques were perfected and as industry developed, the written word came to replace the sign. During the 1600s, newspapers began to appear throughout Europe.

Naturally, early colonists in North America brought with them the advertising techniques they were familiar with in Europe. But it was not until the original thirteen colonies won independence from England that newspapers and newspaper advertising began to develop fully in the United States. Magazines, for the most part, were late in getting started, and their growth as an advertising medium did not come until after the Civil War. The growth of outdoor advertising had to wait on the expansion of the automobile industry and the improvement of roads. By 1926, radio was available as an advertising medium, adding the power of the human voice to advertising messages it carried.

By the end of the 1920s advertising was well on its way to becoming a major industry and a major factor in the growth of all American industry, particularly automobiles and packaged foods. As might be expected, the growth in advertising volume brought about the expansion of the advertising agency business. From mere wholesalers of newspaper and magazine space, advertising agencies have evolved into national organizations that combine the talents of writers, artists, musicians, psychologists, and marketing experts, capable of providing the advertiser with an extensive range of sophisticated services. Advertising volume, slowed in its growth, first by the Great Depression of the 1930s, then by the war years, has, since the end of the Second World War, risen to new peaks.

## QUESTIONS FOR DISCUSSION

**1.** How have technological developments affected the nature of advertising?

**2.** What interest does the study of advertising have for anyone not planning to enter the field?

**3.** From current publications select examples of advertisements that are used to promote:
a. merchandise
b. services
c. ideas

**4.** If advertising were, for any reason, to be prohibited entirely, what could business do to promote its products?

**5.** What makes advertising such a basically American institution?

**6.** In addition to recruitment for the armed forces, what other areas are important in government advertising?

**7.** Do you find any symbols of royalty or nobility used on products or in their promotions today?

### Sources and suggestions for further reading

Elliott, Blanche B. *A History of English Advertising.* London: Business Publications Ltd., 1962.

Foster, G. Allen. *Advertising: Ancient Market Place to Television.* New York: Criterion Books, 1967.

Gloag, John. *Advertising in Modern Life.* London: William Heinemann, Ltd., 1959.

Miller, Clyde R. *The Process of Persuasion.* New York: Crown Publishers Inc., 1946.

Presbrey, Frank. *The History and Development of Advertising.* Garden City: Doubleday, Doran & Company, 1929.

Schumer, Philippe. *History of Advertising.* London: Leisure Arts Ltd., 1966.

Sutphen, Dick. *The Mad Old Ads.* Minneapolis: The Dick Sutphen Studio Inc., 1966.

Watkins, Julian Lewis. *The 100 Greatest Advertisements.* New York: Moore Publishing Co., 1949.

Wood, James Playsted. *The Story of Advertising.* New York: The Ronald Press, 1958.

## THE MARKETING FOUNDATIONS OF ADVERTISING

**Marketing defined**

**Elements of the marketing mix**

The product
Consumer goods
The price
Channels of distribution
Promotional considerations

**What is a market?**

Segmenting the target market

**Conditions that affect marketing success**

The dynamics of consumer tastes
Changes in social and cultural
influences
Changing demographics
Economic conditions
Legal and political climate
Changes in technology
Competitive actions

## WORKING VOCABULARY

| | | |
|---|---|---|
| marketing concept | shopping goods | market segment |
| marketing mix | specialty goods | reference group |
| product | channels of distribution | demographics |
| consumer goods | market | |
| convenience goods | target market | |

CHAPTER

# the marketing foundations of advertising

*This is a world of bustle, of imperfect knowledge, of constantly evolving competitive and other external pressures, and of interrelationships among the company, its ultimate customers, and its middlemen, among elements of its own marketing mix —even among products or services in its line.*

THE CONFERENCE BOARD, INC.
Some Guidelines for Advertising Budgeting

THE BUSINESS WORLD in the United States today operates, as it has operated for the past three decades, under what is known as the marketing concept. Quite simply, the *marketing concept* means that for every seller of goods and services, the prime consideration at every step in that organization's functioning is the satisfaction of the prospective customer. Gone forever is the attitude typified by Henry Ford's dictum that his customers could have their Model T in any color they liked—as long as it was black. In 1977, the Ford Motor Company not only manufactured eighteen

different makes of passenger cars but also offered their customers an extensive choice of styles, colors, and optional features for each. Today, most manufacturers are interested in making the products that people want. Retailers try to stock the product assortment that people will demand and to offer their customers special delivery services and convenient evening shopping hours. Both manufacturers and retailers try to design the product and service mix that will assure their customers maximum satisfaction. Satisfied customers will, in turn, assure these businesses of steady demand.

## Marketing defined

*Marketing* is the process that facilitates the exchange of goods and services between producers and users to the satisfaction of all parties. Note that the word *process* is used to indicate an activity that does not stop. In fact, postsales activity is a very vital part of marketing. The word *consumer* has purposely been omitted from this definition because it has more than one meaning: A steel service supply center is a consumer of steel for a steel rolling mill. A manufacturer of soups is a consumer of the supply center's steel for canning. A homemaker is also called a consumer—of soup—but is in fact "consuming" the steel as well.

Thus, the exchange process involves all of these users and more. The marketing of steel involves the transfer of the sheet steel from the steel mill to the steel supply house to the canner, where it is transformed into a can. That steel, now in the form of a can, goes from the wholesaler of grocery products to the retailer of grocery products to the ultimate purchaser—the housewife who feeds the soup to her family.

Each step involves an exchange, usually the exchange of money for the specific product. Likewise, each step has to provide satisfaction for both parties to the exchange—a profit and a salable product for the rolling mill, the steel supply center, the cannery, the grocery wholesaler, and the retailer; and a tasteful, nutritious soup for the homemaker and her family.

## Elements of the marketing mix

If you were to examine the activities of the soup manufacturer carefully, you would see that several important marketing decisions were made. The soup canner decided on:

1. the product
2. the price of that product
3. the kinds of outlets through which the product would be sold (the channels of distribution, as they are more appropriately described)
4. the promotional activities that will accompany that specific product, at that specific price, through the decided-upon channels of distribution

This group of decisions that is within the control of the producer is known as the *marketing mix*. We will examine each decision in turn.

### The product

In its broadest sense, a *product* is a good or service that an individual or an organization buys in order to obtain a measure of satisfaction. As stated earlier, that satisfaction may range from the profitable, resalable nature of the product to its taste and nutritional value.

The physical attributes of the product—the taste, the aroma, the color, the texture, and the quantity—are important contributions to consumer satisfaction. But, at the same time, every product has a number of psychic attributes that may be major components in the creation of that satisfaction. Such psychic attributes include the *brand name*, the style, the design, the exclusivity, and the *package*. In the selection of such services as restaurants, hairdressers, or retail stores of any kind, customers consider the store's location, reputation, and atmosphere, as well as the *quality* of its service.

In the case of the soup manufacturer, the soup could have been packaged in a glass container. It could have been dehydrated and packaged in foil as individual servings or in a jar to be portioned out by the spoonful. Each packaging decision would make the product different in the eyes of the ultimate purchaser.

Therefore, in addition to the basic characteristics of the soup product such as taste, aroma, quantity of chicken, consistency, etc., the advertiser of that product must also consider such factors as the design or style of the package, the reputation of the manufacturer, the name chosen for the brand, and the convenience of use.

**Consumer goods**    For reference purposes, marketing people usually distinguish between *consumer goods* and *industrial goods.* To be sure, the industrial purchaser is indeed a consumer, but industrial buying activity is prompted by business or organizational needs, not by personal needs. The consumer that interests us is a person who buys products and services for personal and family use. The words *goods* and *products* are, for our purposes, interchangeable and include services and intangible products.

There are no doctrinal rules for classifying consumer products, but we can gain a better understanding of the advertising implications if we classify goods according to the manner in which the consumer buys them.[1] Although we can separate consumer goods from industrial goods, the ad-

---

[1] For a well-written description of consumer goods classification, see David J. Schwartz, *Marketing Today,* 2d ed. (New York: Harcourt Brace Jovanovich, 1977), Chapter 3, "The Marketing Process."

vertising manager finds it helpful to make distinctions between the various categories of consumer goods. Traditionally, consumer goods have been classified as convenience goods, shopping goods, or specialty goods. Each classification has marketing characteristics that help guide the advertising approach.

*Convenience goods*    The term *convenience goods* best describes merchandise that has a low unit price and has little or no fashion connotation. What goods are included in this category? Groceries, drug sundries (such as toothpaste, shaving cream, deodorant, and mouthwash), hardware products (such as light bulbs and flashlight batteries), inexpensive candy, and cigarettes. Convenience goods are not large in physical size, and consumers generally demonstrate a preference for one brand over another. Convenience goods are usually purchased frequently or with some degree of predictable regularity. The consumer purchases this type of goods when needed, as rapidly as possible, and with the greatest convenience—hence the designation. Any savings the consumer might obtain by "shopping around" are usually not worth the effort.

From the advertising viewpoint, the consumer is familiar with the product and its attributes before setting out to buy it. The retail outlet is of little importance. The package and the brand name are of the utmost importance, as are point-of-purchase displays. Retailers, as a rule, carry several brands of any convenience item, and we cannot expect them to advertise such goods, especially when every retailer carries essentially the same assortment. The entire promotional effort is by the manufacturer.

*Shopping goods*    In contrast to convenience goods, *shopping goods* are those for which con-

Compare this ad for high fidelity components with the JVC ad on the opposite page. The tape deck in this ad is more a *shopping good* than a specialty good for several reasons: (1) The price is prominently displayed; no price is shown in the JVC ad. (2) The names of the retail outlets are very prominent. This suggests that the ad was placed by the retailers (it appeared in a newspaper) and that the cost of placing the ad was shared by the manufacturer, who also supplied the copy and the artwork. (3) The copy in this ad is far less technical than that in the JVC ad. The prominence of the price also suggests that the manufacturer is distributing through a selected dealer network that will maintain the advertised price.

sumers are willing to shop around, visiting several stores in order to compare price, quality, and style. Typical shopping goods are women's apparel, men's ready-to-wear clothing, home furnishings, jewelry, and fabrics. In general, shopping goods represent higher unit value than convenience goods. The extent to which consumers will shop around is related to the benefit they believe they will gain from this investment of their time and energy. The consumer does not have extensive product knowledge about shopping goods and seeks to augment that information by visiting different stores and comparing merchandise. Such purchases are made infrequently; otherwise the consumer would be forever busy just shopping.

A marketing consideration for the manufacturer of shopping goods would be to use fewer retail outlets than the manufacturer of convenience goods. Because customers are willing to shop around, and because such purchases are made infrequently, shopping goods are carried in department stores and large retail outlets. These stores are usually located near each other so that people can make comparisons conveniently. Inasmuch as the manufacturer uses fewer retailers, there is also less use of wholesalers and a more direct relationship with retailers. Above all, the store's name and reputation are important attributes, often more important than the manufacturer's name. The store itself becomes a major factor in the consumer's purchasing decision. This fact will affect the promotional effort, in which retailers provide most of the advertising and display.

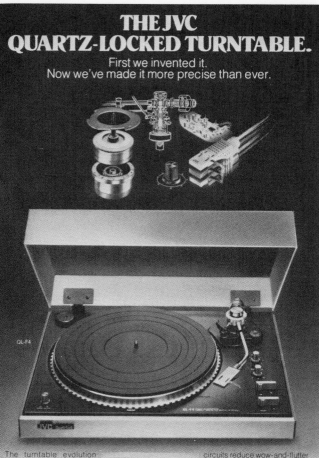
A *specialty good*—the ad provides a wealth of technical data in the jargon that is familiar to readers knowledgeable about this type of product. The target market is high fidelity enthusiasts who will go out of their way to buy this brand, not at just any retail outlet, but at their "JVC dealer." The headline automatically selects the target market.

*Specialty goods*    The consumer's insistence on a specific brand is the distinguishing characteristic of *specialty goods.* Many such goods are the same as shopping goods—expensive wearing apparel, gourmet food products, high fidelity components, cameras, home appliances, and automobiles. As in the case of convenience goods, the consumer usually has a good deal of information about the particular product before setting out to make a purchase. As in the case of shopping goods, but unlike convenience goods, the consumer is willing to make a shopping trip (often at some inconvenience) to buy a desired brand—and *that brand only.*

Manufacturers can therefore be more selective in their choice of retail outlets, often confining their product to a single store in a particular area, as a form of franchise. This establishes a close relationship between the manufacturer and the retailer. The retailer will mention the manufacturer's name prominently in local advertising, and the manufacturer often pays for a portion of the retailer's advertising costs. In a similar manner, manufacturers will often name retailers in their national advertising. The interdependence between manufacturer and retailer is close.

## The price

For good or ill, in American society price is frequently used as an index of quality. When making purchases in the absence of other criteria, many people equate quality with price. They assume that if a product or service costs more, it must be better. The reverse is also considered true—if the product costs less, then obviously, it cannot be as good. To a large extent, of course, the manufacturer's pricing decision is closely related to the quality and quantity of the product. A soup manufacturer who is marketing a chicken noodle soup recognizes the demand of the homemaker for that type of soup at a particular price. Obviously, adding more chicken meat to the soup will increase its cost. And, among the various kinds of soup, lobster bisque will be more expensive than chicken noodle. Even among lobster bisques, there will be variations in price, depending upon the quantity and quality of lobster in the can.

## Channels of distribution

The third decision required of manufacturers is the choice of a distribution network through which they will reach the ultimate purchaser, in this example, the homemaker. There are various channels of distribution available to the manufacturer of such products. Soup, particularly the chicken noodle soup, could be sold through every type of retail food outlet—from supermarkets to corner grocery stores and delicatessens. The lobster bisque, however, might be more appropriately distributed through gourmet food shops and the gourmet food departments of better department stores. Sales of another type or flavor of soup might be helped by distribution through health food stores.

The distribution decisions made by the manufacturer are contingent upon the nature of the product, the price, the channels that are available, and the practices that are common to the industry. Consider some of the options that are available:

1. Selling to retailers through wholesalers
   The manufacturer can sell to merchant wholesalers who will buy in quantity, maintain inventory (taking title to the goods), deliver, extend credit, and provide information and advice. These middlemen are sometimes designated as jobbers, distributors, or full-service wholesalers.

2. Selling to retailers through agents
   Agents do not take title to the goods, do not maintain inventory, and do not extend credit. They rarely perform any service other than selling. They are often designated brokers or manufacturers' representatives, depending on their contractual arrangement with the manufacturer.

3. Selling directly to retailers
   Working through their own sales force, manufacturers will sell to a retailer—a business organization that stocks and displays the goods on the premises and sells them, in turn, to consumers. Depending on the nature of the product, manufacturers have a number of choices—independent retailers, chain stores, supermarkets, department stores, discount stores, and vending machines.

4. Selling directly to the consumer
   Manufacturers may choose to establish their own retail outlets, to recruit a sales force in the field (as Avon and Fuller Brush do), or to sell through mail order. Each manufacturer will make this decision based on the nature of the product, the market, and the manufacturer's own capabilities.

### Promotional considerations

Up to this point, the seller (manufacturer or retailer) has had options as to the form of the product itself, the price of that product, the channels of distribution used (conditioned upon what is available), and the *promotional mix,* meaning the combination of personal selling, advertising, and sales-related activities, such as point-of-purchase displays, coupons, premium offers, special deals, demonstrations, and trade shows. The promotional mix will be explored in detail in Chapter 3.

## What is a market?

Manufacturers use the word *market* very often. They say they will bring a new product "to market." They use research techniques to learn if there is a "market" for a particular product. A market is people—people with the desire for a product, the willingness to buy it, and the ability to pay for it. Of course, there are many markets: An industry may be a market; the government may be a market; schools may be a market; farmers may be a market. The manufacturers of home appliances are a market for the manufacturers of sheet steel. The Department of Defense is a market for the manufacturers of military hardware. A school system is a market for the publishers of textbooks. Our focus in this text is on consumers as a market.

We are probably very accustomed to finding an adjective in front of the word *market.* We often say "mass market" when we mean very large numbers of people. We say "urban market" when we wish to designate consumers who live in cities. We say

"male market" when we wish to define the sex of the consumer. With such adjectives we define more precisely what we mean by a market. We have narrowed the total market—male or female, urban or rural, mass or class—into the most likely prospects for our product. When we have defined those consumers who have a need for our product, a willingness (in our opinion) to buy it, and the ability to pay for it, we have designated our target, or more commonly, our *target market.* Remember this term because we will use it often in preparing our advertising appeal and in selecting our media.

### Segmenting the target market

To be certain that our marketing effort is directed most efficiently—that is, with a minimum of wasted time, effort, and money—we divide our target market into submarkets, called *segments.* For example, if we were planning to market lipstick, our target market would be a female market. But *female market* is not an adequate definition. Not all women wear lipstick. For example, girls under the age of twelve generally do not wear lipstick. Our segment, or submarket, would be females over twelve years of age. That narrows the market for us. But even this description is inadequate. Our final definition would depend upon many different factors, including the price of our lipstick. Lipstick that sells for $5 would appeal to one segment of the market. Lipstick that sells for $1 would appeal to a totally different market segment. These represent logical, identifiable, reasonably homogeneous market segments. They enable us to evaluate the type of package, the preferred channels of distribution, and the appeal and media selection that we would use to market our lipstick.

# Steady as a rock 100 miles at sea.

While a floating drilling rig heaves in a heavy sea, the drill string that reaches down deep beneath the ocean floor is held firm and steady. It's a complex mechanical marvel called a drill string compensator that overcomes wave motion and keeps the drilling bit properly loaded. NL Shaffer, a part of NL Petroleum Services group, developed and produces the compensator systems that are used today on approximately 9 out of 10 floating drilling rigs throughout the world.

NL is a worldwide producer and supplier of petroleum equipment and services, chemicals and metals, with annual sales of about $2 billion.

NL Industries, Inc., 1230 Ave. of the Americas, N.Y., N.Y. 10020

A similar procedure (*called segmentation analysis*) is used for any product or service. An airline that flies overseas will have two basic consumer segments—the tourist on vacation and the business or government executives traveling on business. The tourists can be further segmented into different submarkets—students off for the summer, first-time travelers, and knowledgeable, sophisticated travelers who have been abroad before. Each segment wants something different from the airline. Can you visualize a different advertising appeal for each segment? And perhaps a different "package"?

This ad appeared in the business section of the *New York Times*. At first glance the *target market* appears to be companies that drill for oil. However, placing an ad for that purpose in a New York newspaper would represent a considerable waste of money—there are not many oil wells in Manhattan. The target for this ad is actually the investing public: men and women who are affluent enough to buy the company's stock for their investment portfolios or who are in a position to recommend its purchase by others.

## Conditions that affect marketing success

For a business to enjoy the full benefit of the marketing concept, that concept must be translated into specific activities. Everything that the company does must be directed toward satisfying the customer and, in the process, making a profit or achieving whatever other measure of success is applicable. Remember, advertising is not a science. There are no laws or rules that tell the advertiser what specific combination of price, product, and distribution channel, together with the right amount of advertising, will yield a specific sales result. Our inability to devise a formula for success arises from the fact that a number of critical factors in the marketing of a product are beyond our control—factors that can delay or even completely thwart our hoped-for results.

The success of our marketing effort is affected by changes in:

1. consumer tastes
2. social and cultural influences
3. demographics
4. economic conditions
5. the legal and political climate
6. technology
7. the actions of competitors

Let us consider the ways each of these factors affect our marketing, and help or hinder our advertising plans.

# What price glory?

**Sail Queen Elizabeth 2 to Europe and fly back, all for as little as $695.** Nothing provides such a glorious vacation as the Queen. She's incomparable. Almost a thousand feet of sheer luxury. Thirteen stories devoted to pleasure. Sail the Queen and you'll enjoy superb continental cuisine, nightclubs, bars, a gymnasium, a sauna, a theatre, a shopping arcade, and entertainment featuring movie stars, public figures, and authors.

This year, when you buy a one-way ticket on the Queen to or from Europe, the price includes a British Airways ticket the other way—to or from your hometown. Prices from $695 to $985 in tourist class, from $1,185 to $2,165 in first class.* For details, see your travel agent, call Cunard at (212) 983-2510, or return the coupon.

*Prices per person, double occupancy
*British registry*

## CUNARD
### Queen Elizabeth 2

Cunard, P.O. Box 999
Farmingdale, N.Y. 11735
Please send more facts on the QE 2 experience and Europe.
☐ QE 2 transatlantic air/sea booklet
☐ QE 2 European tours booklet
Name_____
Address_____
City_____State_____Zip_____
My Travel Agent is_____

**For once in your life, live.**

Obviously Cunard does not have passenger space on its *Queen Elizabeth 2* for all 6 million tourists who visit Europe each year. Since the air/sea prices for this trip range from $1,600 to $8,000 per couple, Cunard's *target market* is clearly affluent and interested in the "good life." This advertisement appeared in *Gourmet* magazine. A food publication? Yes, but a food publication that reaches the sophisticated and affluent *market segment* from which the steamship line expects to find its 42,000 passengers.

# In Concert.

"Anyone who really loves to cook will wonder how they ever lived without it. I know I couldn't . . ."
—James Beard in nationally syndicated column

"It has been labeled, not without justice, the 20th Century French Revolution."
—Craig Claiborne with Pierre Franey in The New York Times

"It speedily handles so many time-consuming culinary exercises that it brings epicurean feats frequently into the realm of everyday fare."
—Gourmet Magazine

"Cuisinart® (it's like the Canadian National Tower—there's only one, and its uncopiable) . . ."
—Betty Jane Wylie in The Toronto Star

"Unless you're going to get the top performer (at the top price), stick with your blender and a sharp knife. Second best simply is not good enough, —no matter how hard they've tried."
—Jane Benet in the San Francisco Chronicle

If you are thinking about buying a Cuisinart® food processor, we welcome your questions. If you already own one, we welcome your comments. Write Box MK, Cuisinarts, Inc., 1 Barry Place, Stamford, Conn. 06902.

# Cuisinart® food processor
WE HAVEN'T COMPROMISED. NEITHER SHOULD YOU.

The target market for this ad is *upscale*—that is, well educated and affluent—and has an abiding interest in fine foods and restaurants. The market segment thus identified, with interest in the product *and* the ability to buy it, the advertiser provides the last dollop—a *reference group*—in this case some of the best-known names in haute cuisine. Note the small picture of the product and the complete absence of "nuts-and-bolts" copy.

## The dynamics of consumer tastes

What makes tastes change? No one really knows for sure. Listen to people talk: "That's what they're all buying." "That's what they're wearing this season." Who are *they?* Perhaps *they* are a *reference group*— a group of people to which a person looks for establishing his or her own attitudes or behavior. Common examples are members of work groups, school groups, or social groups who appear to have a life style worth emulating, such as business or government executives, sports or show business stars. The idea for the advertiser is to create an appeal that suggests to the target market that they can be like the athlete or famous person if they use the particular product.

A brief glance at new products introduced to the market in recent years hardly provides a clue to the direction of consumers' fancies. "Natural" foods such as yogurt have increased in popularity, but so have "junk" foods. Eighty percent of the new products introduced do not succeed.[2] Is it because the marketers are so enamored of their products that they do not bother to find out what the market wants? Not at all.

Here is what frequently happens: After a market study has been carefully made, a manufacturer decides that the time is ripe for the introduction of a new product. The manufacturer gears up for a small production run, has a beautiful package designed, selects the most suitable channel of distribution, advertises, and—nothing happens. In the six months that have elapsed since the development of the manufacturer's brainchild, consumer interests have moved on. The failure of the Edsel

[2] Thomas L. Berg, *Mismarketing* (Garden City, N.Y.: Doubleday & Co., Anchor Books, 1971).

provided a multimillion-dollar lesson in the fickleness of consumer tastes.

## Changes in social and cultural influences

Much consumer behavior is culturally determined. Traditional social institutions used to provide guidelines, but the old Puritan ethic of hard work and thrift—saving money, paying cash, living within one's means—has been replaced with a *quality-of-life* ethic. In the last two decades, marketers have experienced a growing demand for gourmet foods, long vacations, fine wines, and fine art. Both men and women pamper themselves with cosmetics, hair dyes, skin-care preparations, and colognes. Tennis has become one of the fastest-growing sports in the United States, and everyone who plays tennis buys a new steel or aluminum racket, a racket bag, and the proper warm-up suit. Can the marketer predict what the next craze will be, or how long the present one will last?

The increased divorce rate has also had an effect on the consumer market. Smaller family groups need smaller apartments with fewer appliances. More working mothers has meant more interest in grooming products for women who now have less leisure time because they spend their daytime hours at the factory or office. Working wives also need another automobile and buy life insurance now that they are an insurable asset. They need food processors, blenders, crockpots, and microwave ovens. Because working women have less time to plan their shopping and rely more and more heavily on impulse buying, manufacturers must design different packaging for their products and, in some cases, different floor displays for retail stores. Do social changes affect our marketing results? And how.

## Changing demographics[3]

As you may have noted, much segmentation analysis is based on observable characteristics of the people who compose our target market. The most obvious of these characteristics are sex, age, income level, marital status, geographic location, and occupation. You can see how the markets for most products are easily segmented by the use of one or more of these characteristics. For certain products, our market is women, but not all women. We may want young women or mature women, single women, married women, or mothers. Doesn't a married woman with two children buy different products than a single woman of the same age? Indeed she does.

You may have noted that we used the word *observable* to describe these characteristics. That means we want to be able to quantify this information, and we can. Census data and other sources provide us with information on the number and location of various segments. Although we have defined the target market as people with the desire for a product and the ability to buy it, we must also determine whether or not enough of these people exist to make our marketing effort profitable.

We must also consider all the changes in the population of the United States that have occurred in the past ten years. People have been moving to the Sunbelt, which means that they spend more time outdoors and therefore buy more patio furniture, barbecue equipment, swimming pools, bathing suits, and suntan lotion and spend less for heavy winter clothing. People in the Sunbelt want brightly colored clothing, too.

[3] *Demography* is the science of vital social statistics (births, deaths, diseases, marriages) of populations.

**You buy the best!**
**the Continental Quilt**
*is next!*

You know who you are and what you want! You seek out quality and you make your investment. You are not fooled by sales, sales, sales, ...so-called sales. But you will pay for excellence. The Continental Quilt or the CQ is not inexpensive, but it will give you years of the best comfort. You know you always wanted one. The Continental Quilt is next! The Continental Quilt is... Down with Love!!

• *filled with dreamy white European goose down*
• *eliminates topsheet, blanket, bedspread and bedmaking*
• *100% Cambric cotton. The only recognized down covering*
• *warm in winter cool in summer saves energy*
• *channel high-loft construction*

Open 10am — 6pm • Only available from:

**the Continental ✥ Quilt shoppe**

610 5th Ave.      129 E. 57 St.
Rockefeller Center (Across from Saks)   235 E. 51 St.   N.Y., N.Y. 10022   10 Littell Rd.   110 E. Oak St.
Street Entrance: 7 W 49 St.   N.Y., N.Y. 10022   212-752-7631   East Hanover, N.J. 07936   Chicago, Ill. 60611
N.Y. 10020 • 212-757-3511   212-688-3882   (Open Sunday)   201-884-1462   312-664-9614
American Express, Bank Americard, Mastercharge welcomed

from $99.95 colors: bone, camel, lt. blue, white, navy, yellow, brown    NYT 6/11

Not satisfied, perhaps, with available channels of distribution, this company sells through its own retail outlets. Its product, as advertised, is a specialty good, and consumers will want this quilt and no other. The target market: people who want something different *and* who are not reluctant to spend more for high quality. *Demographics:* male and female, over twenty-five, and affluent. The placement of the price tells us the product is expensive, and the copy confirms it.

The population is also getting older, and older people want more health-care products, more low-cost travel, more trailers, vans, and mobile homes. They want remote control for their television set so they don't have to get up to change channels. They drink prune juice and eat bran cereals. Many have moved back into the center city from the suburbs. They don't want automobiles. They do want compact kitchens.

## Economic conditions

It is easy to understand how economic conditions can affect our marketing results. The most useful, high-quality, well-priced product or service cannot be sold in an area where the unemployment rate is high. The purchase of expensive items—major appliances, for example—represents confidence in the economy. The prospective purchasers expect that they will have their jobs over the payout period. Rising prices coupled with slower economic growth (stagflation) have prompted shifts in consumer spending patterns. Dry cleaning sales are down. Camera sales are up. As the price of meat and fish goes up, so do sales of macaroni and spa-

ghetti products. What area will suffer major strikes or devasting winter storms that will close factories and stores? These events will drastically affect our marketing plans.

## Legal and political climate

New rules and regulations issued by various agencies of the federal government have had a powerful impact on the advertising business. The ban on cigarette advertising on television caused major shifts in cigarette advertisers' media schedules and forced them to reevaluate the use of print media. The ban on cyclamates sent all the soft-drink companies running to find a substitute. Having found that substitute in saccharin, the bottlers have once again had their marketing plans upset by the government's contentions regarding that sweetener. What will happen to soft-drink sales if nonreturnable bottles are prohibited? What will the sausage and salami makers do if the government should ban the use of sodium nitrate in their products? In anticipation of a ban on aerosols with fluorocarbon propellants, marketers have already started to repackage hair sprays and deodorants.

Marketers and their advertising agencies find it expedient to have copy for their advertisements cleared with their legal staffs to be sure that none of the material contravenes the law. Recent court rulings requiring advertisers to put disclaimers in their present ads have made everyone in the advertising business very circumspect.

## Changes in technology

The development of polyester fiber put many laundries out of business. The drip-dry shirt and the no-iron sheet eliminated the need to send these

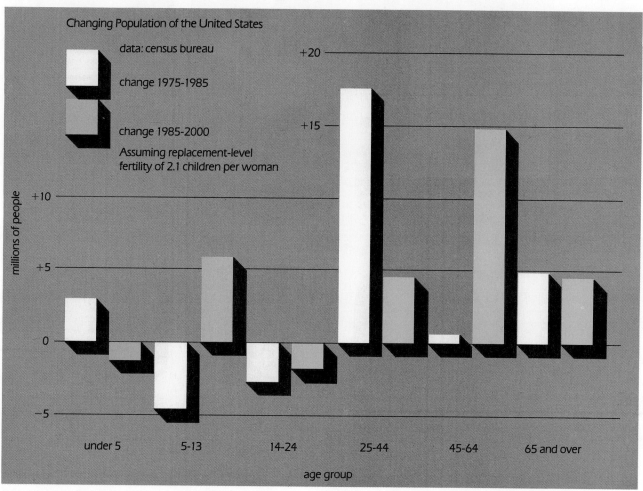

Changing Population of the United States

data: census bureau

change 1975-1985

change 1985-2000
Assuming replacement-level
fertility of 2.1 children per woman

millions of people

+20

+15

+10

+5

0

−5

under 5    5-13    14-24    25-44    45-64    65 and over

age group

The dramatic changes in the population of the United States that are forecast in this chart will have a far-reaching impact on marketing. The continued reduction in the 14 – 24-year-old population group will mean a declining market for many of the products consumed by this group—soft drinks, beer, motorcycles, and snack foods, for example. The sharp drop in the 25 – 44 age group, matched with an increase in the 45 – 64 group, will mean substantial shifts in buying habits. The 45 – 64 age group will want more conservatively styled clothes and cars, more cosmetics, and more health-care products. Publications aimed at the 25 – 44 age group will face declining readership, while the more general and conservative publications will find their audience growing.

The introduction of a new product or an innovative change in an old product can alter consumers' spending patterns. This commercial for Burlington Industries announces a product innovation that helps set Burlington socks apart from their competition. The distinction is emphasized by the bright green stripe for easy visual identification. A clever, light touch makes what might otherwise be an unappealing subject interesting and informative.

**BURLINGTON INDUSTRIES CORPORATE ADVERTISING**
"BIOGUARD SOCKS"
:30 Commercial

SFX: Swamp Sounds

TROOPER: We found the sock. You find the foot that fits it.
SHERIFF: We'll get him.

SHERIFF: Smell, Duke. Now c'mon, smell, boy.
V/O: There's something remarkable about Burlington Socks.

SHERIFF: He's just funnin' here.
V/O: A special treatment called Bioguard

V/O: helps control sock odor.

V/O: That goes for Burlington dress socks... casual socks...

V/O: sports socks... Just look for the green stripe on the toe that says....

V/O: they've been treated with Bioguard, the odor controller. Lasts for the life of the socks.

SHERIFF: I don't know what happened, trooper.
V/O: ONLY BURLINGTON MAKES IT.
SHERIFF: Duke, where'd you go? Duke...

items to the laundry. The old phonograph has been replaced by complex high fidelity systems that include quadraphonic sound, Dolby noise suppression, reel-to-reel tape recorders and decks, and eight-track cassettes. As products have changed, so have marketing opportunities, for the better for some companies, for the worse for others. The blender has given way to the food processor. New cameras, recreation vehicles, jogging shoes, television games, radial tires—every day scores of new products enter the marketplace, thwarting the plans and expectations of others.

### Competitive actions

Competition is like an enemy skirmish line, always searching for a weakness in your front. Chivas Regal competes with Johnnie Walker and with Teacher's

Client: CHURCH & DWIGHT

Product: ARM & HAMMER BAKING SODA

Type: TV

Title: "KITTY PARTY"

Comm'l No.: ZCTB-0237

Length: 30 SECONDS

SFX: MUSIC
1st cat: Lovely party, isn't it?

2nd cat: Yes, but don't you detect an odor?

1st cat: Must be the litter box.

2nd cat: The litter box? Haven't you told our hostess about Arm & Hammer Baking Soda?

It absorbs odor naturally for days and days, so the litter box smells clean.

One part Arm & Hammer...

With three parts cat litter.

The litter lasts longer so she won't have to change it as often.
1st cat: O' Jessica! You're so sophisticated.

SUPER: ARM & HAMMER BAKING SODA. FOR A CLEANER-SMELLING LITTER BOX.

Sodium bicarbonate—baking soda—has been around for a long time. Our grandparents probably used it as an antacid or mouthwash. Of course, it is called *baking soda* because it is used as a leavening agent in cakes and breads. But this advertiser has found a new use for sodium bicarbonate and has thereby increased the range of the product's market. Creative marketing.

and with all the other well-known brands of Scotch whiskey. Each brand tries to increase its market share. Any marketer has five ways to increase sales:

1. by increasing the frequency of product use

2. by increasing the quantity of purchase

3. by increasing the length of the buying season

4. by taking customers from competitors

5. by increasing the range of the total market

But sometimes the attack comes from an unexpected quarter. Who wants to take business away from brand X Scotch? Brands Y and Z to be sure, but also all the vodkas, gins, and rums. Jose Cuervo tequila woos drinkers of Scotch, vodka, rye,

**CONDITIONS THAT AFFECT MARKETING SUCCESS**

## ALBERT D. LASKER

Albert D. Lasker has been called the father of modern advertising. In fact, his story parallels the history of the advertising business itself. In 1898, shortly after graduation from high school in Galveston, Texas, he went to work as an office boy for Lord & Thomas advertising agency in Chicago. Before he was 40, he was earning a million dollars a year and owned the agency, which had become the largest in the United States at that time.

In the early 1900s, most manufacturers considered advertising as merely a way of "keeping your name before the public," but Albert Lasker learned from a copywriter named John E. Kennedy that advertising was really *salesmanship in print*. He came to understand that effective advertising should give its readers reasons why they should buy the goods or services being offered. "Reason why" became the motif of the Lord & Thomas agency and the "salesmanship in print" school of copywriting Albert Lasker started became the training ground for many writers who went on to form their own successful agencies.

Among the well-known accounts for which Albert Lasker worked were Stokley–Van Camp, California Fruit Exchange (later to become Sunkist), Kimberly-Clark, Pepsodent, and Lucky Strike cigarettes. In 1918, he left management of the Lord & Thomas agency in the hands of a great copywriter named Claude C. Hopkins and went to work for the presidential campaign of Warren G. Harding. He was among the first to bring modern advertising techniques to politics.

In 1923, Albert Lasker resumed active management of Lord & Thomas, and during the next two decades applied his ideas to such modern forms of advertising as the radio commercial. It was Lasker who gave a struggling young comedian named Bob Hope a chance to do a radio show for Pepsodent. Then, in 1942 after 44 years in the advertising business, Albert Lasker decided to retire. He turned the agency over to his three branch managers: Emerson Foote in New York, Fairfax M. Cone in Chicago, and Don Belding in Los Angeles. The new agency was named Foote, Cone & Belding and was the fifth largest agency in the United States in 1978.

From his retirement until his death in 1952, Albert Lasker devoted himself and his wealth to an active life of philanthropy. Author John Gunther called Albert Lasker "one of the most extraordinary personalities of our time."

The market for coffee in the United States is a huge prize, well worth striving for. Americans buy about $4.5 billion worth of coffee at retail every year, $3 billion of which is ground coffee; the balance, instant coffee. Sales of both ground and instant coffee to the institutional market account for another $1 billion annually. Therefore, a market share as small as 1 percent represents over $50 million in sales volume.

Among the major brands of coffee in the years 1976 and 1977, General Foods' Maxwell House had a 28 percent share of the total retail market, Procter & Gamble's Folger's had a 23 percent share, followed by Nestle (instant only) with about 15 percent, Hills Brothers with about 5 percent, and Chase & Sanborn with about 1.5 percent.

Folger's strong market base was west of the Mississippi, but in the 1960s it began to expand its distribution eastward, seeking a national market. The extension of its market to the East would mean that Folger's would have complete national distribution, thereby making its advertising on network television more cost-effective.

In 1977, Procter & Gamble launched a program to win a market share for Folger's along the East Coast. P&G's objective was a 12 percent share of the East Coast market, which would have made Folger's the leading national brand. P&G bombarded that market with cents-off coupons and with television commercials featuring their spokeswoman, Mrs. Olsen, who told homemakers how to make their husbands happy: by serving them Folger's coffee, of course. General Foods did not sit back and quietly watch Procter & Gamble's campaign gather momentum. It counterattacked. General Foods quickly increased its advertising for Maxwell House. Maxwell House's spokeswoman, Cora, reassured television viewers who already used the General Foods' brand: "When you find a good thing, stick with it." Maxwell House also reacted elsewhere. In Kansas City and Dallas, traditionally strong markets for Folger's, Maxwell House cut prices.

Although Folger's achieved its market share goals in most major eastern markets, it fell short of them in the New York metropolitan market, the largest single market for coffee in the United States. In New York, Folger's was able to pick up only an additional 8 percent of the market. Local brands, blends of stronger coffees such as Chock Full o' Nuts, Savarin, and Martinson, have managed to maintain their market shares—at least for the present.

As of this writing, both companies express great optimism. Procter & Gamble claims that it will, in time, achieve its projected market share. General Foods is confident that it will retain its market share. The Federal Trade Commission, meanwhile, has entered the fray, very much concerned that this war between the two giant corporations is endangering their smaller competitors.

Source: Hugh D. Menzies, "Why Folger's Is Getting Creamed Back East," *Fortune*, June 17, 1978, pp. 68–76.

# DANNY® FROZEN YOGURT
# THE ICE CREAM ALTERNATIVE

Even as the various brands of ice cream compete among themselves for market share, frozen yogurt comes on the scene to compete with them all. This commercial is aimed directly at the consumer who wants the taste and consistency of ice cream with fewer calories per serving. The woman in the commercial provides a good point of contact for women viewers. She is young, but can still be perceived as a homemaker who would buy Danny frozen yogurt for her family.

I love ice cream. But I've found something with more protein, less fat, and less calories:

Danny Frozen Yogurt. In all kinds of flavors. In a cup.

As a fruit-topped flip...

or on a stick. It's the ice cream alternative.

How about it, ice cream fans?

V.O.: Danny is made from natural Dannon Yogurt.

gin, and rum. Trucking companies compete with each other and with railroads and airlines for freight business. Everyone wants a piece of the pie.

Of course, all brands of electric blankets compete with each other; but consider the other competitors as well: a feather comforter, heavy pajamas, an electric space heater, a heavy woolen blanket, or one could even simply turn up the thermostat. The object of the purchase for the consumer is to keep warm on cold winter nights, and any of these products will serve that need. Therefore, they can all be said to compete with the electric blanket.

## Summary

Advertising is a tool of marketing, and every advertising decision is influenced by the four components of the *marketing mix*. These four components are: the nature of the product, the price of the product, the channels of distribution that take the product to the consumer from the producer, and the promotional activities, including advertising, that are used to help sell the product.

Today, every manufacturer applies the *marketing concept:* the concept that every facet of an organization should be dedicated to satisfying the wants of prospective customers. This concept has led marketers to use *segmentation analysis,* which is the examination of submarkets composed of people with certain attributes who are the most likely purchasers of the product. We call these submarkets our *target market,* and we call the attributes of people that distinguish them as targets or nontargets, *demographics.* Demographic characteristics include sex, age, income, level, and other statistical classifications into which we can separate people for advertising purposes.

We are also aware that products, as well as people, can be separated into categories—for example, *consumer products* and *industrial products* —on the basis of the purpose for which they are bought. We can further divide consumer products into categories based on the *behavior* of the people who buy them. These categories are *convenience goods, shopping goods,* and *specialty goods.* Advertising for a consumer product is influenced by the category the product falls under.

Furthermore, as we prepare our advertising and marketing plans, we are well aware that we do not operate in a vacuum. In the real world, decisions are always influenced by forces beyond our control, such as changes in consumer tastes and life-styles, changes in demographics, the activities of competitive products, changes in technologies, and the pervasive activities of government.

## QUESTIONS FOR DISCUSSION

**1.** What is, or should be, the relationship of the marketing mix to the organization's advertising effort?

**2.** If we could indeed build a better mousetrap, what would we have to do to market it successfully in today's economy?

**3.** Why would a company with no product to sell to the general public advertise?

**4.** What marketing changes can you foresee as a result of
   a. a return deposit being charged on beverage bottles
   b. a ban on the use of fluorocarbon propellant for aerosols
   c. a total ban on artificial sweeteners for soft drinks
   d. a serious shortage of gasoline

**5.** What changes in packaging do you foresee as a result of
   a. an increasing number of working women
   b. a continued trend toward smaller families

**6.** What products would be affected by changing demographic factors such as
   a. age
   b. family size
   c. educational level

**7.** How many segments can you identify in the market for
   a. toothpaste
   b. bottled water
   c. shampoo

**8.** How have the cultural and social changes of the past twenty years affected the marketing of certain products?

**9.** There have been a few noticeable changes in retailing in recent years. What are some of these changes? How have they affected the marketing of some products?

**THE MARKETING FOUNDATIONS OF ADVERTISING**

## Sources and suggestions for further reading

"Americans Change: How Demographic Shifts Affect the Economy." *Business Week*, 20 February 1978.

Bartos, Rena. "The Moving Target: The Impact of Women's Employment on Consumer Behavior." *Journal of Marketing* (July 1977).

Berg, Thomas L. *Mismarketing: Case Histories of Marketing Misfires.* Garden City: Doubleday & Co., Anchor Books, 1971.

Crawford, C. Merle. "The Role of Personal Values in Marketing and Consumer Behavior." *Journal of Marketing* (April 1977).

Cundiff, Edward W.; Still, Richard R.; and Govoni, Norman A. P. *Fundamentals of Modern Marketing.* 2d ed. Englewood Cliffs, N.J.: Prentice-Hall, 1976.

Henry, Walter A. "Cultural Values Do Correlate With Consumer Behavior." *Journal of Market Research* (May 1976).

"How the Changing Age Mix Changes Markets." *Business Week*, 12 January 1976.

Lazer, William, and Smallwood, John E. "The Changing Demographics of Women." *Journal of Marketing* (July 1977).

Levitt, Theodore. "Marketing Myopia." *Harvard Business Review* 53 (September-October 1975).

McCall, Suzanne H. "Meet the 'Workwife.'" *Journal of Marketing* (July 1977).

Robicheaux, Robert A. et al. *Marketing: Contemporary Dimensions.* Boston: Houghton Mifflin, 1976.

Rogers, David S., and Green, Howard L. "Changes in Consumer Food Expenditure Patterns." *Journal of Marketing* (April 1978).

Stanton, William J. *Fundamentals of Marketing.* 5th ed. New York: McGraw-Hill, 1978.

# THE PROMOTIONAL MIX

## The marketing plan and advertising

Marketing objectives
Factors influencing the promotional
mix
    The nature of the market
    The nature of the product
    The life cycle of the product
    The advertiser's financial capabilities

## Advertising as the main thrust

The decision to advertise
Factors influencing the decision to
advertise

    Primary demand
    Brand differentiation
    Market potential
    The advertising budget
    The product must be good
Advertising objectives
Advertising redefined
    Retail and national advertising
    Consumer and business advertising
    Trade advertising
    Industrial advertising
    Professional advertising
    Institutional and public-service
        advertising

## WORKING VOCABULARY

| | | |
|---|---|---|
| promotional mix | national advertising | professional advertising |
| product life cycle | consumer advertising | institutional advertising |
| primary demand | business advertising | public-service advertising |
| selective demand | trade advertising | |
| retail advertising | industrial advertising | |

CHAPTER **3**

# the
# promotional mix

*From the standpoint of the producer, advertising is clearly used because it is thought to be the most efficient marketing technique. If the advertiser knew of a selling tool that promised lower cost or greater return, he'd be irrational to continue advertising.*

HERBERT STEIN
*"Advertising Is Worth Advertising"*

As YOU MAY RECALL from the preceding chapter, the marketing mix consists of four elements: the product (which includes the package), the price, the channels of distribution, and the promotion. The subject of this chapter is promotion—or what is more appropriately termed the *promotional mix.* It is a mix because as marketers we select the combination of advertising, publicity, personal selling, and sales promotion that we believe will best assist us in achieving our overall marketing objectives. Promotion, then, is the term that is used to include all four of these marketing activities.

In keeping with a systems approach, an organization should consider all of its promotional efforts as a complete subsystem within the total marketing system. This means that the activities of the sales force, the advertising and publicity programs, and all other promotional efforts must be coordinated. Technically, promotion is an exercise in communication, the purpose being to provide information, persuade, and influence behavior.

# The marketing plan and advertising

Successful advertising does not exist in a vacuum. It must be part of an overall *marketing program.* Among marketing people, few decisions can more significantly affect the growth and profitability of a business than the formulation of the marketing program. The marketing objectives of the company must be determined product by product together with the marketing activities that will be necessary to achieve those objectives.

The first step in developing the marketing program is to decide on the *marketing plan*—the foundation on which the company's operating plans are based. The marketing plan integrates the four components of the marketing mix into a single comprehensive program designed to achieve the marketing objectives. Wherever possible, these objectives should be defined in quantitative terms so that progress toward them can be measured. There are dollar goals and nondollar goals. Dollar goals may be specific short-term or long-term financial aims such as increased profitability, sales volume, return on investment, and earnings per share of common stock.

Nondollar goals usually lead to dollar goals. Nondollar goals may include developing the company image, attaining a certain standing or reputation in particular markets, supporting community programs, and winning public approval for company programs.

## Marketing objectives

Marketing objectives should be measurable, attainable, and clear; they should be acceptable to the sales department, to the advertising department, and to the various production and operating departments whose cooperation is critical to the achievement of these goals. Marketing objectives should be flexible, challenging, and consistent with each other. If the objectives satisfy these criteria, we are ready to consider how we can use advertising to help achieve the desired results. A countless number of decisions must be made—should more sales people be hired? Can product quality be improved? Can the price be reduced? Should the amount of advertising be increased? These decisions are all related to each other. Low prices will do little good unless we tell people about them through advertising.

When top management states a goal explicitly —for example, "increase profits"—this becomes the implicit goal of every division or department of the organization. Advertising cannot be assigned specific communications tasks that are separate from marketing goals. If the job to be done is a goal of advertising, it *automatically* becomes a goal of marketing. Advertising has no goal of its own, but rather a continuing responsibility to help management attain the higher order company goals. For example, can advertising be used to increase distribution? Will advertising increase market share? Will a media change result in more sales? For every product dozens of questions such as these must be answered.

Advertising's principal task is to make more sales at more profit than would have been made without advertising, just as the job of the sales force is to make more sales at more profit than would have been made without salespeople. In order for advertising to succeed, the product, the price, and the method of distribution must be right. Personal selling and sales promotion strategies must be right. The promotional mix must be right.

## Factors influencing the promotional mix

One of the most difficult jobs in marketing is determining the most effective promotional mix. No one knows exactly how much any one element contributes to the attainment of the sales goals. In general, however, there are four factors that influence management's decision:

1. the nature of the market
2. the nature of the product
3. the stage in the product's life cycle
4. the financial capabilities of the organization

**The nature of the market**    The *nature of the market* has a tremendous bearing on the promotional mix. For an industrial product such as a utility generator, for which there are relatively few customers, the mix will differ considerably from that used to sell a toaster to hundreds of thousands of homes. The manufacturer of a utility generator can use personal selling efforts very extensively, whereas, for the toaster manufacturer, personal selling efforts to reach the ultimate consumer would be prohibitively costly. In fact, some retailers would not even stock the product unless the manufacturer agreed to do a certain amount of advertising. Thus, the number of prospects, the type of customer, and the geographic distribution of the market must all be considered.

**The nature of the product**    Consumer products and industrial goods usually require quite different strategies. Each strategy is based on the *nature of the product.* Within each category, the mix will be different. Capital machinery installations are not promoted in the same way that industrial raw materials are promoted. Sales of convenience goods rely on a heavy advertising investment and on displays at the point of sale, where buying decisions are frequently made. Personal selling activities play a minor role. Many *raw materials* are unbranded, and the products from competing firms may be equally acceptable. In this case, the persuasive efforts of the field sales force may be the most effective influence.

**The life cycle of the product**    Strategy decisions for promoting any product are also influenced considerably by the particular phase of the product's *life cycle.* Products go through a cycle in much the same way people do. We start as infants that need to be carefully nurtured; move on through a vigorous, growing youth; into our mature development to a level of stability; then on to old age and decline. So, too, with a product. Its life begins with an introductory stage (infancy); then the product catches on, and there is a period of vigorous growth (youth), followed by its maintenance of a share of a relatively stable market (maturity). When a product's market share shows signs of decline (old age), we have the choice of putting it to sleep (demarketing) or rejuvenating it (improving, repackaging, and developing a different advertising appeal).

In the introductory, or pioneering, stage of this cycle the manufacturer is concerned with the stimulation of primary demand. The objective of promotion during this stage is to inform and educate the potential customers. The advertiser has to tell the market that the product exists, how it may be used, and the want-satisfying benefits it provides. Simply stated, to stimulate *primary demand* is to stimulate demand for a *type of product.* (In contrast, *selective demand* is demand for a *particular brand.*) For industrial products in the pioneering

# SAY "A BETTER BETAMAX" TEN TIMES FAST.

Practice this tongue twister. You'll be saying it a lot in the near future.

When the leading name in videorecorders announces a better model, it's big news. Especially since videorecorders have become such a big business.

Since we introduced our first Betamax a few years ago, the demand for home videorecorders has been rapidly growing. And it's only the beginning. (Home videorecorders are catching on even faster than color television did in its day!) Now there's a new Betamax.

**New Betamax...new features.**

Once you get the hang of saying "a better Betamax," the rest will be easy. Just tell your customers that Betamax now gives you up to 3 hours recording time on our new L-750 videocassette — which is as long as you're likely to need.

 But recording time isn't the only thing we've added. Now there's a built-in LED digital timer with 24-hour automatic pre-set capability for videotaping when no one is going to be home. And when someone *is* going to be home while videotaping, it has a remote control pause button. The new Betamax is even better-*looking*. More sleek and compact. And, of course, it has all the features that made our Betamax so popular in the first place.

**The respected Sony name.**

Sony's quality image is backed by 20 years

©1978 Sony Corp. of America. SONY and Betamax are registered trademarks of Sony Corp.

of experience and reliability in videorecording. In fact, we've not only sold more videorecorders to consumers, but we've also sold more to broadcasters and industry than any other consumer manufacturer.

What's more, we make our own videorecorders *and* our own parts. And we're the only consumer manufacturer who makes its own tapes. (To show we mean business and to assure a steady supply of blank tapes, we've just built a multimillion-dollar tape plant in Dothan, Alabama.)

**New advertising and promotion campaigns.**

It was our Betamax and our advertising that created most of the excitement about videorecorders.

So get ready.

Because once we introduce the SL-8600 Betamax (with more advertising dollars behind it than we've ever spent to introduce a product) on network and spot television, in national magazines, in newspapers and on radio, you'll be very busy doing what you do best. Selling. Which means now is a good time to start practicing:

"A better Betamax"...
"a better Betamax"...
"a better Betamax"...

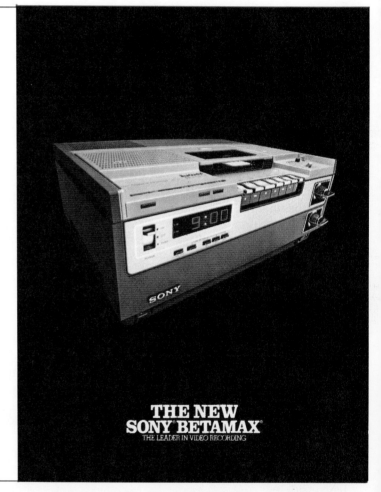

## THE NEW SONY BETAMAX
THE LEADER IN VIDEO RECORDING

---

This ad shows how the nature of the market for videorecorders influences one company's advertising. It is not enough for Sony to advertise to consumers; without a strong network of dealers, its consumer advertising would be wasted. What do prospective dealers want to know?

That "the demand for videorecorders has been rapidly growing"; that the product is a good one and is backed by "the respected Sony name"; and that Sony will back them "with more advertising dollars . . . than we've ever spent to introduce a product."

# The Old Raisin Ploy, Part 2:

1.

"Mom said I could have one Mr. Chunko...

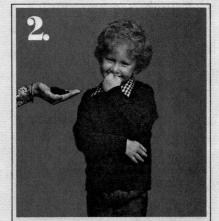

2.

...or a whole handful of raisins.

3.

She can't fool me. I took the raisins!

4.

Now she says I'm getting too smart for her."

This usually successful ploy brought to you by

**Raisins from California. Nature's candy.**

California Raisin Advisory Board

This ad is one in a campaign (see Chapter 18) by the raisin growers of California to stimulate *primary demand* for their product. Each of the individual growers expects to share in the public response to this advertising program. Target market: homemakers with children. The individual producers may also advertise under their own names (Del Monte, SunMaid) in an effort to stimulate *selective demand*, that is, to create a preference, not merely for raisins, but for a particular brand.

47

stage, manufacturers may have to rely heavily on personal selling to get middlemen to handle the product. It is only after customers have become aware of the existence of a product and the way it will satisfy certain wants that advertising moves from providing information to persuasion.

**The advertiser's financial capabilities**  In the final analysis, the determining factor in selecting the most effective promotional mix is the *financial resources* of the company. An organization well endowed with funds can make more effective use of advertising than companies with smaller advertising budgets. Small or financially weak companies are more likely to rely on personal selling or dealer displays. Personal selling may not provide the most efficient means of carrying the product message at the lowest cost, but to do the job with advertising may require more money than is available.

## Advertising as the main thrust

### The decision to advertise

Not every product lends itself to advertising, and not every company needs advertising. For example, the soup company that opts for a private-label operation might sell its product to A&P or Kroger or Jewel Tea or any of the dozens of supermarket chains that exist in the United States. With a store's label on its product, the soup company has nothing to advertise. In fact, the H. J. Heinz Co., the leading producer of private-label canned soups in the United States, does not advertise its soups.

On the other hand, the soup company may concentrate on the institutional market, producing only large cans that are sold exclusively to restaurants, hospitals, and other institutions that prepare food for large numbers of people. In this case, advertising would play a very limited role.

### Factors influencing the decision to advertise

The decision to advertise and the extent of the commitment to advertising are based on specific market and product requirements:

1. Primary demand for the product or product type should be rising.
2. It must be possible to differentiate the brand.
3. Identifiable buying motives must exist.
4. The company must have an advertising budget large enough to purchase a sufficient amount of advertising.
5. The product must be good.

**Primary demand**  The importance of rising primary demand cannot be overstated. Contrary to popular belief, advertising cannot sell a product that people no longer want or did not want in the first place. The advertising graveyard is filled with products that simply died of old age, products that no amount of advertising could rejuvenate.

**Brand differentiation**  There is no purpose in advertising a product that cannot be differentiated or distinguished from others that appear to fill the same need. This is clearly shown by the lack of advertising for such commodities as vegetables, fruit, grains, meat, and natural fibers. Usually, such advertising as exists for these products is sponsored by a trade association, such as the Wool Bureau or the American Dairy Association, that seeks to stimulate primary demand. Manufacturers who cannot brand, label, or otherwise clearly identify their products will gain little, if any, benefit from their advertising.

**Market potential**   We know now that every product, to be successful, must satisfy the want or wants of a market segment. Most products satisfy more than one want. Toothpaste, for example, serves to clean the teeth, to freshen the breath, and, it is hoped, to prevent tooth decay or cavities. When we believe we know the *strongest reason* for the purchase of the product—and that may be price or brand name as well as the physical benefits its use confers—we have developed an *appeal.*

A product without strong, identifiable buying motives offers no appeal to prospective purchasers, and therefore, little opportunity to build such appeal by the use of advertising. It is not difficult to build an advertising appeal for quality luggage, for example, or for shoes or for automobiles. But it is extremely difficult to develop an appeal for men's hose or for towels or for clotheslines.

**The advertising budget**   Without a sufficient advertising budget, however, nothing can be accomplished. Most laymen are unaware of the magnitude of advertising costs today. A single page in *Good Housekeeping* costs $24,000. A single thirty-second television commercial can cost as much as $150,000, and no advertising campaign consists of only one ad in one magazine or one commercial on one television program. Launching an advertising program for a consumer product in just one major market can cost a company hundreds of thousands of dollars.

**The product must be good**   Most important, a product must deliver the benefit its advertising promises. The cost of getting a customer to switch from brand A to brand B is so high that brand B cannot afford to make that investment unless it is sure that the customer will find satisfaction in the product. Is it possible for a company to sell a poor product by means of an intensive advertising campaign? Possible yes; probable no. The American consumer is not fooled that easily. In any event, when a reputable manufacturer makes the sizable investment in advertising required to launch a new product, one can be confident that the product has been tested and retested.

## Advertising objectives

Advertising is one of the tools of marketing, a tool that is composed of many intangible aspects. The fact that we can count or measure the number of advertisements run in newspapers and magazines, the number of commercials played on radio or television in a given period of time, or the number of mailing pieces launched sometimes fools us into thinking that we are measuring the *impact* of our message when we are in fact only examining the means of transmission. What do we want advertising to do? What *can* advertising do?

Let's begin by describing what advertising *has* to do. First, it must *attract the attention* of the target market. If it fails to do this, it can accomplish nothing. Second, it must *interest* the target market to the point where they read, listen to, or watch the message. If it does not succeed in this, the message will not be delivered. Third, advertising must *inform* the people who read it, listen to it, or watch it. The message received must be the message intended by the advertiser. Fourth, to be considered effective, advertising must *stimulate* an economical portion of the target market to act, to change an attitude, or to adopt a new attitude that may lead to action that will be favorable to the advertiser in the future.

The specific objectives of each advertising campaign or program are different from those of every other campaign. Every company derives its objectives from its general marketing plan, and these objectives will vary as the product, competitive situation, economic conditions, company strengths, and other goals of the company change. However, the following are some of the most frequently stated advertising objectives:

1. to get orders

2. to get inquiries

3. to bring a general increase in sales

4. to provide leads for the sales force

5. to help open doors for the sales force[1]

6. to induce a trial use

7. to provide important information

8. to create or to change an attitude or opinion

These objectives are not listed in order of importance. Their importance is decided by each individual firm. Some firms will have only one of

[1] A word of explanation is necessary here to distinguish this objective from the preceding one. It is a fact that in the sale of industrial products there is more than one buying influence; some may be completely unknown to the sales force. We want to obtain a better image for our product and to gain entry for our salespeople to the offices of those buying influences that are ordinarily difficult to see.

them as a goal; others may have several. The choice will be determined by the company's market position at that moment and/or by their overall marketing objectives.

The objective of most retail advertising is to develop sales on the day the advertisement appears or the day after. The objective of the manufacturer is different because it is often difficult to identify orders resulting from advertising alone. The specific sales results stimulated by an advertising campaign generally merge into the flow of orders received by the firm. Coupons and coded addresses or booklet requests are time-honored methods for drawing inquiries that will identify the particular advertisement that triggered the response. Unfortunately, many prospects may not use the coupon or may write without using the key designed to identify the source of information.

## Advertising redefined

In Chapter 1, advertising was defined as the nonpersonal presentation of goods, services, or ideas. Up to this point, we have been considering advertising as an abstract whole. Upon closer inspection, however, we will find that advertising is, in fact, composed of many different segments, some independent, and some closely related.

**Retail and national advertising**   We may first divide advertising into retail advertising and national advertising. The simplest distinction to draw between the two is based on the firm doing the advertising. When a retail organization advertises, it is *retail advertising*. Usually this type of advertising is confined to a particular area. It might be illogical for a large retailer such as Marshall Field in Chicago to advertise in a nationally circulated magazine.

# Introducing new Flip Flash Super 10.
# Now you have two more chances to get it right.

Sylvania has gone the old flip flash two better.
Now, for use in all flip flash cameras, there's Flip Flash Super 10. With ten flashes instead of eight. Which gives you two extra shots at the perfect picture (plus a better match with 10 and 20 exposure films).

What's more, flash for flash, you pay less for Super 10 than you do the old 8-flash unit.*

And when it's time to flip your flash, Super 10 has a red indicator light that tells you so. To keep you from wasting a shot.

New Blue Dot™ Flip Flash Super 10.

Because Sylvania never leaves well enough alone.

**GTE SYLVANIA**

*Based on manufacturer's suggested retail price.

Such advertising would represent waste. Aside from the obvious retail nature of the sponsor, retail advertising can generally be distinguished from national advertising by its emphasis on actual price and its appeal for an immediate response. *Mail-order advertising* is simply a nonstore method of selling at retail. Instead of visiting a store, the consumer is expected to purchase the product through the mail.

When an advertisement is placed and paid for by the manufacturer of the product advertised, it is designated as *national advertising.* For those manufacturers whose distribution is national, their advertisements in a nationally circulated magazine are indeed aimed at a national audience. However, the designation also applies to a regional producer using a regional edition of a national magazine and to a producer of a nationally distributed product whose ads appear in a local newspaper or on a local radio or television station. The designation is determined by the nature of the firm. In fact, the designation, as we shall subsequently learn, is acknowledged by most media in their rate structure. Thus, if Marshall Field department stores were to advertise in a nationally circulated magazine, they would pay the lower *retail rate*, while a national advertiser in that same magazine would pay the higher *national rate.*

The market for Coca-Cola is broad and has two main branches. One goes through retailers who sell the product for home consumption in bottles and cans. The other goes through food service retailers and vending machines for on-premises consumption as a fountain drink. The target markets for this *business ad* are owners and managers of food service outlets and vending companies. The president of a large and well-known organization who endorses the product represents the *reference group* for the target market.

**Van Myers,
President, Wometco Vending**

## "Sure, Coke is a great soft drink. But, that's not enough anymore! People want more for their money."

The marketing specialists from Coca-Cola USA got the message. And went to work with Wometco's management. Van Myers, President of Wometco Vending, pioneered the launching of what turned out to be a very profitable solution to rising soft drink vending costs. The idea was to convert from a 9-oz. cup of Coca-Cola to a 12-oz. cup at 25¢. The 12-oz. size would satisfy larger thirst needs, increase the number of cups vended and give Wometco more profit.

**"The larger 12-ounce cup really caught on! Our unit sales went up 43.7% in the first week — 50.5% in the second."**

Van Myers was also looking for help in implementing the conversion. And that's what he got from Coca-Cola USA. Converting the equipment to accommodate the 12-oz. cup was accomplished by Wometco's engineers. And Coca-Cola USA's promotion experts had the perfect program to help introduce the new idea. A Levi Strauss Promotion that they felt couldn't miss. And they were right! The first week saw an increase of 43.7% in unit sales of those machines vending 12-oz. cups. The second week, the sales figures went up 50.5% over the original base. And the increase in profits was very healthy.

**"The program from Coca-Cola USA to increase profits with 12-oz. vending made everybody happy. Profits and the number of cups vended went up dramatically, even with the price increase."**

All in all, the introduction of the 12-oz. vending cup of Coca-Cola was so successful that now it's a priority consideration for the thousands of vending machines operated by Wometco. Indeed, the 12-oz. vending cup of Coca-Cola proved itself to be full of refreshment and profit. Which is a nice ending to the story.

| Facts about Wometco Enterprises Inc. |
| --- |
| Operates in 19 States, Canada, the Caribbean and South America |
| $280 Million in Sales  6,000 Employees |
| The Vending Division Operates 24,000 Vending Machines and Manual Food Service Centers in Schools, Industrial Plants and Institutions |

**Coke** *adds life* **and more profit to your business.**

Coca-Cola and Coke are registered trademarks which identify the same product of The Coca-Cola Company

**Consumer and business advertising**  The next distinction to be drawn is that between consumer advertising and business advertising. Now, this distinction is derived, not from the sponsor of the advertising, but from the target market. *Consumer advertising* is simply advertising directed to consumers of mass-marketed products. *Business advertising* is directed to people in business who, in their operating capacity, buy and/or specify products or services. Even business advertising on closer inspection can be divided into three areas, areas that occasionally overlap but are nevertheless quite distinct.

**Trade advertising**  is aimed at retailers and wholesalers who buy products or services for resale. Yes,

52

This *trade ad* is particularly interesting because the advertiser has demonstrated two facts to supermarket managers (and to us). First, notice how the advertiser has reminded the audience of the variety of products produced by the Campbell Soup Company. Second, the manufacturer has acknowledged a *demographic change* in the market—growing numbers of singles. To serve that market, Campbell's produces a number of its products in single-serving sizes.

# In four homes out of every ten someone eats alone every day.

Which is why four of our Chunky Soups now also come in cans that are exactly right for exactly one.

And why there are five Franco-American® products available in a size that's perfect for one.

And why there are 36 Swanson® frozen dinners and 11 frozen entrees, plus three meat pies that satisfy one.

And why our tomato juice also comes in a size that fills one juice glass for one juice drinker.

And why Campbell goes to the trouble of packing three varieties of beans in a size to serve one.

And why "V-8®" cocktail vegetable juice comes in a can that's just right for just one person.

And why we think it's worth the effort to make a half dozen varieties of Campbell's Soup for One.™

And why you'd be missing out on lots of additional sales if you weren't featuring Campbell's single serving sizes.

SINGLE SERVING SIZES FROM

*Campbell Soup Company*

HELPING BUILD MARKETS

services too. The insurance field and the travel industry are but two examples of service industries in which "producers" offer their "products" at wholesale prices to "retailers" (insurance agents and travel agents) who sell the "product" at retail.

**Industrial advertising,** another part of the broad category of business advertising, represents advertising of machinery, chemicals, raw materials, components, partially finished products, machine parts, and consumable supplies used by manufacturers in their production processes. Imagine the range of products that are promoted. In order to make refrigerators, for example, a manufacturer must buy steel; nuts and bolts; insulating material; plastic partitions; paints; machinery for bending,

The company that placed this *industrial ad* is well known for its consumer products, but here the emphasis is entirely different. What does the industrial buyer want? Style is not important, but durability and low maintenance are. The photograph and the headline "flag" the target market: any firms that use lift trucks. Note, too, the bold, sturdy looking typeface in the headline.

# FROM THE ENGINE UP

**That's how we build Toyota lift trucks to keep them going strong.**

We design each Toyota lift truck around the remarkable Toyota-built engine. It's what keeps them going strong and on the job. We aim for a harmonious balance between engine, transmission and mast. We produce our own parts and components under the strictest quality control to reduce breakdowns and lower maintenance costs. This detailed manufacturing helps assure you prompt parts supply and reliable after-sales service.

Your Toyota dealer is backed by a nationwide distribution network, and he can offer you a complete line of lift trucks with capacities from 1,200 lbs. to 33,000 lbs.

Let your Toyota dealer show you what owners and operators across the country already know: Toyota lift trucks keep going strong because they're built from the engine up.

**Toyota Industrial Trucks, U.S.A., Inc.** 1041 East 230th Street, Carson, California 90745

welding, and forming; nameplates; and materials for packing and crating. The factory itself needs floor-cleaning compounds, brooms and mops, cutting and lubricating oils. The building must be heated and cooled. The offices need typewriters, adding machines, office furniture, pencils, and floor waxes. As you can see, the list is extensive, and everything this company buys for production, ad-

ministration, and maintenance may be advertised by another company. No wonder there are over 3,000 business publications in the United States.

Somewhere in between trade advertising and industrial advertising lies advertising directed to service people. This market includes plumbers, electricians, auto repair shops, television repair shops, and hairdressers, as well as companies large

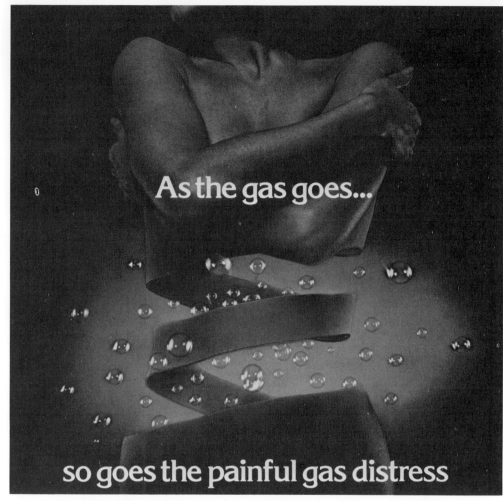

## As the gas goes...

## so goes the painful gas distress

**Mylicon-80 provides prompt and effective antiflatulent activity.**

Alters surface tension of the foam which entraps G.I. gas…causing the bubbles to coalesce.

Gas is then liberated for easier expulsion…by belching or by passing flatus.

## MYLICON®-80 HIGH-CAPACITY ANTIFLATULENT

(simethicone 80 mg.) STUART PHARMACEUTICALS | Division of ICI Americas Inc | Wilmington, DE 19897

and small that sell a service, but that must buy materials in order to perform that service. In order to sell their products to these service producers, manufacturers advertise as a component of their promotional mix.

**Professional advertising** is the term that best describes advertising directed to doctors, dentists, architects, hospitals, nursing homes, lawyers, and accountants. Doctors and dentists buy equipment for their treatment and examination rooms, but, more important, they prescribe the medications, treatments, and devices their patients buy. Accountants recommend financial control systems for their clients. Architects specify building products costing hundreds of thousands of dollars. Hos-

**Horowitz-Live!**
**The New York Philharmonic.**
**Zubin Mehta, conducting.**
**Sunday, September 24,**
**on NBC-TV.**

The concert of the year. The brightest event of the new television season.

It happens Sunday, September 24—live from Lincoln Center—when the legendary pianist Vladimir Horowitz performs Rachmaninoff's Piano Concerto No. 3 in D Minor with the New York Philharmonic under the direction of its new conductor, Zubin Mehta.

This special concert continues the celebration of the 50th anniversary year of Maestro Horowitz's American debut with the Philharmonic. It's part of a tradition of fine music programming by the Bell System that began with sponsorship of the memorable Bell Telephone Hour.

More good news: starting in 1979, and continuing for the next several years, the Bell System will sponsor the tours of some of America's finest symphony orchestras, reaching cities, towns and universities across the land. Watch for performance dates in your area.

And don't forget to be watching Sunday evening for Vladimir Horowitz, the New York Philharmonic and Zubin Mehta. An outstanding television event.

Sunday, Sept. 24, 5-6 p.m., EDT
NBC-TV

⊕ **Bell System**

An *institutional ad* designed to build goodwill for the Bell System. No attempt is made to sell anything. The headline instantly selects the audience: educated, middle class, and sophisticated. The ad is representative of a growing phenomenon in which advertisers use one medium to advertise their programs in another medium.

---

pitals buy furniture, food, equipment, pharmaceuticals—everything necessary to maintain a large, dynamic, complex organization that must care for, clothe, and feed hundreds of people.

We shall examine the interesting ramifications of business advertising in Chapter 20. Our object for the moment is merely to place it in its appropriate relationship with consumer advertising. *Farm advertising*, too, will be discussed in a later chapter. Farmers are both business people who buy machinery (tractors, milking machines, and so on) and chemicals (herbicides, insecticides, fertilizers) and consumers who buy mass-marketed goods such as refrigerators, automobiles, toothpaste, and shampoo.

**Institutional and public-service advertising** Another set of definitions is also called for, describing to a certain extent the *purposes* of the advertising. A firm uses different kinds of advertising for different markets, or it may use different kinds of advertising for the *same* market segments because it has different purposes. These classifications of advertising are not mutually exclusive. The terms are merely "handles" that enable us to understand what the purpose or strategy of the advertising may be. For instance, *institutional advertising* is intended to sell the consumer reasons for patronizing a firm other than the products or services it sells. Although no product may be featured, institutional advertising can do many things to enhance the reputation of

# MAN MADE FIBERS LIFE MADE BETTER

## Introducing the sign most garments are born under.

It's a great sign. Garments born under it can work all day in the fields, or go to a dance in the South of France. They can feel like suede or swing like silk. They can take every color under the sun, and drip-dry overnight. Life made better? The sign should read, "life made *incredibly* better."

If you're a retailer, where would you be if suddenly every garment made with man-made fibers disappeared from your store? Simple. You'd be in a virtually empty store.

If you're a manufacturer, where would you be if suddenly there were no man-made fibers? Simple. You'd be looking for work.

And if you're a consumer? Equally simple. You'd be giving up at least one day of your week to ironing. And all those clothes you love to wear wouldn't wear as long. They'd be tired out before you were tired of them.

It's high time man-made fibers were honored with their own sign. Come to think of it, they ought to have a monument.

**CELANESE**

This *institutional ad* was placed in such publications as *Women's Wear Daily* and *Clothes Magazine*. At the same time, however, it also appeared in *Linen Supply News*, a magazine circulated to laundry plants that rent uniforms to factories. Why would Celanese Corporation want to advertise to a target market several steps removed from the ultimate user of the product? The answer is that Celanese would like the laundry plants to specify garments made of man-made fibers. The manufacturers of such garments would then buy fabrics knit from man-made fibers to make these uniforms. Thus, by stimulating *primary demand*, Celanese hopes to increase the size of the market for man-made fibers.

## FAIRFAX M. CONE

Born in San Francisco in 1903, "Fax" Cone originally planned a career as an English teacher. On graduation from the University of California, however, he went to work for the *San Francisco Examiner*, where he spent the next three years as a want-ad clerk, writer, and illustrator. He then embarked on a new career, leaving the *Examiner* to take a job as an artist with an advertising agency in San Francisco. He soon realized, though, that this career, too, was not for him, since his color blindness would severely limit his success as an artist.

In 1929 he joined the San Francisco office of Lord & Thomas as a copywriter. He was a natural and gifted writer and he accepted the dictum of Albert Lasker, the head of Lord & Thomas, that advertising was *salesmanship in print*. He believed that the purpose of advertising was to deliver a message that was really in the interest of the reader. At Lord & Thomas he was responsible for writing advertising for Southern Pacific Railroad (still a client of Foote, Cone & Belding), the Dollar Steamship Lines, and Sun Maid raisins. He did his job so well that by 1938 he had become the manager of the Lord & Thomas office in San Francisco.

In 1940 Albert Lasker transferred Fairfax Cone to New York to work on the Lucky Strike cigarette account, for which the agency developed the advertising campaign that started with the slogan: LS/MFT—Lucky Strike Means Fine Tobacco. In 1942 Fax went to Chicago as executive vice-president. Three months later, when Albert Lasker retired, he joined with the managers of Lord & Thomas' New York and Los Angeles offices to form Foote, Cone & Belding. In its first year, the new agency had $22 million in billings.

During his active career, Fairfax Cone was involved in the creation of many well-known advertising themes—"When you care enough to send the very best" (Hallmark), "Which twin has the Toni?" and "Aren't you glad you use Dial?"

Fairfax Cone retired from Foote, Cone & Belding in 1970, remaining as a director of the company until 1975. He died in 1977 after a distinguished career that included work as a civic leader in the city of Chicago.

An outspoken critic of the advertising industry as well as a distinguished practitioner of advertising, Fairfax Cone constantly reminded his colleagues that:

> Punishment for sinning is swift and sure. It comes from a public that deeply resents being fooled and will not buy any new product that has failed to live up to its original promise.

One of the many *public-service* posters and advertisements prepared by the Advertising Council. This public-spirited message is trying to sell an idea to the public: "Prevent forest fires." Now in its thirty-eighth year of operation, the Advertising Council is a private, nonprofit corporation that is supported entirely by American business, including the advertising and communications industries. During its lifetime, the Advertising Council has helped to sell such ideas as "register and vote" and "buy U.S. savings bonds." More recently, the council has concerned itself with such issues as drug abuse, pollution, and crime prevention.

the company that, it is hoped, will yield some tangible benefits in the future. For example, some institutional advertising is intended to strengthen the company's image in the financial community. Other programs may help establish an "umbrella," or total product-line, image for the company that will provide support for the introduction of new products. In recent years, many companies have attempted to enhance their image by noncommercial support of cultural programs or by advertising support for social and environmental issues. *Public-service advertising* is advertising intended to sell an idea about a social problem: for instance, to offer citizens free legal assistance, to remind them to "help prevent forest fires," or to ask them to conserve energy. Some of these ads are sponsored by private companies to improve their public image; some by the media as a public service.

# Summary

The *promotional mix* is a combination of advertising, publicity, personal selling, and sales promotion that a company chooses for the purpose of increasing its sales and/or profits. Although our purpose in this textbook is the study of the advertising component, we should be aware that the advertising effort must complement all other marketing efforts. The job of advertising, broadly stated, is to make profitable sales economically and to make more sales than could be made without advertising.

The decision to invest in advertising is contingent upon the nature of the product, the nature of the market, the financial and productive capabilities of the firm, and the stage in the product's life cycle. In the introductory stage of this cycle, advertisers want to stimulate *primary demand* for the product advertised, that is, demand for all products of that type, regardless of brand. Later, they will concentrate on *selective demand,* which is demand for a particular brand. Advertisers attempt to stimulate demand for a product by giving consumers in the target market reasons to buy the product. The reason that they choose to emphasize is known as the *appeal.*

Although each company's advertising program will have unique objectives, the specific emphasis of any program will depend upon the kind of advertising the company is engaged in. Advertising may be divided into three general categories. The first is based on the sponsor of the advertising and includes *national advertising* and *retail advertising.* The second is based on the company's target market and may be divided into *consumer advertising* and *business advertising.* Business advertising may be further broken down into *trade, industrial,* and *professional.* The last category is based on the purpose of the advertising and contains *institutional advertising* and *public-service advertising.*

### QUESTIONS FOR DISCUSSION

1. Describe the relationship between advertising and marketing.

2. Imagine that all advertising has been banned. What alternatives would a manufacturer have to stimulate the sale of goods?

3. Why would a company with no goods to sell at a particular time continue to advertise?

4. Can you name any fruits or vegetables that have been successfully advertised? How did they do it?

5. Find examples of public-service advertising. Who is the advertiser (if identified)? What is the audience expected to do?

6. Find examples of advertising intended to stimulate primary demand.

7. Find an advertisement in which the product is at the beginning of its life cycle. Find an advertisement for a mature product. What differences do you find between the advertisements?

8. How would you approach the market if you were assigned the task of increasing sales for a seasonal food such as turkeys or mince pies, which are usually associated with Thanksgiving and Christmas.

9. Select a product you know, preferably one you like, and specify marketing and advertising objectives.

10. How can advertising be used to promote
    a. conserving energy
    b. increasing attendance at a museum
    c. hiring minority individuals
    d. fund raising for a local charity

### Sources and suggestions for further reading

Chase, Cochrane, and Barasch, Kenneth L. *Marketing Problem Solver.* 2d ed. Radnor, Pa.: Chilton Book Company, 1977.

Cundiff, Edward W.; Still, Richard R.; and Govoni, Norman A. P. *Fundamentals of Modern Marketing.* 2d ed. Englewood Cliffs, N.J.: Prentice-Hall, 1976.

Dunn, S. Watson. *Advertising.* New York: Holt, Rinehart and Winston, 1969.

Fox, Edward J., and Wheatley, Edward W. *Modern Marketing.* Glenview, Ill.: Scott, Foresman and Company, 1978.

Littlefield, James E. *Readings in Advertising.* St. Paul: West Publishing Co., 1975.

Prasad, V. Kanti, and Ring, L. Winston. "Measuring Sales Effects of Some Marketing Mix Variables and Their Interactions." *Journal of Marketing Research* (November 1976).

Pride, William M., and Ferrell, O. C. *Marketing: Basic Concepts and Decisions.* Boston: Houghton Mifflin, 1976.

Stanton, William J. *Fundamentals of Marketing.* 5th ed. New York: McGraw-Hill, 1978.

# THE ADVERTISING BUSINESS

**The advertiser**

Responsibilities of the advertising
manager
The advertising department

**The advertising agency**

The development of the agency
Agency organization
What does an agency do?
Innovations in the agency business

Agency compensation
The commission system
Charges for out-of-pocket expenses
Fee arrangements
Agency recognition
House agencies
More on the fee system
Serving competing advertisers

**Advertising media**

**Ancillary advertising services**

## WORKING VOCABULARY

agency of record
full-service agency
account executive

boutique agency
*a la carte* service
agency network

recognition
house agency

CHAPTER 4

# the advertising business

Advertising agencies develop and prepare advertising. *These are what are customarily called the creative functions of an agency—the glamor areas of a business mythologized by Hollywood and novelists. But for success, advertising agencies must also depend heavily on media planning and placement as well as . . . account development, client contact, new-business-getting, and financial know-how.*

JAMES V. O'GARA
*"The Advertising Agency—What It Is and What It Does"*

VIRTUALLY EVERY BUSINESS ORGANIZATION (and many nonbusiness organizations) uses advertising in one form or another. For the manufacturer of private brands, advertising may be entirely unnecessary. For the corner grocery store, advertising may be precluded by the size and location of the market. For many other companies, a sales letter, a point-of-sale sign, or a simple circular is all the advertising they will do. However, our concern here is with the national advertiser of consumer products. If you will refer to the list of leading advertisers in Chapter 1, you will note that food advertising represents the largest volume of expen-

ditures, followed by drugs and cosmetics, automobiles, soaps and household cleansers, and cigarettes.

## The advertiser

Most modern businesses have an advertising department. The title of the person responsible for managing this department and the exact range of his or her responsibilities will vary from company to company. Some companies have an *advertising manager;* others, a *director of advertising;* still

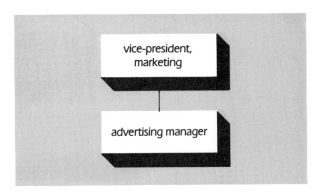

When advertising is grouped with marketing, as it is in most manufacturing companies, the advertising manager reports to the marketing vice-president.

In some companies, the advertising manager may be one additional step removed from the chief marketing executive.

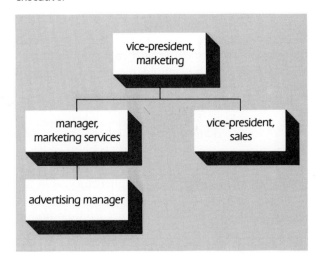

In another variation, the vice-president, sales, is the chief marketing executive. In the field, the terms *vice-president, sales* and *vice-president, marketing* are sometimes used interchangeably.

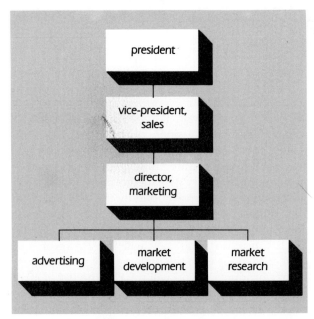

THE ADVERTISING BUSINESS

others, a *vice-president for advertising*. But regardless of title, the person responsible for the firm's advertising effort performs certain functions that are common to all.

## Responsibilities of the advertising manager

The advertising manager is responsible for *planning the company's advertising*. This planning cannot be delegated to the company's advertising agency because the advertising plan is an integral part of the firm's marketing plan. As such, it must be coordinated with all the company's other operations — with production, with finance, and of course, with marketing. Such coordination can only be accomplished by a person *in the company* who has ready access to all the other departments of the company. How high in the corporate hierarchy the advertising manager sits depends on the company and the importance its management attaches to the advertising effort.

If advertising is a subfunction under marketing or sales, the high-level executive is typically a vice-president of marketing or sales or a manager or director of marketing. If advertising lies outside the marketing or sales department, it is most often the responsibility of general management, such as the president or an executive vice-president at corporate headquarters, or of a division manager at that level.[1]

Advertising managers *help select and evaluate the agency.* We say *help select* because in many instances the choice of agency is considered so

important that top management participates in the selection process. Advertising managers then *supervise the execution* of the advertising plan by the agency. They work closely with the agency in the development of the budget, the media schedule, and the creation of the individual advertisements. An important aspect of advertising managers' jobs involves selling the advertising plan to the top management of their firms. They must also work closely with the sales department to be sure that the firm's advertising effort will benefit both the sales force and the distribution network.

Some large companies operate with individual *product managers*, who may also supervise the tasks of advertising under the direction of a general advertising manager. In some organizations, the product manager for a particular brand serves as a liaison between the production department and the sales department. Under such an arrangement, there is a separate advertising manager for each product line who reports to the general advertising manager as well as to the product manager.

## The advertising department

Large national advertisers usually maintain their own fully staffed advertising department as well as retaining the services of an agency. Very large advertisers, in fact, will employ several agencies as well as their own very large advertising department. The *advertising department,* in addition to coordinating and supervising the work of the agency, will tend to work on the myriad of little advertising jobs such as packaging, direct-mail advertising, company house organs, point-of-purchase materials, displays, sales literature, trade shows, and dealer aids that can be done more efficiently within the company.

---

[1] For detailed reporting relationships of the corporate advertising head in a number of companies, see *Top Management Organization in Divisionalized Companies*, Studies in Personnel Policy, no. 195 (New York: National Industrial Conference Board, 1965).

Large advertisers that employ more than one advertising agency will designate one of those agencies as agency of record. The *agency of record* will coordinate the media schedules of the various agencies to be certain that the advertiser is receiving the most advantageous rate. For example, if agency A places six pages of advertising in magazine X and agency B (agency for a different product of the same company) also places six pages in the same magazine X, the advertiser is entitled to receive the rate for twelve pages of advertising, which is lower than the rate for six pages.

## The advertising agency

There are now more than 7,000 advertising agencies in the United States, with headquarters and branch offices in every major city in the country. Although some of these agencies are small, employing only one or two people, many are multinational corporations with thousands of employees in branch offices located throughout the world. In 1978, there were 279 agencies in the United States that reported gross incomes of more than $1 million. In that same year, the twenty-five largest agencies had a combined gross income of more than $2.37 billion.

### The development of the agency

In describing the history of advertising in Chapter 1, we noted that today's full-service agency evolved from the business of the publisher's agent, who had acted as a broker of advertising space in newspapers and magazines. The agent actually represented the media, not the advertisers. There were no published advertising rates until 1875, when N. W. Ayer, working for the advertiser rather than the media, provided information on the rates charged by the newspapers and religious magazines he represented. Gradually, agents began to become less interested in selling advertising space and more interested in helping the advertiser with copy and art services. The space brokerage business was dealt a final blow in 1887, with the establishment of the American Newspaper Publishers Association. Newspapers that joined the ANPA began to publish their advertising rates and to provide advertisers with information about their circulation. The era during which blocks of newspaper space, sold to brokers, were peddled at whatever price they could get had ended.[2]

### Agency organization

Successful advertising agencies, like most business organizations, depend on the efficient operation of such day-to-day internal functions as accounting, personnel, and administrative management. Though most agencies are started and run by creative or marketing people, the agency must succeed as a business, not simply as a "hot shop" or a winner of advertising awards. In fact, after an advertising agency is established, much of its growth comes from the increased advertising expenditures that result from the higher sales volume that it has helped the advertiser achieve. Other growth must come from new business, from mergers, from acquisitions, and from the tremendous expansion of foreign billings. The foreign billings of American agencies have increased over 100 percent in the

[2] Ralph M. Hower, *History of an Advertising Agency* (Cambridge, Mass.: Harvard University Press, 1949), p. 404.

| | | | World Gross Income | | U.S. Gross Income | | World Billing | | U.S. Billing | |
|---|---|---|---|---|---|---|---|---|---|---|

## TOP 25 U.S. ADVERTISING AGENCIES
(World billings)

| 1978 World Income Rank | U.S. Income Rank | Agency | World Gross Income 1978 (millions) | 1977 | U.S. Gross Income 1978 (millions) | 1977 | World Billing 1978 (millions) | 1977 | U.S. Billing 1978 (millions) | 1977 |
|---|---|---|---|---|---|---|---|---|---|---|
| 1 | 2 | J. Walter Thompson Co. | $221.5 | $188.8 | $106.6 | $ 92.8 | $1,476.5 | $1,258.9 | $710.4 | $619.0 |
| 2 | 9 | McCann-Erickson | 210.6 | 162.6 | 59.5 | 51.1 | 1,404.5 | 1,083.5 | 396.5 | 339.6 |
| 3 | 1 | Young & Rubicam | 203.8 | 169.9 | 118.0 | 101.1 | 1,359.5 | 1,133.4 | 787.7 | 674.5 |
| 4 | 6 | Ogilvy & Mather International | 153.9 | 127.7 | 71.4 | 62.9 | 1,003.7 | 872.2 | 472.3 | 450.5 |
| 5 | 4 | BBDO International | 132.4 | 108.6 | 80.1 | 66.9 | 890.0 | 734.3 | 541.5 | 456.5 |
| 6 | 10 | Ted Bates & Co. | 130.9 | 101.0 | 54.9 | 45.4 | 890.0 | 751.2 | 424.8 | 372.3 |
| 7 | 3 | Leo Burnett Co. | 128.2 | 117.3 | 89.0 | 84.3 | 865.1 | 795.1 | 604.0 | 575.0 |
| 8 | 23 | SSC&B | 127.6 | 113.4 | 26.7 | 25.2 | 840.5 | 724.0 | 175.9 | 163.0 |
| 9 | 5 | Foote, Cone & Belding | 111.0 | 85.5 | 75.7 | 59.0 | 740.3 | 540.1 | 504.8 | 393.0 |
| 10 | 13 | D'Arcy-MacManus & Masius | 104.7 | 84.7 | 50.0 | 43.6 | 698.8 | 565.0 | 333.7 | 290.5 |
| 11 | 7 | Grey Advertising | 90.3 | 78.7 | 65.2 | 55.5 | 600.3 | 525.0 | 433.0 | 370.0 |
| 12 | 8 | Doyle Dane Bernbach | 90.0 | 73.4 | 64.5 | 52.3 | 600.0 | 491.0 | 430.0 | 350.0 |
| 13 | 18 | Compton Advertising | 82.7 | *63.7 | 36.0 | 19.9 | 557.4 | 427.5 | 246.2 | 135.0 |
| 14 | 12 | Benton & Bowles | 77.0 | 68.7 | 50.1 | 44.4 | 554.2 | 470.4 | 369.8 | 304.7 |
| 15 | 19 | Campbell-Ewald | 70.0 | 59.5 | 35.0 | 33.5 | 466.7 | 396.9 | 233.1 | 224.0 |
| 16 | 11 | Dancer Fitzgerald Sample | 56.5 | 43.0 | 51.5 | 40.0 | 459.0 | 380.0 | 362.0 | 305.0 |
| 17 | 28 | Norman, Craig & Kummel | 48.2 | 42.5 | 13.6 | 13.9 | 321.2 | 283.3 | 90.4 | 92.6 |
| 18 | 17 | Needham, Harper & Steers | 47.0 | 38.0 | 38.1 | 31.2 | 315.0 | 257.2 | 254.1 | 208.1 |
| 19 | 14 | N W Ayer ABH International | 46.5 | 36.8 | 46.5 | 36.8 | 310.5 | 245.7 | 310.5 | 245.7 |
| 20 | 21 | Marsteller Inc. | 45.9 | 36.0 | 32.9 | 27.1 | 306.2 | 240.2 | 225.0 | 180.6 |
| 21 | 15 | Wells, Rich, Greene | 45.4 | 39.6 | 44.1 | 38.5 | 302.5 | 264.2 | 293.8 | 256.4 |
| 22 | 23 | Kenyon & Eckhardt | 41.7 | 52.3 | 26.7 | 25.3 | 278.3 | 348.0 | 178.3 | 168.6 |
| 23 | 16 | William Esty Co. | 41.2 | 33.0 | 41.2 | 33.0 | 275.0 | 220.0 | 275.0 | 220.0 |
| 24 | 20 | Bozell & Jacobs International | 34.5 | 27.1 | 34.0 | 26.8 | 230.2 | 181.9 | 227.1 | 180.3 |
| 25 | 26 | Ketchum, MacLeod & Grove | 33.0 | 30.0 | 24.5 | 23.0 | 223.6 | 202.4 | 163.2 | 153.6 |

Reprinted with permission from the March 14, 1979 issue of *Advertising Age*. Copyright by Crain Communications, Inc.

Hoffman-York is a *full-service* advertising agency, and in this advertisement, which appeared in *Advertising Age,* they are soliciting new clients. The copy describes the kinds of services that this agency provides and the clients that they now serve.

# Why does Walker, America's best selling muffler, choose to tune in with Hoffman-York?

The answers: total involvement and top-notch creativity.

At Hoffman-York, we believe the same team that plans the overall strategy, creates the advertising and executes the campaigns should show just as much enthusiasm in every facet of the total communications program.

Walker executives like it that way, too.

They like the creative quality of our television and radio commercials. But just as important is that we give top-drawer attention to their trade-paper advertising. Co-op advertising programs. POP materials. Yellow-page programs. Audio-visual presentations. And the field-promotion work needed to help them maintain their leadership position in the marketplace.

We believe full service should mean just that. Full service. Shrewd marketing strategies. Smart media planning and buying, in-depth research. And the willingness to get involved in the tough, unglamorous jobs that giant agencies shy away from.

We feel we owe service like this to all of our clients—and our record of consistent and healthy growth to over $30 million in billings shows our clients believe we're right.

If you'd like to hear more about an agency that looks forward to total involvement in client marketing programs, pick up the phone and call Gene Lawler at (414) 259-2000. He's our president and a very active member of the team. Hoffman-York, Inc., 2300 N. Mayfair Road, Milwaukee, WI 53226.

# HOFFMAN YORK
### Advertising & Public Relations Milwaukee

**CONSUMER CLIENTS**  Amity Leather   Bank of Commerce   Canada Dry   Dubuque Packing   Field Packing   Johnson Outboards   McDonald's   North Central Airlines   OMC Stern Drive   Oster   Sentry Food Stores   Simplicity   Time Insurance   Walker   Wisconsin Public Service

**BUSINESS CLIENTS**  Allen-Bradley   Allis-Chalmers   A.O. Smith   Artos Engineering   Bay West Paper   Bradley   Brillion   Bucyrus-Erie   Fiat-Allis   Hamilton Industries   Harnischfeger   Kimberly-Clark   Rexnord   SPI Lighting

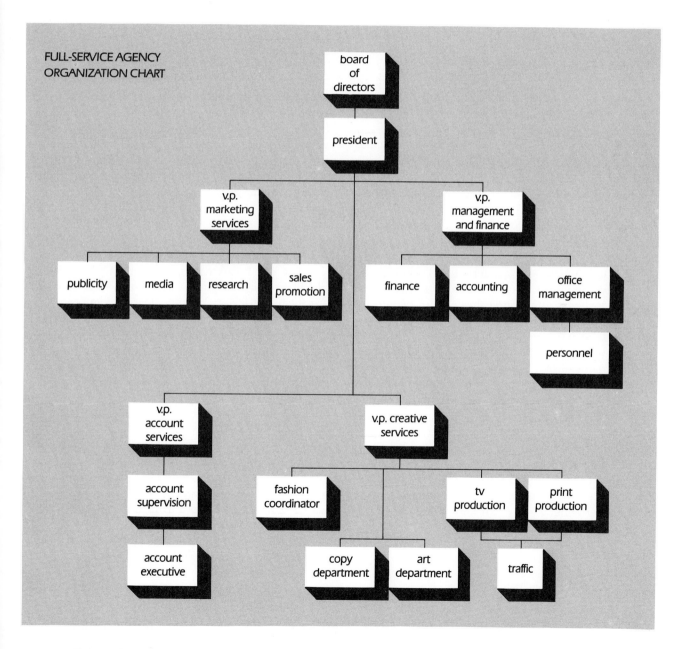

FULL-SERVICE AGENCY
ORGANIZATION CHART

board of directors

president

v.p. marketing services

v.p. management and finance

publicity

media

research

sales promotion

finance

accounting

office management

personnel

v.p. account services

v.p. creative services

account supervision

account executive

fashion coordinator

tv production

print production

copy department

art department

traffic

past ten years. As you can see from the chart on page 67, the largest agency in 1978, J. Walter Thompson Co., received more income from its operations outside the United States ($114.9 million) than it did from its domestic operations ($106.6 million). Today, every major agency in the United States has operating branches in every important world market.[3]

The organization of the agency will differ with its size, the kind of services it provides, and the requirements of its clients. The agency may operate on a departmentalized basis, with the usual departments, including account service, market research, copy, art, media, production, traffic, and public relations.

The account service department consists of account executives, each of whom works with one or more clients on a regular basis. The *account executive* maintains client contact; that is, he or she is the person who provides the liaison between the various departments of the agency and the advertising manager of the client company. This is not to say that other members of the agency staff are not involved in client-agency discussions, but generally only the account executive provides continuous contact. To the agency, account executives bring the objectives desired by the client. To the client, they bring the agency's recommended budget, the proposed media schedules, and the creative suggestions of the agency staff. All the departments of the advertising agency work together toward a common goal—a deadline for the presentation of their recommendations for the client's advertising program.

In recent years, many of the larger agencies have favored a matrix-type organization. Under this arrangement, a creative group is formed by copywriters, artists, television producers, and media buyers, all working as a team under a creative group head and responsible to an account executive who is the liaison between the agency and the client. Sometimes media people may not be included in the group, and the media department will remain as a separate, centralized service unit for the various creative groups. In a similar way, the group can also call on other staff services, such as marketing research, when required.

The Leo Burnett advertising agency, for example, utilizes a matrix organization in which teams are formed to work on one large account or, in some cases, as many as three accounts. The team, which is under the supervision of a senior management member, may consist of an account supervisor and one or more account executives. This group provides client contact and overall supervision of the advertising programs. To make the plans operational, the management group utilizes the services of a media team consisting of space and time buyers supervised by media and program analysts and a creative team of writers and artists. Each account also has a research supervisor and a staff assigned to it. The details of production are taken care of by adding people from broadcast production and print production to the account team and by providing coordinators who oversee traffic (the flow of orders and material) and other financial and administrative details.

The advantage of the group system is the creative growth and stimulation that a group of people experience when working together closely and

---

[3] For example, Grey Advertising, Inc., which ranked eleventh among U.S. advertising agencies for world billings in 1978, has offices in Amsterdam-Baarn, Auckland, Brasilia, Brussels, Buenos Aires, Caracas, Dusseldorf, Gothenburg, Johannesburg, London, Madrid, Milan, Montreal, Oslo, Paris, Rio De Janeiro, Sao Paulo, Stockholm, Sydney, Tokyo, Toronto, and Vienna.

This chart of a *matrix organization* does not show the entire company as most organizational charts do. Instead it shows the group or team that is assembled to "service" one or more accounts, depending on the volume and complexity of the clients' advertising programs.

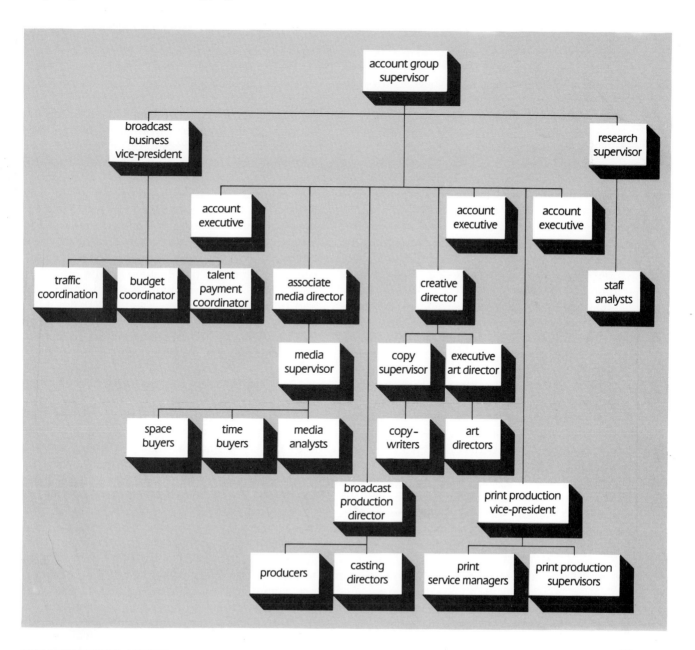

maintaining a continuous relationship with a particular advertiser. But every agency adapts its organizational structure as needed. Some agencies maintain large internal art staffs, whereas others retain a few *art directors* and buy their finished art from studios and free-lance artists as needed.

## What does an agency do?

A *full-service agency* performs creative services, of course, but those creative services incorporate many other important contributions to the advertiser's marketing program as well. The agency begins by providing an *objective viewpoint*. All too often, a firm's marketing problems may be obscured by internal politics, vested interests, and traditional attitudes.

Basically, the full-service agency's marketing experts study the client's product or service and objectively analyze its strengths and weaknesses relative to those of competing products. The media department applies a knowledge of available media that might be utilized to carry the advertiser's message. The creative department develops ideas that will transmit the advertiser's message with persuasive impact and then produces the individual ads and commercials. The media department will analyze the media and select those that will be most effective in delivering the message to the target market. The media department, working with the advertiser's budget, contracts with the various media for space and time. They issue instructions to the media in the form of an insertion order and verify the insertion; that is, they make certain that the ad did appear in print or that the commercial was aired as specified. Administrative services within the agency oversee both the billing to the advertiser and the payment to media and suppliers and perform the other necessary administrative chores common to every business.

For some agencies, these functions may represent only the tip of the iceberg. Many agencies also provide marketing counsel and create brochures, catalogs, and stockholders' reports. They design packages and trademarks. They perform or supervise important market research. They often prepare and implement publicity and public relations programs.

Although the subject of retail advertising will be taken up in Chapter 19, it is appropriate to mention here that, in general, retailers do not employ advertising agencies. There are two reasons for this: (1) the nature of the retail operation—which allows very little time for the creation of the advertisements, and (2) the distinction made by newspapers and other media between retail advertising rates and national rates. Retail rates are lower, and therefore the media do not pay the agency a commission for placing this type of advertisement.

## Innovations in the agency business

Up to this point we have been discussing the full-service agency. Most agencies today are full service—that is, they make available to their clients a *range* of advertising services. Naturally, with the larger agencies, the range is wide indeed. With smaller agencies, the range is narrower, but full service nevertheless for the clients they serve. Recently, small creative services known as *boutique agencies* have come into existence. The word *boutique* derives from the field of retailing. We expect to find a wide range of merchandise in a department store and a wide range of styles, sizes, and colors in every department. But in a *boutique*—a small store—we expect to find only a very narrow

**As we see it, the role advertising agencies play in American business today is to assimilate, interpret, analyze, interrelate and utilize an ever-expanding array of component factors, techniques and procedures, including such diverse items as** R&D, Cost of Goods, A to S ratio, Pipeline, Profitability, Warehousing, Return on Investment, Distribution, Labor Costs, Factory Sales, Unit Cost, Capital Investment, Sales Objectives, Trade Relations, P.E.R.T., Cash Flow, A.D.I., Sales Force, Trade Areas, SAMI, Earnings, Shares, Competition, Corporate Image, Government Regulations, Allowances, Demographics, Psychographics, Usage and Attitude, Aided Awareness, Unaided Awareness, Focus Groups, Recall, Attribute Scale, Questionnaire, Regression Analysis, Index, Mean, Percentile, Mode 1, Norm, Profile, Response, Cross Tabulation, Sample, Market Penetration, Correlation, Top of Mind, Qualitative, Test Market, Ratio Analysis, Market Segmentation, Statistical Significance, Heads of Households, Quantitative, Mall Intercept, Image Perception, Personal Interviews, Marketing Objective, Position Paper, Creative Strategy, Copy Platform, Media Strategy, Frequency, Reach, CPM, Gross Rating Points, Media Allocation, Concept, Space Unit, Spot Buys, Prime Time, Fringe, Regional Buy, Copy, Artwork, Illustration, Comp Layout, Photography, Storyboards, Typography, Timetables, Roughs, Themes, Format, Music, Suppliers, Deadlines, Traffic, Bids, Print Production, Casting, Dailies, Etch Proofs, Engraving, Mnemonic Devices, Screens, Inter-negs, Opticals, VTR, Proofs, Keylines, Answer Prints, Tape Transfers, Recording, Dubbing, Mixing, Veloxes, Release Prints, etc. **and through the application of common sense, intuition and that elusive commodity known as creativity, develop and disseminate**

**The
Selling
Idea.**

**It's that simple.**

# PKG/Cunningham & Walsh Inc.

A new name in the Chicago advertising community resulting from the merger of Post • Keyes • Gardner and Cunningham & Walsh.

875 NORTH MICHIGAN AVENUE, CHICAGO, IL 60611, (312) 943-9400 • NEW YORK • LOS ANGELES • SAN FRANCISCO

Marcoa is an advertising company, but unlike most advertising agencies, this organization does not place advertising in media. Instead, they create advertising that

# We're 5 and growing. By helping

### Encyclopaedia Britannica

"MARCOA has been one of the key factors in creating the effective lead advertising which first <u>successfully introduced Britannica 3 and then built and maintained our current momentum.</u>"

**Ray Markman**
Vice President
Marketing

### Allstate Insurance Company

<u>Direct marketing of insurance gets bigger each year at Allstate.</u> MARCOA's involvement starts with helping in the development of concept and rationale through creative, production and analysis of results. If you want to know more about MARCOA's contribution to Allstate's growth, call (312) 291-5602 and ask for...

**John Flieder**
Asst. Vice President
Direct Response Marketing

### Heath Company (Schlumberger)

"MARCOA helped us reach new levels of understanding in the analysis of 'request' advertising and direct marketing through catalogs—and, more important, in <u>helping us reach new highs in sales from those catalogs.</u> We even converted former customers who hadn't bought for up to eight years into active buyers at an unprecedented rate. If you want to know more about MARCOA's contribution to our growth, call me at (616) 982-3200."

**Bob Gernand**
Director of Advertising

### The Butterfly Group/ World of Beauty (G.R.I. Corp.)

"We've worked with MARCOA from the day they opened their doors five years ago. Since then, <u>more than 10 million beauty-conscious women have joined The Butterfly Group,</u> responding directly to our advertising. Beautiful! That's just one way MARCOA has contributed to our growth..."

### S.A.V.E. (G.R.I. Corp.)

"From scratch, MARCOA helped us launch—and profit from—our package-goods continuity plan. They even named it: S.A.V.E.—Shoppers' Association for Value and Economy. It's now a going enterprise—<u>one of the fastest growing clubs in the country.</u> That's another way MARCOA has contributed to our growth..."

### Homeward House (G.R.I. Corp.)

"MARCOA's believable, effective advertising helps us sell our exclusive Homeward House patterns of Oneida stainless on our exclusive continuity mail order plan. <u>It works, profitably.</u> If you want to know more about MARCOA's contribution to our growth for The Butterfly Group, S.A.V.E., and Homeward House, call me at (312) 977-3780."

**Tony DeNunzio**
Vice President Advertising

**"After five years, we have a lot to smile about!"**

encourages dealers and consumers to order the advertised product directly from the advertiser. This is known as *direct-response advertising.*

---

# our clients grow even more.

### Mercury Marine/ Mercury Outboards (Brunswick Corp.)

"How could direct response disciplines fit into our dealer distribution system? MARCOA showed us—with the most successful dealer traffic and sales campaign we've ever run. Our dealers loved it. And it's all measurable. We know our cost per inquiry and cost per sale for each media source and each dealer. If you want to know more about MARCOA's contribution to our growth, call me at (414) 921-8220."

**Lynn Mellenthien**
Advertising Director

### Mercury Marine/Quicksilver (Brunswick Corp.)

"If MARCOA could help us sell outboard motors through dealers using direct response techniques, could they improve accessories sales too? Yes. . .oils, props, instruments, more. We're building more traffic and sales for our dealers than ever. If you want to know more about MARCOA's contribution to our growth, call me at (414) 921-8220."

**Steve Cummings**
Advertising Manager

### Douglas Dunhill (Cordura Corp.)

"From appliances to fine art, our mail order and space ad merchandising to Gulf, Texaco and other credit card holders makes us one of the country's largest mailers and direct response advertisers. We mail over 150,000,000 pieces a year and advertise in more than 50 different publications. If you want to know more about MARCOA's contribution to our growth, call me at (312) 786-1700."

**Tom McKenna**
Senior Vice President
Creative

### Fashion Finds (Aparacor, Inc.)

"How do you market over-ordered party-plan women's fashions in limited quantities at each season's end? MARCOA helped us turn inventory liquidation into a growing profit center at Aparacor through regular Fashion Finds big sale catalog mailings. If you want to know more about MARCOA's contribution to our growth, call me at (312) 492-1400."

**Jim Davis**
President

### MARCOA'S Fifth Birthday

"For five years, we've measured ourselves by our contributions to our clients' growth. The results speak for themselves. If you'd like to know how MARCOA Direct Advertising can contribute to your company's growth, call me at (312) 454-0660. Or drop me a note on your company letterhead."

**David Hefter**
President

# MARCOA
## DIRECT ADVERTISING, INC.
### 10 South Riverside Plaza, Chicago, Illinois 60606

Although it is not an advertising agency, D. L. Blair provides an important component of the promotional mix—sales promotion. It takes specialized knowledge to organize the sweepstakes and contests that are part of the promotional effort of many companies. Blair works with the advertiser and the advertiser's agency to build a program that, as the ad states, "increases sales, share of market, advertising awareness and accelerated awareness of product and/or package improvement."

# HOW TO RUN A SUCCESSFUL SWEEPSTAKES.

Running a sweepstakes is a lot like entering a Grand Prix Race. Success demands meticulous planning, a well-engineered, perfectly tooled vehicle, experience with the track conditions and an almost palpable desire to succeed. Make no mistake about it. Make a mistake in the planning and design, and you may never get your sweepstakes on the track. Make an error in execution, and you may find yourself behind the wheel of a disaster. But plan and execute carefully, knowledgeably and with some smarts, and you've got a winner.

## Sweepstakes and contests: What they can do and what they can't do.

Sweepstakes and contests have proven themselves as extremely important promotion tools in the hands of capable marketers. Marketers savvy enough to recognize that a sweepstakes isn't intended as a replacement for strong creative advertising, a decent product, media support or as a panacea when all else fails. But, given a good product, decent creative, a fair level of media support and a sensible strategy, sweepstakes and contests can do lots of nice things. Nice things like increasing sales, share of market, advertising awareness and accelerated awareness of product and/or package improvement.

## Where to begin.

If you're thinking of running a sweepstakes or contest, the place to start is with a good sweepstakes company. Without their experience and acumen, chances for success are negligible.

A good consumer sales-promotion company, for example, understands the ins and outs and ups and downs of the various laws and regulations governing sweepstakes, contests and lotteries in each of the 50 states. And, yes, they may markedly differ from state to state. A sales-promotion agency can help untangle the federal red tape. A good consumer sales-promotion company can work with you and your advertising agency to help develop the theme and the structure of your sweepstakes. It should be big enough so it can supply you with: (a) promotion research, (b) creative development, (c) prize selection and structure and (d) complete fulfillment. It should also be smart enough and flexible enough to give you only those elements of a sweepstakes package which you really require.

## Picking a sweepstakes company. Why not the best?

In recommending a company to run your sweepstakes, we'll admit to a bias, here and now. We're D.L. Blair, and since we are paying for this ad, it's not surprising that we recommend (you guessed it) D.L. Blair. But for a more objective viewpoint, let's look where the majority of America's, and the world's, best and brightest marketers look for SWEEPSTAKES help.

## More major package-goods clients than BBDO, SSC&B, Ted Bates and Ogilvy & Mather combined.

When it comes to consumer sales promotion in general, and sweepstakes in particular, more large advertisers come to D.L. Blair than to all other similar companies combined. Of the top Fortune "50," 35 count themselves as clients of D.L. Blair. Of the 10 largest U.S. magazines, 5 are our clients. Worldwide, we are, according to Advertising Age, the second-largest sales-promotion company and by far the world's largest sweepstakes company.

## D.L. Blair. What we can do for you.

If you're thinking of running a sweepstakes or contest, think about this. D.L. Blair has run more successful sweepstakes than all other sweepstake companies combined. If it has to do with sweepstakes, we do it all. Or any part of it. For more information as to what sweepstakes can do for your product and, more specifically, what D.L. Blair can do for your company, get in touch with our president and CEO, Tom Conlon. Drop Tom a note or, better yet, give him a call at (212) 688-1500. He'd love to tell you more about us and how we can help— and all, of course, in the strictest of confidence.

# D.L.BLAIR

**We're number one in more ways than one.**

185 Great Neck Road., Great Neck, N.Y. 11021 • (516) 487-9200    1548 Front St., Blair, Nebraska 68008 • (402) 426-4701

Media Basics, Inc., is an *a la carte* advertising agency that, according to its ad, negotiates for and buys media time and space. Most print media do not have negotiable rates, but television rates are often negotiated. The advertiser may use this organization for media services and hire the services of other agencies for creative work.

range of expensive, highly styled merchandise in a limited size range. So it is with the boutique agency: It offers advertisers very creative, very limited, and very expensive services.

Other agencylike firms include independent *media-buying services*, which purport to obtain the best media buys. There is also *a la carte service*, in which the advertiser negotiates for the use of certain services of a full-service agency, such as a package design or a one-time program. But none of these agency services represent a threat to the full-service agencies, whose billings continue to grow year after year.

Over the years, advertising agencies have organized *networks*—generally loose affiliations of small- and medium-size agencies. Networks were originally founded as trade associations in which small operators could get together to discuss common interests, but the member agencies soon began to trade work assignments, particularly when one agency was involved in buying space in newspapers or time on radio or television in unfamiliar areas. An agency in Minneapolis, for example, might have an assignment that involved advertising in the New York and San Francisco markets. Which newspaper would be most appropriate? Which radio station? Which television station? The local agency, very knowledgeable about local media, could, in effect, become the branch office for the agency in Minneapolis, making that agency's services national in scope.

## Agency compensation

Agencies are compensated for their services in three ways: (1) They receive a commission from most media for advertisements they place, (2) they add a percentage charge to the bill for materials

and services (other than media) that they purchase for their client; and (3) they operate on a fee basis.

**The commission system**   Most agencies derive the greater part of their income from commissions that they receive for placing advertisements in the media. The commission system works as follows: An advertising agency places an advertisement in one of the media, say a local newspaper, at a cost of $100. The agency then bills its client $100 for the cost of running the advertisement. From that $100, the agency then deducts a commission of 15 percent and remits the remainder, in this case $85, to the newspaper. There is usually a 2 percent discount on the net amount for prompt payment that the agency passes along to the advertiser. Although most media pay the agency a 15 percent commission, outdoor media usually pay a 16 2/3 percent commission.

There has been some criticism of the commission system. Misunderstandings arise over what the agency does for its 15 percent, and critics point out that there is at least the potential for abuse in the system. It is conceivable that an agency might be tempted to recommend a program using more expensive media in order to enhance its remuneration. Or that an agency might avoid one program in favor of another that requires less work. Conceivable, yes. Likely, no. Why? An agency's reputation and growth depend on the results it produces for its clients.

**Charges for out-of-pocket expenses**   In preparing advertisements and other material for the advertiser, the agency incurs costs in addition to the cost of time or space. For print media, there may be costs for typography, photography, artwork, and engraving materials. For television, there may be

## DAVID OGILVY

At the age of 38, David Ogilvy founded the advertising agency that was to become Ogilvy & Mather International, the fifth largest agency in the world in 1978, with billings of $1,003.7 million. During his career as an advertising man, David Ogilvy built a reputation as a creator of sophisticated and literate advertising, advertising that his clients also found to be extremely effective. *Time* magazine proclaimed him to be "the most sought after wizard in the advertising business," and *Newsweek* referred to him as "one of the innovative giants of U. S. Advertising."

Born in West Horsley, England, in 1911, David Ogilvy worked as a chef in a Paris Hotel and a stove salesman in Scotland before emigrating to the United States. Soon after arriving in this country, he went to work for Dr. George Gallup's American Institute of Public Opinion, where his first assignment involved measuring the popularity of movie stars and pretesting story ideas for Hollywood motion picture studios. During the Second World War, he joined the British Secret Service and later served as Second Secretary at the British Embassy in Washington.

In the twenty-six years that he headed Ogilvy & Mather, David Ogilvy produced a great number of successful advertising campaigns. For Hathaway shirts he thought of the idea of featuring a model with a black eyepatch; for Rolls-Royce Corporation he wrote the famous headline: "At 60 miles an hour the loudest noise in this new Rolls-Royce comes from the electric clock"; for Dove soap he stressed the fact that "one quarter percent cleansing cream, Dove will cream your skin while you wash." His other clients have included General Foods, Lever Brothers, Sears Roebuck, IBM, Schweppes, Guinness, and Helena Rubinstein. During this period, he somehow found time to write his best-selling book on the advertising industry: *Confessions of an Advertising Man.*

Now living in semi-retirement in the Chateau de Touffou, a castle in the south of France, David Ogilvy has recently written his autobiography: *Blood, Brains, and Beer.* In this book, the following advice heads the list of the "Eleven Lessons I Learned on Madison Avenue."

You can divide advertising people into two groups—the amateurs and the professionals. The amateurs are in the majority. They aren't *students* of advertising. They guess. The Professionals don't guess, so they don't waste so much of their clients' money.

large expenditures for models, actors, studio rental, filming, taping, editing, and special effects. For research mailings, there may be outlays for postage and forms. In charging for such out-of-pocket expenses, agency practice varies. Some add 15 percent to the cost; most add 17.65 percent to the cost. The 17.65 percent on net cost makes the charge to the client equivalent to the 15 percent gross, which is the same percentage they earn on media. Thus, an expense of $85 that the agency incurs for artwork would be billed to the client at $100, the $15 charge representing 17.65 percent of $85, or 15 percent of $100.

**Fee arrangements**   Many agencies, especially those whose major practice is business advertising, have found it advantageous to themselves and to their clients to work on a fee basis. The reason is that, in many cases, the cost for placing advertisements in many business publications may be so small in comparison with the cost of national consumer media that the 15 percent earned by the agency is insufficient compensation for the effort required. For example, the advertisement on page 57 for Celanese Corp. had a rate of $350. The agency's commission was $52.50, for which they had to provide the talents of a copywriter, an artist, a production staff, and bookkeeping and clerical help.

As you can see, the work that is required to produce an effective business ad may often be unprofitable for the agency. The commission may be inadequate compensation. Many advertisers are aware of this problem and willingly pay a special fee or service charge to the agency for work done on business advertising. Some agencies may be willing to absorb the unprofitable aspects of a client's business advertising if the consumer portion of the client's advertising program is large.

## Agency recognition

*Recognition* means that the media will accept advertising placed by that agency. It has nothing to do with the quality of the agency's work. In order to obtain media recognition, an agency generally has to meet a few simple requirements:

1. The agency must be independent and free of control by the advertiser.

2. The agency's financial resources must be adequate to cover the costs of the advertisements they place.

3. The agency people must have a certain amount of measurable experience in the advertising business.

In practice, the financial qualification is the most critical because the media extend credit to the agency and want to be assured of the agency's ability to meet its obligations.

**House agencies**   Theoretically, recognition is granted only to *bona fide* independent agencies, but the temptation is great for advertisers to set up their own agencies. A *house agency*, which may be little more than the advertising department of the company, can be established as a separate entity and then be granted recognition *and* the agency commission. The economics of the concept become apparent when we consider that the commission on $1 million worth of media advertising is $176,500—a handsome contribution toward the support of the advertising department. Needless to say, the house agency cannot provide the objectivity or the scope of services available from an independent full-service agency, and sometimes a company with a house agency uses the services of a regular agency as well.

**More on the fee system**   Another requirement for agency recognition is adherence to the policy that the agency will not *rebate* or *kick back* any of its commission to the advertiser. The rebate is one of the taboos of the agency business. However, under many fee arrangements, the client will be credited with media commissions that the agency earns. For example, if an advertiser pays an agency an annual retainer of $20,000 (plus out-of-pocket expenses that may be charged at cost) and the advertiser's media budget is $50,000, the agency, earning $7,500 in commissions, will credit that amount to the advertiser toward the $20,000 fee. In any case, the *fee system* is in use, and crediting the advertiser as described does not constitute a rebate. However, despite the existence of a fee arrangement, most of the larger agencies continue to work on a commission basis. About 75 percent of the larger agencies' total income is derived from media commissions. The remaining 25 percent comes from fees for work performed and from percentages added to purchases made for the advertiser's account. The fact is that media commissions remain the backbone of the agency business. The system apparently works effectively for both advertiser and agency.

**Serving competing advertisers**

An agency does not normally provide services for competing clients for two reasons. One is the confidential nature of the relationship between the agency and the advertiser. To perform effectively, the agency must have access to a great amount of data on the company's product, sales, and profits —the kind of information that is not divulged to the public and that, in the hands of competitors,

could be detrimental to the client's business. The other reason is the conflict of interest that could occur in the development of advertising ideas. The agency is expected to provide its most effective creative work for each client. No agency can serve two masters. Consider the dilemma that would face an agency representing a major cigarette advertiser and a major brewery that marketed brand A beer. If the cigarette company bought a brewery that made brand B beer, the agency would be forced to drop either the cigarette advertising account or the brand A beer account. In fact, for the large agencies, one of the most serious limits to growth comes from client conflict. Advertisers are diversifying into one another's businesses.

## Advertising media

Although we shall examine in close detail all the media available to national advertisers in Chapters 7 – 12, it is only fitting that we consider the scope of the communications industry as part of our examination of the advertising business.

In the United States there are approximately:

6,450 commercial radio stations
3,300 business publications
1,588 daily newspapers
1,200 consumer magazines
  723 outdoor sign and billboard operators
  560 Sunday newspapers
  539 commercial television stations
  506 Sunday magazine sections
  283 farm publications
  233 color comic sections

This list includes only the *major media* in which advertisers place the greatest volume of their

# Arbitron measures the Orlando-Daytona Beach television audience in 46 different ways.

# Arbitron says we're first in all 46 ways.

The November 1978 Arbitron report for Orlando-Daytona Beach places WFTV in first place in every single demographic category, sign-on to sign-off, all week long. However your buy is made, there's no better choice than WFTV in Orlando, the growing station at the center of growth in Florida.

p.s.: Nielsen says WFTV ranks first in only 44 of 46 categories. Sorry about those other two. Just wait 'til February.

 REPRESENTED BY BLAIR TELEVISION

 WFTV 9 ORLANDO

INFORMATION CONTAINED HEREIN IS BASED ON THE ARBITRON AND NIELSEN REPORTS FOR ORLANDO-DAYTONA BEACH, NOVEMBER 1978, SUNDAY-SATURDAY, SIGN-ON TO SIGN-OFF (ARBITRON) AND 7:00 AM-1:00 AM (NIELSEN), AND IS SUBJECT TO QUALIFICATIONS CONTAINED THEREIN.

As this sampling of ads from an advertising trade publication indicates, advertisers and advertising agencies rely on many ancillary companies to provide the back-up services they need—from creating original musical jingles to skywriting their advertising messages.

# Astro Aerial Ads

## Aerial Advertising Service Offering:

# BANNER TOWING          SKY WRITING
# FLYING NITE-LITES

Aerial banners offer one of the lowest cost-per-thousand rate of any advertising media. Ask us about our 9.7¢ CPM!

Get results! Reach millions of people at amusement parks, beaches, lakes, golf courses, race tracks, stadiums, shopping centers, and housing developments.

Flyng Nite-Lites can be viewed over a 100 square mile area. High intensity lights spell out moving messages at an average rate of 224 times per hour! Copy can be changed automatically in flight.

Full coverage. We can fly your message over millions of consumers almost anywhere in the U.S.

**Aerial banners are the fastest growing advertising medium today. They are being used more than ever before in their entire history. Call or write us now. Let one of our experts prepare a custom package for your business or client. We're the best in the business. We produce results!**

P.O. Box 35, Blackwood, NJ. 08012 · (609) 228-0035

INDOOR OUTDOOR
**FLAGS BANNERS**
SINCE 1886
KRAUS & SONS
23 E. 22ND ST., N.Y.C. N.Y.
(212) 777-1352

**NASHVILLE SOUND STUDIO**

1719 West End Building, Suite 817
Nashville, Tennessee 37203
(615) 242-2551

## The complete in-house production company

- Production services
- Complete custom commercial images for radio and T.V.
- Over 500 existing jingle beds
- Station I.D.'s

**The "NASHVILLE SOUND" — The Sound That Sells**

Demo presentations available upon request

HAMILTON PRODUCTION CENTER

# JINGLES
Original Music Production

- COLOR TELEVISION STUDIO -
- RECORDING STUDIO -
- ART & DESIGN -

HAMILTON PRODUCTIONS, INC.
20001 N.E. 15th Ct., Dept. AA
North Miami Beach, FL 33179
305-651-7576

advertising. Although secondary advertising media represent only a tiny portion of total billings, their range is enormous and includes station posters, matchbooks, car cards, and pennysavers.

The media recognize the value of the advertising agency. The agency relieves the publisher or the broadcaster of the need to prepare advertisements, a service that some media still have to provide for small advertisers. The agency creates more effective advertising and thereby improves the effectiveness of the medium. The agency carries the burden of credit. In short, agencies simplify media's task.

## Ancillary advertising services

There would be no advertising business if it were not for the services of all the technical experts who provide the *physical* components of advertising. Typographers set the type. Engravers provide engravings or film for publications. Film studios prepare and process film and tape for television commercials. Photography studios take the photographs so essential to the message. Sound studios prepare the transcriptions and tapes for radio commercials. Art studios perform specialized services that are needed from time to time. Printers print the catalogs and brochures designed and prepared by the advertising department and the agency. Market research organizations conduct polls and surveys, compile special studies of markets that are of interest to advertisers, and evaluate the effectiveness of advertising compaigns. All these services are part of the advertising business, and all are in the business of advertising.

## Summary

Although the person who is responsible for an organization's advertising may have one of several different titles, the functions are generally the same. The advertising manager is responsible for the planning of the advertising, for the selection of the advertising agency, and for the supervision of the advertising program. Some companies employ product managers who direct the advertising of individual products under the supervision of a general advertising manager. Many large advertisers maintain fully staffed advertising departments in addition to employing the services of one or more advertising agencies. There are over 7,000 agencies in the United States, most of them full-service organizations that provide complete service for advertisers, including copywriting, art, market research, media analysis and scheduling, and the services of creative people in producing print ads and radio and television commercials. The organization of the agency will depend, for the most part, on the size of the agency. Most operate on a departmentalized basis; others work with a matrix-type organization that combines groups of people into teams that provide the talents needed to serve each client. There are also some highly specialized advertising organizations that provide a portion of the advertising service, generally art or media or special promotion. For its work, the advertising agency receives a 15 percent commission from most media. Although most agencies work within the standard agency commission arrangement, others work with clients on a fee basis, particularly when a large portion of the advertising consists of low-cost business advertising. Agencies rarely, if ever, work for competing clients at the same time. In fact, one of the limits to agency growth has been the diversification of many large advertisers. As for media, there are more than 12,000 media to choose from in the United States, ranging from radio stations (more than 6,000) to business publications (more than 3,300) and hundreds of other choices in between, from farm magazines to color comic sections. Nor would there be an advertising business if it were not for the many people, such as typographers, photoengravers, film studios, photographers, and printers, who provide vital services.

## Advertising industry reference guide

*Advertising Associations*

The Advertising Council, 825 Third Avenue, New York, N.Y. 10022

American Association of Advertising Agencies (AAAA), 200 Park Avenue, New York, N.Y. 10017

Advertising Research Foundation (ARF), 3 East 54th Street, New York, N.Y. 10022

American Marketing Association (AMA), 230 North Michigan Avenue, Chicago, Il. 60606

*Media Associations*

American Business Press, Inc. (ABP), 205 East 42nd Street, New York, N.Y. 10017

American Newspaper Publishers Association (ANPA), The Newspaper Center, 11600 Sunrise Valley Drive, Reston, Va. 22091

Audit Bureau of Circulations (ABC), 123 North Wacker Drive, Chicago, Il. 60606

Business Publications Audit of Circulation (BPA), 360 Park Avenue South, New York, N.Y. 10010

Direct Mail Marketing Association, 6 East 43rd Street, New York, N.Y. 10017

Magazine Publishers Association (MPA), 575 Lexington Avenue, New York, N.Y. 10022

Radio Advertising Bureau (RAB), 485 Lexington Avenue, New York, N.Y. 10017

Television Bureau of Advertising, 1345 Avenue of the Americas, New York, N.Y. 10019

*Advertising Publications*

*Advertising Age,* 740 Rush Street, Chicago, Il. 60611

*Advertising News of New York* (ANNY), 230 Park Avenue, New York, N.Y. 10017

*Editor and Publisher,* 575 Lexington Avenue, New York, N.Y. 10022

*Industrial Marketing,* 740 Rush Street, Chicago, Il. 60611

*Media Decisions,* 342 Madison Avenue, New York, N.Y. 10017

*Madison Avenue,* 750 Third Avenue, New York, N.Y. 10017

*Television/Radio Age,* 1270 Avenue of the Americas, New York, N.Y. 10020

*Journal of Marketing,* 222 South Riverside Plaza, Chicago, Il. 60606

*Sales & Marketing Management,* 633 Third Avenue, New York, N.Y. 10017

*Reference Books*

*Ayer Directory of Publications,* N. W. Ayer & Son, Inc., West Washington Square, Philadelphia, Pa. 19106

*Handbook of Advertising Management,* Roger Barton, McGraw-Hill Book Company, New York, 1970.

"Leading National Advertisers," *Advertising Age,* 740 Rush Street, Chicago, Il. 60611

*Standard Directory of Advertisers,* National Register Publishing Co., Inc., 5201 Old Orchard Road, Skokie, Il. 60076

## QUESTIONS FOR DISCUSSION

1. Why would top management insist on participation in the selection of an advertising agency?

2. If you were to consider a fee basis for advertising service, what factors would you have to consider
   a. if you were the advertiser
   b. if you were the agency

3. If you examine the worldwide billings of the leading advertising agencies, what accounts for the remarkable prominence of Japanese advertising agencies?

4. If you were a foreign manufacturer seeking to bring your product to the American market, would you prefer an American advertising agency or one from your own country?

5. What criteria would you set for the selection of an advertising agency? Would the kind of product affect your criteria?

### Sources and suggestions for further reading

Aaker, David A., and Myers, John G. *Advertising Management.* Englewood Cliffs, N.J.: Prentice-Hall, 1975.

Barton, Roger, ed. *Advertising Agency Operations and Management.* New York: McGraw-Hill, 1970.

Hurwood, David L., and Bailey, Earl L. *Advertising, Sales Promotion and Public Relations —Organizational Alternatives.* New York: National Industrial Conference Board, 1968.

Mayer, Martin. *Madison Avenue, U.S.A.* New York: Harper & Row, 1958.

Ogilvy, David. *Confessions of an Advertising Man.* New York: Atheneum Publishers, 1963.

Reeves, Rosser. *Reality in Advertising.* New York: Alfred A. Knopf, 1961.

Stansfield, Richard. *The Dartnell Advertising Manager's Handbook.* Chicago: The Dartnell Corporation, 1969.

# THE PAGEANT OF ADVERTISING

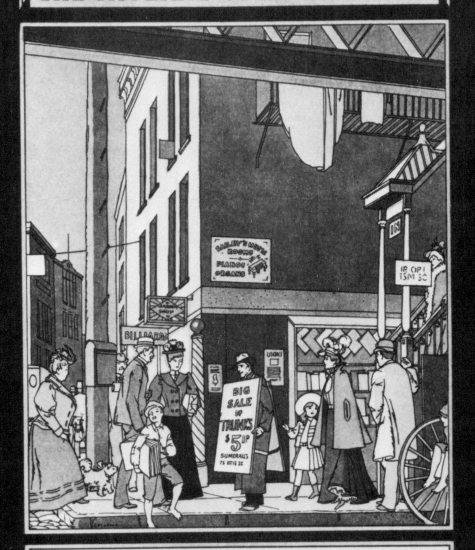

## THE SANDWICH MAN

Here we have motion in advertising used by a resourceful merchant to appeal to his public. Once a frequent figure, but now comparatively rare, the sandwich man adds a curious and picturesque note to the pageant.

## A WESTVACO SURFACE FOR EVERY PRINTING NEED

See reverse side for LIST OF DISTRIBUTORS.

# ADVERTISING DECISIONS

**5**

Marketing intelligence: statistics behind sales

**6**

The budget: investment or expense?

**7**

Advertising media: an overview

# MARKETING INTELLIGENCE: STATISTICS BEHIND SALES

## The role of marketing intelligence

Objectives for marketing
intelligence
Taking aim at sales potential

## Intelligence sources

Secondary data
External sources of secondary data
Internal secondary data
Evaluating secondary data
Primary data

Collecting primary data
Observational method
Survey method
Sampling
Sampling methods

## Motivation research

Psychographics
Copy testing
Media research

## WORKING VOCABULARY

marketing research
market potential
sales potential
secondary data
primary data

panel
sample
motivation research
depth interview
focus group

psychographics
life-style
copy testing

CHAPTER

# marketing intelligence: statistics behind sales

*Commercial propaganda or advertising had its genesis in the need of the mass producer to sell goods in large quantities, and competition of other goods forced him to resort to an anonymous market: an aggregation of people scattered geographically, and unknown and unidentified as individuals.*

EDMUND D. McGARRY
*"The Propaganda Function in Marketing"*

N O EXECUTIVE WOULD MAKE THE DECISION to purchase a multimillion-dollar computer system without first learning as much about that computer system, and computer systems in general, as possible. So it is with the decision to advertise. For many companies advertising is the single largest expenditure in their operating budget. Executives rely on their company's marketing intelligence system to supply them with the information they need to make intelligent advertising decisions.

The scope of marketing intelligence is very wide. In practice it includes the gathering of information on pricing, product mix, product development, sales quotas, sales-force performance, distribution channels, market forecasts, and market share analyses. But for our purposes, we will simply take an overview of marketing intelligence so that you will understand its place—and its importance—in relation to advertising. It is so important that we will deal with other aspects of it in Chapters 14, 18, and 19.

# The role of marketing intelligence

The term *marketing research* is often used interchangeably with marketing intelligence, but a distinction does exist. Marketing intelligence concentrates on the gathering of as much general marketing information as possible, whereas marketing research is a systematic seeking out of facts *related to a specific marketing problem.* Marketing research is concerned with *nonrecurring problems* and is conducted on a project-by-project basis. Marketing intelligence, on the other hand, is concerned with a *continuous flow* of marketing information for use in frequent decision making. Marketing research examines what has already taken place. Marketing intelligence is more *future-oriented.*

## Objectives for marketing intelligence

A marketing intelligence system is similar in many ways to a military intelligence system. Of course, every country would love to have access to information from spies planted in the innermost circles of enemy governments. But this method of intelligence is more frequently encountered in the pages of novels than in real life. For the most part, an effective marketing intelligence system relies on the routine, systematic collection of data. If we are selling a product to women, we want data on how many women in the United States are prospective customers for our product. Of these women, we might want to know, for example, how many of them are married. We do not need spies to obtain this kind of information—just a methodical approach to the gathering of data and a knowledge of potential sources of information.

If our advertising is to achieve its maximum effectiveness, our message must reach the greatest number of potential customers at the lowest possible cost. To help us achieve this objective, our marketing intelligence system must seek the answers to such questions as: Who are our prospective customers? Where are they located? What features do they like in our product? What appeals will be most effective in stimulating them to buy? We also need to obtain information on the most effective advertising strategy. When and how often should our advertisements be run? What will be the best media for carrying our message?

Some of these questions can be refined still further. If we use print media, what layout, style of illustration, and size of type will work best? Should our advertisement be in color or in black and white? If we use broadcast media, what program and format will reach the largest audience? What consumer attitudes already exist with regard to the product? Effective marketing intelligence can supply us with the answers to all these questions.

## Taking aim at sales potential

In Chapter 7 we shall discuss the availability and interpretation of media data. The problems involved in evaluating the effectiveness of any advertising campaign will be investigated in Chapter 18. At present, we are going to concentrate on the methods of obtaining intelligence on our markets.

What is the potential market for our product? *Market potential* is the ability of a market to absorb a specific volume of product sales. If we were manufacturers of toothpaste, for example, our market potential would include every user of toothpaste in the world. Can any company ever hope to achieve such a potential? Of course not. Our *sales potential*

The chart illustrates one of the many demographic changes taking place in the United States. In the New England, Great Lakes, and Far West areas the suburban population is expected to grow at a faster rate than the urban population. In contrast, the urban population is increasing faster in the Plains, Southwest, and Southeast areas. Overall, the metropolitan market areas are growing more slowly. The changes will be reflected in the next decade in driving habits and car use, shopping patterns, clothing styles, and recreation interests.

### REGIONAL PATTERN OF METRO VS. NONMETRO GROWTH

| Region | Projected 1982 total pop. (thous.) | % Change 1977–82 | Projected 1982 metro pop. (thous.) | % Change 1977–82 | Projected 1982 nonmetro pop. (thous.) | % Change 1977–82 |
|---|---|---|---|---|---|---|
| New England | 12,618.8 | + 2.4% | 10,483.5 | + 1.3% | 2,135.3 | + 8.1% |
| Mideast | 43,198.3 | + 1.0 | 37,513.4 | + 0.1 | 5,684.9 | + 7.0 |
| Great Lakes | 41,723.0 | + 1.3 | 33,011.7 | + 0.5 | 8,711.3 | + 4.4 |
| Plains | 17,677.4 | + 3.9 | 9,420.5 | + 4.0 | 8,256.9 | + 3.8 |
| Southeast | 52,596.0 | + 7.0 | 31,756.5 | + 7.2 | 20,839.5 | + 6.6 |
| Southwest | 21,215.4 | +10.2 | 15,668.6 | +10.6 | 5,546.8 | + 9.2 |
| Rocky Mountain | 6,687.8 | +11.5 | 4,101.3 | +11.2 | 2,586.5 | +12.1 |
| Far West | 32,573.7 | + 8.3 | 28,142.5 | + 7.6 | 4,431.2 | +12.6 |
| **U.S.** | **228,290.4** | **+ 4.8%** | **170,098.0** | **+ 4.1%** | **58,192.4** | **+ 6.9%** |

**New England**—Conn., Me., Mass., N.H., R.I., Vt. **Mideast**—Del., D.C., Md., N.J., N.Y., Pa. **Great Lakes**—Ill., Ind., Mich., Ohio, Wis. **Plains**—Iowa, Kan., Minn., Mo., Neb., N.D., S.D. **Southeast**—Ala., Ark., Fla., Ga., Ky., La., Miss., N.C., S.C., Tenn., Va., W. Va. **Southwest**—Ariz., N.M., Okla., Texas. **Rocky Mountain**—Colo., Idaho, Mont., Utah, Wyo. **Far West**—Alaska, Cal., Hawaii, Nev., Ore., Wash.

Source: *Sales & Marketing Management*, October 23, 1978. Reprinted by permission from *Sales & Marketing Management* magazine. Copyright 1978.

is merely the portion or share of the total market that we can reasonably hope to persuade to try our toothpaste.

As we stated in an earlier chapter, for a product to justify an advertising investment, that product must have certain attributes. The product must have an identifiable appeal, and it must be capable of being distinguished by advertising. Now we add one more qualification: that the product's *sales potential* must be worth the cost of its attainment. In addition to providing us with a base for our advertising projections, there are other good reasons to determine sales potential. The sales department needs such information to determine the size of the sales force as well as the quotas and territories to assign to that sales force. The production department will want to know if its manufacturing facilities are adequate.

Returning to our former example, if we examine the total market for toothpaste more closely, we will see that it breaks down into segments for regular toothpaste, toothpaste with fluorides, toothpaste with whiteners, and mint-flavored toothpastes. There are toothpastes for people with sensitive teeth and toothpastes for people with dentures. These are but a few examples of market segments.

If we decide to manufacture fluoride tooth-

The area across the southern tier of the United States—the *Sunbelt*—continues its population growth, but the emphasis is beginning to shift. As the chart shows, in the 1970–77 period the state of Florida exhibited the greatest population growth, led by the cities of Fort Myers, Fort Lauderdale, and Sarasota. The center of population continues to move west. Note the expected growth of Brownsville, Texas; Santa Cruz, California; and Olympia, Washington.

### FAST-GROWING MARKETS SLOWING DOWN

| Rank | S&MM metro market | Annual growth rate 1970–77 | Annual growth rate 1977–82 | 1977–82 rate as ratio of 1970–77 rate | Rank | S&MM metro market | Annual growth rate 1970–77 | Annual growth rate 1977–82 | 1977–82 rate as ratio of 1970–77 rate |
|---|---|---|---|---|---|---|---|---|---|
| 1. | Fort Myers, Fla. | 6.8% | 4.3% | 63% | 15. | Bryan-College Station, Texas | 4.0% | 2.9% | 73% |
| 2. | Anchorage, Alaska | 5.4 | 3.2 | 59 | 15. | Boise, Idaho | 4.0 | 3.0 | 75 |
| 3. | Fort Lauderdale-Hollywood, Fla. | 5.3 | 2.4 | 45 | 15. | Provo-Orem, Utah | 4.0 | 3.6 | 90 |
| 4. | Fort Collins, Colo. | 5.2 | 2.9 | 56 | 15. | McAllen-Pharr-Edinburg, Texas | 4.0 | 3.7 | 93 |
| 5. | Sarasota, Fla. | 4.8 | 2.4 | 50 | 15. | Las Vegas, Nev. | 4.0 | 3.5 | 88 |
| 5. | West Palm Beach-Boca Raton, Fla. | 4.8 | 3.3 | 69 | 15. | Tampa-St. Petersburg, Fla. | 4.0 | 1.9 | 48 |
| 7. | Killeen-Temple, Texas | 4.7 | 2.8 | 60 | 21. | Phoenix, Ariz. | 3.9 | 2.7 | 69 |
| 8. | Brownsville-Harlingen-San Benito, Texas | 4.3 | 4.5 | 105 | 22. | Tallahassee, Fla. | 3.8 | 3.2 | 84 |
| 8. | Santa Cruz, Cal. | 4.3 | 4.1 | 95 | 23. | Reno, Nev. | 3.7 | 2.7 | 73 |
| 8. | Austin, Texas | 4.3 | 3.5 | 81 | 23. | Santa Rosa, Cal. | 3.7 | 2.7 | 73 |
| 8. | Tucson, Ariz. | 4.3 | 2.5 | 58 | 25. | Anaheim-Santa Ana-Garden Grove, Cal. | 3.6 | 2.6 | 72 |
| 12. | Bradenton, Fla. | 4.1 | 2.5 | 61 | | | | | |
| 12. | Orlando, Fla. | 4.1 | 2.4 | 59 | | | | | |
| 12. | Olympia, Wash. | 4.1 | 3.9 | 95 | | | | | |

Note: Growth rates are geometric rates (annual rates, compounded). Source: *Sales & Marketing Management*, October 23, 1978. Reprinted by permission from *Sales & Marketing Management* magazine. Copyright 1978.

paste, we must depend on our marketing intelligence to tell us: (1) how many people currently use fluoride toothpaste, (2) what brands of fluoride toothpaste they now use, and (3) how many of these potential customers we can reasonably expect to buy our new brand.

## Intelligence sources

There are two basic sources of information for companies or advertising agencies that are seeking mar-

keting intelligence. These sources are: secondary data and primary data.

### Secondary data

A foreign government wouldn't send spies into the United States to obtain information that is published every day in our newspapers. Advertisers, too, know that they can obtain much valuable marketing information from *secondary data*—from records that have been compiled and published by someone else.

MARKETING INTELLIGENCE: STATISTICS BEHIND SALES

**External sources of secondary data** The public library is a warehouse of marketing information—most of it provided by the United States government. The Federal Reserve Board, the Department of Commerce, the Department of Agriculture, and the Department of Health, Education and Welfare produce volumes of data on consumers, markets, occupations, and industries. State and county governments provide data on income, housing, education, retail sales, auto registration, alcoholic beverage consumption—the list is almost endless. Publishers of newspapers provide data on retail sales for various segments of their market, trading area, or Standard Metropolitan Statistical Area (SMSA). Trade associations gather much data on their industries and, although most is reserved for their members, in many instances it is made available to interested advertisers. Magazine publishers and television and radio stations are constantly conducting surveys to determine the reading or viewing habits of their audiences, as well as their eating and drinking habits, income and educational levels, and other demographic details. They are always eager to supply advertisers and their agencies with this information.

**Internal secondary data** A well-organized business routinely accumulates substantial amounts of information that an efficient marketing intelligence system can utilize. The sales records of the company, carefully studied, can be a mine of valuable information. From them, researchers can determine, among other things, the season in which the company's sales peak, the regions of the country that offer the best markets for the company's product, and the channels of distribution that are the most effective. Of course, the amount of information collected will vary from company to company,

but certainly there will be enough basic data to provide an important foundation for future advertising decisions.

**Evaluating secondary data** Although the use of secondary data offers savings in time and cost, a word of caution is warranted. Before basing important marketing decisions on such data, we should ask ourselves a number of questions that will help us evaluate the material.

1. *Under what conditions was the data gathered?*
   The data compiled by a well-known market research company offers a greater level of reliability than, for example, statistics quickly assembled by a local chamber of commerce.

2. *Who financed it?*
   Not that anyone would knowingly provide incorrect data, but sometimes a company or business or organization commissions a study to prove that its interpretation of the facts is the correct one. It is simply good business to find out who paid for the data search.

3. *When was the data gathered?*
   We live in a very dynamic world. Last year's figures may be stale, if not suspect. Data gathered five or ten years ago may be all but valueless.

4. *How are the terms defined?*
   A report describing sales of *fresh fruit* is not at all clear. What does "fresh" mean? Not cooked? Is it the same as raw fruit? Are frozen strawberries fresh because they have

The U. S. Department of Commerce, Bureau of the Census, publishes the *Statistical Abstract of the United States*. In the *Abstract* are almost one thousand pages of charts that contain nearly all the demographic information a marketer might want.

## No. 737. MEDIAN FAMILY MONEY INCOME AND PER CAPITA MONEY INCOME—STATES: 1959 TO 1975

[For 1959 and 1969 data, population and families as of **April 1960** and **April 1970**, respectively. For **1975** data, families as of **spring 1976** for median family income, population as of **July 1976** for per capita income. Ranks for the 50 States based on descending order from highest to lowest income. For definition of median, see p. xii. See *Historical Statistics, Colonial Times to 1970*, series G 205–256, for median family income]

### MEDIAN FAMILY INCOME

| STATE RANKED BY 1975 MEDIAN INCOME | 1959 [1] Income | Rank | 1969 [1] Income | Rank | 1975 [2] Income | Rank |
|---|---|---|---|---|---|---|
| **U.S.** | $5,660 | (X) | $9,586 | (X) | $14,094 | (X) |
| **HIGHEST FIFTH** | | | | | | |
| Alaska | 7,305 | 1 | 12,441 | 1 | 22,432 | 1 |
| Hawaii | 6,366 | 8 | 11,552 | 3 | 17,770 | 2 |
| Md | 6,309 | 9 | 11,057 | 5 | 17,556 | 3 |
| N.J. | 6,786 | 3 | 11,403 | 4 | 16,432 | 4 |
| Conn | 6,887 | 2 | 11,808 | 2 | 16,244 | 5 |
| Ill | 6,566 | 6 | 10,957 | 7 | 16,062 | 6 |
| Del | 6,197 | 13 | 10,209 | 14 | 15,732 | 7 |
| Mass | 6,272 | 10 | 10,833 | 8 | 15,531 | 8 |
| Mich | 6,256 | 11 | 11,029 | 6 | 15,385 | 9 |
| N.Y. | 6,371 | 7 | 10,609 | 11 | 15,288 | 10 |
| **FOURTH FIFTH** | | | | | | |
| Calif | 6,726 | 5 | 10,729 | 9 | 15,069 | 11 |
| Wis | 5,926 | 15 | 10,065 | 15 | 15,064 | 12 |
| Colo | 5,780 | 20 | 9,552 | 21 | 14,992 | 13 |
| Wash | 6,225 | 12 | 10,404 | 12 | 14,962 | 14 |
| Nev | 6,736 | 4 | 10,687 | 10 | 14,961 | 15 |
| Ohio | 6,171 | 14 | 10,309 | 13 | 14,822 | 16 |
| Wyo | 5,877 | 18 | 8,944 | 27 | 14,784 | 17 |
| Minn | 5,573 | 24 | 9,928 | | | |
| Va | 4,964 | 32 | 9,044 | 23 | | |
| R.I. | 5,589 | | | | | |
| **THIRD FIFTH** | | | | | | |
| Iowa | 5,069 | | | | | |
| Ind | 5,798 | | | | | |
| Utah | 5,899 | | | | | |
| N.H. | 5,636 | | | | | |
| Nebr | 4,862 | | | | | |
| Pa | 5,719 | | | | | |
| Oreg | 5,892 | | | | | |
| N. Dak | 4,530 | | | | | |
| Mont | 5,403 | | | | | |
| Ariz | 5,568 | | | | | |
| **SECOND FIFTH** | | | | | | |
| Kans | 5,295 | | | | | |
| Mo | 5,127 | | | | | |
| Idaho | 5,259 | | | | | |
| Tex | 4,884 | | | | | |
| La | 4,272 | | | | | |
| Ga | 4,208 | | | | | |
| Vt | 4,890 | | | | | |
| Fla | 4,722 | | | | | |
| S.C. | 3,821 | | | | | |
| Okla | 4,620 | | | | | |
| **LOWEST FIFTH** | | | | | | |
| S. Dak | 4,251 | 42 | | | | |
| W. Va. | 4,572 | 39 | | | | |
| Maine | 4,873 | 35 | | | | |
| N.C. | 3,956 | 45 | | | | |
| N. Mex | 5,371 | 27 | | | | |
| Ala | 3,937 | 47 | | | | |
| Tenn | 3,949 | 46 | | | | |
| Ky | 4,051 | 44 | | | | |
| Ark | 3,184 | 49 | | | | |
| Miss | 2,884 | 50 | | | | |

### PER CAPITA INCOME

| STATE RANKED BY 1975 PER CAPITA INCOME | 1959 [1] Income | Rank | 1969 [1] Income | Rank | 1975 [3] Income | Rank |
|---|---|---|---|---|---|---|
| **U.S.** | $1,850 | (X) | $3,119 | (X) | $4,838 | (X) |
| | | | | | | 1 |
| | | | | | | 2 |
| | | | | | | 3 |
| | | | | | | 4 |
| | | | | | | 5 |
| **HIGHEST FIFTH** | | | | | | |
| Alaska | 2,259 | 5 | 3,725 | 2 | 7,969 | 6 |
| Md | 2,003 | 11 | 3,512 | 7 | 5,626 | 7 |
| N.J. | 2,260 | 4 | 3,674 | 3 | 5,600 | 8 |
| Conn | 2,352 | 2 | 3,885 | 1 | 5,571 | 9 |
| Nev | 2,356 | 1 | 3,554 | 6 | 5,493 | 10 |
| Calif | 2,308 | 10 | 3,614 | 4 | 5,464 | |
| Wash | 2,033 | 7 | 3,357 | 12 | 5,369 | |
| Ill | 2,182 | 17 | 3,495 | 8 | 5,334 | |
| Hawaii | 1,863 | 15 | 3,373 | 10 | 5,259 | |
| Colo | 1,889 | | 3,106 | 17 | 5,193 | |
| **FOURTH FIFTH** | | | | | | |
| N.Y. | 2,236 | 6 | 3,608 | 5 | 5,... | |
| Wyo | 1,888 | 16 | 2,895 | | | |
| Del | 2,086 | 8 | | | | |
| Mass | 2,050 | 13 | | | | |
| Oreg | | 14 | | | | |
| V. | | 15 | | | | |
| | | 16 | | | | |

X Not applicable. [1] From the ... [2] From the 1976 Survey of Income ... sampling variability; for details, see sou... sharing allocations; for details, see sou... est rank equal to number of States sho...

Source: U.S. Bureau of the Census, ... Nos. 110–113; and unpublished data.

## No. 738. MEDIAN FAMILY MONEY INCOME, BY EARNERS AND RACE: 1967 TO 1977

[Beginning 1975, data not strictly comparable with earlier years due to revised procedures. See headnote, table 729. For definition of median, see p. xii]

| YEAR AND NUMBER OF EARNERS | ALL FAMILIES, MEDIAN FAMILY INCOME (dollars) All races [1] | White | Black | FAMILIES WITH HEAD FULL-TIME WORKER [2] Percent of all families All races [1] | White | Black | Median family income (dollars) All races [1] | White | Black | BLACK–WHITE INCOME RATIO All families | Families with head full-time worker [2] |
|---|---|---|---|---|---|---|---|---|---|---|---|
| **All families, 1967** | 7,933 | 8,234 | 4,875 | 67.6 | 68.8 | 55.2 | 9,263 | 9,495 | 6,331 | .59 | .67 |
| No earners | 2,447 | 2,534 | 1,991 | .3 | .3 | .3 | (B) | (B) | (B) | .79 | .57 |
| 1 earner | 6,980 | 7,247 | 3,693 | 70.3 | 71.6 | 53.4 | 7,854 | 8,031 | 4,598 | .51 | .71 |
| 2 earners | 8,931 | 9,214 | 6,275 | 75.2 | 76.1 | 67.3 | 9,693 | 9,931 | 7,043 | .68 | .67 |
| 3 earners | 11,221 | 11,590 | 6,957 | 79.7 | 81.5 | 64.5 | 11,741 | 11,987 | 8,036 | .60 | .67 |
| 4 earners or more | 13,170 | 13,673 | 7,680 | 79.6 | | 59.2 | 13,700 | 14,106 | 9,418 | .56 | |
| **All families, 1970** | 9,867 | 10,236 | 6,279 | 67.3 | 68.8 | 51.4 | 13,790 | | 12,016 | .61 | .74 |
| No earners | 3,289 | 3,489 | 2,235 | 65.2 | | 46.7 | (B) | 9,750 | (B) | .64 | |
| 1 earner | 8,352 | 8,713 | 4,844 | 72.6 | 67.0 | 66.2 | 9,960 | 12,263 | 6,533 | .56 | .78 |
| 2 earners | 11,190 | 11,450 | 10,000 | 78.1 | 73.4 | 64.3 | 12,507 | 15,460 | 9,776 | .74 | .75 |
| 3 earners | 14,438 | 14,795 | 11,112 | 80.9 | 79.4 | 17,689 | 15,828 | 18,066 | 11,839 | .68 | .71 |
| 4 earners or more | 16,888 | 17,311 | | | 83.0 | 64.7 | 18,066 | | 12,806 | .64 | |
| **All families, 1975** [3] | 13,772 | 14,320 | 8,723 | 65.5 | 61.3 | 60.9 | 17,161 | 17,485 | 13,441 | .61 | .77 |
| No earners | 5,232 | 5,645 | 3,511 | 67.0 | 72.1 | 42.3 | (B) | (B) | (B) | .62 | .67 |
| 1 earner | 11,568 | 12,198 | 7,086 | 59.4 | 77.8 | 64.1 | 14,156 | 14,531 | 9,760 | .58 | .84 |
| 2 earners | 16,058 | 16,360 | 12,914 | 71.3 | 81.6 | 65.0 | 17,606 | 17,842 | 14,902 | .79 | .72 |
| 3 earners | 20,383 | 20,748 | 15,808 | 76.5 | | 67.6 | 21,540 | 21,789 | 18,095 | .75 | .73 |
| 4 earners or more | 23,785 | 24,203 | 18,129 | 80.2 | | | 25,054 | 25,229 | 18,933 | | |
| **All families, 1977** [3] | 16,060 | 16,782 | 9,485 | 60.4 | 61.9 | 46.9 | 20,079 | 20,420 | 14,903 | .57 | .73 |
| No earners | 6,019 | 6,608 | 3,669 | 59.5 | 61.0 | 47.6 | (B) | (B) | (B) | .56 | .61 |
| 1 earner | 13,148 | 14,077 | 7,761 | 73.5 | 74.3 | 65.7 | 15,949 | 16,548 | 10,146 | .55 | .85 |
| 2 earners | 18,704 | 19,019 | 14,984 | 76.5 | 77.7 | 62.6 | 20,368 | 20,567 | 17,415 | .79 | .78 |
| 3 earners | 23,511 | 24,058 | 18,222 | 81.7 | 83.5 | 67.1 | 25,089 | 25,308 | 19,679 | .76 | .82 |
| 4 earners or more | 27,236 | 27,089 | 20,629 | | | | 28,087 | 28,439 | 23,263 | .75 | |

— Represents zero or rounds to zero. B Base less than 75,000. X Not applicable. [1] Includes races not shown separately. [2] Employed year-round. [2] Civilian members 14 years old and over.

Source: U.S. Bureau of the Census, *Current Population Reports*, series P-60, No. 116, and earlier issues. ... series P-60, ...

*Sales & Marketing Management* is published monthly except in February, April, July, and October, when it is published twice a month. "The Survey of Buying Power," generally published in one of the July issues, contains a wealth of data: effective buying income (by Metro area), per household retail sales (by Metro area), and retail sales (by store group) for various categories of goods; as well as median income levels and other helpful marketing facts.

## RETAIL SALES BY STORE GROUP 1977

| | Total Retail Sales ($000) | Food ($000) | Eating & Drinking Places ($000) | General Mdse. ($000) | Furniture/ Furnish./ Appliance ($000) | Auto- motive ($000) | Drug ($000) |
|---|---|---|---|---|---|---|---|
| | | | 47,007 | 122,625 | 38,129 | 128,648 | 14,633 |
| | 718,845 | 141,669 | 1,899 | | 35,508 | 122,626 | 11,964 |
| | 5,730 | 1,226 | 39,075 | 105,080 | 35,508 | 122,626 | 11,964 |
| | 616,396 | 107,053 | 39,075 | 105,080 | 2,621 | 6,022 | 2,669 |
| | 616,396 | 107,053 | 6,033 | 17,545 | | | |
| | 96,719 | 33,390 | 7,932 | 17,545 | | | |
| | 102,449 | 34,616 | | | | | |

## POPULATION—12/31/77

**GA. (cont.)**
S&MM ESTIMATES
**METRO AREA**
County
City

| | Total Population (Thou- sands) | % Of U.S. | Median Age of Pop. | % of Population by Age Group | | | | House- holds (Thou- sands) |
|---|---|---|---|---|---|---|---|---|
| | | | | 18–24 Years | 25–34 Years | 35–49 Years | 50 & Over | |
| | | | 25.6 | 17.9 | 16.3 | 15.5 | 19.3 | 72.2 |
| | 227.2 | .1043 | 22.1 | 57.0 | 15.1 | 8.5 | 2.7 | 2.1 |
| | 18.6 | .0085 | 26.8 | 14.9 | 17.0 | 16.3 | 19.8 | 55.5 |
| COLUMBUS | 162.3 | .0745 | 26.8 | 14.9 | 17.0 | 16.3 | 19.8 | 55.5 |
| Chattahoochee | 162.3 | .0745 | 27.7 | 12.7 | 14.6 | 15.6 | 23.7 | 14.6 |
| Columbus | 46.3 | .0213 | 23.9 | 25.3 | 14.8 | 13.6 | 17.7 | 16.7 |
| • Columbus | 64.9 | .0298 | 27.7 | 13.0 | 15.9 | 17.0 | 21.4 | 76.7 |
| Russell, Ala. | 239.9 | .1102 | 29.3 | | | | | |
| SUBURBAN TOTAL | 143.1 | .0657 | | | | | | |
| **MACON** | | | | | | | | |
| Bibb | | | | | | | | |
| • Macon | | | | | | | | |

# PER HOUSEHOLD RETAIL SALES
S&MM METRO MARKET RANKING

| Area | ($) | Rank |
|---|---|---|
| | 19,507 | 1 |
| | 18,577 | 2 |
| | 15,661 | 3 |
| | | 4 |
| Savannah | 10,779 | 104 |
| Eau Claire | 10,771 | 105 |
| Billings | 10,761 | 106 |
| Galveston - Texas City | 10,739 | 107 |
| Omaha | 10,702 | 108 |
| | 10,697 | 109 |
| | 10,686 | 110 |
| | 10,683 | 111 |
| | 10,681 | 112 |
| | | 113 |

| Area | ($) | Rank |
|---|---|---|
| Fort Collins | 9,649 | 205 |
| Albuquerque | 9,642 | 206 |
| Jackson, Mich. | 9,632 | 207 |
| Northeast Pennsylvania | 9,615 | 208 |
| Richland - Kennewick | 9,609 | 209 |
| Worcester - Fitchburg - Leominster | 9,602 | 210 |
| Chattanooga | 9,587 | 211 |
| Allentown - Bethlehem - Easton | 9,585 | 212 |
| △ Anderson, S.C. | 9,578 | 213 |
| Charleston - North Charleston, S.C. | 9,550 | 214 |
| Riverside - San Bernardino - Ontario | 9,538 | 215 |
| | 9,537 | 216 |
| | 9,530 | 217 |
| | 9,512 | 218 |
| | 9,506 | 219 |
| | | 220 |

# EFFECTIVE BUYING INCOME
S&MM METRO MARKET RANKING

| Area | ($000) | Rank | Area | ($000) | Rank | Area | ($000) | Rank |
|---|---|---|---|---|---|---|---|---|
| New York | 65,867,154 | 1 | York | 2,201,946 | 101 | △ Elkhart | 821,073 | 203 |
| Chicago | 51,603,077 | 2 | Albuquerque | 2,186,620 | 102 | Waco | 820,756 | 204 |
| Los Angeles - Long Beach | 48,778,564 | 3 | Lancaster | 2,145,729 | 103 | Tallahassee | 809,089 | 205 |
| Detroit | 32,740,884 | 4 | El Paso | 2,138,826 | 104 | Yakima | 808,011 | 206 |
| Philadelphia | 31,773,741 | 5 | Madison | 2,082,597 | 105 | Wichita Falls | 793,135 | 207 |
| San Francisco - Oakland | 24,969,073 | 6 | Columbia, S.C. | 2,067,554 | 106 | Provo - Orem | 786,096 | 208 |
| Boston - Lowell - Brockton - Lawrence - Haverhill | 24,869,796 | 7 | Mobile | 2,044,579 | 107 | Wilmington, N.C. | 770,908 | 209 |
| Washington | 24,526,767 | 8 | Reading | 2,033,165 | 108 | McAllen - Pharr - Edinburg | 765,494 | 210 |
| Nassau - Suffolk | 19,679,437 | 9 | Ann Arbor | 1,914,201 | 109 | Muncie | 759,764 | 211 |
| Dallas - Fort Worth | 17,916,645 | 10 | Johnson City - Kingsport - Bristol | 1,898,211 | 110 | Vineland - Millville - Bridgeton | 755,041 | 212 |
| Houston | 17,433,280 | 11 | Rockford | 1,887,078 | 111 | Kokomo | 751,031 | 213 |
| Newark, N.J. | 15,081,323 | 12 | Santa Barbara - Santa Maria - Lompoc | 1,871,159 | 112 | Richland - Kennewick | 742,191 | 214 |
| St. Louis | 14,941,529 | 13 | Shreveport | 1,860,576 | 113 | Mansfield | 741,959 | 215 |
| Pittsburgh | 14,229,803 | 14 | Newport News - Hampton | 1,852,179 | 114 | Abilene | 734,227 | 216 |
| Cleveland | 13,473,200 | 15 | Spokane | 1,844,800 | 115 | Fort Collins | 728,069 | 217 |
| Anaheim - Santa Ana - Garden Grove | 13,246,942 | 16 | Charleston - North Charleston, S.C. | 1,809,561 | 116 | △ Jamestown | 727,664 | 218 |
| Minneapolis - St. Paul | 12,926,807 | 17 | Lexington-Fayette | 1,796,761 | 117 | Lafayette, La. | 726,993 | 219 |
| Baltimore | 12,664,084 | 18 | Bakersfield | 1,791,303 | 118 | △ Danville, Ill. | 724,164 | 220 |
| Atlanta | 11,974,685 | 19 | Utica - Rome | 1,709,646 | 119 | Lynchburg | 721,996 | 221 |
| San Diego | 10,544,908 | 20 | Vallejo - Fairfield - Napa | 1,689,864 | 120 | Bradenton | 713,920 | 222 |
| Seattle - Everett | 10,135,755 | 21 | Lorain - Elyria | 1,663,578 | 121 | Bay City | 712,377 | 223 |
| Denver - Boulder | 9,779,863 | 22 | Jackson, Miss. | 1,655,017 | 122 | Longview | 709,090 | 224 |
| Miami | 9,778,144 | 23 | Saginaw | 1,623,258 | 123 | Monroe | 707,129 | 225 |
| San Jose | 9,469,702 | 24 | Appleton - Oshkosh | 1,617,940 | 124 | Brownsville - Harlingen - San Benito | 704,110 | 226 |
| Milwaukee | 9,232,941 | 25 | Stockton | 1,608,055 | 125 | Clarksville - Hopkinsville | 702,502 | 227 |
| Kansas City | 9,018,124 | 26 | Santa Rosa | 1,598,302 | 126 | △ Bangor | 697,098 | 228 |
| Cincinnati | 8,568,625 | 27 | South Bend | 1,590,982 | 127 | Altoona | 694,791 | |
| Buffalo | 7,938,292 | 28 | Charleston, W. Va. | 1,587,714 | 128 | Fargo - Moorhead | | |
| Tampa - St. Petersburg | 7,927,357 | 29 | Salinas - Seaside - Monterey | 1,579,732 | 129 | | | |
| Phoenix | 7,577,507 | | Bingham | 1,578,615 | 130 | | | |
| Riverside - San Bernardino - Ontario | | | | | | | | |

not been cooked? And what fruits have been included in the study? Apples? Peaches? Does "part-time" employment mean five hours a week or twenty-five hours a week? You see the difficulty.

**5.** *Was the sample adequate?*
By "adequate" we mean large enough, representative of the market, randomly selected, or whatever other criteria we value in sampling. We will have more to say about sampling later in this chapter.

## Primary data

When the information we seek is not available from secondary sources—perhaps because it is so specialized that we are the only people interested in it—we must go out and collect the data for ourselves. *Primary data*, as the name implies, is firsthand information, collected according to plan by our procedure and, generally, for our private use. If we want to know, for example, how many females between the ages of 12 and 18 live in Florida, the chances are good that such data have already been compiled. If we want to know what percentage of these females is black and what percentage white, that information, too, should not be difficult to find. But, suppose we want to know how many of them make their own clothes? (Perhaps we are interested in selling them sewing machines or clothing patterns, or perhaps we want to open a chain of fabric stores.) This type of information is not usually available from secondary sources—not from the government, not from a trade association, not from a syndicated service. Therefore, we must obtain our own data.

There are many different ways we could go about gathering the information we want. We always begin our search by obtaining all the related secondary data available. Once we have done this, our next step is to take a sample of our total potential market or universe (in this case, all young women 12 to 18 years old) and find out what percentage of this sample sews their own clothes. We could conduct the survey of our sample by questionnaire, by telephone, or through personal interviews at the local high schools. Each of these methods has advantages and limitations. The formulation of the questionnaire and the selection of the sample demand specialized skills. For that reason, we might want to contract with a market research organization to do the survey for us. Of course, if we did undertake such a survey, we would want, at the same time, to gather additional data about our market. We might want to ask the young women in our sample what kind of fabrics they buy, how often they sew, how many garments they make in a year, and what makes of sewing machines they own. Such information, when gathered and assembled, is very valuable and we would keep it for our exclusive use. But it will be costly to obtain.

## Collecting primary data

**Observational method** The simplest method of gathering primary data is to have a trained observer watch what takes place when a consumer purchases our product. The observer then records particular aspects of the consumer's purchase behavior. How do consumers select a particular type of packaged food? Do they scan all the shelves or do they go straight to the brand they want? Do they read the information on the package to check for weight or contents?

These are representative ads for some of the many marketing research services available. These research companies offer interviewing, focus groups, copy testing, package tests, commercial pretesting, taste testing—in short, everything an advertiser might want to know to make an advertising program successful.

## THE INNOVATIVE MARKETING RESEARCH COMPANY

*Chilton Research Services* developed the first commercially availab[le] Cathode Ray Tube interviewing system that can be used on all telepho[ne] survey research projects.

### IN ADDITION:

**PERSONAL FACE TO FACE INTERVIEWING**

— — over 900 fully trained professional survey research viewers located in 332 counties across the nation

— — a special group of interviewers in major markets to interviews with executives and businessmen

**ON-SITE INTERVIEWING**

— — the ability to conduct on-site interviews in shoppi[ng] located in 30 major markets

**FOCUSED GROUP INTERVIEWING**

— — focused group interviewing facility with moder[n] [fa]cilities located in Radnor, Pa.

**DEPTH INTERVIEWING**

— — highly trained interviewers for tape recorded studies

**CENTRAL LOCATION TELEPHONE INTERVIEWING**

— — one of the largest batteries of WATS lines voted to survey research

**LOCAL TELEPHONE INTERVIEWING**

— — rigidly controlled local telephone inter[viewing] validation to insure that interviews are to specifications

**SPECIALIZED MATHEMATICAL ANALYTICAL P[...]**

— — the development of mathematical mo[dels] in brand share and price elasticity mapping techniques

**Chilton Research**

Chilton Way, Radnor, Pennsylvania 19089 • 215-687-8200

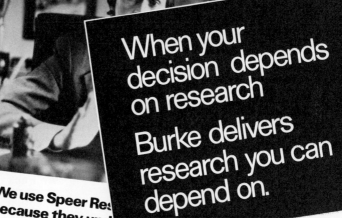

"We use Speer Res[earch]
because they und[erstand]
industrial marketi[ng]

"We're one of the largest advertisin[g] country specializing in industrial and [ ] accounts. To do our job right we've g[ot] understanding of technical language, and the industrial marketplace."

"We look for the same capabilities in a [ ] research supplier, and that's why we us[e Speer.]

"Speer can handle a wide range of resear[ch] personal interviews to multivariate analy[sis] develop the best research format and then [ ] in-house. And they show a healthy respect [ ] and budgets, absolutely essential in my bus[iness.]

Walter T. Queren, Vice-President. Account Supervi[sor]
Michel-Cather Inc., New York

Call Speer. We'll be pleased to send you our b[ ] list of client references, provide further inform[ation] prepare a proposal to your requirements. Cont[act] Raymond Speer, President

We understand industrial marketing.

## Speer Research

Los Angeles: 493 S. Robertson Blvd., CA 90211, (213) 274-2007
New York: 745 Fifth Avenue, NY 10022, (212) 759-6137

When your decision depends on research

Burke delivers research you can depend on.

As full-service specialists in consumer, professional and institutional research, Burke's more than 45 years' experience includes studies in these areas:

- TRADE AREA STUDIES
- NATIONWIDE SURVEYS—NATIONAL WATS CENTER
- CENTRAL LOCATION STUDIES/PERMANENT MALL OFFICES
- GROUP INTERVIEWING
- NATIONAL PROBABILITY SURVEYS
- TV COMMERCIAL TESTING: RCR AND DAR
- PRINT AD TESTING: PRETESTING AND DAR
- CLAIM SUPPORT RESEARCH
- CAMPAIGN TRACKING STUDIES
- AWARENESS, TRIAL, AND USAGE SURVEYS
- PRODUCT AND PACKAGE TESTING: IN-HOME PLACEMENTS, SHOW TESTS, TASTE TESTS
- INTERVIEWING OF PROFESSIONALS— PHYSICIANS, BUSINESSMEN, ETC.

Burke's unique personnel policies and organization contribute to the consistent accuracy of its research:

- All interviews made by Burke employees who work for no one else.
- Burke supervision in the field at the point of interview.
- Telephone interviewing in each city from a central location using local lines or WATS facilities.
- Permanent field offices in 34 cities across the U.S.A.

*Call or write for details or to set up a no-obligation discussion of your needs.*

**Burke Marketing Research, Inc.**
1529 Madison Road, Cincinnati, Ohio 45206
(Phone: 513/961 8000)
• New York (609/665 2000)
• Philadelphia (203/236 5401)
• New England (203/961 8787)
• Cincinnati (513/961 8000)
• Dallas (214/233 5755)
• Detroit (313/559 8160)
• Chicago (312/469 7722)
• San Francisco (415/937 0660)
• Los Angeles (213/393 0477)

This ad is an announcement for an interesting new development in marketing research—tracking *eye movement*. For example, an advertiser might want to know if a new package stands out on the shelf. Is it more visible than competitive packages? Which area of the package catches the eye of the consumer first? The illustration? The name? Which part of an ad does the reader notice first? This company tracks the eye movements of respondents and then interviews them to measure the impact of the message and the brand image conveyed.

The observer may then gather additional information by conducting a personal interview with the customers after they have made their selection. There are many other observational techniques that may be used. Some of them involve nothing more than counting the number of people entering a store or department during a specified period of time, or using a mechanical counter to record the number of cars that pass a given point each day.

But the observational method provides only overt behavioral information. We do not learn why consumers do something, only that they do it. Any other conclusions must be inferred.

**Survey method**  Surveys may be classified by the procedure used to gather the data. These proce-

The illustration below shows a portion of a research questionnaire designed to collect primary data through personal interviews. The interviewer seeks to determine the brand preferences of toothpaste users.

```
6a.  Do you, yourself, use a toothpaste for brushing your teeth?

          Yes   ( )  (ASK Q. 6)    No   ( )  (SKIP TO Q. 7a)

 b.  What brand of toothpaste did you use the last time for brushing your
     teeth?  (RECORD ANSWER BELOW)

 c.  What other brands, if any do you use quite regularly?  (RECORD ANSWER BELOW

 d.  Are there any other brands of toothpaste that any members of your family
     consider to be their regular brands?

          Yes   ( )  (ASK Q. 6e)   No   ( )  (SKIP TO Q. 7a)

 e.  What are these brands?  (RECORD BELOW)
```

| | Q. 6b | Q. 6c | Q. 6e |
| | | | Other Family Members |
| | Last Time | Quite Regularly | Quite Regularly |
|---|---|---|---|
| Aim | ( ) | ( ) | ( ) |
| Close-Up Green | ( ) | ( ) | ( ) |
| Close-Up Red | ( ) | ( ) | ( ) |
| Colgate | ( ) | ( ) | ( ) |
| Crest Regular | ( ) | ( ) | ( ) |
| Crest Mint | ( ) | ( ) | ( ) |
| Gleem II | ( ) | ( ) | ( ) |
| Macleans Regular | ( ) | ( ) | ( ) |
| Macleans Spearmint | ( ) | ( ) | ( ) |
| Peak | ( ) | ( ) | ( ) |
| Pearl Drops | ( ) | ( ) | ( ) |
| Pepsodent | ( ) | ( ) | ( ) |
| Plus White | ( ) | ( ) | ( ) |
| Ultra Brite Regular | ( ) | ( ) | ( ) |
|      Mint | ( ) | ( ) | ( ) |
| Other (SPECIFY) | _____ | _____ | _____ |
| None other | | ( ) | ( ) |

dures include the personal interview, mail survey, and telephone survey.

*The personal interview* is the most costly of all survey procedures. But if it's successful, it can provide us with information critical to the success of our advertising program. We can use personal interviews to obtain information on the consumers' knowledge of our product, their attitudes toward it, their life-styles, and many demographic details. Large amounts of information can be collected in a short time, but the cost of the survey will be ten to twenty times greater than a mail survey.

A *mail survey* typically employs the use of a self-administered questionnaire; the subject answers the questions without help from an interviewer. The procedure is simple and the cost is far less than a personally administered questionnaire. The major drawback of a mail survey is the amount of time required to gather the information. It takes time to get the mailing out, time for the respondent to complete the questionnaire, and then more time for the questionnaire to be returned. In some cases, the time required to complete a mail survey can be as long as two months. Another drawback is the poor rate of return. Many people simply do not take the time to answer and return the questionnaire. Finally, a mail survey generally elicits only very limited types of information.

The *diary* is another form of questionnaire. The subjects of the study are given a diary in which they record their behavior. In some cases they are asked to record their supermarket purchases or their product use. In other cases, they record their reading and/or viewing habits. In this way, we can learn about the consumption of certain products, their frequency of purchase, and frequency of use. We can detect shifts in taste. *A media exposure diary* might provide information about which programs television viewers watch. If the diarists have been carefully selected, the results of such a survey can be projected onto the relevant market.

Obviously, the diary method of survey also has its limitations: It is very expensive; it requires two to three months for completion; and it is difficult to control. Because of the cost and time involved, there are a number of market research organizations that maintain a continuous diary-information service. They in turn make this information available, for a fee, to advertisers and advertising agencies. Most major consumer advertisers make use of diary information.

Somewhere between the personal interview and the mail survey lies the *telephone interview*. The costs are lower than those for personal inter-

views, but higher than those for a mail survey. The interviews can be completed very quickly. Much valuable information can be elicited on the telephone—demographic characteristics, attitudes, and intentions. The amount of such information is restricted, however, because it is difficult to complete a long, detailed interview over the telephone.

Some market research organizations make use of large groups of people that represent cross sections of the entire population of the United States. These groups are known as *panels* and provide a continuous source of consumer purchasing behavior information that the research organization makes available to its subscribers. Sometimes an individual advertiser sets up a panel, but it is difficult to maintain the active participation of its members. To purchase this information from a research firm is, in the long run, cheaper and faster.

## Sampling

A *sample* is a small, but representative, portion of the total. We cut off a small piece of a wheel of cheese in order to *sample* the whole wheel. We receive a small tube of toothpaste in the mail to encourage us to *sample* that brand of toothpaste. We assume that the little bite of cheese or the half ounce of toothpaste will tell us whether or not we like the product well enough to buy it on our own.

It is not necessary to eat a whole wheel of Swiss cheese to see if we like it. Nor is it necessary to brush our teeth with an entire tube of one brand of toothpaste to see if we like its taste. We predicate our decisions to purchase (or not to purchase) on the assumption that the sample truly represents the entire product. But we must take pains to ensure that the sample we are using is truly representative of the product that interests us. Basing

The use of WATS lines permits fast telephone interviewing on a national basis. Careful supervision of the interview process is important to make sure that every interviewer asks the same question in the same manner. This company also offers the national advertiser facilities for focus-group sessions located in strategic areas around the country.

# You're Right On With Walker*

Walker Research has a national network of six data collection offices and a 40 booth WATS Center. This enables us to exercise positive control over the data gathering process. We standardize interviewer training and offer continuous supervision throughout each step of the research process.

Each office offers Focus Group Facilities, Intercept Interviewing, Local Telephone Interviewing and Pre-Scheduled Central Location Studies.

Let us help you pinpoint your advantages.

 **WALKER RESEARCH, INC.**
Data Collection Offices in:
Indianapolis/New York/St. Louis/
Tampa/San Francisco/Phoenix

Utility Research Offices:
Chicago, Denver, Fort Wayne

*If you would like one of our dartboards, drop us a note on your company letterhead.*

decisions on personal samples ("I asked my brother") or on gut reactions ("It *looked* like good cheese") is very dangerous.

In marketing intelligence, sampling is one step in the establishment of a system intended to obtain the most accurate information on our target market as efficiently and as economically as possible. The scope of the information desired and the expense of gathering that information are the important considerations. Let us turn our attention now to the two most crucial aspects of sampling as described above.

*Is the sample representative of the target market?*

The question is: How do we define "representative"? Our target population may have a specified income level or it may have only a typical income range. Or we may want information on a certain age group—over 18, perhaps, or 18 to 34. Such *parameters,* or boundaries, of our sample would depend on the nature of the market and would affect our sampling procedure.

*Is the sample accurate and reliable?*

If we are going to base important advertising decisions on the results of our sample, we must really expect to obtain dependable results.

It is not unlikely that two samples, using the same procedures, could produce two sets of widely differing data. To rely on *either* set of data would be unwise. The reliability of the sample—the amount of confidence we have in it—depends on two things: the sampling procedure applied and, even more important, the size of the sample. A sample of 1,000 will produce more reliable results than a sample of 200. And, it will be more expensive. The importance of the advertising decision that will later be based on the results of the sample should be the guide to determining the size of the sample. Time,

too, is a factor. There is no need to obtain a degree of accuracy that is not warranted by the risk involved in making a particular decision. Data that arrive too late to be useful serve no purpose regardless of their accuracy. Data must be fresh to be valuable.

**Sampling methods**   Our first step, of course, is to define the population from which the sample is to be drawn. This definition must be clear and complete. We must state the attributes of the target population in terms that are as precise as possible. Once we have specified the demographic characteristics of our target population, we can then decide on the method to use for extracting the sample.

An unrestricted probability sample is a sample chosen at random in which every member of the population has an equal chance of being selected. If we were using an unrestricted probability sample to determine the average weight of all the male students at our school, we would choose the students for our sample at random. We could pick the first 100 male students who cross the campus or every nth student who crosses the campus until we have 100. By using random selection we expect, according to the laws of probability, to get a normal distribution of weights in our sample. It is possible that by chance we could pick the fattest 100 men on our campus. It is equally possible that we could draw the skinniest 100. But it is likely that the characteristics of our random sample will cluster around the true mean. We can, in fact, predict our probable error mathematically.

We can obtain more accurate data by using a *restricted,* or stratified, probability sample. In this sampling method we first divide, or stratify, our population into subgroups and then apply an

This research company offers a very large panel. From this panel, the company can compile attitude and image studies through its WATS line facility. It can also provide *tracking*, that is, information on the movement of a product into homes. For instance, an advertiser who is test marketing a product in several areas of the country can have a profile developed of the families that were the first to buy it. This demographic and psychographic information can help guide the creation of an advertising theme before the advertiser embarks on a national program (called a *roll-out* in the trade).

unrestricted sample to each of the subgroups. For example, we might want to specify that our sample of 100 students consists of equal numbers of freshmen, sophomores, juniors, and seniors, or we might want to have numbers proportionate to the percentage these groups represent in the total school population. It is more than likely that freshmen would compose the largest percentage of the student population, with the percentages declining for each higher category. A stratified sample of this kind will make our data more accurate (and at no extra cost).

We encountered an example of a *nonprobability sample* in a different context when we described how research firms use consumer panels to obtain marketing data. They cannot use either random selection *or* a stratified sample to get as wide a cross section, or as representative a panel, as they need. Instead, they use *purposive selection*. They select one household, in Indiana for example, with a predetermined level of income and of a specified family size. Then they add similar households in other areas of the country to their sample. To this mix, they then add some households with no children, also carefully chosen from different areas of the country, some households with higher and lower income levels and so on, for other demographic characteristics. By carefully selecting their "sample" they can, with as few as 1,000 households, project the purchase behavior of the rest of the American population. This technique is called *quota sampling*, because the research firm has specified a *quota* for each household category. This method is widely used in market studies because it is faster and less expensive than a *probability sample.*[1]

[1] David J. Luck, Donald A. Taylor, and Hugh G. Wales, *Marketing Research*, 4th ed. (Englewood Cliffs, N.J.: 1974), p. 187.

Another form of purposive selection is the *judgment* sample. In this procedure, the criteria for selection are specified and population members are sought, who, in the *judgment* of the individual conducting the study, represent the criteria. The procedure is obviously not scientific, but there are situations in which such judgment might be used. If a member of a panel were to drop out, the research director or supervisor might select a replacement who, *in his or her judgment*, had the same attributes. If advertisers wanted to study the attitude of retail store owners carrying their products and wanted to draw a sample for such purpose, the research director might set up criteria that would describe the types of stores (by dollar sales, location, lines of merchandise, number of employees, and so on). Then, by examining a list of stores, he or she could select the retailers that in *his or her judgment* met the criteria. Of course, the individual exercising that judgment is expected to avoid prejudice and personal whim. The method is efficient, and it does avoid the chances, present in a random selection, of drawing a misrepresentative sample from the target population.

## Motivation research

The data we have gathered thus far are all demographic, that is, they have recorded only such information as age, marital status, income, family size, place and type of residence, car ownership, and other similar attributes of our target population. But demographic information alone may be insufficient for the development of advertising strategy and copy. Although our research may describe a potential user of our product as a woman between the ages of 30 and 35, with 2.3 children, living in a home with 5.4 rooms and 2.1 baths, with 0.6 dogs and 1.58 automobiles, we do not meet many women like this in real life. Moreover, after our product has been on the market for some time, we may discover that Mrs. A., 32 years old, 3 children, buys our product and, in fact, is quite "brand loyal" —she buys 32 units of our product every month. Meanwhile, Mrs. B., 32 years old, 3 children, buys only 7 units of our product each month; and Mrs. C., also 32 years old, 3 children, same education and income level as Mrs. A. and Mrs. B., does not buy our product at all—in fact, will not even try it. Why? Obviously, the notion that we will know our target market after we have segmented it by means of clearly discernible demographics is deceiving.

In order to understand the consumers in our target market better—to understand what makes the difference between users of our product and nonusers, between heavy users and light users— we must begin to probe the *reasons why* they buy particular products. By applying the techniques of psychology, sociology, and anthropology, motivation researchers attempt to explain *what makes consumers react to various products and different appeals.* In many cases the consumers themselves are not aware of the reasons for their reactions, or they are unwilling to reveal them. Under carefully controlled conditions, however, researchers may be able to obtain information on the whys of people's purchasing behavior by using projective techniques and depth interviews.

*Projective techniques* are based on the idea that, although individuals may be unable or unwilling to describe their own feelings in a particular situation, they may do so *indirectly* by ascribing to others the emotions or attitudes that underlie their

This research company specializes in focus groups. On commission by an advertiser or an agency, the company will bring to its offices a group of five or six people of specified demographic characteristics. Then, prompted by a skilled group coordinator, these people will discuss (focus on) cosmetics, cakes, dog food, or any other product category that is of interest to the advertiser. Out of the focus group's relaxed discussion, the advertiser may learn more about consumers' attitudes toward a product and their perceptions of brands. The researchers may observe the discussion through a one-way mirror or have the entire discussion videotaped for careful analysis by the advertising staff.

own reactions to a product, idea, or situation. The procedures used include the Thematic Appercep-tion Test (TAT), picture-association test, word asso-ciation and sentence completion tests, and other psychological devices calculated to get the respon-dent to *act out* the idea.

In *depth interviewing*, researchers encourage respondents to freely express their ideas on sub-jects that are important to the area being re-searched. The procedure is slow and expensive. Some researchers use a *focus-group* interview, working with a group of five or six consumers who will speed the process and perhaps even generate more information as a result of their interaction with each other.

## Psychographics

Every day each of us is bombarded by a tremen-dous number of advertising messages; yet at the end of the day we will remember only one or two of these appeals. The others will have vanished from our consciousness as if we had never seen or heard them. We have protected ourselves from being overwhelmed by this flood of product infor-mation by a process psychologists describe as *se-lective perception*. Unconsciously, we filter out words and symbols that we deem unimportant, while allowing those words and symbols we con-sider important to pass through.

As advertisers, once we understand what motivates consumers in our target market to buy, we must supply the copywriters and artists who create our advertising message with detailed information on the words, signs, and symbols that effectively stimulate this purchasing behavior. Otherwise, there is a very real danger that the personal values of our creative staff will dominate the advertisements they create. As a result, our advertising may impress the advertising community but leave the consumer unaffected.

In the attempt to supply creative personnel with all the information they need to create effective advertising, advertising agencies and research firms have developed methods of obtaining psychographic data. *Psychographics* refers to the development of psychological profiles of several dif-

## ERNEST DICHTER

Dr. Ernest Dichter is internationally recognized as the leading exponent and practitioner in the field of motivational research. He is founder of the Institute of Motivational Research and founder and president of Ernest Dichter Associates International, Ltd.

Born and educated in Austria, Dr. Dichter received a Ph.D. in Psychology from the University of Vienna. In 1938, he came to the United States and joined the J. Stirling Getchell advertising agency, where he introduced a new approach in selling Plymouth automobiles for Chrysler Corporation. He found that when married couples were asked who made the decision to buy a car, the men answered, "I did." But when further questioned about how they arrived at a particular choice, the men began to use the plural pronoun "we" in their explanations. This led Dichter to suggest that Chrysler aim some of its advertising at the real decision makers in car buying—women.

Dr. Dichter has developed many psychological and sociological techniques to study consumer buying habits. He introduced depth interviewing into marketing research and adapted numerous clinical techniques to consumer testing. He is the author of numerous books and articles on market research, including *Handbook of Consumer Motivation* and *Motivating Human Behavior.*

His approach to marketing and motivational research is keen and penetrating and he brings a sense of excitement to his work. As he has said:

Any good detective can show you what proper motivational research is. "What's the motive?" Columbo always asks. There must be a motive. He does motivational research. The motive is greed or jealousy or whatever. . . . We do the same thing.

## THE MR. GOODWRENCH STORY—
### Marketing Research Points the Way

Since the early 1960s, General Motors' share of the multibillion dollar market for automobile replacement parts had been shrinking steadily. Two market research surveys, one commissioned by the National Automobile Dealers Association and one by General Motors itself, indicated that the owners of GM automobiles were not returning to their GM dealers for parts and service. In fact, 72 percent of all GM car owners were going to other companies for parts and service within three years of buying their new cars. In the summer of 1974, the General Motors Parts Division invited twenty-five of its key dealers to Detroit to discuss their common problem: stiff competition for service business.

The result was a new marketing program, arrived at with the help of the GM Corporate Service Section and General Motors' advertising agency, D'Arcy-MacManus & Masius. The object of the program was to fight back against Sears, Ward's, K Mart, and other retailers who had moved into the profitable replacement market for shocks, brakes, and tune-up kits.

The study commissioned by the National Automobile Dealers Association had been made by the Harvard Business School, and it cited four main reasons for customer dissatisfaction with dealer service. First, owners said they were treated with indifference. Second, they complained that service work was often not done right the first time. The third reason that they gave was inconvenience—inconvenient service hours, lack of quick service, and lack of alternate transportation. The fourth reason was the belief that GM dealer service was more expensive than that of other companies.

The General Motors Parts Division set up a program that they hoped would increase dealer service and parts volume by building the belief among GM car owners that GM dealers would provide the best parts and service for their cars. At the same time, the program aimed at instilling an attitude of pride in workmanship among GM dealer personnel to improve the quality of service.

The campaign was centered around a trade character—Mr. Goodwrench—a friendly, believable spokesman who, it was hoped, would help improve the image of GM dealers. The concept was tested by research teams in Minneapolis, Minnesota, and Orlando, Florida. The research teams found that the GM spokesman was accepted as a mechanic whose appearance, as judged by consumer panels, promised experience, friendliness, and trustworthiness.

The next step was advertising in the test cities. Advertisements were placed on television and radio, and in newspapers. The object was to reach 95 percent of all homes in the trading areas as often as possible. Results were very positive—every dealership noted an increase in service business. There was also a noticeable improvement among dealership personnel in their attitude toward their work.

GM used the same advertising strategy in their roll-out plan, and on March 1, 1977, Mr. Goodwrench was introduced nationally. Ads were placed in *Time, Newsweek,*

continued

107

Mr. Goodwrench continued

*U. S. News and World Report,* and *Sports Illustrated.* Sunday supplements such as *Parade* and *Family Weekly* were used in over 450 Sunday papers. Sixty-second commercials were aired on 1,988 radio stations. Mr. Goodwrench appeared on every television network—ABC, NBC, and CBS—over 646 stations.

It worked. Mr. Goodwrench continues to help achieve the marketing goals of the GM Parts Division. Research paid off.

Source: D'Arcy-MacManus & Masius, advertising agency for the General Motors Parts Division.

ferent types of "typical" consumers and their life-styles. A consumer's *life-style* is a distinctive pattern of activities, interests, and opinions that often cannot be deduced from other demographic data.

Psychographics had its origins in motivation research and later attempts by psychological researchers to relate these personality variables to product choice. Psychographics may serve to explain and predict consumer behavior when demographic and socioeconomic analyses are not sufficient. Psychographic variables may include *self-concept, life-style, attitudes, interests, and perception of product attributes.* The first national probability sample study of psychographics conducted by *Holiday* magazine showed a strong positive correlation between life-style and self-concept. People who went out often were also heavy buyers of new products. They thought of themselves as more imaginative and more outgoing than others.[2]

The measurement of personality traits is very complex. A trait is a relatively enduring tendency in an individual to respond a certain way in all situations.[3] To measure these traits, researchers administer interviews, tests, scales, and, when possible, direct observation of an individual's behavior.

Scales are psychological tests that are generally divided into three types: agreement-disagreement (or approve-disapprove), rank order, and forced choice.[4] In the *agree-disagree scale* the subject reports his or her reaction to each item by agreeing or disagreeing. Typical items might be:

I believe it is very important to keep the house spotless.
I believe it is necessary to place the needs of the children before my own.

The *rank-order* scale is one in which the subject is asked to rank all the items in a series of value concepts. Typical statements might be:

a comfortable life
a sense of accomplishment
equality
freedom
social recognition

[2] Emanuel Denby, "Psychographics and from Whence It Came," *Life Style and Psychographics,* ed. William D. Wells (Chicago: American Marketing Association, 1974), p. 15.

[3] Fred N. Kerlinger, *Foundations of Behavioral Research,* 2d ed. (New York: Holt, Rinehart and Winston, Inc., 1973), p. 494.

[4] For detailed information on personality scales and tests, *see The Sixth Mental Measurements Yearbook,* ed. O. Buros (Highland Park, N.J.: Gryphon Press, 1965). For much valuable information on the subject of attitudes and behavioral research, *see* Kerlinger, *Behavioral Research;* and M. Rokeach, *Beliefs, Attitudes, and Values* (San Francisco: Jossey-Bass, 1968).

The *forced-choice* method requires the subject to choose among alternatives that appear (on the surface) equally favorable or unfavorable. In this way the preference value of the items is determined. For example, the subject may be asked to choose between two paired statements such as:

getting ahead in the world
enjoying the pleasure of the moment

In some forced-choice scales four statements are presented for which the subject indicates high preference or low preference.
For example:

conscientious
agreeable
responsive
sensitive

The subject chooses two high-preference words and two low-preference words. Of the four words, two are irrelevant. The subject cannot tell which of the words are irrelevant and which are discriminant of a trait.

## Copy testing

Although we will deal with the problem of measuring advertising effectiveness in a later chapter, it is appropriate at this point to consider the *pretesting* of copy. By pretesting we mean we are testing before the advertisement goes into a magazine or on the air.

Many different methods of pretesting have been developed. We can have rough television commercials, called animatics, shot from a series of drawings of the scenes we want to show. A video-tape of the drawings, accompanied by a sound track, can help researchers evaluate the commercial's effectiveness. We can also have our print advertisements inserted into copies of real magazines, and then test them for recall. We can do a headline test, showing people several possible headlines and thereby determining which headline seems to have the greatest stopping power. We can do portfolio tests—making up a booklet of several advertisements, showing them to people, and recording measures of appeal, recall, and understanding.

## Media research

The most carefully created advertisement can get maximum results only if we, the advertiser, have made the wisest media selection. Our advertisement must reach the greatest number of prospective buyers at the lowest possible cost. Every newspaper and magazine, every television and radio station provides data on the size and demographics of the audience it reaches. We must evaluate this information in relation to our product, our market, and our budget. Of course, it is very important to know the *number* of people in the medium's audience, but we would like to know the sex, age, location, income, occupation, and marital status of that audience as well. We also want to know the image projected by the medium itself because that image comprises the environment in which our message must do its job. We shall examine all aspects of media in coming chapters.

One word in closing—we also want to monitor the advertising efforts of our competitors. Fortunately, this information is readily available from a number of syndicated services which provide the advertising schedule for all national advertisers in all well-defined product categories.

The cost of airing a thirty-second television commercial during prime time (7 to 11 PM) is around $60,000. The cost of preparation for such a commercial may range from $30,000 upward. Together, the preparation and airing add up to a large investment. Before making that investment, an advertiser can have its "rough" commercials tested by a company like Westgate Research. The data gathered from this test can then be used to modify the original script before investing in a finished commercial. As the ad says, the advertiser can test five to seven different commercials in animatic form for what it would cost to produce just one finished commercial.

# Summary

Although we are intent on delivering our advertising message to our target market, we have to remember that our prospective customers may have something to tell us, too. Our prospective customers will deliver their message to us by choosing between our product and its alternatives in the marketplace. The failure rate for new products is claimed to be four out of every five. It is probably higher. Therefore, before our product reaches the marketplace, we must obtain as much information as possible about the people who may buy it. We want to know what products they presently buy, what appeals may be effective in convincing them to try our product, and what media we should use to carry our appeals.

Marketing intelligence can be obtained from two basic sources: primary data and secondary data. We can obtain much valuable information from secondary sources—from company records or from data that have already been compiled by someone else. We must collect primary data for ourselves. We may do this through observational methods or through survey methods, which include personal interviews, mail surveys, diaries, telephone interviews, and panels. Naturally, we cannot survey the entire target market; therefore, we must select a representative "sample" of the people we want to reach.

Motivation research and psychographic profiles will give us even more data on our target market. From focus groups, depth interviewing, and psychological tests, we will obtain information that can help us see our prospective customers as individuals, not merely statistical abstracts.

### Marketing intelligence reference guide

**Government Sources**

*Directory of Federal Statistics for States*, Government Printing Office, Washington, D.C. 20402

*Sources of State Information* and *State Industrial Directories*, Chamber of Commerce of the United States, 1615 H Street, NW, Washington, D.C. 20006

*Statistical Abstract of the United States*, Superintendent of Documents, U.S. Government Printing Office, Washington, D.C. 20402

**Publication Sources**

American Newspaper Publishers Association (ANPA), The Newspaper Center, 11600 Sunrise Valley Drive, Reston, Va. 22091

*Advertising Age*, 740 Rush Street, Chicago, Il. 60611

*Editor and Publisher Market Guide*, 575 Lexington Avenue, New York, N.Y. 10022

Magazine Publishers Association, Inc., 575 Lexington Avenue, New York, N.Y. 10022

Radio Advertising Bureau, 485 Lexington Avenue, New York, N.Y. 10017

*Sales & Marketing Management Survey of Buying Power*, 633 Third Avenue, New York, N.Y. 10017

Television Bureau of Advertising, 1345 Avenue of the Americas, New York, N.Y. 10019

*Private Information Sources*

A. C. Nielsen Co., Nielsen Plaza, Northbrook, Il. 60062

The Arbitron Company, 1350 Avenue of the Americas, New York, N.Y. 10019

Burke International Research Corporation, 420 Lexington Avenue, New York, N.Y. 10017

The Conference Board, 845 Third Avenue, New York, N.Y. 10022

Emhart-Babic Associates, Inc., 120 Route 9W, Englewood Cliffs, N.J. 07632

Home Testing Institute, Two 6th Street, Garden City Park, N.Y. 11040

Starch INRA Hooper, Inc., 566 East Boston Post Road, Mamaroneck, N.Y. 10543

W. R. Simmons & Associates Research, Inc., 219 East 42nd Street, New York, N.Y. 10017

## QUESTIONS FOR DISCUSSION

1. Prepare a questionnaire on travel. Your object is to discover themes for travel advertising. Administer the questionnaire to a small sample of people you consider appropriate. Describe the results of your survey. What would be your recommendation for advertising?

2. Why are population figures alone not the best index of market potential? What other information would you want? Where could you find it? Be specific.

3. If you were to be responsible for the advertising of central air-conditioning systems for private homes, what information would you need about
   a. the market
   b. the media
   c. the buying appeal

4. If you were going to advertise a new dog food and wanted to test market the product in two or three cities, how would you select the cities? What information would you need? Where would you find it? Be specific.

5. For a local bank (one office), what marketing intelligence would you need to prepare an advertising plan? Where would you find the information you need? Be specific.

6. The manufacturer of a new shampoo wants to name the product. How would you go about selecting the name? How can you be sure the name would be well received by consumers?

7. Suppose you were hired as an advertising consultant to an importer of French and Italian racing bicycles. What information would you need to prepare an advertising program? Where would you get the information you need? Be specific.

## Sources and suggestions for further reading

Bass, Frank M. "The Theory of Stochastic Preference and Brand Switching." *Journal of Marketing Research* (February 1974).

Bogart, Leo, and Lehmann, Charles. "What Makes a Brand Name Familiar." *Journal of Marketing Research* (February 1973).

Burger, Phillip C., and Schott, Barbara. "Can Private Brand Buyers Be Identified?" *Journal of Marketing Research* (May 1972).

Day, George S. *Buyer Attitudes and Brand Behavior.* New York: Free Press, 1970.

Dichter, Ernest. *Handbook of Consumer Motivation.* New York: McGraw-Hill, 1964.

Engel, James F.; Kollat, David T.; and Blackwell, Roger D. *Consumer Behavior.* 2d ed. New York: Holt, Rinehart and Winston, 1973.

Granger, C. W. J., and Billson, A. "Consumers' Attitudes Toward Package Size and Price." *Journal of Marketing Research* (August 1972).

Holbert, Neil. *Advertising Research.* Monograph Series #1. Chicago: American Marketing Association, 1975.

Kraft, Frederic B.; Granbois, Donald H.; and Summer, John O. "Brand Evaluation and Brand Choice." *Journal of Marketing Research* (August 1973).

Luck, David J.; Wales, Hugh G.; and Taylor, Donald A. *Marketing Research.* 4th ed. Englewood Cliffs, N.J.: Prentice-Hall, 1974.

Martineau, Pierre. *Motivation in Advertising.* New York: McGraw-Hill, 1957.

Morrison, Bruce J., and Darnoff, Marvin J. "Advertisement Complexity and Looking Time." *Journal of Marketing Research* (November 1972).

Newman, Joseph W., and Werbel, Richard A. "Multi-variate Analysis of Brand Loyalty for Major Household Appliances." *Journal of Marketing Research* (November 1973).

Tull, Donald S., and Hawkins, Del I. *Marketing Research.* New York: Macmillan Publishing Co., 1976.

Wasson, Chester R.; Sturdivant, Frederick D.; and McConaughy, David H. *Competition & Human Behavior.* New York: Appleton-Century-Crofts, 1968.

Wells, William D., ed. *Life Style and Psychographics.* Chicago: American Marketing Association, 1974.

## THE ADVERTISING BUDGET: INVESTMENT OR EXPENSE?

**What is the advertising budget?**

How management philosophy
  affects the advertising budget
  The "expense" school of thought
  The "investment" school of thought
The upper hand on the bottom line
  The controllers
  The marketing executives
The advertising–sales relationship
  Advertising is postpurchase
    reassurance
  Advertising wins dealers

**Methods of setting the advertising
  budget**

Influence of the product on the
  appropriation

Stage in the product's life cycle
Type of product
Favorable primary demand
The objective, or task, method
Matching competitors—the
  share-of-the-market method
Percentage-of-sales method
An empirical method
Take your choice

**Time to set the budget**

Budget periods and flexibility

**What belongs in the advertising
  budget?**

### WORKING VOCABULARY

| | | |
|---|---|---|
| budget | share-of-the-market method | empirical method |
| reassurance value | percentage-of-sales method | per-unit assessment |
| objective, or task, method | unit-of-sale method | |

CHAPTER

# the advertising budget: investment or expense?

*A famous company president once said: "Advertising, to me, is really one of the mysteries of American business. . . . I can figure my taxes, estimate my depreciation, determine my sales cost, derive my return per share. Yet there are times when I spend as much as $18,000,000 a year on advertising—and have no idea what I am really getting for my money."*

ROSSER REEVES
*Reality in Advertising*

ONCE WE HAVE MADE THE DECISION that advertising will be a component of our promotional mix, we cannot sit back in our chairs and begin dreaming up ideas for our campaigns. Instead, we must sharpen our pencils and go back to work, seeking the answers to a new set of questions.

1. How much advertising will we need to achieve our agreed-upon *marketing* objectives?

2. How much can we *afford* to spend on advertising and still achieve the agreed-upon *profit* objective?

3. Can we compromise, can we accept less advertising and still achieve our marketing objectives or our profit objective?

4. How much advertising should we devote to each of our company's individual products or to each group of products?

115

**5.** How much advertising should we devote to our new products and how much to our established products?

The answers to these questions will guide us in making one of the most difficult advertising decisions: the setting of our advertising budget.

# What is
# the advertising budget?

In business management, a *budget* is the dollar representation of planned activities over a specified period of time. The advertising budget is a single dollar figure that represents a company's total planned advertising investment, including any reserve for unforeseen expenses. The advertising budget is usually set for a one-year period and contains a detailed breakdown of the advertising activities that the company will spend its money on during that year. In other words, the advertising budget describes proposed advertising activities in terms of dollars.

The benefits of such long-range planning are obvious. It forces advertising and marketing executives to carefully review past and/or proposed results of the company's advertising effort, and it provides management with a standard against which they can judge current performance.

## How management philosophy affects the advertising budget

A company's top management is generally concerned only with setting budget *totals*. The question of how the total advertising budget should be divided among the company's different products is usually left to the discretion of the company's marketing executives. Those questions are considered mere details that can be cleaned up by less than top management.

In setting the total budget for advertising, top management will consider the company's advertising effort in relation to the company's profit objective. For most companies that advertise, a fundamental goal is to increase profits. Among many business executives there exist two schools of thought on how their company's advertising budget relates to their company's profit objective. One school believes that advertising is an expense; the other believes that advertising is an investment. The attitude of a company's top management is important because, in any year, profits can be increased by reducing expenses or by increasing sales volume, or market share. As background to our discussion of how top management sets the advertising budget, we should first examine the philosophies of these two schools.

**The "expense" school of thought**    Management that belongs to the "expense" school believes that their company's advertising, if any, should be kept to a minimum. They begrudge every penny the company spends on advertising. When they must cut expenses, advertising is one of the first things to go. It is an easily reducible expense—that is, cutting back on advertising will not have an immediate impact on the company's operations. Telephone service is an expense, too, but cutting back drastically on the use of telephones will have a dramatic impact on the way the company does business.

**The "investment" school of thought**    Management that belongs to the "investment" school believes that advertising is an investment, and, like any investment made by the company, should have a predictable rate of return. In their minds, advertising is similar to an investment in bonds or in shares of stock. They feel that devoting a certain amount of money to advertising will yield a certain percentage of increased sales volume. Unfortunately, advertising does not lend itself to this sort of evaluation. As we learned in Chapter 2, advertising is only one component of the marketing mix. It is not possible to determine how much of the result of a given marketing program is attributable to advertising alone, because it is difficult to isolate the effect of advertising from such factors as product quality improvements, price changes, or competitive changes. The investment school's attitude might be compared to that of a health food enthusiast who claims that wheat germ mixed with yogurt will make one healthy. Wheat germ and yogurt will *contribute* to a person's health as a component of a program including a balanced diet, adequate rest, and exercise. So, too, will advertising contribute to the success of our marketing program.

### The upper hand on the bottom line

When it is time for a company to set its budget for the coming year, the question of how much money is to be budgeted for advertising may be fiercely debated by representatives of the investment and expense schools of thought. Let us examine the reasoning of members of each school of thought and their methods for setting the advertising budget.

**The controllers**  Controllers, or financial vice-presidents, are not necessarily enthusiastic about allocating monies to achieve an unpredictable result.

Some consider advertising an expense, and their method of setting the advertising budget may be referred to as the "leftover" technique. In simplified form, their method of arriving at an advertising budget is as follows: First, they add up what they consider to be the company's necessary expenses. These include administrative expenses, research and development costs, interest on borrowings, and taxes. Then, they subtract the total of these necessary expenses from the company's estimated gross profit for the coming year, as based on projected sales volume. This gives them a figure for the company's net profit. From the net profit, they subtract the dividend that the company's board of directors wants to pay stockholders. Whatever is left over can be budgeted for advertising. It is really a very simple method, requiring only the most ordinary arithmetical skills for which a pocket calculator may be substituted. Some controllers do not appreciate the fact that there *may be* a correlation between the advertising budget and sales volume.

**The marketing executives**  In contrast, the company's marketing vice-president believes that there is some relationship between advertising expenditures and sales volume. The marketing executive wants to increase the company's profit by increasing sales volume rather than by decreasing expenses. In setting the advertising budget, the marketing vice-president relies on a method that might be termed the "intuitive" technique. This method relies on the judgment of the company's marketing executives. These executives are familiar with the company's past advertising expenditures and past sales volume. They reason thus: If next year we hope to increase our sales by 10 percent, we should also increase our advertising expenditures by 10 percent. In other words, a 10 percent increase in the advertising budget should yield a 10 percent increase in sales. These marketing executives also take competitive activities into consideration. If, they reason, one of our competitors is spending 5 percent more than we are now on a sales volume no greater than our own, we had better increase our appropriation by an additional 5 percent—no, make it 10 percent—in order to offset the competitive factor.

Executives who think in this way *assume* there is a relationship between advertising expenditures and sales volume, but they really *do not know*. Some critics of this technique say it is nothing more than guessing. It is. If we did know that every $x$ dollars' worth of advertising would produce $y$ dollars in sales, all we would have to do to achieve unlimited sales is continue to increase our advertising budget.

Some controllers do not credit advertising with any productive role, however, and do not recognize any relationship at all between advertising expenditures and sales results. Marketing executives like those described above recognize the existence of a relationship, but have made no attempt to relate advertising expenditures to the attainment of specific objectives. Let us attempt to determine just what the relationship of advertising to sales is.

### The advertising–sales relationship

The value of advertising lies in its ability to persuade a sufficient number of prospects to do what it says or to buy what it sells. Much advertising is designed to assist the sales force. It makes it easier for a salesperson to sell consumers something at some future time. Advertising on radio and television, the food pages in newspapers, and the array of ads in magazines are all designed not to make a sale but to make the prospect *aware* of a product or a service, *to stimulate interest, to develop desire,* and *to secure an inquiry or "lead,"* thereby making it possible for the actual sale to be consummated at some other place and time.

Of course, today in so many buying transactions the salesperson has disappeared. Self-service is the practice. Here advertising fills a critical role. It preinforms and presells customers to such an extent that when they enter the place where the purchase will actually be made—the supermarket, for example—the necessity for personal salesmanship has entirely disappeared. Advertising, then, works six ways to help make sales:

1. Advertising makes the prospect familiar with the product.

2. Advertising reminds the prospect about the product.

3. Advertising brings news of new products.

4. Advertising adds a value not intrinsic to the product.

5. Advertising reassures and helps retain present customers.

6. Advertising increases the confidence and enthusiasm of the people engaged in the marketing process of that product.

**Advertising is postpurchase reassurance**  Research into advertising indicates that consumers read the advertising for a product *after* they have bought it as carefully as they do *before* they buy it. This is particularly true with regard to major purchases such as an automobile or a major appliance. Having made a serious buying decision, the buyers want reassurance that they have acted wisely and

THE ADVERTISING BUDGET: INVESTMENT OR EXPENSE?

bought well. They find that reassurance in the advertising for the product. There they find a reaffirmation of the values that induced the purchase in the first place. The continued appearance of advertising for that product is testimony to the wisdom of the buyers. They are, therefore, very likely to buy the same product again when the need arises.

Few businesses can operate successfully without sales to customers who are satisfied enough to repeat their purchases. This *reassurance value* is one of advertising's most important contributions to sales. The postpurchase impact of advertising explains in large measure why no major advertiser ever stops or sharply curtails advertising.

**Advertising wins dealers**   Retailers find their image enhanced by the brands they sell. It is difficult to imagine the disorientation consumers would feel if they entered a supermarket and found no familiar brands. The chances are they would do little, if any, shopping in that store. Therefore, retailers prefer to stock well-known, fast-moving, nationally advertised brands. Shelf space is at a premium. Retailers are most reluctant to make room for an unknown brand. Once again, we see the relationship between advertising and sales. A company must invest in advertising to build an effective distribution network. Without a network of dealers, sales would be unobtainable.

We have examined two procedures for arriving at the advertising budget. Today, most knowledgeable executives are aware of the relationship between advertising and sales. At the same time, they know that it is impossible to isolate the effect of advertising on their company's sales volume. As advertisers, we must approach the problem of budget allocation in a businesslike manner. We want to

protect the profits that are the concern of the company controllers and presidents, and, at the same time, we want to make a sufficient investment in advertising to insure the growth and stability of our company. We must balance need against affordability.

# Methods of setting the advertising budget

We can develop our advertising budget in several different ways. We can ask ourselves:

1. How much money must we spend on advertising in order to meet our marketing objectives?

2. What does our nearest competitor spend on advertising?

3. What percentage of sales, or what percentage of the price of each unit we sell, should we set aside for advertising?

Before we examine each of these three methods in detail, however, we should remind ourselves of an important fact: Our ultimate choice of a method to use will depend on our company's objectives, its financial capabilities, its philosophy of management, and, perhaps most important of all, its product.

## Influence of the product on the appropriation

**Stage in the product's life cycle**   It takes substantially more advertising money to launch a new

# ESTIMATED ADVERTISING PERCENTAGES IN SELECTED INDUSTRIES

| Industry sector | Advertising as % of net sales 1977 |
|---|---|
| **FOOD PRODUCTS** | |
| Food & kindred products | 2.9 |
| Meat products | 1.1 |
| Dairy products | 2.0 |
| Canned foods | 2.6 |
| Flour & other grain mill products | 2.1 |
| Bakery products | 2.2 |
| Malt beverages | 5.1 |
| **TOBACCO PRODUCTS** | |
| Cigarettes | 5.4 |
| Cigars | 2.0 |
| **TEXTILE MILL PRODUCTS** | |
| Textile products | 0.3 |
| Floor covering mills | 6.0 |
| **APPAREL PRODUCTS** | |
| Apparel & finished products | 1.3 |
| **MANUFACTURERS OF FURNITURE & FIXTURES** | |
| Household furniture | 1.6 |
| Office furniture | 0.2 |
| **PAPER** | |
| Paper products | 0.5 |
| **PRINTING & PUBLISHING** | |
| Publishing | 2.9 |
| Newspapers | 0.9 |
| Periodicals | 4.1 |
| Books | 4.2 |
| **CHEMICALS & ALLIED PRODUCTS** | |
| Chemicals | 1.6 |
| Industrial inorganic chemicals | 0.4 |
| Plastics materials & synthetic resins | 0.4 |
| Ethical drugs | 5.7 |
| Soap & other detergents | 7.2 |
| Paints, varnishes & lacquers | 1.6 |

| Industry sector | Advertising as % of net sales 1977 |
|---|---|
| **PETROLEUM & COAL PRODUCTS** | |
| Petroleum refining | 0.3 |
| Paving & roofing materials | 0.5 |
| **RUBBER & MISC. PLASTICS PRODUCTS** | |
| Rubber products | 1.1 |
| Misc. plastic products | 0.8 |
| Footwear, except rubber | 1.9 |
| **STONE, CLAY & GLASS PRODUCTS** | |
| Glass containers | 0.2 |
| Pottery & china | 3.6 |
| **FOUNDRIES** | |
| Blast furnaces | 0.1 |
| **FABRICATED METALS** | |
| Heating equipment & plumbing fixtures | 1.8 |
| **MACHINERY & EQUIPMENT** | |
| Farm & garden machinery & equipment | 1.2 |
| Metalworking equipment | 0.5 |
| Office computing & accounting machines | 1.5 |
| Refrigeration & service industry equipment | 1.1 |
| **ELECTRIC & ELECTRONIC EQUIPMENT** | |
| Household appliances | 2.5 |
| Radio, TV sets & home entertainment | 3.0 |
| **TRANSPORTATION EQUIPMENT** | |
| Automotive vehicles | 0.8 |
| Travel trailers & campers | 1.4 |

| Industry sector | Advertising as % of net sales 1977 |
|---|---|
| **MISC. MANUFACTURING INDUSTRIES** | |
| Jewelry & silverware | 4.6 |
| Musical instruments | 3.6 |
| Toys, games & sporting goods | 5.4 |
| Pens & other writing instruments | 4.7 |
| **COMMUNICATIONS** | |
| Radio-TV broadcasters | 2.3 |
| CATV companies | 1.2 |
| **WHOLESALING** | |
| Auto parts | 0.5 |
| Sporting & recreational goods | 6.9 |
| Drugs | 2.5 |
| Food | 0.9 |
| **RETAILING** | |
| Lumber | 1.6 |
| Department stores | 2.6 |
| Variety stores | 2.2 |
| Grocery store chains | 0.8 |
| Automotive dealers & supplies | 2.8 |
| Apparel | 2.1 |
| Women's ready-to-wear | 0.7 |
| Shoes | 1.8 |
| Furniture stores | 5.7 |
| Household appliances | 5.2 |
| Restaurants & fast food chains | 2.6 |
| Mail-order houses | 16.6 |
| **FINANCIAL** | |
| Savings & loan | 0.7 |
| Consumer finance | 1.0 |
| Financial service | 0.8 |
| **MISC. SERVICE INDUSTRIES** | |
| Hotels & motels | 2.0 |
| Personal & family services | 3.9 |
| Motion pictures | 7.0 |
| Educational services | 4.9 |

Source: Schonfeld & Associates, Inc., Chicago.

Note that advertising ratios for CHEMICALS AND ALLIED PRODUCTS may vary widely: the ratio of advertising to sales for soaps and detergents (consumer products) is 18 times that for industrial inorganic chemicals. Consumer products traditionally show higher ratios of advertising to sales than do industrial goods. (Consider this chart only a general guide, because what companies consider advertising may vary, and data from advertisers involved in several industries may be derived from all or merely one of their fields.)

Although the data used to fill out the form below is fictitious, the task method can be used to determine the advertising budget for any company or product line. In addition to the advertising objectives listed below, a company might have the hiring of more people for its sales force as an objective. In order to hire more salespeople, the company has to find and interview applicants. Advertising could be used to draw applications and to improve the image of the company in order to help its recruiters on college campuses.

| TASK METHOD BUDGET FORM | | | |
|---|---|---|---|
| **Objective** | **Subobjectives** | **Strategy** | **Budget** |
| Increase number of inquiries | 1. From retailers <br> 2. From consumers | Trade advertising <br> Print advertising | $ 25,000 <br> $100,000 |
| Improve image | 1. As a modern company <br> 2. For a quality product | Television advertising <br> Publicity program | $500,000 <br> $ 60,000 |
| Stimulate sales volume | 1. For purchase of larger sizes among present users <br> 2. For new tries | Television advertising <br> Newspaper coupons <br> Cooperative advertising and dealer aids | $100,000 <br> $100,000 <br> $ 50,000 |

product than it does to keep an old one going. Most companies do not expect to make a profit during the introductory period of a product's life cycle. During that period advertising dollars should come from capital rather than from income, as should all the other costs that are incurred in getting a new product ready for market.

**Type of product**     As the chart on the opposite page shows, there are wide variations from product to product in the percentage of sales invested in advertising. To what can we attribute the variations? An examination of the table reveals that products more capable of being differentiated seem to justify a greater advertising investment. Products that are sold primarily on the basis of price do not justify the expenditure of many advertising dollars to create a brand preference in consumers. Price is relatively unimportant for *Soaps and Detergents* but is an important factor for *Industrial Chemicals.* Note

that the figures in the chart are *averages* and may themselves include wide variations.

**Favorable primary demand**     Advertising intended to stimulate *brand preference* is much more effective if the product classification is in demand. No matter how many millions of dollars we spend on advertising our brand of 78 RPM records, we shall never succeed in substantially increasing our sales because most turntables manufactured today do not play records of this type.

### The objective, or task, method

If we define the budget as a plan to achieve certain marketing objectives, we are using advertising as a tool. What must we spend to have a program adequate for the job? With this method, we begin by stating our objectives. What do we want our advertising to do? *Stimulate* leads for the sales force?

*Force* a level of brand awareness among a specific group of consumers? *Force* distribution of our product through particular channels? Once these goals are set, we can go on to determine how many ads in which magazines or how many commercials on which radio or television stations it will take to stimulate the leads or force the distribution we seek. If the selection of the type and quantity of advertisements is the *art* of advertising, then budget development is the *science,* because clearly defined objectives make measuring the effectiveness of the advertising much more accurate.

Of course, once we have determined the final costs, management must decide if the company can afford them. If the company is not able to invest the amount of money called for in our plan, then we must determine which of our objectives can be modified or sacrificed to bring the budget within reasonable limits. In any case, the *task, or objective, method* precludes hasty judgments.

> Advertising managers are generally in agreement that, in theory, the ad budget should be determined only after the objectives have been approved and the program for achieving these objectives has been worked out. However, most of them find that, in practice, management has strong views on how much the company can "afford" to spend on advertising, either in dollars or as a percentage of either total sales revenues or total marketing costs.[1]

## Matching competitors— the share-of-the-market method

A simple way for us to establish our advertising budget is to take the budget of a company that al-

[1] Saul S. Sands, "Setting Advertising Objectives," *Strides in Business Policy*, National Industrial Conference Board, no. 18 (1966), p. 15.

ready has a market share and match those figures or exceed them. We assume that our competitor must be doing something right to have achieved its market share, and that it has learned from experience what its promotional mix should be. The concept is intriguing but hardly sound management. Of course, we should consider the competition in calculating our budget, but we must keep in mind the fact that their figures are derived for *their* company, with *their* objectives— and *before* we came on the scene. Now it's a new ball game.

## Percentage-of-sales method

Nothing could be easier than to take a specific percentage of the sales of our product and apply that sum to advertising. What percentage? The percentage can be based on the industry average or on the percentage the company applied the preceding year. Notice that we suggested the use of the industry average, which is an excellent guide if the *range* of percentages that compose that average is not too large.

But even if the range is small, there are other pitfalls that we must avoid. Imagine an industry in which the top spender uses 6 percent of sales for its advertising budget, while the stingiest uses 1 percent of its sales. We can take a mean percentage and spend 3.5 percent of our sales on advertising. But suppose the industry in our example is the computer industry, and the stingiest spender is International Business Machines Corporation? Even with only 1 percent of their total sales from computers budgeted for advertising, IBM will no doubt have a lot more money to spend than our 3.5 percent will allow us. We have to consider the other companies in our industry in terms of their profitability, their length of time in the industry, their market share, and their marketing objectives.

THE ADVERTISING BUDGET: INVESTMENT OR EXPENSE?

| MEDIA | JANUARY Space | JANUARY Dollars | FEBRUARY Space | FEBRUARY Dollars | CUMULATIVE Pages | CUMULATIVE Dollars | MARCH Space | MARCH Dollars | APRIL Space | APRIL Dollars |
|---|---|---|---|---|---|---|---|---|---|---|
| **TOBACCO & TOBACCO PRODUCTS** | | | | | | | | | **G110** | |
| **PHILIP MORRIS, INC., New York, N. Y.** | | | | | | | | | | |
| **MERIT FILTER CIGARETTES** | | | | | | | | | **G111** | |
| Business Week (420) | 1 P4s | 2,570 | 1 P4s | 1,710 | .08 | 4,280 | | | | |
| **PHILIP MORRIS, INC., New York, N. Y.** | | | | | | | | | | |
| **MERIT KINGS & 100'S REGULAR & MENTHOL FILTER CIGARETTES** | | | | | | | **$10,323,077 (1977) G111** | | | |
| Atlantic (420) | | | 1 P4 | 6,260 | 1.00 | 6,260 | | | | |
| Better Homes & Gar. (429) | 1 P4 | 43,995 | 1 P4 | 46,850 | 2.00 | 90,845 | | | | |
| Book Digest (182) | 1 P4 | 10,500 | 1 P4 | 10,500 | 2.00 | 21,000 | | | | |
| Cosmopolitan (429) | | | 1 P4 | 18,595 | 1.00 | 18,595 | | | | |
| Cue (429) | | | 2 C42 | 6,400 | 1.00 | 6,400 | | | | |
| Esquire (420) | | | 4 C4 | 17,500 | 1.00 | 17,500 | | | | |
| Family Circle (429) | | | 1 P4 | 46,100 | 1.00 | 46,100 | | | | |
| Glamour (429) | 1 P4 | 15,300 | | | 1.00 | 15,300 | | | | |
| Golf (429) | 1 P4 | 12,770 | | | 1.00 | 12,770 | | | | |
| Golf Digest (420) | 3 C4 | 17,690 | | | 1.00 | 17,690 | | | | |
| Harper's Bazaar (429) | 4 C4 | 12,500 | 1 P4 | 10,550 | 2.00 | 23,050 | | | | |
| Harper's Magazine (420) | | | 1 P4 | 6,260 | 1.00 | 6,260 | | | | |
| House Beautiful (429) | 1 P4 | 13,300 | | | 1.00 | 13,300 | | | | |
| House & Garden (429) | 1 P4 | 16,360 | | | 1.00 | 16,360 | | | | |
| Ladies' Home Jrl. (429) | 1 P4 | 32,890 | 1 P4 | 36,180 | 2.00 | 69,070 | | | | |
| Mademoiselle (429) | 1 P4 | 8,950 | | | 1.00 | 8,950 | | | | |
| McCall's Magazine (429) | | | 1 P4 | 41,600 | 1.00 | 41,600 | | | | |
| Money (420) | 2 C4 | 13,555 | 4 C4 | 17,140 | 2.00 | 30,695 | | | | |
| New West (420) | 1 P4l | 6,500 | 4 C4l | 8,480 | 2.00 | 14,980 | | | | |
| New York Magazine (420) | 2 C4l | 8,900 | 3 C42 | 9,440 | 2.00 | 18,340 | | | | |
| Newsweek (420) | 1 P42 | 41,590 | | | . . . | . . . | | | | |
| Newsweek (420) | 1 P44 | 41,590 | | | | | | | | |
| Newsweek (420) | 2 C45 | 41,590 | 1 P43 | 41,590 | 4.00 | 166,360 | | | | |
| Oui (420) | 1 P4 | 11,900 | | | 1.00 | 11,900 | | | | |
| Penthouse (420) | 1 P4 | 31,085 | | | 1.00 | 31,085 | | | | |
| People Weekly (420) | | | 1 P4l | 18,950 | | | | | | |
| People Weekly (420) | 1 P42 | 18,950 | 4 C42 | 24,650 | | | | | | |
| People Weekly (420) | 1 P44 | 18,950 | 1 P44 | 18,950 | 5.00 | 100,450 | | | | |
| Playboy (420) | | | 1 P4 | 36,675 | 1.00 | 36,675 | | | | |
| Psychology Today (420) | | | 1 P4 | 19,090 | 1.00 | 19,090 | | | | |
| Redbook Magazine (429) | 1 P4 | 28,735 | 1 P4 | 29,525 | 2.00 | 58,260 | | | | |
| Saturday Review (420) | | | 4 C4l | 9,920 | 1.00 | 9,920 | | | | |
| Signature (420) | 4 C4 | 7,145 | 4 C4 | 7,145 | 2.00 | 14,290 | | | | |
| Southern Living (420) | 1 P4 | 15,390 | | | 1.00 | 15,390 | | | | |
| Sports Illustrated (420) | 2 Pl | 47,740 | | | . . . | . . . . | | | | |
| Sports Illustrated (420) | 1 P4l | 37,235 | | | . . . | . . . . | | | | |
| Sports Illustrated (420) | 4 C4l | 47,995 | 1 P43 | 37,235 | | | | | | |
| Sports Illustrated (420) | 1 P45 | 37,235 | 1 P44 | 37,235 | 7.00 | 244,675 | | | | |
| TV Guide (182) | 1 P4l | 56,500 | | | | | | | | |
| TV Guide (182) | 4 C43 | 70,200 | 1 P42 | 56,500 | 3.00 | 183,200 | | | | |
| Time (420) | 4 C43 | 75,330 | | | . . . | . . . . | | | | |
| Time (420) | 1 P45 | 58,755 | 3 C43 | 58,755 | 3.00 | 192,840 | | | | |
| Travel & Leisure (420) | | | 2 C4 | 11,070 | 1.00 | 11,070 | | | | |
| U.S.News&World Rep. (420) | 1 P42 | 28,800 | 1 P4l | 28,800 | | | | | | |
| U.S.News&World Rep. (420) | 4 C43 | 36,760 | 1 P43 | 28,800 | 4.00 | 123,160 | | | | |
| Us (420) | 1 P42 | 3,725 | | | 1.00 | 3,725 | | | | |
| Vogue (429) | | | 1 P4 | 11,800 | 1.00 | 11,800 | | | | |
| Woman's Day (429) | 1 P4 | 43,920 | 1 P4 | 43,920 | 2.00 | 87,840 | | | | |
| **Total** | | 1,014,330 | | 802,465 | 68.00 | 1,816,795 | | | | |
| Family Weekly (850) | 1 P42 | 65,430 | | | . . . | . . . . | | | | |
| Family Weekly (850) | 1 P44 | 65,430 | | | | | | | | |
| Family Weekly (850) | 1 P45 | 65,430 | 1 P43 | 65,430 | 4.00 | 261,720 | | | | |
| New York Times Mag. (850) | 1 P42 | 11,605 | | | . . . | . . . . | | | | |
| New York Times Mag. (850) | 1 P44 | 11,605 | | | | | | | | |
| New York Times Mag. (850) | 3 C45 | 11,605 | 1 P43 | 11,605 | 4.00 | 46,420 | | | | |
| Parade (850) | 1 P42 | 125,050 | | | | | | | | |
| Parade (850) | 1 P44 | 125,050 | | | | | | | | |
| Parade (850) | 1 P45 | 125,050 | 1 P42 | 125,050 | 4.00 | 500,200 | | | | |
| Sunday News Mag. (850) | 1 P42 | 21,310 | 1 P4l | 21,310 | | | | | | |
| Sunday News Mag. (850) | 4 C44 | 22,310 | 1 P42 | 21,310 | 4.00 | 86,240 | | | | |
| **Total** | | 649,875 | | 244,705 | 16.00 | 894,580 | | | | |
| **Grand Total** | | 1,664,205 | | 1,047,170 | 84.00 | 2,711,375 | | | | |

## SPLIT-RUN AND PARTIAL-RUN ADVERTISING

Split-run advertising is identified by the following superior-letter codes: "d"—geographical split-run advertising using full circulation; "a"—numerical, alternate copy or newsstand-subscription splits using full circulation. Partial-run advertising is identified by: "b"— partial circulation on a national distribution basis; "s"—sectional advertising and partial circulation on a geographical basis: "k"—demographic editions.

## 100 LEADERS' ADVERTISING AS PERCENT OF SALES

Covering total 1976 ad expenditures, including measured and unmeasured media

| Ad rank | Company | Advertising | Sales | Adv. as % of sales |
|---|---|---|---|---|
| **CARS** | | | | |
| 2 | General Motors Corp. | $287,000,000 | $47,181,000,000 | 0.6 |
| 7 | Ford Motor Co. | 162,000,000 | 28,839,661,000 | 0.5 |
| 19 | Chrysler Corp. | 110,000,000 | 15,537,800,000 | 0.7 |
| 48 | Volkswagen of America | 60,500,000 | 8,900,000,000 | 0.7 |
| 67 | Toyota Motor Sales, U.S.A. | 42,418,000 | 7,173,911,000 | 0.6 |
| 72 | Nissan Motor Corp. in U.S.A. | 40,000,000 | 7,362,200,000 | 0.5 |
| 74 | American Motors Corp. | 38,535,400 | 2,315,470,000 | 1.6 |
| 99 | American Honda Motor Co. | 19,928,300 | 2,927,600,000 | 0.7 |
| 100 | British Leyland Motors Corp. | 18,349,000 | 385,000,000 | 4.8 |
| **FOOD** | | | | |
| 3 | General Foods Corp. | 275,000,000 | 3,641,600,000 | 7.6 |
| 13 | General Mills | 131,600,000 | 2,909,404,000 | 4.5 |
| 20 | McDonald's Corp. | 105,000,000 | 3,063,000,000 | 3.4 |
| 25 | Norton Simon Inc. | 91,634,000 | 1,342,491,000 | 6.8 |
| 27 | Nabisco Inc. | 90,100,000 | 2,027,300,000 | 4.4 |
| 31 | Ralston Purina Co. | 87,780,000 | 3,393,800,000 | 2.6 |
| 33 | Kraft Inc. | 82,800,000 | 4,226,788,000 | 2.0 |
| 36 | Beatrice Foods Co. | 76,800,000 | 5,288,000,000 | 1.5 |
| 39 | Pillsbury Co. | 74,000,000 | 1,460,826,000 | 5.1 |
| 42 | Campbell Soup Co. | 69,000,000 | 1,634,762,000 | 4.2 |
| 44 | Kellogg Co. | 67,200,000 | 1,385,446,000 | 4.9 |
| 52 | Borden Inc. | 58,700,000 | 3,381,075,000 | 1.7 |
| 58 | Nestle Co. | 50,000,000 | 1,000,000,000 | 5.0 |
| 61 | CPC International | 48,700,000 | 1,165,870,000 | 4.2 |
| 62 | H. J. Heinz Co. | 47,000,000 | 1,868,820,000 | 2.5 |
| 64 | Standard Brands Inc. | 47,000,000 | 1,200,000,000 | 3.9 |
| 70 | Quaker Oats Co. | 41,252,300 | 1,473,052,000 | 2.8 |
| 79 | Carnation Co. | 33,069,300 | 2,166,957,121 | 1.5 |
| 96 | Consolidated Foods Corp. | 22,600,000 | 2,892,000,000 | 0.8 |
| **SOAPS, CLEANSERS (AND ALLIED)** | | | | |
| 1 | Procter & Gamble Co. | 445,000,000 | 5,300,000,000 | 8.4 |
| 12 | Unilever | 135,000,000 | 1,226,504,000 | 10.7 |
| 15 | Colgate-Palmolive Co. | 118,000,000 | 3,511,492,000 | 3.4 |
| 68 | S. C. Johnson & Son | 42,000,000 | 315,000,000 | 13.3 |
| 69 | Clorox Co. | 42,000,000 | 822,101,000 | 5.1 |

| Ad rank | Company | Advertising | Sales | Adv. as % of sales |
|---|---|---|---|---|
| **TOBACCO** | | | | |
| 9 | Philip Morris Inc. | $149,000,000 | $4,293,782,000 | 3.5 |
| 11 | R. J. Reynolds Industries Inc. | 140,276,400 | 5,753,568,000 | 2.4 |
| 32 | American Brands | 87,000,000 | 4,125,800,000 | 2.1 |
| 34 | B.A.T. Industries Ltd. | 82,000,000 | 2,025,723,000 | 4.0 |
| 55 | Liggett Group Inc. | 53,209,000 | 851,877,100 | 6.2 |
| **DRUGS AND COSMETICS** | | | | |
| 5 | Warner-Lambert Co. | 199,000,000 | 1,300,000,000 | 15.3 |
| 6 | Bristol-Myers Co. | 189,000,000 | 1,986,370,000 | 9.5 |
| 8 | American Home Products Corp. | 158,000,000 | 1,800,000,000 | 8.8 |
| 16 | Richardson-Merrell | 115,507,000 | 745,877,000 | 15.5 |
| 24 | Gillette Co. | 94,000,000 | 1,491,506,000 | 6.3 |
| 41 | Sterling Drug Inc. | 70,000,000 | 638,938,000 | 11.0 |
| 43 | Johnson & Johnson | 68,900,000 | 1,493,172,000 | 4.6 |
| 47 | Revlon Inc. | 61,000,000 | 600,000,000 | 10.2 |
| 49 | Chesebrough-Pond's Inc. | 60,000,000 | 746,986,000 | 8.0 |
| 50 | Schering-Plough Corp. | 60,000,000 | 871,537,000 | 6.9 |
| 56 | SmithKline Corp. | 51,644,000 | 673,501,000 | 7.7 |
| 60 | Miles Laboratories | 49,000,000 | 315,186,000 | 15.5 |
| 65 | Avon Products Inc. | 46,000,000 | 1,434,374,000 | 3.2 |
| 75 | Morton-Norwich | 36,400,000 | 563,710,000 | 6.5 |
| 81 | Pfizer Inc. | 32,960,000 | 869,400,000 | 3.8 |
| 84 | Block Drug Co. | 30,000,000 | 127,186,000 | 23.6 |
| 86 | A. H. Robins Co. | 28,331,000 | 284,925,000 | 9.9 |
| 90 | Squibb Corp. | 26,500,000 | 1,214,509,000 | 2.2 |
| 93 | Noxell Corp. | 25,350,000 | 122,167,000 | 20.7 |
| 94 | Merck & Co. | 24,000,000 | 1,661,514,000 | 1.4 |
| **GUM AND CANDY** | | | | |
| 71 | Mars Inc. | 40,850,000 | 735,000,000 | 5.6 |
| 82 | Wm. Wrigley Jr. Co. | 32,529,000 | 370,198,000 | 8.8 |
| **LIQUOR** | | | | |
| 14 | Heublein Inc. | 29,143,000 | 1,550,902,000 | 8.3 |
| 45 | Seagram Co. Ltd. | 66,000,000 | 2,048,970,000 | 3.2 |
| 92 | Hiram Walker-Gooderham & Worts Ltd. | 26,000,000 | 875,000,000 | 3.0 |
| **BEER** | | | | |
| 57 | Jos. Schlitz Brewing Co. | 50,950,000 | 1,214,662,000 | 4.2 |
| 59 | Anheuser-Busch Inc. | 49,021,000 | 1,752,998,000 | 2.7 |

| | | Advertising | Sales | % |
|---|---|---|---|---|
| **OIL** | | | | |
| 10 | Mobil Corp. | $146,500,000 | $28,046,467,000 | 0.5 |
| 83 | Exxon Corp. | 32,000,000 | 52,626,000,000 | 0.1 |
| 98 | Shell Oil Co. | 21,000,000 | 9,309,000,000 | 0.2 |
| **AIRLINES** | | | | |
| 85 | Trans World Airlines | 28,400,000 | 2,970,453,000 | 1.0 |
| 88 | Eastern Airlines | 27,800,000 | 1,825,475,000 | 1.5 |
| 89 | UAL Inc. | 27,199,000 | 2,929,637,000 | 0.9 |
| 91 | American Airlines | 26,250,000 | 2,007,883,000 | 1.3 |
| 97 | Delta Air Lines | 21,735,800 | 1,616,089,000 | 1.3 |
| **SOFT DRINKS** | | | | |
| 23 | PepsiCo Inc. | 95,000,000 | 2,727,455,000 | 3.5 |
| 26 | Coca-Cola Co. | 91,334,540 | 1,698,000,000 | 5.3 |
| 87 | Royal Crown Cola Co. | 28,000,000 | 281,995,000 | 9.9 |
| **APPLIANCES, TV, RADIO** | | | | |
| 21 | RCA Corp. | 100,000,000 | 5,363,600,000 | 1.9 |
| 28 | General Electric Co. | 90,000,000 | 15,697,000,000 | 0.6 |
| **RETAIL CHAINS** | | | | |
| 4 | Sears, Roebuck & Co.† | 245,000,000 | 12,535,000,000 | 2.0 |
| 35 | J. C. Penney Co. | 81,600,000 | 8,353,800,000 | 1.0 |
| **CHEMICALS** | | | | |
| 22 | American Cyanamid Co. | 95,880,300 | 732,835,250 | 13.0 |
| 66 | Union Carbide Corp. | 42,458,000 | 6,342,700,000 | 0.7 |
| **PHOTOGRAPHIC EQUIPMENT** | | | | |
| 37 | Eastman Kodak Co. | 74,332,000 | 4,000,000,000* | 1.9 |
| 77 | Polaroid Corp. | 35,316,300 | 950,032,000 | 3.7 |
| **TELEPHONE SERVICE, EQUIPMENT** | | | | |
| 18 | American Telephone & Telegraph Co. | $112,762,700 | $32,815,000,000 | 0.3 |
| 30 | International Telephone & Telegraph Co. | 87,842,000 | 11,764,106,000 | 0.7 |
| **MISCELLANEOUS** | | | | |
| 17 | U. S. Government | 112,996,000 | — | — |
| 29 | Gulf & Western Industries Inc. | 90,000,000 | 3,508,430,000 | 2.6 |
| 38 | Goodyear Tire & Rubber Co. | 74,000,000 | 5,791,500,000 | 1.3 |
| 40 | CBS Inc. | 73,251,000 | 1,904,654,000 | 3.8 |
| 46 | Loews Corp. | 64,275,000 | 2,901,454,000 | 2.2 |
| 51 | Hanes Corp. | 59,000,000 | 372,317,000 | 15.8 |
| 53 | Esmark Inc. | 54,800,000 | 5,300,566,000 | 1.0 |
| 54 | Greyhound Corp. | 53,500,000 | 3,738,147,000 | 1.4 |
| 63 | Rapid-American Corp. | 47,000,000 | 2,346,125,000 | 2.0 |
| 73 | North American Philips Co. | 40,000,000 | 1,723,672,000 | 2.3 |
| 76 | Time Inc. | 35,752,000 | 1,038,242,000 | 3.4 |
| 78 | American Express | 34,250,000 | 2,948,865,000 | 1.2 |
| 80 | Mattel Inc. | 33,000,000 | 386,273,000 | 8.5 |
| 95 | Scott Paper Co. | 23,534,000 | 1,373,770,000 | 1.7 |

† Percentage shown would be two and a half times more if Sears' $298,000,000 in local advertising were added to the $245,000,000 national total. The other retail chain (J. C. Penney) ad total also does not include local advertising.

* U.S. only, estimated by AA.

Note: All ad totals are domestic. Whenever possible, AA has reported the company's domestic sales figure in this table, although for some companies only a worldwide sales total was available.

Reprinted with permission from the August 29, 1977 issue of Advertising Age. Copyright by Crain Communications, Inc.

It is interesting to note that among food companies the range of the percentage of sales allocated to advertising ranges from 0.8 percent to 7.6 percent. Campbell Soup spends a larger percentage on advertising than H. J. Heinz, although Heinz's sales are higher. The difference can be attributed to marketing considerations. For example, Heinz is very active in the institutional food supply field. The need for advertising and the cost of advertising in this market are far less than in the consumer market.

The basic strength of the *percentage-of-sales method* is that it recognizes that a relationship exists between advertising and sales. The basic weakness is obvious: *We are basing the budget for this year's advertising on last year's sales.* If our sales were up sharply last year owing to certain market conditions that may or may not have been within our control, we would have loads of money to spend. On the other hand, if sales were down sharply, also for reasons that may have been beyond our control, we would have less to spend, perhaps at a time when we need more. We must remember that the market is dynamic and that products change, as do customers and their tastes.

The *unit-of-sales method* is a variation of the percentage-of-sales method. A specific number of

| NEW-CAR MARKET SHARES IN U. S. 1977 vs. 1976 | | | | | |
|---|---|---|---|---|---|
| | Regis. 1977 | Percent share of market | Regis. 1976 | Percent share of market | Pct. pt. change '77 vs. '76 |
| Chevrolet | 2,189,542 | 20.36 | 2,035,858 | 20.88 | −0.52 |
| Ford | 1,775,663 | 16.52 | 1,665,619 | 17.08 | −0.56 |
| Oldsmobile | 946,777 | 8.81 | 867,485 | 8.90 | −0.09 |
| Pontiac | 794,170 | 7.39 | 706,460 | 7.24 | +0.15 |
| Buick | 730,806 | 6.80 | 700,778 | 7.19 | −0.39 |
| Mercury | 484,327 | 4.50 | 408,121 | 4.19 | +0.31 |
| Dodge | 445,504 | 4.14 | 460,547 | 4.72 | −0.58 |
| Cadillac | 323,855 | 3.01 | 293,716 | 3.01 | . . . . . |
| Plymouth | 434,193 | 4.04 | 526,957 | 5.40 | −1.36 |
| Chrysler | 301,443 | 2.80 | 271,472 | 2.78 | −0.02 |
| AMC | 171,136 | 1.59 | 115,801 | 1.19 | +0.40 |
| Lincoln | 181,433 | 1.69 | 247,032 | 2.53 | −0.84 |
| General Motors | 4,985,150 | 46.37 | 4,604,297 | 47.22 | −0.85 |
| Ford Motor Co. | 2,431,126 | 22.61 | 2,189,541 | 22.45 | +0.16 |
| Chrysler Corp. | 1,181,140 | 10.98 | 1,259,076 | 12.91 | −1.93 |
| American Motors | 181,433 | 1.69 | 247,032 | 2.53 | −0.84 |
| Imports | 1,985,150 | 18.30 | 1,446,637 | 14.84 | +3.46 |
| Miscellaneous | 5,316 | 0.05 | 4,902 | 0.05 | . . . . . |
| **Total** | **10,751,924** | | **9,751,485** | | |

Automotive News analysis of new-car registrations based on R. L. Polk & Co. statistical report.

Reprinted with permission from *Automotive News.* Copyright 1978.

If we examine market shares by corporation and by brand, and then examine the advertising expenditures of these companies, we can see more clearly the problem of getting a foothold in this market. American Motors Corporation, with less than 2 percent of the market, has to spend 1.6 percent of sales to hold that market. General Motors, with 47 percent of the auto market, spends only 0.6 percent on advertising. These figures do not tell us if this is the manner in which these companies in fact establish their advertising appropriation. It is simply an after-the-fact statistic.

dollars (or cents) for each unit produced is allocated to the advertising budget. The same criticisms may be applied to this method that were applied to the percentage-of-sales method: That is, we have not considered the individual advertising *requirements* for our particular product, and we have made our assessment based on *last year's* sales or production. The unit-of-sales method is not truly

formulated to meet the challenges of a dynamic business world.

## An empirical method

One method that has been suggested for determining an optimum advertising budget is an empirical method based on trial and error. The idea of the

---

### WILLIAM BERNBACH

Perhaps advertising would have reached new creative heights in the 'fifties and 'sixties without William Bernbach, but since 1949, when he and Ned Doyle and Maxwell Dane founded the Doyle Dane Bernbach agency, advertising has never been the same. William Bernbach is credited with having started a revolution on Madison Avenue.

He believed that there was far more power in a simple message that was artfully and provocatively stated than in a loud and cluttered presentation. His belief that advertising should be uncluttered and built on simple ideas led him to create such successful advertising as the "Think small" campaign for Volkswagen and the "We try harder because we're only number two" campaign for Avis Rent a Car. He has also created well-known campaigns for such clients as Polaroid, Levy's Jewish Rye Bread, Mobil Oil, American Airlines, and Colombian Coffee.

A native New Yorker, William Bernbach attended New York University. After service in the Army during the Second World War, he became a copywriter, soon rising to become vice-president in charge of art and copy at Grey Advertising Company. When Doyle Dane Bernbach, Inc. opened its doors in 1949, it had only $500,000 in billings; but by 1978 the agency had grown to more than $600 million in billings and had offices in Europe, Canada, Mexico, and Australia.

In recognition of his creative contributions to the advertising industry, William Bernbach has received numerous awards, including the Parsons School of Design Diamond Jubilee Award for "his creative contribution to the graphics communications industry." In 1977, he was inaugurated into the Advertising Hall of Fame. At 68, he is still active in the famous agency that he helped found.

---

Business publications compete vigorously for a share of the budget that many advertisers devote to the business and industrial market. It is curious that all three of these publications used transit posters on a suburban railroad to carry their message to the target market: commuting executives. Perhaps they were "matching the competition."

method is to advertise at varying levels of expenditure, using the same medium in different test cities to see if sales results will vary with the level of advertising. After a series of such trials, the most productive level of advertising expenditure should be readily identifiable.

There are several flaws in this concept. The first is that any sales results will be entirely attributable to the advertising. The second flaw is that there are variables that can cause a difference in results between one test city and another, no matter how carefully we try to match cities in terms of demographic characteristics. Finally, although the tests use the same *type* of medium, there may be differences in the impact of *specific media* in the different test cities.

## Take your choice

If all the methods we have described have weaknesses, which method is *best?* The reply to that question is that there is no single best method. Most companies use a percentage-of-sales method, and that method appears to work. Many companies use the unit-of-sale method (*per-unit assessment*), and this method is particularly suitable for determining cooperative budgets. For example, if the manufacturers of cotton fabrics were to combine their efforts to stimulate the sale of cotton apparel and linens, each member might contribute $x$ cents per yard or per pound or per whatever unit amount would be most convenient for all. The manufacturers of new products can also use the

THE ADVERTISING BUDGET: INVESTMENT OR EXPENSE?

unit-of-sales method by basing it on *anticipated* sales. Of course, to a degree this is merely an educated guess, and, if optimistic, the result may be more money budgeted for advertising than is needed. If pessimistic, however, the budget may be inadequate and thereby become a self-fulfilling prophecy.

## Time to set the budget

Budgets are usually set for one year at a time. For large advertisers whose fiscal year coincides with the calendar year, budget preparation often starts in July. Preparation begins so far in advance of the end of the year because it may take months to work out and revise the details of all the various alloca-

tions. In addition, advertisers must be particularly careful to have their budgets completed in time to meet deadlines for media commitments. To place an advertisement in the March issue of a consumer publication, advertisers must order the space they need in December, and supply the publication with copy or artwork for the ad in early January. Therefore, budget preparation can hardly take place in a flurry of activity during the last few weeks of the year.

### Budget periods and flexibility

Advertisers can maintain budget flexibility by monthly planning and by relating expenditures to objectives. In most instances, the changes that take

"Love the apple.
Love the snake.
Love the whole concept.
Shoot the works!"

Drawing by Lorenz; © 1979
The New Yorker Magazine, Inc.

place during the operational year will involve a *reduction* in budget. However, to take advantage of opportunities for which *additional* funds might be needed, a certain amount for contingencies—not earmarked for any specific purpose—would be included in the total budget.

Top management wants to know how the company's money will be spent. Therefore, we should itemize our budget by products, by markets, and by objectives. We should break down costs by individual projects so that if we must make cuts in the course of the program, executives in the organization will be able to cut projects, not merely dollars. Monthly planning is also an indication to management that the advertising program is flexible, designed to meet changes in marketing conditions, and adaptable to fast-breaking situations.

Sometimes we may have to revise our budget to bring total costs within the limits dictated by management. The amount of money available may be restricted by other, more critical, financial needs.

Once our budget has been approved, it is the job of the advertising manager to supervise expenditures so that costs remain within the amounts specified. The advertising manager's supervision of the budget would certainly include controls over media schedules and contracts as well as cost estimates and expenditures for materials and services; a system to assure that all goods and services have been provided as specified and paid for promptly; and a method for comparing actual costs against budget estimates.

## What belongs in the advertising budget?

If we are going to judge the effectiveness of the advertising appropriation, we want to be certain that the budget does not include costs for activities that are not directly related to that effectiveness. In some firms, the advertising budget becomes a catchall for expenses that cannot be classified elsewhere. For example, is the cost of a pair of tickets to the World Series for a good customer an advertising expense? Hardly. Here is what properly belongs in the advertising budget:

1. Paid advertising space and time in all recognized media

2. Literature intended to perform a selling function, such as brochures, circulars, catalogs, and package inserts used for advertising, not for directions on product use

3. The salaries and operating expenses of the advertising department

4. Fees paid to advertising agencies, writers, artists, and for other ancillary *advertising* services

5. Mechanical costs involved in the preparation of advertising material such as photography, typography, artwork, engravings, radio transcriptions, television films, etc.

Some of the many items that may be charged against the advertising budget but do not belong there include: cartons, labels, packaging, house organs, sample portfolios for the sales force; company stationery, charitable contributions, annual reports, display signs on the factory building, premiums, showrooms, and booths at trade shows.

## Summary

A company's advertising budget is a plan that defines its proposed advertising activities in dollar amounts. The budget is usually set for one year. Although advertising costs are listed as an expense on a company's balance sheet, today most executives are aware that advertising can more properly be viewed as an investment. They know that advertising will influence their company's sales, and therefore its profitability.

There are four principal methods in use for determining the amount of money to allocate to advertising. These are: the objective, or task, method, the share-of-the-market method, the percentage-of-sales method, and the unit-of-sales method. These classifications of the approaches to budget determination are useful only as a general guide, however. There will always be certain arbitrary elements factored into any budgetary decision. Marketing and advertising requirements vary greatly, for example, as a product moves through its life cycle. A new product may call for much higher levels of advertising than are needed for an established product. The degree of product differentiation probably has the greatest influence on the need for advertising dollars: a well-differentiated product being able to achieve a positive market share more easily, and with fewer dollars, than one with little to distinguish it from the competition.

If a company decides to allocate a certain percentage of its sales to advertising (*percentage-of-sales method*), it still has to determine the exact percentage to use and what items to include in the advertising budget. This method also has a major weakness in that its future advertising needs are being based on its *past sales*. This same weakness also exists in the *unit-of-sales method*, by which an advertiser allows a certain amount of the sale price of each unit of its product for advertising.

The activities of competitors have an important influence on the need for advertising dollars. Few advertisers arrive at their final appropriation without being very mindful of competitors' levels of appropriation. In fact, some companies set their appropriation by merely matching or exceeding the budget of a competitor with a similar market share (*share-of-the-market method*). However, this method does not take into account the unique strengths and weaknesses of each company.

The specific goals assigned to advertising during the budget period will also influence the size of the advertising appropriation. To *increase* market share may require more dollars than to maintain market share. The budget needed to win *new* users may be substantially greater than that needed to increase frequency of use or size of purchase among present users. The expense of introducing a new product, of shifting people's buying habits, or of providing them with the information they need to evaluate the new product will be considerably greater than the cost of maintaining a mature product's share of the market. Determining how much money the company must spend to achieve each of its advertising goals (the *task, or objective, method*) is probably the most effective way of setting its advertising budget.

The dollar level for advertising may also be influenced by the profits we expect to generate. A high volume of sales may support a larger advertising appropriation because it generates a greater amount of revenue to finance the appropriation. Nor can the appropriation decision be separated from the long-range profit picture of the firm. A company operating with a high fixed cost may find that extra advertising will increase sales so that the fixed costs are spread over a larger number of units, thereby reducing the per-unit cost. Under such conditions, increased advertising expenditures may be well-justified. Every advertising budget will ultimately be reflected in the profit and loss statement, no matter what the nondollar goals of advertising may be.

## QUESTIONS FOR DISCUSSION

**1.** What is an advertising budget? What purpose does it serve?

**2.** What are some of the ways advertising contributes to the achievement of sales volume?

**3.** The advertising budget as a percentage of sales tends to be lower for industrial products than for consumer products. Why do you think this is so?

**4.** In what ways might cyclical fluctuations in business affect the advertising budget?

**5.** What relationships exist between marketing intelligence and the advertising budget?

**6.** What budget procedure would you recommend for
a. a new prescription drug
b. a household plant food for regional distribution
c. a line of children's sweaters
Justify your recommendations.

**7.** What is the role of sales forecasting in the preparation of the advertising budget?

**8.** Why do opportunities for product differentiation make such a difference in the advertising budget?

### Sources and suggestions for further reading

Chase, Cochrane, and Barsch, Kenneth L. *Marketing Problem Solver.* 2d ed. Radnor, Pa.: Chilton Book Co., 1977.

Crawford, John W. *Advertising*, 2d ed. Boston: Allyn and Bacon, 1965.

Dunn, S. Watson. *Advertising.* 2d ed. New York: Holt, Rinehart and Winston, 1969.

Hurwood, David L., and Brown, James K. *Some Guidelines for Advertising Budgeting.* New York: The Conference Board, 1972.

Littlefield, James E. *Readings in Advertising.* St. Paul, Minn.: West Publishing Co., 1975. Part IV.

Longman, Kenneth A. *Advertising.* New York: Harcourt Brace Jovanovich, 1971.

Sissors, Jack Z., and Petray, E. Reynold. *Advertising Media Planning.* Chicago: Crain Books, 1976.

Stansfield, Richard H. *The Dartnell Advertising Manager's Handbook.* Chicago: The Dartnell Corporation, 1969.

Weinberg, Robert S. *An Analytical Approach to Advertising Expenditure Strategy.* New York: Association of National Advertisers, 1960.

# ADVERTISING MEDIA: AN OVERVIEW

**Looking at the media**

Media strategy

**Media selection factors**

Cost
Matching media and market
Geographical selectivity
Medium and product
Program objectives
Other factors that influence media
    selection
  Editorial environment
  Flexibility and frequency
  Durability of the message
  Retail impact

**Measuring the medium's audience**

Circulation and coverage
Refining circulation data

**The media mix**

Reasons for a mix
Duplication
Gross audience

**The role of the media planner**

Cumulative audience
Seasonal concentration
Scheduling
The use of computers in media
    selection
Media buying procedures

**People in media**

The media rep

## WORKING VOCABULARY

| | | |
|---|---|---|
| medium | coverage | duplication |
| cost per thousand (CPM) | circulation | flighting |
| selectivity | secondary circulation | blitz schedule |
| frequency | media mix | insertion order |
| | reach | |

# advertising
# media:
# an overview

*The salesman in the Sumerian market place of 3,000 B.C. had three advertising media: his voice, perhaps a few tricks and his merchandise display. . . . Today, the advertising agency has such a wide range of media that planning an advertising campaign for a new product requires a tremendous amount of judgment, experience, and research.*

G. ALLEN FOSTER
*Advertising: Ancient Market Place to Television*

T HE MEDIA OFFER US *reach*—the opportunity to communicate with people who are the target market for our product. Some of the responsibility for the effectiveness of any advertising program is shared by both the advertising message and the medium that carries it. The ability to develop a *favorable attitude* toward a product is a shared responsibility. The ability to *stimulate action* on the part of the individual consumer is a shared responsibility. And the ability to develop *additional sales* of a product is also a shared responsi-

bility. It is important, therefore, that we study the characteristics of each of our partners in the advertising process.

## Looking at the media

A *medium* (singular of "media") is a vehicle that conveys information or entertainment to the general public. People buy, subscribe to, turn on, or tune in a medium for the informative articles or the entering programs contained in that medium's editorial or program format. At the same time, each medium is used as a vehicle to distribute commercial messages. The newspaper that we purchase at the newsstand for news of the world is also a vehicle for hundreds of advertisements. The magazine that we subscribe to for news of sports events is a vehicle for advertisements. The radio station we turn on for music and the television program we tune in for news or entertainment are all vehicles for advertising.

You will note that we have omitted transit and outdoor from our general description of media because, although advertising people generally refer to them as media, they are not media in a true sense. They do not have either editorial or program formats. No one turns to, buys, or subscribes to the posters in a bus or a train. No one purposefully seeks out billboards along the highway (unless they want to know how far it is to the next Howard Johnson's). However, outdoor and transit are considered media by advertising professionals and are therefore included in this chapter and in subsequent discussions of media. Nonmedia advertising refers to persuasive communications that, instead of being transmitted by one of the media, are distributed through the mails or by various other means—everything from stuffing the advertisements into mailboxes and under front doors to handing them out on street corners.

The general categories of media, then, are:

### PRINT

| | |
|---|---|
| Newspapers | Magazines |
| Daily | Consumer |
| Weekly | General interest |
| Sunday | Special interest |
| Sunday supplements | Demographic editions |

| | |
|---|---|
| Business | Farm |
| General | National |
| Industrial | State or regional |
| Trade | Agricultural product |
| Professional | |
| Institutional | |

### BROADCAST

| | |
|---|---|
| Radio | Television |
| Network | Network |
| Spot | Spot |

### TRANSIT

### OUTDOOR

## Media strategy

The media strategy is part of the marketing plan. The broad media decisions are:

1. What general category of available media will serve our advertising needs best?

2. Which individual medium in each category will provide the best vehicle for our advertising?

3. What combination, or mix, of media might we use?

4. What would be the best specific schedule for the appearance of our advertisements in each of these media?

## Media selection factors

With an appropriation for media expenses in hand, we are faced with the problem of allocating that budget, first among the various categories of media,

This table reveals that the percentages of advertising budgets allocated to the various media remained reasonably constant in 1977 and 1978. The overall increase in volume does not represent a surge in national advertisers' interest in advertising, but rather the general cost increases in space and time charges by the media.

## ADVERTISING VOLUME IN THE U.S. IN 1977 AND 1978

| Medium | 1977 | | 1978 (Preliminary) | | |
| --- | --- | --- | --- | --- | --- |
| | Millions | Percent of total | Millions | Percent of total | Percent of change |
| **Newspapers** | | | | | |
| Total | $11,132 | 29.2 | $12,690 | 29.0 | +14.0 |
| National | 1,677 | 4.4 | 1,810 | 4.1 | + 8.0 |
| Local | 9,455 | 24.8 | 10,880 | 24.9 | +15.0 |
| **Magazines** | | | | | |
| Total | 2,162 | 5.7 | 2,595 | 5.9 | +20.0 |
| Weeklies | 903 | 2.4 | 1,165 | 2.7 | +29.0 |
| Women's | 565 | 1.5 | 670 | 1.5 | +19.0 |
| Monthlies | 694 | 1.8 | 760 | 1.7 | +10.0 |
| **Farm Publications** | 90 | 0.2 | 105 | 0.2 | +14.0 |
| **Television** | | | | | |
| Total | 7,612 | 20.0 | 8,850 | 20.2 | +16.0 |
| Network | 3,460 | 9.1 | 3,910 | 8.9 | +13.0 |
| Spot | 2,204 | 5.8 | 2,600 | 5.9 | +18.0 |
| Local | 1,948 | 5.1 | 2,340 | 5.4 | +20.0 |
| **Radio** | | | | | |
| Total | 2,634 | 6.9 | 2,955 | 6.8 | +12.0 |
| Network | 137 | 0.4 | 160 | 0.4 | +16.0 |
| Spot | 546 | 1.4 | 610 | 1.4 | +12.0 |
| Local | 1,951 | 5.1 | 2,185 | 5.0 | +12.0 |
| **Direct Mail** | 5,333 | 14.0 | 6,030 | 13.8 | +13.0 |
| **Business Publications** | 1,221 | 3.2 | 1,420 | 3.3 | +16.0 |
| **Outdoor** | | | | | |
| Total | 418 | 1.1 | 465 | 1.1 | +11.0 |
| National | 290 | 0.8 | 310 | 0.7 | + 7.0 |
| Local | 128 | 0.3 | 155 | 0.4 | +21.0 |
| **Miscellaneous** | | | | | |
| Total | 7,518 | 19.7 | 8,630 | 19.7 | +15.0 |
| National | 3,935 | 10.3 | 4,495 | 10.3 | +15.0 |
| Local | 3,583 | 9.4 | 4,135 | 9.4 | +15.0 |
| **Total** | | | | | |
| National | 21,055 | 55.2 | 24,045 | 55.0 | +14.2 |
| Local | 17,065 | 44.8 | 19,695 | 45.0 | +15.4 |
| **GRAND TOTAL** | 38,120 | 100.0 | 43,740 | 100.0 | +14.7 |

Note: Data reflect final revisions for 1977 and preliminary figures for 1978.

Reprinted with permission from the January 9, 1979 issue of *Advertising Age*. Copyright by Crain Communications, Inc.

and then among the specific media in each category. Our first decision—what general category of available media will serve our advertising needs best?—is influenced by several factors. Among these are (1) cost, (2) the nature of our target market, (3) our method of distribution, (4) our product, (5) the objectives of our advertising program, and (6) special media characteristics such as editorial environment, flexibility, frequency, and durability.

## Cost

The most important consideration when comparing media is cost. Media charges, in fact, are usually the largest single item in advertising budgets. Our concern is *not* with absolute cost, but with *cost effectiveness*, that is, with the ability of the medium to deliver our advertising message to the largest number of prospective customers at the lowest possible price. Some of the media number their audiences in the millions, but not all of these people will be prospective customers for our product. A medium with a small audience that has a high concentration of product users is a more economical buy than another medium with a much larger audience, but a low percentage of prospects.

One simple ratio used frequently for comparing media charges is *cost per thousand*, usually abbreviated as *CPM*. For print media, the formula for determining CPM is:

$$\text{CPM} = \frac{\text{cost of 1 black and white page} \times 1,000}{\text{circulation}}$$

For broadcast media, the formula is:

$$\text{CPM} = \frac{\text{cost of 1 unit of time} \times 1,000}{\substack{\text{number of homes reached by} \\ \text{a given program or time}}}$$

When data are available from the medium detailing the demographic characteristics of its audiences, advertisers can use the figures for the specific market segment they want to reach to replace total circulation or audience figures. For example, if magazine A had a total circulation of 50,000 and charged $500 for a single page, black and white advertisement, its CPM would be $10. But, if the advertiser only wanted to reach males over 35 years of age, and a detailed analysis of the magazine's circulation showed that it reached 14,000 men in this demographic segment, the advertiser could derive a new CPM. The CPM based on this figure would be: $500 \times 1,000 \div 14,000$, or $36.

## Matching media and market

To increase the cost effectiveness of our advertising, we must attempt to match the profile of our target market, supplied to us by our marketing intelligence system, with the demographic characteristics of a given medium's audience. If our product is cigars, for example, our marketing intelligence may tell us that our target market is men 35 to 70 years old. Therefore, we might consider placing our advertisements in a special-interest magazine that appeals to an all-male audience. But, even if we were to choose a magazine with a 100 percent male audience, part of this audience would consist of younger men (18 to 34), part of the audience would be nonsmokers, and part of the audience would be addicted to cigarettes and would rather fight than switch. We are still paying for a large amount of waste circulation. But at least by placing our advertising in a men's magazine we have held the waste to a minimum.

Some media—such as network radio and television, general-interest consumer magazines, and

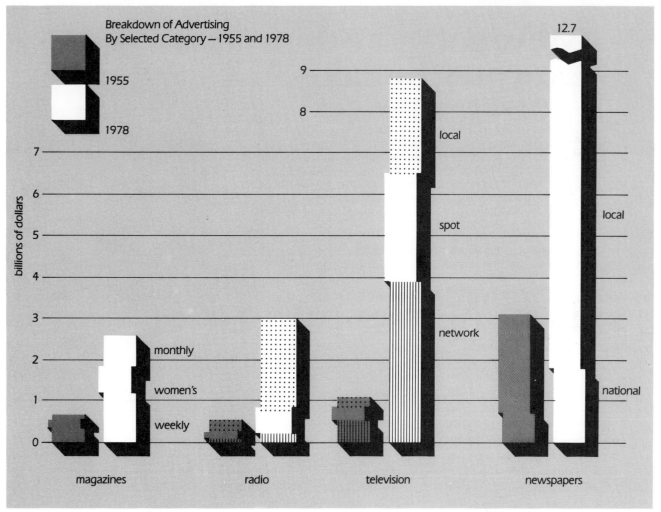

Breakdown of Advertising
By Selected Category — 1955 and 1978

1955

1978

billions of dollars

9
8
7
6
5
4
3
2
1
0

12.7

local

spot

network

local

national

magazines

monthly

women's

weekly

radio

television

newspapers

This chart shows the increase in advertising expenditures over 23 years.
The total growth in advertising volume was more than 6-fold, but it was
spread unevenly among the various media. Television made the largest
gains, as advertisers took advantage of its ability to provide
demonstration as well as to deliver a spoken message. Note the
remarkable growth of local radio. How do you account for this increase?

This advertisement was placed by the *Buffalo Evening News* in an advertising trade publication. It tells advertisers about some of the characteristics of the male audience that the *Evening News* attracts with its Saturday sports magazine section. The city of Buffalo does not have a population of 3 million, but the newspaper claims circulation not only in its home county but in eleven adjacent counties as well.

# We've got more than news reaching Buffalo's ADI.

**We've got Saturday's Sports.**

Not just the athletic world's schedules and scores, but a study of teams, individuals and the hows and whys that make the sports world tick. Sports Magazine is structured for this region's 3 million consumers with an annual Effective Buying Income of 8 billion dollars. And they aren't sitting around.

They want to know of the athletic events and are involved in both this area's major and minor sports activities.

They are the kind of consumer you are looking for. And they have an avid interest in us.

So put your media message in front of an active consumer. Put it into Sports and the Buffalo Evening News.

For more information, call Hugh G. Monaghan at (716) 849-3422.

**We deliver. 7 days a week.**

## BUFFALO EVENING NEWS

One News Plaza, Buffalo, New York 14240
Represented nationally by Story & Kelly-Smith

newspapers—offer us the means to transmit our advertising message to a cross section of the consumer market. They appeal to people of all income levels, ages, sexes, and occupations. Other media— such as spot radio and television, special-interest magazines, and business and farm publications— offer us *selectivity*: the ability to aim our appeal at a distinct target market or a particular area of the country. As part of their effort to sell us time or space, the media themselves will supply us with a great deal of information on the demographic char-

acteristics of their audience. More specific details can be obtained for a fee from media research organizations such as the Arbitron Company and W. R. Simmons & Associates Research.

## Geographical selectivity

The previous example of an all-male target market is one of *class selectivity*, class being an abbreviation for demographic classification, such as sex, age, marital status, and occupation. We will find, however, that the subscribers to the men's magazine in which we have considered placing our advertisements are scattered throughout the country. If we only distribute our cigars on a regional basis, many of the men who are stimulated to buy our product will find that it is not available in their local stores. These men will add to the amount of waste circulation that we must pay for. We may find, therefore, that we would like to obtain a degree of *geographic selectivity* as well as class selectivity.

It is often difficult for regional or local manufacturers to find a magazine that will reach only the limited geographic area in which their product is distributed. It is difficult, but not impossible now that more national consumer magazines offer demographic editions. But, unless the demographic

## JOHN PHILIP CUNNINGHAM

An all-around advertising man, John Philip Cunningham could write copy, draw illustrations, conduct research, select media, and plan campaigns. From the time he graduated from Harvard in 1919 until he retired from the active management of Cunningham & Walsh, Inc. in 1961, he spent his entire life in the advertising business. His first job was as an artist and layout man at the Newell–Emmett agency in New York. Newell–Emmett became Cunningham & Walsh in 1950, at which time John Cunningham was elected executive vice-president. He was elected president of the agency in 1954 and chairman of the board in 1958. In 1978, Cunningham & Walsh was the twenty-sixth largest agency in the world with billings of $222.6 million.

In 1934, when the agency was appointed to the Texaco account, John Cunningham put on a service attendant's uniform and for two weeks he pumped gasoline and made oil changes in a Texaco service station. He learned at first hand that a clean rest room and cheerful attendants are sometimes more important to motorists than the brand name of the gasoline they buy. From this experience he developed a unique concept for his agency—account executives, artists, and copywriters spent a week a year working in the field for their clients, learning at the point of sale what the consumer wanted. Other well-known accounts on which he personally worked included Johns–Manville industrial products, Sunshine Biscuits, and Chesterfield cigarettes.

John Philip Cunningham worked hard to raise the standards of creativity in the advertising industry. During the Second World War he was active in the creation of advertising campaigns for the Red Cross, the U.S.O., and the United States Treasury's war bond drive. In 1973, he was elected to the American Advertising Association's Hall of Fame—the first living advertising executive to be so honored.

For regional advertisers with product distribution exclusively in the Southwest, or for national advertisers seeking extra advertising impact in this area, *Houston Magazine* offers a very affluent readership. Notice that the magazine does not reveal its circulation figures in this advertisement but prefers to emphasize the impressive demographic characteristics of its readers, such as a median income of $54,700.

**Houston readers are the cream of the crop.**

Houston Magazine is fertile ground for advertisers who wish to cultivate a very affluent market.

Houston readers earn a median income of $54,700. 68% are in top management. 72% are college graduates.

Our readers appreciate the difference between the ordinary and the extraordinary. They spend their money willingly, but wisely, on the best of products.

Our comprehensive reader profile* further illustrates that Houston readers are Houston's leaders.

Call Mike Marshall at (713) 651-1313. Or write 1100 Milam, Suite 2500, Houston, Texas 77002.

**Houston** MAGAZINE

* Source: Marplan Research, Inc., 1978

edition is distributed only in areas that coincide exactly with the manufacturers' areas of product distribution, there will always be some waste. Local radio and television, newspapers, transit, and outdoor media provide exceptional opportunities for geographic selectivity. They can be used to carry our message to certain states, to certain counties in that state, to certain cities in that county or even to specific neighborhoods in each city.

### Medium and product

The nature of our product will also exert an influence on our choice of medium. Perhaps our product requires demonstration. Only television offers us the ability to transmit both sound and motion. Perhaps color is an important aspect of our product's appeal. The high-quality color reproduction available in magazines is superior to that offered by television. In Chapters 8–12, we will discuss the unique advantages and limitations of each of the categories of media.

Advertisers of consumer products of an intimate nature may not be able to use certain types of media for fear of offending portions of the public. Although media in general have become more broad-minded, some media still do not accept advertising for certain products. Some publications do not accept liquor or cigarette advertising, just as television stations will not accept whiskey or cigarette advertising. Even more important, the image of the product may be enhanced or distorted by certain publications or broadcast programs. Stock brokerage companies do not advertise in *Playboy* magazine, or in the entertainment section of a newspaper, or during a Saturday-morning children's television program.

## Program objectives

The objectives of the advertising program also influence media selection. A company that wants to build an "image" with an institutional campaign might use high-quality television programs to carry primarily institutional messages. It might also use general-interest magazines to carry the same messages, even though it would not find such magazines the best vehicles for its product advertising. The advertisement by Mobil on page 4 is a good example of this type of promotion.

## Other factors that influence media selection

**Editorial environment**  The editorial content of some media can be an important consideration in our analysis. Some media command great loyalty from their audiences, particularly radio and television programs that feature popular local personalities, disc jockeys, and commentators. Similarly, the authority and prestige of certain publications can lend greater impact to the advertisements that appear in them.

**Flexibility and frequency**  A very broad comparison of media can be made on the basis of *flexibility*, that is, the speed with which changes can be made in an advertising schedule for a particular medium. If we would like to advertise our snow tires just as the first snow of winter hits, we will find this much easier to do through newspaper or local radio advertising than through a consumer magazine. Why? With a newspaper or radio station, we can schedule our ads to run on the day or even within hours of the first snowfall. With a magazine, our ads may run only within a week or a month of the first snow.

Flexibility may not be important for some products, but it is critical for others.

Frequency is another time-related characteristic of any medium. *Frequency* refers to the number of times we can use a medium to present our message to an audience within a fixed amount of time. Radio is a high-frequency medium; we could have our commercial aired several times every hour if we could afford it. Newspapers offer us lower frequency: once a day or once a week. Magazines offer even lower frequency: weekly, monthly, or even quarter annually.

**Durability of the message**  The *durability* of the message, that is, the opportunity to deliver the same message more than once, is a characteristic of certain media. It is not critical, except where repetition would help strengthen the selling impact of our message. Clearly, the broadcast media do not offer us durability. Our message appears or is spoken and then vanishes. The viewer or listener cannot refer to it again. Daily newspapers, on the other hand, offer some durability, and weekly magazines offer even more. The greatest durability, however, is offered by monthly magazines that the reader will pick up and read several times during the life of each issue.

**Retail impact**  Another factor we must consider is the importance of a given medium in the minds of the retailers and wholesalers who are responsible for the distribution of our product. Advertisers often feature their national consumer advertising schedules prominently in their trade advertising. In this way they hope to convince retailers that it is to their advantage not only to stock but to push a nationally advertised brand.

## Measuring the medium's audience

As we compare media types according to such characteristics as class and geographic selectivity, we will also consider the size of each medium's audience. Data on audience size are available from a number of different sources, including the media themselves, who have their figures verified by independent auditing organizations. Buyers of advertising space or time are understandably concerned with obtaining reliable figures. We need accurate information to help guide us in making the second media decision—which individual medium in each general category will provide the best vehicle for our advertising?

### Circulation and coverage

Different media use different methods to measure the size of their audiences. If, for example, we are interested in telling the consumers in Boondock County about our product, this is how the different media there will describe the size of their audiences to us.

Radio and television stations will tell us about their *coverage,* that is, about the number of homes in Boondock County that can receive their stations' transmission signals clearly. One radio station may then claim that 80 percent of the homes in its coverage actually listen to its morning news program, and a television station may claim that the same percentage actually watches its Friday evening movie. Out of all the homes that can *receive* these stations' signals (their *coverage*), the number of homes that *actually tune in* is their *circulation.*

Newspapers and magazines will also use the word *circulation* to describe the number of copies they sell in Boondock County, either at newsstands or by subscription. The *Boondock Bugle* may have an audited circulation of 80,000 copies, and a national consumer magazine such as *Time* may have 5,000 subscribers in Boondock County and newsstand sales there of another 15,000 copies. These figures represent each publication's *primary circulation.*

Outdoor and transit media in Boondock County will also offer to sell us a certain amount of *coverage.* Their data on coverage will tell us what percentage of all the people living in Boondock County will pass by or be exposed to all of our outdoor or transit advertising during a thirty-day period. For example, they may promise us that during the month of November 200,000 people will drive by our billboard on the outskirts of Boondock City. If the total population of Boondock County is one million, then our billboard gives us 20 percent coverage.

### Refining circulation data

In describing their circulation, the broadcast media in Boondock County have used the term "homes" or "households." Not all members of a family or household are prospective purchasers of our product, however. Some purchases are indeed "family" purchases. The household collectively establishes buying potential for many products, such as automobiles, washing machines, and color television sets; and the decision to purchase these products may be made by the entire household, though the actual purchase may be made by the family's "buying agent." But most advertisers would prefer to have demographic information on all the individuals in a home or household.

Magazines and newspapers usually describe their audiences in terms of individuals. In addition

# S&MM's SURVEY OF TELEVISION MARKETS

### S&MM ESTIMATES 1977

| STATE S&MM/ARB TV(ADI) MARKET | POPULATION—12/31/77 | | | EFFECTIVE BUYING INCOME | RETAIL SALES BY STORE GROUP | | | | | | |
|---|---|---|---|---|---|---|---|---|---|---|---|
| | Total Pop. (Thous.) | Total House-holds (Thous.) | Black Pop. (Thous.) | Total EBI ($000) | Total Retail Sales ($000) | Food ($000) | General Merchandise ($000) | Furniture/ Furnish./ Appliance ($000) | Automotive ($000) | Drug ($000) | Buying Power Index |
| **KANSAS** | | | | | | | | | | | |
| TOPEKA | 392.9 | 136.4 | 22.0 | 2,202,924 | 1,347,872 | 248,934 | 181,550 | 60,224 | 282,515 | 33,378 | .1764 |
| WICHITA-HUTCHINSON | 1,094.4 | 396.7 | 41.8 | 6,580,289 | 3,838,135 | 699,219 | 462,090 | 200,146 | 963,472 | 112,278 | .5116 |
| **KENTUCKY** | | | | | | | | | | | |
| BOWLING GREEN | 95.7 | 32.3 | 7.4 | 461,996 | 315,254 | 80,073 | 35,566 | 9,577 | 51,550 | 9,878 | .0395 |
| LEXINGTON | 654.1 | 215.2 | 45.2 | 3,169,789 | 1,912,486 | 454,295 | 318,587 | 60,305 | 341,526 | 63,434 | .2612 |
| LOUISVILLE | 1,364.1 | 453.1 | 122.4 | 7,886,418 | 4,298,699 | 922,353 | 747,621 | 159,420 | 913,175 | 144,648 | .6056 |
| PADUCAH-CAPE GIRARDEAU-HARRISBURG | 770.7 | 283.7 | 56.3 | 3,697,008 | 2,499,196 | 569,385 | 271,444 | 125,133 | 561,223 | 81,659 | .3164 |
| **LOUISIANA** | | | | | | | | | | | |
| ALEXANDRIA | 220.5 | 66.1 | 55.6 | 926,184 | 538,150 | 139,054 | 84,074 | 22,455 | 119,531 | 14,883 | .0782 |
| BATON ROUGE | 630.7 | 196.7 | 209.0 | 3,349,962 | 1,738,241 | 464,841 | 254,429 | 81,817 | 371,920 | 52,909 | .2582 |
| LAFAYETTE | 497.7 | 153.0 | 136.1 | 2,125,785 | 1,361,605 | 398,949 | 142,211 | 54,386 | 261,014 | 45,226 | .1835 |
| LAKE CHARLES | 192.4 | 62.5 | 41.8 | 986,940 | 612,830 | 122,295 | 95,344 | 21,882 | 142,171 | 25,636 | .0808 |
| MONROE-EL DORADO | 534.5 | 175.1 | 193.0 | 2,360,788 | 1,518,107 | 416,420 | 161,530 | 65,428 | 345,132 | 54,403 | .2024 |
| NEW ORLEANS | 1,569.9 | 513.8 | 445.4 | 8,829,939 | 5,017,846 | 1,241,773 | 638,107 | 243,663 | 901,143 | 187,129 | .6907 |
| SHREVEPORT-TEXARKANA | 1,068.9 | 369.3 | 317.1 | 4,973,371 | 3,257,238 | 788,353 | 350,791 | 152,502 | 765,953 | 100,991 | .4242 |
| **MAINE** | | | | | | | | | | | |
| BANGOR | 340.0 | 114.7 | .8 | 1,667,497 | 997,976 | 246,653 | 114,669 | 30,663 | 218,746 | 26,327 | .1364 |
| PORTLAND-POLAND SPRING | 789.8 | 271.8 | 2.8 | 4,261,768 | 2,611,885 | 608,235 | 318,861 | 83,095 | 555,788 | 65,856 | .3443 |
| PRESQUE ISLE | 98.4 | 29.6 | 1.2 | 417,411 | 253,960 | 64,443 | 34,560 | 7,920 | 54,836 | 7,221 | .0356 |
| **MARYLAND** | | | | | | | | | | | |
| BALTIMORE | 2,337.2 | 791.9 | 555.7 | 13,497,534 | 6,572,491 | 1,563,431 | 997,861 | 310,628 | 1,049,528 | 253,109 | 1.0042 |
| SALISBURY | 198.0 | 70.7 | 49.5 | 1,011,264 | 748,816 | 190,008 | 73,096 | 35,884 | 122,394 | 23,648 | .0879 |
| **MASSACHUSETTS** | | | | | | | | | | | |
| BOSTON | 5,323.8 | 1,816.3 | 168.9 | 32,874,033 | 18,030,333 | 4,001,003 | 2,452,173 | 835,979 | 3,162,445 | 416,952 | 2.4966 |
| SPRINGFIELD | 659.4 | 224.6 | 28.9 | 3,697,790 | 1,924,221 | 385,817 | 259,092 | 91,237 | 341,678 | 51,117 | .2822 |
| **MICHIGAN** | | | | | | | | | | | |
| ALPENA | 42.9 | 14.4 | .3 | 195,670 | 146,376 | 31,800 | 14,399 | 9,431 | 33,382 | 3,111 | .0176 |
| DETROIT | 4,807.0 | 1,606.6 | 757.1 | 35,695,042 | 15,705,291 | 3,420,705 | 2,052,775 | 851,845 | 3,531,566 | 604,617 | 2.4612 |
| FLINT-SAGINAW-BAY CITY | 1,197.2 | 387.0 | 100.1 | 7,734,326 | 3,848,757 | 884,978 | 443,179 | 203,037 | 948,378 | 116,749 | .5662 |
| GRAND RAPIDS-KALAMAZOO-BATTLE CREEK | 1,435.5 | 476.5 | 83.2 | 7,861,795 | 4,298,718 | 1,090,138 | 347,341 | 225,140 | 1,082,735 | 96,331 | .6120 |
| LANSING | 592.2 | 198.2 | 28.7 | 4,009,775 | 1,903,403 | 354,175 | 291,728 | 106,447 | 477,360 | 45,122 | .2867 |
| MARQUETTE | 152.5 | 51.7 | 2.2 | 636,898 | 378,115 | 90,489 | 20,526 | 19,357 | 90,276 | 7,303 | .0540 |
| TRAVERSE CITY-CADILLAC | 441.9 | 150.6 | 4.6 | 1,903,010 | 1,430,706 | 380,793 | 111,139 | 53,379 | 255,204 | 33,371 | .1726 |
| **MINNESOTA** | | | | | | | | | | | |
| ALEXANDRIA | 296.3 | 103.1 | .0 | 1,342,794 | 809,170 | 169,831 | 59,920 | 38,085 | 136,833 | 25,826 | .1121 |
| DULUTH-SUPERIOR | 465.0 | 166.3 | 1.3 | 2,316,004 | 1,578,964 | 310,674 | 226,841 | 61,498 | 255,070 | 39,632 | .1971 |
| MANKATO | 137.0 | 47.1 | .3 | 757,034 | 410,913 | 83,130 | 57,860 | 21,311 | 98,033 | 12,311 | .0587 |
| MINNEAPOLIS-ST. PAUL | 2,882.6 | 966.3 | 31.8 | 16,893,710 | 10,192,318 | 1,925,015 | 1,546,706 | 476,759 | 1,927,495 | 247,915 | 1.3355 |
| ROCHESTER-MASON CITY-AUSTIN | 385.9 | 133.9 | .9 | 2,170,810 | 1,220,032 | 236,268 | 171,682 | 60,778 | 263,329 | 36,832 | .1692 |
| **MISSISSIPPI** | | | | | | | | | | | |
| BILOXI-GULFPORT-PASCAGOULA | 159.2 | 48.9 | 29.0 | 763,848 | 553,383 | 107,309 | 95,569 | 28,627 | 105,753 | 16,969 | .0670 |
| COLUMBUS-TUPELO | 407.8 | 134.4 | 121.2 | 1,774,051 | 1,110,115 | 292,774 | 146,093 | 48,216 | 260,265 | 32,618 | .1518 |
| GREENWOOD-GREENVILLE | 132.2 | 38.5 | 79.6 | 473,044 | 270,834 | 82,675 | 19,650 | 12,833 | 65,780 | 11,518 | .0414 |
| JACKSON | 774.8 | 243.6 | 340.7 | 3,490,735 | 2,269,563 | 541,593 | 358,829 | 92,449 | 532,829 | 65,692 | .2989 |

The advantage of local television is the geographical selectivity it offers—we can choose the counties or regions to which our message can be directed. Before we can even consider the number of homes that may be tuned into any station, we want to know the areas in which the station signal can be received—its coverage. Television and radio stations provide advertisers with maps such as this, showing their strongest signal areas (Grade A) and weaker signal areas (Grade B). You will find a more detailed map for this station on page 227.

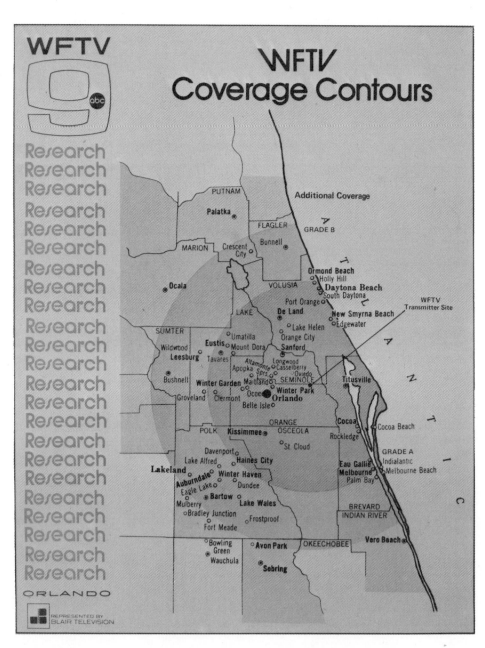

to data on their primary circulation, however, *Time* and the *Bugle* will also supply us with information on their *secondary circulation,* or pass-along readers. Secondary readers do not purchase or subscribe to a publication, but pick up and read copies in barbershops, beauty salons, doctors' waiting rooms, offices, and libraries. For some publications, pass-along readership can be two to three times greater than their primary circulation.

## The media mix

Each of the major media has certain characteristics that we must consider before we make the third media decision: What combination, or *mix,* of media might we use? The logical media combination will be arrived at by examining our company's marketing objectives and target market, and then by matching, as far as possible, the gross audience of our media mix to our target market. We say "as far as possible" because, although the ideal combination would be one that reached only prospective customers (no waste), at a low cost, and with maximum impact, we can rarely obtain such an ideal in practice.

Although we will consider each media category in detail in Chapters 8—12, at this point we should briefly examine the characteristics of each major class of media.

*Magazines* offer audience selectivity, length of life, editorial climate, high-quality color reproduction, and, in many cases, opportunities for regional coverage.

*Newspapers* can deliver our message to the target market daily. They offer exceptional geographic selectivity that we can tailor to meet our specific market needs. However, newspapers are not very selective as to audience.

*Television's* greatest attribute is its ability to provide an active demonstration of our product. Over 94 percent of all the homes in the United States have one or more television sets. This makes television the most efficient means of reaching a large, national audience. If local coverage is an objective, we can buy television time on a station-by-station basis.

*Radio's* principal advantage is its ability to deliver an advertising message at a low cost per thousand. Its major weakness is its inability to provide a visual presentation of our product. Because radio audiences are so dispersed and fragmented (there are over 6,000 commercial radio stations in the United States), radio is generally considered a supplementary medium.

*Outdoor* and *transit* can be used on a national basis or on a local basis, depending on the market coverage desired. However, outdoor and transit are, for the most part, nonselective, providing exposure to all economic and social classes.

### Reasons for a mix

As we have said, the media strategy we pursue will be determined by our advertising objectives. If our general advertising objective were to provide leads for our sales force, then our most important criterion for setting our media strategy might be *reach* —that is, bringing our message to as many people as possible. To achieve this goal, we might use a media mix of 60 percent television, 30 percent magazines, and 10 percent newspapers. A percentage of the audience of each of these three media will be people who have not been exposed to our message through either of the other two. If, on the other hand, our objective were to provide important new information, we would want *frequency*—that is, the ability to deliver our message as often as possible within a given period of time. In this case, our choice might be 100 percent television, 100 percent newspapers, or a combination of the two. Both of these media offer us high frequency and large audiences. The most important concept in evaluating a possible media mix is *balance.* Does the mix strike the best possible balance among all the media selection factors that are important to us? Does it offer us a balance between the reach we want and the frequency we want? Between the reach, frequency, and degree of demographic selectivity that we desire? And so on, until we have considered all the factors that are important to us.

Finally, the most important consideration in choosing the proper media mix is cost. Some media are more expensive than others on an absolute cost basis. For example, we might consider allocating half our budget to television and half to magazines, or half to newspapers and half to magazines. Although we are spending the same amount of money—half our budget—on each medium, that money will buy far less in television than it will in magazines, and less in magazines than it will in newspapers. Of course, we must weigh the cost against how well the media type will match the needs of our product and of our market.

A media mix may distribute our budget among various types of media, or it may concentrate our budget on one media type. In recent years there has been an observable trend toward *concentration,* particularly among large advertisers. Concentration offers us the opportunity to obtain great impact on a specific market segment. We may even be able to dominate competitive advertising in one

particular medium. Advertising our brand in such a manner will create an impression of its widespread acceptance by consumers across the nation. Furthermore, that impression will carry over to dealers. "Look at the way we back you up," we can say to the retailers who carry our brand. If they are impressed, they may increase their support of our brand. We may be able to obtain preferential positioning on store shelves and to negotiate favorable rates and discounts.

In contrast, some advertisers prefer a widely varied media mix. By choosing an assortment of media, we can deliver different messages about the same product to different market segments. This is of great importance to advertisers who have more than one target market. An advertiser may use Saturday morning television to reach children and *Good Housekeeping* or *Woman's Day* magazines to reach their mothers.

Furthermore, a mix of media enables us to reach the same prospects in different "climates" or editorial environments. The difference in "climate" will help prevent early "wear-out" of our message. "Wear-out" is the time it takes for people to become bored with an ad or commercial.

With a media mix of several different types of media, we can also increase the reach of our message beyond what we can obtain through concentration, since a certain percentage of each medium's audience is not reached by any other medium. When we considered the advantages of concentration, we listed its strong impact. But that impact tends to be uneven. If we concentrate our advertising in television, for example, we reach both heavy viewers *and* light viewers. Heavy television viewers tend to be light readers of magazines, while light television viewers tend to be heavy magazine readers. Thus, we are making more impact on the heavy viewers and little impact on the light viewers, leaving weak areas in our message exposure potential. A media mix that devotes some of our budget to magazines will level out the imbalance caused by our heavy schedule in television. But a mix of two or more types of media will require that a larger portion of our budget be invested in the costs of preparing our advertising copy and artwork. And then, of course, there will be fewer dollars available for time and space. Therefore, advertisers must beware media mixes that spread their budgets too thin.

## Duplication

Advertisers who use a media mix are necessarily concerned with duplication. *Duplication* is the number of prospects who are reached by more than one of the media in a mix. Many executives who read *Fortune* magazine, for example, also read the *Wall Street Journal.* These executives are counted in the circulation figures of both publications, and the advertiser who buys space in both publications pays to reach some of the prospects twice.

In theory, every advertiser would like to have unduplicated reach among its best prospects, but in practice this may be very expensive, or impossible, to obtain. As total reach of our media mix approaches 100 percent of our target market, any new vehicle we add to it will pick up relatively few new prospects. Most of the cost of advertising in each new medium after this point will be for duplicate coverage.

Data on audience or circulation duplication can be obtained from audience studies made by research firms or by the media themselves. If we know how much overlap there is among the audiences of various vehicles, we can place our advertisements in those media that will provide us with the greatest number of exposures per audience member. This can be especially important during critical periods of an advertising campaign—the months before Christmas, for example. We can analyze many alternative vehicles until we find the best combination in terms of the size of the exclusive audience each medium contributes to the mix.

## Gross audience

The term *gross audience* refers to the total number of people exposed to *all* the forms of advertising used in a single campaign. This may include the audiences for radio and television programs, outdoor and transit displays, circulation figures for various publications, and the number of people attending trade shows. Some advertisers want to know the size of the gross audiences offered by alternative campaigns so that they can choose the mix that delivers the greatest number of exposure alternatives.

# The role of the media planner

The media planner has responsibility for making the fourth media decision: What would be the best specific schedule for the appearance of our advertisements in each medium? In working out the fine details of the media schedule, the media planner must seek the answers to such preliminary questions as: How many times shall we deliver the same

This well-known media research organization will tell any advertiser who wants to know what his or her competitors are doing in 75 different markets. By matching the competition's schedules with Arbitron or Nielsen ratings (measures of popularity or viewing), knowledgeable advertisers can then punch up their own media schedules in weak areas, goad their sales forces into more aggressive action, or do whatever else they think is necessary to meet and beat their competitors.

message to the same audience? During what months or on what days should our advertisements appear? At what location within the magazine or newspaper do we want to place our advertisements? Should our broadcast or newspaper advertisements appear in the morning or in the evening? Media planners use media research and market research, as well as their experience and intuition, to shape the final media plan.

## Cumulative audience

When arranging for a series of advertisements to appear in a single medium, a media planner must take into account the vehicle's cumulative audience, or cumulative reach. The *cumulative audience* is the number of people exposed to the medium over a given period of time. For example, Mr. Smith, Mrs. Jones, and Mr. Cleary may read the November issue of a magazine in which we have placed our advertisement. If we also place our ad in the December issue of the same magazine, that issue may be read by Mr. Smith, Mrs. Jones, and Mr. Cresap. Therefore, although each issue was read by only three people, if we placed our advertisements in both issues, we reached a cumulative audience of four people: Smith, Jones, Cleary, and Cresap. In the same way each episode of a radio or television program will be seen or heard by a certain number of people who did not tune in to the previous episode. For national television shows and for some mass magazines, the cumulative reach of four or five programs may be two or three times that of any single program or issue.

## Seasonal concentration

Because consumers purchase many products only at certain times of the year, it is usually very diffi-

This table deserves careful examination. Note, for example, that advertising in women's magazines peaked in March, while newspaper advertising peaked in August. Spot television advertising peaked in October, as did network television. Is October the best month for TV?

## NATIONAL ADVERTISING INDEX
### First 10 months, 1978

| | General index | Net tv | Spot tv | All magazines | Weeklies | Women's | Monthlies | Newspapers |
|---|---|---|---|---|---|---|---|---|
| Jan. | 226 | 247 | 267 | 182 | 149 | 216 | 219 | 211 |
| Feb. | 215 | 234 | 250 | 188 | 155 | 210 | 235 | 212 |
| March | 223 | 235 | 260 | 203 | 158 | 281 | 227 | 189 |
| April | 234 | 261 | 257 | 196 | 153 | 238 | 246 | 218 |
| May | 238 | 271 | 269 | 197 | 169 | 221 | 234 | 207 |
| June | 247 | 274 | 281 | 216 | 183 | 256 | 250 | 208 |
| July | 244 | 267 | 277 | 212 | 181 | 239 | 252 | 212 |
| Aug. | 257 | 288 | 265 | 228 | 208 | 237 | 260 | 236 |
| Sept. | 248 | 286 | 259 | 224 | 191 | 269 | 253 | 205 |
| Oct. | 252 | 291 | 284 | 204 | 168 | 241 | 246 | 217 |
| Change to date | +14 | +13 | +18 | +20 | +28 | +18 | +10 | +7 |

All indexes have been seasonally adjusted. The index shown for each medium is based on estimated total advertising investments in the medium, including talent, production and media costs. For each medium, the base (100) is an average of total investments in 1967.

Reprinted with permission from the January 9, 1979 issue of *Advertising Age.* Copyright by Crain Communications, Inc.

cult to persuade them to buy these products out of season. In order to maximize the effectiveness of the media, our advertising should be concentrated at the time when product interest is highest. Temperature and weather conditions affect the sales of many products. Swim suits, water skis, and soft drinks are sold most heavily during the warm summer months. Snow tires, antifreeze, and sleds are sold at the onset of winter. Certain food products tend to be consumed more heavily at specific times of the year. The wide variations in weather and temperature across the nation must also be taken into account.

Holidays are a seasonal variation offering special opportunities for media concentration. The Christmas season, which begins about mid-November and extends almost to December 25, is a period when many products are advertised much more heavily than usual. Toys, gift items, small appliances, and alcoholic beverages are intensively promoted at this time. Other holidays and commemorative days are very important for some products—for example, champagne around New Year's Day; pens, watches, and cameras around graduation time. Mother's Day, Father's Day, and Easter are traditional periods when certain products sell at greater volume than usual. The knowledgeable media planner will take advantage of this kind of consumer interest when arranging media schedules for these products.

## Scheduling

Having taken into account the seasonal demand for our product (if any) and the cumulative reach of the media we are using, the media planner determines a schedule for the appearance of our advertisements. This *schedule* shows the number of advertisements that are to appear in each medium, the size of the advertisements, and the dates on which they are to appear. There are many different ways to schedule any advertising program. No single type of schedule is best for all advertisers. Each company must arrange its schedule to suit its market and its advertising objectives. What may be best for one company or product may be bad for another.

For example, an advertiser may decide to buy six pages in a monthly consumer magazine. The media planner may arrange for a one-page advertisement for that firm's product to appear in every other issue of that magazine for a year. Or, the media planner may decide to have a one-page advertisement run in every issue of the magazine for three months, followed by a period of no advertising, followed by the reappearance of one-page advertisements in the next three issues. The latter schedule is a wave strategy called *flighting.* Flighting simply bunches the advertising—in print or broadcast media—to provide a concentrated impact. At the same time, flighting allows advertisers to take advantage of seasonal demand for their products.

Sometimes—particularly for the introduction of a new product or the implementation of a new marketing strategy—a media planner might use a *blitz schedule.* Taking the six pages described in the example above, a media planner might arrange a blitz schedule calling for the insertion of two double-page advertisements in three consecutive issues of a magazine.

One of the more recent innovations in print advertising is called bunching. In *bunching*, several different versions of the same advertisement are run on three to five consecutive right-hand pages of a magazine. Bunching provides concentrated impact within a single issue of a publication.

## The use of computers in media selection

Several years ago many of the largest advertising agencies turned to computers in their search for a more scientific approach to media selection. Much effort (and much publicity) was devoted to the development of models that would enable a load of relevant data to be processed. The computer would then churn out the optimum media *selection* along with the best media *schedule.* Computers, alas, merely process data, and much media analysis is qualitative rather than quantitative. Computer technology can certainly be utilized to analyze quantitative data, but the qualitative aspects are subject to many widely differing interpretations. Media decisions continue to require the exercise of experience and judgment.

## Media buying procedures

The actual purchase of time and space is made by the advertising agency's media department or—for the small agency that does not have a department —by the media person. Broadcast purchasing often involves negotiation of rates and schedules. Orders for space in newspapers and magazines are almost always made from the publisher's rate card, which lists the entire rate structure. Once the

In 1975, Magic Mountain Tea Company was a small San Francisco based producer of herbal teas with sales of about $4,000 a month. At that time, the company distributed its products through health and specialty food stores. In order to grow, Magic Mountain knew that it had to begin supermarket distribution; however, it had to be prepared for tough competition in this area from Thomas J. Lipton Inc., the country's largest tea marketer, and from R. C. Bigelow Inc., a well-entrenched producer of specialty teas.

To prepare for supermarket distribution, Magic Mountain developed a new package —similar to one already offered by Lipton—that contained 16 tea bags. The results of a market test had indicated that the mood names, such as Foggy Morning, that Magic Mountain had originally considered for its new line would not be as well accepted as descriptive names, such as Peppermint Spice, Sweet Orange Spice, and Wild Red Mint. As a result, the company decided to feature such descriptive names prominently on the new package.

The market for the company's products consisted of young people, women between the ages of 18 and 49, and older people who wanted a warm drink that was caffeine-free. Media selection presented a problem, however, because distribution of the product was not yet nationwide. In order to reach only those areas of the country where Magic Mountain teas were sold, the company would have to use such geographically selective media as spot television, spot radio, newspapers, or regional editions of magazines. The company also wanted a high-frequency medium, thus eliminating magazines from consideration. This preference also made spot radio a more attractive medium than spot television, since the lower costs of radio would allow Magic Mountain to run a greater number of commercials. At first, however, the company was reluctant to use radio because it offered no opportunity to display the package it had so carefully developed. At last, the recommendation of a media consultant convinced Magic Mountain to develop a media mix of high-frequency spot radio and Sunday supplement ads with coupons. A radio commercial was created around the message that herbal tea tastes like regular tea but is not bitter. The headline in print advertisements asked: "What would tea taste like without caffeine or bitterness?"

The media mix appeared to work well. In 1979, the company was expected to gross more than $1 million a month in sales.

Source: John J. O'Connor, "Berliner Brewing Up a Marketing Marvel," *Advertising Age*, September 4, 1978, p. 4.

media buy has been decided upon, a contract will be issued by the agency on behalf of the client to cover the rate and the frequency discounts. Then, when the schedule has been worked out, the agency will issue individual *insertion orders* to specify the particular date and space, or time and position, for each advertisement or commercial.

# People in media

Print media are organized somewhat differently from other businesses with which we may be familiar. The publications deliver to the advertiser a not-quite-tangible product—the attention of people, customers and prospects. So the medium must first sell itself, through its editorial contents, to people. That is the job of the editorial department, of the editors, writers, and artists who create and assemble the articles and illustrations that make up a publication. The circulation department is actively involved in getting as many people as possible to buy the publication, either by subscription or at the newsstand. The job of the advertising department, on the other hand, is to *sell* the publication as an advertising vehicle to advertisers and their agencies. All three of these departments contribute to the success of the publication. However, it is not on the income from subscriptions or newsstand sales, but on the revenue from sales of advertising space, that the publication will make its profit. Without the audience, there would be nothing to sell.

Broadcast sales are simpler, but the principle is the same. It is the program or editorial format of the radio or television station that attracts the audience. That is the job of the producers, directors, writers, announcers, and disc jockeys—to give the station a "personality" that attracts a consistent audience. This consistent audience is "sold" by the station's advertising department to potential advertisers. There is no circulation department to promote purchase of anything—radio and television programs are free. Also, it is very interesting to note the extensive use of the print media (newspapers usually) to boost the audience for a television broadcast and the frequent use of radio to sell magazine readership. Outdoor, of course, has no editorial format. Outdoor advertising companies are known as *plants*, which sell and install, or "post," the available locations.

## The media rep

Since most newspapers and radio stations are local in scope, their sales force tends to be limited to home base. But the radio station in Council Bluffs or Wichita Falls wants to solicit advertising from the large national advertisers as well as the local retail business organizations that are its main source of revenue. Out of this need there has developed the media sales representative—an individual or a firm that represents a number of noncompetitive media. Located in major marketing centers, the representative organization or *rep*, as it is called, makes frequent and regular contact with the national advertisers and the agencies responsible for buying time and space. For national advertisers and their agencies, the rep provides a local source of information regarding media in other areas of the country. For example, by contacting one of any number of rep organizations in Atlanta, an agency in that city can obtain current information about newspapers, television, or radio in most other parts of the United States and frequently in Canada.

An actual insertion order sent by a well-known agency to a major magazine. Space is provided on the form for all the instructions necessary. In this case, the agency has specified that the ad be placed on the inside back cover (3rd Cover) of the magazine. The ad will be printed in four colors (4/C) and will "bleed" (Bld.), that is, it will extend out to the edges of the page. Notice that certain position requirements are standard with this agency and are printed on the form.

---

## Cunningham & Walsh Inc.

260 Madison Avenue, New York, N.Y. 10016 Telephone: 212·683·4900

### *INSERTION ORDER*

**PUBLISHER**

Fortune
Time & Life Bldg.
1271 Ave. of America
New York, N.Y.   10020

DATE ____April 17, 1979____

RE Contract # ____65710____

Dated ____12/11____

Please insert ☐ National / ☐ Regional  Advertising as follows for:   St. Regis Paper Co. - Corp. '79

and charge in accordance with contract now in your possession. Unless otherwise noted, issues and tear sheets containing advertisements **must be sent to Client and to this office.**

| ISSUE | SIZE & COLOR | AD NO. & TITLE | JOB NO. |
|---|---|---|---|
| April 9, 1979 | 3rd Cover Bld. 4/C | We drove this 2½ ton (Bridge ad) (Rpt. of Jan. 16, 1978) | 46425 |

A copy of this issue must be mailed to Mr. Tino Pelino, V.P. Director of Traffic & Production immediately upon completion of this printing.

**NOTE:** This advertising is not to appear on page with, page facing, or backed up by the advertising of any similar product.
This advertising is not to be backed up by coupon.
See contract for position request, competitive clause, and other pertinent data.

**COPY:** You have.

**CUTS:**

BY      Frank Mathisen

**TRAFFIC DEPARTMENT**
**Cunningham & Walsh Inc.**

**Magazine Note:** Proofs must be submitted to us for OK before insertion!

Any insertion made to the contrary of this insertion order will be disallowed!

# Summary

If advertisers had unlimited amounts of money to spend, then media decisions would present no problems. But no advertiser, not even the United States Government, has an unlimited advertising budget. Therefore, advertisers (and their agencies) must carefully select the medium or combination of media that will reach the greatest number of prospective customers with their advertising message at the lowest possible cost.

In planning a media schedule, advertisers have to consider several factors in addition to the all-important one of cost. These factors include the nature of their product's target market and its method of distribution, since each medium is aimed at particular demographic and geographic market segments; the nature of their product, since it may require active demonstration (television) or high-quality color reproduction (magazines); and the overall objectives of their advertising program. As they examine the media, advertisers will also consider the length of time people can spend in examining the advertisement (*durability*), the *frequency* with which the medium can repeat the advertisement, and the editorial contents of the medium, because the editorial environment has an important effect on the way in which the audience responds to the actual advertising message.

An advertiser can reach the same audience repeatedly because of the audience's loyalty to their favorite medium—although the advertiser knows that most audiences, particularly those for the mass media, do not buy, watch, or read a medium for the advertisements it carries. Broadcast media are rarely looked to for their advertising. Quite the contrary, the advertising is an interruption of the viewer's enjoyment, breaking into the action of the program. Outdoor billboards, car cards, and train posters carry no editorial matter and are neither bought nor requested by their readers. Readers of magazines, for the most part, read them because they are looking for articles that will inform and entertain them. However, special-interest magazines and newspapers are often read as much for the product advertisements as for the editorial contents.

In choosing among the various media available in each media category, advertisers work with circulation figures and costs, with audience research data and market research data. For broadcast media, they measure *coverage*, the number of homes that can receive a station's broadcast signals, and *circulation*, the number of homes that actually tune in. For print media they measure circulation as the number of copies of the publication sold on the newsstand or by subscription. Publications will sometimes emphasize their pass-along readership, or *secondary circulation.* This is the number of people who read a publication without having purchased it.

*Balance* is the most important consideration for advertisers who place their messages in a combination, or mix, of media. Does the media mix achieve the best possible balance among all the important media selection factors? For example, if timeliness is important, radio or television lend urgency to the advertising message. So do newspapers, and the newspaper message will be longer lasting and permit more reflection on the part of the prospect. If this durability is also an important factor, the advertiser might want to consider a mix of radio and newspapers. If the product requires demonstration, television may be added to the mix. And so on. In using a media mix, however, an advertiser also pays for a certain amount of duplication. A message is reinforced by duplication, but the advertiser may want to trade some of this duplication for greater frequency or more reach.

To analyze all the various combinations of media, some advertisers and their agencies have used computers in the hope of obtaining the optimum prospect exposure. But the computer has proven more useful in performing clerical functions, storing and retrieving large quantities of data efficiently, than in performing analytic functions. In the complex process of weighing both the quantitative and the qualitative factors involved in media selection, the computer has not been able to replace the experience and intuitive judgment of the media buyer.

## Media reference guide

*Circulation Data*

Audit Bureau of Circulations, 420 Lexington Avenue, New York, N.Y. 10017

Business Publications Audit of Circulation, Inc., 360 Park Avenue South, New York, N.Y. 10022

Canadian Circulations Audit Board, 44 Eglinton Avenue, Suite 705, West Toronto M4R 1A1, Ont.

Standard Rate & Data Service, Inc., 866 Third Avenue, New York, N.Y. 10022

Traffic Audit Bureau, 708 Third Ave., New York, N.Y. 10017

Verified Audit Circulation Corporation, 1413 Seventh Street, Santa Monica, Ca. 90401

*Media Associations*

Agricultural Publisher's Association, 111 East Wacker Drive, Chicago, Ill. 60601.

American Business Press, Inc., 205 East 42nd Street, New York, N.Y. 10017

American Newspaper Publishers Association, The Newspaper Center, 11600 Sunrise Valley Drive, Reston, Va. 22091

Institute of Outdoor Advertising, 485 Lexington Avenue, New York, N.Y. 10017

Magazine Publishers Association, Inc., 575 Lexington Avenue, New York, N.Y. 10022

Society of National Association Publications, 3 Executive Terrace, National Press Building, Washington, D.C. 20045

Radio Advertising Bureau, 485 Lexington Avenue, New York, N.Y. 10017

Television Bureau of Advertising, 1345 Avenue of the Americas, New York, N.Y. 10019

Transit Advertising Association, 1725 "K" Street NW, Washington, D.C. 20006

*Independent Research Organizations*

A. C. Nielsen Company, Nielsen Plaza, Northbrook, Il. 60062

Advertising Research Foundation, 3 East 54th Street, New York, N.Y. 10022

American Research Bureau, Inc., 1350 Avenue of the Americas, New York, N.Y. 10019

The Arbitron Company, Inc., 1350 Avenue of the Americas, New York, N.Y. 10019

Broadcast Advertisers Reports, Inc., 500 Fifth Avenue, New York, N.Y. 10036

Media Records, 370 Seventh Avenue, New York, N.Y. 10001

N. C. Rorabaugh Co., 347 Madison Avenue, New York, N.Y. 10017

Publishers Information Bureau, 575 Lexington Avenue, New York, N.Y. 10022

The Pulse, Inc., 1212 Avenue of the Americas, New York, N.Y. 10036

Starch INRA Hooper, Inc., 566 East Boston Post Road, Mamaroneck, N.Y. 10543

Trendex, Inc., 800 Third Avenue, New York, N.Y. 10022

W. R. Simmons & Associates Research, Inc., 219 East 42nd Street, New York, N.Y. 10017

## QUESTIONS FOR DISCUSSION

1. What is the importance of *selectivity* in media planning?

2. How do *reach* and *frequency* relate to each other?

3. What benefits does the advertiser derive from *flighting?*

4. Can you find examples in which media cooperate with one another to boost audience?

5. Newspapers appear to dominate in total media expenditures. How do you account for this?

6. For what classes or types of products would editorial environment be very important?

7. For what products do you think cost might not be the most important factor in media evaluation?

8. Based upon what you've learned so far, what media recommendations would you make for
   a. cold cereal
   b. men's deodorant
   c. expensive cigars

## Sources and suggestions for further reading

Barban, Arnold M.; Cristol, Stephen M.; and Kopec, Frank J. *Essentials of Media Planning.* Chicago: Crain Books, 1976.

Barton, Roger. *Media in Advertising.* New York: McGraw-Hill, 1964.

Chase, Cochrane, and Barasch, Kenneth L. *Market Problem Solver.* 2d ed. Radnor, Pa.: Chilton Book Co., 1977.

Frey, Albert Wesley, and Halterman, Jean C. *Advertising.* 4th ed. New York: The Ronald Press Co., 1970.

Littlefield, James E. *Readings in Advertising.* St. Paul: West Publishing Co., 1975. Part 5.

Sissors, Jack Z., and Petray, E. Reynold. *Advertising Media Planning.* Chicago: Crain Books, 1976.

Ulanoff, Stanley M. *Advertising in America.* New York: Hastings House, 1977.

Wolfe, Harry Deane; Brown, James K.; Thompson, G. Clark; and Greenberg, Stephen H. *Evaluating Media.* Business Policy Study no. 121. New York: National Industrial Conference Board, 1966.

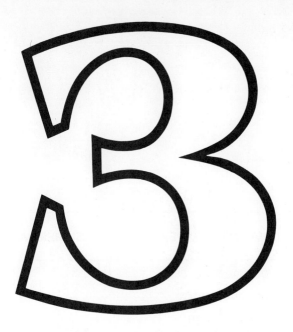

# GUIDE TO ADVERTISING MEDIA

**8**
Print media: newspapers and consumer magazines

**9**
Print media: business and farm publications

**10**
The broadcast media

**11**
Outdoor, transit, and directories

**12**
Nonmedia advertising

Although you can't tell it from this black-and-white photograph, this balloon is very colorful. Sponsored by Anheuser-Busch, it flies in balloon races. When it does, its picture appears in newspapers and on television, and millions of people get the Budweiser message. The balloon is advertising that begets publicity.

## PRINT MEDIA: NEWSPAPERS AND CONSUMER MAGAZINES

**Newspapers: advertising workhorse**

Advantages of newspapers as an
    advertising medium
Limitations of newspapers
Tear sheets and checking copies
Newspapers by type
    Daily newspapers—morning and
        evening
    Weekly newspapers
    Sunday newspapers
    Sunday supplements
    Ethnic and foreign-language papers
Buying newspaper space
Newspaper rates
    Positions and premiums
    ROP color

Rate comparisons
Combination buys
Special newspapers

**Consumer magazines**

Types of consumer magazines
Advantages of magazines
Magazine circulations
Magazine space and rates
Demographic editions
Comparing magazines

## WORKING VOCABULARY

| | | | |
|---|---|---|---|
| closing date | square third | open rate | milline rate |
| tear sheet | matched color | contract rate | combination rate |
| checking copy | rotosection | short rate | rate base |
| make-good | agate line | split run | island half |

CHAPTER 8

# print media: newspapers and consumer magazines

*While one might compare the circulation of a newspaper with coverage of a radio station, these intermedia comparisons cannot be made on a statistical basis and instead would have to be made on some subjective basis.*

*The bases of these latter comparisons, however, are not entirely subjective. They are founded on the idea that all media have inherent qualities that make them desirable.*

JACK Z. SISSORS and E. REYNOLD PETRAY
*Advertising Media Planning*

IN 1976, advertising volume in the United States on all media totaled more than $33.7 billion. Of this amount, newspapers received the largest single share—$9.9 billion. But, although in recent years the volume of newspaper advertising has steadily increased, the percentage of total advertising volume committed to newspapers has declined, from 34 percent in 1955 to 29.4 percent in 1976. This decline occurred at the same time that total advertising volume almost quadrupled, and while television was increasing its share of total volume from 11 percent to 19.9 percent. Although newspapers still command the largest share of all advertising dollars, the bulk of it is in local, not national, advertising.

## Newspapers: advertising workhorse

### Advantages of newspapers as an advertising medium

*Newspapers provide intensive coverage of specific geographic markets.* By using newspapers, advertisers can obtain the high degree of geographical

163

A newspaper advertises itself in a major advertising trade publication. What do advertisers want to know about the *Orlando Sentinel Star?* They want to know that it is located in a growing area—as evidenced by the 89 percent increase in food sales over the past five years. They want to know that it reaches 79 percent of the population every week. They want to know that it carries a large volume of advertising from local food stores, which is an indicator of value to national advertisers of food products.

# Orlando: A super market for food advertisers.

Orlando's appetite is ravenous. Last year alone, the Orlando area carted from food store shelves over $470 million in groceries—up a hearty 89% in only 5 years.

And if you'd like the Orlando market handed to you on a plat-ter, nobody can do it like the Sentinel Star. Because, of all the print and broadcast media in town, we're the one way your advertising can tempt 73% of Orlando every Sunday, and 79% every week.

No wonder advertisers handed us such a huge helping of retail food ad linage last year —the second largest in the entire state. So, if you'd like a bigger slice of the Orlando and Central Florida market, satisfy your hunger with the Sentinel Star: Florida's No. 1 medium in market penetration.

## Orlando Sentinel Star
## Florida's Shopping Center

Represented by: Cresmer, Woodward, O'Mara & Ormsbee, Inc.
Source: 1978 Belden CMS, (Orange, Seminole, Osceola and Lake Counties);
1977 Sales Management Survey of Buying Power.

selectivity they need to meet a number of marketing and advertising objectives. Newspapers provide the most cost-efficient medium for advertising when product distribution is regional. National advertisers who are slowly building a distribution network can use newspapers to introduce their products to the major metropolitan markets, one market at a time. National advertisers can also use newspapers to meet competition from local or regional products.

*Newspapers have very short deadlines.* Most metropolitan daily papers have a *closing date* —that is, a deadline by which they must receive advertising copy—of only forty-eight hours in advance of publication. In contrast, consumer magazines have closing dates three months or more in advance of publication. Thus, newspapers' comparatively short deadlines allow advertisers the freedom to alter their copy to tie in with current events, fast-breaking discoveries, or sudden changes in the weather.

*Newspapers are local.* Newspapers are filled with local news and local advertising. Local advertising offers the national advertiser excellent opportunities for cooperative advertising with local retailers.

Cooperative advertising is advertising placed by retailers in their local newspapers, the cost of which is *shared* by the national advertiser. The subject of vertical cooperative advertising is dealt with more fully in Chapter 19.

*Newspapers offer excellent opportunity for frequency.* Published daily, with loyal readers comprising the bulk of their circulation, newspapers can deliver an advertising message day after day— five, six, or seven times a week.

*Newspapers reach a well-educated audience.* Eighty-seven percent of all college graduates read a newspaper every day. Eighty-three percent of high-school graduates read a newspaper. Only 64 percent of the people who have *not* completed high school read a daily paper. We also know from market surveys that regular newspaper readers have higher incomes than occasional readers. Almost 90 percent of families with annual incomes of $15,000 or more read a newspaper regularly.

*Newspapers contain a wide range of editorial material aimed at a broad audience.* Whatever the interest of the readers may be—finance, sports, homemaking, fashion, politics—their newspapers will contain news and editorial features that hold their attention and expose them to the advertising message.

*Newspapers offer great flexibility in terms of the size of the advertisements, from a few inches to a full page.*

## Limitations of newspapers

Some of the advantages of newspapers can, however, be considered detriments by some advertisers. Newspapers do indeed have a *short deadline.* They also have a very short life. Not many people will read a two- or three-day-old newspaper. Of course, readers may always return to an article or review that they missed; but when they do so, there is very little chance that they will also look over the paper's advertisements again. Usually, if the reader missed the message on the first go-round, *the message will not get a second chance.*

Daily newspapers are able to produce a new issue every twenty-four hours only by using a high-speed rotary printing process. But, because the papers are printed rapidly on coarse wood pulp paper called newsprint, the reproduction of fine detail in photographs or drawings is impossible.

Therefore, although advertisers enjoy the speed with which their advertising message is produced, *the quality of reproduction leaves much to be desired.*

Newspapers are demographically selective only to a limited extent. Men and women read the same newspaper. Old people and young people read the same newspaper. Rich and poor and those in between read the same newspaper.

National advertisers who commit themselves to the use of a large volume of newspaper advertising also commit themselves to the completion of a large volume of paperwork. To place an advertisement in *TV Guide* that will reach 20 million readers, agency personnel must fill out one insertion order, one invoice, and check one copy of the magazine to verify the appearance of the ad. A newspaper schedule with only a fraction of *TV Guide*'s reach requires agency personnel to: make dozens of phone calls for space reservations; fill out dozens of insertion orders; arrange for the delivery of reproduction materials to dozens of cities; check dozens of tear sheets; and check, verify, and pay dozens of invoices.

## Tear sheets and checking copies

A few words in explanation of the process of verifying the appearance of an ad in the print media are appropriate here. A *tear sheet* is a copy of the page on which an advertisement was printed that has been cut (or torn) from the particular edition in which it appeared. A newspaper will enclose a tear sheet along with its invoice for the space cost as a verification of the appearance of the ad. A *checking copy* is a copy of the entire newspaper or magazine that contained the ad. Advertisers, or their agencies, use the checking copies to examine the edito-

rial climate of the newspaper and, perhaps, to see what competitive products were advertised in that issue. Magazines generally follow the same practice, sending a tear sheet with their invoice to the agency's accounting department and a checking copy to the media department. Checking copies are often sent to the account executive at the agency and to the advertiser.

What happens if the newspaper or magazine made a mistake in running an ad? What if they inserted an incorrect ad or placed an ad in the wrong issue of the publication? Perhaps, as very rarely happens, an ad was poorly printed. If the error is the fault of the publication, they will rerun the ad in the first available issue. This rerun ad is commonly called a *make-good.*

National advertisers also want to verify the appearance of newspaper and magazine advertisements placed by their dealers in order to answer the following questions:

**1.** Are dealers featuring my products or those of my competitors?

**2.** Are dealers passing my price reductions on to consumers or taking them as additional profits for themselves?

**3.** Which products in my line are being featured most frequently?

**4.** Are the dealers tieing in with our national advertising?

To get the answers to these and many other questions regarding newspaper and local broadcast advertising, many national advertisers use the services of the Advertising Checking Bureau, Inc. The ACB, as it is usually called, was established in 1917 to act as a clearinghouse for newspaper pub-

## TOP 15 NEWSPAPERS IN THE UNITED STATES
### (in circulation)

| | Morning | Evening | Total | Sunday |
|---|---|---|---|---|
| 1. New York News | 1,824,836 | — | 1,824,836 | 2,656,981 |
| 2. Los Angeles Times | 1,020,208 | — | 1,020,208 | 1,315,051 |
| 3. New York Times | 878,714 | — | 878,714 | 1,486,662 |
| 4. Chicago Tribune | 762,810 | — | 762,810 | 1,155,687 |
| 5. San Francisco Chronicle/Examiner | 488,782 | 156,083 | 644,865 | 668,550 |
| 6. Detroit News | — | 633,708 | 633,708 | 826,111 |
| 7. New York Post | — | 621,564 | 621,564 | 457,087 |
| 8. Kansas City Star/Times | 322,800 | 295,606 | 618,406 | 403,851 |
| 9. Chicago Sun-Times | 611,135 | — | 611,135 | 704,358 |
| 10. Detroit Free Press | 608,987 | — | 608,987 | 716,107 |
| 11. Washington Post | 561,640 | — | 561,640 | 801,035 |
| 12. Miami Herald/News | 447,057 | 71,743 | 518,800 | 551,593 |
| 13. Philadelphia Bulletin | — | 516,872 | 516,872 | 610,898 |
| 14. Milwaukee Journal/Sentinel | 161,310 | 334,167 | 495,477 | 532,692 |
| 15. Boston Globe | 306,114 | 160,569 | 466,683 | 660,428 |

Source: 1979 edition of *Information Please Almanac*, pp. 638–640.

lishers in the distribution of checking copies to agencies and national advertisers throughout the country. ACB *reads* virtually every daily newspaper in the country and the more important weeklies. They provide tear sheet service and verification of cooperative ads. For subscribers who are interested, they report on secondary brand mentions, as when an appliance is advertised as "powered by a General Electric motor." ACB also reports on the use of material provided by the national advertiser as it is used in ads placed by retailers. These reports tell the national advertiser which models or styles appear to be most popular with dealers.

## Newspapers by type

To understand the use and value of newspapers, we will find it helpful to separate them into five categories:

1. *Daily newspapers* publish morning and/or evening editions in cities or large metropolitan areas.

2. *Weekly newspapers*, or country newspapers as they are often called, are usually published in small towns, and their circulation is predominantly rural and suburban.

3. *Sunday newspapers* are the large Sunday editions of daily papers and often include a *Sunday supplement.*

4. *Ethnic and foreign-language newspapers* are directed to various ethnic groups in the population of the United States and are circulated nationally, or, in some cases, only in the ethnic communities of metropolitan areas.

5. *National newspapers* are distributed nationwide. There are seven: the *Christian Science Monitor*, the only daily national consumer newspaper; the *Wall Street Journal, Journal of Commerce*, and *American Banker*, which are daily business newspapers; and *Grit*, the *National Enquirer*, and the *National Star*, which are weeklies.

**Daily newspapers—morning and evening**  About 1,800 newspapers in the United States issue daily editions. The majority, roughly 80 percent, are evening papers; a few papers print both morning and evening editions. Many advertisers believe that a morning paper enjoys a shorter period of readership and fewer secondary readers than an afternoon paper. They argue that the afternoon paper, purchased by a commuter during the ride home, or delivered to the home in the afternoon, is then perused in a leisurely manner at home by all the members of the family or household. They believe that the morning paper, however, leaves the house with one of the members of the family, is taken on the train or bus, is read in transit, and is often left at the station or at work. Although there is some logic to this analysis, many readers also bring their morning paper home with them to finish their reading. One final note: According to a Simmons study in 1978, each newspaper is read by 2.2 people.

**Weekly newspapers**  There are over 9,000 weekly newspapers in the United States, most of which circulate in small towns. Published once a week, these newspapers cannot compete with big-city dailies or broadcast media for coverage of national, or even state, news events. Their existence is justified by the publication of hometown news that is neither carried in big-city papers nor delivered over broadcast media. The local news is of interest to local readers, and these papers are an excellent medium for local retailers. When national advertisers choose to include these publications in a national advertising program, they usually arrange to place their ads through a representative organization that will accept one insertion order from the agency and will then distribute copy to the weekly papers involved.

The task of ordering, checking, and billing would be so onerous without the aid of the representative organization that few agencies would bother, particularly considering the marginal coverage such papers offer.

**Sunday newspapers**  Newspaper editions that are published on Sunday have larger circulations than the daily editions. In 1977, the daily circulation of *The New York Times* was 835,700; the circulation of the Sunday edition, 1,436,768. The Sunday edition is read at home by all the members of the family. The Sunday edition usually provides in-depth coverage of a wide range of subjects. Advertisers may choose the section that provides the most appropriate editorial environment. The advertiser expects greater effectiveness because the reader has more time on Sunday; other members of the household have an opportunity to read; and the interest-focused sections enhance the impact of the selling message.

Most Sunday papers include a comics section, which is a syndicated section. Once, advertisers seeking to reach young people—children and adolescents—placed ads in these sections. Today, however, advertisers use other media, notably television, to reach this market. As a result, the amount of advertising in comic sections declined. Advertisers must remember, however, that about 70 percent of the comics section's audience are adults, not children.

**Sunday supplements**  The magazine or *rotosection* of the Sunday paper is not truly a magazine, nor is it properly a section of the newspaper. Standard Rate & Data Service (SRDS) carries the listing for Sunday supplements in its *Consumer Magazine and Farm Publication Rates and Data* book, as well

# THE GLOBE-DEMOCRAT IS FIRST IN ST. LOUIS

# EVERY MORNING

## FIRST in circulation

| Globe-Democrat | **271,755** |
|---|---|
| Post-Dispatch | 262,707 |

Audit Bureau of Circulations, March 31, 1978

## FIRST in readership

| Globe-Democrat | **561,400** |
|---|---|
| Post-Dispatch | 553,800 |

Three Sigma Research Center, Inc., 1978

For demographics, psychographics and on-line media mixes, call Ian Cohen at 314/342-1460 and ask about the Market Audience Potential of St. Louis as revealed by the new Three Sigma Research study.

# GLOBE-DEMOCRAT

Another newspaper advertises itself to national advertisers, this time by making direct comparison with its competitor. Note the reference to the Audit Bureau of Circulations, the independent organization that verifies the circulation of newspapers all over the country. The *Globe-Democrat* claims, however, a *readership* that is more than double its circulation, indicating about 2.1 readers per copy. The source for this information is a private research organization.

as in its *Newspaper Rates and Data* book. The Sunday supplement has the characteristics of a consumer magazine, but it does not have the same length of life. It offers advertisers the same depth of local market coverage that a newspaper offers plus excellent four-color reproduction. Sunday supplements do have long closing dates, however; some may be even longer than those of many consumer magazines.

Today, about 456 newspapers include either *Parade* or *Family Weekly* magazines in their Sunday editions. The newspaper contracts for the supplement, and it is delivered in bulk. The paper then simply inserts the supplement into its Sunday edition as a self-contained section. The name of the paper is carried on the masthead of the magazine, and to the reader it looks like a section of the newspaper. *Parade* is distributed through more than 100 of the larger newspapers with a circulation of 21 million copies. *Family Weekly* distributes through some 250 smaller newspapers with a total circulation of over 11 million copies. Another supplement, *Sunday,* is distributed through 50 newspapers, including such large and well-known papers as the *New York Daily News* and the *Chicago Tribune. The New York Times* and the *Los Angeles Times* publish their own independent Sunday magazines.

**Ethnic and foreign-language papers**   The difference between ethnic and foreign-language newspapers is that foreign-language papers are directed to members of ethnic groups that do not read the English language press. New York's Chinatown, for example, boasts four Chinese-language newspapers. But, as dependence on the former native language has lessened, so has dependence on foreign-language media.

On the other hand, there are more than 200 newspapers in America that are basically reflective of—and primarily oriented to—the distinct needs and problems of black Americans. These papers reach black consumers at a sales identification level comparable to that of papers primarily oriented to white Americans.

While in the past the bulk of the advertising in most ethnic and foreign-language newspapers has come from local retailers or regional distributors of specialty products, national advertising in these media is increasing.

## Buying newspaper space

Newspaper space is sold in units of measurement called agate lines. An *agate line* is 1/14 of an inch deep and one column wide. Advertising space is generally specified by stating both the number of agate lines and the number of columns. For example, we can order space as *70 × 2* or *70 on 2,* which means 70 agate lines on 2 columns—a total of 140 lines. Or we can order 140 lines (10 inches) as 140 × 1. Some newspapers may not permit us to order space in the form of 47 × 3 (141 lines) because they have restrictions on the dimensions of the ads they will accept. Each newspaper has its own set of restrictions. For instance, *The New York Times* requires a 3-column ad to be a minimum of 56 agate lines in depth; the *New York Daily News* requires a 3-column ad to be at least 50 lines in depth.

Most papers will not sell display space measuring less than 14 agate lines. Most will not accept advertisements measuring less than 28 × 2, which means that in order to have an ad on 2 columns, minimum depth must be 28 lines (a total of 56 lines). Such specifications are listed by Standard Rate & Data Service and on the newspaper's rate card.

A standard-size paper has a column of 300 agate lines. A tabloid paper has 200 lines to a column. Most newspapers will charge us for a full column if our ad is *almost* a full column. For example, we may want to run a column ad in a tabloid newspaper that will fit in 190 lines. The newspaper will, however, insist upon billing us for 200 lines (a full column), so we might as well increase the size of our ad if we can, because we will have to pay for 200 lines of space anyway.

Most standard-size newspapers have an 8-column format with 2,400 agate lines to a full page (300 × 8). Some have adopted a 6-column format, and others a 9-column format. Tabloid newspapers are 5 columns wide and offer a full page as 200 × 5 or 1,000 lines. In some cases, weekly newspapers sell their advertising space by the column inch rather than the agate line. The lower rates for space in these papers make measurements by the inch more practical.

## Newspaper rates

Newspaper rates are listed on the rate card as either open or contract rate. An *open rate* is the highest rate quoted for a national advertiser and involves no commitment beyond a single insertion. However, if an advertiser plans to run a series of ads in the newspaper over a one-year period, most papers will offer that advertiser a lower rate based either on total linage used or on frequency. These lower rates are called *contract rates*.

If a newspaper offers a contract rate structure, it will be based on the total linage used during the contract year. If a newspaper offers a rate structure based on frequency of insertion, the bases are usually thirteen or twenty-six insertions, or more, over the course of the contract year. Some newspapers offer a rate structure based on both linage and frequency. For a national advertiser, all the rates are subject to the 15 percent agency commission. Local retail advertising is offered at a lower rate, with reductions for quantity and/or frequency, and it is not subject to agency commission. A *flat rate* is one that provides for neither frequency nor volume reductions.

If we (or our agency) issue a contract calling for a specified quantity of space at the contract rate and then fail to fulfill the schedule, the newspaper has the right to bill us at the rate actually earned. The difference between the *contract rate* and the *earned rate* is called the *short rate*. The procedure for determining the short rate is simple. Suppose our agency had planned a series of ten ads in a particular newspaper, each ad 100 × 4 (400 lines). The open rate might be $5.00 an agate line, the 2,000-line rate $4.80, and the 4,000-line rate $4.60 a line. The agency contracts for the program at the $4.60 rate. If, after only five insertions, we have to cancel our program, the newspaper would send us a *short-rate invoice* for the 2,000 lines we used at 20¢ a line—the difference between the rate at which we were billed and the rate that we earned. On the other hand, if the contract had originally called for only five insertions at the 2,000-line rate of $4.80, and after six months we decided to use five additional insertions, we would be entitled to a *rebate*. We would receive credit at 20¢ a line for the 2,000 lines used at the $4.80 rate and the newspaper would bill us for the succeeding five insertions at the lower $4.60 rate.

**Positions and premiums**  Unless we specify where we want our advertisement to appear within a newspaper, the publisher may place it wherever it happens to fit. Newspaper insertions placed in this

To be sure that this message reached its target market—men—the advertiser had the ad placed in the sports section of the paper. This advertiser pays a higher rate than retailers pay for the same amount of space. In addition, the advertiser pays a special charge, called a *premium*, for placement in the sports section.

manner are described as *ROP*, meaning *run of paper*. Specific positions within the newspaper, on the other hand, offer the advertiser a number of advantages. In a standard-size newspaper, the top of the page generally has a better opportunity for readership than the bottom of the page. In making up the page, the publisher usually places the large ads at the top of the page and the small ads at the bottom. We may request *top-of-the-page position* and hope for the best. But to be sure of obtaining a top-of-the-page position, our insertion order should specify *top of the page paid*. The publisher will then guarantee us that our ad will appear at the top of the page and will add a standard extra charge to our bill for that *premium position*.

Top or bottom location on a page is not the only position some advertisers are willing to pay extra for. Some may want to place their ad on page 2, or in the back of the first section, or on the editorial page. For men's products, advertisers frequently specify the sports section. For women's products, the fashion page or the food page may be most desirable. Such specific positioning of the ad within the paper improves the demographic selectivity.

Many newspapers offer split-run facilities. The *split run* is a process by which alternate copies of the same newspaper are printed with different ads for the same product. We can use this technique to test the appeal of our ad, the copy, the illustration, or any of the other elements that can be varied. By tabulating the response to different ads—through reader letters, phone calls, or coupon redemptions —we can select the most effective for use in other papers, or we can adapt the most effective ad for use in other media. Of course, newspapers will charge us extra for the use of their split-run service.

**ROP color**  Today, more than a thousand newspapers can reproduce four-color ads in full-page size only; another few hundred can print ads in black plus one color, also in full-page size only. We can increase the readership of our ads by using color, and when it is used functionally in reproducing the package or the trademark, for example, extra impact is added.

In certain cities it is possible for newspapers to offer their advertisers very high-quality color reproduction with the use of HiFi or SpectaColor rotogravure preprinted paper.[1] The advertiser or the

[1] HiFi and SpectaColor are produced by Standard Gravure Corporation, Louisville, Kentucky. About 1,750 newspapers offer HiFi and about 300 newspapers offer SpectaColor.

A typical HiFi newspaper ad. As you can see, no matter where the ad is cut off, the message will be complete. In fact, the repetition of some portions of the ad simply makes it more interesting.

agency provides the artwork, the list of newspapers that will carry the ad, and the insertion date. The producers of HiFi or SpectaColor do the rest. By means of rotogravure, the advertisement is printed on only one side of a roll of paper. Rotogravure printing provides very high-fidelity color reproduction, which is an important factor in the promotion of many products.

After printing one side, the paper is rerolled and shipped to the local newspapers that will carry the ad. When the preprinted roll reaches the newspaper plant it is placed on the newspaper press just like a blank roll of newsprint. Current news and advertising is printed on the blank, or back, side of the roll as it runs through the newspaper press and the HiFi or SpectaColor ad becomes an integral part of that day's edition of that newspaper.

SpectaColor is designed for a registered cutoff. This means that each page will be cut off in exactly the same spot so that it is the same size as a full newspaper page. To do this, the SpectaColor rolls are printed with "eye marks" positioned along the edge of the roll at the top and bottom of the ad. Electronic inset equipment on the newspaper press "reads" these eye marks so that the paper is always cut off in the right spot.

HiFi is designed for those newspapers that do not have inset equipment on their presses to control the cutoff of the page. Without this equipment, the paper would stretch a few thousandths of an inch with each repeat, and the image would "creep," allowing the cut to occur anywhere on the page. This means that the HiFi ad must be designed in a continuous or wallpaper pattern, so that the full advertising message will be delivered no matter where the cut occurs.

**Rate comparisons** The space rates for different newspapers are difficult to compare because they are based on circulation, which will vary from one paper to the next. Advertisers have, however, developed a formula to help them determine the cost effectiveness of their newspaper advertising. The formula is:

$$\frac{\text{line rate} \times 1{,}000{,}000}{\text{actual circulation}} = \text{milline rate}$$

Newspapers do not have a milline rate that they charge for space. It merely serves as a standard for comparison. For example, let us suppose that the *Boondock Times* has an open rate of $4.00 a line and a circulation of 625,000, but the *Boondock Bugle* has an open rate of $3.20 and a circulation of 425,000. Which is the better buy? To find out, we convert their circulation and rate figures to milline rates:

$$Times: \frac{4.00 \times 1,000,000}{625,000} = 6.4$$

$$Bugle: \frac{3.20 \times 1,000,000}{425,000} = 7.53$$

Now, when we compare the *Boondock Times* with the *Boondock Bugle* we see that, even with a higher open rate, the *Times* is a better buy. Similar comparisons can be made between all newspapers.[2] Of course, if the milline rate were the sole criterion, the *Times* would have all the advertising and the *Bugle* would quickly have to reduce its rate to make its milline more favorable. Therefore, we must assume that there are certain demographic differences between the audiences of the two fictitious papers that advertisers consider important. If the demographic characteristics of their target market match those of the *Bugle*'s audience, advertisers will buy the *Bugle* regardless of the milline rate. You must weigh *all* the factors in light of your advertising objectives.

A final word about newspaper rates and national advertising: The cost of achieving national coverage through newspapers is very high. For this reason, advertisers usually buy only limited coverage, concentrating, for example, on their top ten markets. These top ten markets may be of the advertiser's own designation, based perhaps on product distribution, or they may be the ten largest markets in the United States as shown in the "Survey of Buying Power" published by *Sales & Marketing Management*.[3]

**Combination buys** In areas where the same publisher owns one or more newspapers, an advertiser may buy space in all of them at a special *combination rate*. If the publisher owns both the morning and evening newspapers in a city, advertisers may place their ads in both papers for a combination rate that is little more than the open rate for one paper. A publisher might, on the other hand, own several newspapers in different cities scattered throughout a geographic area. The combination rate for these papers is usually far less than the total of the individual rates for each of these papers.

## Special newspapers

Most high schools and colleges issue a weekly newspaper. Why should any national advertiser consider such media? High-school and college students represent a very selective market for phonograph records, soft drinks, beer, cigarettes, and books. The U.S. government uses these papers for recruiting for the military. Magazines also use these newspapers to solicit subscriptions.

Union newspapers, religious newspapers, and military newspapers are usually of little or no interest to national advertisers. SRDS carries listings for such papers in its magazine edition. The shopping news, or pennysaver as it is commonly called, is not

---

[2] When newspaper rates are compared on the basis of their open rate, the index is known as the *maximil*. A *minimil* is the index used when the comparison is made on the basis of the lowest contract rate.

[3] The "Survey of Buying Power" is contained each year in one of the July issues of *Sales & Marketing Management,* a marketing magazine published by Bill Communications, Inc., New York. In February, April, July, and October the magazine publishes an extra issue that contains a special survey feature.

PRINT MEDIA: NEWSPAPERS AND CONSUMER MAGAZINES

For national advertisers, this newspaper publisher offers a *combination* of two newspapers that serves a geographic area in northern New Jersey. Note the reference to the exclusivity of the combined newspapers' readership, an important benefit. A local retailer may buy either paper, according to the trading area that suits his or her particular needs best.

a newspaper. Generally it contains no news and little, if any, editorial content. Pennysavers are rarely used as a vehicle for national advertising.

## Consumer magazines

About 1,200 consumer magazines are published in the United States. It is very difficult to consider their value as advertising vehicles without separating them into categories based on the type of audience they appeal to. The question of clarification is made more complicated by the magazines' frequency of issue and method of distribution—some are weeklies, some are monthlies. There are even some bimonthlies and a few quarterlies. Some magazines are distributed only by mail subscription; some are sold on the newsstand; others, at the supermarket.

In recent years, the problems of profitable publication have been exacerbated by rising costs of

*McCall's* magazine provides an appropriate editorial climate for all advertisers who want to reach women. It contains a wide range of articles that are of interest to this specific demographic group: from cosmetics and fashions to business and politics.

paper and printing and by repeated increases in postage rates. The competition of television has also changed the character of many magazines: Their editorial emphasis is no longer on fiction— television provides enough of that—but, rather, on news and informative articles.

## Types of consumer magazines

The first choice that advertisers face in selecting a consumer magazine as a vehicle for their advertising is whether to use a *mass*, or general-interest, magazine or a *class*, or special-interest, magazine. Mass circulation magazines today include *People*, *TV Guide*, and *Reader's Digest*. These publications contain reading matter for the entire family with editorial contents of broad general interest. Among class magazines, we find such widely diverse publications as *Time, Better Homes & Gardens, Sports Illustrated*, and *Woman's Day*. These publications are aimed at specific demographic groups or at groups with certain fairly well-defined interests. There are probably no subject areas of interest to a sizeable group of people that are not reached by a special-interest magazine. There are magazines for horse lovers, stamp collectors, do-it-yourselfers, tennis players, even model-railroad buffs. Class magazines aimed at groups with certain demographic characteristics, such as age or sex, include *Seventeen* for teenage girls, *Good Housekeeping* for homemakers, and *Retirement Living* for senior citizens.

Most consumer magazines are issued monthly. In order to keep current, newsmagazines, emphasizing not the reporting of news, but analysis and comment on the news, are issued weekly. A few publications are issued quarterly. The editorial approach of quarterly magazines is generally highly selective and of interest only to a well-defined social or demographic group. Quarterly magazines may be of more importance to an advertiser than their usually low circulation figures indicate, however. If the demographic characteristics of an advertiser's target market match those of a specific quarterly magazine's audience, advertising in that magazine will be exceptionally cost effective.

## Advantages of magazines

*Most magazines offer high-fidelity color reproduction*—an important factor when a product's color provides much of its appeal.

*Magazines offer an exceptional range of selectivity.* We have earlier lamented the fact that much of our advertising is wasted. If we advertise a detergent for dishwashing machines on an evening television program, for example, we will find the majority of the program's audience do not own a dishwasher. In contrast, magazines, through their editorial content and format, aim at certain people. The media analyst's task is to find the magazines whose audiences correspond closest to the target market for the advertiser's product. Women's magazines for women; men's magazines for men. But, merely specifying women's magazines is not enough. We can select a women's magazine where the editorial emphasis is on fashion. Or we can select a women's magazine where the editorial emphasis is on home, beauty, and furnishings. Still others deal with homemaking, cleaning, cooking, and family health care.

*Magazines have a long life.* The television commercial is over in sixty seconds or less—if you missed it, you missed it. The newspaper might linger in the home an extra day or two after it is pub-

# You just <u>know</u> it's McCall's.

Beauty, fashion, exercise—time-saving regimens that reflect the way the New Suburban Woman wants to look and feel. With graphics as clean, bold and bright as her own clear-eyed view of the beauty world. An editorial package tailored to the reader gives McCall's the edge.

## McCall's. You just know it's for you.

*Bon Appetit* is a magazine aimed at a well-educated, affluent group of readers who are linked by a shared interest in fine food. The audience is a natural market for wines, liqueurs, travel, luxury automobiles, fine china, silverware, and decorative accessories for the home. Filled with recipes, the magazine is probably saved by many readers and referred to again and again, thereby providing further opportunities to deliver the advertiser's message.

In this advertisement, advertisers are offered a medium to reach a specific demographic segment—men and women 50 years of age and older. What do these older people buy that younger people do not? Well, their families are grown so they are freer to travel. They are probably at their peak earning power so they are more interested in financial services. They are also more concerned with health care. Thus, advertisers for any of these services will reach a receptive market through this medium and find their messages enhanced by the magazine's appropriate editorial climate.

lished. A monthly magazine has at least a month of *life*, that is, it offers a month-long opportunity for the readers to receive the message. As a matter of fact, monthly magazines have a life span of more than a month. The October issue, for example, is usually in the mail or on the newsstand toward the end of September. Readers may even pick up a weekly newsmagazine weeks after it is published and read or glance through it again. This long life is an important advantage because it gives the reader time to read slowly, to return to the advertisement a second time, and to reflect on the product—a valuable factor if we are selling a complex or expensive product.

*Magazines enable the advertiser to use some artistic variety.* Although space is sold in standard units, design possibilities include bleeds, spreads, gatefolds, inserts, multiple pages, return cards, and pop-ups.

Many magazines offer demographic editions that enable the advertiser to buy circulation only in certain sections of the country or only for certain sections of the audience based on socioeconomic or occupational attributes. *Time* magazine offers a *Time B* demographic edition that circulates in the United States solely to business readers who are qualified by job title and industry. *Sports Illustrated* offers *SI Select*, a demographic edition of upscale readers as based on the ZIP codes of the most affluent communities in the United States. There are also about thirty magazines that circulate only in a particular metropolitan area—from *Boston Magazine* to *Gold Coast of Florida*, from *Houston* to *Honolulu*, and many cities in between.

*Magazines have a considerable amount of secondary readership.* The original subscribers or purchasers may pass the magazine to other members of their family or to friends. In professional offices,

# THIS THANKSGIVING, WE CREATED THE RECIPE FOR A MILLION.

**Our Editorial Staff:** Paige Rense, Pat Brown, Alan Deakins, Arline Inge, Philip Kaplan, Judi Kaufman, Linda Lang, Joanne O'Donnell, Bernard Rotondo, Natalie Schram and Jan Thiesen.

*Bon Appétit* will soon be serving 1,000,000 in circulation. Double our March '77 rate base.

But we're not surprised. We started with a great concept for a food magazine. Added a generous helping of dedication. More than enough know-how. Plus a lot of just plain hard work.

So naturally we're really dishing it out.

Why not follow our recipe for success and take advantage of our special offer.

Contact our Advertising Staff to buy a space contract before September '78 for your November and December advertising and they'll give you the 800,000 circulation rate. Making a delicious bonus circulation of 200,000. We think that's a nice way to celebrate

our first million.

Maybe it's time you started cooking with us. After all, 1,000,000 Americans can't be wrong.

## Bon Appétit
### Just the right mix made us a million.

**Advertising Offices:** Los Angeles, Calif. (213) 937-1025  New York, N.Y. (212) 765-3610  San Francisco, Calif. (415) 781-6449  Chicago, Illinois (312) 861-1786
Representatives: Rowayton, Conn. (203) 838-3501  Southfield, Mich. (313) 352-8333 · Marietta, Ga. (404) 973-1977

barbershops, and beauty parlors, the volume of secondary readership is tremendous.

*Magazines, because they are selective in their editorial contents, tend to build a loyal body of readers who value the magazines as sources of information.* A good deal of this prestige spills over to the advertising, and readers tend to believe that any advertiser in their favorite magazine is a reliable company with a quality product. An added value accrues to the advertiser from the stimulation of interest that the editorial contents arouse. An article on redecorating a nursery or playroom may prompt a reader to consider the ideas presented in the article for his or her own home and to read with more interest advertisements for decorating materials.

*Magazines offer a convenient means to obtain national coverage.* One insertion order to magazine X buys millions of readers all over the country. With a careful mix of magazines, advertisers can reach unduplicated segments of the market with a minimum amount of paperwork and mechanical preparation.

The only real general limitation that applies to magazines as a vehicle is their long deadlines. Advertisers are required to provide printed copy and art for their ads two months or more in advance of publication. This limits the advertisers' flexibility; they cannot make quick shifts in appeal that may be needed to meet changes in competition, market conditions, or legal restrictions. Nor can advertisers capitalize as quickly as they might like on some unique discovery or product innovation. Some advertisers consider magazines' lack of localized appeal to be a limitation, but such a limitation is highly subjective and of importance only to certain types of advertising campaigns.

## Magazine circulations

All major publications provide advertisers with audited circulation figures. Any one issue may, however, experience a substantial increase or decrease in its circulation: An issue with an unusual editorial feature may spark sales one month, while a particularly dull issue may result in poorer than average sales. Therefore, publishers always describe their rate base. The *rate base* represents the circulation that is *guaranteed* by the publisher and on which the publisher's advertising rates are determined. If the circulation exceeds the rate base, the magazine's advertisers receive the additional circulation as a bonus. If the circulation falls below the rate base, the advertisers will receive a rebate. Most publications set a conservative rate base, however, so that a bonus is more likely than a rebate. But the circulation of a publication that depends heavily on subscription varies little from month to month.

## Magazine space and rates

Consumer magazines offer advertising space in standard size units. This means that advertisers will not have as wide a choice of advertisement size in a consumer magazine as in a newspaper. The units of space depend on the format of the magazine. A standard magazine uses an advertising page that measures 7 × 10 inches. That is not the size of the entire page, but the amount of space that is available for advertisements. Most magazines have a 3-column format that permits an advertiser to buy fractional space in the form of either a half-page, a two-thirds page, a one-third page, or a one-sixth page vertically, half the page horizontally, or what

House Beautiful subscribers spend $380,000,000 each month merely to make their houses beautiful.

# THINK HOW MUCH THEY SPEND A MONTH TO EAT.

## HOUSE BEAUTIFUL.
## IMMENSE BUYING POWER
## LOOKING FOR THINGS TO BUY.

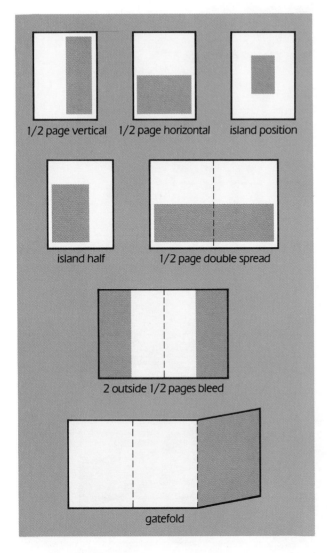

1/2 page vertical     1/2 page horizontal     island position

island half     1/2 page double spread

2 outside 1/2 pages bleed

gatefold

is called an *island half*— a space 2 columns wide by 7 1/2 inches deep. A one-third page may be ordered as a single column or as a *square third*— 2 columns wide by 4 7/8 inches deep. In some instances, the island half carries a slightly higher rate because it is usually surrounded by editorial material and therefore offers improved visibility. Other publications range from a tabloid size, such as *Rolling Stone*, to a digest size, such as *Reader's Digest*. Magazines that maintain a two-column format offer a vertical or horizontal half-page, quarter page, or eighth of a page. Tabloid-size magazines offer space in a wider variety of shapes that are based on the number of columns in their format.

A *bleed page* advertisement is one in which the copy runs off the edges of the paper. In addition to providing more message space (it utilizes the white border that normally frames a full-page advertisement), a bleed ad offers greater impact. For a bleed page, most publications add an extra charge, usually 15 percent, to the space cost. Bleed may be permitted in some magazines in less than full-page space; it is used quite often in two-thirds page and half-page spaces.

A *spread* is an ad run on two facing pages, and the rate for a spread is simply that for two pages. In most cases a spread entitles the advertiser to a *gutter bleed* at no charge. The gutter is the border of white paper that appears in the center of the magazine between the two facing pages. The gutter bleed adds to the uniformity and impact of a spread. If any of the copy runs off the paper in any *other* direction, however, the magazine will add a bleed charge. Magazines that are bound together with staples offer advertisers a particularly desirable position known as a center spread. The *center spread* refers to the two pages that appear in the exact middle of the magazine. With a binding of this type, the magazine tends to spring open at the center, luring readers into that particular ad and thereby adding to its readership. Magazines charge a sizeable premium for a center spread.

Charges for other special positions are generally stated on the magazine's rate card. The inside front cover (also called the second cover), the inside back cover (the third cover), and the outside back cover (fourth cover) all carry sizeable premiums, with the fourth cover being the most expensive. Other special positions—page 1, opposite the table of contents, or next to a particular edito-

**Houston**
MAGAZINE

**Rate Card #24**
Effective January 1st, 1979

*Houston Magazine* is one of a growing number of city magazines. Most of these magazines are circulated in larger, affluent cities. The circulation of *Houston* is small — about 16,700 — 90 percent male, and very affluent, with a median income of more than $54,700 a year. Who can advertise to these readers in this magazine rather than in a national magazine to reach a similar demographic segment? Local banks, local insurance companies, local residence and office facilities, local contracting organizations. Expensive rates for the quantity of circulation, but what an upscale market!

## Mechanical Requirements

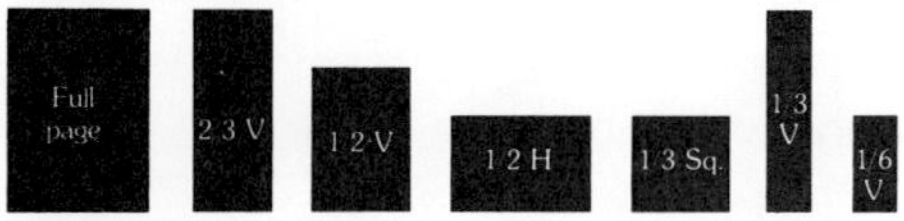

Full page / 2 3 V / 1 2 V / 1 2 H / 1 3 Sq. / 1/3 V / 1 6 V

Spread, bleed .................................. 17¼ x 11½
Spread, non-bleed ............................... 15 x 9⅞
Full page, bleed ................................. 8⅜ x 11½
Full page, non-bleed ............................ 6¾ x 9⅞
2/3 page, V ..................................... 4⅜ x 9⅞
1/2 page, V ..................................... 4⅜ x 7¼
1/2 page, H ..................................... 6¾ x 4¾
1/3 page, V ................................. 2 1/16 x 9⅞
1/3 page, SQ ................................... 4⅜ x 4¾
1/6 page, V ................................. 2 1/6 x 4¾
Trim size: 8-1/4″ x 11-1/4″; vital advertising matter should be kept 3/8″ from trim. Inserts: 8-3/8″ x 11-5/8″ to allow for trim to 8-1/4″ to 11-1/4″.

## Printing Specifications

Printed offset, sheet fed. Paper stock: 60# Lithofect Suede; Cover: 100# black and white gloss. Pressed-glue, slotted binding.
Prefer 133 line screen; maximum—150, minimum—110.
Prefer one piece offset negative, right reading, emulsion side down. Acceptable copy, velox, Scotchprints, camera-ready artwork, repro proof. Proof shown only on request.
Progressive proofs required for 4-color ads.

## Shipping Instructions

All space reservations, insertion orders, negatives, acceptable copy, payments and other correspondence should be addressed to:
Advertising Department
HOUSTON Magazine
25th Floor, 1100 Milam Building
Houston, Texas 77002

## Houston readers are the juiciest slice of the Texas market.

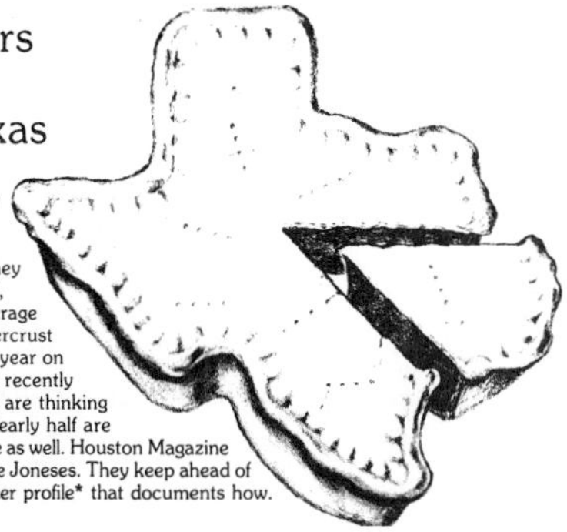

Houston Magazine readers earn a median annual income of $54,700, more than that of any other major Texas magazine. They live in homes valued at $105,000, nearly twice the value of the average new home in Houston. Our uppercrust readers spend over $1,000 each year on gifts for their spouses. 31% have recently vacationed in Europe. Over 60% are thinking of buying a new car this year. Nearly half are considering a new home purchase as well. Houston Magazine readers don't just keep up with the Joneses. They keep ahead of them. Ask for our new 1979 reader profile* that documents how.

*Source: Marplan Research Inc., January, 1979.

## General Rate Policy

Advertising must be inserted within 12 months to earn frequency discounts. Should new rates be announced, current contract advertisers will be protected for four months.
The contract rate will be adjusted to the earned rate in case of contract cancellation or additional space purchased.
Space order may not be cancelled after closing deadline. All advertising orders and copy subject to approval of publisher.

## Payments & Commissions

Payment due 10 days following invoice. No cash discount.
A 15% commission to all recognized advertising agencies on space, color, bleed and position charges only.

## Issue & Closing Dates

Published monthly: Issued first of publication month
Advertising space reservation deadline: 1st of month prior to month of cover date
Advertising copy deadline: 5th of month prior to month of cover date for all negatives and final copy.

## Advertising Rates

| | Page size | 1 time | 3 time | 6 time | 12 time |
|---|---|---|---|---|---|
| Black & White | Full page | 890 | 845 | 770 | 660 |
| | 2/3 vertical | 630 | 600 | 545 | 460 |
| | 1/2 vertical | 575 | 545 | 495 | 420 |
| | 1/2 horizontal | 485 | 445 | 410 | 360 |
| | 1/3 vert. or square | 335 | 315 | 285 | 250 |
| | 1/6 vertical | 215 | 200 | 185 | 165 |
| | 24 time rate (full page only) 545 | | | | |
| Covers | Cover II | 1200 | 1165 | 1125 | 1040 |
| | Cover III | 1075 | 1045 | 1030 | 930 |
| | Cover IV | 1495 | 1450 | 1390 | 1230 |
| Position | Special positions, add 15% to gross space cost. | | | | |
| Color | Any one AAAA color or matched color: $250 plus black and white space charge. Four-color process: $600 plus black and white space charge. | | | | |
| Bleed | Add $40 to black and white space charge. Available for full and 1/2 page horizontal ads only. | | | | |
| Inserts | Pre-printed inserts furnished to printer. Back-up printing, inserting and handling charges, if any, on request. | 1 page $1045 6 pages $2,510 | 2 pages $1,450 8 pages $3,350 | 4 pages $1,840 | |
| Production Charges | Art, photostats, special typesetting, sizing, conversions and layout service supplied by publisher may be charged additionally to the advertiser or agency. | | | | |

This ad for *Sports Illustrated* appeared in *Advertising Age* and informs advertisers and their agencies that *Sports Illustrated* reaches more upscale males 18–49 at a lower CPM than any other major weekly magazine. *Sports Illustrated* also offers geographic editions based on 104 district marketing areas—an important factor for a regional advertiser who wants the prestige of advertising in a national magazine but whose distribution is confined to only a portion of the country. Advertisers can also have their ads appear in an edition that is circulated only to homeowners. Why talk about a new heating system to an apartment dweller? And, if the advertiser wants to reach the cream of *SI* circulation, the magazine offers an edition that is delivered only to the ZIP codes that represent the most affluent communities in the United States.

rial feature of the magazine—also carry premium charges.

A magazine's *card rate* is always quoted for a black and white ad only. If advertisers want to use color, they must pay a standard charge usually described in the publication's rate card as *AAAA color.* The AAAA designation is applied to a group of standardized colors established some years ago by the American Association of Advertising Agencies. Standard AAAA colors are generally red, blue, yellow, green, and orange. Any color other than those standard colors will represent a *matched color*—that is, a color matched to the advertiser's specifications. A matched color is usually charged at a higher rate. If we want our ad to be printed in blue, whether AAAA or matched blue, we will pay for space cost plus one additional color—blue. A four-color ad carries a rate of its own; it is not calculated simply by adding the cost of three colors to the space cost, but is considerably more expensive. Black ink is all advertisers are entitled to for the space charge.

Just as newspapers charge advertisers an open rate for a single insertion and contract rates for two or more insertions, magazines offer one-time rates and volume rates. Advertisers planning to run a series of ads in one magazine can obtain reduced rates for *frequency contracts*—for three, six, twelve, or more, insertions, depending on the magazine's frequency of issue. A space contract covers a twelve-month period, just as a newspaper contract does, with similar provisions for short rate. On application to the publisher, advertisers can make use of such innovative space options as fold-out pages, inserts, reply cards, and tipped-in coupons. An *insert* represents advertising material that has been printed by the advertiser and delivered to the publisher for binding (insertion) into the magazine.

When the material is to be glued to a page, it is said to be *tipped* in—that is, a thin line of adhesive is run along the edge of the advertising matter.

Advertisers (or their agencies) are required to provide a publisher with copies of their ads ready for printing in accordance with the specifications of the magazine.

## Demographic editions

As mentioned earlier, many major publications today offer demographic editions that enable advertisers to select the geographical market that they wish to reach. Demographic availability makes it possible for regional marketers, and for national marketers expanding their distribution in stages, to use important consumer magazines. Some consumer magazines can also provide split-run facilities. *Time* magazine offers demographic editions based on income, class, and occupation. *Sports Illustrated* offers a "market track system" that permits the advertiser to choose any one, or any combination, of fifty metro markets. *Sports Illustrated* also has a homeowners' edition that reaches 640,000 households.

## Comparing magazines

Magazines are difficult to compare in some ways and simple in others. In comparing two publications reaching the same market segment—for example, the homemaker—an advertiser might want to compare *Family Circle* with *Woman's Day.* The first basis for comparison would be CPM—cost per thousand. For such comparisons, we use the two magazines' primary circulation figures. Secondary readers must be considered a bonus. But CPM is not enough. For instance, in making a comparison

# HOW SPORTS ILLUSTRATED HELPS YOU COMPETE.

In today's highly competitive marketplace, Sports Illustrated offers you dozens of ways to reach your best customers, and special extras to drive your advertising home. Here are a few of the options:

**SI's National Edition reaches upscale males with the lowest CPM of any major newsweekly.**

The national edition of Sports Illustrated is the most powerful, efficient newsweekly you can buy to reach upscale American males 18-49. Not only does Sports Illustrated offer the lowest CPM* among major newsweeklies for reaching this audience, it also offers a wide choice of the *best* ways to reach it.

**You can hit your marketing target with precision.**

Every week SI offers marketers and media planners literally hundreds of editions of Sports Illustrated that pinpoint almost every target group or market an advertiser could be competing for. *Market Track System*, or *MTS* for short, divides the country into 104 distinct marketing areas and lets you choose from 4 regions, 50 states, and 50 metro markets. You can run your campaign in any one of them or all of them or in any combination.

You can buy a special *homeowners'* edition that puts your ad in 640,000 subscriber households. Or you can buy exactly *half* the SI circulation on a random 50/50 split. We even have *split runs* for ads as small as one column.

**Sports Illustrated Select takes you to the nicest neighborhoods.**

SI Select means just that. This select edition puts your ad campaign in the homes of 700,000 of our most upscale readers according to ZIP Codes. These 2,200 ZIP Codes (out of a total of 36,000) are culled from America's most affluent communities.

**Our direct response cards bring results directly to you.**

Another feature of SI is our "For More Information" card—FMI—that we insert in the back of the magazine. These cards direct the reader to write to you for more information, and channel all reader inquiries right to you.

**Merchandising: We take your campaign right to your sales people, distributors, and best prospects.**

Sports Illustrated has the largest, most unique merchandising department in the business. We can support your advertising campaign with everything from guest sports celebrities for your sales meetings to retail displays, direct mailings and sales incentives. We'll even put together complete golf tournaments for your sales staff and their customers.

By providing our advertisers with the right audience, the right environment, and the right efficiency, Sports Illustrated became America's fourth largest magazine in advertising revenues.

And by providing all kinds of different ways to use our magazine in media planning, we now plan to become America's most flexible media tool. For more information on any of the options listed below, call a Sports Illustrated representative.

• National Edition • SI Select Edition • Homeowners' Edition
• Market Track System • 50% SI Edition • Split Runs
• Merchandising • Direct Response Cards (FMI) • Special Event Inserts • Regional Editions

# AN OPTION FOR EVERY GAME PLAN.

# LEO BURNETT

In 1935, Leo Burnett and eight associates founded Leo Burnett Company. In its first year, this new advertising agency had billings of $600,000; in 1978, the agency's billings were $865.1 million, making it the eighth largest advertising agency in the world.

After graduation from the University of Michigan in 1914, Leo Burnett worked for a short period as a newspaper reporter before starting his advertising career as editor of the Cadillac Motor Company's house magazine. Later, he moved to the Homer McKee advertising agency in Indianapolis, where he spent the next ten years fulfilling both creative and executive duties. After moving to Chicago to take a job as vice-president and creative head of Erwin Wasey & Company, he decided to found his own agency in that city "because there was nobody else here in Chicago."

The Leo Burnett agency is probably best known for its famous Marlboro cigarette ads, for which it developed the symbol of the tattooed cowboy. Today, the company still serves the Green Giant Company of LeSueur, Minnesota, for whom it created the Jolly Green Giant. Some other well-known accounts on which Leo Burnett worked included Schlitz beer, Maytag washers, Pillsbury cake mixes, Kellogg's cereals, and Campbell's soups.

When he retired in 1967, Leo Burnett left behind not only a worldwide agency that employs more than three thousand people but a major imprint on the creative thinking that helps shape the advertising business. He played a dominant role in the development of a creative approach that some advertising people have called "the Chicago school of advertising." It was Leo Burnett's idea to look for the inherent drama in a product and to write the advertising copy based on that drama. *Inherent drama,* he said, is "what the manufacturer had in mind . . . when he conceived the product." This drama, he believed, can be found in all good advertising. As he explained:

> . . . it gives the effect of news, even in an old product, and has about it a feeling of naturalness which gives the reader an emotional reward and makes him feel good about it.

Among the many honors that came to Leo Burnett were election to the Copywriters Hall of Fame, the special merit award of the New York Art Directors Club, and election as Marketing Man of the Year in 1966 by the American Marketing Association.

between *TV Guide* and *Business Week* magazines, we could make the following notes:

| TV GUIDE | | BUSINESS WEEK | |
|---|---|---|---|
| circulation: | 20,443,000 | circulation: | 761,000 |
| cost for 1 | | cost for 1 | |
| b & w page: | $51,300 | b & w page: | $14,200 |

Comparison of cost per page would be meaningless, but when we reduce these figures to CPM, we see that:

CPM: $1.19                              CPM: $5.27

But even these CPM figures are misleading, because we haven't taken the demographic characteristics of each medium's audience into account.

*TV Guide*, for example, reaches a 45 percent male audience, while *Business Week*'s audience is 76 percent male. Also, on the basis of a household income index of $25,000 or more, *TV Guide*'s audience achieves a 73 rating and *Business Week*'s a 233 rating. This tells us that an advertisement in *Business Week* will reach a much more affluent market segment. If our product were a very expensive luxury item, we would buy *Business Week,* even though its CPM is much higher than *TV Guide's.*

Other factors we must consider include our competition's magazine schedules and the editorial contents of each magazine. What kind of editorial climate does each magazine provide for our product? Also, how does each publication obtain its circulation—through subscription or through newsstand sales? Is the yearly subscriber a more valuable reader than the newsstand or supermarket purchaser? The magazine's publisher may claim that the reader who buys the magazine on the newsstand does so because he or she *wanted* to read it. This expression of interest is expected to spill over to the magazine's advertising. Mail subscribers who paid for several months' or years' issues in advance were obviously interested at the time they subscribed. But is the interest still there? If it is, we have reached an interested and steady audience.

The ability to reach specific geographic areas is an important consideration in an advertiser's choice of consumer magazines. Some magazines have greater circulation in cities. Some are stronger in certain regions of the country. All the data that advertisers and their agencies can obtain must be evaluated in making specific media decisions.

## Summary

The print media category is composed of newspapers and magazines. In terms of delivery of an advertising message, the benefits that each vehicle in this category provides are dependent upon the advertiser's product, the nature of the advertiser's target market, and the distribution of the advertiser's product. Newspapers offer advertisers immediacy—instant access to local markets in an editorial environment that is local and current. Although the quality of reproduction in newspapers is not as good as may be desired, the short closing date enables advertisers to tie in with fast-breaking news or to take advantage of weather or seasons that may have an important bearing on the sale of a particular product. Air conditioners, for example, should be advertised with the advent of summer heat.

Newspapers provide a high degree of geographical selectivity; advertisers can choose to reach only selected cities or metros. In this way, advertisers can use newspapers to keep pace with expanding distribution and to provide strong dealer support at the local level. Advertisers can also obtain some measure of demographic selectivity through the use of preferred positions within a newspaper. Generally speaking, newspaper reading peaks in middle-age groups, when people's interest in news and civic affairs runs highest. Readership is also greatest among upper socioeconomic groups in large metropolitan and suburban areas.

The cost of running an ad in a newspaper depends on its frequency of insertion, size, and position. ROP color adds to the cost, but studies have found that color advertising pays for itself by attracting additional readership. Comparisons in costs between newspapers with different circulation bases is made with the use of an index known as the milline rate. Advertisers of automobiles and foods are the heaviest users of national newspaper advertising, but the bulk of the advertising in newspapers is sponsored by local retail firms. Over the years, though total national advertising expenditures have increased, the percentage devoted to newspapers has declined.

The greatest advantage of magazines is heightened demographic selectivity. Depending on the editorial scope of the magazine, advertisers can reach both men and women, women only, men only, young women, married women, older people, health food addicts, gourmets, travel enthusiasts, sports fans, yachting enthusiasts, and so on. Each magazine delivers a market segment interested in that magazine's editorial content, and that interest spills over to the advertising. Advertisers can deliver their messages with beautiful color in a vehicle that the reader can examine slowly, digest, and reflect on. Furthermore, the issue can be referred to again and again and is often passed along to other members of the family or friends. Sometimes the secondary readership of a magazine will be two to three times the circulation that the publisher promises an advertiser as a rate base or guarantee.

The only disadvantage of magazines is their long deadline for the submission of advertising copy: usually about eight weeks prior to publication. The long closing hinders flexibility and demands long-range planning, which is difficult to revise quickly enough to meet changing market conditions.

Comparisons between magazines reaching the same market segment are difficult to make. CPM (cost per thousand) is a good starting point, but media planners are also concerned with a magazine's editorial climate, frequency of issue, and the buying habits and life-styles of its audience.

## QUESTIONS FOR DISCUSSION

**1.** Why is primary audience more important than secondary audience?

**2.** What kinds of magazines would you specify for reach? What kinds for frequency?

**3.** What are some of the ways you could utilize demographic editions of consumer magazines?

**4.** Can you suggest any types of products for which newspapers would be the best medium? For which magazines would be best?

**5.** How does the editorial climate of a magazine affect the advertising message?

**6.** If circulations were about equal, what factors would you consider in choosing between a morning paper and an evening paper?

**7.** Would the size of the publication format have a bearing on your choice of medium? For example, on what grounds would you base a choice between a tabloid newspaper and a standard newspaper, or between a digest magazine and a standard-size magazine?

## Sources and suggestions for further reading

Barban, Arnold M.; Cristol, Stephen M.; and Kopec, Frank G. *Essentials of Media Planning.* Chicago: Crain Books, 1976.

Frey, Albert Wesley, and Halterman, Jean C. *Advertising.* 4th ed. New York: The Ronald Press Co. 1970.

Littlefield, James. *Readings in Advertising.* St. Paul: West Publishing Co., 1975. Part III.

Sissors, Jack Z., and Petray, E. Reynold. *Advertising Media Planning.* Chicago: Crain Books, 1976.

Ulanoff, Stanley M. *Advertising in America.* New York: Hastings House, 1977.

Wolfe, Harry Deane; Brown, James K.; Thompson, G. Clark; and Greenberg, Stephen H. *Evaluating Media.* Business Policy Study no. 121, New York: National Industrial Conference Board, 1966.

## PRINT MEDIA: BUSINESS AND FARM PUBLICATIONS

**Selling the decision makers**

Buying power
The audience for business
    publications
General business publications
Industrial publications
Trade publications
Institutional publications
Professional publications
Rates and spaces

Media decisions for business
advertisers

**Farm publications**

National farm publications
    Progressive Farmer
    Farm Journal
    Successful Farming
State and regional publications
Specialized farm publications

## WORKING VOCABULARY

| | | |
|---|---|---|
| buying power | horizontal publications | reader service card |
| paid circulation | vertical publications | crop editions |
| controlled circulation | inserts | |

CHAPTER

# print media: business and farm publications

*There is no question about business publications being read —by the people the supplier's salesmen call upon (and sometimes don't get to see) and uncounted others the salesmen don't know about, but who have a say in the selection of vendors.*

HOWARD G. "SCOTTY" SAWYER
*Business-to-Business Advertising*

STANDARD RATE & DATA SERVICE INC. lists about 3,300 publications under more than 175 different market categories in its *SRDS Business Publication Rates and Data* book. The number of business publications changes from year to year as some publications disappear and new ones spring up. Some business publications disappear because the industry or market they serve has dwindled or disappeared. New publications are introduced as new industries are created or mature industries expand. Although the percentage of the total advertising volume in the United States that is invested in business publications is far less than that devoted to television or consumer magazines, the total outlay for business advertising was well over $1 billion in 1977. Business advertising is a rapidly growing segment of the advertising industry.

## Selling the decision makers

Business publications are distinguished from consumer publications by their editorial focus, and by

191

the fact that the information in the advertisements they carry is often as important to the readers as the magazine's editorial contents. In fact, it is quite common for companies to expect their managers and technicians to read pertinent business publications on company time. Very often the company itself pays for subscriptions to certain business publications. It then circulates each issue among its employees with an attached routing slip that indicates to whom readers should pass the magazine once they have read it. Reading business publications is one way the company's decision makers keep abreast of developments in their industry.

Business publications may be divided into five categories:

1. general business publications

2. industrial publications

3. trade publications

4. professional publications

5. institutional publications

The distinctions between these types of business publications are not always clear; a magazine will often exhibit characteristics of two or three categories. But the above list will serve as a rough map to help guide us over the topography of the world of the business press.

## Buying power

Unlike advertisers in national consumer magazines, who analyze their audience in terms of demographic characteristics such as age, sex, marital status, and level of education, advertisers in business publications are interested in the buying power of their audience. *Buying power* is the amount of money, or budget, that potential customers for our product have to spend on goods and services. In his book *Marketing Strategies*, P. Dudley Kaley points out the differences in buying power of the consumer and the industrial customer.

> In developing segmentation strategies, it is worthwhile to consider some differences between market segments for consumer products and for industrial products. In the consumer market, no one customer for toothpaste has enough buying potential to warrant consideration as a market. If there were not tens of thousands of these individuals with similar desires in the marketplace, no company would find it profitable to market such a product. At the other extreme, however, one industrial customer might have enough purchasing potential to comprise a market segment unto itself. Take, for example, fiber glass insulation. United States Steel Corporation's 64-story office building in Pittsburgh required carloads of insulation. So did the new World Trade Center in downtown New York. In such cases, each building can represent a market segment, but with a very definite time relationship—a segment opportunity that exists only once.[1]

## The audience for business publications

Business publications also differ from consumer publications in the way they build their audiences. Few specialized business publications are sold on newsstands. If we place an advertisement in one of these magazines for machinery costing hundreds of thousands of dollars, then obviously we are not interested in reaching the random or occasional

[1] P. Dudley Kaley, *Marketing Strategies* (New York: The Conference Board, 1974), pp. 56–57.

This ad contains an unusual combination of factors. It appeared on the back cover of *Fast Service*—a business magazine serving, as you might imagine from the name, the fast-food restaurant industry. Potatoes, being a commodity, are not branded, but distinctions do exist between potatoes from different areas of the country. The objective of this ad, sponsored by the state of Washington, is to stimulate primary demand. The advertiser is not concerned with how restaurants use the potatoes as long as they insist upon Washington potatoes.

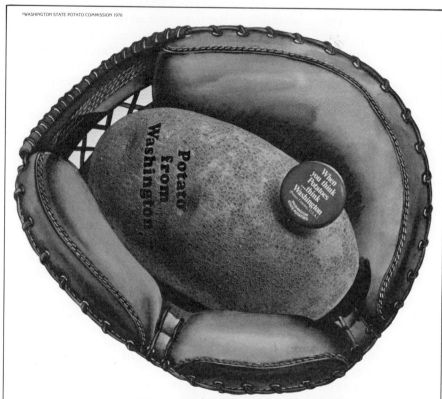

# HOT POTATO!

When you're hot, you're hot, and the potato that's really on the move these days is the Russet Burbank from Washington. With a longer growing season, ideal climate and controlled irrigation, Washington has doubled the yield for Russet Burbanks. If you're looking for a consistent supply of the highest quality, look to Potato Country, U.S.A.™ for the Washington Russet Burbank. It's the hot one.

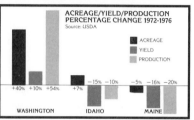

**ACREAGE/YIELD/PRODUCTION PERCENTAGE CHANGE 1972-1976**
Source: USDA

ACREAGE
YIELD
PRODUCTION

| WASHINGTON | IDAHO | MAINE |
|---|---|---|
| +40% +10% +54% | +7% −15% −10% | −5% −16% −20% |

**Washington State Potatoes from Potato Country, U.S.A.™**
For information write: Potato Country, U.S.A.,™ 108 Interlake, Moses Lake, WA 98837

reader. The stakes are high. We want to reach the people who buy, specify, and make decisions for their companies that involve very substantial amounts of money. We are interested in learning what companies each business publication's readers work for and what their job titles are within those companies. In the *SRDS Business Publication Rates and Data* book and in their own circulation documentation, business publications list the kinds and sizes of the companies they reach—by Standard Industrial Classification (SIC) number and by size of plant in number of employees. As you can see, comparing business publications is as complicated as comparing consumer magazines. We want to know how many plants the publication reaches and how many people work in each plant because we know that pass-along readership of business publications is very high.

Although many business publications build their circulations by selling subscriptions, the readers of many important business publications receive copies of the magazine free. The number of readers who buy subscriptions is known as *paid circulation;* the number of readers who receive free copies is known as *controlled circulation.* Some magazines have circulations that are part paid and part controlled. Others, usually magazines published by a trade or professional association, have circulations that are entirely controlled. (Each member of the society or association is given a subscription to the magazine as part of his or her membership rights.) For publications with circulations based primarily on paid subscriptions, the Audit Bureau of Circulations (ABC) provides verification of audience. In order to build its audience, a controlled-circulation publication sends subscription request forms to members of the industry it serves. Recipients of this form can obtain a free subscription to the magazine merely by filling out the form and sending it in. Publishers obtain the names of prospective subscribers from trade associations, from professional organizations, and from industry directories. Controlled circulation publications are audited by Business Publications Audit (BPA) or Verified Audit Circulation (VAC). All major business publications are audited. The auditing organization verifies the magazine's circulation through post office mailing receipts and also verifies that the recipients, either as companies or as individuals, are *qualified* to receive that publication on the basis of product, line of business, SIC category, plant size, job title, job function, or any other combination of attributes that the publisher sets. For example, *Industrial Maintenance and Plant Operation,* a BPA-audited magazine, states that "recipients must be employed in plants with 50 or more employees, or with a minimum Dun & Bradstreet rating of $50,000."

## General business publications

General business publications have no specific editorial focus; like mass-circulation consumer magazines, they try to have something for everyone. The total thrust is usually all business. A quick glance at the table of contents of such general business publications as *Business Week, Dun's Review,* or *Fortune* will reveal an editorial mix of current business news plus features that include in-depth reports on companies, individuals, and industries. Some general business publications that are published by well-known business schools tend more toward analysis of trends and ideas in their editorial mix.

The *Wall Street Journal* is essentially a *business newspaper,* that is, it contains only news of the world of business. Published every weekday, the

*Barron's* is a business publication whose editorial scope is the business of finance and investments. It is issued every Monday to a circulation base of 231,000, but the publication claims a *readership* of 1.2 million, owing to a very sizeable pass-along readership. Their reader profile claims an average income of $45,565, with an average net worth of $250,000. These readers are corporate executives and individual investors.

*Wall Street Journal* has become "must" reading for 1,493,387 people. It is available nationally and in five demographic editions—an Eastern, a Midwestern, a Western, a Southwestern, and (published in Hong Kong) an Asian. The publication claims that one out of every twenty subscribers is a millionaire!

Advertisers in these general publications may have several objectives. They may want to reach hidden influences their salesmen cannot see—top executives of companies who can affect the sale of their product. The Paper Mill Study[2] revealed, for example, that for suppliers of chemical products, only seventeen of the forty identified buying influences were on their customer lists. Suppliers of process machinery learned that of the forty-five identified buying influences, only three were on their lists.

Advertisers frequently want to influence the financial community—either to enhance the value of their company's stock or to build their company's image in preparation for the time when it may want to go to the market for funds. Another important objective is the stimulation of executive thinking in new directions—perhaps to suggest the purchase of a company airplane, a site for the location of a new plant, the installation of a data processing system, or the purchase of a fleet of company cars. Business publications offer advertisers the opportunity to reach business executives in a business environment with a minimum of waste. Advertisers of consumer products have also turned to the use of general business publications to reach upscale men and women who buy automobiles, whiskey, cigarettes, and other personal products.

[2] "The Paper Mill Study," Commissioned by Miller Freeman Publications (New York: American Business Press, 1975).

## Industrial publications

Industrial publications are read by people in manufacturing industries that change the shape or form of a product, convert raw materials into semifinished or finished goods, or assemble components or semifinished products into finished goods. In any particular plant, people in different job capacities will read those business publications that are related to their work.

For example, in a company that manufactures hi-fidelity amplifiers, the electronics engineers might read *Electronic Design, Electronics, Electronic Component News*, or any of the more than twenty publications covering some part of the industry. The person responsible for the maintenance and operation of the factory might read *Plant Engineering* or *Industrial Maintenance and Plant Operation*. The purchasing agent might read *New Equipment Digest, Industrial Bulletin, Purchasing Magazine, Purchasing World*, or any of the many publications serving his or her interests. The top brass might read *Electronic Business, Electronic News*, and other publications related to the hi-fidelity business in general, as well as general business publications. All of these people want to keep up with the industry, to learn quickly about new developments that may affect their work and their company's future.

The importance of industrial magazines and the advertisements they carry becomes obvious once we realize that in 1977 the cost for an industrial salesman to make one face-to-face sales call was estimated to be $96.79.[3] Often, however, an industrial purchase involves the participation of several operating people, many of whom our salespeople will not know or could not call on even if they did know them. Advertising in an industrial publication enables the advertiser to reach the engineer who specifies the product, the purchasing agent who buys it, and the manager who must pass on it. Industrial products are not bought on the basis of emotional appeal. The buyers are hard-nosed people with sharp pencils who want reliability first.

There are two types of industrial publications: horizontal publications and vertical publications. *Horizontal publications* reach several specific categories of job function across many different industries. *Industrial Maintenance and Plant Operation*, for example, reaches 105,000 people in 68,756 plants. The publisher's statement of editorial policy will give us a better understanding of their focus:

> Editorial purpose: provide recipients with news on new and improved products and methods used in maintaining and operating plant equipment, buildings, facilities, and grounds.

The editorial content of this type of magazine provides information of interest to many people in many plants that all have common problems. If we are advertising a product that is used in several different industries, we would want to use a horizontal publication to get maximum reach.

On the other hand, if the product advertised is designed for a very clearly delineated industry, we would want to use a vertical publication.

A publication is described as *vertical* when it reaches various segments in the *same* industry. If our product were printing presses or printing ink, for example, we might advertise in *Graphic Arts Monthly*, which reaches 76,419 people in the print-

---

[3] "The Cost of an Industrial Sales Call Climbs to $96.79," Laboratory of Advertising Performance, Bulletin no. 8013.4 (New York: McGraw-Hill, 1977).

# electronic products

September 1977      Volume 20 Number 4

**Outlook**    **15**

High density recorder head • Solor cells — the wet look • Mass market microcomputer • Floppy sales to soar • Backtalk

**Feature Articles**

The SMA Connection    **25**
Semi-precision rf coaxial connectors provide outstanding service at relatively low cost in high frequency communication systems. But watch out for cost/performance tradeoffs.

Micro Muddle    **35**
Fifteen of the most misunderstood microprocessor terms defined and explained so you can keep up with the experts.

Selecting a Power Transformer    **45**
When it comes to buying transformers, it's knowing what **not** to specify that counts.

Product Quiz on IC Logic Families    **111**
Are you rational? Take this self-test and find out.

**IC Update**    **55**

Special Report on EAROM's    **57**
Electrically alterable ROM's are coming of age. Here's how they operate, what's available and what's coming.

Product Perspectives    **64**
Should the larger RAM's be fully or partially static? Two industry experts present their cases.

**WESCON 77**    **87**

San Francisco is the site of the bigger than ever WESCON show this year. In case you can't make it, here's a sampling of the new products introduced there.

**New Products**

Highlights    **117**
Circuit Components    **127**
Packaging & Interconnections    **143**
Controls, Drives & Switches    **154**
Power Sources    **168**
Test & Measurement    **181**
Computers & Peripherals    **197**
Displays & Subassemblies    **208**

**Product Planning Directory**    **219**

**Advertisers' Index**    **247**

COVER: Cover design by Joan Shearer.

The table of contents for this publication, which serves the electronics industry, reveals the kind of editorial mix that readers demand: factual, technical, and informative. The one-third page ad that is positioned with the table of contents enjoys the added readership that usually goes with such a favored position. Note the message in the ad is couched in the same technical and informative language used in the table of contents. The advertisements in business publications are often just as important to the reader as the editorial contents.

This technical ad is aimed at several people involved in the manufacture of coatings—the plant manager concerned with efficiency and cost reduction, the research chemist concerned with product improvements, and the purchasing agent who is expected to be alert to cost-cutting opportunities. Frequently, the decision to change from one raw material to another involves reaching many people. The supplier's sales force can often see only the purchasing agent. It is the supplier's advertising that informs and persuades the other hidden influences to switch—to replace, in this ad, half of their titanium dioxide with Min-U-Sil.

# Replace half your TiO₂ with economical Min-U-Sil.®

Now, you have an economical alternative to costly TiO₂ powder coating fillers. It's PGS Min-U-Sil.

Min-U-Sil is a high-purity silica, available in four uniform micron sizes and meshes. You can use it to replace 50% of the titanium dioxide in powder coating formulations with no loss in hiding power. Even higher replacement rates are possible with adjusted formulations.

Since TiO₂ costs about 47¢ a pound and Min-U-Sil costs only 5¢ a pound, changing to Min-U-Sil can save you tons of money. Savings that become profits at the sales end.

Min-U-Sil also offers important benefits to your customers. Like greater film thickness per coat, resulting in higher productivity than TiO₂ in fluid bed applications. And it's totally compatible with every known powder coating formulation. Epoxy, acrylics, polyesters. You name it.

Replace half the TiO₂ in your powder coatings with eco-nomical Min-U-Sil. Your customers will like the change. And so will you.

For a free sample of Min-U-Sil and more information, contact Pennsylvania Glass Sand Corporation, Dept. A-3, Three Penn Center, Pittsburgh, PA 15235. Telephone: (412) 243-7500.

**PGS**
A Subsidiary of ITT

## Pound-wise, it's penny wise.

**1 lb. TiO₂**
(Approx.Cost)

**1 lb. Min-U-Sil**
(Approx.Cost)

ing industry. The printing industry is composed of many segments, each producing or marketing a different product, but *all related* to printing processes and the printing business. Thus *Graphic Arts Monthly* could be used to advertise inks, presses, bindery equipment, engraving and platemaking equipment, paper, photography, and typesetting and numbering devices. The advertiser interested in marketing any of the products mentioned would find *Graphic Arts Monthly* and other publications in that category very efficient.

Advertisers will pay for a certain amount of waste circulation in both horizontal and vertical publications, however, because not every product is suitable for every factory or every type of manufacturing operation. Horizontal publications may

## WILLIAM A. MARSTELLER

William Marsteller founded the agency that bears his name in 1951. In 1978, with billings of more than $306.2 million, Marsteller, Inc., was among the twenty-five largest advertising agencies in the world. Originally started as an industrial advertising agency, the agency today serves mostly consumer accounts, but it is still the largest industrial agency in the United States. The agency's public relations subsidiary, Burson–Marsteller, is one of the largest public relations firms in the country. The phenomenal growth of these companies is a tribute to the skill and drive of one man—William A. Marsteller.

William Marsteller was born in Champaign, Illinois, in 1914. While majoring in journalism at the University of Illinois, he worked as a reporter for the *Champaign News Gazette* and later, from 1937 to 1941, as an insurance agent for the Massachusetts Mutual Life Insurance Company. In 1941, he obtained a position in the advertising department of a manufacturing company, Edward's Valves, leaving this company in 1945 to join Rockwell Manufacturing Company as advertising manager, a newly created position. By 1949, he was vice-president for marketing at Rockwell, and two years later he followed up a suggestion that he start his own advertising/market research agency. The new agency had two accounts—Rockwell Manufacturing and Clark Equipment.

In the field of advertising, William Marsteller believes in "total communications with all publics." He is considered a pioneer in the development of the editorial evaluation concept of media selection. In 1979, William Marsteller was elected to the Advertising Hall of Fame, an honor reserved for men and women who have made significant contributions to the field.

From Standard Rate & Data Service's *Business Publications Rates and Data* book, this is a listing for *Graphic Arts Monthly*, a vertical publication. Note the business analysis of circulation, BPA audited and controlled, and of interest only to people in the printing industry—business management, production, and sales.

---

## 118—Printing & Printing Processes

# Graphic Arts Monthly

**A Technical Publishing Company Publication**

▽BPA ☆ABP

## mcc
### Media Data Form

Media Code 7 680 1600 8.00

Published monthly by Technical Publishing Co., a Dun & Bradstreet Company, 666 Fifth Ave., New York, N. Y. 10019. Phone 212-489-2200.

**PUBLISHER'S EDITORIAL STATEMENT**
GRAPHIC ARTS MONTHLY'S editorial purpose is to provide readers with information to help them lower costs, increase productivity, enhance quality and maximize safety. Articles on methods, materials, equipment and techniques are published and balanced with news and interpretative reports. Rec'd 12/18/78.

**1. PERSONNEL**
Publisher—Robert T. Brawn, 489-3450.
Associate Publisher—R. E. Lewis, 312-648-5914.
Editor—Bert Chapman, 489-2503.
Production Manager—Robert J. Gaydos, 489-2500.

**2. REPRESENTATIVES and/or BRANCH OFFICES**
New York 10019—R. R. Berliner, Ron Andriani, Thomas S. Melchers, 666 Fifth Ave. Phone 212-489-4640.
Chicago 60606—Mike O'Hara, Emidio L. Gaspari, 222 S. Riverside Plaza. Phone 312-648-5903.
Atlanta 30359—Robert Powell, P. O. Box 49087. Phone 404-633-8296.
Cleveland 44114—Paul Holder, Suite 1617, Superior Bldg., 815 Superior Ave. Phone 216-696-4492.
Garland (Dallas), Tex. 75041—Dick Eldredge, 1580 Eastgate Dr. Phone 214-270-6461.
Missouri City (Houston) Tex. 77459—Richard W. Sheehan, 3114 Springhill Dr. Phone 713-499-8352.
Los Angeles 90035—Patricia M. Sweet, 1801 S. La Cienega Blvd. Phone 213-559-5111.

**3. COMMISSION AND CASH DISCOUNT**
15% of gross billing to agencies for display advertising space, color, special position premium, provided account is paid within 30 days of invoice date.

### ADVERTISING RATES
Effective October, 1978 issue.
NOTE: Effective October, 1978 issue for new advertisers, January 1, 1979 for all advertisers. Rates received August 1, 1978.

**5. BLACK/WHITE RATES**

|  | 1 ti | 3 ti | 6 ti | 12 ti | 18 ti |
|---|---|---|---|---|---|
| 1 page | 2080. | 2040. | 1950. | 1860. | 1800. |
| 2/3 page | 1640. | 1610. | 1560. | 1470. | 1435. |
| 1/2 page (island) | 1370. | 1340. | 1295. | 1240. | 1215. |
| 1/2 page | 1205. | 1185. | 1165. | 1090. | 1040. |
| 1/3 page | 860. | 840. | 805. | 755. | 735. |
| 1/4 page | 655. | 635. | 605. | 575. | 560. |
| 1/6 page | 485. | 465. | 440. | 415. | 395. |
| 1/8 page | 395. | 385. | 365. | 340. | 340. |

|  | 24 ti | 36 ti | 48 ti | 60 ti |
|---|---|---|---|---|
| 1 page | 1740. | 1680. | 1630. | 1570. |
| 2/3 page | 1395. | 1355. | 1315. | 1285. |
| 1/2 page (island) | 1180. | 1150. | 1120. | 1090. |
| 1/2 page | 1000. | 970. | 940. | 915. |
| 1/3 page | 720. | 705. | 690. | 675. |
| 1/4 page | 540. | 520. | 500. | 480. |
| 1/6 page | 380. | 365. | 350. | 340. |
| 1/8 page | 340. | 340. | 340. | 340. |

**5a COMBINATION RATES**
Combination rates for ads placed in Graphic Arts Monthly and In-Plant Printing Section of Graphic Arts Monthly available.

**6. COLOR RATES**
Standard AAAA colors, red, blue, yellow, green, per page, or fractional page ... 235.
Per spread, or fractional page spread ... 370.
3 or 4 color process, earned black/white rate plus:
Full or fractional page ... 700.
2 page or fractional page spread ... 920.
Matched color, per page or fraction thereof ... 325.
Per page or fractional page spread ... 600.

**7. COVERS**
Non-cancellable.

|  | 6 ti | 12 ti |
|---|---|---|
| 2nd cover | 2725. | 2615. |
| 3rd cover | 2585. | 2475. |
| 4th cover | 2780. | 2675. |

Cover rates shown include premium position charge, bleed and standard 2nd process color.
3 or 4-color ads on cover extra ... 465.
Matched color available.

**8. INSERTS**
Standard sized inserts furnished ready for binding, which do not require back up or other handling, regular black/white space rates apply.
Back-up charge:
Page ... 400.
Spread ... 500.

**9. BLEED**
No extra charge.

**11. CLASSIFIED AND READING NOTICES**

|  | 1 ti | 12 ti |
|---|---|---|
| Per agate line (4 line min.) | 6.00 | 5.00 |
| Per inch | 82.00 | 72.00 |
| 3" to 5" per inch | 80.00 | 70.00 |
| 6" or more, per inch | 78.00 | 68.00 |

For payment in advance of issue closing, deduct 5%.
Box number service: 4.00 per ad insertion.
Non-commissionable.
Display spaces may run in classified. Display rates and policies apply.

**13a GEOGRAPHIC and/or DEMOGRAPHIC EDITIONS**
IN-PLANT PRINTING SECTION

| Rates: | 1 ti | 3 ti | 6 ti | 12 ti | 18 ti | 24 ti | 36 ti | 48 ti |
|---|---|---|---|---|---|---|---|---|
| 1 pg | 895. | 865. | 840. | 800. | 755. | 725. | 700. | 675. |
| 2/3 pg | 715. | 695. | 665. | 625. | 595. | 575. | 550. | 530. |
| *1/2 pg | 630. | 610. | 585. | 550. | 525. | 500. | 485. | 470. |
| †1/2 pg | 585. | 565. | 545. | 525. | 505. | 485. | 465. | 445. |
| 1/3 pg | 470. | 460. | 445. | 425. | 410. | 395. | 380. | 365. |
| 1/6 pg | 250. | 245. | 240. | 235. | 230. | 225. | 220. | 215. |

(*) Island.
(†) Only horizontal ads accepted.
Inserts: Black/white rates apply.
Circulation:
Publisher states: Effective with May, 1975 issue, guaranteed non-paid circulation average of 15,000.

**14. CONTRACT AND COPY REGULATIONS**
See Contents page for location—items 1, 3 thru 35.

**15. MECH. REQUIREMENTS (Web Offset)**
For complete, detailed production information, see SRDS Print Media Production Data.
Trim size: 8-1/8 x 10-7/8; No./Cols. 2&3.
Binding method: Perfect.
Colors available: AAAA/ABP; Matched; 4-Color Process (AAAA/MPA).
Cover colors available: AAAA/ABP (Red, Blue, Green, Yellow); Matched; 4-Color Process (AAAA/MPA).

DIMENSIONS—AD PAGE

| 1 | 7 | x 10 | 1/4 | 3-3/8 | x 4-3/4 |
|---|---|---|---|---|---|
| 2/3 | 4-1/2 | x 10 | 1/4 | 7 | x 2-1/4 |
| (*) | 4-1/2 | x 7-1/2 | 1/6 | 2-1/8 | x 4-3/4 |
| 1/2 | 7 | x 4-3/4 | 1/8 | 3-3/8 | x 2-1/4 |
| 1/2 | 3-3/8 | x 10 | | Merchandiser. | |
| 1/3 | 4-1/2 | x 4-3/4 | | 2-1/8 | x 1-3/8 |
| 1/3 | 2-1/8 | x 10 | (*) | Island half. | |

**16. ISSUE AND CLOSING DATES**
Published monthly; issued 5th of publication month. Closing date—5th of month preceding month of publication.
Inserts due 10th of month preceding publication. If new copy is not provided, publisher reserves right to repeat last ad, of same size as space reserved. Cancellation of space reservations must be made before closing date of any issue.

**17. SPECIAL SERVICES**
MCC Media Data Form registered 8/21/78.
Direct Response Service.
Annual Buyer's Guide/Directory.
BPA Unit Audit released Nov/77.

**18. CIRCULATION**
Established 1929. Single copy 2.00; per year 18.00. Summary data—for detail see Publisher's Statement.
B.P.A. 12-31-78 (6 mos. aver. qualified)

| Total | Non-Pd | Paid |
|---|---|---|
| 76,969 | 76,969 | ....... |

Average Non-Qualified (not included above):
Total 7,362

TERRITORIAL DISTRIBUTION 11/78—77,019

| N.Eng. | Mid.Atl. | E.N.Cen. | W.N.Cen. | S.Atl. | E.S.Cen. |
|---|---|---|---|---|---|
| 5,142 | 14,143 | 16,702 | 6,957 | 10,320 | 2,943 |
| W.S.Cen. | Mtn.St. | Pac.St. | Canada | Foreign | Other |
| 4,913 | 2,904 | 9,536 | 3,307 | 59 | 93 |

BUSINESS ANALYSIS OF CIRCULATION
1 —Commercial printers.
1-1—General commercial printers.
1-2—Publication printers.
1-3—Rotary business forms printers.
1-4—Book printers—mfrs.
1-5—Converters—packaging, carton & paper box envelope tag & ticket, tape & label printers.
2 —Newspapers.
2-1—Dailies without commercial printing dept.

indeed reach nonprospects. Vertical publications, reaching all the job functions and different levels of management in a single industry, will also include a number of readers in their circulation figures who will not be prospective customers for a given product. For example, *Graphic Arts Monthly* will reach commercial printers, converters who make packaging materials, noncommercial printers (internal operations in businesses, government, or schools,) typesetters, plate makers, and binderies. However, only the commercial or noncommercial printers would be prospective customers for the manufacturers of printing presses or printing ink. The readers in other areas of the printing industry would represent waste circulation.

## Trade publications

Trade magazines contain news and advertising of interest to people employed in both the wholesale and retail distribution of specific lines of consumer goods and services. Virtually every retail field is covered by one or more trade magazines such as *Snack Food, Music Retailer, American Drycleaner,* and *Supermarketing.* Although the editorial focus of trade magazines is aimed predominately at retailers, most of them tend to reach a vertical audience. For example, a grocery magazine such as *Supermarketing* would reach independent grocers, chain supermarket managers and executives, and food wholesalers, as well as the manufacturers of many products *sold through* supermarkets or *used by* supermarkets in their operations. In addition, many regional trade publications are available. The manufacturers of hardware products can reach their regional markets through such publications as *Southern Hardware, Northern Hardware Trade,* and *New England Hardware.*

## Institutional publications

Institutional publications circulate to executives, managers, and supervisors in organizations that provide a service to the public on their premises— such as hotels, hospitals, nursing homes, schools, and resorts. These institutions represent tremendous buying power—for furniture, linens, uniforms, food, and cleaning and maintenance supplies. Publications in this category include *Hospitals, Modern Healthcare, Club Management, Hotel & Motel Management, Resort Management,* and *Ski Area Management.* The titles are indicative of their areas of editorial interest.

## Professional publications

When we think of professionals, the people that come to mind are physicians, lawyers, architects, veterinarians, accountants, and engineers. They are professionals by training, and the journals they read are written with an editorial focus that is often very specialized. The professional market is important to advertisers because these are the people who influence the purchases others make and who, in many cases, write the actual specifications. Advertisers would want to place their ads in the *American Bar Association Journal* to reach attorneys who may influence plant location or method of financing; *Engineering News-Record* to reach civil engineers who specify the machinery and materials used in highway construction; *Dental Management* to reach dentists who prescribe medication and dentures; *Medical Economics* to reach physicians who prescribe drugs; *Architectural Digest* to reach architects who specify the materials used in building construction. The medical field alone is covered by over 200 specialized publica-

Detergents for use in a commercial laundry are sold on a different basis than those for use at home. This ad appeared in a magazine circulated to laundries that specialize in cleaning industrial uniforms. The copy does not contain consumer appeals such as whiteness or clean smell; these laundries want to know that the product will work on greasy, heavily soiled uniforms and that it will suspend and *deflocculate** the grease and dirt—all at a reasonable cost.

* deflocculate: to cause to disperse

# Do we have to spend a lot of money to get good work?

# Not when there's PQ's economical ENERDET™ detergent.

PQ's new, improved ENERDET phosphorus-free built detergent is formulated especially for the cost-conscious laundry manager. It's been thoroughly proven in independent lab tests run at an energy-saving 140°F, and in several leading laundries.

ENERDET removes stubborn oil and grease stains; it's well suited to industrial service as well as other soil classifications.

ENERDET's secret? Its formulation! ENERDET has silicated alkali to provide just the right level of alka-

linity, plus selected additives to give you good surface activity, suspension, deflocculation, and whitening action. Nothing beats economical ENERDET in its price range.

Let a PQ Systems Service Technician show you how ENERDET can give you great cost/performance action in your laundry. Contact him, or call Philadelphia Quartz Company, Valley Forge, PA 19482. 215-293-7200.

**Detergents for the quality-conscious who are cost-conscious, too.**

PQ CHEMICALS

# Before they ask you about dental care programs, ask us. Last year 4,114 benefit managers did.

A most unusual ad, sponsored by the American Dental Association, appeared in *The Personnel Administrator*, a professional publication for personnel managers and other company officers concerned with the personnel function. In this ad, the ADA is seeking to build good will, out of which might develop more programs covering dental benefits. Here we see one group of professionals (dentists) addressing another group of professionals (personnel people) who have the ability to specify and choose for their companies dental programs that can amount to millions of dollars of business.

Last year thousands of employee benefit managers contacted the American Dental Association for information on dental benefit plans. Why?

Dental care plans are a rapidly growing employee benefit—from two million people covered in 1965 to an estimated 48 million today. Employers and union officials recognize dental plans as a worthwhile employee benefit.

Further, the American Dental Association has experience gained from longstanding cooperation with the nation's largest carriers and purchasers of dental insurance.

We can help you better understand dental care and make the right decisions for your company and your employees.

Return this coupon, and we'll send you a package of useful background information on dental prepayment.

If you are considering a dental plan for your company, or presently have coverage,

we believe you will find this information important. Please send the coupon to: James Y. Marshall, Council on Dental Care Programs, American Dental Association, 211 East Chicago Avenue, Chicago, Illinois 60611.

---

For your information kit send this coupon to:

James Y. Marshall
Council on Dental Care Programs
American Dental Association
211 East Chicago Avenue
Chicago, Illinois 60611

| Name | | |
| Title | Phone | |
| Company | | |
| Address | | |
| City | State | Zip |
| Number of employees | | |
| Presently have a dental plan? Yes | No | |

tions ranging from *The American Journal of Cardiology* to *Urology*. As in many industrial publications, the advertising is very important to the readers. It is often through the advertising pages that professionals learn of new products and new techniques. Such interest adds impact to the advertisers' message and demands advertising that is very informative. Consider the statement by P. Dudley Kaley earlier in this chapter. An architect or engineer involved in the design and construction of the 64-story office building he mentioned specified the use of glass fiber insulation, a sale amounting to several hundred thousand dollars.

## Rates and spaces

Business publications vary in size and format in the same way that consumer magazines do. There are tabloids, standards, and digests. They also vary in their editorial approach, with some emphasizing, or devoted entirely to, new product information. Others may contain a mix of new product information and feature articles. Space is sold in full pages or in the same range of fractional space available in consumer magazines. Most business publications sell cover positions; some even sell the front cover positions. Contract rates and color rates are similar to those of consumer publications. Business paper advertisers make frequent use of *inserts.* An insert is an advertisement, one page or more, that is prepared and printed by the advertiser and then bound into the magazine by the publisher. The publisher charges the advertiser the black and white earned rate plus a binding charge, which is noncommissionable to the advertiser's agency. The use of inserts offers advertisers several benefits. If they use the same insert in several magazines, the cost for color printing can be kept relatively low. By printing their inserts on a paper that is different in weight and texture from the paper used in the rest of the magazine, advertisers can add impact to their message. The advertiser can also get extra mileage from copies of the insert material by using them for direct mailings or by distributing them at trade shows.

Another unique feature of many business publications is the reader service card, commonly known as a "bingo card." A *reader service card* is a postage-paid postcard that is bound into every copy of the magazine. One side of the card bears the name and address of the publication; the other side contains a series of numbers. Each of these numbers corresponds to a service key number that the publisher has placed below the copy of every advertisement in the magazine. The purpose of the reader service card is to stimulate inquiries by making it easy for readers to request more information. Rather than sending in a coupon or writing a letter, busy readers simply circle the numbers on the service card that correspond to the advertised products or services that interest them. They then fill in their names and addresses and drop the postage-free card into the mail. The publisher sorts the cards and sends each advertiser the names and addresses of those who inquired. The advertisers then send these readers more information on their product or have one of their salespeople call on the prospect. In this way, the advertisers will receive clear feedback on the effectiveness of their activity by counting the number of inquiries obtained from a specific advertisement in a specific publication.

## Media decisions for business advertisers

Although there are thousands of business publications from which to choose, the nature of our prod-

# Industrial Maintenance and Plant Operation

**An Ames Publishing Co. Publication**

BPA

**Media Code 7 652 3600 5.00**

Published monthly by Ames Publishing Co., One West Olney Ave., Philadelphia, Pa. 19120. Phone 215-224-7000.

For shipping info., see Print Media Production Data.

**PUBLISHER'S EDITORIAL STATEMENT**

INDUSTRIAL MAINTENANCE AND PLANT OPERATION, a newstabloid magazine for those responsible for maintenance and operation of industrial plants. Editorial purpose: provide recipients with news on new and improved products and methods used in maintaining and operating plant equipment, buildings, facilities and grounds. Product news, new literature, and capsule news present overall picture of what's new in industrial product mix. Feature stories provide more depth information on specific areas of maintenance/plant operations—i.e., materials handling, corrosion control, grounds maintenance, lubrication, plant safety.

**1. PERSONNEL**

Publisher—F. E. Milner.
General Manager—B. J. Wasserbly.
Editor, Publisher—L. M. Wasserbly.
Marketing Director—E. M. Marks.

**2. REPRESENTATIVES and/or BRANCH OFFICES**

Chicago—Jack Farley, Craig Pitcher, Jean Hoover, Jake Brown, Jim Barrett, The Farley Co., 35 E. Wacker Dr., Suite 2700. Phone 312-346-3074.
Pittsburgh 15219—John Barnes, Jr., 550 Grant St., Rm. 204. Phone 412-281-3398.
Philadelphia 19120—Robert Frey, Greg Cassidy, One West Olney Ave. Phone 215-224-7000.
New York 10017—Stanley Greenfield, 101 Park Ave., Suite 1430 N. Phone 212-683-6711.
Highland Beach, Fla. 33431—F. S. Osgood, 3212 S. Ocean Blvd., Suite 808. Phone 305-278-4593.
Rochester, N. Y. 14619—Neil Seymour, P. O. Box 8504. Phone 716-325-4090.
Cleveland 44115—Nick LaRich, Joe Drochak, The Farley Co., The Hanna Bldg., Rm. 605. Phone 216-621-1919.
Caldwell, N. J. 07006—John McGrane, 285 Bloomfield Ave. Phone 201-783-7355.
Beverly Hills, Calif. 90211—E. I. Brand, Fox-Wilshire Theatre Bldg., 202 S. Hamilton Dr. Phone 213-651-0612.
Dallas 75201—Don Moeller, Media Company, 2017 Cedar Springs. Phone 214-651-0297.
Southington, Conn. 06189—William P. Hickey, P. O. Box 602. Phone 203-621-4009.

**3. COMMISSION AND CASH DISCOUNT**

15% to agencies on space, color, bleed and position; 2% 10 days from invoice date.

**ADVERTISING RATES**

Effective January, 1979 issue. (Card No. 17.)
Card received October 9, 1978.

**5. BLACK/WHITE RATES**

| Tabloid: | 1 ti | 6 ti | 12 ti | 18 ti | 24 ti | 36 ti |
|---|---|---|---|---|---|---|
| 1 page | 4420. | 4170. | 3835. | 3790. | 3710. | 3610. |
| 2/3 page | 3685. | 3500. | 3330. | 3170. | 3010. | 2860. |
| 1/2 page | 2945. | 2800. | 2660. | 2590. | 2545. | 2490. |
| 1/3 page | 1850. | 1755. | 1670. | 1600. | 1515. | 1440. |
| Standard: | | | | | | |
| 1 page | 2945. | 2800. | 2660. | 2590. | 2545. | 2490. |
| 2/3 page | 2065. | 1985. | 1920. | 1860. | 1850. | 1830. |
| 1/2 page | 1525. | 1475. | 1445. | 1410. | 1385. | 1315. |
| 1/3 page | 1075. | 1025. | 1000. | 990. | 970. | 965. |
| 1/4 page | 765. | 745. | 725. | 710. | 695. | 660. |

Rates are based on the number of insertions contracted for and used within a 12-month period from the first insertion. Each page or fractional page counts as one insertion. Thus, a spread is figured as two insertions. The combination of various space units is a factor in determining the frequency rate. Therefore, advertising schedules composed of mixed with one exception. The exception is a mixed schedule in which the use of the smaller unit lowers the total cost of the campaign below the amount which the larger units taken alone would cost. Example: Addition of a 1/3 page unit to 11 full pages to earn the 12-time rate on the full pages.

**5a COMBINATION RATES**

Insertions in Industrial Distributor News and/or Safety Product News may be added to insertions in Industrial Maintenance and Plant Operation to earn combined frequency rates.

**6. COLOR RATES**

Color rates based on the use of 1 color in addition to black. Specified colors (matched or standard) cannot be guaranteed for a fixed position except on covers. Standard colors, AAAA red, blue, green, orange, yellow.

| | |
|---|---|
| Standard 2nd color, per page, extra | 200. |
| Standard 2nd color, per spread, extra | 350. |
| Matched 2nd color, per page, extra | 280. |
| Matched 2nd color, per spread, extra | 470. |
| Standard 2nd and 3rd color, per page, extra | 500. |
| 4-color process, per page, extra | 700. |
| 4-color process, per spread, extra | 1250. |

**7. COVERS**

1st cover—not sold.
2nd, 3rd and 4th covers available on non-cancellable basis.

**8. INSERTS**

Supplied complete by advertiser take black and white space rates. Inserts not exceeding 8-1/2" x 12" will take regular 7" x 10" page rates. Inserts larger than 8-1/2" x 12", or exceeding either of these dimensions will take full page rates.

Binding charges: No binding charge for inserts that take space rate of 2 or more pages. For inserts that take space rate of less than 2 pages, add the following binding charges:

| | |
|---|---|
| Stitch-in, per M | 5.00 |
| Tip-in, per M | 11.00 |

All binding charges are net (non-commissionable).


impo

Industrial Maintenance and Plant Operation

*plant operating products, equipment and systems*

## IMPO's QUALITY CIRCULATION

INDUSTRIAL MAINTENANCE AND PLANT OPERATION delivers over 68,576 BPA Audited units* — more than any other publication in this classification of SRDS.

These units are analyzed by 4-digit SIC; and by employee plant size. Recipients must be employed in plants with 50 or more employees, or with a minimum D&B rating of $50,000. In the chemical SIC 28 and metal-working SIC's 33-39, recipients must be employed in plants with 20 or more employees, or with a minimum D&B rating of $50,000.

*November 1977 BPA Unit Audit

## IMPO's QUALITY PLANT COVERAGE

INDUSTRIAL MAINTENANCE AND PLANT OPERATION delivers over 105,000 BPA-audited recipients* with titles in the following areas: Plant Engineering, Plant Utilities Operation; Purchasing; Maintenance; Engineering; Plant Safety; Production; Administration.

IMPO's circulation standards are among the highest in the industry: 78.7% of the circulation has been qualified in the past year and 91.9% of the circulation has been qualified by personal written request.*

*December 1978 BPA Statement

## IMPO's QUALITY INQUIRIES

In 1977, IMPO readers circled an average of 4.6 items per Reader Service Card — an indication of quality sales leads from potential buyers.

Responses to follow-up studies conducted by the Ames Research Department in 1977 indicated that an average of 70.4% of all inquiries came from "identified buyers".‡

Inquiries are qualified by SIC, employee plant size, title, address and telephone number (if supplied). And, advertisers receive two sets of inquiries — one on pre-gummed labels for fast handling; the second set for follow-up and reference. The second set of IMPO inquiries also have mini "call report" forms printed on reverse side for easy sales follow-up.

‡Based on over 200 research studies. An "identified buyer" is an inquirer who bought the product he inquired about, bought a competitive product, or was still considering purchase at the time of the survey.

## IMPO's QUALITY MARKETING PACKAGE

- Individual Marketing Counseling
- IMPO ACTION CARDS
- Direct Mail Capabilities — IMPO's list may be selected by state, zip code, 4-digit SIC, basic title group, employee plant size or any combination thereof.
- APMP Program — Ames' Precision Marketing Program — all of the versatility of direct mail with the prestige of an advertising insert in a national publication. Split-runs also available.
- Readership Studies — to help advertisers determine the effectiveness of their ads; the importance of color, size, position, frequency, etc.
- Product Area Research Surveys — to help advertisers pinpoint their market.
- Ad Volume Reports
- Inquiry Analyses
- Custom Merchandising Services
- Instant Hotline Coupons — for quick advertiser response to readers with an immediate need for a product or service.


**9. BLEED**

| | |
|---|---|
| Per page, extra | 100. |
| Bleed spreads | 120. |

No charge for gutter bleed only on spreads.

**10. SPECIAL POSITION**

Available at additional premium position charge, which depends on location and mechanical considerations.

**12. SPLIT RUN**

Available.

**13a GEOGRAPHIC and/or DEMOGRAPHIC EDITIONS**

AMES PRECISION MARKETING PLAN

An insert program, or split-run advertising program or a combination of both can be used in conjunction with a national advertising program. APMP utilizes one or more of the following options: Zip Code, SIC, Plant Size, Units, Recipient Title, and/or Sales Volume.

INSERT SPACE RATES

Per thousand (commissionable):

| | |
|---|---|
| *Tabloid page | 110.00 |
| *Up to standard 7 x 10 page | 82.50 |
| Production charges: | |
| Binding or Zip Code Break (min. 2 breaks) | 55.00 |
| Tip-in binding, per M | 11.00 |
| Stitch-in binding, per M | 5.00 |
| Per computer selection after 1st selection | 110.00 |

Multiple page insert rates available.
Minimum charges (not including Production charges) .......... 500.00
APMP rates do not apply for national inserts.
(*) Inserts may be printed on both sides at no additional cost.

SPLIT RUN SPACE RATE

Per thousand rates:

| Names: | (*) | (†) | Names: | (*) | (†) |
|---|---|---|---|---|---|
| 10 | 83. | 117. | 45 | 48. | 79. |
| 20 | 73. | 107. | 50 | 45. | 71. |
| 30 | 66. | 99. | 55 | 42. | 63. |
| 35 | 59. | 91. | 60 | 39. | 59. |
| 40 | 53. | 83. | 65 | 37. | 56. |

Per thousand rates:

| Names: | (*) | (†) | Names: | (*) | (†) |
|---|---|---|---|---|---|
| 70 | 35. | 53. | 90 | 30. | 45. |
| 75 | 34. | 51. | 95 | 29. | 44. |
| 80 | 32. | 49. | 100 | 28. | 43. |
| 85 | 31. | 47. | | | |

(*) 7 x 10 CPM.
(†) Tabloid CPM.

Plate Removal and Substitution:

| | |
|---|---|
| 1 color (black) | 220. |
| 2 colors | 365. |
| 3 colors | 505. |
| 4 colors | 650. |
| ZIP code breaks (min. 2 breaks) | 55. |

Minimum quantity for split runs is 10,000 names

**14. CONTRACT AND COPY REGULATIONS**

See Contents page for location—items 1 through 31.

**15. MECH. REQUIREMENTS (Web Offset)**

For complete, detailed production information, see SRDS Print Media Production Data.

Trim size: 11 x 16-1/8; No./Cols. 3.
Binding method: Saddle Stitched.
Colors available: AAAA/ABP; Matched; 4-Color Process (AAAA/MPA); Metallic; Simulated Metallic.

DIMENSIONS—AD PAGE

| | | | | | |
|---|---|---|---|---|---|
| Tabloid: | | | 1/2 | 7 | x 4-3/4 |
| 1 | 10-1/4 | x 15 | 1/2 | 4-9/16 | x 7-3/8 |
| 2/3 | 7 | x 15 | 1/2 | 7-1/2 | x 10 |
| 1/2 | 10 | x 7-1/2 | 1/3 | 3-1/4 | x 15 |
| 1/3 | 3-1/4 | x 15 | 1/2 | 3-1/4 | x 9-5/8 |
| Standard: | | | 1/3 | 4-9/16 | x 4-3/4 |
| 1 | 7 | x 10 | 1/3 | 2-1/8 | x 9-5/8 |
| 2/3 | 4-9/16 | x 9-5/8 | 1/4 | 3-1/4 | x 4-3/4 |

**16. ISSUE AND CLOSING DATES**

Published monthly: issued 1st week of month.

Last forms close 1st of preceding month. If proofs are required, copy must be received 1st of preceding month.

Complete plates: 5th of month preceding. Inserts due 15th of month preceding. 10th of month preceding for inserts to be backed-up. All space reservations due 1st of month preceding. Cancellations not acceptable after 5 p.m. of 1st of month preceding date of publication. Contracts may be cancelled by advertiser or publisher on written notice 30 days in advance of closing date.

SPECIAL FEATURE ISSUES

June/79—Plant Storage Issue.
July/79—Western PE&M Show Issue.
Aug/79—Fall Maintenance Issue.
Sept/79—Material Handling Show Issue.
Oct/79—Pumps & Compressors Issue.
Nov/79—Machinery Maintenance Issue.
Dec/79—Air Pollution Control Issue.

**17. SPECIAL SERVICES**

MCC/Media Data form registered 6/5/78.
Received 7/31/78.
1979 Ad Readership Studies—Jan., Apr., Aug., Nov.
BPA Unit Audit Report released Nov/77.
Reprints.

**18. CIRCULATION**

Summary data—for detail see Publisher's Statement.

**B.P.A. 12-31-78 (6 mos. aver. qualified)**

| Total | Non-Pd | Paid |
|---|---|---|
| 105,571 | 105,571 | ........ |

Average Non-Qualified (not included above):
Total 5,015

TERRITORIAL DISTRIBUTION 11/78—105,525

| N.Eng. | Mid.Atl. | E.N.Cen. | W.N.Cen. | S.Atl. | E.S.Cen. |
|---|---|---|---|---|---|
| 7,323 | 21,294 | 27,980 | 8,070 | 13,019 | 5,527 |
| W.S.Cen. | Mtn.St. | Pac.St. | Canada | Foreign | Other |
| 7,646 | 2,877 | 11,572 | ........ | ........ | 217 |

uct limits the number which we have seriously to consider. In many cases, however, there may still be too many publications in the field for us to think of using them all. To narrow the choice, we need to make a simple media analysis by asking ourselves a few pertinent questions:

1. *Is circulation paid or nonpaid?*
   Some media analysts believe that paid circulation indicates greater interest on the part of the reader because the reader was willing to pay for the subscription. This is not necessarily true in practice. Often the reader's company has paid for the subscription.

2. *Is the editorial content of value to the type of person we want to reach?*
   Remember, we are looking not only for the individual who signs the purchase orders, but also for the many others who influence the buying decision.

3. *Is the publication a weekly or a monthly?*
   Publishers of monthly magazines argue that each issue has a longer life with more opportunity to make contact with the audience. Publishers of weekly magazines claim that their timeliness is important to keep readers abreast of the latest news of the industry. Both are correct, but media decisions should be based on editorial content, circulation, and rates—not frequency of issue. If the publication serves its audience properly, it will be read regardless of its publication schedule.

4. *How often are the readers of a publication qualified?*

How frequently does the publication update its circulation list to prune out individuals who have left the business (moved, retired, deceased)? If they don't do it every year, the list will be out of date.

5. *What is the inquiry average?*
   Publications have data on inquiries, particularly when they employ reader service cards. Needless to say, we should maintain a record of our experience with every publication.

## Farm publications

Although Standard Rate & Data Service Inc. lists farm publications as a section in its *Consumer Magazine and Farm Publication Rates and Data* book, these publications are a cross between business publications and consumer publications. To be sure, farmers and their families are consumers, buying most of the products bought by consumers everywhere. At the same time, farmers operate a business—an agricultural business. For the operation of their agricultural enterprise, they buy seeds, machinery, chemicals, and buildings. For the family-run farm, farming is more than business; it is a way of life.

The total farm population in the United States at the end of 1977 was 7,829,400.[4] The total farm income for that year was reported as a bit over $104 billion. The United States Department of Agriculture figures for 1974 (the latest available) show that there were 2,314,036 farms in this country at that

[4] *SRDS Consumer Magazine and Farm Publication Rates and Data* (February 1, 1979), p. 56.

CASE HISTORY

**MARKETING A
REPAIR
METHOD
FOR HOSPITAL
LINENS**

Although hospitals have for many years sent their linens and staff uniforms to commercial laundries for washing, today an increasing number of hospitals operate their own laundry facilities. This enables them to control the quality of the washing operations and, equally important, to assure themselves of laundry service twenty-four hours a day, seven days a week.

The most critical area in the operation of a hospital laundry is the handling of surgical linen. Because these linens are in constant contact with sharp-edged equipment and instruments, they are often damaged. But, years ago, it was determined that such linen should not be repaired by sewing because the needle holes created breeding places for bacteria. Fortunately, Thermopatch Corporation developed a procedure for the heat-seal mending of linen. With this method a tiny hole or a long slit in a piece of linen could be covered completely with a fabric of the same physical characteristics as the original. Tests proved that the heat-seal repairs maintained the highest level of sterility.

The advertising objective of the Thermopatch Corporation was to bring its technique to the attention of both hospitals and commercial laundries. For those hospitals that operated their own laundries, the advertising was intended to generate sales leads. At the same time, the advertising would seek to make such mending desirable for hospitals that sent their linen to commercial laundries. The company also wanted to stimulate sales inquiries from commercial laundries of all kinds because many other linen services could use the Thermopatch process for mending.

To reach the two basic market categories (commercial laundries and hospitals) for the Thermopatch process, the company's advertising agency specified a mix of business publications that included: *Hospitals, Modern Healthcare, Executive Housekeeper,* and *American Laundry Digest.*

*Hospitals* magazine was selected to reach hospital administrators, the executives responsible for the business side of hospital operations. *Modern Healthcare* was chosen to reach the owners and managers of nursing homes, and *Executive Housekeeper* was chosen to reach the people responsible for linen service in hospitals, nursing homes, and hotels. To reach laundry plants and their management, the agency placed ads for Thermopatch in *American Laundry Digest.* All these publications carried Business Publications Audit (BPA) circulation, an important qualification for an advertiser seeking assured circulation values.

Calculation of CPM for two of these publications proved to be an interesting exercise. *Hospitals,* for example, with a circulation of approximately 77,000 and a black and white page rate of $1,570, had a CPM of $20. *American Laundry Digest,* on the other hand, with a circulation of only 16,000 and a page rate of $965, had a CPM of $60. On the face value of CPM, there would seem to be a considerable difference in cost between the two publications. But *Hospitals,* with its larger circulation, reaches many

continued

Thermopatch continued

people who are not involved in hospital laundry operations, especially since many hospitals do not even operate their own laundry facilities. Thus, subtracting unwanted circulation leaves *Hospitals* with an effective reach of about 10,000 and a CPM of about $160. Therefore, the laundry magazine, with virtually 100 percent effective circulation, proved to be the better buy when all factors were considered.

Thermopatch's advertising program proved to be an outstanding success. The company received many requests for information on its heat-sealing process and continues to increase its sales of patches.

This case courtesy of Richard-Lewis Corp., Scarsdale, New York, advertising agency for Thermopatch Corporation.

time. That number has been dropping steadily over the past fifty years. The number of family farms has been declining even more rapidly. While in 1900 one out of every three Americans lived on a farm, today it is only one out of thirty. At the same time, many of the farms that remain have become larger. However, the volume of farm advertising in 1978, estimated at $105 million, was up 14 percent over the preceding year.[5]

Do farmers and their families also read consumer magazines? Of course they do, and national advertisers reach farm family consumers through most of the usual consumer media. The value of farm publications lies in their unique editorial climates—climates that are just right for the advertisers of products farmers buy to run their agricultural businesses. A family farm today may consist of 4,000 acres of farm land, with over $1 million invested in farm machinery and equipment. The farm will spend over $250,000 a year on chemicals and fertilizers and over $60,000 a year on seed.[6]

Farm publications are a very selective medium. When farmers and their families read farm publications, they are farmers first and consumers second.

For media consideration, farm publications are usually grouped into three types:

**1.** national publications

**2.** state or regional publications

**3.** specialized publications

### National farm publications

The term "national" is somewhat misleading because the coverage of these publications is not truly national. *Farm Journal* has a circulation of 1,410,677 farm families. *Progressive Farmer* has a circulation of 900,000 families, and *Successful Farming* has a circulation of 752,774.

**Progressive Farmer,** for example, is not circulated all over the United States. It reaches the southern farm market—fifteen states in a broad belt stretch-

[5] *Advertising Age* (January 8, 1979), p. S8.
[6] *Ibid.,* (March 19, 1979), p. S1.

# MOTHER'S DAY STARTS NOW!

Mother's Day in the cattle business is the day a cow drops her calf. It starts *now* because the size of a calf dropped in spring or summer depends on what you do for its mother earlier. For example, when you worm pregnant cows now, with TBZ®, the No-Setback Cattle Wormer, you help them get these five important benefits:

**5 benefits of worming with TBZ**

**1. Helps prevent damage** to digestive system and loss of feed efficiency.

**2. Helps "stretch" pasture.** Wormed cattle are more efficient, make better use of scarce grass.

**3. Helps cattle resist stresses** such as cold weather and poor pastures.

**4. Helps cattle stay stronger** to resist other diseases.

**5. Helps cows drop better calves,** nurse them better, too.

And remember, yearlings, stockers, and heifers...*all* cattle...need no-setback worming *now* for better performance in the months ahead.

**Merck Animal Health Division,**
Merck & Co., Inc., P.O. Box 2000,
Rahway, New Jersey 07065

TBZ comes as a paste, bolus, and
in cattle cubes and pellets, for one-time
feeding in your supplement program.

TBZ (thiabendazole) is a registered trademark of Merck & Co., Inc.

Pharmaceuticals for cattle? Yes, indeed. An important part of a farmer's business is practicing animal husbandry. Therefore, pharmaceutical manufacturers with highly specialized products use farm publications to bring important information about their products to farmers.

ing from Maryland to Arizona. The advertiser may buy advertising in the "national" edition or in any of seventeen demographic editions that may be bought singly or in combinations that best meet the advertiser's sales and distribution objectives. Rates for a black and white page range from $12,075 for the southwide edition (circulation: 900,000 families) to $940 for the Florida edition (circulation: 30,000 families).

**Farm Journal** offers a national edition and a wide range of demographic options. There are four regional editions—east, central, west, and south—with any combination of these editions also available. The advertiser may buy *crop editions* for corn, soybeans, wheat, sorghum, or cotton to reach those farms that comprise a very particular market segment for some herbicide or piece of machinery. There are state editions and livestock editions for beef, hogs, or dairy.

**Successful Farming** is circulated in all fifty states, but 79 percent of the magazine's circulation is concentrated in the north central region. In addition to providing thirteen individual editions, certain editions are combined to make an eastern edition, a western edition, and a southern edition. There are also editions directed toward the beef market, dairy market, hog market, and the corn, rootworm, and sunflower markets.

What are the interests of the readers? We can understand the value of these publications by studying this sample of articles from an issue of *Progressive Farmer:*[7]

[7] *Progressive Farmer*, East Texas edition, vol. 94, no. 3 (March 1979).

Baits lure worms to a deadly feast
Forage sorghums and millet—fast summer feeds
Weed shifts cause new headaches
Should you lease your next tractor?
Muskrat control for your farm pond
How to avoid a grain bin explosion

This same issue contains articles on the home vegetable patch, recipes for cookies, spring menus with pork, recipes for cooking carrots, how to make a boot cleaner, and sewing patterns for a collection of dresses and blouses.

## State and regional publications

The opportunities for geographic selectivity are limitless because there are farm publications issued in most states and regions of the country. Typical of such publications are *Hoosier Farmer* (Indiana), *Iowa Farm Bureau Spokesman*, *Kansas Farm Bureau News*, and *The Grange News* (Washington and Oregon).

## Specialized farm publications

The use of specialized farm magazines related to very specific reader interest, such as peanuts or poultry or hogs, provides the advertiser with a unique editorial climate. *Poultry Tribune, Shorthorn World, The Sunflower, Sugarbeet Grower, Spudman,* and *Rice Farming* attract readers who subscribe to the magazine not only for the editorial matter, but for the information contained in the advertisements. Rates vary widely. A black and white page in *Soybean Digest* costs $2,200. A page in *Rice Farming* costs $585. *Sunsweet Standard* (for prune growers) costs $230 a page. These publications are, in every sense, business publications.

A well-known chemical company uses a farm publication
to tell peanut farmers about a very special herbicide.
Notice how specific the copy is and how the illustration
of the peanut is used to "flag" the peanut farmer.

# A great tank mix doesn't have to cost a great deal.

# PREMERGE 3

The first thing that a great tank mix for peanuts should give you is good control of seedling broadleaf weeds and problem grasses. The second is economy. You get both when your tank mix contains PREMERGE*3 Dinitro Amine Herbicide. PREMERGE 3 is a highly-effective broadleaf herbicide. And it's cheap.

Tank mix PREMERGE 3 with Lasso† and apply in peanuts at the cracking stage for control of cocklebur, beggarweed, morningglory, teaweed, pigweed, common ragweed, lambsquarters and other broadleaf weeds. On contact. You'll get good control of problem grasses, too. Just be sure to read and follow all label directions and precautions.

To control Florida beggarweed in Georgia peanuts, team PREMERGE 3 in a tank mix with AMIBEN‡ and apply at cracking. PREMERGE 3 knocks out emerged broadleaf weeds. AMIBEN controls the later germinating annual grasses and broadleaf weeds. Be sure to read and follow all directions and precautions on the supplemental AMIBEN label, available for Georgia only.

Ask your dealer just how economical a great PREMERGE 3 tank mix can be. Then put it to work for you. Agricultural Products Department, Midland, Michigan 48640.

**DOW CHEMICAL U.S.A.**

*Trademark of The Dow Chemical Company
†Trademark of Monsanto Company
‡Trademark of Amchem Products, Inc.

# Summary

Management's *need to know* has been well served by the business press—with 3,300 publications serving over 175 business categories. There is, in fact, no business, industry, trade, or profession that does not have at least one publication to provide news and information to its practitioners and to serve as a highly selective vehicle for the delivery of important advertising messages. And the advertising messages are important—important enough for executives, technicians, and professionals to read them at work as part of their responsibility to keep up with developments in their fields.

The various types of business publications can be roughly divided into five categories, based on the kind of business market the publication serves. The categories are: (1) general business publications, (2) industrial publications, (3) trade publications, (4) professional publications, and (5) institutional publications. Some business publications span many industries with a focus on subjects of common interest and with an appeal to readers with similar job functions. These are *horizontal publications.* The readers of *vertical publications*, on the other hand, often run a gamut of job functions, but are confined within a single industry. Some business publications are distributed as consumer magazines are—on the basis of paid subscriptions. There are, however, many which are distributed to controlled groups of people qualified to receive the publication by virtue of their job titles or functions.

Business publications come in all sizes from tabloid to digest size and their frequency of issue ranges from daily to monthly. These publications sell space to advertisers in standard size units—and offer contract and color rates—similar to those of consumer magazines.

Farm publications serve the nation's farm population in two ways—as business magazines and as consumer publications—in recognition of the dual role of the American farmer. These publications are usually divided into three categories: (1) national publications, (2) state or regional publications, and (3) specialized publications, which are devoted to particular crops or to particular breeds of livestock.

## QUESTIONS FOR DISCUSSION

1. Is it possible for an industrial manufacturer to discontinue all business paper advertising and put the money into the sales force? What advantages or disadvantages would result from such a decision?

2. A manufacturer of mouthwash advertises in three general magazines in the belief that these publications adequately cover the country. What reasons can you provide for adding farm magazines to this schedule?

3. If you were considering a media schedule for advertising a company jet, what publications would you recommend and why?

4. Why do advertisers use inserts more frequently in business publications than in consumer media?

5. Why would a manufacturer of consumer products advertise in business publications? Why would a manufacturer of industrial products advertise in consumer magazines? Can you find some examples of both?

6. What are some of the demographic breakdowns that are commonly used by business publications?

7. What does a publisher mean by "qualified" circulation?

### Sources and suggestions for further reading

Arthur D. Little, Inc. "An Evaluation of 1100 Research Studies on the Effectiveness of Industrial Advertising." New York: American Business Press, May 1971.

Bailey, Earl L., ed. *Marketing Strategies.* New York: The Conference Board, 1974.

"Industrial Advertising Effectively Reaches Buying Influences at Low Cost." Report by U. S. Steel. New York: American Business Press, 1969.

Morrill, John D. "How Advertising Helps Sell Industrial Products." Report commissioned by Westinghouse. New York: American Business Press, 1975.

Yankelovich, Shelly and White, Inc. "A Study of Corporate Advertising Effectiveness." Prepared for *Time* magazine, 1978.

## THE BROADCAST MEDIA

**Radio**

Where it all came from
AM and FM radio
Radio as an advertising medium
Spot radio
Network radio
Radio audiences
    GRPs: gross rating points
Buying radio time

**Television**

UHF, VHF, and cable
The television audience
Network television
Spot television
Buying time
    GRPs again
Audience ratings
    Gross impressions
    Reach and frequency
    Flighting

## WORKING VOCABULARY

| | | |
|---|---|---|
| spot radio | gross rating points | package house |
| network radio | package plan | participations |
| drive time | run of station | adjacencies |
| cume | prime time | gross impressions |

# 10

the
broadcast
media

*Especially through the medium of television, advertising has brought to millions of Americans new ideas, not only about which soap to buy, but where to live, for which goals in life to aspire, what jobs to seek, and what to do with their increasing amounts of leisure time.*

SAM J. ERVIN, JR.
*Advertising Age*

T HE BROADCAST MEDIA are the media of the twentieth century. Less than sixty years ago, radio was first made available to advertisers as a commercial medium; and it is only within the past thirty-five years that commercial television has become a national medium. In a relatively short time, these media have made a profound impact, not only on the advertising industry, but on almost every facet of our society.

## Radio

In 1948, advertisers in the United States were spending $408 million on radio advertising while devoting only $9 million to television. But in the early 1950s, radio station owners saw one advertiser after another defect to the new medium, until, in 1959, advertising expenditures for television were $1,164 million, and radio's were only $506 million. By 1960, however, radio station operators saw an opportunity to take advantage of changing lifestyles and demographics. The renaissance started with adolescents and rock music. Today, of course, radio has something for everybody—the listener *and* the advertiser. And the statistics are impressive:[1]

1. The public spends more on radio sets than on many other categories of leisure/entertainment/knowledge expenditures. Since 1952, the number of radio sets in use has more than tripled. The average household has 5.7 sets. Sixty percent of all homes wake up to radio.

2. 95 percent of all cars have a radio.

3. Radio battery sales have increased by 2,000 percent since 1952.

4. 95.8 percent of the population of the United States listen to radio. People over twelve years of age spend three hours and twenty-four minutes a day listening to their radios. The average college student spends two hours and forty-five minutes a day with a radio, but only thirty-one minutes a day with a newspaper.

## Where it all came from

Although a number of physicists had been working on the use of electromagnetic energy, it was an Italian engineer, Guglielmo Marconi, who transmitted the first radio signal in 1895. Only twenty-five years later the first commercial radio station, KDKA

in Pittsburgh, was opened by the Westinghouse Broadcasting Company. In 1922, several radio stations broadcast the World Series and by 1926 the National Broadcasting Company had established a network of twenty-four stations, which was followed by the establishment of the Columbia Broadcasting System the next year. And so the radio industry grew. Today, there are over 7,300 radio stations. Each station is licensed by the Federal Communications Commission (FCC) and assigned call letters for national identification. Stations west of the Mississippi use call letters beginning with K. Stations east of the Mississippi use call letters beginning with W. Call letters that were assigned in the early days of radio, such as KDKA, present some exceptions to this rule.

## AM and FM radio

Radio stations transmit the sound of voices or musical instruments from their broadcasting studios to your radio receiver by means of electromagnetic waves. These electromagnetic waves, like waves of water on a pond, have both height, or *amplitude*, and width. The width of the wave determines its *frequency*. The narrower the waves are, the greater the number that can pass by a fixed point in a second—or the higher their frequency; the broader the wave, the lower the frequency.

The designation AM is derived from the term *amplitude modulation*. An AM radio station broadcasts its programs by varying the height, or amplitude, of the electromagnetic waves that it radiates from its transmitting tower. Some of these waves follow the contour of the ground, and are therefore called *ground waves*; others radiate upward into the sky, and are known as *sky waves*. During the daytime, radio receivers pick up only the ground

---

[1] Data compiled by Radio Advertising Bureau, Inc.

waves; the sky waves travel through the earth's atmosphere and out into space. At night, however, the sky waves bounce back to earth and can be picked up by receivers far beyond the range of the station's ground waves.

The strength of the AM signal, expressed in watts, is assigned by the FCC. The stronger the signal, the greater the distance it will travel. On the basis of strength of signal, there are three kinds of stations. First, there is the local station with a broadcast range of about twenty-five miles. Second, there is the regional station, which may cover an entire state. Last, there is the clear-channel station with up to 50,000 watts. Stations that broadcast with that range are few and no other station is permitted to operate on the same frequency during evening hours. Generally, the lower the frequency, the farther the signal will travel. The signal of a 1,000-watt station at the lower end of the radio dial will cover a greater territory than a station with equal power (watts) at the top of the dial.

FM stands for *frequency modulation.* An FM radio station broadcasts its programs by varying the width, or frequency, of the electromagnetic waves that it radiates from its transmitting tower. FM transmission follows the line of sight, and the distance for which reception is satisfactory depends on the height of the antenna. For this reason, many FM transmitting towers are located on tall buildings or mountains. But as a rule, FM signals cannot be received over great distances.

When a group of two or more stations broadcast the same program simultaneously (as is done on radio networks), the program is transmitted from the originating station over telephone lines. The other stations in the group receive the program from the originating station over the telephone and rebroadcast it from their transmitting towers.

## Radio as an advertising medium

Radio is a *high-frequency* medium. If we think that we need to repeat our advertising message often, radio is the ideal medium for us. The total cost is relatively low, and there are many stations to choose from with time available to build a high-frequency plan.

Radio is a good *supporting* medium. We can use radio to support the other media in our media mix because its cost is low. And it can provide us with good reach into selected target markets.

Radio is very *selective.* It enables us to reach a wide range of geographical markets—city, metro, state, and national. It also offers us a remarkable degree of demographic selectivity. We can use drive time—the hours in the morning and afternoon when people are on their way to and from work—to reach workers who commute. Daytime radio, on the other hand, accompanies people on their shopping trips. The last advertising message they receive before they enter the supermarket or department store may be delivered to them over their car radio.

Radio offers us great *flexibility.* Fast, low-cost production can meet changing market conditions and make it possible for us to tie our advertisements in with current news events. Pepsi Cola's use of radio is an excellent example of the way one company utilizes the medium's flexibility. Several commercials are distributed to each station with instructions to use a particular commercial when the temperature reaches ninety degrees. Radio lends itself equally well to the advertiser who wants to tie in with a particular event. For example, a commercial could be delivered to the stations waiting only for the name of the winner of the Indy 500 or the Daytona race to be dropped in.

Radio offers us many opportunities for low-cost *market testing*. For example, the advertiser makes an offer over the radio—for a sample or a booklet, some reason for the listener to write or telephone. Such an offer provides a quick way to determine the interest in a product. There are no long deadlines or extended preparation time for announcements. By using *spot radio* in different markets, the advertiser can obtain a low-cost market test.

But radio has limitations that the media analyst must weigh. In some markets there are so many competing stations that no one station can achieve dominance. In New York City, for example, there are twenty-nine stations (AM and FM) plus thirty-four in the surrounding metro areas. The audiences for these stations tend to be segmented—which is great if we want to reach a particular segment, but frustrating if we want a mass audience.

Since radio appeals to only one sense, it is of limited value to us if our product needs to be seen or demonstrated. What's more, consumers often listen to their radios while reading, working, or driving. Under such conditions, it may be difficult for us to get our message across.

The low costs for radio time yield very little revenue in media commissions for the advertising agency. Therefore, many agencies are reluctant to assign their best, highly paid creative personnel to work on a client's radio advertisements. Also, handling the paper work involved in spot radio buys—with thousands of stations to choose from, many with 24-hour broadcast days—is economically unfeasible for some agencies.

## Spot radio

When we say we are using *spot radio* it means that we are contracting with individual radio stations to carry our advertising message. The word *spot* distinguishes a radio advertisement broadcast on separately owned radio stations from advertising on *network radio*, which involves the simultaneous broadcast of a program over a group of stations. A *radio spot* is a short commercial, sometimes called a spot announcement. The term radio spot represents a time unit. The term spot radio represents a geographical unit.

The importance of spot radio is clear: It permits us to deliver our sales message area by area, city by city. This can be particularly useful if we do not have national distribution. We can also use spot radio to tie in local retailers in specific market areas. Spot radio is also extremely flexible, enabling us to take advantage of local conditions, fast-breaking news, or competitive activities.

Above all, spot radio is beautifully segmented: Its wide variety of programming attracts sharply defined audiences. In such major markets as New York, Chicago, and Los Angeles, there are forty or more stations available, most covering vertical programming. *Vertical programming* refers to a particular listening segment of people who prefer a certain kind of program—all news, hard rock, country, soul, Spanish (and other ethnics), good music, classical, and so on. Radio stations promote themselves every few minutes by mentioning their call letters. This allows listeners to switch around to whatever programming suits them—to an all-news station or to a station that broadcasts traffic reports every fifteen minutes.

Thus, we can gear our message to the listening habits and the living habits of our target market. The time periods 6 to 10 in the morning and 4 to 7 in the evening Monday through Friday are known as *drive time* and are to radio what *prime time* (7:30 to 11 in the evening) is to television. After the

We have said that radio is a limited medium—limited to just the one sense of hearing. But this advertisement, sponsored by the NBC radio network, is intended to provoke the imagination of advertisers and their agencies to the creative possibilities of radio. Couldn't the sound of a child drinking a soda be more effective in catching an audience's attention than a picture of a child drinking a soda? How about the crunching sound of a fresh apple when we bite into it? Or the distinctive sound of a champagne bottle being opened, an auto starter when the car won't start, or a busy airport terminal? A little imagination is all it takes to make effective use of this medium.

## Slurp.

## One sound is often worth 2,000 pictures.

Do you feel you shouldn't advertise on radio because people have to see your product? Try this test. Buy your child a chocolate shake. Then cover your ears and *watch* him/her drink the shake. Next, treat your child to another chocolate shake. This time, close your eyes and *listen* to him/her drink the shake.

If you don't have a child, borrow one from your neighbor, or drop us a line and ask to hear the "Slurp" commercial, just one of an unforgettable series of radio commercials that demonstrate

radio's power. What do they talk about? Chocolate shakes. Plus some incredible facts that will make you wonder why you don't advertise on radio. Write to Advertising and Promotion, NBC Radio Network, 30 Rockefeller Plaza, NY, NY 10020

**NBC Radio Network**

## WBMX (FM)
### 1950
### OAK PARK

**Bernard Howard & Co., Inc.**
**Independent Black**

A Sonderling Station

(This is a paid duplicate of the listing appearing under Chicago Urban Area.)
Media Code 4 214 2887 1.00
Sonderling Broadcasting Corp., 408 S. Oak Park Ave., Oak Park, Ill. 60302. Phone 312-626-1030.

**STATION'S PROGRAMMING DESCRIPTION**
WBMX (FM): Programmed for adults.
MUSIC: Contemporary black album cuts & singles 6-4 am M-Sa, Su noon-midnight. Public affairs 9 am-noon Sun. Gospel 4-6 am M-Sa, 6-9 am Sun.
NEWS: 3 min at :50 6:50 am-7:50 pm M-Sa. UPI, city bureau. Editorials 25x/wk. COMMERCIAL POLICY: 10 minutes in 4 stop sets per hour. Contact Representative for further details. Rec'd 5/24/77.

**1. PERSONNEL**
President—Egmont Sonderling.
General Manager—Ronald K. Craven.
General Sales Manager—Cooke Bausman.
**2. REPRESENTATIVES**
Bernard Howard & Co., Inc.
**3. FACILITIES**
ERP 6,000 w. (horiz.), 6,000 w. (vert.); 102.7 mc. Stereo.
Operating schedule: 24 hours daily. CST.
Antenna ht.: 1,170 ft. above average terrain.
**4. AGENCY COMMISSION**
15/0 time and spots only.
**5. GENERAL ADVERTISING See coded regulations**
Rate Protection: 10g.
AM facilities: WOPA.
Affiliated with Bernard Howard Black Radio Network.

**TIME RATES**
No. 16 Eff 10/1/78—Rec'd 10/2/78.
AA—Mon thru Fri 5:30-10 am & 3-8 pm; Sat 10 am-7 pm.
A—All other times.

**6. SPOT ANNOUNCEMENTS**

| CLASS AA | | | | | | | |
|---|---|---|---|---|---|---|---|
| | | 1 min | | | | 30 sec | |
| | 6 ti | 12 ti | 18 ti | 24 ti | 6 ti | 12 ti | 18 ti | 24 ti |
| 1 wk. | 125 | 120 | 115 | 110 | 100 | 96 | 92 | 88 |
| 13 wk. | 120 | 115 | 110 | 105 | 96 | 92 | 88 | 84 |
| 26-52 | 115 | 110 | 105 | 100 | 92 | 88 | 84 | 80 |
| CLASS A | | | | | | | |
| 1 wk. | 110 | 105 | 100 | 95 | 88 | 84 | 80 | 76 |
| 13 wk. | 105 | 100 | 95 | 90 | 84 | 80 | 76 | 72 |
| 26-52 | 95 | 90 | 85 | 80 | 76 | 72 | 68 | 64 |

Submitted by Cooke Bausman III. (D)

## WCFL AM 10
### 1926

**MAJOR MARKET RADIO, INC.**
**Personality Entertainment Radio**

Media Code 4 214 1760 1.00
Chicago Federation of Labor Industrial Union Council, Marina City Commercial Bldg., 300 N. State St., Chicago, Ill. 60610. Phone 312-222-1000

---

**1. PERSONNEL**
Pres. & Gen'l Mgr.—William A. Lee.
Station Manager—William J. Lemanski.
General Sales Manager—Bob Pates.
**2. REPRESENTATIVES**
Major Market Radio, Inc.
**3. FACILITIES**
50,000 w.; 1000 kc. Directional—separate patterns day and night.
Operating schedule: 24 hours daily. CST.
**4. AGENCY COMMISSION**
15/0 time and announ. only; payable when rendered
**5. GENERAL ADVERTISING See coded regulations**
General: 2a, 3a, 4a, 4d, 5, 8.
Rate Protection: (*)
Basic Rates: 20a, 23a, 25a.
Contracts: 40a, 42a, 45, 46, 48.
Comb.; Cont. Discounts: 60a, 60e, 60f.
Cancellation: 70c, 73a.

*RATE PROTECTION
Rates quoted herein are guaranteed for a period of 4 weeks from the effective date of any increase in these rates, provided that advertising equalling a weekly expenditure of 100.00 is actually running at the time of effective date of increase, and providing that these broadcasts continue without interruption during rate protection period.
Affiliated with MBS.

**TIME RATES**
No. L Eff 3/1/78—Rec'd 3/3/78.
AAA—Mon thru Fri 5:30-10 am & 3-8 pm.
AA—Mon thru Fri 10 am-3 pm; Sat 5:30 am-8 pm; Sun 11 am-8 pm.
A—Mon thru Sat 8 pm-midnight.

**6. SPOT ANNOUNCEMENTS**

| | 1 min | | | | 30 sec | | | |
|---|---|---|---|---|---|---|---|---|
| | 1 ti | 6 ti | 12 ti | 18 ti | 1 ti | 6 ti | 12 ti | 18 ti |
| AAA | 105 | 115 | 95 | 95 | 84 | 80 | 76 | 76 |
| AA | 90 | 85 | 80 | 75 | 72 | 68 | 64 | 60 |
| A | 75 | 70 | 65 | 60 | 60 | 56 | 52 | 48 |

10 sec: 50% of 1-min.

**7. PACKAGE PLANS**
WEEKLY ENTERTAINMENT PLAN I—
1/2AAA, 1/2AA

| | 10 ti | 16 ti | 20 ti | 24 ti |
|---|---|---|---|---|
| 1 min | 90 | 80 | 70 | 60 |
| 30 sec | 72 | 64 | 56 | 48 |

WEEKLY ENTERTAINMENT PLAN II—
1/3AAA, 1/3AA, 1/3A

| | 12 ti | 15 ti | 21 ti | 24 ti |
|---|---|---|---|---|
| 1 min | 80 | 70 | 60 | 50 |
| 30 sec | 64 | 56 | 48 | 40 |

10 sec: 50% of 1-min. Preemptible.

**8. PARTICIPATING PROGRAMS**
LARRY KING SHOW—MON-FRI 11 PM-4:30 AM

| | 1 ti | 6 ti | 12 ti |
|---|---|---|---|
| 1 min | | 30 | 28 | 25 |
| 30 sec | | 24 | 22 | 20 |

Submitted by William J. Lemanski.

### 1961
### SKOKIE

**Torbet Radio**

(This is a paid duplicate of the listing appearing under Chicago Urban Area.)
Media Code 4 214 2940 8.00
Radio Skokie Valley, Inc., A Bonneville Station. 4849 Golf Rd., Skokie, Ill. 60076. Phone 312-677-5900.
Send all copy to Skokie address.
Sales Office: John Hancock Center, 875 N. Michigan Ave., Chicago, Ill. 60611. Phone 312-787-4226.

**STATION'S PROGRAMMING DESCRIPTION**
WCLR: Programmed for adults.
MUSIC: foreground MOR presented by AIR PERSONALITIES. Contact Representative for further details. Rec'd 7/27/78.

---

**1. PERSONNEL**
President—Miller R. Gardner.
General Sales Manager—Chet Redpath.
National Sales Manager—Chuck Tweedle.
**2. REPRESENTATIVES**
Torbet Radio, Inc.
**3. FACILITIES**
ERP 3,000 w. (horiz.), 3,000 w. (vert.); 101.9 mc. Stereo.
Operating schedule: 24 hours daily. CST.
Antenna ht.: 1,500 ft. above average terrain.
**4. AGENCY COMMISSION**
15/0 time only.
**5. GENERAL ADVERTISING See coded regulations**
General: 2a.
*Rate Protection: 10, 11, 12, 13, 14.
Cancellation: 70c.
(*) 60 days.
Affiliated with Torbet Network.

**TIME RATES**
NATIONAL AND LOCAL RATES SAME
No. 5 Eff 5/26/78—Rec'd 7/27/78.
AAA—Mon thru Sun 5:30 am-8 pm.
AA—Mon thru Sun 8 pm-1 am.
A—Mon thru Sun 1-5:30 am.

**6. SPOT ANNOUNCEMENTS**

| PER WK: | 1 min | | | 30 sec | | |
|---|---|---|---|---|---|---|
| | 12 ti | 18 ti | 24 ti | 12 ti | 18 ti | 24 ti |
| AAA | 120 | 105 | 96 | 84 | 72 |
| AA | 50 | 45 | 40 | 40 | 36 | 32 |
| A | 20 | 18 | 17 | 16 | 14 | 13 |

| | 10 sec | | |
|---|---|---|---|
| | 12 ti | 18 ti | 24 ti |
| AAA | 60 | 53 | 45 |
| AA | 25 | 23 | 20 |
| AA | 10 | 9 | 8 |

Fixed position, extra 25%.
Subject to short rate if frequency not earned.
Higher unit rate preempts TAP.

**7. PACKAGE PLANS**
TAP—1/2AAA, 1/2AA:

| | 1 min | 30 sec | 10 sec |
|---|---|---|---|
| 12 ti | 720 | 576 | 360 |
| 18 ti | 990 | 792 | 504 |
| 24 ti | 1200 | 960 | 600 |

Fixed position, extra 25%.
Subject to short rate if frequency not earned.
Higher unit rate preempts TAP.

**10. SPECIAL FEATURES**
Newscasts—1-1/2x 1-min.
Submitted by Chuck Tweedle.

(D)

## WCRW
### 1926

Media Code 4 214 1815 3.00
WCRW, Inc., Embassy Hotel, 2756 Pine Grove Ave Chicago, Ill. 60614. Phone 312-327-6860.
1 min rate 1x: 15.00.

**AN ABC OWNED RADIO STATION**

### WDAI (FM)
### 1946

**Katz Radio**

An ABC Station
Media Code 4 214 1835 1.00
American Broadcasting Co., Inc., a division of American Broadcasting Companies, Inc., 360 N. Michigan Ave., Chicago, Ill. 60601. Phone 312-782-6811. TWX 910-221-0243.
See affiliated AM station for additional information.
AM facilities: WLS.

(This listing continued on next page)

---

These listings appeared in Standard Rate & Data Service's *Spot Radio Rates and Data.* This book contains profiles of approximately 4,350 AM stations and 2,100 FM stations, including basic buying information on program types, special features, rates, commissions, and representatives. In addition, state, county, city, and metro area data are given, along with market data on population, households, income, and retail sales. There are also market maps and information on farm, foreign-language, and black programming.

drivers get to work, we can concentrate on reaching people who are getting ready for the day's shopping. Late afternoon is prime time for FM progressive rock when young listeners are out of school. In agricultural areas, farmers listen early in the morning for news of livestock and grain prices.

## Network radio

A network is a group of radio stations permanently connected by telephone lines. This connection makes it possible for the advertiser's message to be broadcast simultaneously over all the stations in the network. The network may be national or regional and is usually composed of a number of company-owned stations together with independent stations that have contracted for network programming. There are four national radio networks —Columbia Broadcasting System, National Broadcasting Company, Mutual Broadcasting System, and American Broadcasting Company. Some regional networks are the Beck-Ross Group, the Groskin Group, and the Intermountain Network. Most of the state networks are rural and, for the most part, specialize in farm news. These are not true networks as we use the term to describe the CBS network or the NBC network. Regional networks are groups of independent stations that are assembled as a "package" by a station representative as a convenience for advertisers. These stations are not linked together electronically.

Local stations that affiliate with a network enjoy the benefit of programs generated by the network—sponsored as well as sustaining—often featuring top talent. A sponsored program is one that is paid for by one or more advertisers. A sustaining program is one that has no advertisers; it is generally provided by a network to build an audience

in the expectation that a sponsor will become interested. In return, the network has an option on part of the local station's time, generally the choicest hours. Network radio programming consists primarily of news-on-the-hour, although some sports programming and some personality programming is available. Network programming is generally adult-oriented. Network radio carries only 4.3 percent of all radio advertising, while spot radio accounts for 95.7 percent.

Network radio is not as selective as spot radio, but it does offer greater reach. The CBS radio network, for example, claims an audience of 2,400,130 adults (18+) from 6 to 10 AM every weekday. From 7 PM to midnight on Saturday night, which is the least listened to time period, a spot on CBS will still reach 475,000 adults (18+). This reach makes network radio very attractive to national advertisers. Food, automobile, and drug manufacturers are the primary users of network radio. Food, automotive service, and travel companies are the heaviest users of spot radio.

## Radio audiences

In examining a description of the audience for any particular radio station, the advertiser is most interested in the station's *coverage*—the number of homes that can pick up the station clearly. *Circulation* represents the number of homes that *actually tune in* to that station. *Coverage* depends on the power of the station's transmitter, the location and height of its antenna, the transmission frequency, and the terrain. Although at night AM radio covers a larger area owing to the effect of sky waves, no advertiser can count on this circulation. The national advertiser can only consider it a bonus. The *circulation* of a program depends on whether it is broad-

Group W is not a network but a group of radio stations owned by the same management. In this ad, Group W points out that in a survey of listeners made by the Advertising Research Bureau, six of their stations appeared among the most listened to radio stations during drive time. Drive time is radio's most important time period.

cast during the day or at night, the nature of the program, and the nature of competitive programs (including those on television) in the same time slot.

A media analyst wants to be able to compare and evaluate alternative station mixes. One of the factors that any analyst must consider in evaluating a mix is the *cumulative audience* of each station. The *cume,* as it is usually called, is a term devised by the Nielsen service to describe the net cumulative audience of a single program or of an entire spot schedule over a four-week period. The idea is that if a person tunes in to station Y every morning, he or she will be counted only *once.* Audience accumulation measures the number of different people that are exposed to the program. Some media people describe this factor as the station's reach. *Reach* generally refers to the net unduplicated audience of a campaign. In practice, however, both cume and reach are used interchangeably to indicate the number of people covered by a station or a program.

### GRPs: gross rating points

In an effort to simplify comparison between stations and station combinations, media planners use a measurement system known as *gross rating points* (GRPs). A gross rating point is an index figure that represents 1 percent of the total audience of radio listeners (or television viewers) within a specified market area or geographical area. If, for example, a particular program were heard by 10 percent of all the radio listeners in San Francisco, a commercial that ran on that program would have a rating of 10 GRPs. If the program were broadcast twice a week, the GRPs for that commercial would be 20. GRPs provide us with a method for measuring the *weight* of our broadcast campaign. For example, if we were considering

using a media package consisting of 1 commercial on 3 different programs, each with a 12-point rating, and 1 commercial on 4 different programs with 6-point ratings each, we can calculate its weight as:

$$
\begin{aligned}
3 \text{ commercials} \times 12 \text{ rating} &= 36 \text{ GRPs} \\
4 \text{ commercials} \times \phantom{0}6 \text{ rating} &= 24 \text{ GRPs} \\
\text{TOTAL} &= \overline{60 \text{ GRPs}}
\end{aligned}
$$

We can then compare the total GRPs offered by this package to those offered by alternate combinations. Please note that a total rating of 60 GRPs does not mean that we will reach 60 percent of the audience; GRPs measure *gross*, not *net* audience. That is, the GRP figures contain duplications: listeners who tuned in to two, three, or even all seven of the programs. The package's unduplicated audience will be indicated by its cume.

### Buying radio time

Compared to the cost of other media, radio time is inexpensive. If we can buy time on programs that reach our target market, then spot radio is exceptionally cost efficient. A sixty-second network commercial during drive time might cost from $2,200 to $3,400 and might be broadcast over as many as 200 stations, mostly adult oriented. Compare that figure with a cost of approximately $60,000 for a sixty-second commercial on prime time television or about $75,000 for the cost of a four-color page in a leading consumer magazine.

Stations generally have about eighteen minutes an hour available for advertising. Time is sold, for the most part, on the basis of spot announcements in units of sixty, thirty, twenty, or ten seconds. Stations offer quantity discounts with rates based on the total number of announcements

A rate card for a radio station. Notice how WMAQ has broken up the day into parts and has provided discounts for specific frequency contracts (6X, 12X, 18X, 24X). Notice, too, the difference between AM DRIVE rates and OVERNIGHT rates, based on the size of the listening audience.

# WMAQ Radio 670

Merchandise Mart / Chicago. Ill. 60654 / 312-861-5555

WMAQ

### RATE CARD #35        EFFECTIVE 1/1/79

Announcement Rates (One-Minute/150 Word Commercials)

| FREQUENCY:<br>LENGTH: | 1X<br>:60 | 1X<br>:30 | 6X<br>:60 | 6X<br>:30 | 12X<br>:60 | 12X<br>:30 | 18X<br>:60 | 18X<br>:30 | 24X<br>:60 | 24X<br>:30 |
|---|---|---|---|---|---|---|---|---|---|---|
| AM DRIVE (5:30-10AM MON-SAT) | 285 | 215 | 272 | 217 | 260 | 208 | 246 | 196 | | |
| PM DRIVE (3PM-7PM MON-FRI) | 259 | 208 | 246 | 197 | 233 | 188 | 220 | 175 | | |
| MIDDAY/WK-ND DRIVE M-F(10AM-3PM)<br>(10AM-7PM SAT & SUN) | 221 | 178 | 208 | 166 | 194 | 156 | 181 | 145 | 168 | 134 |
| EVENING (7PM-12MID MON-SUN) | 168 | 136 | 156 | 124 | 143 | 114 | 130 | 103 | 116 | 94 |
| OVERNIGHT (12MID-5AM TUE-SAT) | 97 | 78 | 86 | 70 | 76 | 60 | 65 | 52 | 54 | 43 |

TOTAL AUDIENCE PLANS: (Limited Substitutions as Availabilities Permit)

| FREQUENCY:<br>LENGTH: | 6X<br>:60 | 6X<br>:30 | 12X<br>:60 | 12X<br>:30 | 18X<br>:60 | 18X<br>:30 | 24X<br>:60 | 24X<br>:30 |
|---|---|---|---|---|---|---|---|---|
| AM DRIVE | 1@ 217 | 174 | 2@ 206 | 166 | 3@ 197 | 158 | 4@ 197 | 158 |
| PM DRIVE | 1@ 197 | 158 | 2@ 187 | 150 | 3@ 175 | 140 | 4@ 175 | 140 |
| MIDDAY/WEEKEND DRIVE | 2@ 166 | 132 | 4@ 156 | 124 | 6@ 145 | 116 | 8@ 134 | 108 |
| EVENING | 2@ 124 | 100 | 4@ 114 | 90 | 6@ 103 | 83 | 8@ 93 | 74 |

| WEEKLY TOTALS | 994 | 796 | 1866 | 1488 | 2604 | 2088 | 3304 | 2648 |
|---|---|---|---|---|---|---|---|---|

WEEKEND DRIVE PLANS (ROS 7PM FRI - 7PM MON)

| | | | | | | | | | | | |
|---|---|---|---|---|---|---|---|---|---|---|---|
| 60's | 10X | @ | 156 | = | $1,560 | 20X | @ | 130 | = | $2,600 | 30X @ 97 = $2,910 |
| 30's | 10X | @ | 124 | = | $1,240 | 20X | @ | 103 | = | $2,060 | 30X @ 78 = $2,340 |

SPONSORSHIPS                 30 SECOND RATES ARE 80% OF MINUTE RATES.
NEWS
SPORTS                         10 SECOND RATES ARE 60% OF MINUTE RATES.
WEATHER
TRAFFIC                       CANCELLATION REQUIRES 2 WEEKS NOTICE.

RATES FURNISHED UPON REQUEST

scheduled during the year. Rates vary with the time of day, and stations designate their time periods as Class AA, Class A, Class B, and so on. The most expensive time, Class AA, might be 6 to 10 AM, Monday through Friday. That's drive time. Class C might be 7 PM to midnight. Each station determines its own classes, basing them on the listening characteristics of its audience. A classical music FM station might find its major audience from 7 to 11 PM, Monday through Friday. A farm station might find its prime time very early in the morning when its audience tunes in for weather, crop, and livestock reports.

Most stations offer *package plans* that represent a number of spots broadcast within a consecutive seven-day period on an *ROS*, or *run of station*, schedule. ROS is for radio what ROP is for newspapers: radio station programmers may schedule the commercial at whatever time is most convenient for them. For the advertiser who wants to specify the program, stations offer special features with high audience attention, such as five-minute news reports, late headlines, stock market reports, traffic 'copter reports, or time signal announcements (IDs). The ID (station identification) consists of twelve words or six seconds. Many time slot arrangements are not listed on a station's rate card and very often radio time is negotiated.

# Television

Although there were five television stations in the United States that regularly broadcast programs in the late 1930s, the Federal Trade Commission did not authorize the use of television as an advertising medium until 1941. In 1941 there were only about 10,000 television sets in use. By 1978, however, 72.9 million homes had television, and 46 percent of those had more than one set. Television has become the favorite medium of national advertisers, receiving 75.3 percent of *their* advertising dollars. This percentage amounts to well over $4 billion, or almost half of the $8.8 billion invested in television advertising in 1978.

The rapid rise of the television industry and its continued success today are for the most part due to the characteristics of the medium itself. Television delivers sight, sound, motion, and color. The television set is, for many families, the focal point of the living room. The average household spends six hours and forty-nine minutes a day viewing television.[2] Television also demands and usually receives the full attention of its audience. Radio listeners sometimes work, drive, or study (if possible) while listening. Not so with television. In short, television offers advertisers impact, the power to stimulate people to take action.

## UHF, VHF, and cable

VHF (Very High Frequency) television is represented by channels 2–13. UHF (Ultra High Frequency) channels are 14–74. VHF stations usually have a greater range of broadcast coverage. UHF stations cover a smaller area. There are 515 VHF stations and 210 UHF stations in the United States.

The problem of clear reception has been solved for many viewers through the use of cable television, which uses telephone transmission lines to bring excellent viewing to nearly 13 million subscribers—about 18 percent of all television homes.

---

[2] "TV Basics 21," Television Bureau of Advertising, 1977.

The concentric circles on this coverage map for a television station in Orlando, Florida, show the broadcast range of the station. The circle defines the station's Grade A area, and the outer circle, Grade B. Notice that the Area of Dominant Influence (ADI) for the Orlando—Daytona Beach Market is larger than the Metro area. Notice also that the lower left-hand portion of the station's Grade B area is not included in the ADI. That area is probably included in the Tampa—St. Petersburg ADI.

## The television audience

The terms used to describe the television audience are the same as those used for the radio audience. *Coverage* refers to the number of homes that *receive* the television signal. *Circulation* describes the number of homes that *actually tune in* on the signal. The ability of any station to provide coverage depends on the power of its transmitter, the height of its transmitter antenna, the kind of terrain over which the signal must pass, and the frequency of the signal. The lower the frequency, the greater the carrying power. Coverage for cable TV is limited to the number of its subscribers.

Television stations usually provide advertisers with a map indicating their signal strength in a market. The strongest signal is designated *Grade A,* generally the primary market area surrounding the station. The secondary area coverage is designated *Grade B.* These measurements (of signal strength) are useful in determining coverage. Another way to gauge coverage is to mail a questionnaire to a selected sample of homes within, and outside of, a station's A and B areas. The questionnaire asks respondents to list the stations they view regularly. From the replies, estimates are made of how many homes in each area are covered by the station's signal. *Gross rating points* are another criterion advertisers use to determine the size of the audience within a specified market area or geographic region.

The characteristics of the station's audience are determined by the program, the time of day, the time of the year, and the competing programs. Television today is received by 98 percent of all households in the United States. The most popular viewing time—*prime time*—is between the hours of 7:30 and 11 PM, Monday through Sunday. The next most popular time is 4:30 to 7:30 PM, Monday through Sunday. Third most popular is 7:00 AM to 4:30 PM, Monday through Friday. Although the demographics may vary somewhat, specific time slots will deliver a predictable audience.

Like the editorial content of a magazine, the program format of a television station to a large extent determines its audience. In fact, individual programs may have their viewing audiences enhanced by carry-overs from the previous programs. But, unlike the reader of a magazine or newspaper, who may be exposed to all the messages in a single issue, the television viewer can watch only one program at a time. A popular program on one station may reduce the size of the audience on another station. Although the size of the potential audience is very large, each program will attract only a modest percentage of the total. When advertisers use television to reach only certain segments, they pay for considerable waste. Nevertheless, on a CPM basis, television is not expensive. The calculation of CPM is as follows:

**1.** when based on homes

$$CPM = \frac{\text{cost of 1 unit of time} \times 1{,}000}{\substack{\text{number of homes reached by} \\ \text{a program or time period}}}$$

**2.** when based on audience

$$CPM = \frac{\text{cost of 1 unit of time} \times 1{,}000}{\substack{\text{number of prospects reached by} \\ \text{a program or time period}}}$$

As was the case in describing a radio station's audience, we are concerned here with a television program's *cumulative audience.* The value of the term may be clarified with an explanation. If a

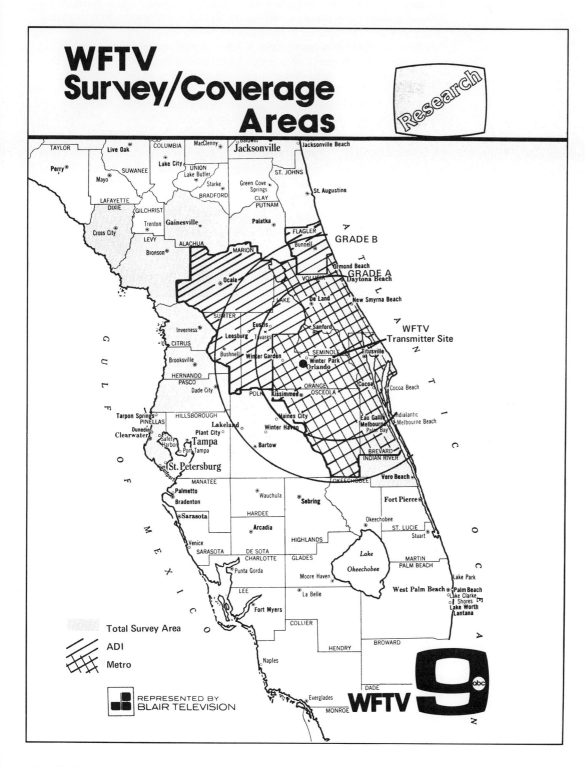

# WFTV Survey/Coverage Areas

Research

WFTV 9 abc
WFTV
REPRESENTED BY BLAIR TELEVISION

Total Survey Area
ADI
Metro

woman reading *Good Housekeeping* looks into the same issue fifteen different times in a month, she is counted only once.[3] Magazine audience accumulation is measured by total audience—the *number of people* who buy or subscribe to the magazine. In broadcast we measure the *number of households* that tuned in to a program at least once over a four-week period. The figure may be expressed as a percentage of all television homes or as the number of homes tuned in during the four-week period. What the figure tells us is the *reach* of the program (how many homes) as well as the frequency (how often the same people are reached).

## Network television

There are three national television networks—the American Broadcasting Company, the Columbia Broadcasting System, and the National Broadcasting Company. Unlike radio programming, most television prime-time programming is network. The three networks themselves own a total of fifteen stations; the remainder of the stations in the networks are affiliates. Network television offers its advertisers several advantages. Buying network time allows the advertiser to control the commercial so that it is delivered uniformly and efficiently to all the stations in the network. Network programs enhance the images of their advertisers. The network may not have the strongest station or affiliate in each market, but it will favor advertisers who buy the full network lineup with preference in choice of time slots and, in some cases, better rates. However, network television does have one major

limitation. Unlike print media, which can expand their publications to accommodate more advertisers, network television has only a certain amount of time per hour available for advertising. If advertiser A buys the 8 PM slot, there is no other 8 PM slot for advertiser B on that network.

Programs today are either developed by the network or bought by the network from a package house. A *package house* is an independent movie-producing company that creates and produces television shows—from a single special to an entire series.

Few advertisers today can afford to be the sole sponsor of a television program. Most buy *participations*, which means that the available commercial time on one program is divided up among a number of different advertisers in thirty- and sixty-second units. The announcements are made within the context of the program instead of between programs at station-break times. It is better to have the commercial aired *during* the program. The most popular time unit with advertisers is thirty seconds, because it enables them to spread their media budget over several different programs to reach different segments of the population. It is also possible to buy ten-, twenty-, or thirty-second spots on programs initiated by local stations. The ten-second spot is merely an ID (station identification). Of the time periods that precede and follow a regular network television program, usually two minutes are available for local or spot advertisers. These time slots are called *adjacencies.*

## Spot television

Spot television is local station programming for sale in local markets. These stations may be affiliated with a network and carry network programming at

---

[3] A study by Target Group Index in 1977 indicated that the average time spent reading *Good Housekeeping* was about ninety-five minutes.

# Georgia  —CONTINUED

| COUNTY NAME | TOTAL HOUSEHOLDS | TELEVISION HOUSEHOLDS | TV % | CTY SZE | ADI MARKET ASSIGNMENT |
|---|---|---|---|---|---|
| DOOLY | 3,500 | 3,300 | 95 | D | COLUMBUS, GA |
| DOUGHERTY | 28,700 | 27,800 | 97 | C | ALBANY, GA |
| DOUGLAS | 15,800 | 15,500 | 98 | A | ATLANTA |
| EARLY | 4,100 | 3,900 | 94 | D | DOTHAN |
| ECHOLS | 500 | 500 | 92 | D | TALLAHASSEE |
| EFFINGHAM | 4,700 | 4,500 | 96 | B | SAVANNAH |
| ELBERT | 6,100 | 5,900 | 97 | D | GREENVILLE-SPARTANBURG-ASHEVILLE |
| EMANUEL | 6,800 | 6,400 | 95 | D | AUGUSTA |
| EVANS | 2,900 | 2,800 | 96 | D | SAVANNAH |
| FANNIN | 4,800 | 4,600 | 95 | D | CHATTANOOGA |
| FAYETTE | 5,900 | 5,700 | 97 | A | ATLANTA |
| FLOYD | 26,700 | 26,000 | 97 | B | ATLANTA |
| FORSYTH | 7,100 | 7,000 | 98 | A | ATLANTA |
| FRANKLIN | 4,700 | 4,600 | 97 | D | GREENVILLE-SPARTANBURG-ASHEVILLE |
| FULTON | 212,300 | 208,400 | 98 | A | ATLANTA |
| GILMER | 3,500 | 3,300 | 95 | D | ATLANTA |
| GLASCOCK | 700 | 700 | 95 | D | AUGUSTA |
| GLYNN | 15,500 | 15,000 | 97 | C | JACKSONVILLE |
| GORDON | 9,600 | 9,300 | 97 | D | ATLANTA |
| GRADY | 6,400 | 6,200 | 96 | D | TALLAHASSEE |
| GREENE | 3,300 | 3,100 | 95 | D | ATLANTA |
| GWINNETT | 42,200 | 41,400 | 98 | A | ATLANTA |
| HABERSHAM | 7,900 | 7,600 | 96 | D | ATLANTA |
| HALL | 22,700 | 22,100 | 97 | C | ATLANTA |
| HANCOCK | 2,600 | 2,400 | 92 | D | AUGUSTA |
| HARALSON | 6,300 | 6,100 | 97 | D | ATLANTA |
| HARRIS | 3,700 | 3,500 | 95 | C | COLUMBUS, GA |
| HART | 5,500 | 5,300 | 97 | D | GREENVILLE-SPARTANBURG-ASHEVILLE |
| HEARD | 2,100 | 2,000 | 96 | D | ATLANTA |
| HENRY | 9,200 | 8,900 | 96 | A | ATLANTA |
| HOUSTON | 23,000 | 22,500 | 98 | C | MACON |
| IRWIN | 2,800 | 2,700 | 95 | D | ALBANY, GA |
| JACKSON | 8,100 | 7,800 | 97 | D | ATLANTA |
| JASPER | 2,200 | 2,100 | 94 | D | ATLANTA |
| JEFF DAVIS | 3,600 | 3,400 | 95 | D | SAVANNAH |
| JEFFERSON | 5,000 | 4,700 | 95 | D | AUGUSTA |
| JENKINS | 2,800 | 2,700 | 95 | D | AUGUSTA |
| JOHNSON | 2,300 | 2,200 | 96 | D | AUGUSTA |
| JONES | 4,800 | 4,600 | 96 | B | MACON |
| LAMAR | 3,500 | 3,400 | 96 | D | ATLANTA |
| LANIER | 1,800 | 1,700 | 94 | D | ALBANY, GA |
| LAURENS | 11,500 | 10,900 | 94 | D | MACON |
| LEE | 2,900 | 2,700 | 95 | C | ALBANY, GA |
| LIBERTY | 5,300 | 5,100 | 96 | D | SAVANNAH |
| LINCOLN | 1,900 | 1,800 | 96 | D | AUGUSTA |
| LONG | 1,000 | 900 | 94 | D | SAVANNAH |
| LOWNDES | 20,200 | 19,300 | 96 | C | ALBANY, GA |
| LUMPKIN | 2,700 | 2,600 | 97 | D | ATLANTA |
| MC DUFFIE | 5,700 | 5,500 | 96 | D | AUGUSTA |
| MC INTOSH | 2,700 | 2,600 | 94 | D | SAVANNAH |
| MACON | 3,900 | 3,700 | 94 | D | COLUMBUS, GA |
| MADISON | 5,200 | 5,000 | 96 | D | GREENVILLE-SPARTANBURG-ASHEVILLE |
| MARION | 2,000 | 1,800 | 92 | D | COLUMBUS, GA |
| MERIWETHER | 5,900 | 5,600 | 95 | D | ATLANTA |
| MILLER | 1,800 | 1,700 | 94 | D | DOTHAN |
| MITCHELL | 5,900 | 5,600 | 95 | D | ALBANY, GA |
| MONROE | 3,500 | 3,400 | 96 | D | ATLANTA |
| MONTGOMERY | 1,900 | 1,700 | 92 | D | SAVANNAH |
| MORGAN | 3,000 | 2,800 | 95 | D | ATLANTA |
| MURRAY | 5,900 | 5,700 | 96 | D | CHATTANOOGA |
| MUSCOGEE | 56,200 | 55,000 | 98 | B | COLUMBUS, GA |
| NEWTON | 10,100 | 9,800 | 97 | A | ATLANTA |
| OCONEE | 3,100 | 3,000 | 98 | D | ATLANTA |
| OGLETHORPE | 2,400 | 2,300 | 95 | D | ATLANTA |
| PAULDING | 7,900 | 7,700 | 98 | A | ATLANTA |
| PEACH | 6,100 | 5,900 | 96 | D | MACON |
| PICKENS | 3,400 | 3,300 | 97 | D | ATLANTA |
| PIERCE | 3,200 | 3,000 | 95 | D | JACKSONVILLE |
| PIKE | 2,400 | 2,300 | 94 | D | ATLANTA |
| POLK | 10,700 | 10,400 | 97 | D | ATLANTA |
| PULASKI | 2,800 | 2,600 | 94 | D | MACON |
| PUTNAM | 2,600 | 2,500 | 96 | D | ATLANTA |
| QUITMAN | 600 | 600 | 94 | D | COLUMBUS, GA |
| RABUN | 3,300 | 3,100 | 95 | D | GREENVILLE-SPARTANBURG-ASHEVILLE |
| RANDOLPH | 3,000 | 2,800 | 94 | D | COLUMBUS, GA |

certain times of the day, or they may be independent stations that program their own day entirely. Costs for local spots will vary from market to market, depending on the size of the audience the station delivers. As a rule, spots in New York, Chicago, and Los Angeles are more expensive because of the size of the circulation in these markets. For example, in New York City a daytime spot (7 AM — 4:30 PM) costs $100 for thirty seconds, and a prime time spot (7:30 — 11 PM) costs $375 for thirty seconds. In Salt Lake City, however, a thirty-second daytime spot costs $8 and a thirty-second prime time spot costs $34. Even within prime time and daytime programming by networks, there are segments of the day set aside for local sale. There are, in any case, numerous opportunities for an advertiser to select specific time slots to reach the target audience.

Spot television is used by both national advertisers and regional advertisers. National advertisers use spot television to supplement their national programming, and regional advertisers use it because it is not practical for them to use network television. In 1977 national advertisers spent over $4.3 billion for television commercial time, with $2.7 billion for network television and $1.6 billion for spot television—roughly 63 percent network to 37 percent spot. A network advertiser can also use spot television to add extra weight to campaigns in certain markets that may not be satisfactorily covered by the network. Or they may use it to meet unique competitive situations—perhaps to add a certain local appeal that might be needed in some markets. Or, the advertiser may not be able to afford network television time and can use spot television to buy the top fifty markets that will reach 70 percent of the television homes in the country. Of course, the advertiser will not actually reach 70 percent of the homes; that figure represents the *poten-*

*tial.* It is also possible that a network program may not be as popular in some places as a local program on which spot time is available.

## Buying time

There are certain parts of the broadcast day that are programmed by the networks, which serve from 150 to 225 stations. The networks sell time to advertisers to run with specific programs. These programs are broadcast during various parts of the day, generally described as daytime, prime time, or late night.

Prime time (7:30 to 11 PM) is so called because of the large number of sets in use during this period. This time period tends to reach a family audience. Media costs for prime time are generally the highest of all three time periods. Individual program costs will vary, depending on the rating of the program. Prime time cost per thirty seconds is around $60,000.

Daytime network television (7 AM to 4:30 PM) is the least costly of network time periods. Cost per thirty seconds is in the range of $9,000—a very efficient cost for buying a largely female audience. Late night network programming generally consists of movies or talk shows. Rates for such programs— around $16,000 for thirty seconds—are much lower than for prime time programs. Although rating levels for late night programs are about the same as those for daytime, rates are higher because the audience consists of approximately equal numbers of men and women.

Sports programming, aimed at a primarily male market, often dominates network television on weekends. Beer, automobiles, and men's grooming aids are usually heavily advertised on weekend sports programs.

## Chicago—W L S-TV—Continued

Non-Orbit Spots: Advertisers purchasing non-orbit spots in positions which are part of an orbit, may be preempted by an orbit advertiser.
Splicing cost—15.00 net for each splicing request.

**Product Protection**
Station will endeavor to secure an 8 minute separation between competitive products, but no guarantees are made. Makegoods will only be offered to competitive advertisers running within the same commercial break. Under no circumstances will credit be given for a product conflict.

**6. TIME RATES**
Rates have been temporarily withdrawn by station.

**11. SPECIAL FEATURES**
COMMERCIALS ON VIDEO TAPE
45.00 charge for each duplicate made from master tape. Station will destroy video commercial material unless otherwise directed, 30 days after the last air date for that commercial.
COLOR
Schedules network color programs, film, tape and live. Equipped with high and low band VTR.

**13. CLOSING TIME**
72 hours prior film, slides and artwork.
Submitted by Constance Saville.

### W M A Q-TV
(Airdate October 3, 1948)

An NBC Station
Subscriber to the NAB Television Code
Media Code 6 214 0350 0.00
National Broadcasting Co., Inc., Merchandise Mart Plaza, Chicago, Ill. 60654. Phone 312-861-5555. TWX 312-222-0207.

**1. PERSONNEL**
Vice-Pres. & Gen'l Mgr.—Robert Walsh.
Station Manager—Albert Jerome.
Director of Sales—Jim Zafiros.
National Sales Manager—John Llewellyn.
Local Sales Manager—Richard Daggett.

**2. REPRESENTATIVES**
NBC Spot Television Sales.
Atlanta, Dallas, St. Louis — Bomar Lowrance & Associates, Inc.
Eastern Canada—NBC Spot Television Sales. (N. Y. office)
Oregon, Washington, Idaho & British Columbia—Katz Television, American.

**3. FACILITIES**
Video 40,100 w. (maximum power), audio 10,250 w. (maximum power); ch. 5.
Antenna ht.: 1,320 ft. above average terrain.
Operating schedule: Mon thru Sun. CST.

**4. AGENCY COMMISSION**
15% to recognized agencies on net time charges, studio charges, production services and station-built programs.

**5. GENERAL ADVERTISING See ceded regulations**
Rate Protection: 13 weeks rate protection from date of announcement of revised rates. 4 weeks rate protection from date of announcement on reclassification of Class AA time.
Notice of Renewal: An advertiser must notify the station of intent to renew 28 days prior to the expiration of a schedule.
Cancellation: Contracts for announcements are firm for the first 4 weeks. Contract subject to cancellation on 4 weeks or 4 telecasts prior notice.
Product Protection
While we strive to maintain 10-minute separation between competitive announcements, makegoods will only be offered to competitive advertisers running within the same commercial break. Protection is limited only to competitive products, or in the case of retail stores—only to competitive departments. In no case will credit be given for a product conflict—suitable makegoods will be offered. Station retains right to make final determination as to whether products or services are competitive.

**6. TIME RATES**
Rates have been temporarily withdrawn by station.

**11. SPECIAL FEATURES**
COLOR
Schedules network color, film, slides, tape and live. Equipped with high and low band VTR.

**13. CLOSING TIME**
All commercial materials, including copy, film, slides and artwork must be received 48 hours prior to air. Revisions become effective 24 working hours after receipt.

---

*Cross references, call letter or representative logotypes, corporate or network identification logotypes, boldface title headings (group or programming or network identification) are paid advertising services.*

R-TV-36z

---

### W S N S-TV
(Airdate date April 5, 1970)

**BB** Bolton Broadcasting Ltd.

A HarriScope Station
Media Code 6 214 0375 7.00
Video 44. A Joint Venture between Harriscope of Chicago, Inc. & Rivergrove Theatre Corp., Velma Entertainment Corp., Riverdale Drive-In. Inc., 430 W. Grant Place, Chicago, Ill. 60614. Phone 312-929-1200. TWX 910-221-1407.

**1. PERSONNEL**
Vice-Pres. & Gen'l Mgr.—Edward Morris.
Assistant General Manager—Mal Wyman.
Sales Manager—Dan Maslan.
Program Director—Peter Strand.

**2. REPRESENTATIVES**
Bolton Broadcasting, Ltd.
Canada—Andy McDermott Broadcast Sales Ltd.

**3. FACILITIES**
Video 2,500,000 w., audio 500,000 w.: ch 44.
Antenna ht. 1456 ft. above average terrain.
Operating schedule: 9 am-midnight Mon; 9:15 am-midnight Tues; 9:30-12:30 am Wed; 9-12:30 am Thurs; 9:15-1:30 am Fri; 6:30-1:30 am Sat; 7:30-12:30 am Sun. CST.

**4. AGENCY COMMISSION**
15% on time. Bills payable 15th of month following broadcast.

**5. GENERAL ADVERTISING See ceded regulations**
General: 1b, 2a, 2b, 3a, 3b, 3c, 3d, 4a, 5, 8.
Rate Protection: 10f, 11f, 12c, 13c, 14f.
Contracts: 20b, 21, 22b, 22c, 24b, 25, 29, 31b, 32d.
Basic Rates: 40a, 41b, 41c, 41d, 42, 43a, 45a, 46, 50.
Comb.. Cont. Discounts: 60a, 61b.
Cancellation: 70b, 70e, 71, 72.
Prod. Services: 80, 81, 82, 83, 84, 85, 86.
While the station will attempt to provide an 8 minute separation between competitive products, makegoods will only be offered to competitive products running within the same break. Protection is limited only to competitive products, or in the case of retail stores, only to competitive departments. In no case will credit be given for a product conflict, suitable makegoods will be offered. The station retains the right to make final determination as to whether products or services are competitive.
No product protection is granted in children's programming.

**6. TIME RATES**
No. 31 Eff 1/8/79—Rec'd 3/8/79.

**7. SPOT ANNOUNCEMENTS**

SECTION I

| | A | B | C | D | E | F |
|---|---|---|---|---|---|---|
| 60 sec | 580 | 540 | 500 | 460 | 420 | 380 |
| 30 sec | 300 | 280 | 260 | 240 | 220 | 200 |
| 10 sec | 160 | 150 | 140 | 130 | 120 | 110 |

SECTION II

| | A | B | C | D | E | F |
|---|---|---|---|---|---|---|
| 60 sec | 480 | 440 | 400 | 360 | 320 | 280 |
| 30 sec | 250 | 230 | 210 | 190 | 170 | 150 |
| 10 sec | 135 | 125 | 115 | 105 | 95 | 85 |

SECTION III

| | A | B | C | D | E | F |
|---|---|---|---|---|---|---|
| 60 sec | 380 | 340 | 300 | 260 | 220 | 180 |
| 30 sec | 200 | 180 | 160 | 140 | 120 | 100 |
| 10 sec | 110 | 100 | 90 | 80 | 70 | 60 |

Section I—Fixed.
Section II—Subject to preemption on 1 week notice by section I.
Section III—Subject to immediate preemption without notice.

**8. PARTICIPATING ANNOUNCEMENT PROGRAMS**
Rec'd 3/8/79.

| MON THRU FRI, PM: | Code |
|---|---|
| Munsters—noon-12:30 | D |
| I Love Lucy—12:30-1 | A |
| One O'Clock Movie—1-3 | C |
| The Beatles—3-3:30 | B |
| Fun World of Hanna Barbera—3:30-4 | A |
| Spectrum—4-4:30 | A |
| Speed Racer—4:30-5 | A |
| Rookies—5-6 | A |
| Bonanza—6-7 | A |
| Hazel—7-7:30 | A |
| Gomer Pyle—7:30-8 | A |
| Room 222—9:30-10 Tues, Thurs & Fri | C |
| Coping—9:30-10, 1 per mo (Mon) | C |
| Dimensions—9:30-10 Wed | C |
| Get Smart—10-10:30 | A |
| Untouchables—10:30-11 Mon thru Thurs | A |
| Monster Rally Movie—10:30-concl Fri | A |
| Burns & Allen—11:30 pm-midnight Mon thru Thurs | A |
| SAT, PM: | |
| Monster Movie 1—1-2:30 | B |
| Monster Movie 2—2:30-4 | B |
| It Takes a Thief—4-5 | B |
| Bonanza—5-6 | A |
| Dragnet—6-6:30 | A |
| Science Fiction Theatre—6:30-7 | A |
| Seven O'Clock Movie—7-9 | B |
| Journey to Adventure—9:30-10 | C |
| Get Smart—10-10:30 | B |
| Saturday Night Movie—10:30 pm-12:30 am | B |
| SUN: | |
| Wrestling—11 am-noon | B |
| PM: | |
| Outer Limits—noon-1 | B |
| Thing Theatre—1-3 | B |
| Capt. Fathom—3-3:30 | B |
| Popeye—3:30-4 | B |
| New 3 Stooges—4-4:30 | B |
| The Beatles—4:30-5 | B |
| King Kong—5-5:30 | B |
| Mighty Hercules—5:30-6 | B |
| Sunday Night Movie—10:30 pm-12:30 am | B |

**11. SPECIAL FEATURES**
COLOR
Schedules film slides, tape and live.
Equipped with high and low band VTR.

---

**13. CLOSING TIME**
1 work week preceding 1st broadcast for film, copy, slides and artwork.
Submitted by Dan F. Maslan.

### DANVILLE
Vermilion County—Map Location G-6
See SRDS consumer market map and data at beginning of the State.

## See Champaign-Urbana-Springfield-Decatur-Danville Area

### DECATUR
Macon County—Map Location E-6
See SRDS consumer market map and data at beginning of the State.

## See Champaign-Urbana-Springfield-Decatur-Danville Area

### FREEPORT
Stephenson County—Map Location D-2.
See SRDS consumer market map and data at beginning of the State.

## See Rockford (including Freeport)

### HARRISBURG
Saline County—Map Location F-10
See SRDS consumer market map and data at beginning of the State.

## See Paducah (Ky.)-Cape Girardeau (Mo.)-Harrisburg (Ill.) Area

### MOLINE
(3 Paid Cross References)
Rock Island County—Map Location C-3
See SRDS consumer market map and data at beginning of the State.

## See Davenport (Iowa)-Rock Island-Moline (Ill.)

### W H B F-TV
City of license, Rock Island, Ill.
Affiliated with CBS Television Network.
See listing under Davenport (Iowa)-Rock Island-Moline (Ill.), Iowa.

### W O C-TV
City of license, Davenport, Iowa.
Considered by NBC Television Network as their Davenport-Rock Island-Moline outlet.
See listing under Davenport (Iowa)-Rock Island-Moline (Ill.), Iowa.

### W Q A D-TV
City of license, Moline, Illinois.
Considered by ABC Television Network as their Davenport, Rock Island, Moline outlet.
See listing under Davenport (Iowa)-Rock Island-Moline (Ill.), Iowa.

### PEORIA (3 Stations)
Peoria County—Map Location D-5
See SRDS consumer market map and data at beginning of the State.

### W E E K-TV
(Airdate February 1, 1953)

NBC Television Network

A Mid America Television Co. Station
Subscriber to the NAB Television Code
Media Code 6 214 0400 3.00
Mid-America Television Co., 2907 Springfield Rd., East Peoria, Ill. 61611. Phone 309-699-3961. TWX 910-652-4455.

**1. PERSONNEL**
President—William A. Bates.
General Manager—William E. Adams.
National Sales Manager—Sam Taylor.

**2. REPRESENTATIVES**
Katz Television, Continental.

**3. FACILITIES**
Video 1,000,000 w. audio 200,000 w.; ch 25
Antenna ht.: 710 ft. above average terrain.
Operating schedule: 7 am-midnight. CST.

## TOP 100 NATIONAL AND REGIONAL SPOT TELEVISION ADVERTISERS
### 1977

| 1977 rank | | Est. net time sales 1977 | 1977 rank | | Est. net time sales 1977 | 1977 rank | | Est. net time sales 1977 |
|---|---|---|---|---|---|---|---|---|
| 1. | Procter & Gamble | $114,624,600 | 41. | Philip Morris Inc. | $10,376,200 | 81. | GRT Corp. | $5,663,300 |
| 2. | General Foods | 67,561,200 | 42. | RCA Corp. | 10,211,200 | 82. | H&R Block | 5,571,900 |
| 3. | PepsiCo Inc. | 37,762,100 | 43. | Esmark | 9,972,800 | 83. | Crane-Norris Marketing | 5,558,600 |
| 4. | General Mills | 36,205,000 | 44. | K-Tel International | 9,944,800 | 84. | Stroh Brewery | 5,472,900 |
| 5. | Lever Bros. | 35,926,400 | 45. | Volkswagenwerk A.G. | 9,588,500 | 85. | Oldsmobile Auto Dlrs. Assn. | 5,467,200 |
| 6. | American Home Prod. | 35,248,200 | 46. | American Dairy Assn. | 9,470,800 | 86. | Kimberly Clark Corp. | 5,426,500 |
| 7. | Colgate-Palmolive | 34,256,100 | 47. | Standard Oil (Ind.) | 8,865,000 | 87. | Union Oil Co. of Calif. | 5,410,000 |
| 8. | Wm. Wrigley Jr. Co. | 31,978,900 | 48. | CBS Inc. | 8,814,700 | 88. | E. & J. Gallo Winery | 5,395,100 |
| 9. | Chrysler Corp. | 29,790,200 | 49. | Ford Auto Dlrs. Assn. | 8,809,100 | 89. | American Motors | 5,313,900 |
| 10. | AT&T | 28,970,700 | 50. | Sterling Drug | 8,677,900 | 90. | H. J. Heinz Co. | 5,262,900 |
| 11. | Kraftco Corp. | 28,330,200 | 51. | Audio Research | 8,660,800 | 91. | Clorox Co. | 5,120,100 |
| 12. | Ford Motor Co. | 28,033,600 | 52. | Ralston Purina | 8,524,600 | 92. | American Express Co. | 5,095,600 |
| 13. | Coca-Cola Co. | 27,263,400 | 53. | Consolidated Foods | 8,388,800 | 93. | Dodge Auto Dlrs. Assn. | 5,087,600 |
| 14. | General Motors | 26,713,400 | 54. | Ideal Toy Corp. | 8,366,000 | 94. | Olympia Brewing Co. | 4,994,500 |
| 15. | ITT | 26,427,900 | 55. | Ronco Teleproducts | 8,109,600 | 95. | Pillsbury Co. | 4,946,200 |
| 16. | A. H. Robins Co. | 21,880,600 | 56. | American Can | 8,052,800 | 96. | Phillips Petroleum Co. | 4,942,900 |
| 17. | Nestle Co. | 21,530,600 | 57. | Richardson-Merrell | 7,996,500 | 97. | Heublein Inc. | 4,940,900 |
| 18. | Warner-Lambert | 20,158,600 | 58. | Anheuser-Busch Inc. | 7,995,500 | 98. | Dr. Pepper Co. | 4,873,200 |
| 19. | Bristol-Myers Co. | 18,940,800 | 59. | Campbell Soup Co. | 7,844,700 | 99. | Melville Corp. | 4,761,200 |
| 20. | Mattel | 18,813,500 | 60. | Seven-Up Co. | 7,794,700 | 100. | Squibb Corp. | 4,686,200 |
| 21. | Time Inc. | 18,225,000 | 61. | Trans World Airlines | 7,739,300 | | | |
| 22. | Mars Inc. | 18,129,300 | 62. | Royal Crown Cola | 7,643,900 | | | |
| 23. | Borden Inc. | 17,221,000 | 63. | Chesebrough-Pond's | 7,368,100 | | | |
| 24. | Kellogg Co. | 17,122,700 | 64. | Carnation Co. | 7,366,400 | | | |
| 25. | Quaker Oats Co. | 17,016,900 | 65. | Standard Brands | 7,202,400 | | | |
| 26. | Triangle Publications | 14,954,400 | 66. | UAL Inc. | 7,043,700 | | | |
| 27. | Dial Media | 14,176,100 | 67. | Alberto-Culver | 6,930,200 | | | |
| 28. | Beatrice Foods | 13,725,100 | 68. | Standard Oil Co. (Cal.) | 6,896,100 | | | |
| 29. | Scott Paper Co. | 13,527,100 | 69. | Block Drug Co. | 6,840,700 | | | |
| 30. | Toyota Motor Dist. | 13,294,800 | 70. | Schering-Plough | 6,618,900 | | | |
| 31. | Milton Bradley Co. | 13,228,400 | 71. | Hasbro Industries | 6,447,300 | | | |
| 32. | Mego International | 12,902,300 | 72. | Liggett Group | 6,308,200 | | | |
| 33. | Nissan Motor Corp. USA | 12,836,500 | 73. | Eastern Airlines | 6,273,800 | | | |
| 34. | CPC International | 12,789,900 | 74. | Jos. Schlitz Brewing | 6,196,400 | | | |
| 35. | Norton Simon Inc. | 12,520,300 | 75. | K. Hattori & Co. Ltd. | 6,182,000 | | | |
| 36. | Revlon Inc. | 12,463,500 | 76. | Miles Labs. | 6,091,600 | | | |
| 37. | Nabisco Inc. | 12,080,300 | 77. | Chevrolet Auto Dlrs. Assn. | 5,999,300 | | | |
| 38. | North American Philips | 11,942,000 | 78. | American Airlines | 5,963,800 | | | |
| 39. | Gillette Co. | 11,857,500 | 79. | FAS International | 5,820,000 | | | |
| 40. | General Electric | 10,664,600 | 80. | Action Marketing | 5,706,100 | | | |

Source: Television Bureau of Advertising from Broadcast Advertisers Reports monitoring 263 stations in 75 major markets.

Note: Investments classified as "Retail/Local" by BAR (i.e. General Foods' investment for Burger Chef, investments by J. C. Penney Co. Inc., Sears, Roebuck & Co., etc.) are not included in the above.

Reprinted with permission from the April 3, 1978 issue of *Advertising Age*. Copyright by Crain Communications, Inc.

There are several interesting points to note in this listing. Clearly food and household products companies are the big spenders in the television medium. Chrysler Corporation (no. 9) appears to have outspent General Motors (no. 14), despite the much smaller share of the market controlled by Chrysler. But, in considering General Motor's advertising, we must also take into account the Chevrolet Auto Dealers Assn. (no. 77) and the Oldsmobile Auto Dealers Assn. (no. 85). Chrysler comes back with its Dodge Dealers Assn. (no. 93). Finally, we see American Motors (no. 89), which spends less than the Chevrolet Dealers Assn. Among the big spenders on television, we also note two major publishers—Time Inc. (no. 21) and Triangle Publications (no. 26).

During prime time, network stations are permitted to sell up to nine and a half minutes of commercial time per sixty-minute broadcast period. Independent stations are permitted to sell up to twelve minutes in any sixty-minute period. In non-prime time, all stations are permitted up to sixteen minutes of commercial time per hour. Advertisers with more than one product often buy sixty seconds and run two thirty-second commercials for different products back to back. This practice, called *piggybacking*, saves money because sixty seconds is cheaper than two thirty-second slots.

Sole sponsorship of a program is rare, usually limited to specials—one-shot programs related to a seasonal promotion. Advertisers who cannot afford participation in national network programs often buy spots that are available between programs in ten-, twenty-, thirty-, or sixty-second units. The stations sell these units as *preemptible* or *nonpreemptible* time. The preemptible spot is lower in price, but can be dropped by the station if some other advertiser is willing to pay nonpreemptible rates for that time slot. Occasionally, a special event, such as a speech by the President of the United States, will preempt a commercial. When that happens, the advertiser receives a credit, a make-good, or an extension of the contract.

**GRPs again**    A media planner is often given the objective of obtaining a weekly level of GRPs for the number of dollars budgeted. For example, an advertiser may believe that to keep up with competition, 80 GRPs a week are required. To meet this objective, a media planner could buy time for one spot on four programs with ratings of 20, or on ten programs with ratings of 8. Either way, the total GRPs will meet the objective. Cost and the demo-graphic characteristics of the audience for each program will determine which schedule the media planner will buy.

## Audience ratings

Rating services (there are several) do not measure the *quality* of a television show—only the quantity of its audience. As a word, *rating* is a misnomer. Programs are rated because networks are in the entertainment business. If the stations did not provide programs that please people, if they did not respond to people's tastes, they would not remain in business very long. When the viewer tunes in a program, he or she is stating a preference for that program over all other programs aired at the same hour. Ratings are the way the preferences are added up. A program that is tuned in by the greatest number of viewers isn't necessarily the best program offered.

The *Nielsen rating* you may see reported in your newspaper is simply a statistical estimate of the number of homes tuned in to a program. A rating of 20 for a network TV program means that 20 percent of the television homes in the United States are estimated to have tuned in to that program. Since about 76 million households now have television sets, a rating of 20 means that an estimated 15.2 million households were tuned in. The Nielsen rating is just one of several rating methods used in the evaluation of advertising.

Another rating service is offered by the Arbitron Company. Arbitron uses a television meter to monitor set tuning and transmits the information to a computer. The service is currently available for the New York and Los Angeles markets with approximately 450 metered households in each mar-

This is a sample of a Nielsen monthly report on television viewing for one of the 220+ markets serviced by A. C. Nielsen Company. Careful reading of the report will reveal how many men, women, teens, and children were watching each television program. Reports of this kind permit advertisers and their agencies to make advertising and programming decisions quickly.

**234**

SAN FRANCISCO–OAKLAND, CA  WK1 9/28-10/4  WK2 10/5 -10/11  WK3 10/12-10/18  WK4 10/19-10/25

WEDNESDAY 10.30PM-12.15AM

For explanation of symbols, see page 3.
For RSE explanations, see page 2.

| Time | Station | Program | RATINGS WK1 | WK2 | WK3 | WK4 | MW AVG RTG | MW AVG SHR | SHARE MAY78 | FEB78 | OCT77 | HH | W18+ | W18-34 | W18-49 | W25-49 | W25-54 | WKG | M18+ | M18-34 | M18-49 | M25-49 | M25-54 | C2-11 | C6-11 |
|---|---|---|---|---|---|---|---|---|---|---|---|---|---|---|---|---|---|---|---|---|---|---|---|---|---|
| | | R.S.E. THRESHOLDS 25+% | 5 | 5 | 5 | 5 | 1 | | | | | 26 | 24 | 23 | 24 | 21 | 22 | 23 | 25 | 27 | 27 | 23 | 23 | 37 | 33 |
| | | (1 S.E.) 4 WK AVG/50+% | 1 | 1 | 1 | 1 | LT | | | | | 7 | 6 | 6 | 6 | 6 | 5 | 5 | 6 | 7 | 7 | 6 | 6 | 10 | 9 |
| 10.30PM | KBHK | HOGANS HEROES | << | << | << | << | 1 | | | | 1 | 3 | 4 | 1 | 1 | 1 | | | 4 | 2 | 2 | 1 | 1 | 11 | 7 |
| | KGO | #VEGA$ | 5 | | | | 14 | 27 | 26X | 35 | 29 | 258 | 221 | 84 | 130 | 92 | 117 | 63 | 155 | 65 | 91 | 59 | 69 | | |
| | | WED MOV | 5 | | | | 5 | 10 | | | | 99 | 54 | 4 | 4 | 13 | 27 | | 42 | 9 | 9 | 9 | 16 | | |
| | | VEGA$ | | 17 | 20 | 13 | 17 | 33 | | | | 311 | 276 | 110 | 172 | 123 | 151 | 74 | 193 | 83 | 118 | 75 | 86 | 15 | 9 |
| | KGSC | MERV GRIFFIN | << | << | 1 | << | 1 | 1 | NR | | NR | 13 | 6 | 6 | 6 | 1 | 1 | 2 | 3 | 3 | 1 | 1 | | |
| | KPIX | #CBS WED-MOV | | | | | 16 | 31 | 27X | 29 | 28 | 301 | 247 | 119 | 183 | 143 | 157 | 94 | 182 | 74 | 138 | 116 | 123 | 16 | 11 |
| | | CBS WED MV SPC | 19 | | | | 19 | 35 | | | | 362 | 318 | 124 | 240 | 198 | 218 | 122 | 213 | 132 | 178 | 125 | 125 | 6 | |
| | | CBS WED-MOV | | 15 | 9 | | 12 | 25 | | | | 225 | 155 | 94 | 125 | 96 | 100 | 63 | 140 | 52 | 109 | 95 | 101 | 20 | 20 |
| | | GRASS-GREENER | | | | 21 | 21 | 40 | | | | 391 | 361 | 162 | 242 | 182 | 209 | 128 | 235 | 61 | 155 | 149 | 166 | 17 | 5 |
| | KQED | VARIOUS | | | | | 1 | 2 | 7X | 1 | 4 | 23 | 24 | 5 | 16 | 16 | 16 | 9 | 14 | 3 | 11 | 10 | 12 | | |
| | | LINCOLN CENTER | 1 | | | | 1 | 2 | | | | 22 | 23 | 4 | 9 | 9 | 9 | 6 | 7 | 4 | 7 | 7 | 7 | | |
| | | PRFRM-WLF TRAP | | 4 | | | 4 | 7 | | | | 66 | 70 | 13 | 54 | 54 | 54 | 28 | 43 | 9 | 32 | 28 | 34 | | |
| | | GOSPEL-AWARDS | | | << | | << | | | | | << | 2 | 2 | 2 | 2 | 2 | | 2 | | 2 | 2 | 2 | | |
| | | GRT PERFRMNCES | | | | << | << | | | | | << | 2 | | 2 | | | | | | | | | | |
| | KRON | #NBC WED-MOV | | | | | 10 | 19 | 24X | 18 | 19 | 194 | 156 | 70 | 100 | 70 | 80 | 38 | 130 | 49 | 94 | 83 | 92 | 12 | 7 |
| | | NBC WED-MOV | 19 | | 4 | | 13 | 25 | | | | 259 | 208 | 105 | 141 | 93 | 105 | 56 | 179 | 68 | 132 | 119 | 133 | 19 | 11 |
| | | CHARLEY PRIDE | | 4 | | | 4 | 7 | | | | 69 | 63 | | 17 | 17 | 29 | | 29 | | 14 | 14 | 14 | | |
| | | SPTSWRLD FEAT | | | 6 | | 6 | 14 | | | | 119 | 72 | 28 | 52 | 52 | 52 | 22 | 86 | 48 | 59 | 36 | 42 | | |
| | KTVU | 10 OCLOCK NWS | 5 | 4 | 4 | 4 | 4 | 8 | 10X | 9 | 14 | 108 | 75 | 8 | 26 | 22 | 23 | 24 | 69 | 12 | 31 | 25 | 26 | | |
| | | HUT/PUT/TOTALS * | 55 | 49 | 48 | 53 | 51 | | 44 | 44 | 45 | 900 | 733 | 293 | 462 | 344 | 394 | 231 | 557 | 207 | 370 | 295 | 324 | 39 | 25 |
| 11.00PM | KBHK | GONG SHW | << | 2 | 2 | 1 | 1 | 11 | | 4 | 6 | 23 | 16 | 15 | 15 | 1 | 1 | 5 | 15 | 15 | 13 | 14 | 1 | | |
| | KGO | LATE NWS SCENE | 9 | 16 | 14 | 11 | 13 | 33 | 32X | 41 | 37 | 244 | 181 | 47 | 98 | 75 | 93 | 35 | 156 | 50 | 86 | 68 | 76 | 4 | 3 |
| | KGSC | CINEMA-NITECAP | << | 1 | << | 1 | 1 | | NR | | NR | 13 | 4 | 3 | | | 9 | | 8 | | | | | | |
| | KPIX | #EY NWS-11 | | | | | 12 | 31 | 16 | 24 | 23 | 223 | 187 | 68 | 119 | 102 | 106 | 52 | 144 | 55 | 99 | 85 | 88 | 9 | 6 |
| | | CBS WED MV SPC | 19 | | | | 19 | 48 | | | | 358 | 333 | 130 | 253 | 235 | 243 | 92 | 234 | 136 | 180 | 139 | 139 | 10 | |
| | | EY NWS-11 | | 5 | | 15 | 10 | 28 | | | | 190 | 142 | 31 | 62 | 46 | 50 | 37 | 116 | 21 | 63 | 55 | 60 | | |
| | | CBS WED-MOV | | | 8 | | 8 | 22 | | | | 155 | 133 | 79 | 100 | 82 | 82 | 43 | 105 | 43 | 89 | 89 | 89 | 22 | 22 |
| | KQED | DICK CAVETT | << | 1 | << | 1 | 1 | | 2 | 3 | 2 | 6 | 11 | 9 | 5 | 6 | 6 | 6 | 4 | 6 | 3 | 5 | 5 | 6 | |
| | KRON | #NWSCENTER 4-11 | | | | | 6 | 16 | 22 | 15 | 15 | 117 | 109 | 41 | 64 | 51 | 59 | 38 | 66 | 18 | 37 | 34 | 42 | 10 | 5 |
| | | NWSCENTER 4-11 | 9 | | 8 | 6 | 7 | 19 | | | | 140 | 129 | 50 | 77 | 60 | 68 | 47 | 76 | 19 | 42 | 40 | 48 | 13 | 6 |
| | | CHARLEY PRIDE | | | 3 | | 3 | 8 | | | | 51 | 47 | 12 | 22 | 22 | 11 | | 33 | 12 | 21 | 16 | 22 | | |
| | KTVU | LOVE EXPERTS | 3 | 2 | 2 | 2 | 2 | 6 | 11 | 8 | 9 | 50 | 43 | 20 | 26 | 7 | 10 | 11 | 24 | 17 | 17 | 9 | 11 | | |
| | | HUT/PUT/TOTALS * | 40 | 34 | 38 | 39 | 38 | | 27 | 30 | 31 | 681 | 549 | 199 | 331 | 242 | 276 | 148 | 415 | 160 | 262 | 216 | 239 | 24 | 14 |
| 11.15PM | KBHK | GONG SHW | << | 2 | 2 | 1 | 1 | | 1 | 14 | 2 | 23 | 17 | 16 | 16 | 1 | 1 | | 15 | 15 | 13 | 14 | 1 | | |
| | KGO | LATE NWS SCENE | 10 | 14 | 12 | 9 | 11 | 34 | 33X | 41 | 37 | 216 | 156 | 41 | 87 | 67 | 84 | 29 | 138 | 45 | 77 | 62 | 70 | 4 | 3 |
| | KGSC | CINEMA-NITECAP | << | << | << | 1 | 1 | | NR | | NR | 14 | 4 | 3 | 3 | | 1 | 3 | 4 | 4 | 4 | 2 | | | |
| | KPIX | #EY NWS-11 | | | | | 9 | 28 | 15 | 22 | 23 | 223 | 144 | 51 | 86 | 74 | 78 | 40 | 108 | 33 | 74 | 66 | 68 | 6 | 6 |
| | | WED SP/EY NWS | 12 | | | | 12 | 38 | | | | 230 | 199 | 73 | 136 | 127 | 135 | 55 | 134 | 64 | 102 | 83 | 83 | | |
| | | EY NWS-11 | | 5 | | 12 | 8 | 26 | | | | 155 | 117 | 23 | 51 | 42 | 46 | 28 | 99 | 17 | 55 | 48 | 53 | | |
| | | CBS WED-MOV | | | 9 | | 9 | 25 | | | | 163 | 143 | 83 | 106 | 86 | 86 | 48 | 106 | 37 | 88 | 88 | 88 | 24 | 24 |
| | KQED | DICK CAVETT | << | << | 1 | 1 | << | | 2 | 2 | 6 | 8 | 7 | 3 | 4 | 4 | 4 | 2 | 4 | 2 | 3 | 3 | 4 | | |
| | KRON | NWSCENTER 4-11 | 7 | 3 | 8 | 6 | 6 | 17 | 21X | 16 | 15 | 106 | 97 | 34 | 57 | 48 | 56 | 32 | 60 | 18 | 35 | 33 | 40 | 8 | 4 |
| | KTVU | LOVE EXPERTS | 3 | 2 | 2 | 2 | 2 | 7 | 11 | 8 | 9 | 51 | 45 | 21 | 28 | 9 | 12 | 10 | 24 | 15 | 15 | 5 | 8 | | |
| | | HUT/PUT/TOTALS * | 32 | 29 | 35 | 34 | 33 | | 26 | 29 | 29 | 593 | 470 | 169 | 281 | 203 | 236 | 122 | 353 | 130 | 222 | 184 | 206 | 19 | 13 |
| 11.30PM | KBHK | MAVERICK | << | 1 | << | << | 1 | | 2 | 7X | | 10 | 3 | 2 | 3 | 1 | 1 | | 8 | | 8 | 8 | 8 | | |
| | KGO | POLICE WOMAN | 7 | 9 | 9 | 5 | 7 | 31 | 20 | 28 | 21 | 145 | 105 | 45 | 67 | 45 | 56 | 31 | 81 | 24 | 36 | 23 | 28 | | |
| | KGSC | CINEMA-NITECAP | << | << | << | << | << | | NR | | | 5 | 5 | 4 | 4 | 1 | 2 | | 5 | | 4 | 4 | 2 | | |
| | KPIX | #CBS LATE MOV | | | | | 6 | 24 | 19 | 17 | 19 | 106 | 80 | 34 | 50 | 35 | 35 | 18 | 71 | 37 | 52 | 40 | 42 | | |
| | | EY NWS-11 LATE | 9 | | | | 9 | 37 | | | | 166 | 130 | 67 | 93 | 81 | 81 | 35 | 117 | 65 | 92 | 80 | 80 | | |
| | | CBS LATE MOV | | 5 | | 7 | 6 | 25 | | | | 110 | 83 | 30 | 50 | 26 | 26 | 19 | 69 | 33 | 47 | 29 | 33 | | |
| | | EY NWS-WED LT | | | 2 | | 2 | 8 | X | | | 38 | 22 | 7 | 7 | 7 | | | 29 | 17 | 21 | 21 | 21 | | |
| | KQED | BLITHE+BLCK N | OFF | OFF | | | << | | | | | 7 | | | | | | | 4 | 4 | 1 | 1 | 1 | 1 | |
| | | BLITHE SPIRIT | | | << | | << | | | | 7 | | 4 | 4 | 3 | 3 | 4 | | | | | | | | |
| | | BLCK NARCISSUS | | | | << | << | | | | 7 | 8 | | | | | | | | | | | | | |
| | KRON | #TONITE SHW | | | | | 7 | 28 | 34 | 34 | 34 | 124 | 90 | 31 | 51 | 42 | 46 | 26 | 87 | 47 | 64 | 45 | 51 | 9 | 5 |
| | | TONITE SHW | 7 | | 8 | 8 | 8 | 32 | | | | 144 | 110 | 38 | 62 | 52 | 55 | 32 | 102 | 59 | 81 | 56 | 61 | 11 | 6 |
| | | NWSCENTER 4-11 | | 4 | | | 4 | 15 | | | | 66 | 34 | 9 | 8 | 12 | | | 37 | 10 | 10 | 7 | 15 | | |
| | KTVU | ROOKIES | << | 2 | 2 | 1 | 1 | 6 | 8 | 7 | 12 | 27 | 23 | 9 | 14 | 8 | 9 | 10 | 11 | 10 | 10 | | | | |
| | | HUT/PUT/TOTALS * | 24 | 24 | 24 | 24 | 24 | | 16 | 17 | 18 | 425 | 306 | 125 | 189 | 132 | 149 | 87 | 262 | 122 | 174 | 119 | 132 | 9 | 5 |
| 11.45PM | KBHK | MAVERICK | << | << | << | << | | | 5X | | | 6 | 3 | 2 | 1 | 1 | | | 4 | 4 | 4 | 4 | | | |
| | KGO | POLICE WOMAN | 5 | 7 | 6 | 4 | 6 | 29 | 17 | 24 | 19 | 114 | 79 | 32 | 49 | 31 | 41 | 21 | 59 | 23 | 32 | 20 | 26 | | |
| | KGSC | CINEMA-NITECAP | << | << | << | << | << | | NR | | NR | 7 | 5 | 4 | 4 | 1 | 2 | | 3 | 3 | 3 | 2 | | | |
| | KPIX | #CBS LATE MOV | | | | | 4 | 22 | 22 | 16 | 18 | 81 | 72 | 16 | 30 | 18 | 18 | 15 | 43 | 15 | 21 | 13 | 14 | | |
| | | CBS LATE MOV | 6 | 4 | | 5 | 5 | 27 | | | | 97 | 91 | 19 | 38 | 22 | 22 | 20 | 47 | 14 | 20 | 9 | 11 | | |
| | | EY NWS-WED LT | | | 2 | | 2 | 8 | X | | | 30 | 15 | 7 | 7 | 7 | | | 29 | 17 | 21 | 21 | 21 | | |
| | KQED | BLITHE+BLCK N | OFF | OFF | | | << | | | | | 4 | | | | | | | 4 | 4 | 1 | 1 | 1 | 1 | |
| | | BLITHE SPIRIT | | | << | | << | | | | 6 | 8 | | | | | | | | | | | | | |
| | | BLCK NARCISSUS | | | | << | << | | | | | 8 | | | | | | | | | | | | | |
| | KRON | TONITE SHW | 7 | 4 | 6 | 5 | 5 | 28 | 35X | 40 | 36 | 102 | 75 | 29 | 48 | 39 | 42 | 24 | 71 | 48 | 59 | 38 | 43 | | |
| | KTVU | ROOKIES | << | 2 | 2 | 1 | 1 | 7 | 9 | 8 | 12 | 20 | 20 | 4 | 9 | 8 | 9 | | 11 | 10 | 10 | 7 | | | |
| | | HUT/PUT/TOTALS * | 21 | 20 | 21 | 17 | 20 | | 14 | 14 | 16 | 341 | 254 | 87 | 143 | 98 | 113 | 68 | 190 | 98 | 128 | 78 | 90 | | |
| 12.00MD | KBHK | MAVERICK | << | 1 | << | << | 1 | | 3 | 5X | | 10 | 4 | 2 | 4 | 2 | | | 8 | | 8 | 8 | 8 | | |
| | KGO | POLICE WOMAN | 3 | 6 | 4 | 4 | 4 | 25 | 16 | 27 | 23 | 88 | 54 | 19 | 31 | 20 | 28 | 11 | 54 | 23 | 34 | 24 | 31 | | |
| | KGSC | CINEMA-NITECAP | 1 | << | << | << | << | | NR | | NR | 9 | 5 | 4 | 1 | 1 | 2 | | 3 | 3 | 3 | 2 | | | |
| | KPIX | CBS LATE MOV | 5 | 4 | 1 | 4 | 4 | 21 | 24X | 15 | 19 | 68 | 87 | 11 | 18 | 9 | 9 | 11 | 25 | 7 | 9 | 6 | 7 | | |
| | KQED | BLITHE+BLCK N | OFF | OFF | | | << | | | | | 4 | | | | | 4 | | 4 | 4 | 1 | 1 | 1 | 1 | |
| | | BLITHE SPIRIT | | | << | | << | | X | | | 7 | | | | | | | | | | | | | |
| | | BLCK NARCISSUS | | | | << | << | | | | | 8 | | | | | | | | | | | | | |
| | KRON | TONITE SHW | 7 | 3 | 6 | 4 | 5 | 28 | 38X | 45 | 43 | 91 | 69 | 19 | 36 | 29 | 33 | 24 | 70 | 45 | 57 | 32 | 34 | | |
| | KTVU | ROOKIES | << | 2 | 1 | 1 | 1 | 7 | 6 | | | 25 | 18 | 3 | 8 | 7 | 8 | | 9 | 8 | 8 | | | | |
| | | HUT/PUT/TOTALS * | 18 | 17 | 17 | 16 | 17 | | 11 | 10 | 12 | 295 | 237 | 58 | 101 | 68 | 82 | 54 | 170 | 89 | 120 | 73 | 83 | | |
| | | | 3 | 4 | 5 | 6 | 7 | 8 | 9 | 10 | 11 | 12 | 13 | 14 | 15 | 16 | 17 | 18 | 19 | 20 | 21 | 22 | 23 | 24 | 25 |

## Lois Wyse

Lois Wyse is president of Wyse Advertising, the agency she and her husband, Marc A. Wyse, the agency's chairman, founded in Cleveland, Ohio, in 1951. A former newspaper reporter and magazine writer, Lois Wyse was born in Cleveland and attended Case Western Reserve University. She now commutes between the Wyses' home in Cleveland's Pepper Pike and New York City, where Wyse Advertising opened an office in 1967.

Wyse Advertising is a full-service agency that provides account and creative services, media planning and execution, marketing services, sales promotion, and merchandising material, including direct mail and brochures. It has particular expertise in package goods and retail services and is well known for its work with consumer products. Clients of Wyse Advertising include American Express, the Sherwin-Williams Corporation, Stouffer Corporation, the Tappan Company, Union Dime Savings Bank, Bristol-Myers Company, and the J. M. Smucker Company.

Lois Wyse has long been associated with the agency's advertising for the J. M. Smucker Company. For this client, she wrote the line: "With a name like Smucker's it has to be good." She is actively involved with the agency's campaigns for Bristol-Myers' Clairol products and the Union Dime Savings Bank. She also works on a special women's editorial supplement for East/West Network.

Lois Wyse is a director of the Higbee Company, a Cleveland-based department store, and a director of the Consolidated Natural Gas Company Pittsburgh. She has published more than forty books, including poetry, fiction, nonfiction, and children's books. She has received many major advertising awards, including the Clio.

ket. Subscribers can use the information to aid them in their programming and media-buying decisions.

The Arbitron Company also offers a television market report that provides ratings of the audiences for each broadcast period. The ratings are either a percentage of the total number of television households in an area, generally a cluster of counties called an Area of Dominant Influence (ADI),[4] or a percentage of persons in a particular sex—age

[4] The Area of Dominant Influence (ADI) is a concept developed by the Arbitron Company in 1966. It is a geographic market designation that defines all the counties in which home-market stations capture the greatest amount of total viewing hours. Each county in the United States, excluding Hawaii and portions of Alaska, is allocated exclusively to one ADI.

category in the area. An ADI rating of 10 for women 18—49 means that an estimated 10 percent of women 18—49 in the ADI were watching a particular station during an average quarter-hour of the reported time period.

A rating's value lies in its utility as a yardstick by which the advertiser may compare the relative sizes of audiences on different stations or in different time periods. It would be unfair, for example, to compare the number of households viewing a station in a large market with the number viewing a station in a small market. But a rating of 25 for each station would indicate a strong program in each market, regardless of the size of the market.

Other methods used in the evaluation of advertising will be mentioned in Chapter 18.

**Gross impressions** Network advertisers who use spot television to beef up certain key markets must be able to measure the ratings of their spot program market by market. To do this, the advertisers' media analysts will examine the network ratings in each key market to see how well the local network station rates. If the network is below the level set for the market (as determined by competitive GRPs), then the media analyst will have to add more GRPs with spot buys. Media planners use the term *gross impressions* to describe the entire audience delivered by a media plan in one figure. One impression equals one exposure by one media vehicle.

For example, if the advertiser buys ten commercials on a network program, and the rating for the show is 20:

$$76{,}000{,}000 \times .20 \times 10 = 152{,}000{,}000$$
gross impressions

Calculated in this way, however, gross impressions will represent duplicated exposures.

**Reach and frequency** Reach and frequency are measurements that tell advertisers and media planners about the size and viewing habits of a program's audience. Reach is the number who tuned in at least once during a specified period of time. Frequency is the number of times during that period the viewers tuned in. Reach and frequency take place at the same time, but generally in inverse proportion. If a program develops a large reach, it will have a relatively small frequency. If it has repeat viewers—that is, large frequency—chances are its reach will be relatively small. Programs that develop reach are those that change their content from week to week. A news analysis program or a special are good examples of this type of program. As the contents of the program change, so do the people who watch. There is, of course, an overlap, but in general such programs develop more reach than frequency. A regular program—a situation comedy; or the ultimate, a soap opera on five days a week, same time, same station—will develop a small audience with large frequency.

**Flighting** *Flighting* is a method of scheduling in which a period of advertising is followed by a blank period, which is followed by a period of advertising, and so on. The objective of this *wave strategy*, as it is sometimes called, is to give advertisers with a limited budget the means to add greater impact to their messages by concentrating them within a short period of time. To spread those messages out over the entire budget period would reduce their impact. A limited budget might permit us only twenty-six weeks of advertising, but by advertising only every other week, we can keep our product in front of the market for a full year. Some advertisers add impact using periods of frequency, as in radio, alternating with blank periods.

MEDIA PROFILE

**WIND 56
CHICAGO**

WIND is Chicago's only news and talk radio station. From 5 to 9 in the morning the station broadcasts news and information with frequent traffic, weather, and sports reports. Midday, the programming is all talk shows. In the evening, it is in-depth talk shows with listener participation by means of telephone call-in. Late night, there are more talk programs until 5 in the morning, when the morning programming of news and traffic information resumes. On the weekends, the station broadcasts news reports and talk shows with a two-hour listener participation program that allows sports fans the opportunity to talk about their favorite teams. The station also broadcasts all the Chicago Bulls basketball games play-by-play.

The station's ratings indicate that it reaches 784,000 adults (12 +) each week. Advertising rates for the various time periods during the day are based on the time of year and availabilities. Rates for morning drive time range from $120 to $200 for a sixty-second commercial. Evening drive time ranges from $50 to $90. The high end of these ranges indicates the rates charged during the most desirable seasons of the year. Evening time, 8 PM to midnight, ranges from $30 to $60 per minute. For a commercial broadcast from midnight to 5 AM, the cost per minute may be as low as $7.

## Summary

No matter how excellently prepared the advertising message, that message must be delivered—and to the right audience. Broadcast media have distinct characteristics that affect their ability to reach certain audiences and affect the cost advertisers must pay to reach those audiences.

Because a great number of radio stations are available in every market in the United States, radio offers advertisers a high degree of geographical selectivity. Demographic selectivity is also available, since the type of program, to a very large extent, determines the demographics of the audience. Radio is also flexible, permitting quick changes of copy in order to match competitive and seasonal conditions. The relatively low cost of radio advertising enables advertisers to bring their messages before their target markets with great frequency. Its major limitation is that it appeals to only one sense.

Television, on the other hand, appeals to both the senses of sight and sound. Television enables advertisers to show their products in action and to demonstrate their use, an ability no other medium can match. Television is *the* mass audience vehicle—ubiquitous and pervasive; it offers advertisers the ability to reach millions of viewers. Television is expensive, but only in absolute terms because of the large numbers of viewers it delivers. On a *cost per thousand* (CPM) basis, television probably delivers more people at a lower cost than any other medium.

In measuring the audience of one of the broadcast media, advertisers consider the station's coverage (the number of people who can receive the station's signals) and its circulation (the number of people who actually tune in those signals). Unlike magazines, where advertisers can easily count the number of copies sold on the newsstand or delivered via mail subscription, the size and nature of broadcast audiences are established by a sampling procedure. Also, the individual magazine audience is a net audience. The broadcast audience, however, is a gross audience: listeners and viewers may tune in to the same program regularly and, hence, be counted more than once.

The cost of a radio or television commercial is affected by both the length of the commercial and the time of day at which it is to be broadcast. Broadcast commercials are generally sold in units of ten, twenty, thirty, and sixty seconds. On radio, commercials broadcast during *drive time* (6 to 10 in the morning and 4 to 7 in the evening) are generally more expensive than those broadcast at other times during the day, because that is when radio stations reach their largest audiences. On television, commercials broadcast during *prime time* (7:30 to 11 in the evening) reach the largest audiences of the day. Advertisers use an index figure known as a *gross rating point* (GRP) to measure the percentage of a specified market area that they reach with one commercial.

## QUESTIONS FOR DISCUSSION

1. How can spot radio advertising be best utilized for products with seasonal variations?

2. Would you recommend radio advertising for the following? Justify your recommendations.

a. a children's toothpaste
b. an overseas airline.
c. a domestic airline
d. women's high-fashion sweaters
e. mattresses

**3.** For the products listed in the preceding question, would you recommend television advertising? Justify your recommendations.

**4.** If you were assigned to develop an advertising program for your school, what would your media plan include? Justify your recommendations.

**5.** What media plan would you recommend to reach the black market?

**6.** Suppose you developed an excellent media plan for an advertiser, but the total cost was more than the budget allowed for. What steps could you take to solve the problem?

**7.** Why is flexibility so important in media planning?

**8.** What are the advantages in buying a network radio package instead of individual spots? Any disadvantages or limitations?

**9.** Watch a television station for one hour during prime time. List the commercials you viewed. Which took advantage of the characteristics of the medium? Explain your answer. Were there any products advertised that other media might promote more effectively?

### Sources and suggestions for further reading

Barban, Arnold M.; Cristol, Stephen M.; and Kopec, Frank J. *Essentials of Media Planning*. Chicago: Crain Books, 1976.

Littlefield, James E. *Readings in Advertising*. St. Paul: West Publishing Co., 1975.

Sissors, Jack Z., and Petray, E. Reynold. *Advertising Media Planning*. Chicago: Crain Books, 1976.

Stanley, Richard E. *Promotion*. Englewood Cliffs, N.J.: Prentice-Hall, 1977.

Ulanoff, Stanley M. *Advertising in America*. New York: Hastings House, 1977.

"Radio Facts," published by Radio Advertising Bureau, Inc., April 1979.

"TV Basics 21," published by Television Bureau of Advertising, 1977.

## Outdoor, transit, and directories

### The story of outdoor advertising

Outdoor compared with other
media
Billboards—an old friend
Who uses outdoor?
Advantages of outdoor
Limitations of outdoor
Types of outdoor
  Posters
  Painted bulletins
  Spectaculars
Measuring the audience
Buying outdoor
  How paper is sold
  The rotary plan
  Buying paint
  OHMS
  Space position value

### Transit advertising

Transit media
Advantages of transit
There are limitations
The transit advertising business
Buying transit: forms and rates
  Car cards
  Exterior, or traveling, displays
  Station posters
  Other transit displays

### Directories

Yellow Pages

### Miscellany media

### WORKING VOCABULARY

| | | |
|---|---|---|
| snipes | paint | half run |
| coverage | embellish | basic bus |
| plant | spectacular | take-ones |
| plant operator | Traffic Audit Bureau | taillight spectacular |
| 24-sheet poster | 100 showing | total bus |
| 30-sheet poster | rotary plan | clock spectacular |
| junior panel | space position value | |
| 3-sheet poster | full run | |

# 11

## outdoor, transit, and directories

*With outdoor, you have only seconds to reach your mobile audience. "A poster should be to the eye what a shouted demand is to the ear," said poster artist C. B. Falls. The only shout it will hear is one big idea.*

KENNETH ROMAN and JANE MAAS
*How to Advertise*

THE TOP 100 ADVERTISERS in the United States, who spend well over $4 billion a year in advertising, invested about 1.1 percent of that amount in outdoor advertising in 1977 and 1978, of which 0.7 percent was national and 0.4 percent was local—not a very impressive figure, compared with the almost 80 percent spent on television advertising. However, in absolute dollars, the $418 million spent on outdoor in 1977 and the $465 million spent in 1978 are not small numbers.[1] And these

figures may very well be understated because companies with small investments in outdoor tend to report them under *miscellaneous.*

Outdoor advertising appears to be most popular with cigarette manufacturers. During the years 1977−78, R. J. Reynolds Industries, Inc. was by far the largest user of outdoor, followed by Philip Morris, Inc., and British-American Tobacco Co., Ltd.

## The story of outdoor advertising

Outdoor advertising is the oldest form of advertising. The signs described in Chapter 1, for example,

---

[1] "Advertising Volume in the U.S. in 1977 and 1978," *Advertising Age,* January 9, 1979. For an interesting breakdown see also "TV Basics 21," issued by the Television Bureau of Advertising, Inc., 1978.

date back to the days of ancient Rome and Greece. Today, however, business signs are *not* considered part of the outdoor medium. The distinction was drawn by the industry organization, the Outdoor Advertising Association of America, in an effort to limit criticism against all outdoor advertising. The organized industry conforms with the law[2] using uniform panels, the required set-back (the distance of the sign structure from the highway as measured from the center of the structure to the line of travel), and installations in appropriately zoned areas in cities.

Nevertheless, many states have limited the number of billboards that may be placed along highways, and pressure from environmentalists has caused thousands of billboards to be removed. Certainly, some of the criticism may have been provoked by the excessive number of signs, by signs in poor taste, or by physically unattractive signs in some areas. Supporters of the industry argue, however, that signs along the highway can hold a driver's interest, preventing him or her from becoming bored or hypnotized and falling asleep at the wheel.

Regardless of its merits or defects, outdoor is here to stay. It is one of the most important media options available to any national advertiser. The increase in the number of automobiles in use, the extension of our network of highways, the dispersion of population to the suburbs, and the general mobility of Americans have all spurred the growth of the outdoor medium. The more people travel, the more they are exposed to the advertising messages carried by outdoor advertising.

[2] The Federal Highway Act of 1958 and the Highway Beautification Act of 1965.

## Outdoor compared with other media

Outdoor conforms to our definition of a medium; it is addressed to people—large groups of people. There are some basic differences, however, between outdoor advertising and the media we have previously examined. Outdoor is literally out of doors—it is out of the home or place of business. There is no editorial vehicle to carry our message. The consumer makes no expenditure for, nor exerts any effort to see, our outdoor advertising. Our message is not brought to the audience; the audience goes to the message, passing it in the course of other activities. The audience has little, if any, opportunity to dwell or to reflect on our message. However, outdoor does provide its audience with repeat opportunities to see our message— either at the same display or on an identical billboard at another location.

## Billboards—an old friend

Curious word, "billboard." To promote attendance at a theatrical performance, theater managers posted a playbill outside the theater. These "bills" were later tacked or pasted to the walls of other buildings around town. It was primitive advertising and it still exists. Fences around vacant lots and buildings with a usable wall are often plastered with posters, unless the owner puts up a sign of equally ancient origin: Post No Bills.

Today, the word *poster* is used to describe an advertising message that is *posted* on a structure built for that purpose. The original poster was one sheet of paper, 28 inches by 41 inches. Several "one-sheets" could be combined to make larger posters to fit different frames. Then, as presses were developed to reproduce larger sheet sizes, the meaning of the original term became obsolete, but the word *sheet* continued to be used to indicate the relative size of the poster to be placed inside a frame.

## Who uses outdoor?

As we have already indicated, cigarette companies are the largest users of outdoor advertising. What is the characteristic of cigarettes that enables them to benefit from outdoor advertising? Cigarettes are impulse goods, intensively distributed, sold everywhere, bought by brand name—as are chewing gum, soft drinks, and beer. Outdoor is also great for automobiles and car after-market products such as gas, oil, batteries, tires, and waxes. What better time to reach your audience with a message about car care than while it is driving? Airlines use outdoor advertising along the roads that lead *out of town* to the airport. Local hotels, restaurants, and service stations use outdoor along the roads that lead *into town* in order to reach tourists.

The more the audience drives, the greater the opportunity for exposure to outdoor advertising. Although outdoor is nonselective (because people of every demographic category drive), drivers are generally considered upscale. Most high-mileage drivers (with more opportunities for exposure) are men in the higher income and educational brackets. These people are the natural targets for many products such as whiskey, automobiles, and, of course, products related to highway use.

## Advantages of outdoor

Outdoor offers us *geographic selectivity*. Billboards are well-suited for spot coverage of specific mar-

kets: They permit us to vary our message to suit particular ethnic communities, areas of the country, or types of traffic. National advertisers can have the names and addresses of their local dealers added to the bottom of their posters. These dealer imprint strips are known as *snipes*. However, billboards are relatively expensive for a national advertiser, particularly when multiple markets are involved.

Outdoor offers us *long life*. The standard posting period for our message is thirty days, which provides us with opportunities for repetition.

Outdoor offers us *impact*. Since shoppers on their way to stores or shopping centers are exposed to outdoor advertising, it can serve as an important last-minute reminder of our product. Our outdoor displays' large physical size—larger than life—and bright colors will add drama and recognition to our message. And because billboards are not usually erected in groups, our message will not have to compete for attention with other billboards in the same location.

## Limitations of outdoor

The limitations of outdoor are inherent in the medium. Since readers will be driving past billboards at highway speeds, copy must be brief—the briefer the better. Dramatic artwork is often used to get the message across. Because of this need for brevity, most advertisers use outdoor as a supplementary medium, relying on print or broadcast media to deliver longer messages.

Outdoor is nonselective. The audience is a mass audience whose members share only one characteristic: They are all riding in motor vehicles. People of every age, sex, educational and socioeconomic level make up this audience. The only type of outdoor that offers selectivity is the 3-sheet poster that is available on a neighborhood-by-neighborhood basis.

Using billboards on a national basis is relatively expensive. When expressed in CPM, the cost for outdoor is low, but the brevity of the message and the fact that the driver may not have time to comprehend it tend to make this medium more expensive than mere CPM comparisons would indicate. It is not the nature of the medium to build recall.[3]

## Types of outdoor

There are three types of outdoor advertising: posters, painted displays, and spectaculars. A *plant* refers to all of the outdoor advertising structures in a given city, town, or area operated by a single outdoor company, or *plant operator*. Plant operators own or lease the land or locations on which the structures are erected, build and maintain the structures, and operate the trucks and other equipment necessary for mounting the posters, painting the displays, or installing the spectaculars. There are about 1,100 plant operators in the United States.[4]

**Posters**    Outdoor posters are printed on sheets of paper that, when assembled and mounted, form an outdoor sign, or, as it is often called, a *paper*. Traditionally, the most popular size has been the *24-sheet poster*, so-called because years ago, before the development of giant litho printing presses, 24 separate printed sheets were required to make a poster. Today, presses accept larger sheets, and the 24-sheet poster now consists of only 10 sheets.

Faster-moving traffic has stimulated the development and use of the *30-sheet poster*, which measures about 21 1/2 feet wide by 9 1/2 feet high. The 30-sheet poster usually consists of 14 sheets, and, if we include the white margin of paper that surrounds the copy area, its full dimensions are 25 feet by 12 feet. Many posters today use bleed sheets, which eliminate the white margin and extend the copy area to the full dimensions of the poster. Plant operators do not charge extra for posters that bleed since they fit on the same frame as posters with the white paper border. Thirty-sheet posters provide greater visibility and improved legibility and thereby greater readership.

The *junior panel* is a 6-sheet poster similar in proportion to the 24-sheet poster. It is used where space is not available for the full-size posters.

*Three-sheet posters* are mounted on the walls of buildings, particularly in shopping areas. The overall dimensions for the copy area are 42 inches by 84 inches. The basic purpose of the 3-sheet poster is to remind pedestrians of a product as close as possible to the point of purchase.

Poster panels may be regular or illuminated. Where there is a high volume of night traffic, outdoor advertisers may obtain several additional hours of use by lighting their posters until midnight or even all night. The hours of illumination will be determined by the volume of nighttime traffic in the area and by the legal restrictions of the city or municipality.

**Painted bulletins**    Painted bulletins may be either painted walls or large bulletin board structures composed of panels that are individually painted.

[3] For a particularly interesting experiment, see "What One Little Showing Can Do," by Wendell C. Hewett, *Journal of Advertising Research*, 12, no. 5 (October 1972).

[4] *The First Medium.* (New York: Institute of Outdoor Advertising, 1975).

The 24-sheet poster (below) consists, in fact, of 10 sheets of printed paper. The 30-sheet poster consists of 14 sheets and, within the same frame that contained the 24-sheet poster, provides a large image that improves the visibility of the message. The 30-sheet bleed poster may consist of up to 20 sheets of paper. It utilizes every available inch of space on the frame.

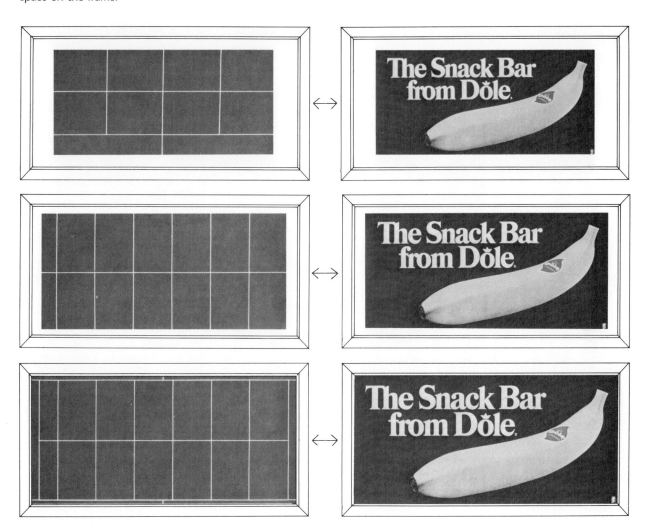

The latter are generally larger than posters; the most common size is 14 by 48 feet. The copy is reproduced by painting directly on the surface. When painting is the method of reproduction, the bulletin is called a *paint*. The most inexpensive *paint* is an advertisement painted directly on the wall of a building. It is the most inexpensive because it requires no structure. The size of the advertisement depends on the size of the wall available. The cost will vary with the location.

The *3-sheet poster* in this illustration is placed horizontally instead of in the more usual vertical position. Mounted on the side of a building at pedestrian eye level, this form of outdoor makes its impact close to the point of sale.

Painted bulletins are sold on contract. Contracts can run from one to three years and generally provide for two repaintings. Changes of copy are permitted at repaint time. A painted bulletin is usually illuminated and is often *embellished* with extensions or cut-outs that protrude from the top or sides of the bulletin's frame.

**Spectaculars** A *spectacular* is an outdoor advertising display built with structural steel and designed for a particular advertiser on a long-term contract.

The advertising copy is presented in a "spectacular" fashion with lights, flashers (the lights go off and on), or a chaser border (the lights go on in sequence around the border, giving the impression of movement), as well as any combination of flashing or moving electrical devices. These displays are very expensive to erect and are usually used in areas that attract both pedestrian and vehicular traffic during the day and after dark. The cost of a spectacular can run as high as $500,000. The big spectaculars at Times Square in New York City are

246

This painted bulletin (above) for a local restaurant is cleverly *embellished* by having the claw and the tail of the lobster protrude beyond the frame.

A clever play on words (below) adds a light touch. Buyers do want to customize their vans. Why not a picture of Vincent? Note how four words say it all.

probably the most widely known in the country. Other well-known spectaculars are located on Michigan Avenue in Chicago and Public Square in Cleveland.

Less elaborate spectaculars are known as semispectaculars. They utilize flashers and mechanical devices to draw the public's attention, but are smaller in size and less expensive to build.

## Measuring the audience

Advertisers can obtain circulation figures for a plant or for each of the individual locations within a plant from several different sources. The most important of these is the *Traffic Audit Bureau, Inc.* (TAB). The Traffic Bureau does not merely audit circulation figures supplied by plant operators, but actually gathers some circulation data on its own.

All traffic circulation figures are obtained either from official traffic counts or from manual counts. Usually state highway commissions oversee programs of continuous traffic count sampling. These counts are generally obtained by mechanical counting instruments that are moved from location to location throughout the state, and the results are made available to advertisers. The resulting counts are adjusted to reflect a yearly estimate of average daily traffic, taking into account seasonal factors, weekly variations, and other variables. The traffic count is converted into potential viewers by counting 1.75 persons per car. The hours of exposure may be from 6 AM to midnight (eighteen hours for an illuminated display) or from 6 AM to 6 PM (twelve hours for nonilluminated display). Actually, traffic volume consists of three modes of transportation: automobiles, pedestrians, and mass-transit vehicles. For the most part, outdoor circulation figures report only the number of people in automobiles.

A number of studies have indicated that outdoor offers high levels of both reach and frequency. For all practical purposes, outdoor reach is the same thing as coverage, because both measure exposure to the medium. *Coverage* is the number and percent of people who pass, and are exposed to, a given showing of billboards during a thirty-day period. *Circulation* represents the gross potential audience and does not assume exposure.

## Buying outdoor

**How paper is sold**  Plant operators set up their panels in high-traffic areas of individual markets. Advertisers will "buy" a group of these panels in order to obtain exposure for their message in that market. The basic unit of sale is still often referred to as a *100 showing*, although in 1973 the Outdoor Advertising Association of America, Inc., adopted the term *100 gross rating points daily*, or 100 GRPs. The new designation was adopted so that plant operators and advertisers could describe the weight of exposure opportunities offered by their panels in the same units that are used by other media.

In outdoor advertising, one rating point is equal to one percent of a specified market population. If we buy a 100-GRP showing, that does not mean that our message will appear on 100 billboards in our target market. Instead, it means that our message will appear on as many panels as is needed to provide a *daily* exposure equal to 100 percent of the market population. For example, in a market with a population of one million, a 100-GRP showing would deliver a circulation of one million each day. A panel distribution that provided 50 GRPs in this market would deliver a circulation of 500,000. Actually, a 100-GRP showing is not passed by 100 percent of the market's mobile population,

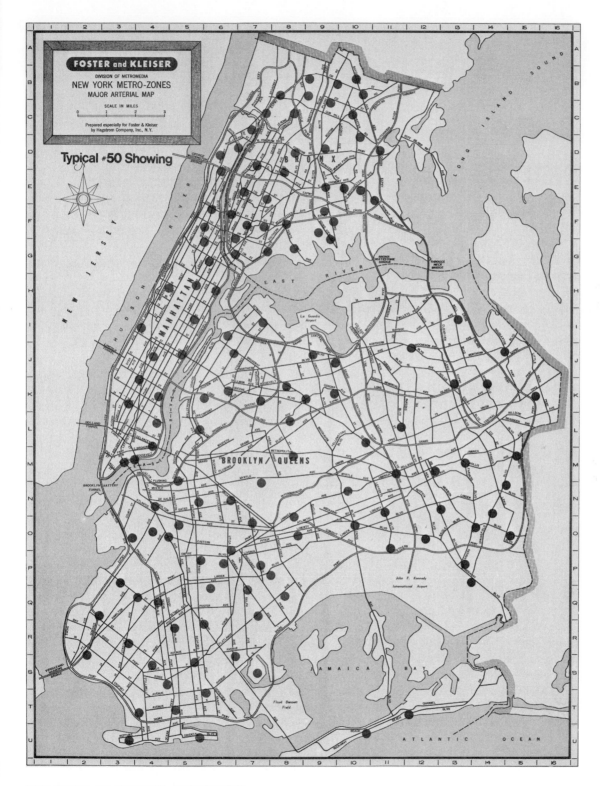

but by a percentage somewhere between 90 and 100 percent, which is quite acceptable.

Rates for paper are based on the number of GRPs bought for a thirty-day period. Rates will differ from plant to plant, depending on the size of the market, the number of panels needed, and the costs incurred by the plant operator. Since the number of panels needed to obtain a 100-GRP showing will vary from city to city, the cost of the showing will vary accordingly. A 100-showing package in Los Angeles, for example, requires 594 panels. The cost for this showing is in the neighborhood of $121,106 a month. A 100-showing package in greater New York City consists of 1,185 panels and costs about $226,777 a month. In Cincinnati, a 100 showing requires only 242 panels and costs $32,045 a month. In a small town, it might consist of only two panels—one where the highway enters the town, and the other where the highway exits.

Advertisers can compare the rates offered by different plant operators on the same basis that they use for other media: CPM, or cost per thousand. Plant operators offer discounts for longer contracts much the same as those offered by the owners and operators of other media.

**The rotary plan**　The *rotary plan* is a simple concept. An advertiser may buy just one poster panel, for example, for a full-year contract. After two months in one location, the poster is moved to a second location for the next two months. By the end of the year, that same poster has appeared in six different locations in the market selected by the advertiser. For variety, the advertiser could buy two posters and have both of them rotated every month —or the advertiser could substitute a new poster design every month.

**Buying paint**　Painted bulletins are bought by a different arrangement. There are far fewer paint locations in a market than poster locations, and each is selected individually, not on the basis of showings or GRPs. There are about 36,000 painted displays in the United States. Paint is more expensive than paper and the usual buy is for a one-year period. The copy is expected to last a year. If it deteriorates, the plant operator bears the responsibility of repainting it. If the advertiser wants to change the copy, the change will be made by the operator, but at the expense of the advertiser.

**OHMS**　Until the end of 1977, much outdoor advertising and billing services were provided through the National Outdoor Advertising Bureau (NOAB). NOAB had been owned by twenty advertising agencies for whom it made outdoor advertising "buys." In 1978, OHMS (Out of Home Media Service) replaced NOAB. OHMS is not owned by advertising agencies, but is a privately held employee-owned organization. The usual advertising agency commission for outdoor media is 16 2/3 percent. OHMS charges an agency a 2 percent fee for its buying services.

**Space position value**　Most cities have only one plant; some of the larger cities have several. When buying a showing, advertisers must consider the distribution and the coverage of the panel locations, particularly as they apply to the advertisers' products. Suntan lotions, such as Coppertone, would benefit most by being advertised at the seashore or in resort areas. Not that people do not sun themselves in North Dakota or Wyoming, but the cost of reaching prospects would be far higher in those areas than in Florida where more people sun

Working from the original photograph, this artist is painting a bulletin in the studios of a plant operator. The finished bulletin will be prepared in sections and transported by truck to the location where it will be installed. The final size of the bulletin can be estimated by comparing the size of the artist to the size of the face he is painting.

themselves during the longer sunny seasons. Similarly, airlines (heavy users of outdoor) would want to be sure that their outdoor advertising messages are placed along roads leading to airports. For a product with regional distribution, the advertiser would want to be certain that coverage was heavy in, or leading to, those areas where the product was available. Any other locations would be wasteful. Other considerations affecting the relative value of a given location include the number of illuminated panels, the traffic flows, and the visibility of the panels.

The latter factor, the visibility of the panels, is of considerable importance in determining the value of the showing. *Space position value* (SPV) is an index of a poster panel's visibility based on the length of the approach, the speed of travel, the angle of the panel to its circulation, and its space relationship to adjacent panels. The longer the approach, the longer the panel is visible. The slower the traffic, the easier it is to see and read the message. The closer the approach is to head-on, the better the visibility. A panel standing alone has the best chance of being seen. A cluster of panels reduces the chances of any single panel to make an impression. The Traffic Audit Bureau assesses all of these factors and arrives at an individual rating for each location.

# Transit advertising

## Transit media

Transit media include interior displays in mass-transit vehicles, exterior displays on mass-transit vehicles, and terminal and station-platform displays. These media offer the advertiser a number of advantages similar to those of outdoor. Transit can provide mass coverage of a metropolitan area. For the most part, it reaches adults on their way to and returning from work. Demographically, transit reaches more women than men but is evenly split between white-collar and blue-collar workers.

## Advantages of transit

Transit is primarily an urban medium with little or no reach in rural or small-town areas. But in metropolitan areas, its reach is great. Because the travel patterns of the audience are repeated five days a week, fifty-two weeks a year, there is an excellent opportunity for repeat delivery of the message. Transit is a *high-frequency* medium. Transit is very useful to local advertisers who want to reach consumers in their shopping areas. Transit advertising may be, for some consumers, the last advertising message they receive before they make a purchase in the marketplace.

Transit is also selective. Advertisers can select the train or bus routes that expose their messages to demographically defined groups. Some advertisers may want to reach the mass market of an entire transit system, and they can do that, too. Others can select the ethnic markets or certain upscale markets that are most appropriate for their products.

## There are limitations

Like outdoor, transit media have a limited amount of message space available, but this is not as critical as it is in outdoor because the audience has more time to absorb the message. The reader often has ample time to read all the copy; in fact, exposure time for transit advertisements averages twenty to thirty minutes. Transit is, nevertheless, not intended for long or complex selling messages. Competition for attention is high. Transit is not intrusive. It must compete with other displays, other reading material, people, and scenery outside the vehicle. Also, people who travel the same route day after day tend to become less attentive to the transit advertising on that route.

## The transit advertising business

Commuter trains, subways, and bus lines are the means of transportation between suburban areas and urban centers. The advertising in and on these transit lines is operated by about 70 companies organized into 380 designated markets. The transit advertising operator places and maintains transit

## KARL ELLER

Karl Eller grew up in Tucson, Arizona, and began his working career there as a billboard salesman for Foster & Kleiser, the largest outdoor advertising company in the United States. By the time he was twenty-nine, he was a vice-president in charge of Foster & Kleiser's Chicago office. When he was passed over for the presidency in 1959, he left Foster & Kleiser and went to work for a Chicago advertising agency: Needham, Louis and Brorby. Three years later, he was offered a chance to buy Foster & Kleiser's outdoor plants in Phoenix and Fresno for $5 million, and, in 1962, he formed the Eller Outdoor Advertising Company of Arizona.

Perceiving that billboards could be sold as an adjunct to other media, rather than as their competitor, Karl Eller merged his billboard company with radio and television stations in Phoenix in 1968. His choice of Combined Communications as the name for his new company represented his belief that a successful marketing campaign involves advertising in media that reinforce each other. In 1978, Combined Communications Corporation operated seven television stations, six radio stations, two newspapers and approximately 28,000 billboards. Its revenues for that year were more than $289 million.

In the early 1970s, outdoor advertising companies were concerned by the environmentalists' intense attacks on the industry, but Karl Eller believed that the industry could survive by improving the attractiveness of its signs through new construction techniques and better landscaping. As he has said:

> If they are done right, billboards can be as beautiful as buildings or anything else. . . . [They are] another economic use of property, another choice to tell a message.

These *car cards* had a two-fold objective: to encourage use of buses on holidays and to stimulate attendance at Chicago's cultural and educational institutions. A very efficient use of transit media, since the target market is people who ride public transportation.

advertisements on the vehicles or lines for which the advertiser contracts. The printed advertisements themselves are supplied and paid for by the advertiser. The operators pay the standard 15 percent agency commission.

Total expenditures in the transit medium in 1977 amounted to about $70 million, including both national and local advertising.[5] National advertisers accounted for 42 percent of the volume and local advertisers 58 percent. Compared with the $11 billion spent in 1977 on national and local newspaper advertising, and the nearly $8 billion spent on national and local television, $70 million is not an impressive figure. Although many national advertisers have used transit advertising consistently for many years, the bulk of transit advertising is used by local advertisers. For national advertisers, transit particularly lends itself to the advertising of low-priced convenience goods that are widely distributed. Transit is a supplementary component in many advertisers' media mix, used to add extra weight to urban markets. Local advertisers can use transit advantageously by taking space only on those transit lines that serve their trading areas.

### Buying transit: forms and rates

**Car cards**   A *car card* is a standard size piece of lightweight cardboard that is printed on one side and mounted in a retaining frame on the interior walls of a train or bus. Car-card space is sold on the basis of a *run* or *service*. A *full run* would indicate one card in every vehicle or every train car of the transit system. A *half run* means one card in half of the line's vehicles. A *double run* indicates two cards

in every vehicle. Some markets, generally the larger ones, also offer a *quarter run*, but the half run is the service most frequently bought. In the New York City subway system, a full run consists of two cards in every car, because the size of the cars makes it possible that many riders would not be exposed to only one card.

Rates are usually based on monthly service, with reduced rates for contracts of three, six, or twelve months. The cards are supplied by the advertiser and installed by the operator. Cards are usually changed once a month, but the frequency of change is up to the advertiser; some leave the cards unchanged for longer periods. The advertiser usually provides more cards than are needed so the operator can replace those that have become soiled, that fall down, or are defaced. In large cities, a full run on buses can cost more than $2,000 a month. CPM runs about 14 cents in large metropolitan markets.

*Positions*   Car cards are 11 inches high by 28 inches wide. But greater visibility can be obtained with oversized cards 42 inches wide or 56 inches wide. All cards are 11 inches high, which is standard for both buses and train cars. Premium positions, available at extra cost, include *square-end* cards 22 inches by 21 inches, *top-end* cards 16 inches by 44 inches, and *over-door* positions. A relatively new idea in transit advertising is the *basic bus*, which consists of *all* the advertising space on the inside of a specified number of regularly scheduled buses.

*Take-ones*   *Take-ones* are perforated postcards or leaflets that are attached to a pad and fastened to the bottom or corner of a car card. The postcards or leaflets are easily detached by the viewers, who are

---

[5] As reported by the Transit Advertising Association, Inc., Washington D.C.

invited to send for information or to take home the leaflet and read it more carefully in private. There is an additional charge of about 10 percent for the use of take-ones.

**Exterior, or traveling, displays**    Exterior displays are carried on both sides of the bus as well as front and rear. Sizes vary, but the most common is 21 inches high by 44 inches wide. Other display sizes include the *king size* (30 inches by 144 inches), the *queen size* (30 inches by 88 inches), and the *taillight spectacular* (21 inches by 72 inches). Exterior king-size posters are sold in *showings*. A *100 showing* represents multiple coverage on every base route in the market. Contracts for showings are made by the month, with discounts for consecutive showing periods of up to twelve months.

Other variations available to advertisers include a rooftop backlighted display, called a *busorama*, that is 22 inches high by 144 inches wide. One busorama is available on each side of the bus. Some operators also sell the *total bus*—that is, all the exterior advertising on the bus. The advertiser using the basic bus *and* the total bus buys the *total, total bus.*

**Station posters**    Station posters are displayed in and on stations of subways, bus lines, and commuter railroads. They are generally available in a one-sheet size (30 inches wide by 46 inches high), a two-sheet size (60 inches wide by 46 inches high), or a three-sheet size (42 inches wide by 84 inches high—the same size as a 3-sheet poster used in outdoor advertising).

**Other transit displays**    Transit advertising operators also offer floor displays, diorama displays, and clock spectaculars in train, bus, and airline termi-

nals. A *clock spectacular* consists of a large electric clock set in a display framework that may include a moving message. Most of the other displays are custom designed and include many of the same components as outdoor spectaculars. Other transit media available include displays on the roofs and rear decks of taxicabs, but these displays are used mostly by local advertisers.

## Directories

There are more than 4,000 directories published in the United States, many of which sell advertising space in the pages of their listings. These directories are published by directory publishers, magazines, trade associations, chambers of commerce, and government agencies at all levels. Most directories are published to serve business—trade, industrial, and professional. For many buyers of industrial products, the industrial directory is a valuable tool for locating sources of supply. Chief among industrial directories is the *Thomas Register,* which is a general industrial directory. In addition, there are numerous directories known as vertical directories that are designed to serve the needs of a single industry.

The use of an industrial directory by a national industrial advertiser does not replace the need to advertise in an industrial publication. Directories work hand in hand with the advertiser's other promotional activities. The company's advertisements in industrial and business publications are designed to provoke interest in the advertiser's product, while the directory, in effect, completes the selling cycle by providing would-be purchasers with information about the product and where to

# COMMUTER CARDS Standard Showings

## "A" PACKAGE

consists of 21″ × 33″ carcards in prime end positions in New York and Philadelphia; 21″ × 22″ carcards in prime end positions in Chicago and Washington Metro in D.C.

### Monthly Rates for 12 Consecutive Months

|  | New York District | Philadelphia District | Chicago District | Washington District |
|---|---|---|---|---|
| FULL RUN | $22,396. | $2,213. | $6,345. | $3,776. |
| ¾ RUN | 17,596. | 1,739. | 5,038. | 2,832. |
| HALF RUN | 12,797. | 1,265. | 3,789. | 1,888. |
| QUARTER RUN | 7,679. | 759. | 1,868. | — |
| **Number of Cards Displayed** | | | | |
| FULL RUN | 3,692. | 356. | 700. | 236. |
| ¾ RUN | 3,077. | 297. | 525. | 177. |
| HALF RUN | 2,051. | 198. | 350. | 118. |
| QUARTER RUN | 1,026. | 99. | 175. | — |
| **Number of Vehicles** | | | | |
| FULL RUN | 2,629. | 356. | 700. | 236. |
| ¾ RUN | 2,190. | 297. | 525. | 177. |
| HALF RUN | 1,460. | 198. | 350. | 118. |
| QUARTER RUN | 730. | 99. | 175. | — |
| Potential Monthly Exposure | 19,734,926 | 2,791,000 | 11,901,384 | 5,000,000 |

"A" Package includes displays in Long Island, New Haven, New York Central, Pennsylvania, Erie-Lackawanna, Jersey Central, Reading, PATH and Staten Island Ferry System in New York. In Chicago, it's the Illinois Central, Rock Island, Burlington Northern and North Western … Pennsylvania and Reading in Philadelphia and the METRO System in Washington, D.C.

## "C" PACKAGE

in New York only comprises showing of 21″ × 33″ carcards in side of door and compartment positions of MTA and similarly appointed equipment.

|  | Monthly Rate 12 Month Basis | Number of Cards Displayed | Number of Vehicles |
|---|---|---|---|
| FULL RUN | $10,325. | 2,264. | 1,282 |
| ¾ RUN | 8,113. | 1,887. | 1,068 |
| HALF RUN | 5,900. | 1,258. | 712 |
| QUARTER RUN | 3,540. | 629. | 356 |
| Potential Monthly Exposure | 10,230,149 | | |

"C" Package incudes the Long Island, New Haven, New York Central, Pennsylvania railroads and PATH System.

## TERMS AND CONDITION:

**RATES:** All rates quoted are monthly for periods of 12 consecutive months. Showings for shorter consecutive months are subject to short term rates as follows: for 9 to 11 months, add 5%; for 6 to 8 months, add 10%; for 3 to 5 months, add 15%; for 1 or 2 months, add 20% per month.

**DISCOUNTS:** Deduct 15% from Philadelphia and/or Chicago rates when added to New York showings. Deduct 10% from Philadelphia rate when added to Chicago District showing.

**PRODUCTION:** Rates do not include production of cards which are to be supplied by advertiser on 5-ply stock with vertical grain for end spaces with ½″ free margin on all sides shipped prepaid to designated TDI service points at least 10 days prior to showing date. Production assistance is available through TDI.

**COPY CHANGES AND SERVICE CHARGES:** Advertisers are entitled to a change of copy once in any contract month without charge, with non-commissionable service charge of 15¢ per card for each additional change, 30¢ per card per month for "take-one" service.

**CORPORATE PURCHASES:** Multiple products that are wholly owned by any advertiser within the same industrial category are entitled to interchangeability of space use within the same media and to rate benefits applicable to continuity and size of showing.

**AVERAGE MONTHLY CIRCULATION** is total passengers carried in an average month by all commuter railroad cars and ferries serving New York including Long Island, New Haven, Pennsylvania, New York Central, Erie-Lackawanna, Jersey Central, PATH, Reading, Staten Island and City Ferries. In Chicago, the Illinois Central and Rock Island Railroads. In Philadelphia, the Penn Central and Reading Railroads.

**TERMS:** Bills are rendered in advance as of 1st day of service and are due and payable in 30 days.

**COMMISSIONS:** Standard 15% commission is allowed to all recognized advertising agents.

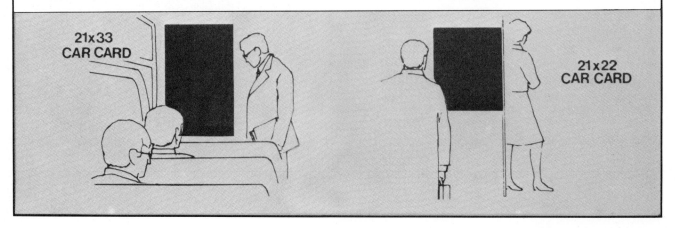

21x33 CAR CARD

21x22 CAR CARD

(Opposite) Notice the great difference in costs between districts shown on this rate sheet for end car cards on suburban commuter lines. These differences reflect number of displays in each car, total number of commuter cars in system, and number of passengers carried. Ordinary cars cards, which are displayed in the side panels of the vehicle, offer much less visibility and are therefore cheaper than end cards, which are visible to most of the occupants of the car.

An *end card* is used in transit advertising. It is much larger than the ordinary car card and, since it appears at the ends of the aisles in railroad cars or buses, enjoys much greater visibility.

An *exterior bus display* is a form of transit advertising. In this case, it is being used to promote a radio station and has been photographed in front of the station's studios.

*Clock spectaculars* (above) are very effective eye-catchers in subway and railroad stations, bus depots, and airline terminals, where people are anxious to know the correct time. As they check the time, they are exposed to the sales message in the display.

*Illuminated dioramas* (below) particularly lend themselves to advertising by auto rental companies, real estate developers, and hotels. They are usually placed in airline and railroad terminals to provide information to arriving visitors.

buy it *when the need arises.* The directory is meant to be used, not read.

One of the most widely used directories is the *U.S. Industrial Directory.* This directory is issued in sets of four: a telephone/address directory, a product directory, a literature directory, and a "new ideas for industry" directory. The *telephone/address directory* is just that—an alphabetical listing of industrial suppliers of virtually every category of product. The *product directory* carries listings by product category so that a prospective buyer is able to learn which companies make a particular product. The *literature directory* carries listings, again by product category, of the literature that each supplier has available on request. The *new ideas directory* contains a copy of the advertiser's own printed material—a circular, a catalogue, even a sample, if feasible—which, together with the literature of other advertisers, is bound into one volume.

The circulation of the *U.S. Industrial Directory* is 32,459 manufacturing plants. Advertising costs range from $1,640 for a full page to $100 for a one-inch display card, with ten other sizes in between. The publisher claims 8.7 users per set.

## Yellow Pages

The most commonly used consumer directory is the Yellow Pages issued by the telephone companies. The Yellow Pages provides national advertisers with an opportunity to make a tie-in with their local dealers at a time when the consumer is interested in buying. Every household and business receives a Yellow Pages directory either as a separate book or bound together with the White Pages.

National Yellow Pages Service Association is a sales organization that enables advertisers to make one contract for as many as 5,000 different Yellow Pages sections. It has been found that 82 percent of the adult (over 20 years of age) consumer population refers to the Yellow Pages an average of 116 times a year. Industrial buyers refer to the Yellow Pages 67 times a year.[6] Ryder Truck Rental claims, for example, that it gets 80 percent of its consumer business from national Yellow Pages advertising. The company rents and leases 50,000 trucks out of 500 company-owned locations and 2,500 authorized dealers in the United States and Canada. The company uses national advertising to develop long-term leasing business with business firms, but uses the Yellow Pages to reach the occasional renter.

The National Yellow Pages Service Association issues a monthly publication of up-to-date computerized information on closing and publication dates, length of issue, population of covered area, advertising rates, and additional technical information.

## Miscellany media

Local as well as national advertisers are constantly being solicited by various charitable, religious, or philanthropic organizations to advertise in their bulletins, journals, or newsletters. Such publications have little or no advertising value, and any advertising considered for such media properly belongs in the public relations budget, not in the advertising budget. The decision to "advertise" in such publications is not the decision of the advertising manager, but of the executive of the company responsible for charitable contributions.

[6] Study for American Telephone and Telegraph Company.

Like any directory, Yellow Pages are organized to be used—and, as the dog-eared copy in this ad suggests, used frequently. Of course, consumers use Yellow Pages often for needed products and services. A business organization will use the Yellow Pages far more frequently for the same purpose—to fill their needs for *nonrecurring items from a local source.*

# THE COMPANY WORKHORSE.
Use. Consult. Trust. The complete purchasing guide for American business.

Bell System Yellow Pages

When you need to know who, what, where, when, why.

260

CASE HISTORY

**HOW
OUTDOOR
BROUGHT
MILES
LABORATORIES
FAST RELIEF**

In 1977, strong competition was causing sales problems for one of Miles Laboratories' largest-selling products, Alka-Seltzer. The problems were particularly acute in Alka-Seltzer's top ten major metro sales markets, where it had been five years since Alka-Seltzer had received local media support.

In an attempt to remedy this situation, Miles Laboratories turned to outdoor advertising. It contracted for a 50 GRP daily showing in Alka-Seltzer's top ten markets during the months of April and May 1977. Within sixty days, these showings began to produce results. Alka-Seltzer's sales volume in retail food and drug stores showed high gains in all ten markets. For example, in the three districts where sales had previously declined most drastically, gains of 17, 23, and 16 percent were reported for the months of July and August.

Mitchell B. Streicker, vice-president of marketing services for Miles Laboratories, attributed the impressive results of Alka-Seltzer's advertising to outdoor's ability to deliver heavy frequency within a short period of time at a lower CPM than either spot television or newspapers. He also believed that outdoor gave "a tremendous boost for our sales force, our management, and our retailers." In fact, the results of these showings convinced Miles Laboratories to expand its outdoor advertising into 101 markets at an investment of more than $2 million.

# Summary

Outdoor advertising represents about 1 percent of the total advertising expenditures in the United States. It is not a major outlet for national advertisers, but it is of value as a helpful supplementary medium for certain types of products. Most outdoor advertising consists of printed paper mounted on panels. The most common sizes are either 24-sheet or 30-sheet posters. Other forms of outdoor include large painted bulletins, one-of-a-kind spectaculars, and smaller paper posters known as 3-sheet posters. Outdoor delivers a brief message to motorists who pass the display one or more times a day. As a medium, it is for the most part nonselective and conveys only a brief advertising message.

Outdoor displays are bought on the basis of showings—a designation representing a specific number of locations offered by a plant operator in a particular city or market. A 100 showing indicates that a message will appear on as many panels as needed in a given market to provide a daily exposure equal to 100 percent of that market's population. Painted bulletins are bought on an individual basis.

Outdoor is suited to impulse goods, intensively distributed and bought by consumers by brand name. Because the audience is most often exposed to the displays while passing by them in an automobile, outdoor is also a very appropriate medium for advertising products related to automobiles.

Transit advertising is an urban medium of limited value for some national advertisers, of excellent supplementary value for others, and of great usefulness to local advertisers. Transit is nonselective with a basically urban reach that delivers adult men and women, white-collar as well as blue-collar.

Directories are another supplementary advertising medium. For the most part, they serve business advertisers. The most widely used consumer directory is the Yellow Pages issued by the telephone company. The national advertiser can use the Yellow Pages to tie in with local dealers at the precise moment when the consumer is ready to buy.

## QUESTIONS FOR DISCUSSION

1. What is the difference between an outdoor poster and a painted bulletin?

2. Why would an advertiser use transit advertising?

3. Briefly describe three different kinds of transit advertising.

4. What is the meaning of a showing?

5. What are the benefits of outdoor advertising? What are its limitations?

6. For what products would you recommend outdoor advertising? Justify your answer.

### Sources and suggestions for further reading

Hewett, Wendell C. "What One Little Showing Can Do." *Journal of Advertising Research*, October 1972.

Sissors, Jack Z., and Petray, E. Reynold. *Advertising Media Planning*. Chicago: Crain Books, 1976.

Stanley, Richard E. *Promotion*. Englewood Cliffs, N.J.: Prentice-Hall, Inc., 1977.

Ulanoff, Stanley M. *Advertising in America*. New York: Hastings House, 1977.

# Nonmedia advertising

## Direct advertising

Direct-mail advertising
Advantages of direct mail
Limitations
Circulation
Mailing lists
    Buying mailing lists
    Keeping the lists up to date
Forms of direct mail
Postal regulations
Advertising specialties
Premiums
External house organs

## Point-of-purchase promotion (POP)

Forms of POP
Attributes of POP
Who benefits from POP?
Distribution of POP
Last word on POP

## Trade shows

The advantages
But is it worth the cost?

## WORKING VOCABULARY

| | | |
|---|---|---|
| package inserts | self-mailer | external house organ |
| direct mail | bulk mail | POP |
| list house | remembrance advertising | merchandiser |
| list broker | specialty advertising | trade show |
| statement stuffer | premiums | |

# 12

## nonmedia advertising

*Specialty advertising can be especially useful in complementing the concept of market segmentation. The key to segmentation analysis lies in differences that exist between groups making up the general population. Once these groups are isolated, then each segment can be investigated separately with a view to finding the precise ad specialty item and message to appeal to that particular group.*

GEORGE L. HERPEL and RICHARD A. COLLINS
*Specialty Advertising in Marketing*

IN USING ANY OF THE MEDIA we have discussed so far, advertisers surrender much of their control over their advertising message. They have to accept the fact that the medium controls the informational environment in which their message will appear. They have to accept the characteristics of the medium's audience. They have to accept the medium's schedule for delivery of their message. They even have to accept the medium's restrictions on the size and format of their message. But now we are going to discuss a form of advertising that is controlled almost exclusively by the advertiser.

## Direct advertising

*Direct advertising is advertising that uses no medium.* Direct advertising is a printed message that is delivered directly to prospective customers by the advertiser. The advertiser selects the prospect and the advertiser determines the timing of delivery. How is it done? Circulars distributed on a street corner to passersby. Circulars stuffed under doors or placed in the mail boxes of prospects. Circulars distributed by salespeople. Circulars packed with the product (package inserts). And, of course,

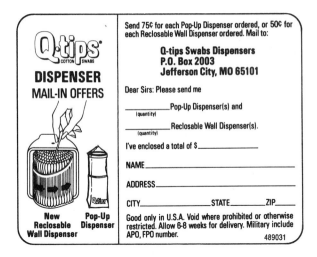

Send 75¢ for each Pop-Up Dispenser ordered, or 50¢ for each Reclosable Wall Dispenser ordered. Mail to:

**Q-tips Swabs Dispensers
P.O. Box 2003
Jefferson City, MO 65101**

Dear Sirs: Please send me

_____Pop-Up Dispenser(s) and
(quantity)

_____Reclosable Wall Dispenser(s).
(quantity)

I've enclosed a total of $_____

NAME_____

ADDRESS_____

CITY_____STATE_____ZIP_____

Good only in U.S.A. Void where prohibited or otherwise restricted. Allow 6-8 weeks for delivery. Military include APO, FPO number.                                    489031

Package inserts may range from multiple page folders to a simple slip of paper printed on one side, such as the insert for Q-TIPS® Cotton Swabs shown at the left. Package inserts may be used to provide more information about the use and benefits of the product than can be accommodated on the product's package, or, as in this example, they may be used to promote a premium offer.

through a wide range of circulars, catalogues, brochures, leaflets, and other printed material sent by way of the post office to prospects selected by the advertiser—*direct mail.*

Not all of the many kinds of direct advertising are suitable for a national advertiser: It is inconceivable that any major national advertiser would have printed advertising handed out on street corners or delivered door to door.[1] The cost would be prohibitive. Such methods are most frequently used by local retailers, generally with limited trading areas. However, package inserts, literature distributed by and through retail outlets, and direct-mail advertising are used extensively by national advertisers. Direct-mail expenditures in 1977 amounted to nearly $7 billion[2]—double the amount spent on direct mail in 1967. Direct mail represents, in fact—after newspapers and television—the third largest share of advertising investment in the United States.

### Direct-mail advertising

Available since the establishment of the postal service in 1775, direct-mail advertising is the most used, and so the most important, form of direct promotion. Direct-mail advertising should not be confused with mail-order selling, which is a form of retailing. The goods offered for sale by mail-order retailers are distributed by mail. Direct-mail advertising promotes the sale of goods available through other channels of distribution. Here are some of the advantages that direct-mail advertising offers the national advertiser.

### Advantages of direct mail

Direct mail is *flexible.* We can mail out our circulars at any time we choose. And we can assemble a mailing quickly to take advantage of unexpected situations. The *frequency* is also of our own choosing. We can send out mailings once a month or once a day. We are independent of publication dates. And direct mail is *selective,* both demographically and geographically. We can send out mailings to a specific city, county, or state—to a hundred names or to a hundred thousand.

*Selectivity* means a minimum of waste. If we were advertising a product that was of value only to home owners, even if we advertised in a homemaking magazine we would still reach a large amount of waste circulation. We would not want to reach readers of the magazine who are apartment house dwellers, for example. In contrast, we can direct our mailing almost *exclusively* to home owners with little or no waste.

Direct mail is *personal,* yet still within our definition of advertising. It is personal to the extent that it is received personally. A prospective customer opens a mailed letter or circular at his or her convenience. Direct mail is not an interruption the way an advertisement in a newspaper or a magazine is when it breaks into an article that a reader is trying

[1] Although that is exactly the way samples are often distributed —on a street corner or stuffed in a letter box or hung on a doorknob.
[2] *Fact Book on Direct Response Marketing.* (New York: The Direct Mail Marketing Association, Inc., 1979), p. 3.

Nonprofit organizations use direct mail extensively for their fund-raising activities. This attractive piece is noteworthy for two reasons: (1) the envelope is used to carry part of the message, and (2) the message has been printed in an unusual combination of typefaces. The envelope, after all, is an expense, and it is logical to use it for more than merely the vehicle for the message. As for the typefaces, note the use of the tall, light face for the words "CRESCENDO III" and the condensed, heavy face for the disco beat line.

to focus on. Nor does a direct-mail piece represent the kind of intrusion demonstrated by a television or radio commercial. The direct-mail advertising message is private and personal.

Advertising through the mail can generate leads for our sales force, and it can prepare the way for the salespeople's personal visits as a form of preselling. Advertising through the mail is also used as a follow-up to the salesperson's call; this follow-up enables advertisers to keep in touch with prospective customers, to supply additional information, and to build and maintain goodwill.

We can also use direct mail to appeal to prospects not reached by other media. How do we reach the homemaker who does not read any magazine at all? We can use television, of course, but even if we have made our media selection carefully,

there will still be waste. We can also use direct mail to reach difficult-to-see business executives who might exert an important influence in the decision to purchase certain business and industrial goods. Direct mail is not a substitute for media advertising, however, but a supplementary means of promotion that we can use to reach business buyers as well as consumers. We can also use direct mail to reach the retailers who will sell our product to consumers. In fact, direct mail is, for many manufacturers, by far the most important means they have to reach middlemen, purchasing agents, and other professional people.

Direct mail can also be used as a research tool. Because the audience is carefully selected, direct mail can be used to test different appeals, illustrations, or product innovations. Information gathered in this way can then be used to make our media advertising more effective.

## Limitations

With all its important advantages, why is direct mail only in third place among advertising techniques? The answer is cost. Even with no waste at all, direct mail is expensive. Costs include: the preparation and printing of the mailing piece and the envelope (if one is used); the cost of the mailing list, if it is rented or purchased; the cost of labor for stuffing and addressing envelopes; and the cost of the postage. At present, bulk-rate postage—the lowest rate for an advertiser—is 8.4 cents each. The postage cost of a thousand circulars is $84. For a million pieces, the postage alone would cost $84,000. In contrast, a full-page, four-color advertisement in *TV Guide* costs $61,000 and reaches an audience of 20,433,000. Consequently, if we want to use direct mail, our target market must be very clearly defined and the expense must be justified by results that cannot be obtained by other means.

In order to reduce the high cost of direct-mail advertising, groups of national advertisers occasionally band together to produce a single mailing. These mailings may contain coupons or inserts from five to ten different manufacturers—noncompetitive to be sure—of household or food products. By sharing the cost of postage, envelopes, lists, and labor, these advertisers can reduce their individual expenses substantially.

One of the most important advantages of direct mail—its personal reception—has its reverse side as well. It is true that a direct-mail piece is personal and private, and that it commands the full attention of the reader—*if the reader reads it.* But many Americans derogatorily refer to direct mailings as

"junk mail" and either ignore the message or throw the mail away unopened. If the mailed piece cannot make an immediately favorable impact, it is lost. The absence of an editorial climate—described as an advantage a few pages ago—can also work against the advertiser, since the mailed message receives no editorial assistance. Overcoming these disadvantages presents a tremendous challenge to the writers and designers of direct-mail advertising.

## Circulation

A magazine is mailed to its list of subscribers and is bought at the newsstand by people who find its editorial contents to their liking. The CPM is relatively low and the advertiser can tolerate the waste that is bound to occur. But direct mail is expensive unless it is successful, and it can only be successful if the audience is right, the timing is right, and the message is right. The most important of these considerations is the audience, because even the best designed message and the most carefully planned timing will be fruitless if the message is directed to the wrong people.

The perfect audience would consist only of people who are interested in, and can afford to buy, the product being promoted. That means we must know the demographic attributes of the target audience as well as their correct names, their correct addresses, and (for a business mailing) their correct job titles. Our list of names must be up to date.

It is possible to categorize lists by credit rating; age; sex; city, neighborhood, suburban, or rural area; customer or noncustomer status; and active customer or inactive customer status. Of course, not all lists need to be broken down in this way, but many should be if the advertiser is to obtain the

greatest amount of selectivity possible from this very selective medium.

## Mailing lists

One of the most productive mailing lists for most advertisers is their own customer list. All the needed information is available, and the customers are already familiar with the product and the company. Advertisers can also compile mailing lists of people or companies who respond to advertisements offering further product information. Lists of likely prospects are also often obtained at trade shows, either from registers of people who visited the advertiser's booth seeking specific information or from lists of registrants compiled by the management of the exhibition. Either way, such lists are current and contain names of people who are interested, if not in the advertiser's specific product, at least in the industry.

Mailing lists can be compiled, with some effort of course, from the White Pages of telephone directories, from Yellow Pages, and from trade directories. County tract maps can be used to develop lists for mailings not addressed to individuals but to the occupants of specific street addresses. Public records are another good source of lists. Records of births, deaths, marriages, home purchases, and auto registrations can be used to obtain names. New parents, for instance, are logical prospects for baby paraphernalia and insurance.

**Buying mailing lists**   Advertisers who do not have the time or the resources to compile their own mailing lists may buy or rent them. The cost of the list will vary according to its quality, completeness, and degree of selectivity, as well as to the difficulty of obtaining the information it contains. A list of corporate presidents will be more expensive than a list of motorcycle owners. Lists may be bought from compilers known as *list houses*, which generally offer business lists. Business names are bought in this way more often than consumer names are.

Business publications are another excellent source of names and addresses. Many trade, industrial, and professional publications allow advertisers to use their circulation lists for direct mailings. Generally, the publications do not deliver the list to the advertiser; the advertiser is required to send its mailing pieces to the publisher, who then addresses and mails them for a specified charge per thousand names. Such charges range from $40 to $100 per thousand.

A very useful source is the *list broker*, who acts as rental agent for list owners. For example, a magazine might rent its subscriber list to a manufacturer, another (noncompetitive) magazine, or a book club or record club. A subscriber to *National Geographic* is a likely prospect for a book club or a travel service. Noncompetitive publications might exchange lists, so that each could solicit new subscriptions.

Retailers are an excellent list source—their charge-account customers make excellent targets for manufacturers of certain products sold through their stores. In fact, a statement stuffer is one of the most frequently used direct-mail pieces. The *statement stuffer* is an advertising leaflet that is mailed to charge-account customers along with their monthly statements. The retailers enjoy the extra business stimulated by the leaflet, the cost of which was borne by the manufacturers of the products advertised. The retailers' only expenses are for the envelopes and the postage, which would have been incurred anyway. It is a cooperative effort in which everyone gains.

| QUANT. | LIST | S.I.C. |
|---|---|---|
| 1,740 | Professional, Scientific. Inst. Mfrs. | 38XX |
| 2,430 | Misc. Mfr. Industries | 39XX |

**By No. of Employees**

| Range | Cos. | Ind. |
|---|---|---|
| N.A. | 2,030 | 3,500 |
| Under 10 | 0 | 0 |
| 10 to 19 | 4 | 10 |
| 20 to 49 | 16,570 | 42,290 |
| 50 to 99 | 8,890 | 27,140 |
| 100 to 499 | 10,250 | 35,920 |
| 500 to 999 | 1,470 | 5,480 |
| Over 1,000 | 1,100 | 4,150 |
| Total | 40,310 | 118,470 |

**Executives** *For State Counts See Page 23*

| QUANT. | LIST | |
|---|---|---|
| 39,540 | General Manager | |
| 34,800 | Purchasing Manager | |
| 30,570 | Engineering Manager | |
| 34,640 | Production Manager | |
| 2,100 | Metal Coating & Allied | 3479+ |
| 4,760 | | |
| 30 | | |
| 450 | | |
| 8,200 | | |
| 500 | | |
| 37,200 | | |
| 2,100 | | |

| QUANT. | LIST | S.I.C. |
|---|---|---|
| 2,840 | Big Business Cos. | |
| 18,160 | Executives of | |
| 100 | Anthracite Coal | 1100 |
| 2,750 | Bituminous & Lignite Coal | 1200 |
| 500 | Metal | 1000 |
| 15,940 | Oil & Gas Extraction | 1300 |
| 3,200 | Quarries & Mines (Non-Metallic) | 1400 |
| 10,700 | Mining & Constr. Mach. Whls. | 5082+ |
| 250 | Mining Machinery Mfrs. | 3532 |
| 2,700 | Minority Groups Dirs. | |
| 5,700 | Minority-Owned Bus. Firms | |
| 13,800 | Mirror & Picture Frame Stores | 5271+ |
| 11,400 | Mobile Home Dealers | 5271+ |
| 600 | Mobile Home Mfrs. | 2451 |
| 13,500 | Mobile Home & Trailer Parks | 6515 |
| 5,550 | Model & Hobby Suppl. Stores | 5945B+ |

| QUANT. | LIST | S.I.C. |
|---|---|---|
| 17,900 | Music Stores | 5733+ |
| | **Musical** | |
| 3,930 | Instruction & Fine Arts Schools | 8299F |
| 8,120 | Instrument Dealers | 5733A+ |
| 400 | Instrument Mfrs. | 3931 |
| 2,600 | Instrument Repair Serv. | 7699X+ |
| 400 | Instrument Whls. | 5099D+ |
| 250 | Mutual Funds | |

# N

| QUANT. | LIST | S.I.C. |
|---|---|---|
| 240 | Nails, Spikes & Wire Mfrs., Steel | 3315 |
| 220 | Nameplate Makers | 3993E |
| 2,000 | National Assn. of Business Economists | |
| 3,580 | Natural Gas & Crude Oil Operations | 1311 |

# COMPUTER LIST OF BUSINESS BY STANDARD INDUSTRIAL CLASSIFICATION (S.I.C.)

| | S.I.C. No. | Page No. |
|---|---|---|
| Accounting Services | 8931 | 65 |
| Advertising Agencies | 7311 | 61 |
| **AGRICULTURE, FORESTRY & FISHERIES** | 0270-0900 | 46 |
| Air Conditioning, Etc. Contractors | 1711C | 47 |
| Air Conditioning Wholesalers | 5075 | 54 |
| Aircraft—Eqpt. Mfrs. | 3721-9 | 52 |
| Amusement Services | 7700 | 62 |
| Apparel Mfrs. | 2300 | 48 |
| Appliance Stores (Household) | 5722 | 58 |
| Architectural Services | 8911 | 65 |
| Associations | 8611 | 64 |
| Attorneys | 8111 | 64 |
| **Automobile Sales & Service—** | | |
| Accessory & Equip.— Wholesalers | 5013 | 53 |
| Battery & Ignition Repair | 7538 | 62 |
| Tire, Battery & Accessory Stores | 5531 | 57 |
| Gasoline Service Stations | 5541 | 57 |
| Glass Replacement & Repair | 7539C | 62 |
| New & Used Car Dealers | 5511 & 21 | 57 |
| Paint Shops | 7535 | 62 |
| Radiator Repair | 7539F | 62 |
| Repair Garages | 7538 | 62 |
| Top & Body Repair | 7531 | 62 |
| Used Car Dealers | 5521 | 57 |
| Automotive—Eqpt.—Mfrs. | 3711-5 | 52 |
| Automotive Services | 7500-7542 | 62 |
| Bakery Prods., Mfrs. | 2051-2 | 48 |
| Bakeries, Retail | 5460 | 57 |
| Banks | 6020 | 60 |
| Barber Shops | 7241 | 60 |
| Bars & Taverns | 5823 | 58 |
| Beauty Shops | 7231 | 60 |
| Beer & Alcoholic Beverage Wholesalers | 5180 | 56 |
| Beverage Inds.—Mfrs. | 2080 | 48 |
| Bituminous Coal Mining | 1200 | 46 |

| | S.I.C. No. | Page No. |
|---|---|---|
| Department Stores | 5311 | 56 |
| Dies & Tools Mfrs. | 3544 | 51 |
| Drive-In Theatres | 7833 | 63 |
| Drugs, Chemicals, etc.— Wholesalers | 5122 | 55 |
| Drug & Proprietary Stores | 5912 | 59 |
| Dry Goods & Gen'l Mdse. Stores | 5311 | 56 |
| Dyeing & Finishing Textiles— Mfrs. | 2261-9 | 48 |
| Educational Institutions (Schools) | 8210-33 | 64 |
| Electrical Goods— Wholesalers | 5060 | 54 |
| Electrical Machinery Mfrs. | 3600 | 51 |
| Electrical Work Contractors | 1731 | 47 |
| Electronics | 3670 | 51 |
| Employment Agencies | 7360 | 61 |
| Engineering Services | 8911 | 65 |
| Excavation & Foundation Contractors | 1794 | 47 |
| Exterminators | 7342 | 61 |
| Fabric Mills Mfrs. | 2211-41 | 48 |
| Family Clothing Stores | 5651 | 57 |
| Farm Equipment Retail Dealers | 5083 | 54 |
| Farm & Garden Supply Stores | 5261 | 56 |
| Farm Products, Raw Materials, Whol. | 5159 | 55 |
| Farms, Commercial | 0270 | 46 |
| **FINANCE & REAL ESTATE— SERVICES** | 6000-6553 | 60 |
| Fish & Sea Foods Wholesalers | 5146 | 55 |
| Floor Covering Stores | 5713 | 58 |
| Floor Laying Contractors | 1752 | 47 |
| Florists | 5992 | 59 |
| Food Products Manufacturers | 2010 | 48 |

| | S.I.C. No. | Page No. |
|---|---|---|
| Jewelry Stores | 5944 | 59 |
| Knitting Mills—Mfrs. | 2251-9 | 48 |
| Labor Organizations | 8631 | 64 |
| Laundries | 7211-5 | 60 |
| Lawyers | 8111 | 64 |
| Leather & Leather Products Mfrs. | 3100 | 50 |
| Legal Services (Lawyers) | 8111 | 64 |
| Libraries | 8231 | 64 |
| Liquor Stores | 5921 | 59 |
| Loan Companies | 6145 | 60 |
| Lumber & Building Material Dealers | 5210 | 56 |
| Lumber & Bldg. Matls.— Wholesale | 5030 | 53 |
| Lumber & Wood Products Mfrs. | 2400 | 48 |
| Machinery & Commercial Equip. Whol. | 5081 | 54 |
| Machinery, Except Electrical Mfrs. | 3500 | 51 |
| Machinery—Electrical—Equpt. Mfrs. | 3600 | 51 |
| Machine Shops | 3599 | 51 |
| **MANUFACTURING INDUSTRIES** | 1900-3999 | 48 |
| Meat Products—Mfrs. | 2011-17 | 48 |
| Meat Wholesalers | 5147 | 55 |
| Medical Equipment Wholesalers | 5086 | 54 |
| Medical Services | 8000-91 | 63 |
| Medical Laboratories | 8071 | 63 |
| Men's & Boys' Apparel—Mfrs. | 2311-29 | 48 |
| Men's & Boys' Stores | 5611-3 | 57 |
| Metal Products (Primary) Mfrs. | 3300 | 50 |
| Metal Prods. (Fabricated) | | |

| | S.I.C. No. | Page No. |
|---|---|---|
| Photography Studios | 7221 | 60 |
| Plastic Products Mfrs. | 3079 | 50 |
| Plumbing, Heating, Air Cond. etc., Contr. | 1711 | 47 |
| Plumbing & Heating Equip't Whol. | 5074 | 54 |
| Poultry and Poultry Prods.— Whol. | 5144 | 55 |
| Primary Metal Industries | 3300 | 50 |
| Printing & Publishing | 2700 | 49 |
| Public Elem. & Secondary Schools | 8210-23 | 64 |
| Quarries | 1400 | 46 |
| Radio Stations | 4832 | 53 |
| Radio & Television Stores | 5732 | 58 |
| Ready Mixed Concrete | 3273 | 50 |
| Real Estate Agencies | 6531 | 60 |
| Restaurants | 5810 | 58 |
| **RETAIL TRADE** | 5200-5999 | 56 |
| Roofing & Sheet Metal Contractors | 1761 | 47 |
| Rubber & Plastic Products Mfrs. | 3000 | 50 |
| Savings & Loan Institutions | 6120 | 60 |
| Sawmills & Planning Mills | 2421 | 49 |
| Schools & School Districts | 8200-33 | 64 |
| Scrap & Waste Mat'ls— Wholesalers | 5093 | 54 |
| Security Dealers | 6211 | 60 |
| **SERVICES** | 7000-8999 | 60 |
| Sheet Metal & Roofing Contractors | 1761 | 47 |
| Ships & Boats—Mfrs. | 3731-2 | 52 |
| Shoe Stores, Mens & Family | 5661 | 57 |
| Signs & Ad. Display Mfrs. | 3993 | 52 |
| Social Service Organizations | 8300 | 64 |

This is a *statement stuffer*, so called because it is literally stuffed into the envelope in which a monthly billing statement is mailed. It is also a superb example of cooperative advertising. Organized by the retailer, several manufacturers probably shared the costs of producing this direct-mail piece. The retailer, with a ready-made mailing list of active charge-card customers, pays only for the added postage and the handling costs (for the labor of stuffing the envelopes).

**Keeping the lists up to date**   Mailing lists are highly perishable items. Women marry and change their names; firms merge; people change jobs; people move, die, disappear. The rate of change is usually in excess of 20 percent each year. To put it another way, a magazine with a subscription circulation of only one million is required to make more than 200,000 changes to its list every year. What can advertisers do to avoid waste if they use rented or purchased lists? Nothing. Publications find that merely keeping up with changes in their subscription lists requires a good-sized staff. In many cases, the work is farmed out to organizations that specialize in maintaining mailing lists.

The post office helps keep mailing lists current by returning undelivered or undeliverable mail to the sender for a small charge. It's an excellent way to keep lists up to date. Many companies that use direct mail to reach their business customers will ask their salespeople to check the names and addresses of the people who live in their individual territories.

Another problem that arises from the use of mailing lists is duplication. If an advertiser rents lists for the same, or similar, target segments from two different sources, the chances are good that some names will appear on both lists. Such duplication is not only wasteful, but might even be responsible for negative reactions from the prospects. It is not unusual for advertisers using rented lists to include a statement of apology in the event of duplication. It is often impossible to cross-check lists.

The use of computers and ZIP codes has been of great help to the users of direct mail. You may recall from our discussion of the demographic editions of magazines in Chapter 8 that *Time* and *Sports Illustrated* both offer demographic editions based on ZIP codes. We can reach the most affluent

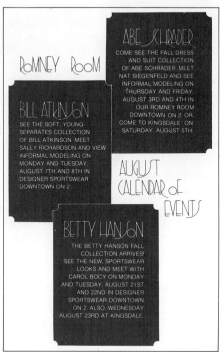

A *self-mailer* is simply a circular or brochure that has been designed to be mailed without the use of an envelope. The addressee's name and address are written, printed, or pasted on the mailing piece itself. In addition to saving the cost of an envelope, postage is reduced and the labor cost for stuffing the piece into an envelope is eliminated.

communities in our market by buying lists of addresses with the ZIP codes for those areas. What is the ZIP code for the most affluent community in your area? In the same way, we can specify the ZIP codes of ethnic neighborhoods. Computers permit the use of any number of break-outs. A *break-out* is any of the various categories into which the names on our list can be separated by the computer. From our total list of names, we could break out men or women or doctors or home owners and so forth. If we wanted to sell automobiles, for instance, we could break out the names of all automobile owners with three-year-old cars.

### Forms of direct mail

Almost any type of material can be sent through the mail. But, in fact, the most frequently used form of direct-mail promotion is the letter. Letters are sim-

ple, direct, and inexpensive to produce, even in small quantities. Today, advertisers can use word-processing systems to customize thousands of copies of a form letter by programming the systems to make small changes in the body of the letter automatically.

Obtaining variety is not a problem for advertisers who use printed direct-mail pieces. They can have their messages printed in one to four colors, on paper of different weights, finishes, and sizes, and in many different sizes and styles of type. If the direct-mail piece is so designed that it does not require an envelope, the address of the prospect being printed or typed directly on the piece itself, it is known as a *self-mailer*.

Designers of direct-mail pieces can also use such special printing production techniques as die cuts and pop-ups. If a three-dimensional paper biplane appears when prospects open a direct-mail

*These ads, culled from the pages of Advertising Age, may serve to suggest the wide range of advertising specialties that are available to an advertiser. Ties, coffee mugs, belt buckles, key rings, luggage tags, print-ons for T-shirts, slide-charts, tote bags—the list of possibilities is almost endless. Would advertisers want to see a few hundred thousand people wearing a T-shirt with their brand's name boldly displayed? Yes indeed, particularly if the people who wear the shirts paid for that privilege.*

piece (a pop-up), or if prospects see the outline of a company's product or trademark cut into the cover of a brochure (die cut), won't they be intrigued enough to read the advertising message? Since the success or failure of the piece depends on that all-important initial impact, such special effects can be well worth their extra cost. For this reason, direct-mail advertisers often include gadgets (small gifts such as coins or key rings) and free samples in their direct-mail pieces.

## Postal regulations

Mail in the United States is divided into four classes. *First-class* mail includes letters, written postcards, air mail under eight ounces, sealed matter, and all matter containing written material. *Second-class* rates apply only to publications and do not pertain to areas of direct mail. *Third class* represents the bulk of direct-mail advertising material. The savings over first class are substantial. As of this writing, first class postage is 15 cents, while third class is 8.4 cents.

To qualify as third-class mail, the mailing piece must be printed; however, printed pieces and retail-store statements may be sent at the third-class rates, provided twenty or more identical pieces are presented at a time to the post office. The *bulk-mail* user pays the post office an annual fee of $30, exclusive of postage. For that annual fee, the advertiser is permitted to enjoy the bulk rate. The mailing pieces must be separately addressed, and the advertiser must send not less than 200 pieces at a time. Postage is paid by the pound, but it will not be less than the 8.4 cent minimum. The words BULK RATE must be printed on the envelope or address side adjacent to the permit imprint or the meter stamp. All mail must be sorted and bundled by ZIP codes.

If consumers are expected to respond to a direct mailing, advertisers must provide them with the means to mail in their reply. They may require the prospect to affix postage to an enclosed reply card or envelope. They may provide a stamped card or envelope. Or, they may use a printed business reply card or envelope. When the prospect is asked to apply the postage, the response tends to be drastically reduced. Providing a stamped return card or envelope, on the other hand, can be very wasteful, for the advertiser pays postage on a certain amount of material that will never be returned —usually the largest portion of the mailing. Printed business reply cards or envelopes are usually the best method of handling reply mail. A permit to use business reply mail can be obtained without cost. Responders use specially printed cards or envelopes to mail in their replies, and the advertiser pays only for each reply that is received. No prepayment is required.

## Advertising specialties

Advertising specialties include an endless variety of useful items that are given to target prospects without charge. Usually the advertiser's name, address, and telephone number, and perhaps a short sales message or slogan, are imprinted on the item. The advertiser's goal is to give the recipients something that will remind them of the advertiser's company and/or product every time they use it, pick it up, or look at it. It is often called *remembrance advertising*. The ultimate goal, of course, is to stimulate sales.

The greatest advantage of the advertising specialty is its long life: The prospect is exposed to the advertiser's name or message again and again. In fact, the most widely distributed advertising spe-

275

cialty is the calendar, which the prospect may see as often as 365 days a year. Other specialties include pencils, pens, books of matches, key rings, memo pads, cigarette lighters, letter openers, shopping bags, and ashtrays. There are literally thousands of items to choose from. Specialty advertising, like direct mail, is highly selective, but it is costly and is a supplementary tool at best. For specialty advertising to be of value, advertisers must have carefully defined objectives, carefully defined targets, a suitable theme, and, if possible, an advertising specialty that bears a logical relationship to their product.

The major disadvantage of most specialties is the limited amount of space available for a message. In some cases there is just enough room for the advertiser's name and address. Also, the cost of the specialty and the cost of distribution tend to limit the size of the target market that can be reached economically. Certain specialty items, such as calendars, are so popular with advertisers that, as the year ends, prospective customers often receive many more than they can use.

## Premiums

A *premium* is an article of merchandise that is offered in addition to, or in combination with, the advertiser's product. The purpose of the premium is to attract (and sell) people who do not usually buy the advertiser's product or who do not buy it very often. Premiums are different from specialties in that they carry no sales message or identification with the advertiser. Unlike the specialties, which are given away without cost or obligation, premiums may be obtained only under conditions specified by the advertiser. The strength of the premium lies in its value as a useful gift. The value

would be reduced or destroyed by imprinting an advertising message on it. Therefore, premiums are not really advertising tools but rather sales promotion devices that require the support of advertising for their success.

## External house organs

Many companies publish on a regular basis a company magazine that is distributed to customers, prospects, distributors, and dealers without charge. This *external house organ* will feature articles of interest to members of the industry. Although they carry no advertising, these publications do help to build goodwill and to enhance the prestige of the company.

The external house organ is included in the advertising budget of some companies or in the public relations budget (where it belongs) of others. External house organs do not qualify as an advertising medium, but rather as a piece of direct mail that does not contain a selling message. The entire magazine (and some are quite expensively produced) is simply one large advertisement for the company.

## Point-of-purchase promotion (POP)

*Point-of-purchase* advertising is promotional material located in, at, or on retail stores and is designed, produced, and supplied by national advertisers. Point-of-purchase advertising has become increasingly important in the past twenty-five years because of the growth of self-service retailing. Point-of-purchase advertising cannot be used in place of print and broadcast advertising but must

To induce prospective customers to try a new brand, advertisers will sometimes offer them a *premium*. The advertiser hopes that after the trial use induced by the premium, the purchasers will contine to buy and use the product. In this advertisement, the advertiser charges the consumer 75 cents for shipping and handling. If the price that an advertiser charges for a premium covers all of the advertiser's costs, it is said to be *self-liquidating*.

Point-of-purchase displays offer advertisers the opportunity to present their products to the consumer at the time he or she is about to make a purchase. The free-standing Coke® display and merchandiser not only helps stimulate sale of the product, but other products that "go with Coke"—in this photo, potato chips. Nabisco uses a giant cookie jar, which is related to the theme of their entire promotion—"America's Cookie Jar."

be used to reinforce the advertising messages placed in those media. The sales messages placed in newspapers, magazines, radio, television, outdoor, and transit must make the initial impact, bringing brand awareness to the consumer, stimulating interest, and conveying information. Then, at the point of purchase—inside the retail store—the advertiser has one final opportunity to influence consumers who are actually making a buying decision in the marketplace.

### Forms of POP

Point-of-purchase materials can be divided into two broad categories—interior and exterior. Gasoline retailers make extensive use of exterior signs, displays, and banners. Other retailers use interior point-of-purchase materials in store windows, on counters, and on shelves; they can hang displays

from the ceiling or mount them on the floor. Much of this point-of-purchase material is of a temporary nature, such as cardboard display cards for the counter; paper shelf strips; paper streamers to be suspended from the ceiling or hung in the window; wall posters; and shipping cartons designed to do double duty as display cases. Other displays, much more permanent, include exterior store signs, interior clock displays, racks and merchandisers that store self-service goods, and decals for doors or windows.

### Attributes of POP

The strength of point-of-purchase advertising is its impact on the consumer at the time and in the place where he or she is physically and psychologically ready to buy. No other form of promotion or advertising enjoys such combination of time and

278

place. It is a unique attribute of POP. Another important attribute of POP is its ability to please two different groups of people: the retailer who will use it and the consumer who will see it. But retailers must be convinced that the POP material they are offered will enhance the appearance of their stores, or be effective in selling, or both. Otherwise, they will not use it, install it, or accept it no matter how much care, effort, and cost the advertisers have put into it. In designing their POP material, advertisers must consider the kind of retail outlets it is intended for and the space requirements of these outlets. Still, all retailers have their own ideas about what fits and what works in their stores. To all of these difficulties, add the fact that hundreds of different POP items are supplied to retailers by hundreds of manufacturers in every field.

### Who benefits from POP?

Everyone benefits from good POP. POP reinforces the manufacturer's advertising in all other media. It is the advertiser's final chance to tie together all the selling efforts that have been made before the consumer entered the store. In order to use manufacturers' POP materials, a retailer must stock their products. What greater benefit could the manufacturers desire?

As for small retailers, they cannot possibly design, produce, or even buy the kinds of POP material they receive, often without charge, from manufacturers. For more elaborate and expensive POP, such as merchandise racks, retailers may be required to pay an amount that is substantially less than their actual cost. This token payment is a subtle request for support. If the retailers pay for a POP display, they are more likely to use it. Sometimes the price of the display may not be specified in dol-

lars, but in units of reorder. The point-of-purchase material thus becomes an inducement to buy. But competition among manufacturers for good display locations in stores limits their ability to pass along to retailers high charges for POP material. There are preferred spaces in every store—in the windows, at the cash register, near the wrapping desk in a department store, at the aisle ends in a supermarket, at the check-out counter or behind the counter in a restaurant or bar.

But retailers benefit greatly from the increased sales that POP materials can stimulate. Good displays convert customers who are "just looking" into customers who buy. Some displays also serve as a source of product information for retail sales people. Point-of-purchase is of benefit to consumers, too. It frequently supplies them with information they need to make a buying decision. And, it does indeed speed up the shopping process, converting street traffic into store traffic.

### Distribution of POP

Unlike other advertising methods, it is difficult to get point-of-purchase materials into the hands of the retailers. Often, manufacturers merely ship the display to the retailer at the most appropriate time and hope that the retailer will be pleased and install it promptly. Some manufacturers have field personnel deliver and install their POP material. For more complicated installations, the manufacturer may contract with a local firm to do the installation work.

### Last word on POP

Point-of-purchase is, by its nature, not truly advertising, but in many instances it is listed within the advertising budget.[3] It should, however, be classified as a sales promotion activity or tool, not an advertising activity. We have discussed the subject of POP here because in many companies it is the job of the advertising manager to plan, select, and buy POP material. Needless to say, advertising managers must coordinate their activities with those of

[3] "100 Leading POP Advertisers," *Advertising Age*, September 18, 1972, p. 98

## JOHN CAPLES

Often called "the father of direct response advertising," John Caples is a man about whom David Ogilvy has said: "He knows more about the *realities* of advertising than anybody else." Caples' knowledge comes from more than 53 years of experience in the advertising business. As a mail-order copywriter, he learned at the very start of his career that every direct-response advertisement must pay its own way. It cannot rely on the cumulative effect of an entire advertising program. As he has said himself: "If you run an ad in a Sunday newspaper, you know by Wednesday whether it is a success or a failure." Every word has to work.

Many of the advertisements written by John Caples are classics in their field, including one which begins with what is probably the most often quoted headline in the history of advertising: "They laughed when I sat down at the piano, but when I started to play!—" John Caples wrote that advertisement in 1925 when he was a cub copywriter in the Ruthrauff & Ryan advertising agency. Three years later he joined Batten, Barton, Durstine, & Osborn (BBDO), where he became a vice-president in 1941. While at BBDO he has become well known for his development of copy-testing methods for such clients as Du Pont, United States Steel, General Electric, and United Fruit. He has also found time to write four very influential books on advertising, including *Tested Advertising Methods* and *Making Ads Pay*.

After more than half a century of writing effective advertisements, John Caples is still hard at work. Why?

I think the reason is because I enjoy my work. I have had fun. In my school days, I liked writing and I liked science. Direct marketing advertising has enabled me to combine the best of both worlds—writing and scientific methods of testing what kinds of ads are successful and what kind are failures.

I have probably written more failures than successes. But every failure has taught me a lesson.

the sales promotion managers to make effective use of this promotional device.

# Trade shows

A *trade show* is an exhibition of the products and services of a particular market or industry, and attendance is usually restricted to members of the "trade." In the United States, nearly 6,000 trade shows, exhibits, and conventions are held each year. Visitors flock to consumer and industrial exhibits to see demonstrations of new products and to learn of innovations within their industry.

## The advantages

For some manufacturers the value of a trade show is excellent. It exposes the firm and its products to many potential customers in a very short time. It enables sales, advertising, and technical people to meet prospective buyers face to face. It is one of the few occasions when the buyers come to the sellers. The advantages of the trade show are many. It can:

1. reinforce the company image

2. provide an opportunity to demonstrate a product that cannot easily be demonstrated by the sales force

3. provide an opportunity to supply in-depth information to a live prospect

4. help build a mailing list

5. generate sales leads for further follow-up

6. provide an opportunity to study industry interest

There are, however, a few disadvantages to exhibiting at a trade show. Attendance at the exhibit takes salesmen out of the field. Many times the most frequent visitor to the exhibit booth is not a new prospect but an old customer. And, exhibiting at a trade show is expensive. Although trade shows are not properly an advertising expense, many companies often include them in their advertising budgets.

## But is it worth the cost?

When exhibiting at a trade show is considered an advertising expense, the advertising manager should monitor these expenses closely. The fee for rental of exhibit space, the expense of flying sales personnel to the exhibit location and paying for their hotel rooms and meals, the cost of setting up the exhibit, the expense of transporting the product or equipment being displayed, and the cost of the executive time needed to supervise the entire procedure—all add up to a very sizeable dollar investment. Would that money be better spent in buying more advertising pages?

To make participation in a trade show productive, the advertising manager must determine what the desired objectives of the exhibit should be and then weigh them against alternative expenditures. What can exhibiting at a trade show do that print advertising cannot do at least as well?

1. Introduce a new product
   Demonstrating a product is often the most effective way to sell it. At a trade show, a prospect can not only see a demonstration of the product, but touch, try, smell, or taste it. For test marketing, a trade show provides instant feedback.

**2.** Bring together key dealers

Company salespeople are always calling on dealers. But bringing most or all of the key dealers together permits the company to build morale and to transmit new-product or policy information to them with unsurpassed opportunities for feedback.

**3.** Enhance the company's image

The advertising that the company places in trade, industrial, or professional journals does indeed build an image, but it is a distant image. No amount of carefully designed and well-written advertising copy can take the place of a handshake from key personnel or a few explanations delivered with a friendly smile.

**4.** Improve the distribution network

The trade show is one place where the dealers and distributors *come to the company.* Dealers or distributors who are willing to fly a thousand or more miles at their own expense to attend a trade show are active and aggressive business people— the kind we want to add to our network.

**5.** Help build a mailing list

It is customary to ask visitors for their name and affiliation[4] at a trade show, so that advertisers can build lists of interested people on the spot to whom they can send catalogues or whom they can have salespeople contact.

[4] In fact, it is not even necessary to ask. Most visitors are required to wear a badge with their name and company printed on it.

## Summary

The national advertiser has, in addition to the big guns of broadcast and print advertising, an arsenal of small arms for the assault on the consumer and on the dealers who serve that consumer. Direct advertising and, more important, direct-mail advertising, the most selective of all advertising procedures, offer a rifle approach after the scatter-fire of the big media barrage. Unless we aim for important targets or unless our percentage of "hits" is high, however, direct-mail advertising can be very expensive. Direct mail is a particularly effective way to reach key prospects in industry and business who are difficult, expensive, or impossible to reach through print media except with great waste. Direct mail demands not only the careful compilation of lists of targets, but the constant maintenance of that list. Mailing lists may also be purchased or rented from list houses or list brokers.

The advertiser may also choose to use specialty advertising and point-of-purchase advertising. The former is usually used to remind the business customer, the latter to remind the general consumer. The great asset of POP is that it reaches the consumer at a very important time and place—in the retail store at the time of purchase decision.

Lastly, we recognize the advertising value of trade shows, which are organized primarily to reach manufacturers who buy our products or the dealers and distributors who are our conduit to the consumer. However, an advertiser must determine whether the considerable expenses involved in participating in a trade show might yield greater returns if invested in another form of advertising.

## QUESTIONS FOR DISCUSSION

**1.** What is the difference between direct advertising and direct-mail advertising? Between mail-order operations and direct-mail advertising?

**2.** What are the strengths and limitations of direct-mail advertising?

**3.** What purposes can be served by package inserts?

**4.** Name some sources for building a mailing list.

**5.** What are some uses of specialty advertising?

**6.** How does an advertising specialty differ from a premium?

**7.** Why is point-of-purchase valuable to the manufacturer of consumer products? What are some of the problems that may be encountered?

**8.** What are some benefits an advertiser might seek from participation in a trade show or exhibition?

### Sources and suggestions for further reading

Gaw, Walter A. *Advertising: Methods and Media.* San Francisco: Wadsworth Publishing Co., 1961.

*Factbook on Direct Response Marketing.* New York: The Direct Mail Marketing Association, 1979.

Hanlon, Al. *Creative Selling Through Trade Shows.* New York: Hawthorn Books, 1977.

Harpel, George L., and Collins, Richard A. *Specialty Advertising in Marketing.* Homewood, Il.: Dow Jones-Irwin, 1972.

Stanley, Richard E. *Promotion.* Englewood Cliffs, N.J.: Prentice-Hall, 1977.

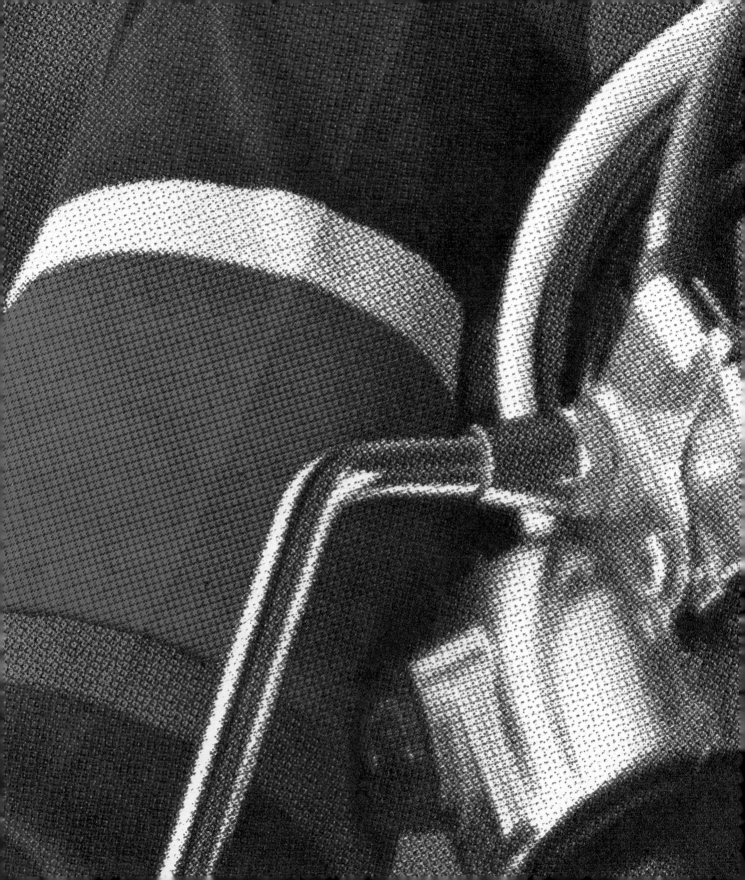

# 4

# CREATIVE ASPECTS

**13**
Product identification: branding and packaging

**14**
Creative strategies

**15**
Copy for advertising

**16**
Advertising art

**17**
Reproduction processes

Of course, when any picture is greatly enlarged, we lose the image. If you look carefully, you can see some of the frame of a motorcycle. This is a detail from a 24-sheet poster for Honda that was reproduced by the silk-screen process.

# PRODUCT IDENTIFICATION: BRANDING AND PACKAGING

**Trademarks and brand names**

Identifying the product
Trade names
Identifying the brand
Legalities
    Exclusions
    Registering the trademark
Objectives in trademarks
Choosing a trademark or brand
    name
    Historical names
    The personal name of the company's
      founder
    Fictitious names
    Foreign words
    Coined words and dictionary words
    Initials and letters
    Places and institutions, real or
      fictional
Attributes of a trademark or brand
    Distinctive

    Suggestive
    Appropriate
    Easy to remember
Family names
What's in a name
Trade characters
Other advertising marks

**Packaging**

Essentials of package design
Dealer requirements
Packaging is advertising
    Packaging is POP
    Packaging can increase the unit of
      sale
    Packaging can stimulate gift sales
    Packaging can convey quality

**Slogans**

---

## WORKING VOCABULARY

| | | |
|---|---|---|
| trade name | private brand | collective mark |
| family name | Lanham Act | certification mark |
| trademark | Principal Register | service mark |
| brand name | Supplemental Register | logotype |
| national brand | trade character | slogan |

# 13

# product identification: branding and packaging

*The old adage "Build a better mousetrap and the world will beat a path to your door" assumes that no one else has an improved mousetrap and that your potential customers know your improved version is available. In the real world, even a superior product may not succeed if its manufacturer fails to use every means possible to distinguish it from its competitors.*

*"The Nielsen Researcher"*

SINCE TRADING AMONG CIVILIZED PEOPLES BEGAN, artisans and craftsmen have placed their name, mark, or brand on the products they have created. The object of these marks was to identify the manufacturer—who would be held responsible for a poor product, of course—but basically it was to assure buyers that they were in fact getting what they bargained for. A trademark or brand name is used today in very much the same way: to facilitate selection of a particular product that has been distinguished or presold through advertising or some other means of promotion.

## Trademarks and brand names

### Identifying the product

If a company is to benefit from its advertising investment, consumers must be able to identify that company's products and to specify them when

purchasing. We have earlier acknowledged that each product has a different set of attributes—either inherent in the product, or existing only in the minds of consumers. For consumers, the ability to identify the product of their choice and to receive that product consistently adds to their satisfaction. As consumers, we have, in most cases, singled out a product that provides us with the most satisfying combination of taste, smell, design and *image*.

There are, you will agree, relatively few products today that are not clearly identified by a brand name. The most notable examples are agricultural products. We do not buy such products as corn, potatoes, or apples by specifying the grower. We do indeed recognize the difference between Long Island potatoes and Idaho potatoes, but that is a basic difference for which Nature is responsible, not the farm or the farmer who grew them. A similar comparison can be made between Florida's Indian River oranges and California's Sunkist oranges. Indian River and Sunkist represent cooperative efforts by growers to identify a *type* of agricultural product. They are not brand names for the produce of individual growers. When the oranges are processed, they become Tropicana, Minute Maid, or Snow Crop brand orange juice. Only when agricultural products are processed are the producers or processors required to identify themselves. Wheat is wheat, but Hecker's Flour is not Pillsbury's. Grapes may be grapes, but Gallo wine is not Taylor wine. When we want to buy a pound of potatoes, we ask for a pound of potatoes, but when we want a bag of potato chips, we specify Pringle's or Lay's.

## Trade names

Many companies, particularly those that manufacture different products, adopt a *trade name*. Such a name might be compared to the "stage" names that movie stars or musicians might adopt because the stage names are more easily remembered by the public than their real names. In a similar fashion, companies adopt their trade names or commercial names. Consider the many famous names in American industry that are not the names of products, but of the companies producing the products: Kimberly-Clark, Bristol-Myers, General Foods, Union Carbide, Minnesota Mining and Manufacturing. Do you know the names of some of the well-known products of these companies? Sometimes a company will change its corporate name to match its more famous trade name. For years, the National Biscuit Company was best known for its Nabisco brand of cookies, crackers, and baked goods. The company ultimately changed its name to Nabisco, Inc.

Companies that produce an extensive line of products use their trade name as a *family name* to help build strong identification among their entire "family" of products. The value of the family or trade name becomes more apparent as the company adds new products to its line and wants consumers to have as much confidence in the new product as in the old. This is particularly valuable for product lines related to health care, such as pharmaceuticals.

## Identifying the brand

In marketing, the words *trademark* and *brand name* are sometimes used interchangeably, but they do not always refer to the same thing. A *trademark* is a pictorial device, number, letter, or other symbol used to identify a product or product family, and under law it may perform no function other than identification. A *brand name* is used to iden-

288

Though many consumers may not be familiar with the name Norton Simon, Inc., one of the largest advertisers in the country, everyone knows Canada Dry. Canada Dry is the family name for a line of soft drinks produced by Canada Dry Corporation, a subsidiary of Norton Simon.

Although each product bears its own distinctive registered brand name—OREO®, RITZ®, TRISCUIT®—all of the products in this illustration are tied together and enhanced by the use of the Nabisco symbol. Consumers recognize the Nabisco trademark as identifying a good, reliable product. This makes it easier for Nabisco to introduce new products to its line—not necessarily new brands of cookies and crackers, but also products such as its cheese spreads and pitted dates.

**PRODUCT IDENTIFICATION: BRANDING AND PACKAGING**

tify a specific product and is a variety of trademark. For example, the word NABISCO set inside an oval surmounted by a cross is the trademark for the Nabisco corporation's line of food products. NILLA ® wafers is the brand name of one of those products; when the word NILLA is printed in the distinctive style of type shown on the package at the left, it is also that product's trademark. Manufacturers may thus identify their products with both a trademark and a brand name—or the trademark and brand name may be identical.

The use of brand names and trademarks is not confined to manufacturers. They are also used extensively by retailers and wholesalers. A manufacturer's brands are usually called *national brands;* a middleman's brands are called *private brands, store brands,* or *distributor brands.* Kenmore products from Sears and Ann Page products from A & P are well-known store brands.

## Legalities

The Lanham Act of 1946[1] defines a trademark as any word, name, symbol, device, or any combination of these elements used by a company to identify its goods and distinguish them from those manufactured or sold by others. Brand names and trademarks are considered synonymous in law. The American Marketing Association considers a brand name a name that can be stated or spoken orally and a trademark a word or symbol that can be visualized.[2]

Brands are registered with the United States Patent and Trademark Office. In fact, about 20,000 trademarks are registered each year. Although recognized by common law, the brand enjoys added protection when it is registered.

**Exclusions**    The registration of a brand name or trademark is good for twenty years and may be renewed every twenty years indefinitely. If abandoned, the brand name or trademark becomes public domain. The Lanham Act specifically *excludes* registration of four types of names and marks:

1. names and marks that so resemble existing ones for the same generic product as to be likely to confuse or mislead the consumer[3]

2. any word or symbol that is merely descriptive, geographically descriptive, or deceptive and misleading

3. surnames that are the same as brands already in use

4. anything contrary to good taste or anything contrary to public policy, which means anything disparaging to people, beliefs, or institutions; flags, coats of arms, or insignia of the United States or any state, municipality, or foreign country; or the name, portrait, or signature of any living person without written permission

**Registering the trademark**    A brand must be used in interstate commerce before it can be registered. To

[1] The Lanham Trade-Mark Act of 1946, 15 U.S.C.A. 1051 *et seq.*
[2] "Report of the Brand Names Committee," *Journal of Marketing* (October 1948), pp. 205–206.

[3] Section 2 of the Lanham Act states the exclusion in no uncertain terms: ". . . consists of or comprises a mark which so resembles a mark registered in the Patent Office or a mark or trade name previously used in the United States by another and not abandoned, is to be likely, when applied to the goods of the applicant, to cause confusion, or mistake or to deceive purchasers."

When a product becomes successful, the manufacturer wants to be sure that its carefully promoted brand name does not become generic and used by the public to describe a type of product or process.

# What the world needed. An ad written by lawyers.

Ahem.
We hate to be stuffy; but legally speaking, please remember that Xerox is a registered trademark. It identifies our products. It should never be used for anything anybody else makes.
You remember that, and we won't write any more ads.

## XEROX

meet that requirement, the name can be used on the product's package or in its national advertising. A trademark is not like a patent; it confers no ownership. Trademark rights are recognized as common-law rights, based on priority of use, continuous use, and diligence in proper use and defense. Registration of a trademark is a validation, an official recognition of what is already in use.

Primary registration of a trademark is accomplished by registering it in the *Principal Register,* which is considered evidence of exclusive ownership of that trademark for products sold in the United States. The registration may be challenged by a person or company claiming prior use of the trademark. After five years on the Register without challenge, permanent legal right is recognized.

There is also a *Supplemental Register* used for the registration of names and symbols that cannot be registered in the Principal Register because they are descriptive words, surnames, or geographical names. Such words must be in use for at least one year prior to registration. The law recognizes that such words take on a secondary meaning after they have been used for five years or more to identify and distinguish products from a particular source. The Supplemental Register was created by the Lanham Act.

Trademark law offers the advertiser three methods of indicating that a trademark or brand has been registered:

**1.** Registered in U.S. Patent Office

**2.** Reg. U.S. Pat. Off.

**3.** ®

® is the most convenient and practical way to indicate registration. Of course, companies must take care not to represent their trademarks as registered before they actually are; the courts may interpret such an act as a false claim. Before a trademark has been legally registered, companies usually use the notation "trademark" or "TM." Copies of material supporting the claim to first use in commerce must be presented to support the registration.

## Objectives in trademarks

National advertisers want their trademarks to be easily and quickly identifiable through the senses of sight and sound. When manufacturers identify one of their products most closely by its brand name, they will stress that word or phrase in their advertisements. Where visual identification is most important, the advertiser will use symbols, designs, pictures, or shapes because they are easily memorized. This means of identification is very important because many people read poorly and some may not even be able to read at all.

For advertisers, there are several benefits to be gained from clear identification of their products. Strong brand recognition protects them from unfair competition by distinguishing their products from products of lesser quality. Strong brand recognition offers manufacturers improved control over the channels of distribution and deflects attempts by retailers to substitute private or house brands. Strong brand recognition helps add a psychic appeal to their advertising. Strong brand recognition helps establish sales preference and may, if possible, give their products the character of specialty goods.

Brand names also help make life simpler for consumers. When making repeat purchases, consumers can avoid the brands that did not satisfy or insist upon the brands that did. And, when consumers are unfamiliar with a certain category of products, they can reduce the chance of making an unsatisfactory purchase by specifying a recognizable brand name. To the consumer, the brand name is an indicator of product quality. The name transmits an image of the product.

## Choosing a trademark or brand name

A trademark cannot be deceptive and cannot be confusingly similar to an existing trademark. Del Monte, for example, is a well-known and respected brand name. For a canner of fruits and vegetables to use a name such as Bel Monti is so obviously deceptive as to be indefensible in a court of law. Descriptive words such as *good, large, rich, thick,* and *better* are also not permitted. Where do manufacturers find brand names for their products, then?

**Historical names**   Prince Albert, Martha Washington, George Washington, Lincoln, John Hancock, and Napoleon are just a few of the many famous names that now identify a wide range of products. Can you name these products?

**The personal name of the company's founder**   Ford, Westinghouse, Coty, Taylor, Heinz, Lipton, and hundreds of thousands of lesser-known names are used to identify both manufactured products and retail stores alike.

**Fictitious names**   Jack Frost, Betty Crocker, and Skippy.

**Foreign words**   Ma Griffe, Tueros, Le Mans, Progresso, Lowenbrau, Goya, Chun King, Kikkoman, and Sabra add a touch of glamour or a hint of different flavor or exotic aroma.

**Coined words and dictionary words**   Whirlpool, Arrow, Carnation, Acme, Premium, and Crest are all dictionary words given a new meaning by the advertiser. Supermarkets and department stores are filled with products that are branded with coined words such as Hotpoint, Frigidaire, Kodak, RIT, Kimbies, O-Cedar, Listerine, and Chux, to name only a few.

**Initials and letters**   Names like Preparation H, 4711, STP, Formula 9, and ZBT have become increasingly popular, perhaps because they suggest some secret ingredient or formula.

**Places and institutions, real or fictional**   Maxwell House, Pepperidge Farm, Parker House, Vermont Maid, French Market, Carolina Rice, and Maryland Club benefit from the reputation that grows up around a hotel, inn, or region of the country for a particular food specialty. The name French Market coffee suggests that it is the same blend that is served in the old French quarter of New Orleans; Vermont Maid suggests the famous maple syrup from Vermont. The names of many products have been chosen to benefit from such implications.

## Attributes of a trademark or brand

**Distinctive**   Because the main purpose of the brand or trademark is to identify or distinguish the product, the name or mark chosen should be as distinctive as possible. The marketplace is filled with such overworked names as Royal, Prince, Standard, Crown, and General, as well as such overused symbols as circles, crosses, diamonds, and triangles. A distinctive name or symbol is not only more easily remembered, but it offers better graphic opportunities for print and television advertising.

**Suggestive**   A well-chosen name may have a suggestive quality that ties in with the advertising theme of the product or with a particular product attribute. Jell-O (gelatin dessert), Chux (disposable diapers), Brown Gold (coffee), and Beautyrest (mattresses) are a few well-known brands whose names contributed to the marketing success of the product.

**Appropriate**   Many products are surrounded by a certain mystique in the minds of American consumers, and the brand names chosen for these products should take these preconceptions into account. Many people think cigars should have Spanish names. Most do. They think perfumes should have French-sounding names. Most do. Vodka needs a Russian-sounding name such as Smirnoff or Popov. Imagine a tequila called Smirnoff or a vodka called Jose Cuervo! Names that conform to the consumer's expectations contribute to the image of the product.

**Easy to remember**   The name or the trademark must not only be easy to remember but easy to read, easy to spell, and easy to pronounce. Consumers will not want to embarrass themselves in front of a salesperson by mispronouncing a name. Some companies take great care to make sure that consumers do not mispronounce their products' names. Baume Bengue is a classic case in which a company simply changed the spelling of the brand name to Ben—Gay to preclude any misunderstanding. In its advertising, Dewar's Scotch reminds us to pronounce its brand name *do—ers.* One company began marketing a brand of cheese called Pollio, apparently named after the founder of the company. Consumers thought the name was pronounced *polio*! It was not long before the company precluded any problems by spelling the brand name *Polly-O* and using a parrot for a symbol. The point is: if any unpleasant association can be attached to a brand name, don't use it.

Often, consumers themselves will refer to a product by a shortened name or nickname, and advertisers usually find it expedient to adopt the abbreviated version and to register it. Consider: *Luckies* for Lucky Strike, *Pepsi* for Pepsi-Cola, *Coke* for Coca-Cola, *Bud* for Budweiser, and *Chevy* for Chevrolet. On the other hand, though a driver may refer affectionately to his or her car as a "Caddy," the advertiser has chosen to maintain the name Cadillac on the grounds that it lends more dignity to the product.

## Family names

One of the most important branding decisions an advertiser has to make is whether to use an individual brand name for each product in a product line or to group all the products together under a single *family name.* General Motors uses a different name for each of its automobile lines. So do Chrysler and Ford. But Lever Brothers and Procter & Gamble give each of their products an individual brand name.

Many companies market their products under family names. The family name lends itself to insti-

tutional advertising. The good will built by the reputation of each product spreads to all the others in the family line. The H. J. Heinz Company, for example, merely names its products Heinz soups, Heinz beans, Heinz ketchup, Heinz pickles, and so forth. Estee Lauder markets an extensive line of fine cosmetics, all clearly identified as Estee Lauder lipshine, Estee Lauder body lotion, and Estee Lauder fragrance spray. The use of family names also simplifies the launching of a new product because the problem of selecting a name for the new product is eliminated. Of course, when products are completely unrelated, they do not benefit from a common identity and may even, in some cases, be handicapped. Procter & Gamble, for example, names each of its products individually: Ivory soap (bath soap), Ivory Snow (laundry soap), and Downy (fabric softener). Although most consumers do not know the corporate name behind these products, they do know that Procter & Gamble stands for soap products. Therefore, it might be difficult for Procter & Gamble to market other types of products under its company name. People might not find Procter & Gamble cake mix or Procter & Gamble peanut butter very appetizing. Duncan Hines or JIF would be much more appealing.

## What's in a name

Every now and then manufacturers give one of their products a name similar to a nationally known brand name. Such imitation may be merely flattery or it may be intended to cause confusion in the mind of the consumer. In either case, it is illegal and constitutes a patent infringement. It doesn't matter if your name really *is* Pillsbury; you cannot market flour or a line of cake mixes under that name. Manufacturers go to great trouble and ex-

pense to build a trademark or brand name—and to protect it.

One of the problems that plagues advertisers is the public's tendency to use a brand name to refer to *a type of product.* A classic example is *cellophane,* which was developed by Du Pont Corporation and registered as a brand name. But Du Pont failed to prevent widespread misuse of the word *cellophane* as a name for all brands of transparent tape, and, consequently, it became generic. Now Du Pont and other companies with valuable brand names are careful to defend them. They are quick to point out to consumers that Kleenex is a brand of tissues, that Frigidaire is a brand of refrigerator, that Dacron is a brand of polyester, that Band—Aid is a brand of adhesive bandage, and that Scotch Tape is a brand of cellophane tape.

To protect their trademarks, some manufacturers add a descriptive word or phrase after their trademark or brand. It's not just Q-Tips, it's "Q-Tips ® cotton swabs." If the public develops an abbreviation for a brand name, such as Coke for Coca-Cola, most manufacturers will register the abbreviated form as a separate and additional brand name. They also try to educate company personnel, product users, and the news media regarding the proper use of their brand names or trademarks. The most important step a company can take to protect its trademark is to police the market vigorously, taking legal action where necessary.

## Trade characters

*Trade characters* are real or fictional people or animals that can be as important as brand names and trademarks in identifying products or product families. Consumers will associate a good trade character with a particular manufacturer or prod-

Of course everyone recognizes the Jolly Green Giant and Chiquita Banana, but how many remember Bert and Harry, the Piel brothers, as they delivered their clever and funny beer commercials?

uct, and, whenever they see that character, they will also think of that manufacturer or that product. Where possible, advertisers have taken advantage of the popularity of an existing "character" to augment recognition of their product. Mickey Mouse watches? Of course. And Mickey is joined by Betty Crocker, Mr. Clean, the Jolly Green Giant, the Red Baron, Bert and Harry, the White Rock Girl, the Pillsbury doughboy, Mr. Peanut, and hundreds of others.

In the mind of the consumer, a trade character may stand for a particular attribute of a product or may provide a general image that enhances the product. The Jolly Green Giant, representing canned and frozen vegetables and other frozen foods, adds a whimsical touch to the company's advertising as well as a nostalgic reminder of childhood and the long-forgotten story of Jack and the Beanstalk. Mr. Clean represents a clean, pleasant, friendly person who is willing to help the homemaker with the thankless task of housecleaning. Not a woman and not an ordinary man, Mr. Clean is dressed in a sailor's clothes because sailors are accustomed to scrubbing decks (floors) and polishing the brass (household appliances). The earring that Mr. Clean wears tells consumers that he is a genie—a fantasy character who does their bidding. Mr. Clean is a good trade character, and the public has accepted both the image and the product.

## Other advertising marks

A *collective mark* is a trademark or service mark used by members of a cooperative, an association, or some other collective group. Collective marks also include marks used to indicate membership in a union. The Cotton Council's mark is an example of a collective mark.

**PURE WOOL**

**THE TRAVELERS**

When groups of producers plan an advertising program to stimulate primary demand for a type of product, the use of a distinctive emblem fosters recognition by the public. At the same time, the development of an identifying symbol or word provides cooperative promotion opportunities that extend the communication.

A *certification mark* is a mark used to certify a product's origin, mode of manufacture, quality, or accuracy; it may also indicate that the product was made by members of a particular organization or association. Such marks include the Wool Bureau's pure-wool mark.

A *service mark* is used in the sale and advertising of services and includes symbols, names, titles, designations, slogans, characters, and other distinctive features. Such marks include the Travelers Insurance Company's red umbrella mark.

A *logotype* is a representation of the brand name or trade name in an advertisement. The word is also used to designate the company name that appears at the bottom of its print advertisements. It is frequently referred to as the *logo.*

## Packaging

Carefully planned packaging, like carefully planned products, can benefit the manufacturer, the dealer, and the consumer. The package is often considered by consumers as a component of product quality and in this sense a change in packaging becomes a meaningful product improvement.[4]

### Essentials of package design

Packages are forms of advertising at the point of sale. They have become an integral part of most products and may be, for many, one of their most important attributes. The pump-spray container in which a deodorant or hair spray is packaged is—in

[4] Albert W. Frey and Jean Halterman, *Advertising,* 4th ed. (New York: Ronald Press, 1970), p. 23.

view of the potential dangers of pressurized sprays —an added quality feature. Other products offer shatterproof containers; built-in spouts for better pouring; tab-lock tops for easier closing; cutting edges; and "mix-in," "bake-in," or "cook-in" features. In many instances, the package is what keeps the product sold; that is, it helps to keep the consumer brand loyal. When consumers encounter a leaking container or a box that is difficult to open and even more difficult to reclose, the blame falls on the product, not the package. These consumers are not likely to develop loyalty to the brand despite the fact that they may have been satisfied with the product itself. A case in point is the safety cap on aspirin and cold tablet containers that many people find difficult to open. Because of consumer dissatisfaction with this type of package, a number of firms now provide bottles with ordinary caps as well as the safety caps. Consider, too, the tremendous advertising effort behind the flip-top cigarette box. Since good packaging is so important, advertisers must keep in mind the characteristics that consumers look for in a package:

1. Product protection
   Consumers want the package to protect the product against spoilage, leakage, evaporation, and breakage.

2. Convenience
   Consumers want the package to be easy to open and easy to reclose. They want it to be easy to hold and easy to pour. They want it to fit in their pantries or in their medicine cabinets, in their refrigerators or under their sinks. Odd shapes, designed to be cute or appealing, end up unused because they cannot be easily stored. The package should also be disposable. And, perhaps

**PRODUCT IDENTIFICATION: BRANDING AND PACKAGING**

These are some of the many packages produced by Container Corporation of America—food products, household cleansers, ready-to-wear, industrial components, cosmetics—a vast range of products. Often overlooked when consumers think about food and drugs is the informative role played by packaging in the use of household and garden chemicals, hardware items, games, appliances, and so many other products. At a time when self-service is so widespread, it is difficult to imagine how a consumer could make an intelligent purchasing decision without the benefit of information on the package that gives product details, methods of use, and often describes other products that can extend the application and use of the initial item.

The evolution of the distinctive bottle for Coca-Cola is shown in the photographs at the right. The bottle itself became an important identification of the product. The ad below was one of the first to introduce the new bottle to America. Though advertising styles have changed over the years, the bottle for Coca-Cola has not. The bottle says ''consistency'' in a changing and unpredictable world, like a familiar friend.

| 1894–1899 | 1900–1916 | 1916–1956 | 1956–1976 |

most important, all the contents should be removable. Nothing makes consumers feel cheated more than not being able to remove part of the contents of a jar, bottle, or tube. They want that last drop.

3. Identification

Consumers do not want to search for hours to find their favorite brands on the shelf. The package must join with the brand name, the trademark, and the trade character in identifying the product. Consumers want to be able to distinguish their preferred brands from among the competing brands without difficulty. And they want to be able to identify the product easily again once it is in their medicine cabinets or pantries. No mistakes wanted.

4. Information

Consumers want product information. They want a fair and accurate representation of the product and of the results they can expect from the product. Consumers want all the necessary directions for opening, closing, mixing, cooking, and pouring. They have certain preconceptions

**PRODUCT IDENTIFICATION: BRANDING AND PACKAGING**

The type style and the design of a product's label must keep up with the changing tastes and styles of consumers. It is one thing to purposefully give a package or a label an old-fashioned look—if it is part of the product's image, the consumer will understand. But, to maintain a label or package design that is out of fashion can lead customers to question the modernity of the product. Campbell's soup is an old and trusted friend in a new dress. Why didn't Campbell's retain the old package the way Coca-Cola has retained the shape of its bottle for the past sixty-four years? Because the shape of the bottle is distinctive in itself, the can is not. It is the label on the can that distinguishes it from other canned products.

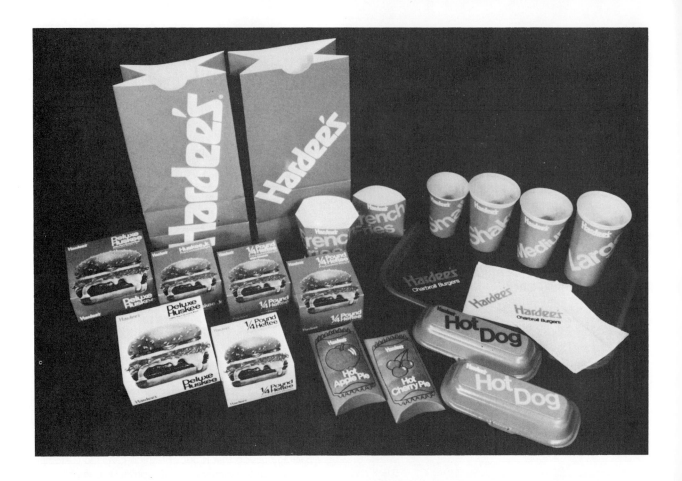

about the type of packaging appropriate for a product, and manufacturers cannot violate these preconceptions. In Europe, condiments are commonly packaged in collapsible tubes. Such packaging can only be utilized for toothpastes and other personal care products in the United States. Jams and jellies cannot be packaged in cans. Baking powder is always in round cans.

## Dealer requirements

Retailers want the packages of the goods they stock to have many of the same characteristics that their customers want. Retailers want the package to protect the product against leakage and spoilage, to be sure. But, in addition, they want the package to be pilfer-proof. They want packages that can easily be coded and that will avoid looking shelf-worn. Dealers want to be sure that the packages will fit on their shelves or in their refrigerators or in their freezer showcases. Good packaging should also make it easier for retailers to sell more efficiently.

To the packaging characteristics demanded by consumers and retailers, manufacturers will add a few requirements of their own. The package should be economical to produce. Since the cost of the package is included in the price the retailers and the consumers pay, manufacturers do not want the package to add unduly to that price. Manufacturers want the package to have sales appeal. The package should be attractive; the style, the design, and the colors should be as eye-catching, as appropriate, and as functional as possible. Also, the product identification should be highly visible on all sides, so that if store clerks do not place the package cor-

A family of packages that enhances the image of the products. Although designed to be used, for the most part, in on-premises consumption, the packages are attractive and functional. Note the manner in which all the packages tie together and tie in too with the napkins, the paper bags, and the carrying tray.

rectly on the shelf, the customer will still be able to spot it.

Briefly, then, the package should be easily identifiable and related, if possible, to the packages of all the other products in the family. It should fit well on retailers' shelves, be easy to price mark, and protect the product thoroughly. The package should conform to all the rules of the FTC, the FDA, the USDA, and all other state, federal, or local regulations that pertain. For drug products these regulations often present packaging problems. A small jar of tablets will often have barely enough room for all the necessary dosage, formula, and precautionary information that is required. These problems have often been solved with great imagination. In some cases, it has been necessary to package the labeled bottle into a paperboard carton and to enclose a printed insert as well.

CASE HISTORY

**A NEW CORPORATE IMAGE STARTS WITH A NEW NAME**

Every company has many "publics" who should be able not only to recognize its name but to correctly identify its industry and its product line. These publics include present customers and stockholders as well as banks, insurance companies, stockbrokers, and securities analysts who supply the company with essential services and capital.

The corporate names of many well-established companies can be a source of misinformation, thereby limiting communication with their publics. This was the problem that faced Michigan Seamless Tube Company—a company with sales of $128 million a year. At first glance, the company's name tells us that it is located in Michigan and that it manufactures seamless tubing. What the name does not convey to most people is the fact that Michigan Seamless Tube also has operations in five other states and has a varied product line—specialty forgings, broaching machines, tools, and steel bars—in addition to seamless tubing. The problem was compounded by the company's subsidiaries, which operated under their own names and were not clearly identified with the parent company.

Customers, suppliers, and the financial community did not see Michigan Seamless Tube as a broadly based metals producer. They perceived it only as a small, specialized, regional manufacturing company. In order to overcome this problem, the company's management decided to adopt a new corporate identity.

The starting point for this change was the company name. The new name had to be one that could encompass all of the company's products and subsidiaries, a name that would correctly project the image of a diversified corporation. After considering many different possibilities, management decided on a coined word: Quanex—a name derived from a combination of the first three letters of the word "QUAlity" and the first three letters of the Latin word "NEXus," which

continued

means connection. The name met all the qualifications that management had set for it: it was short, memorable, contemporary, and not restrictive to one industry, product line, or region. It was unique. An additional benefit was the fact that very few companies listed on stock and bond exchanges have names that begin with the letter Q.

A distinctive logotype was designed for the new corporate name and was applied consistently to all company signs, vehicles, stationery, business forms, and uniforms. It appeared on promotional and technical literature that the sales force carried into the marketplace and it opened up the possibility for the former Michigan Seamless Tube Company to launch a corporate advertising program.

The impact of the name change and promotional campaign quickly became apparent within the company itself, most noticeably at the marketing and sales levels. But the new corporate image soon appeared to yield results in the financial community, where the price/earnings ratio of Quanex's common stock almost doubled.

Source: Walter P. Margulies, "All-Around Facelift Hikes Price/Earnings Ratio for Mid-sized Industrial Company," *Advertising Age*, August 1, 1977, pp. 49–50.

The principal federal agencies that regulate packaging are:

1. the Federal Trade Commission (FTC), which regulates deceptive packaging and labeling as it relates to unfair trade practices

2. the Environmental Protection Agency (EPA), which regulates packaging and use of insecticides, pesticides, and rodenticides

3. the Consumer Product Safety Commission (CPSC), which regulates household products, flammable fabrics, and children's toys

4. the Department of Agriculture (USDA), which regulates fresh and processed meats and poultry

5. the Department of the Treasury, which regulates alcohol, tobacco, firearms, explosives, and imported goods

6. the Department of Health, Education & Welfare (HEW)

7. the Food & Drug Administration (FDA), which regulates foods, drugs, cosmetics, and medical devices

### Packaging is advertising

Is packaging a component of advertising? Or is it really a component of the product? The answer to both these questions is yes. The package, as we have already discovered, is an integral part of the product. But the package also plays an extremely important role in the promotion of the product. The package has evolved from merely a cover to protect the product to a means of making an active contribution to the marketing of that product. Advertisements for the product will strongly feature the package, and the picture of the product conjured up in the minds of consumers is, in many instances, really that of its package. In fact, when different brands of the same type of product all look, feel, taste, smell, and sound alike, the differences in the packaging of each brand becomes the basis for consumer preference.

Here are some of the promotional functions that a product's package can fulfill:

**Packaging is POP**   The package can be a product's most important form of point-of-purchase advertising. In many areas of marketing, the package is also expected to do the work that was formerly performed by the salespeople in a store. The package can provide consumers with a demonstration and an explanation of the product.

**Packaging can increase the unit of sale**   Light bulbs are sold in four-bulb packages, soft drinks in six-packs, chewing gum in "family packs." All of these packages were designed to increase the size of the sale. Two or more different products in the same product family can also be packaged and sold together; or, a sample supply of one product can be packaged with another product in the same family.

**Packaging can stimulate gift sales**   A special package design can appeal to consumers who are shopping for a gift for a holiday or special occasion. However, the package must also be designed so that units that remain unsold after the "special occasion" can be kept on the shelves.

**Packaging can convey quality**   In this respect the color of a package and the style of the type used to print information on it are critical. Consumers may believe that a detergent that comes packaged in a red box will be "too strong" for their needs. The same detergent packaged in a yellow box might impress them as too weak, while the same detergent in a blue or a green box might be just right. The design of a package can also convey a modern, home-style, country-style, or old-fashioned image to consumers. But even packages that want to have that "old-fashioned look" have to be modernized from time to time so that they are in keeping with contemporary ideas of what looks old-fashioned.

No, it is not a label recently designed to look old-fashioned. It *is* an old-fashioned label, and so is the product. But this label is still in use today on a product that is bought and used by consumers who don't go in for "new-fangled products."

# ROGER FERRITER

In creating the name, package, and display unit for L'eggs panty hose, Roger Ferriter combined form and function so perfectly that the product ensemble became a packaging classic almost overnight. In fact, when the product was first test marketed in 1970, the results were 1,500 times greater than the manufacturer expected. From that beginning, L'eggs went on to become the best-selling brand of panty hose in the world—from a standing start to annual sales of almost $400 million in less than five years. One of the most influential publications in the advertising field, *Advertising Age*, described the name L'eggs as "the fastest 'trigger' on a package in the twentieth century."

What sort of man conceives such unique and effective packaging designs? Roger Ferriter studied illustration as an undergraduate student at Rhode Island School of Design, became interested in typography while serving in the Marine Corps and studied photography and printmaking as a graduate student at Yale University. With this well-rounded background, he was able to land a job as an art director with the Young & Rubicam agency in New York soon after graduating from Yale. He was a corporate vice-president and creative director for Metromedia, Inc. in 1972, when he decided to go into business for himself, first in partnership with another famous designer, Herb Lubalin, and later as the president of his own corporation, Roger Ferriter, Inc. He has designed packages, trademarks, and magazine logos and formats for such clients as Westinghouse, Barron's, and the World Trade Center.

In discussing the development of the L'eggs' packaging, Mr. Ferriter has confessed that he was hampered by the lack of some very fundamental information. His solution to the problem was characteristically inventive:

> No one could tell me what size to make the egg. Solution: the L'eggs' egg is exactly the size of my left fist. I could 'squonsch' up the panty hose in that fist—measured it, and made the egg that size.

When asked what were the most important skills college students should acquire if they plan to enter advertising, Mr. Ferriter replied:

> It is hard to give priorities, but here is a list based on my experience: (1) drawing, (2) painting, (3) photography, (4) two- and three-dimensional space division, (5) fundamentals in typography, production, math, and ENGLISH!

Finally, Mr. Ferriter says: "After you secure your first job, change jobs as soon as you are not in a learning experience—whether it's six months or six years."

Redesigned by the internationally famous design firm of Lippincott & Margulies, the cans in the *after* photograph show improved advertising power. Rather than leave so much space at the top of the can blank as in the original design, the new design puts the name of the company, Kendall, at the top of the can in order to achieve maximum visibility. The use of capitals and lower case letters instead of all capitals as on the earlier cans improves legibility. Once Kendall is placed at the top of the can, there is more room below to clearly identify the product. There was nothing ''wrong'' with the old package, but most people will agree that the new package has a cleaner, more modern look.

## Slogans

A *slogan* is a phrase or a sentence that describes either the benefit derived from a product or one of the product's most important attributes. The slogan may be a permanent (relatively) addition to the advertiser's promotion or a temporary expression that captures the essence of a campaign theme. Permanent or temporary, the slogan is a carefully polished group of words intended to be repeated by consumers verbatim and to be remembered by them with a favorable reaction.

No slogan attains wide popularity at once. Promotion over a period of time is required to establish the slogan. Although some slogans may seem to have been around for ages, they were developed diligently over many years at the cost of many dollars. To be successful, a slogan should be built on one idea. A slogan should be brief (about four words), well-balanced, and easy to say. Consider some well-known slogans and see if they satisfy all the criteria:

> WE TRY HARDER
> IT FLOATS
> WHEN IT RAINS IT POURS
> THINGS GO BETTER WITH COKE

Today, slogans are not used as frequently as they once were. The reason may be the growth of television: it is no longer necessary to create some mnemonic phrase when a live demonstration of the product will promote the product far better. Some very old slogans are still around, but have more nostalgic value than selling power.

## Summary

The advertiser works within the framework of the marketing mix: the product; the price; the channels of distribution; the promotion. Although the role of the advertising manager is usually limited to promotion, that promotional effort is critically mixed with the product itself. The item to be sold consists not merely of the physical product, but also of the product's brand name and its package. For the consumer, the brand name or trademark is virtually indispensable in identifying the company's products and in distinguishing them from competing goods. A great deal of thought must go into the creation of a brand name or a trademark: it must enhance the product's image and it must lend itself to use both graphically and orally in advertising and promotion. Legal regulations protect the brand name or trademark against infringement or against adoption as a generic term.

Packaging benefits the consumer and the dealer; it provides protection for the product, eye-catching appeal, convenience, easy identification, and information on the proper use of the product. The package may enhance sales by representing point-of-purchase impact, by stimulating trial usage, and by increasing multiple-unit purchases.

The overall packaging characteristics are determined for the most part by the size, construction, shape, material, closure, and design. The size of the package is determined by the physical characteristics of the product, the machinery available for filling and sealing the package, the custom of the trade, the price of the product to the consumer, and the quantity that the consumer might purchase at one time. Sizes too large to fit the retailer's normal display facilities will meet resistance. Small sizes are subject to shoplifting—a serious problem today in retailing. However, it may be wise to package new products in containers that hold small amounts to stimulate trial purchases. Large sizes stimulate sales among heavy-users; large sizes are more economical and may convert light-users to heavy-users. The increase in the number of women working outside the home tends to stimulate sales of multiple packs, as they often prefer to shop less frequently.

## QUESTIONS FOR DISCUSSION

1. What are the benefits of using different brand names for products of different quality within the same product family? Are there any disadvantages?

2. What are the qualities the advertiser wants in a package?

3. What are the characteristics of a good trademark or brand name?

4. Can you think of several well-known products for which the original brand name has become generic?

5. What is a service mark? Under what conditions is it used?

6. What is the purpose of a label? How does the label or package benefit the consumer?

### Sources and suggestions for further reading

Engel, James F.; Kollat, David T.; and Blackwell, Roger D. *Consumer Behavior.* 2d ed. New York: Holt, Rinehart and Winston, 1973.

Kelsey, Robert J. *Packaging in Today's Society.* New York: St. Regis Paper Company, 1978.

Stanley, Richard E. *Promotion.* Englewood Cliffs, N.J.: Prentice-Hall, 1977.

"The Name Game." *Forbes*, November 15, 1973.

## CREATIVE STRATEGIES

**Developing the appeal**

The purchasing decision

**What does the product offer?**

How the product's life cycle affects
creative strategy

Uncovering the product's subjective
appeal

**Consumer perceptions**

Reference groups
The diffusion process
From innovators to laggards

Attitudes, customs, and habits
Application of psychographics to
advertising
Positioning the product
Competing for space in the
consumer's brain
Trends in positioning

**Media considerations**

**Brainstorming**

## WORKING VOCABULARY

| | | |
|---|---|---|
| appeal | disassociative reference groups | early majority |
| creative strategy | | late majority |
| purchasing decision | diffusion process | laggards |
| competitive strategy | artificially new | rate of adoption |
| frame of reference | marginally new | positioning |
| membership reference groups | genuinely new | brainstorming |
| aspiration reference groups | innovators | |
| | early adopters | |

CHAPTER

# 14

## creative strategies

*We like to put expensive food on our tables, not always because it tastes better than cheap food, but because it tells our guests that we like them, or, just as often, because it tells them that we are well fixed financially.*

S. I. HAYAKAWA
*Language in Action*

WE HAVE ALREADY MADE SEVERAL IMPORTANT DECISIONS—to advertise in the first place, to set up a budget or allocation of money, and to select a media plan after a careful analysis of all the pros and cons of the various media available to us. We have branded our product and registered the trademark we so carefully conceived. Now we are ready to create the actual advertisements that we will have printed in newspapers and magazines, posted on billboards and on the sides of buses, and broadcast on radio and television. We sharpen our pencils or turn to our typewriters; we are ready to begin—but what are we going to say? What words are we going to use? What pictures are we going to show?

## Developing the appeal

We can begin our search for the right words and pictures for our ads by reviewing our advertising goals. Each of our advertisements must contribute to the achievement of one or more of these goals. If our goal is to increase the quantity of purchase, what reasons can we give the members of our target market for buying more of our product? If our goal is to take customers from competing brands, what reasons can we give consumers for switching from their present brand to ours? If we want to stimulate a portion of our target market to act or to change an old attitude and adopt a new one that will lead to action in the future, we must supply them with a reason for doing so. This reason is our *appeal*. The appeal (or appeals) we choose and the combination of words and images that we use to convey it to our target market form our *creative strategy*.

## The purchasing decision

In Chapter 3, we noted that advertising's principal task is to make more sales than would have been made without advertising. For this reason, most creative strategies are designed to influence consumers' *purchasing decisions*. Because it is important to understand how consumers arrive at a purchasing decision, let's take a moment now to examine the process in detail:

1. Awareness of a need
   At this point a consumer's awareness may very well be unfocused. Perhaps the oven is not as clean as it should be or the bathtub has some stains on it that do not seem to come off. The consumer wants to remedy these problems, but does not know how.

2. Awareness of a product—generic
   The consumer learns about a *kind of product* from advertising, from general reading, or from a friend—no matter what the means, the consumer now knows that a product type exists that may remedy his or her problems. The consumer *may* then begin an active search for the product by asking about it in a store or by carefully watching for an advertisement for such a product. Here, our advertising has one major function: to *teach* the consumer about the product. This teaching role is

critical because the consumer's decision to purchase the product will depend on his or her knowledge and perception of the product. The consumer's *perception* of any product is purely subjective and based on the way the consumer sees the product satisfying a very personal need. The consumer does not want a remedy that relieves the discomfort of colds, but one that is perceived as having the power to relieve "my cold," "my headache," and "my running nose."

3. Awareness of a specific brand
   With or without an active search, the consumer becomes aware that a specific brand (or brands) exist that may meet his or her needs. When there are several brands of the same type of product on the market, our advertising must take a competitive approach. We want to show the consumer not only that the generic product cleans the oven or removes the stains from the bathtub, but that *our brand* does it better, faster, or cheaper.

4. Making a purchasing decision
   Two things can happen here. First, the consumer may not believe any of the ads, may be unwilling to spend the money for the product, or may be too lethargic to change existing buying habits. Result: no purchase behavior. Or, second, after consideration, the consumer may decide that one specific brand (we hope that it is *our brand*) will suit his or her requirements best. The consumer buys that brand and actually *tries* it. The consumer has, at long last, made a purchasing decision.

**5.** Adopting a brand loyalty

If *our brand* has lived up to expectations, the consumer will repeat this purchase behavior and become one of our favorite people—brand-loyal customers. At this point, our advertising should reinforce the consumer's decision to stay with us. If *our brand* has not satisfied the consumer, however, the consumer will try another brand and keep switching until a satisfactory one is found.

By reaching prospective customers with appropriate messages at each stage in the purchasing decision, our creative strategy can persuade them to try *our brand.* In general, there are three basic types of creative strategies: the first emphasizes *product features* and *customer benefits;* the second emphasizes the product's or company's *image;* and the third attempts to *position* the product in the minds of our target market. The type of strategy that is best for us will depend on our advertising goals and our choice of appeal. We may, in fact, want to use a combination of any two, or even of all three, of these approaches.

## What does the product offer?

Our search for the most effective creative strategy should begin with what we know best—our product. Our product has a number of physical attributes—such as taste, color, aroma, and texture—that can form the basis of our appeal. Very simply, then, we can list our product's features in one column and, next to each, the translation of that feature into a potential benefit for the prospective buyer. Then, we do the same, as far as we can determine, for our competitors. What do they have that we don't? What do we have that they don't?

If our product were chocolate chip cookies, for example, we might want to point out in our advertisements that the chips in our brand are made from a much richer chocolate than that used in any other brand. Perhaps our cookies are 50 percent larger than those of competing brands, or perhaps they are packaged in a special container that keeps them fresher longer than those of any other brand. For other types of products, we may want to call the consumer's attention to a unique feature of our brand, perhaps a patented device or an innovation not available from competitors.

We must take care, however, to translate the special features of our product into benefits for the consumer. A mere physical description of our product will not convince many people to buy it. Prospective purchasers are more interested in the results or benefits they will obtain from using our product. A jar of cold cream is not just a batch of chemicals; it is a smoother skin. A television set is not merely an elaborate assembly of electronic components; it is entertainment. In every case, we are selling something of interest to the buyer: fast relief; strong cleaning action; reliable service; or social success.

What if we were planning to promote a product for which there is no competition? No such thing. When the first electric slicing knife came to market, the competition was an ordinary slicing knife. At the time the first electric blanket came to market, people slept with plain wool blankets or down comforters. Many still do. If, in fact, our competition is the customary way something is done, then that type of competition demands a different strategy.

What does the homemaker want from a kitchen cleanser? Power! Notice how the advertiser has used *power* as a verb: Ajax "powers out" the stains and does it "faster than Comet." The consumer accepts the claim without requiring to know the particulars. It is enough for them to know that Ajax can power out stains faster than Comet because it has "three special bleaching and grease-cutting ingredients." This ad is purely competitive. The advertiser wants to enlarge its market share by taking customers from competing products. Note, too, that the advertiser's family name appears in small type in the lower left-hand corner of the ad. No one would want to think that Colgate toothpaste had *power* or that Palmolive soap had *power.*

# AJAX TURNS YOUR SPONGE INTO A SCRUB BRUSH...

## ...POWERS OUT THE TOUGHEST GREASY FOOD STAINS FASTER THAN COMET.

The Ajax power formula, with its 3 special bleaching and grease-cutting ingredients...

gives you immediate scrubbing action as it powers out the toughest greasy food stains.

There, a bright, sparkling clean sink. It's easy. And fast. Faster than Comet. Ajax turns your sponge into a scrub brush.

©1978, Colgate-Palmolive Company.

## How the product's life cycle affects creative strategy

As we have already learned, every product has a life cycle. In developing our creative strategy, we must take into consideration the position of our product in this cycle. In the introductory stage of the cycle, our appeal should be directed toward the stimulation of primary demand. At this point the goal of our advertising should be to teach consumers about the product. We have to give them a reason to try our brand by explaining the uses, features, and benefits of all products of this type, regardless of brand. In the growth phase, after the market accepts our product, we can shift our emphasis to a *competitive strategy*—one emphasing the benefits of our brand over those of competing brands. As our product reaches the mature phase, the total market for the product becomes saturated, and our promotional effort must be directed toward maintaining our market share. In the mature phase, we are concerned with the fight for shelf space in retail outlets and with the prevention of the substitution of private brands for our own. At this stage our advertising should be designed to keep our brand name constantly before the public and to give brand-loyal consumers a reason to continue using our product.

## Uncovering the product's subjective appeal

When we examine the actual words and pictures that compose many successful advertisements, we often find that they tell us very little about the product's physical attributes. Consider the ads for Coca-Cola. Do they ever tell us that Coke is better than Pepsi because it contains 37 percent more kola nuts? Or consider the ads for Winston cigarettes: "I

like the box," says the man in the ad. Is that a reason for us to buy that brand of cigarette? Drink Stolichnaya, "the only vodka imported from Russia." Did they tell you it tastes better than American vodka? Or that it is more mellow than Polish vodka? Not at all. What are they trying to communicate?

In our definition of a product in Chapter 2, we pointed out that, in addition to its physical attributes, every product has a number of psychic attributes. In many cases, a product's psychic attributes are the major sources of consumer satisfaction. In order to develop the most effective creative strategy, we, as advertisers, have to understand what the customer wants and expects from our product. Motivation research can supply us with information that can help us understand the minds and psyches of the consumers in our target market. A cloud of meanings, some positive, some negative, surrounds every product. Once we learn to recognize the positive psychic attributes of our product, we can use them to form the basis of our appeal.

Most consumers find it hard to explain exactly why they buy a particular product. Either they don't really know why they made the purchase or they are reluctant to explain their motives to others. Cadillac's greatest sales asset is its symbolic association with achievement and financial success. But very few Cadillac owners would tell you that they bought the car for that reason. There is nothing wrong with a T-shirt and blue jeans. Yet, if you went to a doctor's office where the doctor and nurses were wearing faded jeans and T-shirts, you might have second thoughts about their professional skill. Most people consider this outfit as casual dress or as student dress. Worn by a professional in a professional setting, it represents arrested mental development. Such is the kind of meaning we attach to clothes. A dark suit and a

Ads for imported products are usually very careful to tell readers how to pronounce the product's name. No one wants to look foolish by fumbling over the pronunciation. The ad is meant to project an image of the product. There is very little copy. What image would best represent *Russian* to American consumers? A red flag with the hammer and sickle? A symbol with bad connotations. The Kremlin walls? Not instantly recognizable. A borzoi hound? A symbol that has already been used by similar products. The advertiser has exercised considerable ingenuity in concocting an appropriate image. The bottle encased in a block of ice reminds us of the cold of the Russian climate, and the hammer with the Russian inscription reminds us of the traditional hammer and sickle symbol of Soviet Russia.

**CREATIVE STRATEGIES**

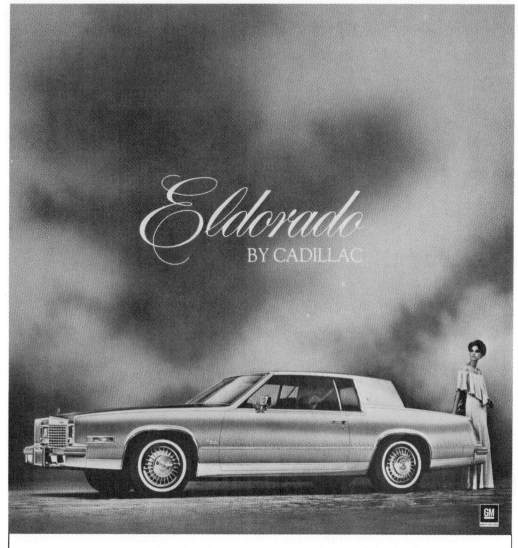

Every element in this ad is designed to add to an image that appeals to an upscale audience. The type script for the name *Eldorado*, the royal style of the crest, the elegant-looking woman—every word, every symbol reinforces the image of elegance and class.

## Unique in features. World-class in engineering. Cadillac in luxury.

This magnificent new Eldorado offers you an unprecedented combination of features found on no other U.S. car. Including "the big five": front-wheel drive...four-wheel independent suspension...electronic fuel injection...

four-wheel disc brakes...electronic level control. All standard. Even side-window defoggers. But you may choose it simply because it's so beautiful. It's at your Cadillac dealer's now. At least once in a lifetime, drive a great car like this.

white shirt with a tie convey a mature, responsible, serious image. A picture of the Eiffel Tower evokes France. The sound of Bouzouki music calls up images of Greece. We all recognize certain symbolic gestures that convey their meanings without words. A handshake, a pat on the back, and a wink all say something to us.

In similar fashion, special symbolism is attached to many products. Coffee represents friendliness and hospitality. Cigarette smoking has traditionally represented masculinity, virility, energy, and accomplishment. The advertisers of Marlboro cigarettes base their appeal on these psychic attributes of their product. The tattooed man in the original Marlboro ads and the cowboys and horses in the more recent ones say to the prospect: "This is a man's cigarette." To convey the appeal, the advertisements do not rely on words alone—often there is no printed message at all—but on nonverbal symbols. Recognizing the masculine symbolism attached to cigarettes, other advertisers saw that when a woman smokes, she is taking some masculine prerogatives and is demonstrating self-assertion, independence, and sophistication. The advertisers of Virginia Slims cigarettes made these aspects of cigarette smoking the basis of their appeal and emphasized those qualities in their advertisements.

# Consumer perceptions

We must always remember that advertising is communication with people—persuasive communication. We want to persuade consumers to do something after they have received our message. In order to get across the most effective message, we should know as much as possible about its receiver. Let's take a moment to examine the communication process.

First, we encode a message—putting it into the words, phrases, and illustrations that we believe convey our message best. The message is then transmitted to consumers by one of the mass media available. When consumers receive our message, they decode it into their own words, according to their *frames of reference*. The decoding is also affected by the receivers' *perceptions of the sender*. This is why many companies consider institutional advertising such an important part of their advertising efforts. By improving the image of a company as a whole, advertisers can improve the reception of the sales messages for that company's products.

We said earlier that consumers interpret the advertising message according to their *frames of reference*. What is a consumer's frame of reference? It is the cultural and social forces that have acted, and are always acting, on that individual. The cultural and social groups to which the consumer belongs affect the way he or she does things, sees things, uses things, and judges things. They help to determine what products consumers will buy and what newspapers and magazines they will read.

## Reference groups

A person is a member of many different groups at the same time. Of all the face-to-face groups, the family is usually the most important influence on an individual's choice of many products. Even if the individual acquires the symbols of another class, latent family influences will remain to affect his or her perceptions. *Membership reference groups*, to which a person automatically belongs because of

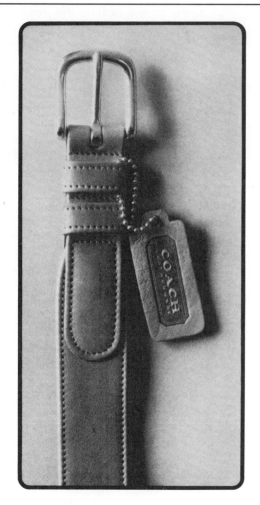

**This is a Coach® Belt.**

Coach® Bags and Belts are made in New York City and sold in selected stores throughout the country. For catalogue write:
Coach Leatherware, 516 West 34th Street, New York 10001.

Coach Leatherware has done a superb job of image building through ads such as this one. Notice that there is no description of the attributes of the product, such as the type of leather that is used to make the belt or the way the belt is stitched together. The entire approach of this ad suggests a product whose quality speaks for itself. The advertiser has built identification for its entire line of leather products by using the same ad format for its bags and belts.

sex, race, income, age, and marital status, also influence the way that person interprets an advertising message. *Aspiration reference groups* are those groups to which a person does not in fact belong, but which he or she wants to join. People will use the behavior and the purchasing decisions of their aspiration reference groups as models for their own actions. *Disassociative reference groups* are those groups to which a person *does not belong and does not want to belong.* No one wants to be fat or old or bald or grey.

Reference groups are important to advertisers because members of any one group tend to be highly resistant to appeals that conflict with that group's beliefs. People are, of course, positively influenced by what others buy, particularly when those "others" belong to a membership or aspiration reference group. "Keeping up with the Joneses" still applies. The reference group can influence the purchase of a product or the choice of a brand. The reference group is the anonymous "they"—as in "that's what *they're* wearing" or "that's what *they're* buying." And the more expensive the purchase, the greater the influence of the reference group.

## The diffusion process

The *diffusion process* is the process by which the acceptance of a new product, new service, or new idea spreads to the target market within a certain period of time. The process involves four elements:

1. the innovation itself

2. the channels of communication

3. the social system in which the innovation takes place

4. the period of time the innovation requires to penetrate the target market

The "newness" of a product may be defined by its physical features and the manner in which it satisfies the user that it is different from the old product or the old way of doing things. Some products are *artificially new,* that is, the product merely appears to be new because of some cosmetic change. Designing a new package for an old product is an example of this type of change. Other products may be *marginally new,* that is, they may contain an added ingredient or have a modified design. Still others may be *genuinely new;* they may be entirely different from older products of the same type or from older ways of doing something. A soup that can be heated in the plastic pouch in which it is packaged is genuinely new. It is a new way of doing something. A laundry detergent that contains a bluing agent is only marginally new. All of these definitions are obviously subjective and based on the consumer's perception of newness.

As advertisers, our main concern is the speed with which the product achieves sales penetration. If we knew how consumers would react to our product, if we could anticipate what features or what advertising approach would speed or retard its acceptance, then we would not have any advertising or marketing problems. Although there are no magic formulas for success, the diffusion process does demonstrate that some of a product's characteristics appear to influence the consumer's acceptance of that product. Such characteristics include: the degree to which the new product is consistent with present practices; the complexity of the product; the cost of trying a new product (the amount of money required to try a new package of chewing gum, for example, as compared with that

Calvin Klein Jeans

An illustration and three words of copy are all that is needed to convey the appeal of this product. For many consumers, the designer's name and the model's style of dress represent values of their *aspiration reference group.* They will interpret the message, in effect, as: "Calvin Klein jeans, that's what they're all wearing."

required for a new microwave oven); and finally the extent of social visibility of the product (a tangible product is more easily communicated than an intangible service or a product used very privately). A tennis racket is more easily diffused than a new checking account service.

**From innovators to laggards** Consumers themselves can be divided into categories based on their willingness to try a new product. Most books on consumer behavior describe product adopters as innovators, early adopters, early majority, late majority, and laggards. The distribution of each type of purchase behavior in the population usually follows a pattern represented by the typical bell curve. A few people, the *innovators*, are willing to take risks and try a new product as soon as it reaches the market. *Early adopters*, a somewhat larger group, discover the product after the innovators and serve as role models for the early majority. The *early majority* is slow to adopt the product, waiting for the innovators and early adopters to do so first. The *late majority* needs considerable peer pressure to stimulate them to adopt a new product; and a few individuals, the *laggards*, are very conservative and tend to remain rooted in past practice.

The *rate of adoption* measures how long it takes for a new product to be adopted. The rate of adoption is contingent upon the factors previously described—the price, the social visibility, the complexity of the product, and the means that are used to communicate news of the innovation (mass media, personal selling) to the target market.

### Attitudes, customs, and habits

Most consumers' habits, customs, and attitudes are derived from their culture and from the social groups to which they belong; they are largely the result of social conditioning. We know that much behavior is habitual. Some people automatically reach for the salt or the mustard or the ketchup. Some people buy the same product or shop in the same store out of habit. And these habits are hard for the individual—and for the advertiser—to break.

Sometimes consumer behavior is affected by customs. For example, orange juice is considered a breakfast drink. Tomato juice can be served at breakfast, lunch, or dinner—but not orange juice. Turkey is served at Thanksgiving and Christmas. Why not on the Fourth of July, too? Custom. There's no logical reason for it, and it will be extremely difficult (perhaps impossible) and extremely expensive to alter a custom through advertising. Cranberry growers tried to induce people to eat cranberry sauce throughout the year, but how often do Americans eat cranberry sauce? Probably only with their turkey dinners at Christmas and Thanksgiving. However, a successful advertising campaign to change a custom of this kind can greatly expand the market for a product.

People's purchasing behavior is also influenced by certain attitudes, that is, by states of judgment that exist before new information is received. Instant coffee suffers from a negative attitude. Most homemakers would apologize to their guests when they served it. Can you imagine a truck driver drinking a cup of instant coffee? Fortunately, attitudes can be changed, but we had better know what attitudes affect the use of our product before we roll out our advertising program.

In this same context, advertisers must also be aware of some taboos that exist. In general, explicit references to sex are not in good taste. Children smoking, women drinking beer, and satires of religious or certain social groups are all taboo. Sex reversal roles, unless clearly spoofs, are also considered to be in bad taste.

## Application of psychographics to advertising

We can use psychographics to help us develop more effective appeals and creative strategies than would be possible if we relied solely on more traditional forms of research. Let us caution the student that psychographics are, however, not a substitute for demographics; and *neither* is a substitute for creativity. Psychographics are simply another tool. How, then, shall we use it?

Psychographic life-style data can provide us with a more lifelike picture of our target consumer. The more we know about the *kind of person*, the more we can fine tune our appeal, aiming it directly at just that portion of our target market that includes our best prospects. All working women are not alike. All older people are not alike. It is a myth that individual demographic groups are relatively homogeneous entities. From life-style data (gathered from marketing research) we can get ideas for the proper settings for our advertisements, the physical appearance of the characters shown, the nature of the art work, the kind of music to use, and the most appealing colors. We can also learn how much fantasy consumers will accept in our advertisements.

The creative people in an advertising agency learn from psychographic data what tone to give to the advertising. They learn whether the most effective message will be serious, humorous, authoritative, traditional, or contemporary. One very interesting application of psychographics is described by a research expert in a major advertising agency.

Seeking to develop a new approach for a beer client, the agency obtained a psychographic profile of the client's target consumer.[1] The demographic data showed the target market as middle-income, male, young, blue-collar, with a high school education. He was the heavy beer drinker—part of the 20 percent of all beer drinkers who consume 80 percent of all the beer sold in the United States. The agency discovered that this consumer believed:

> beer a man's drink
> he liked a physical, male-oriented world
> he loved sports
> he did not object to danger
>
> The resulting campaign was built around the imagery of the sea to dramatize the adventure of one of the last frontiers. The focus of the campaign was on the "life style" of the men of the sea—men who lived their lives with gusto and who enjoyed a "gusto brew."[2]

Another excellent study made by the same agency (Leo Burnett) will serve as an example of the use of psychographics for an entirely different product: heavy-duty hand soap. The heavy-users of this product were downscale—that is, their income and educational levels were low and they were for the most part older people. This is a very static market segment. One of the advertising objectives for the marketers of this soap was to attract new users.

Life-style findings indicated that this new target consumer was a homemaker in the most tradi-

[1] Joseph Plummer, "Applications of Life-Style Research to the Creation of Advertising Campaigns," in *Life-Style and Psychographics*, William D. Wells, ed. (Chicago: American Marketing Association, 1974), pp. 159–169.

[2] Ibid., p. 165.

This ad makes an interesting contrast to the Cadillac ad on page 317. The Cadillac ad is addressed to men. This ad is addressed to women and clearly indicates the reference group—young, married, suburban, two children. The target consumer is a sensible, no-nonsense kind of woman who wants practicality with her style, and that is what the advertiser tells her that the Pacer offers. The lady in the Cadillac ad does not expect to drive in her evening gown.

## When she gave in to practicality, she didn't give up her individuality.

The first baby moved her to the suburbs. The second one moved her out of her beloved sports car. But not into something square. In fact, into something rather well-rounded. The wide stance AMC Pacer Wagon.

Because a woman who knows anything about cars knows that wide is wonderful. The Pacer Wagon's extra width makes it extra efficient. So you get large size room and comfort in a sensibly sized car. And something even more important, extra stability, to make it ride and handle like a much larger car.

And she doesn't mind that the Pacer Wagon's unique wide design makes it look a little different. That's the way a woman with her own style likes to look.

*The exclusive AMC BUYER PROTECTION PLAN® : AMC will fix, or replace free, any part except tires for 12 months or 12,000 miles, whether the part is defective, or just plain wears out under normal use and service.*

### AMC ◢◣ Pacer

The room and ride Americans want. The size America needs.

THE AMC PACER WAGON IS A PRODUCT OF AMERICAN MOTORS CORP. ALSO AVAILABLE IN 2-DOOR HATCHBACK
® BUYER PROTECTION PLAN is reg. U.S. Pat. and Tm. Off.

## AMERICA'S BEST KNOWN BEER DRINKERS TALK ABOUT **Lite** BEER...

Title: "Martin/Steinbrenner"

Comm'l. No.: MOTH0530

George: You know a lot of people think Billy and I argue all the time. Actually, we agree on just about everything. Right, Bill?
Billy: You betcha, George.

George: We even drink the same beer.
Billy: Lite Beer from Miller. Lite's got a third less calories than their regular beer and it's less filling.

George: And the best thing is it tastes so great.
Billy: No George. The best thing, it's less filling.

George: No, Bill it tastes great.
Billy: Less filling, George!

George: Billy it tastes great.
Billy: Less filling! George!

George: Billy!
Billy: Yeh, George?
George: You're fired.

Billy: Oh, not again!

ANNCR: Lite Beer from Miller. Everything you always wanted in a beer.

And less.

Since the target market for beer is primarily male, Miller Brewing Company uses two famous sports personalities in this commercial to capture the attention of the male audience. Billy Martin or George Steinbrenner delivering a straight commercial message by himself might not provide the authenticity (and the interest) that their dialogue provides. Their argument over whether Lite Beer is better because it tastes good or because it has fewer calories emphasizes the product's double appeal.

tional sense of the word—comfortable in her role as a housewife and mother, confident, and conservative. She was very concerned about cleanliness. She wanted her home to be clean, really clean. How could she be persuaded to use a heavy-duty hand soap? You guessed it—the advertisers suggested that she use it on her children. This soap would get their hands clean, really clean, for the first time. The campaign was built around children and placed the mother in the authoritative role suggested by her psychographic profile. As Mr. Plummer stated, "It is accomplishing both the objective of obtaining new users and the objective of increasing usage among current users."[3]

One final word on life-style data—they can also be valuable guides for media selection. We can examine the characteristics of a medium's audience and compare them with the characteristics of the people who do *not* compose the audience for that medium. We can, for example, compare readers with nonreaders, viewers with nonviewers, for each specific medium. We might assume that what turns a viewer on or off a particular program might well be related to his or her life-style. Such a consideration can be an important factor in our media evaluation as well as our creative approach.

## Positioning the product

One of the newest creative strategies advertisers have developed is positioning. *Positioning* refers to the "position" our product occupies in a prospect's mind in relation to the competition—its quality, value, shape, price, and function as compared with those of competing products. To develop a positioning strategy, however, we must take into account more than just the strengths and weaknesses of our own product and those of the competition. We must remember that in today's world our advertising message is competing for the consumer's attention with the messages of tens of thousands of products. We are struggling to reach consumers who are bombarded with advertising messages from every direction.

In order to cope with a tremendous volume of information, people reduce everything to indexes, or the simplest descriptions. When we ask our friends, for example, how they are doing in school, they don't tell us what their grades were on every test and paper they completed for every course they have taken since their first semester. They give us their "cume." The "cume" provides us with a simple means of comparing their positions in school with those of other students. A 3.7 is great. A 2.7 is not great, but it's better than a 2.0 This process is called ranking. And that is what consumers do with all advertising information. How is restaurant A? *It's okay, better than restaurant B, but not as good as restaurant C.* What the consumer has done in response to our question is to position restaurant A in our mind. That position is based not merely on what the chef has done with the veal marsala, but on the total impression of that restaurant—the food, the service, the decor, the price, and the atmosphere.

As consumers, we rank products and brands in our minds. If advertisers are to increase preference (and sales) for their brands, they must convince a certain percentage of consumers that their brands deserve to be moved to a higher level in the ranking game. When advertisers introduce totally new products, they create a new game; and it is sometimes difficult for these new products to get started because consumers do not know where to

[3] Ibid., p. 167.

place them. Consider the many new products that had to be related (positioned) to old products in order to gain acceptance: horseless carriage, food processor, talking picture, pressure cooker. . . .

**Competing for space in the consumer's brain**   There is, however, another phenomenon of consumer psychology that will affect our positioning strategy. The consumer's mind is like a data bank in a com-

## JERRY DELLA FEMINA

Jerry Della Femina works at a desk that was once a dining room table that he salvaged from a trash pile. The room also contains a battered, old-fashioned typewriter, an ancient Zenith radio, and a poster for a movie from the 1930s. He describes the room's decor as "early poverty," but Della Femina, Travisano and Partners gained $23 million in billings in 1977 alone. Total billings for this agency, described as one of the "hot shops" in the Big Apple, now total more than $93 million.

In a field populated by MBAs, Jerry Della Femina has achieved a phenomenal success without the benefit of a college education. He started by writing sample ads and sending them to Daniel & Charles, a New York advertising agency. After sending in five ads, he was hired as a junior copywriter at a salary of $100 a week. He subsequently worked for several other well-known agencies—always provocative, developing and flexing his creative muscle. He left the Ted Bates agency in 1967 to found his own shop, taking with him the creative group he had assembled at Ted Bates to work on the Panasonic account. Among the team's first clients was Squire for Men, a maker of hair pieces for whom Jerry Della Femina created the line: "Are you still combing your memories?" Typically, he made a lot of noise on Madison Avenue in 1970 with his caustic book about the advertising business, *From Those Wonderful Folks Who Gave You Pearl Harbor.*

When the *New York Times Magazine* wanted to do a profile on an advertising agency to spotlight the phenomenon of modern advertising agency growth, it sent its reporters to Della Femina, Travisano and Partners. Apparently the story appealed to Schieffelin & Company, because it prompted them to visit Della Femina and to leave behind a little Blue Nun. The successful advertising that Jerry Della Femina created for Blue Nun wine contributed greatly to the creative reputation of his agency.

puter with a "position," or location, for bits of information it has decided to retain. A computer accepts whatever information is fed into it. It stores everything in its memory. But the consumer's mind has a filter that screens out and rejects much information. It accepts new information that is compatible with its prior knowledge or experience and refuses to accept information that seriously conflicts with its prior knowledge.

For example, when we talk about computers, the first name that most people think of is International Business Machines Corporation: IBM. When we read an advertisement or see a television commercial that tells us that RCA stands for computers, we reject it. We know that RCA means records or television sets. IBM means computers. The computer position in our minds is occupied by IBM. For a competing computer company to obtain a favorable position in our mind, it must relate its name and its product to International Business Machine's position.

**Trends in positioning**  Consider the advertising campaigns for beer. In the 1950s and 1960s, advertising copywriters came up with such slogans as "cold-brewed Ballantine," "real-draft Piels," "just the kiss of the hops," and "the beer that made Milwaukee famous." But in the late 1970s, a new trend developed and beer was positioned, as "Michelob —first class" and "of all imported beers, only one could be number one" demonstrate.

In 1957, Lever Brothers introduced Dove soap —not as another soap to get you clean, but as a complexion bar for dry skin. The oval shape was more feminine than the traditional rectangular soap. Dove came in a box, like a cosmetic, not in the paper wrapper of an ordinary soap. Dove's advertising promised that it would "cream your skin while you wash." In this way, Dove positioned itself as a unique brand.

## Media considerations

Our advertising goals, the phase of the product life cycle, and the nature of the market all affect our creative efforts. A final consideration in the selection of a creative strategy is the suitability of the various media to our purpose. For example, if we want to build primary demand, seeking to influence early adopters by imparting detailed product information, which medium will best serve our needs? Will the thirty seconds available on television be long enough to do a teaching job? Do early adopters watch television?

In the early stages of the product life cycle, reach will be more important than frequency. Therefore, we may want to establish a reach objective that enables us to deliver our new product story to the largest possible percentage of the target market. The creative approach to reach will be different from the creative approach to frequency. If we mean to communicate with as many people as possible, our message must contain as much information as we can squeeze in. Each prospect will seek a different benefit. We would therefore prefer to use *more* magazines or *more* televison programs, as we want more people to be aware of our product. We want *reach*.

A product need not be new for media considerations to affect the creative approach. Consider the sale of baby food: no matter how popular or successful the product, purchasers will only use it for about two years. Therefore, our media strategy should emphasize reach, not frequency, since

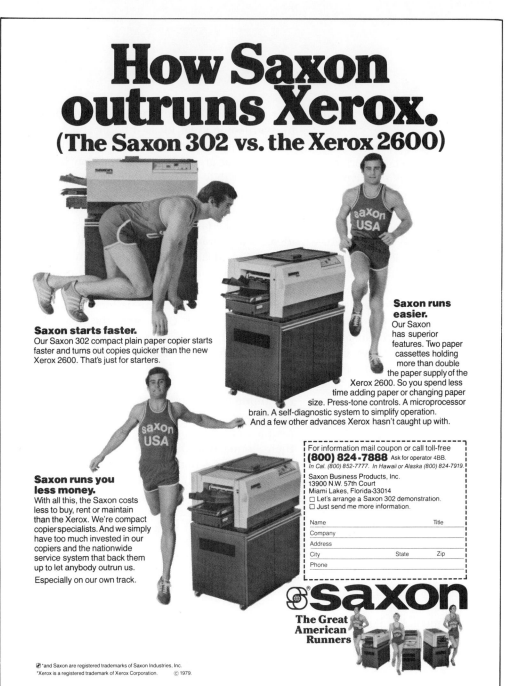

**How Saxon outruns Xerox.**

**(The Saxon 302 vs. the Xerox 2600)**

**Saxon starts faster.**
Our Saxon 302 compact plain paper copier starts faster and turns out copies quicker than the new Xerox 2600. That's just for starters.

**Saxon runs easier.**
Our Saxon has superior features. Two paper cassettes holding more than double the paper supply of the Xerox 2600. So you spend less time adding paper or changing paper size. Press-tone controls. A microprocessor brain. A self-diagnostic system to simplify operation. And a few other advances Xerox hasn't caught up with.

**Saxon runs you less money.**
With all this, the Saxon costs less to buy, rent or maintain than the Xerox. We're compact copier specialists. And we simply have too much invested in our copiers and the nationwide service system that back them up to let anybody outrun us.

Especially on our own track.

For information mail coupon or call toll-free
**(800) 824-7888** Ask for operator 4BB.
In Cal. (800) 852-7777. In Hawaii or Alaska (800) 824-7919.

Saxon Business Products, Inc.
13900 N.W. 57th Court
Miami Lakes, Florida-33014
☐ Let's arrange a Saxon 302 demonstration.
☐ Just send me more information.

Name _____ Title _____
Company _____
Address _____
City _____ State _____ Zip _____
Phone _____

**saxon**
**The Great American Runners**

*and Saxon are registered trademarks of Saxon Industries, Inc.
*Xerox is a registered trademark of Xerox Corporation.     © 1979.

---

When anyone mentions copying, the name that springs to most lips is Xerox. The Xerox name is almost synonymous with copying. If Saxon merely stated that it made copiers, we would not give much weight to its claims for quality, speed, or economy. What does Saxon do? It relates its copier to the Xerox copier and *positions* the Saxon in the mind of the prospective purchaser.

there will always be an influx of new prospects into the target market.

If our product is not new and we plan to position it head-on against the market leader, our media strategy will change; and our creative approach will again be affected. If we mean to be competitive, we will stress our strengths against those of other brands. We can do this best by hammering away at our target market. This time, we want frequency, not reach. We may find—depending on our product and its distribution—that television offers us the greatest opportunity for frequency. On the other hand, certain products may require more selectivity than television offers. In this case, magazines with sharply defined audiences are most suitable. A heavy schedule—one that will give us as much frequency as possible—in a few carefully chosen magazines may be best.

## Brainstorming

We have all heard the word brainstorming[4] before and chances are we have all done it without realizing it. *Brainstorming* is the most familiar and widely used technique for prodding creativity, and advertisers employ it in their search for the proper appeal and creative strategy. There are probably as many different definitions of brainstorming as there are advertising agencies and advertising departments, but the basic concept behind this technique is as follows:

A group of people with knowledge of a product and of the market for that product get together to search for creative ways to bring that product to that market. Of course, any individual could come up with some great ideas if he or she could think about the problem for a long time. But we are in a hurry, so our group of people—it may be only two or three, it may be more—begins to discuss ways to advertise the product. In ordinary conversation or discussion, the group's thoughts would tend to get sidetracked into tangential discussions of initial ideas. But in brainstorming no critical evaluation of any of the ideas expressed at the meeting is allowed, and no negative responses are permitted either. The prime consideration is the generation of ideas, no matter how unusual or impractical they may at first seem. Only after the group has exhausted all its thoughts on the subject are the ideas evaluated and the actual advertising plans determined.

As you can see, brainstorming is primarily a technique to encourage people to get their ideas—all their ideas—out in the open. Of course, the people in the brainstorming group must have done their homework; they must have studied all the available data—demographic, psychographic, motivational research, and media research. As one famous advertising man, David Ogilvy, has revealed in a discussion of a Hathaway shirt campaign:

> I happened to have some research which showed that a wonderful factor to have in the illustration of any advertisement was 'story appeal'. So I thought of 22 different story-appeal elements to put in the photograph of the Hathaway shirts. The twenty-second of them was the eyepatch. It turned out to be a good idea. *But I would not have gone looking for it if I didn't know the research.*[5]

---

[4] The concept originated with Alex F. Osborn, the "O" in BBDO, still one of the country's leading advertising agencies.

[5] Kenneth Roman and Jane Maas, *How to Advertise* (New York: St. Martin's Press, 1976), p. xi.

# Summary

In order to achieve our advertising goals, we must first make consumers aware of our product and then persuade them to try it, either now or in the near future. Naturally, we must give them a good reason for doing the things we desire. This reason is our *appeal,* and our appeal and the words and images that convey it to the target market are our *creative strategy.* In general, there are three types of creative strategies: one focuses on product features and customer benefits, one on product or company image, and one on positioning the product.

Before we can begin to write copy, design a television commercial, or lay out an advertisement, we want to know as much as possible about the people who will see or hear our message. What preconceptions do they bring with them? We will, of course, have as much demographic data as we can gather. We have to know the age, income, education, sex, and marital status of our target market. We cannot even start the creative process without such information.

In recent years, many advertising people have come to believe, however, that demographic data are not sufficient. They understand that a particular segment delineated by a set of demographic statistics is not a homogeneous group of people. Psychological research is also a valuable aid in determining the true reasons why people buy certain products. When we know their purchasing motives, we can emphasize those motives in the advertising for our brand.

We have also learned that consumers with identical demographic characteristics may have entirely different life-styles. An understanding of various life-styles can help us position our product in the consumers' minds — that is, to position the *image* of our brand in comparison to those of competing brands. If we cannot differentiate our brand from its competitors in the eyes of our most likely prospects, our advertising investment may be very unrewarding. If, however, we come armed with all the data we can assemble about our product, about its position in its life cycle, and about our target market, we can begin the creative process. Brainstorming, or the exchange of ideas among interested and knowledgeable people, is not restricted to the creation of advertising. It has come to be associated with many creative efforts, but no matter what the context, the creative process rests on a foundation of information and demands time and effort.

## QUESTIONS FOR DISCUSSION

**1.** What are the steps in a consumer's purchasing decision?

**2.** What is the role of advertising in each step of the purchasing decision?

**3.** What is meant by positioning the product?

**4.** What is meant by a consumer's frame of reference? What effect does it have on the advertising message?

**5.** Why are reference groups important to the consumer?

**6.** How does the position of a product in its life cycle affect the creative strategy?

**7.** How does the product life cycle affect media strategy?

**8.** What is motivation research? Can you suggest the motivation for the purchase of toothpaste? For cranberry juice? For a Mercedes?

**9.** What benefits can the advertiser obtain from a psychographic profile of the target market?

### Sources and suggestions for further reading

Dichter, Ernst. *Handbook of Consumer Motivations.* New York: McGraw-Hill, 1964.

Engel, James F.; Kollat, David T.; and Blackwell, Roger D. *Consumer Behavior.* 2d ed. New York: Holt, Rinehart and Winston, 1973.

Hanan, M. *Life-Styled Marketing.* New York: American Management Association, 1972.

Martineau, Pierre. *Motivation in Advertising.* New York: McGraw-Hill, 1957.

Reynolds, Fred D.; Crask, Melvin R.; and Wells, William D. "The Modern Feminine Life-Style." *Journal of Marketing*, vol. 41, no. 3. July 1977.

Richards, Elizabeth A., and Sturman, Stephen S. "Life-Style Segmentation in Apparel Marketing." *Journal of Marketing*, vol. 41, no. 4. October 1977.

Vinson, Donald W.; Scott, Jerome E.; and Lamont, Lawrence M. "The Role of Personal Values in Marketing and Consumer Behavior." *Journal of Marketing*, vol. 41, no. 2. April 1977.

Wasson, Chester R.; Sturdivant, Frederick D.; and McConaughy, David H. *Competition and Human Behavior.* New York: Appleton-Century-Crofts, 1968.

Wells, William D., ed. *Life-Style and Psychographics.* Chicago: American Marketing Association, 1974.

Ziff, Ruth. *Closing the Consumer-Advertising Gap Through Psychographics.* Combined Proceedings Series, no. 34. American Marketing Association, spring and fall conferences, 1972.

# COPY FOR ADVERTISING

**The function of copy**

Fact finding
Style
Writing rules
    Is it readable?
    Is it believable?
    Does it have interest?

**Ideas for individual media**

Writing for magazines
    The importance of the headline
    Long copy or short copy

Writing the newspaper
    advertisement
    How does a news environment
      affect advertising?
    Learning to write copy for
      newspaper ads
Copy for radio
Writing for television
Writing copy for direct mail
Writing copy for outdoor
The last word

# WORKING VOCABULARY

| puff | blind headline | fact sheet |
| pride foods | story headline | AIDA |

# 15

## copy for advertising

*Copy must foster action—the mental action and the physical action which lead to the purchase of our wares. Therefore, copy must suggest action. But our manner of telling our story can include the suggestion of action.*

AESOP GLIM
*How Advertising Is Written—And Why*

YEARS AGO, before radio and television became important advertising media and before improved graphic arts technology made exciting new printing techniques available, advertisers had to rely on the written word to carry their advertising messages. Today, however, advertisers know that words are only one form of the language of advertising. They have discovered ways of conveying their ideas through form, color, and design. Nevertheless, in the majority of advertisements in both print and broadcast media, the written word remains the most important means of conveying the sales message to the target market.

We do not mean that written advertising copy alone is responsible for the success of any advertising program. Much of a program's success depends on the plans that are carefully formulated before the first word is written. Moreover, the success of the advertising program is contingent upon other variables, many of which are beyond the control of the marketing organization. Advertising may have the ability to draw the customer into the retail outlet, but if that outlet does not enhance the image of the product or if it fails to provide the after-sale service required in some cases, even the best-written advertising will be wasted. The phrases that proved

335

successful last year may be inadequate in the face of changing economic conditions (such as inflation) or changing social conditions (such as smaller families).

## The function of copy

Advertising is used to help sell products. The purpose of copy is to provide information that will stimulate the prospects to buy our product. The illustration and/or the headline will have captured their attention, generated enough interest to start the prospect reading. But it is the copy, the written or spoken words, that will influence and persuade —or fall flat. It is the copy that makes the claims, points out the advantages, explains, emphasizes, teaches, proves—in short, gives the prospect reasons, implicit as well as explicit, for buying our product. And, for buying it *soon.*

### Fact finding

If our copy is going to do all the wonderful things we want it to do, we had better be sure that what we say is the truth. Believability is the key word. We can all think of an advertisement or two that, every time we see it or hear it, we think "baloney." To achieve believability for our ads, we had better do our homework. Study the product. Surely there is something about our product that is unique, different—wanted. White-O may be a powerful bleach. It may wash out the stains ordinary detergents can't handle. Speedyrin is aspirin with antacids added. It acts as fast as ordinary aspirin to relieve pain without stomach upset. From these facts, we can build the sentences of our copy.

Where does the information come from? Copywriters study research reports from secondary sources—psychographic studies and market reports that are available from research organizations. In addition, copywriters search out firsthand sources for information. They talk to people on the streets and ask them questions about the product. They try the product themselves: they bake it, cook it, eat it, drink it, or use it in their homes. They talk to retailers about the product. They visit supermarkets and observe the shoppers. They visit department stores and watch the customers buying or trying the product. They read the magazines, such as *Reader's Digest* and *Good Housekeeping*, in which the product may be advertised. They listen to several different radio stations. They pay attention to what people—prospective customers for the products they must write about—say and do. Their copy must talk the language of the prospect; it must be written in terms the audience will understand.

What are some of the things that a copywriter will want to know?

1. *What is the product made of?*
   What colors, flavors, or shapes are available?
   How is it packaged?
   Is the product well made?

2. *What is the product used for?*
   What problems does it solve?
   What problems does it prevent?
   What emotional needs does it satisfy?

3. *How often is the product used?*
   How often is it bought?
   Who buys it?
   Where is it used?

## Lemon.

This Volkswagen missed the boat.

The chrome strip on the glove compartment is blemished and must be replaced. Chances are you wouldn't have noticed it; Inspector Kurt Kroner did.

There are 3,389 men at our Wolfsburg factory with only one job: to inspect Volkswagens at each stage of production. (3000 Volkswagens are produced daily; there are more inspectors than cars.)

Every shock absorber is tested (spot checking won't do), every windshield is scanned. VWs have been rejected for surface scratches barely visible to the eye.

Final inspection is really something! VW inspectors run each car off the line onto the Funktionsprüfstand (car test stand), tote up 189 check points, gun ahead to the automatic brake stand, and say "no" to one VW out of fifty.

This preoccupation with detail means the VW lasts longer and requires less maintenance, by and large, than other cars. (It also means a used VW depreciates less than any other car.)

We pluck the lemons; you get the plums.

This ad is a classic. Since auto manufacturers would ordinarily never use the word *lemon* to describe their product, the use of the word in the headline is arresting. "What do they mean by lemon?" consumers ask themselves—and then read the body copy to find out. This gives the advertiser an opportunity to tell them how carefully Volkswagen inspected every vehicle.

**4.** *What is the product like?*

Is it like another product on the market?

Does it have masculine or feminine qualities?

Is it modern, old-fashioned, futuristic?

Is it for pleasure or for serious purpose?

**5.** *Who uses the product?*

Men or women or both?

Is age a factor?

Is income a factor?

Is education or occupation a factor?

You cannot know too much. Examine the competing products. Learn how important the price is to consumers. Find out where they usually purchase the product, and how important the dealer is. Most products provide satisfaction to the user in more than one way. An electric blanket may keep us warm on cold nights. But, so will a wool blanket. The electric blanket, however, is lighter. The electric blanket permits us to control the degree of warmth. The electric blanket is attractive. The electric blanket is washable. All of these attributes are benefits. It is the copywriter's task to sort them out and determine which one is the primary reason for the purchase.

How does our product compare with those of the competition? Sometimes one of their strong points is our weakness. We should know about it and evaluate its importance to the prospect. A medicine bottle with a child-proof closure may be important for people with kids around the house. For an all-adult household, it's not a selling feature —it's an inconvenience.

## Style

People do not open a magazine or newspaper to read advertisements. They do not flip the switch on their television sets to watch the commercials. People do read and watch things that interest and stimulate them. The purpose of advertising is to persuade, and the test of good advertising copy is not its grammar, but its effectiveness.

The style of the copy is determined by the writer. There is a big difference between literary style and copywriting style, and it is important to note this distinction. In literary writing the author's personality comes through. We expect it. Dickens, Hemingway, Cheever, Kerouac—we recognize their individual styles immediately. But in writing advertising copy, the copywriter's personality must remain in the background. It is the personality of the product that must come through.

Style is the result of careful word selection. We know that verbs and nouns have more power than adjectives and adverbs. Compare the statement: "she cleaned the room fast" with "she breezed through the cleaning." One places the emphasis on the adverb *fast*, the other on the verb *breezed;* one suggests speed, the other speed *and* ease. Nouns and verbs give impact to a statement. Note also that *breeze through* is an idiomatic expression. That's the way we talk to one another. Why should our copywriting style be stilted or formal? Remember, the purpose of our advertisement is to *communicate* with people—perhaps several millions of them. The best way to do this is to use simple, easy-to-understand words.

Words can also be used to appeal to the senses. Cigars have an aroma. Wine has a bouquet. Garbage has an odor. Perfume has a seductive fragrance. Look at the many ways we can convey an olfactory sensation with words. And in our copy we should use words that involve as many senses as possible. The words we use can evoke images in the mind of the reader or listener: the *blast* of a fog-

## AN IRISH MIST SETTLED OVER THE EVENING.

*The hills roll forever. The lakes radiate light. The dew kisses each morning. The mist settles every evening. You can taste it all, and more.*

*Irish Mist is the legendary, centuries old drink made from all this and sweetened with just a wisp of heather honey. Irish Mist can be enjoyed anytime, or place, or way: on the rocks; neat; or mixed with anything you like.*

*It's a pleasing land. It's a pleasing drink.*

## IRISH MIST. THE LEGENDARY SPIRIT.

The words in this advertisement have been carefully chosen to convey a romantic mood. Such phrases as "the dew kisses each morning," a "centuries old drink," and "a wisp of heather honey" that appear in the body copy reinforce, and are reinforced by, the illustration: a romantic background of misty hills and a castle at twilight.

horn, the *wail* of the police car siren, the *salty smell* of the sea, the *clean look* of new snow. Colors, too, have meanings of their own. Sometimes we are *blue;* sometimes we are *bright, sunny,* or *yellow;* and sometimes we are *green* with envy. Purple connotes majesty, royalty. Blue, authority or masculinity. White is for doctors and nurses.

### Writing rules

The first rule in writing copy is that there are no rules. If there were rules, writing would be no more than following a prescription. There is no prescription for writing effective copy, but there are a few points to consider as the words begin to flow.

**Is it readable?**   We have pointed out before that advertising is often an intrusion. Having interrupted our prospects' entertainment with our advertisement, we must be sure that they can understand what we are saying quickly and easily. Think of some of your textbooks. You don't *read* them, you study them: you may have to struggle to get the meaning. But the readers or viewers of our advertisements won't do that. They will turn the page or mentally tune us out. They don't have to *study* our advertising. Therefore, it must be easily readable, listenable, or viewable.

**Is it believable?**   Much advertising is pure puff. We all know that the word *puff* means a short blast of air. In advertising, the term has come to mean exaggerated commendation. The generous use of such words as *the finest, the best, the most popular,* and *natural goodness* puff out the advertiser's claims. To a certain degree such words may succeed in attracting the reader's attention or in conveying a sense of the quality of a product. But if our adver-

tisements contain too much puff, consumers will begin to question even the most valid claims. Do you believe, for example, that an instant soup has "home-style stock that brings out all the natural flavors of the meat and vegetable ingredients"? Or that a lipstick is "drenched with moisturizers"? Or that a dishwashing liquid has "the power to lift away grease, and keep it away"? Our copy must be believable.

**Does it have interest?**   Does the copy touch the main interest of the prospects who will buy the product? People do not buy cake mixes because a cake made from a mix is more nutritious than a ready made cake. And no advertisements for a cake mix will ever say so. Nor will the advertisements ever tell prospects that they can save money by using a cake mix. Homemakers use cake mixes because they want to demonstrate their cooking skills and to fish for compliments. A person may scrub the bathroom until it sparkles, but other members of the family will hardly ever remark on the sparkle of the bathtub or of the toilet bowl. They *will,* however, remark on how much they like the cake or cookies. No wonder such products are called *pride foods.* The point is, our copy must touch the reader's real interest—health, pride, safety, sex, economy, or any of the other drives that motivate people to try a product and to repeat their purchase behavior.

## Ideas for individual media

### Writing for magazines

Stimulated by competition from television, magazines have increased in number and in circulation.

As we noted in our discussion of media, magazines are, for the most part, selective. People pay to read them. They are also long-lived; they lie around the house for a week or a month. They are read at leisure, at the readers' own pace, and at a time of their choosing. The very specialized appeal of each magazine requires copywriters to tailor their copy carefully to fit the editorial environment.

Leaf through a few of today's magazines and see what their contents are all about. They are filled with information—"how to," "what to," and "why you should" articles. These magazines are *communicating* with their readers; they are printing the types of articles that provoke responses from their audiences. If they were not, they would not grow. What does this mean for advertisers? It means that their advertisements must be as good as the magazine's editorial content. It means that their advertisements must be interesting, informative, and helpful. It means that advertisers cannot rely on tired, meaningless cliches. Expressions such as *new and improved; engineered better; fast, fast, fast; tradition of excellence;* and *created with care* have all been overworked. So has the use of words ending in *ity*, such as *quality, reliability, dependability,* and *uniformity.*

Writing for magazines is easier than writing for radio or television. We can use more complicated words and phrases, if need be, because the reader will have time to dwell on them in order to grasp the full meaning. We start with one important idea. We say it, simply. That one memorable phrase or sentence is the headline.

**The importance of the headline**   The headline of an advertisement is like a flag used to signal a train. It catches the attention of the engineer. The headline is expected to do two things: *select* from the total readership of the magazine those readers interested in the subject of the advertisement; then *promise* them a reward for reading the rest of the copy. There are two kinds of rewards:

1. The reader will gain, save, or accomplish something through the use of our product. It will increase his or her mental, physical, financial, social, emotional, or psychic satisfaction, well-being, or security.

2. The reader will avoid, reduce, or eliminate risks, worries, losses, mistakes, embarrassment, unnecessary work, or some other undesirable condition. The product will decrease fear of poverty, illness, accident, discomfort, boredom, and the loss of business advancement or social prestige.

If possible, the headline will also tell the reader how quickly, easily, or inexpensively the promise will be fulfilled. Your purpose here should be to give readers who refuse to read your body copy a memorable message in the headline alone. Remember, only a small percentage of the audience will read most of your copy. And, besides, an advertisement with a blind headline can be a great waste. A *blind headline* is one that does not reveal to readers a benefit of product use. It requires the reader to read the body copy in order to receive the sales message. Compare these two headlines, for example:

"Revere Ware. They last so long we made their beauty timeless."
"A great Italian meal you can make in 15 minutes. It'll taste like it took hours."

Consider the words of the Revere headline, "they last so long." What do these words convey? What

This *story headline* should arrest the attention of every dog lover. Was the dog lost? How did they find him again? What did they find out about Gaines-burgers? Read the copy and all your questions will be answered. The benefit: *he loves it.*

## When we finally found our dog Skipper, we also found out something about Gaines·burgers.® He loves it.

Our dog Skipper had been missing for three days when the Harrisons found him.

I hadn't slept at all. I'd been so worried that he hadn't eaten. He's so fussy, he won't eat anything that doesn't come out of a can.

Well, there he was at the Harrisons! The fussiest dog in the world, devouring a bowl of Gaines·burgers like he'd been eating it all his life.

Then Mrs. Harrison explained that not only is Gaines·burgers® dog food nutritionally balanced, but it's moist and meaty like canned dog food, too. And it was obvious from Skipper's clean bowl that it must taste terrific.

Anyway, Skipper doesn't stray too far away from home anymore. He doesn't want to get that far away from his Gaines·burgers.

### The canned dog food without the can.
A nutritious combination of meat by-products, vegetables, vitamins and minerals.

Gaines

**COPY FOR ADVERTISING**

# The most effective moisturizer in the world.

# Water.

# If you know how to use it.

Your dry skin is thirsty. Literally. Thirsty for water. So all you need to do is soak in a tub for an hour, right? Wrong. Because although your skin soaks up needed moisture in the tub or shower, it's lost too easily from evaporation once you get out.

But we can make water work for you. Neutrogena® Body Oil was specifically formulated to maximize the moisturizing effects of your bath or shower. It's a pure, light sesame-oil-formula which is applied *after* you bathe, while your skin is still wet, to hold in the moisture.

Does it feel greasy? No, because sesame oil is so light that it seems to disappear on your skin, although it really forms an invisible moisture-holding film. But it won't stain your clothes, either.

Put the world's most effective moisturizer to work for your dry skin. Keep it there with our help.

## Neutrogena® Body Oil
### Use it every day.

A *blind headline*, that is, the headline does not tell the reader what type of product is being advertised or what the brand name is. But the headline is very rational and promises a benefit to the consumer. Notice the effective use of questions and answers in the body copy, including the anticipated question: ''Does it feel greasy?'' Note, too, the frequent use of the words *you* and *your skin*. The advertiser is not talking to women in general, but to ''you.''

does "beauty timeless" convey? Puff. Compare these phrases with the wording of the second headline. Even if consumers never read a word of the body copy, they see benefits—good taste, speed, and pride ("It'll taste like it took hours")—in the headline alone. The second headline promises a benefit even if you never read another word. And, if you did glance at the bottom of each advertisement, just below the illustration, you would find that the Revere ad said:

"A heritage of excellence from Paul Revere."

While the Chef Boy-ar-dee ad told its readers:

"Nothing to add."

Okay? Good headlines make you want to read more. Fortunately for the Revere ad, the product's name was in the headline. That's the best we can say about it.

**Long copy or short copy**   Body copy is the meat of an advertisement—our opportunity to say what must be said. Your readers have the time to read all the copy you can write; the trick is to get them started. Many times we write short copy because we believe people won't read long copy. Sometimes we write long copy because it looks impressive. Neither approach is correct. Write your first sentence so that it fulfills the promise offered in the headline. Write that sentence very carefully and write it so that you are sure the reader will want to read on to the second sentence. Write the second sentence the same way. Continue until you have said all that you promised in the headline, until you have made the reader want to own your product. That's how long the copy should be. More

important than the length of the copy are the *kinds of words* that you use. Remember to use verbs and nouns, few adjectives and adverbs, and short, simple, easy-to-understand words that are just right for the *readers of your advertisement in that particular magazine.*

To sum up, our body copy must *explain* the product's benefits, must *support* the claims we make, must *provide* the reasons needed to convince our readers to spend their money for our product. The appeal we make may be objective or emotional. We know that most products are bought in response to an emotional appeal; we have to touch the right emotional button. Finally, we want the readers to do something; we want them to *accept* the idea, to *visit* their dealers, to *insist* upon our brand by name, to *send for* samples, or to *mail* in a coupon.

Of course, in much advertising our call to action is implicit, not explicit. No one needs to be told where to buy cigarettes, nor do people usually send in for samples or write for additional information. We are instead—particularly with a strong representation of the package—indirectly asking readers to remember our brand, to keep it in mind next time they go shopping, or, if they are already buying our product, to remain loyal.

## Writing the newspaper advertisement

The daily newspaper is the *news medium.* It is current and it is fresh. It changes every day. It is *now.* Like a radio station's musical format, a newspaper's editorial environment has a strong influence on the nature of the advertising it carries. A newspaper is filled with news, facts, data, and information. Most newspapers feature local gossip, giving it the heaviest proportion of their news space. Many

## The legend continues...

# Introducing the world's most sophisticated Diesel passenger car. The new Mercedes-Benz 300D.

*The new, 5-passenger Mercedes-Benz 300D — the state of the Diesel passenger car art.*

 **Here is a most ingenious alternative to the conventional automobile. A truly remarkable new Mercedes-Benz. With a contemporary new look. With ample room for five people, an astonishing 5-cylinder engine and an unusually complete array of luxurious appointments and safety systems. The new 300D. The most sophisticated Diesel passenger car the world has ever seen.**

For years, you've heard about exotic and promising alternatives to the conventional automobile engine. To date, only one alternative has kept its promise: the Diesel engine — for over 60 years, the most efficient combustion power plant in use.

Now Mercedes-Benz has synthesized its proven, 5-cylinder Diesel engine with new, technologically advanced body design, suspension, steering and safety systems to produce the most ingenious alternative to the conventional automobile.

### A matter of taste

Though only a trim 190.9 inches from bumper to bumper, the new 300D is an honest 5-passenger sedan. The secret of its spaciousness lies in new Mercedes-Benz technology that puts the room in the car *in the car* — with-

out adding bulk or sacrificing safety.

Enter a new 300D and you're surrounded by a complete array of security and convenience features. All are standard equipment. Such things as cruise control, bi-level climate control, electric windows, AM/FM radio, central locking system, 3-speed windshield wipers.

The new 300D is not an exercise in opulence. But it does exhibit meticulous taste. And as your senses will tell you, there's quite a difference between the two ideas.

### Sports car handling

The new 300D is one of the most sparkling road cars Mercedes-Benz has ever engineered. Its sophisticated power train, suspension and steering are those of a sports car. And that is why the new 300D handles like one.

The new 300D's unique, 5-cylinder engine is the most powerful, the smoothest Diesel yet engineered into a passenger car. But you pay no penalty for this performance bonus. The EPA estimates that the new 300D should deliver up to 28 mpg on the highway, 23 mpg in town. (Your mileage will depend on how and where you drive and the condition and equipment of your car.)

### The state of the art

For over 40 years, Mercedes-Benz has pioneered many of the major advances in Diesel passenger car engineering. The new 300D is the culmination of that experience. It is the state of the Diesel passenger car art.

Test drive the new 300D. Experience the most ingenious alternative to the conventional automobile. The most sophisticated Diesel passenger car in the world.

## Mercedes-Benz
**Engineered like no other car in the world.**

©Mercedes-Benz, 1977

This ad appeared as a one-sixth page ad (half column) in the *New Yorker* magazine. With very little space to work with, the copywriter wrote a provocative headline that stimulates the reader's curiosity and two tight sentences of body copy to explain the headline.

Every word and inch of space in a mail order ad must work. Notice the promise of the headline, reinforced by the photograph. This ad does not solicit an order. Rather, it offers the reader a free catalog about the product. Inquiries convert a high percentage of the prospects to buyers.

# Perk™ picks you up by the nose!

One whiff of Perk Smelling Salts revives, refreshes and perks you up—naturally. Keep Perk in your office, purse, car or anywhere you feel drowsy, dizzy, faint, or fatigued.

Perk™ is a registered trademark of Gary Farn, Ltd., Stamford, Conn. 06902

# Carry TEN TIMES a Wheelbarrow Load with INCREDIBLE EASE!

These BIG, strong carts are **perfectly** balanced on two huge wheels — roll easily over lawns and gardens — carry up to 400 lbs. of load — huge volume capacity means you make fewer trips — you'll save time **and** steps.

If you are **still** struggling with a wheelbarrow or inadequate cart (with tiny wheels) send for FREE Cart Catalog. Build-it-yourself kits, too.

**GARDEN WAY RESEARCH**
**Charlotte,**
**Vermont**
**05445**

©1979 Garden Way, Inc.

**GARDEN WAY RESEARCH**
**Dept. 94493C**
**Charlotte, Vermont 05445**
    Please send FREE CART CATALOG.

Name ...........................................................

Address ........................................................

City ..............................................................

State ........................................ Zip ................

other sections of the paper consist merely of tabular listings of data, such as the stock market reports and the television program guide. The function of the newspaper is to *inform* us. We do not turn to it for entertainment as we do with radio or television. It is not written just for us the way our favorite magazine is. We buy it and read it when we want to know.

**How does a news environment affect advertising?** Readers of newspapers seek out the ads. Studies show that (for women) display ads are the second most intensively read portion of the newspaper. Newspaper readers are accustomed to act fast—to call the employment agency, to visit the store, to phone for information. They are generally in a decisive mood. They are ready to act.

**Learning to write copy for newspaper ads** Study the classified ads. Realtors really know how to squeeze the strongest appeal into the fewest words. "Good schools. Convenient shopping. View. Low taxes." They know what the prospects want. The trick, then, in newspaper advertising is to be specific. This *now* medium can take advantage of new developments, new processes, and new technologies. Tie your copy in with current news events. A small-space ad with a high-impact headline and copy that concentrates on one strong selling idea can be very successful. We must remember that since newspapers are not selective, our headline has to be. "Now, prompt relief from hemorrhoids with Preparation H" flags its market instantly.

## Copy for radio

Each radio commercial, usually one minute in length, is a sales message. Our commercial is an interruption of the listener's entertainment, so we may want to embellish our selling idea with music or sound effects or we may deliver it in a skit or a jingle. But it is important always to keep in mind the advertising objectives that our commercial must meet. These objectives may be to build the product image, to introduce the product, to stimulate usage, or to position the product against competition. We do not want the entertainment value of our commercial to obscure the sales message we must deliver.

As we have already learned, radio is our most highly segmented medium. People who like rock or contemporary music like a complementary pace in the talk and news on that station. People who like "top tunes" like the announcers that go with them, and so on. When writing copy for a radio commercial, we must take into account the particular context in which our message will appear and write for the type of audience a given station attracts. One of the most popular ways to get a message across is to provide a product information sheet for local announcers or disc jockeys and let them ad-lib the commercial with the *fact sheet* as a guide. Since listeners like and trust the personalities that they listen to regularly, our message gains believability when these announcers read it.

Often, however, radio commercials are recorded announcements. These commercials are read from prepared scripts by professional announcers or actors and sometimes include special sound effects and music. These prerecorded commercials may take several different formats:

*The skit.* A short "play" will hold the attention of the listeners and often entertain them while delivering the message. The clever skits for *Time* magazine and the skits for Blue Nun wine that feature Stiller and Meara are examples of this type of commercial.

*The problem and solution.* The dead battery that won't start the car, the raspy cough that won't go away, the aches of arthritis—all are problems that might be remedied by our product.

*The testimonial.* The basketball star or movie star who uses the product and delivers the message. We can also have average consumers endorse the product as they are being interviewed by an announcer.

*The slice of life.* An apparently unrehearsed dialogue between friends, mother and child, or retailer and customer must be delivered in an everyday context with background sounds that evoke a realistic setting. The situation may be funny or serious. If we use dialogue, however, it must sound like the speech of real people, but it must not wander so aimlessly that we lose the sales message.

*A fantasy story.* This can be somewhat humorous. We can use a talking animal, an elf, or a person from the pages of history.

*A singing commercial.* When well done, a singing or musical commercial is memorable and "sweetens" the selling message.

None of these formats is exclusive; they may be combined in an endless variety of ways. The most important thing to remember in creating a prerecorded commercial is that we have to rely on sounds—the human voice and musical instruments—to convey the message *and* the mood. We have to think of sounds that are appropriate to our message and that the listener can easily identify. Sounds can evoke pictures in the audience's mind. The roar of the wind, the grinding of an automobile starter, the rattle of dishes and trays in a restaurant, the crackle of flames—all are clearly identifiable sounds that can be used to set a background for our words. A simple but effective use of background sounds can be heard in a commercial for Rioja

wines of Spain. A Spanish-accented voice delivers the commercial message while a flamenco guitar plays in the background. The sound of the guitar conjures up images of Spain more effectively than any words, and possibly any pictures, could.

In general, be specific—remember this is the spoken word. There will be no opportunity for the listeners to refer to the copy later as they might on a printed page. Involve the imagination of the listening audience. Conjure up images with your words and with the sound effects that you use. The opening words are critical—you have ten seconds to catch the prospects' attention. If you can't, the rest of the commercial is wasted. Try for something that will stick in their memory, such as the insistent child demanding "more Park's sausages, Mom." Repetition is also important. If written carefully, you can say the same thing two, three, and even four times in that one minute. Every word must say something to, and be understood by, the audience.

## Writing for television

What an opportunity television offers—sight, sound, color, motion! Yet, with all these opportunities to be truly creative, so many of the commercials are wearying—four, five, six in a row, with people talking to each other or to us in stilted, artificial language. The friendly auto mechanic in his spotless uniform, the nurse or doctor type telling us about cold remedies or chapped hands; the list is endless. What's wrong?

If we want to communicate the benefit, or benefits, of our product to our prospects, the first step is to demonstrate it. Television is demonstration. All we need to do is show prospective customers what the product's main value to them is. Unfortunately, the best attributes of some products

| CLIENT | TIME, INC. |
| PRODUCT | TIME MAGAZINE |
| MEDIA/LENGTH | RADIO :30 |
| TITLE | BANANA BOAT |
| DATE | 11/18/77 WRITER |

**YOUNG & RUBICAM INC.**

285 MADISON AVENUE • NEW YORK, NEW YORK 10017

| | |
|---|---|
| 1ST VOICE: | All you have to do is pull the switch and raise the bridge and you were trained to raise bridges. You said I'm sorry. As commissioner of bridges and sidewalks it is my duty to -------. What? |
| 2ND VOICE: | I was reading a magazine. Not just any magazine. A TIME Magazine. You know you just don't look up when you're reading a TIME Magazine. |
| 1ST VOICE: | Here's a 40-ton banana boat from Guatamala. |
| 2ND VOICE: | I didn't see it. |
| 1ST VOICE: | When it sits in front of a bridge for an hour and a half... |
| 2ND VOICE: | You get caught up in a TIME Magazine. What are your interests -- theater, art, music, books? It's all there in TIME Magazine. |
| 1ST VOICE: | It's taxidermy. |
| 2ND VOICE: | Well, TIME has a lot more colorful photography. Maybe there's a picture of something being stuffed. Let's take a look here. |
| 1ST VOICE: | It is my duty... |
| 2ND VOICE: | TIME Magazine -- it's not like I was caught with my hands in the till. |
| 1ST VOICE: | Good grief, man, the boat had to turn away. It'll go all the way back to Guatamala. |
| 2ND VOICE: | You know I've had a perfect record for 11 years... |
| 1ST VOICE: | We haven't had a boat here in Herndon, Iowa for 11 years. |
| 2ND VOICE: | Well, that's being picky... |
| 1ST VOICE: | It is my duty... |
| 2ND VOICE: | TIME Magazine, the most colorful coverage of the week. Pick up a copy. |

One of a series of very well-known radio commercials in *skit* form that were produced for *Time* magazine. The humor of the dialogue holds the listener, brings a smile, and, at the same time, conveys the sales message. By rotating a series of these commercials, the agency developed continuity and audience recognition.

**IDEAS FOR INDIVIDUAL MEDIA**

can't be demonstrated (the taste of beer or the pain-relieving qualities of headache remedies and cold tablets). That's where the need for creative writing comes in. Analogies, skits, testimonials, and slice-of-life situations can help us prove our claim. What about humor? The use of humor can sometimes be effective, but, unless the humor has a relationship to the subject, it will entertain the viewer and leave no message.

A television commercial conveys both sight and sound. In writing advertising copy for television, then, the copywriter must write the words of the message with the accompanying pictures, or video, in mind. A good example of the effective use of both sight and sound is a television commercial for American Tourister Luggage showing one of that company's suitcases in a cage with a gorilla. As the gorilla throws the suitcase against the walls and jumps on it, an announcer's voice describes the sturdiness of the luggage. The words were reinforced by the video. The commercial is simple, believable, and interesting. And it makes its point in thirty seconds. Another effective television commercial shows a man driving a Volkswagen in the dark along a snow-covered road. The VW stops; a man gets out, opens a garage, and gets ready to climb into a huge tractor that will plow the snow from the roads. The announcer simply asks us: "How does the man who drives the snowplow *get* to the snowplow?" Again, a simple, believable, interesting commercial.

Most copywriting courses stress the AIDA of television copy, which is an acronym for *Attention, Interest, Desire, Action.* To these qualities, we must add the word *quick* because we have to do it all in thirty seconds. Because time is at such a premium, every word must pull its weight; every scene must contribute.

In a way, a television commercial is like a play. There has to be a plot with a beginning, a middle, and an end. Each part of the story must relate to and follow what precedes it. The writer builds interest and sustains that interest until the conclusion of the play. It must have pace and the audience must be able to relate to it. Unlike a play which the audience attends voluntarily, however, the opening sequence of the television commercial must instantly capture the attention of the audience. The audience must be prepared for the situation. We have caught their **A**ttention and built their **I**nterest. The action that follows presents the benefits of the product that *relate to the situation* and thus builds **D**esire and, it is hoped, **A**ction in the form of subsequent purchase behavior.

## Writing copy for direct mail

Think of direct-mail advertising as a rifle aimed at the target market, in contrast to the shotguns of other advertising techniques. If we only have one shot, we had better be sure we have loaded our rifle with an effective bullet. With direct mail, we want to stimulate direct, measurable action, more so than with any other medium. To get results, we must be prepared to prove every claim.

The first line of our letter is like the headline of an ad. It has to insure that the rest of the letter will be read. The copy of the direct-mail piece must be sincere. The personal way in which direct mail reaches prospects makes them very sensitive to phony appeals. They receive countless letters and circulars inviting them to join a select group, urging them to take quick action because the supply is limited, or warning them that the offer will be withdrawn soon. You cannot make the message sound sincere unless you are.

This television commercial does its job of delivering a message very well. The recognizable voice of Karl Malden captures the attention of the audience at the very beginning of the commercial with the provocative statement: "You are about to witness a crime." The scene is now set for the story that unfolds, and the story relates the benefit that is offered by the product.

---

**OGILVY & MATHER INC.**

2 EAST 48 STREET, NEW YORK 10017

MURRAY HILL 8-6100

| | |
|---|---|
| **Client:** | AMERICAN EXPRESS |
| **Product:** | TRAVELERS CHEQUES |
| **Title:** | "DUNE BUGGY" |
| **Commercial No.:** | XAPT 7033 |
| **Date Approved:** | APRIL 4, 1977 |

1. KARL MALDEN: (VO) You are about to witness a crime.

2. (SFX: DUNE BUGGY)

3. A couple on their honeymoon.

4. (SFX: DUNE BUGGY)

5. MAN: Hey. Hey Kathy, what's the guy doing?

6. WOMAN: (VO) He's taking all our stuff.

7. MAN: (VO) He's got my wallet with all our money.

8. (DV) Hey, come back, hey, come back. KARL MALDEN: (VO) Protect your trip.

9. (DV) Carry American Express Travelers Cheques.

10. If they're stolen, you can get a full refund

11. usually on the same day.

12. American Express Travelers Cheques. Don't leave home without them.

# JOHN O'TOOLE

After graduating from journalism school (Northwestern University) and completing a stint in the Marines, John O'Toole decided he would rather write advertising copy than newspaper stories. So, in 1953 he joined Batten, Barton, Durstine, & Osborn, Inc. in New York as a copywriter, moving the next year to the Chicago office of Foote, Cone & Belding Communications, Inc. There, under the tutelage of the legendary adman, Fairfax Mastick Cone, John O'Toole polished and perfected his writing skill. Apparently he learned his craft well, because he was quickly promoted from copywriter to copy supervisor and then to associate copy director. From Chicago, O'Toole was sent to Foote, Cone & Belding's Los Angeles office as creative director and later asked to return to Chicago as senior vice-president and director of the company. Ultimately, he moved to the New York headquarters of Foote, Cone & Belding as president of this prospering international agency, the eleventh largest in the world with billings of $740.3 million.

Outside the agency, John O'Toole is active in many civic and professional organizations. He is a member of the board of directors of the American Association of Advertising Agencies and of the board of directors of the Advertising Council. He is a trustee of the Greenwich Academy and the American Ballet Theatre. John O'Toole also finds time in his active life to write poetry. He has published a book of poetry, and a number of his poems have appeared in various magazines.

In a recent interview, portions of which were quoted in advertisements for *The Wall Street Journal*, John O'Toole offered these thoughts on today's consumers and the copywriters who write for them:

> If I want to write to individual consumers, then I must know how they think, and live, and buy. So I believe it's essential to go beyond the statistics of public opinion, to look at what's happening in the real world. For example, you might see today as a time of reassuring quiet after the turbulence of the 'sixties. But that's only the surface. There's a new spirit of individualism; people seeking to satisfy their own goals, serve their ambitions, feed their individual appetites, find life styles to suit their needs. Small wonder there's such distrust of advertising that treats people as a homogeneous mass. Today's great advertising speaks to individual needs—to the strong drive to be yourself.

**COPY FOR ADVERTISING**

The one advantage direct mail has over other forms of advertising is the virtually unrestricted creativity permitted in the design of the shape or form of the direct-mail piece. The copy is still the most important factor in the message, but variations in form add interest and enhance the impact of any direct-mail piece you create.

## Writing copy for outdoor

Outdoor is basically a graphic artist's medium. At best, the copywriter can hope only to convey one major idea on the billboard. The target audience merely glances at the poster and cannot stop to read it carefully. The reader must grasp the entire message at once. Eliminate all unnecessary words and details. If the message cannot be read and understood in ten seconds, do it over. The copy must be simple, direct, compact. The ideal poster is one that uses symbols so universal that everyone recognizes them. The symbol must evoke a response that will remain in the viewer's memory. The major difficulty is in pruning. The more you know about the product and the target market, the more difficult it is to restrain yourself. A good outdoor poster will involve the audience. Remember the Volkswagen poster that showed a VW driving off the left side of sheet with the caption: "Everyone's getting the bug"? What a friendly feeling the reader got when even the company admitted that its car had been nicknamed the "bug."

## The last word

All advertising copy is the result of a collaboration between the copywriter, the artist, and the market researcher. Within the short time permitted for its creation, the copy must be crafted to fit the requirements of the medium and the client company. That so much imaginative and effective copy has been written and is being written is a credit to the advertising copywriter.

## Summary

Advertising copy is not literary copy. Quite the contrary. The writer of advertising copy is self-effacing; his or her art must be transparent. The object is to sell a product. To do this effectively, the writer must know all the facts about the product—its strengths and its weaknesses, if any. The writer must also know the facts about competitive products. Armed with facts, and only then, is the writer ready to match the attributes of the product with the real wants of the target customer. What do customers want in the product? What appeal will make them buy it?

Advertisers must always remember that they are uninvited guests—interrupting viewing and listening, interfering with reading. The reader has bought the publication for news and information. The reader has turned on the radio or television for entertainment, but will watch and listen to our sales message if we say something of interest using words and symbols that are understood and believed. Therein lies the art of copywriting. The headline must stimulate attention and interest. The body copy must develop desire and action. And the writer must do these things within the framework of the media.

Each medium has attributes that, if used properly, enhance the message; when improperly used, advertising money is wasted. Magazines are a selective medium, appealing to readers seeking information on specific subjects. Newspapers create an atmosphere of speed and immediacy. Radio adds to our message the quality and warmth of a human voice and personality. Television puts it all together—the voice, the color, the action—but within a time frame of thirty seconds. There's the rub.

What does a copywriter need? Knowledge of the product, knowledge of the target market, knowledge of the media, and above all, an understanding of the use of words to convey images and information.

## QUESTIONS FOR DISCUSSION

1. What kinds of factual material are needed to formulate copy ideas?

2. What is the main difference between print and television copy? Between print and radio copy?

3. List ten words that have several different meanings. List five pairs of words that have similar meanings.

4. Draw up a set of guidelines for copywriters to follow when writing headlines.

5. Find five samples of magazine ads for which you consider the headlines poor or weak. Rewrite the headlines and justify your changes.

6. List a dozen words that can be used to evoke images.

7. Write three headlines for a breakfast cereal, each using a different appeal to the senses.

8. Choose a product with which you are familiar. Make up two lists, one that indicates what the product offers, the other what the customer wants. Do your lists match?

### Sources and suggestions for further reading

Book, Albert C., and Cary, Norman D. *The Radio and Television Commercial.* Chicago: Crain Books, 1978.

Glim, Aesop. *How Advertising Is Written — And Why.* New York: Dover Publications, 1961.

Hayakawa, S. I. *Language in Action.* New York: Harcourt, Brace and Co., 1941.

Hotchkiss, George Burton. *Advertising Copy.* 3d ed. New York: Harper & Brothers, 1949.

Littlefield, James E., and Kirkpatrick, C. A. *Advertising.* Boston: Houghton Mifflin Co., 1970.

Norins, Hanley. *The Compleat Copywriter.* New York: McGraw-Hill, 1966.

Ris, Thomas F. *Promotional & Advertising Copywriter's Handbook.* Blue Ridge Summit, Pa.: Tab Books, 1971.

Schwab, Victor D. *How to Write A Good Advertisement.* New York: Harper & Brothers, 1962.

# ADVERTISING ART

## The illustration

### Layout

Creating the layout
Principles of design
    Balance
    Movement
    Unity
    Focus
Constraints
Getting attention
Make the message easy to read
Color
Small space ads

### Subjects for illustration

Kinds of art work
    Photography
    Drawings or paintings
    Stock art

## The television commercial

How a television commercial is
    produced
Filmed, videotaped, and live
    commercials
    Film
    Tape
    Live
Restrictions
Terms used in radio and television
    commercial production

## WORKING VOCABULARY

| | | | |
|---|---|---|---|
| visualization | balance | tight | production house |
| layout | optical center | loose | take |
| thumbnail | copy block | line drawing | dailies |
| rough | gaze motion | scratchboard | work print |
| tissues | tempera | stock art | answer print |
| comprehensive | wash | storyboard | mini-cams |

# 16

## advertising art

*Advertising art is also comparable to folk art in the sense that its esthetic meaning is created unconsciously and perceived unconsciously. Whereas the serious painter thinks that he has a message, the advertising artist . . . is unconsciously creating esthetic meanings which are communicable and enjoyable to his audience, meanings with which they want to identify.*

PIERRE MARTINEAU
*Motivation in Advertising*

THE MOST EFFECTIVE ADS are not dreamed up by a writer sitting alone or by a group of writers brainstorming. Most good ads are conceived as a totality—a combination of words, shapes, illustrations, and perhaps color—all planned to produce a certain effect, usually to sell a product or an idea. Radio advertising is the only medium that does not appeal to our sense of sight. We call the presentation of our advertising message in its visual form the *visualization.* The person who designs our ad will give the words of the copywriter visual form to enhance their effect and then combine the words with a form of illustration to *add* to the message, to *underscore* the message, or often, especially in the case of outdoor, to *be* the message.

## The illustration

The centerpiece of most printed advertisements is an illustration. Later in this chapter we will discuss the various methods of producing a suitable illustration, but, for the moment, we should consider its function in our advertisements. The illustration, or illustrations, may serve one or more purposes. It may:

1. attract attention

2. emphasize a fact about the product or its use

3. transmit an idea of the product in use

357

**4.** create an atmosphere

**5.** reinforce the image of the package

**6.** clarify the headline or copy

**7.** stimulate the audience's desire for the product

Like the headline, the illustration also serves as a "flag" to attract the attention of our target market. For example, we know from research that women show *high interest* in illustrations of:

**1.** fashions and wearing apparel

**2.** "pride" foods such as pie and cake mixes

**3.** cosmetics and beauty products

**4.** pharmaceuticals that improve the appearance

**5.** certain types of home furnishings, such as living-room furniture, silverware, rugs, and dishes, that are highly visible and that reflect good taste

**6.** children

**7.** appliances such as freezers, refrigerators, and toasters

Of *medium interest* are basic foods, ordinary home furnishings, household supplies, travel, books, and records.

Illustrations that are of *high interest* to a male audience include:

**1.** machinery

**2.** automobiles

**3.** boats

**4.** whiskey and beer

**5.** electronic products

**6.** cigarettes

**7.** entertainment

**8.** wearing apparel

Readers of both sexes are attracted to illustrations of puppies, kittens, horses, beautiful scenery, food, vacations, and exotic locations.

By carefully selecting an illustration that will most appeal to the members of our target market, then, we can increase the readership and the effectiveness of our advertisements.

# Layout

A *layout* is the arrangement of elements in a printed advertisement—the headline, the illustration, the body copy, the subsidiary illustrations, the border, and the logotype. The layout represents a pattern, formed by these elements, that is intended to attract the reader, enhance the sales message, create an impression, make the message easy to read, direct the eye of the reader, and stimulate action. If all this sounds like a tall order, it really isn't. Every layout does all these things—some do them well, some do not.

## Creating the layout

Artists seek ideas for the layout of an advertisement in much the same way that copywriters seek ideas for the headline and body copy. They begin by immersing themselves in facts about the product and the advertiser. In addition, the artists must learn what the advertiser expects to accomplish, what the constraints are, and, of course, what medium will be used.

The first tentative designs that the artist makes are usually very small—only a fraction of the actual size. Because of their size, these sketches are called *thumbnails*. They include rough approximations of all the elements that must be incorporated into the finished ad. Thumbnails are generally not shown to anyone outside the agency, and certainly not to the advertiser. The purpose of these small sketches is to work up quickly a number of possible designs for the layout. That's why they are small. Once the ideas begin to crystallize, the artist will make full-size sketches of the best designs.

The full-size sketches are called *roughs*, because they are very unfinished, or *tissues*, because they are usually drawn on textured white tracing paper, called tissue. Roughs may be done in pencil or felt-tip pen and, again, are intended for internal agency use only. The artist will include just enough detail to show the other people involved (the copywriter, the art supervisor, the creative director, and the account executive) the style of the ad, the arrangement of the elements, and the type of illustration. Sometimes the artist will turn out as few as two or three, sometimes as many as a dozen, roughs to find the best possible combination of the various elements. After eliminating the unsatisfactory designs, the artist may do two more roughs—a little more detailed than the previous ones. When everyone at the agency approves one of these designs, the artist prepares a *comprehensive*. The *comp*, as it is called, is prepared with great care. The style and size of headline type is precisely indicated, the illustration is carefully delineated; every element of the ad is shown in place. Frequently, the

headline is actually set in type and pasted onto the artist's drawing. If the illustration is a photograph, an actual print of that photograph may be added to the comp. The agency wants the comp to look as much like the finished advertisement as possible, because this is the layout that is shown to the advertiser for final approval.

## Principles of design

The number of possible arrangements of the elements in any advertisement is almost limitless—in theory, at least. Although advertising design is purposeful, it utilizes the same structural principles found in fine art. These principles include balance, movement, unity, and focus.

**Balance**   The advertising designer achieves balance in the layout by placing the elements so that they complement each other in terms of size and weight. Balance may be formal and symmetrical or informal and asymmetrical. Some products, by their nature, demand a very formal balance. One consideration in determining the balance of an advertisement is what is known as the *optical center*. The optical center is a point about three-fifths of the distance up from the bottom of an advertisement. The eye seems to be naturally attracted to this point and, where possible, the designer gives it a pivotal position in the advertisement.

**Movement**   It is important to lead the reader through the ad so that our message is delivered in its most effective sequence. An ad is given motion by the juxtaposition of the elements, using, as far as possible, the illustration or illustrations. The direction in which a model is looking or the direction in which an arm, hand, or finger is point-

The artist's *rough* of an idea for a Hathaway shirt ad. The baby deer symbolizes softness; the trees, the power of nature. Together, these two images transmit a message of ruggedness and warmth. The eye patch identifies the shirt as a Hathaway.

Hathaway's Loch lana
A warm, rugged shirt that's still blissfully soft.

A more careful rendering of the layout for the Hathaway shirt ad. This version, usually described as a *comp* (short for *comprehensive*), contains a more refined suggestion of the size and style of type to be used for the headline. This time the artist visualized the building in the background as a mansion.

The Hathaway ad as it finally appeared. The illustration shows a winter scene with bare trees but no building. The bare trees reinforce the image of winter, whereas the evergreen trees shown in the preceding sketches would have contributed a note of ambiguity. The bare trees also form a contrasting background for the colorful plaid shirt. Notice that the copy has been arranged into three equal blocks of type, probably to improve readability.

## Hathaway's Lochlana.
### A tough, rugged shirt that's still blissfully soft.

Hathaway's Lochlana is so soft, your skin will think you've invested in cashmere. The imported fabric is of incredibly smooth texture. The purest combed cotton and just the "tops"—the softest part—of wool are spun together in every strand.

Two of the finest mills in the world developed special dyes to achieve Lochlana's exclusive patterns. The colors are woven into the cloth, not printed on it. The tartans snap. The solids project a rich, uniform glow.

And of course, every Hathaway Lochlana shirt is crafted with the same thorough attention to detail we lavish on our dress shirts.

Unfortunately, there is one problem. Like fine wines, only so much Lochlana is created each year. What's more, men who refuse to settle for less do hoard the shirts. We recommend haste, while your haberdasher still has your favorite color.

ing gives motion to the ad. The shape of the *copy block*, the break in the headline when it runs to more than one line—these, too, can be utilized to provide the *gaze motion* that subtly directs the reader's eyes.

**Unity**   We often speak of the unity of a painting—which means that all the elements work well together. We have all seen ads at one time or another that looked as if the advertiser had merely thrown all the different elements together to fit whatever space was available. Unfortunately, a jumbled ad conveys a jumbled impression of its message to prospective customers. Without being able to say why, they find the ad confusing, and they either will not read it at all or, reading it, will not be convinced by its appeal.

**Focus**   Just as copywriters emphasize a product's most important selling idea in their copy, designers must create a focus in each of their layouts that will emphasize one or more of the design's elements. Designers can develop *focus* by using any of a number of simple tricks. They can place a round or oval illustration among a group of square ones. They can *reverse* a line of type (that is, have the type printed white against a dark background) on a page of black type. They can add a spot of color to highlight one of the elements or they can use a generous amount of white space to emphasize the body copy. They can set a few words in a bold type or specify an oversize illustration. There are countless ways to create a focus for the ad.

## Constraints

Keep in mind that we are not after ''art for art's sake.'' Our art has a purpose and with it go numer-ous constraints. The copy must fit the available space. The advertiser's name and package must be included. We may have full color to enhance our message—but more often we will have only black and white. Nor do we always have a full page. We have, then, the natural limits of our message, as well as the limits imposed by our advertising budget and by the characteristics of the medium. We can do things in a slick magazine that will simply not turn out well on the coarse, rough texture of a newspaper.

## Getting attention

Unless the ad catches the attention of the reader, it will not be read. Remember, we have said before that an ad is often an intrusion into the reader's concentration on the contents of the publication. How we catch the reader's attention is an art, and some methods of emphasizing one or more elements of an ad will be discussed in Chapter 17. The attention-getting tricks we use, however—the size of the headline, the layout, the format of the ad itself—must call the reader's attention to the whole ad, not just to one of its elements.

## Make the message easy to read

The eye moves in a natural way. We read from left to right, from top to bottom. Effectivement placement of the elements of an ad can facilitate the reader's movement through it, leading the eye from top to bottom, idea by idea, to the ad's conclusion. Our choice of typeface, type size, and arrangement can make the text easy to read and enhance the psychic value of the message. Heavy type is masculine. Light type is feminine. Long blocks of copy are not comfortable to the reader. We have to break the

**The English look is the Burberry look.**

Lord Lichfield is wearing a classic raglan raincoat, the Piccadilly. It comes in a variety of cloths, and in the Shearford version with a detachable lining. It is priced from $95. Available from the finest shops and stores throughout the United States. For further details contact: Burberrys Limited,* Sales Office, Suite 1710, 1290 Avenue of the Americas, New York NY 10019. Tel. (212) 582 3870.

*A New York Corporation. Burberry and Burberrys are registered trade marks of Burberrys Limited.

**Burberrys** OF LONDON

**Jeep Wagoneer, rugged, versatile, accomplished, ...like its owner.**

Jeep Wagoneer, built for a very special individual. An outdoorsman who demands quality and performance from his vehicle no matter what the weather or road conditions. He relies on Wagoneer for everyday transportation or to take him to the special off-road retreats so important to his lifestyle. And since he insists on quality in every aspect of his life, he appreciates Jeep Wagoneer's reputation for consistent performance; its roomy comfort and conveniences like automatic transmission, Quadra-Trac* automatic 4-wheel drive, power front disc brakes, powerful 360 V-8 engine—all standard, of course. Jeep Wagoneer—like its owner—rugged, versatile, accomplished.

◢ **Jeep**
we wrote the book on 4-wheel drive

Jeep Corporation, a subsidiary of American Motors Corporation

*Formal balance*  All the elements of this ad are centered in a very *formal balance.* The model is in the middle of a square photograph that is framed with a thin black line; the unequal lines of copy are all centered above the photograph, provide a contrast to the square photograph, and add interest to the copy. The ad projects a *conservative* image that is very English in the minds of the American audience to whom it is addressed. To reinforce the image, the designer included an English constable.

*Informal balance*  This ad is an excellent example of *informal balance,* well suited to the image of a rugged, four-wheel vehicle such as the Jeep. Notice how the elements enhance the message—the weather-beaten house, the rough terrain, the sea, the hills in the distance. Yet, the vehicle itself is level—stable, dependable, sturdy. Even the type has been carefully arranged to enhance the rugged image; the left side of the type block is uneven, but the right side is straight to contrast with the irregular outline of the house and trees.

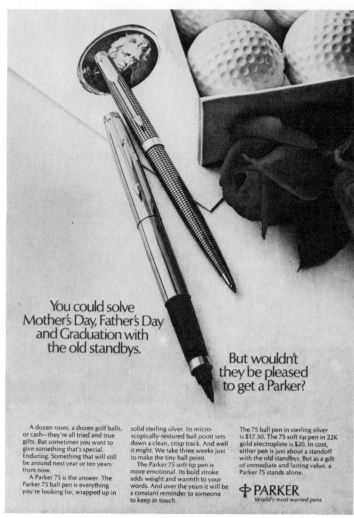

You could solve
Mother's Day, Father's Day
and Graduation with
the old standbys.

But wouldn't
they be pleased
to get a Parker?

A dozen roses, a dozen golf balls, or cash—they're all tried and true gifts. But sometimes you want to give something that's special. Enduring. Something that will still be around next year or ten years from now.

A Parker 75 is the answer. The Parker 75 ball pen is everything you're looking for, wrapped up in

solid sterling silver. Its microscopically-textured ball point sets down a clean, crisp track. And well it might. We take three weeks just to make the tiny ball point.

The Parker 75 soft tip pen is more emotional. Its bold stroke adds weight and warmth to your words. And over the years it will be a constant reminder to someone to keep in touch.

The 75 ball pen in sterling silver is $17.50. The 75 soft tip pen in 22K gold electroplate is $20. In cost, either pen is just about a standoff with the old standbys. But as a gift of immediate and lasting value, a Parker 75 stands alone.

✦ PARKER
*World's most wanted pens*

HEUBLEIN COCKTAILS

THE LIQUOR'S IN IT

PEEL ONE OPEN.
Heublein Banana Colada

HEUBLEIN

BANANA COLADA

Peel yourself a great drink. Creamy bananas and coconut. We added the rum. All you add is ice. You'll go bananas.

Banana Colada. Made with Rum, Natural Flavors, Simulated Cream Base & Certified Color added. 30 proof. ©Heublein, Inc., Hartford, CT.

*Movement*   The designer of this full-page ad has used the two pens as pointers to bring our eyes down to the word "Parker." This *gaze motion* is reinforced by the eyes on the face of the twenty-dollar bill peeking through the window of the gift envelope and also by the angle of the box of golf balls. The juxtaposition of the various components in this ad, as in any well-designed ad, makes for the kind of unity that is pleasing to the eye. At the same time, the elements have been arranged to facilitate the reading of the sales message, which is, after all, the purpose of the ad.

Everything about this ad says "lively." To convey this feeling, the copywriter told the reader to "peel one open." The artist gave the ad *movement*, with material moving in three directions. The bottle is in one plane, the headline another, and the glass, beaded with moisture, is vertical. The headline offers no benefit; the emphasis is on brand and product name.

copy into shorter units. Wide blocks of copy are also hard to read, and so we must split them into columns or hold them to a maximum of three inches. The use of generous amounts of white space adds air, openness, and delicacy.

We also want the reader to do something— *order* the product, *send* for the catalog, *visit* one of our dealers, *write* for a sample. That incentive can be strengthened by the position of a coupon in the layout: in the middle, at the top, or at the bottom right corner (the customary place). Where the coupon goes, or whether or not we use a coupon, depends on what we want to achieve and how we will measure that achievement.

## Color

In addition to adding emphasis, colors have the ability to communicate an idea or an emotion.

1. Blue represents the law, authority, the sea. It is cool. It is masculine.

2. Green represents country, earth, fruitfulness, richness, and "go."

3. Red represents fire, passion, excitement, "stop."

4. White represents cleanliness, hospitals, doctors, and nurses.

5. Purple represents royalty.

6. Yellow represents sunlight, heat, caution, cheerfulness.

Mass markets prefer brighter, simpler colors. Sophisticated markets prefer "different" colors. Size is often enhanced by color—yellow packages seem larger, while dark packages appear heavier.

## Small space ads

Not every ad is a four-color bleed page. There are many small but hardworking ads; ads that are often no more than three inches deep and two inches wide. Your newspaper is filled with them. The same principles that apply to the design of a large ad apply to the design of a small one—but with the added necessity of greater imagination. The designer of a small newspaper ad usually does not have the option of color to add emphasis; instead, the designer may have to use an unusual typeface or confine the message to the single most important fact.

# Subjects for illustration

Since it is the physical representation of what the customer will buy, the product is always the most obvious choice for illustration. The illustration of the product, however, can take any one of several different formats:

1. product alone

2. product in a setting

3. product in use

4. benefit from the product

5. explanation of product use

6. dramatization of the need for the product

7. detail of the product

8. comparison of the product with its competition

9. display of test evidence concerning the product

Small-space ads challenge the copywriter and designer. Copy for the car compass ad is tight. There are no superfluous adjectives; every word counts. No space is wasted, but the ad does not look crowded. On the contrary, it has a quality look that serves to enhance the value of the product. In the ad for paperweights, copy is held to a minimum. The odd shapes of the items and the use of white type on a black background distinguish the ad on a crowded page.

The nature of what is being advertised helps to determine the content of the illustration. A glass of whiskey will look like a glass of brown liquid no matter what brand it is, so whiskey advertisers also include a small photograph of the bottle and its label in their ads. An illustration of a cake mix package alone, however, is hardly adequate. Consumers want to see what the finished cake will look like. On the other hand, showing personal-care products outside their packages would be in poor taste and probably offensive.

Showing the product in a carefully selected setting can enhance its prestige or can suggest a quality of its appeal. Notice how often Lincolns or Cadillacs are depicted parked in front of a mansion or some other elegant building. Note, too, the frequent use of a purple or blue background in these ads. Royalty and masculinity are suggested in this way. Compact cars, in contrast, are generally illustrated in motion—either going uphill or driving across rugged terrain. The illustration is meant to suggest that this compact car has the power and stamina for great driving.

If there were one basic rule to guide the advertiser in the use of illustration, it would be that the illustration must be *believable.* An illustration showing a housewife who looks like a fashion model or like a Hollywood starlet does not ring true. We all know Hollywood actresses do not wax floors or clean kitchen sinks. A mechanic in a business suit, a banker with a beard, or a doctor in blue jeans—all these models would be unbelievable because they are contrary to our expectations. "Cheesecake" photos of models in bikinis say nothing to women, and, although they might catch the attention of male readers, do not enhance the impression of the product's quality or the prestige of the company.

This storyboard does not show all the scenes in the commercial, but enough to give us an idea of the clever, creative thinking that went into it. Who can resist a cute little girl in the opening scene? The farm people are a spoof of the Grant Wood painting. The man in the formal outfit tells us that even the rich enjoy Danny. What better way to demonstrate a three-pack than to show triplets eating the product? Then the final spoof on the Georgians, who are supposedly famous for their long life (from eating yogurt). Eight models, with costumes and props, were required for this thirty-second commercial. Quite an undertaking. And do note the number of times the VO says "all natural."

# DANNY®
## THE DANNON® OF FROZEN YOGURT

ANNCR (VO): There's something very special about all natural Danny Frozen Yogurt In-A-Cup.

About all natural Danny Frozen Yogurt On-A-Stick.

About all natural Danny Frozen Yogurt Flips.

And about all natural Danny Sampler three packs, that make them different from every other frozen yogurt.

They're made with all natural Dannon Yogurt. And no other frozen yogurt's got it.

Danny. The Dannon of frozen yogurt.

## Kinds of art work

Once we have decided *what* we are going to illustrate, our next step is to decide *how* we are going to create the art for that illustration. The choice depends on the cost, the subject, time, and the production requirements of the medium. There are two basic categories of illustration: photography and art. Some ads may use only photography, some only art, and many will use a combination of the two.

**Photography**   Photographs will lend an air of authenticity to our illustration. The people in a photograph are real. The scenery is real. The reader can relate to the photograph. High-quality photographs are not cheap, but, depending on what is wanted, they may be the most economical way to show a product or its use.

One of the limitations of photography is that it is sometimes unable to translate the most attractive features of a three-dimensional product into two dimensions. Sometimes a successful photo of this type requires "interesting" techniques. For example, Campbell Soup Company had a problem in photographing one of its vegetable soups. The soup is indeed full of vegetables, but, when it is poured into a bowl, the vegetables settle to the bottom and all the camera catches is the liquid soup. To overcome this problem a clever photographer hit on the idea of putting marbles on the bottom of the bowl. Then, when the soup was poured into the bowl, the vegetables, resting on the base of marbles, protruded through the soup's surface. Clever? Yes, indeed, but the Federal Trade Commission found the photograph and the ad misleading.

The use of photographs for illustration presents other, not insurmountable, problems—but problems nonetheless. Foods look real and tempting, when photographed in color. But, the cake and the pudding must be prepared just right, and the props that go with the cake and the pudding must look just right. Because such careful preparations must be made, major photography studios have completely equipped kitchens. Even when the greatest care is taken, however, the beads of moisture on the cold bottle may not glisten as we would wish, or the color of the product can be off a shade. Expert retouching is usually required to add what the camera could not pick up.

Finding the "right" models is also a problem: their age and appearance must be appropriate for the product and for the medium. A housewife must look like the kind of woman to whom prospective customers can relate. The photographer and models often must work on location to take advantage of settings that add to the image being projected. Nothing can be substituted for the Trevi Fountain in Rome, the Tower of London, or other sites that are readily recognized.

**Drawings or paintings**   Some subjects simply cannot be photographed. Fictitious or historical people or scenes, mythological animals, pain relievers racing through the bloodstream, or the inside of a healthy hair follicle do not lend themselves to photography. Other subjects—construction details of appliances and machines, for example—are better illustrated by drawings. For such illustrations, an artist can use one of many different techniques.

*Tempera* (opaque watercolor) drawings are frequently used where bright colors or heightened realism is the desired effect. When the illustration will be used in black and white, a wash drawing can be used instead of a tempera drawing. A *wash drawing* is made from either India ink or black wa-

Turn back to page 362 and compare the finished advertisement with this unretouched photograph. The camera did not catch the rump of the deer or enough trees to fill the width required by the ad. An expert photo retoucher patched in more trees (see if you can spot them on the finished ad) and air-brushed the hind quarters of the deer. What the camera misses, retouchers can add and improve upon.

### Hathaway's Lochlana.
### A tough, rugged shirt that's still blissfully soft.

Hathaway's Lochlana is so soft, your skin will think you've invested in cashmere. The imported fabric is of incredibly smooth texture. The purest combed cotton and just the "tops"—the softest part—of wool are spun together in every strand.

Two of the finest mills in the world developed special dyes to achieve Lochlana's exclusive patterns. The colors are woven into the cloth, not printed on it. The tartans snap. The solids project a rich, uniform glow.

And of course, every Hathaway Lochlana shirt is crafted with the same thorough attention to detail we lavish on our dress shirts.

Unfortunately, there is one problem. Like fine wines, only so much Lochlana is created each year. What's more, men who refuse to settle for less do hoard the shirts. We recommend haste, while your haberdasher still has your favorite color.

tercolor that has been mixed with water to provide a "wash." By using more or less water, an artist can obtain various shades: from intense black to the palest of greys to the pure white of the paper. Most of the illustrations used in retail newspaper advertising are wash drawings. Illustrations of furniture or machinery are drawn with great precision and detail—very *tight*. High-fashion illustrations are drawn in a much more imprecise (informal or *loose*) way, intended to provide the reader with only a *suggestion* of the style of the clothing. Retailers may not want customers coming to the store for the particular dress or coat in the ad; obscuring details helps sell the general style and induces the customer to visit the store.

We can obtain simpler and less expensive pen-and-ink drawings—called *line drawings*—that show the product's features in outline only. Often a combination of wash and line can be used with great effect to provide both the crispness and precision of the pen line and the touch of grey color tone that adds style. Other textures and effects can be obtained with pencil, charcoal, or scratchboard. *Scratchboard* gets its name from the procedure in which a clay-coated cardboard is covered with black India ink, and a drawing is then scratched into the board with a stylus or knife. This results in a drawing composed of extremely fine lines. The effect is similar to, but much finer than, that of an old woodcut.

**Stock art**  Very often we will need a photo or a drawing for an illustration but we do not have enough money (or time) to have an original photograph taken or an original drawing made. In this case, we may be able to obtain what we need from a company that maintains files of photographs or drawings illustrating a variety of subjects. There

are, for example, several well-known sources for stock photographs. For only a fraction of what it would cost to have a photograph taken, we can buy a photograph of a doctor, a hospital scene, a family, a sexy model, a beach party, a puppy, or a lion. The list is virtually endless. We can buy a bird's-eye view of Manhattan, the wheat fields of Kansas, or the Florida swamps. We can buy the photographs in black and white or in color.

If we prefer drawings, we can buy very tight drawings of heads, people, things—or loose drawings in line or wash. We can buy ready made emblems, designs, outlines, symbols, motifs, and cartoons, as well as drawings of George Washington, Abe Lincoln, or Santa Claus to tie in with holiday seasons. All this art is ready to use and very inexpensive. Of course, it is possible that another advertiser may use the same illustration in the same publication, but the likelihood of such an occurrence is so small that, when there are budget constraints, stock art or photography should definitely be considered.

## The television commercial

Designing a television commercial is considerably different from designing a print ad. A commercial consists not only of sound but of a continuous series of scenes. The artist must coordinate the sound or narrative with the photography or animation sequences. The design of the commercial is mapped out by means of a *storyboard*—a set of shapes resembling a television screen on which artists sketch the number and content of the scenes they envision as conveying the sales message. The number of sequences can vary from six to as many as thirty-six.

A tight drawing in which every detail is shown very realistically, and with great precision.

# Our Plans Or Yours?

**"ON YOUR LOT" CUSTOM HOME BUILDER OFFERS SAVINGS WITH QUALITY.** Patrick Shelter Group will build your mountain or desert retreat or a custom home that is personalized to your lifestyle. For those who want to save money by doing part of the work themselves, we build to three stages of construction: A shell stage, liveable shell and a completed home. For a complimentary site inspection and estimate, call now at 276-2266.

## PATRICK SHELTER GROUP

1891 Bonus Drive
San Diego, California 92110

372

# focus: the dinner suit

A loose drawing with a minimum of detail, not very realistic. Details are merely suggested with a line or a tone.

**The seductive black suit**

casts its spell upon the night in delicate ripples of crepe.
Sleek, supple and bared with a peplumed camisole of violet tissue faille, subtly striped in black.
Leo Narducci's easy elegance in rayon, 4 to 12, 158.00  Third Floor.
Lord & Taylor, Fifth Avenue at 39th Street—call (212) 391-3300. Open daily 10 to 6, Thursday 10 to 8.
And at Manhasset, Westchester, Garden City, Millburn, Ridgewood-Paramus and Stamford.

**LEO de WYS, INC.**
Photo Agency
60 East 42nd Street
New York, New York 10017
(212) 986-3190

Black & white and color.
Picture Editor for Sports and Recreation: Victoria Brown
Write or call for our free sample catalogue showing pictures
from our files on travel, industry, the environment, human
beings and their emotions.

Imagine how expensive it would be to hire a photographer to fly down to the Gulf Coast, rent a boat, and sail to an offshore oil rig to shoot photographs. Instead of venturing out to sea for a needed photograph, an art director can select a *stock photograph* for prices that range from $400 to $1,500 for one-time use in a black-and-white consumer ad (half that price for a trade-paper ad). Shown is a sample page from the catalogue of Leo de Wys, Inc., New York, a well-known supplier of stock photography. As you can see, a wide range of subjects is available.

113

114

115

116

118

117

119

| Video: | OPEN ON FOOTAGE OF NETTLES ACTION. SUPER: GRAIG NETTLES. | Video: | CUT TO NETTLES RUNNING BASES. CARS LINED UP ON FIELD. SUPER: TOYOTA NY, ETC. | Video: | HE CONTINUES RUNNING BASES | Video: | CONTINUE ACTION |
|---|---|---|---|---|---|---|---|
| Audio: | ANNCR: Another home run for Graig Nettles. He's having a great day. | Audio: | NETTLES: I'm Graig Nettles -- and you'll have a great day, too, at your greater New York dealer. | Audio: | He's dealing like never before on Celica...the car of the 80's, | Audio: | on Corolla the world's best selling car model and the lowest-priced Toyota, at only $3748. |
| ① | | ② | | ③ | | ④ | |

| Video: | HE ROUNDS THIRD BASE | Video: | HE STOPS AT SUPRA AT HOME PLATE | Video: | START PULL BACK | Video: | WIDEN TO SHOW FULL LINE. SUPER AS SHOWN. |
|---|---|---|---|---|---|---|---|
| Audio: | He's dealing on Corona...with the all-new 5-door Liftback. | Audio: | DV: And don't go home without test-driving Supra... | Audio: | the longer, wider, more powerful Celica. | Audio: | ANNCR: See your greater New York Toyota dealer today! |
| ⑤ | | ⑥ | | ⑦ | | ⑧ | |

Dancer-Fitzgerald-Sample / 347 Madison Avenue / New York, New York 10017

| Client: | TDA/N.Y. | Date: | 2/27/79 |
|---|---|---|---|
| Product: | ALL | Film # | TYAM-1270 |
| Title: | NETTLES FULL LINE | Traffic # | TD-31-79 |
| Time: | :30 | Page # | 1, 2 |
| | | | Wd. Ch |

This is a rough storyboard prepared by the Dancer-Fitzgerald-Sample advertising agency for the Toyota Dealers Association of New York. The commercial featured a personality well known to baseball fans in the New York area (a predominantly male audience that the advertiser considers to be its target market). The interest of the audience is caught by the crack of the bat as this star player hits a home run; attention is sustained as his voice delivers the sales message while he runs around the bases. Notice the interesting use of superimposed images in the first, second, and eighth frames.

The storyboard is designed in much the same way as a print ad. Usually the agency's copywriter provides the art director with an initial draft of the copy for the sound portion of the commercial, together with suggestions for how the visual action might be shown. The art director then prepares a rough storyboard that shows the pictures that might accompany the copy. There is generally a close working relationship between these two people. The art director may have an idea for copy while the copywriter may dream up some clever visual ideas. Once the basic sequence for the words and action has been decided upon, the client is shown a copy of the rough storyboard. If the client approves, a comprehensive storyboard that is almost a scene by scene breakdown of the commercial is prepared. This storyboard indicates precisely which words go with which pictures. The commercial is now ready for production.

## How a television commercial is produced

From the moment that the comprehensive storyboard is produced, all work on the production of the commercial is directed toward a deadline—the first air date. It becomes the job of the agency's traffic department to supervise the flow of production from the time the storyboard is assigned a job number to the time the film print of the completed commercial arrives at the television station for broadcast. Most networks require prints of all commercials expected to appear on a particular program at least four weeks ahead of the program's air date.

One of the first steps in the actual production of the commercial is the preparation of a budget. To arrive at firm figures for the cost of production, the producer of the commercial will submit the

storyboard to companies (called *production houses*) for an estimate. The producer is an experienced person who is familiar with the capabilities of the various production houses. After the estimates have been received, the producer, representing the agency, will contract with one of the production houses for production of the commercial. The contract specifies costs, number of prints, and scheduled delivery dates.

A conference is then held, attended by the various agency people involved—the copywriter, the art director, the account executive, and some of the staff of the production house. Details concerning the types of actors, sound effects, and music to be used are then worked out. Every detail is considered. The actors must project an image appropriate to the message the commercial is supposed to transmit. For that reason, many agencies maintain their own casting departments for the audition and selection of actors.[1]

The production house prepares any sets or costumes that will be needed for the commercials. Rehearsals are scheduled; lighting and camera angles are worked out just as they would be for a feature-length movie. The audio portion of the commercial may be recorded simultaneously with the video or some of the sound may be recorded before the actual filming of the commercial begins. Then the takes are made. Each *take* is a filming of an individual scene. The next day, the *dailies*—the takes that have been developed and printed—are

---

[1] All talent is paid for actual time spent in taping, filming, or recording the commercial. In addition, contracts with talent unions provide for the payment of specific schedules of fees to all talent when the commercial is actually broadcast. These fees are known as *residuals*. The principal unions involved in regulating talent payments are the Screen Actors Guild (SAG) and the American Federation of Television and Radio Artists (AFTRA).

**Cunningham & Walsh Inc.**

Television Radio Department/260 Madison Avenue, New York, N.Y. 10016   212 683 4900

FINAL APPROVED FOR PRODUCTION – 4/5/78                              4.5.78

VIDEO                                    AUDIO


EST. HUSBAND, WIFE AND MRS. OLSON         MRS. OLSON:  How beautiful!
IN FLORIST SHOP. WOMAN IS JUST
FINISHING A FLORAL ARRANGEMENT.           WIFE:  Thanks, Mrs. Olson.
ALL HAVE COFFEE.

EST. MAN AS HE COMPLIMENTS WIFE            HUSBAND:  This coffee's beautiful too, honey.
ON COFFEE.                                (HUSBAND SIPS HIS COFFEE)  Tastes delicious.

EST. WIFE'S PLEASED SURPRISE.             WIFE:  Hallelujah!  Dan loves our new coffee.

EST. WIFE PICKING UP FOLGER'S             You said Folger's is different.
CAN.
                                          MRS. OLSON:  Yes.  It's a special blend.
                                          Best I've ever tasted.

EST. CU "MOUNTAIN GROWN."                 MRS. OLSON:  And Folger's is mountain grown --

EST. CU MRS. OLSON.                        the richest most aromatic kind of coffee.

EST. HUSBAND ENTERING ROOM.               HUSBAND:  Your flower arrangements really take the
                                          prize.  And so does your coffee.

EST. PACKAGE AND PEAKING SUPER.           ANNCR:  Delicious mountain grown Folger's.


CLIENT:   Folger Coffee Co.              TITLE:   Florist Shop
PRODUCT:  Vacuum Folger's                LENGTH:  :30
JOB NO:   T47319                         FILM NO: PGVF 3353

The sequence of work for a 30-second commercial is shown in the three illustrations that begin on this page. The first shows the script for the commercial, which contains the writer's ideas for the spoken lines and matching scenes for the video. Next, the preproduction storyboard combines the script with an artist's rough sketches of the scenes to be shown. Finally, the postproduction photoboard shows scenes from the completed commercial. Notice that only modest changes were made to the commercial during production. Skilled copywriters and art directors know how to visualize an effective commercial before it is put on film.

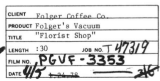

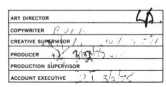

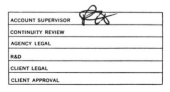

| | | | |
|---|---|---|---|
| EST. HUSBAND, WIFE AND MRS. OLSON [1] IN FLORIST SHOP. WOMAN IS JUST FINISHING A FLORAL ARRANGEMENT. ALL HAVE COFFEE.<br><br>MRS. OLSON: How beautiful!<br>WIFE:  Thanks, Mrs. Olson.<br><br>WORDS 5  FRAME TIME  CUM. TIME | 2.<br>EST. MAN AS HE COMPLIMENTS WIFE ON COFFEE.<br><br>HUSBAND: This coffee's beautiful too, honey. (HUSBAND SIPS HIS COFFEE) tastes delicious.<br><br>WORDS 11  FRAME TIME  CUM. TIME | 3.<br>EST. WIFE'S PLEASED SURPRISE.<br><br>WIFE:  Hallelujah!  Dan loves our new coffee.<br><br>WORDS 6  FRAME TIME  CUM. TIME | 4<br>EST. WIFE PICKING UP FOLGER'S CAN.<br><br>You said Folger's is different.<br>MRS. OLSON:  Yes.  It's a special blend.  Best I've ever tasted.<br><br>WORDS 14  FRAME TIME  CUM. TIME |

| | | | |
|---|---|---|---|
| 5<br>EST.CU "MOUNTAIN GROWN".<br><br>MRS. OLSON:  And Folger's is mountain grown --<br><br>WORDS 5  FRAME TIME  CUM. TIME | 6<br>EST. CU MRS. OLSON<br><br>the richest most aromatic kind of coffee.<br><br>WORDS 7  FRAME TIME  CUM. TIME | 7<br>EST. HUSBAND ENTERING ROOM.<br><br>HUSBAND:  Your flower arrangements really take the prize.  And so does your coffee.<br><br>WORDS 12  FRAME TIME  CUM. TIME | 8<br>EST. PACKAGE AND PEAKING SUPER.<br><br>ANNCR:  Delicious mountain grown Folger's.<br><br>WORDS  FRAME TIME  CUM. TIME |

# CUNNINGHAM & WALSH INC.

**CLIENT:** FOLGER COFFEE COMPANY  **PRODUCT:** FOLGER'S VACUUM  **DATE:** 7/14/78

**FILM TITLE:** "FLORIST SHOP"  **FILM NO.:** PGVF 3353  **FILM LENGTH:** 30 SEC.

1. WIFE: There.
MRS. OLSON: Oh, how beautiful.

2. HUSBAND: Hey, and your coffee's beautiful too, honey. (HUSBAND SIPS HIS COFFEE) Tastes delicious.

3. WIFE: Hallelujah! Mrs. Olson, Dan loves our new coffee.

4. You said Folger's is different. MRS. OLSON: Yah. It's a special blend. Best I've ever tasted.

5. MRS. OLSON: And Folger's is Mountain Grown --

6. the richest most aromatic kind of coffee.

7. HUSBAND: Your flower arrangements really take the prize. MRS. OLSON: Ahh. HUSBAND: And so does your coffee.

8. ANNCR: Delicious Mountain Grown Folger's.

ready for approval. The best take of each scene is chosen as the *work print.* The sound track is synchronized to the work prints and the laboratory work begins. Special effects, titles, and dissolves are added. The final film is called the *answer print.* Color and sound levels are checked and corrected once more on the answer print, and then, when final approvals have been received, the print is ready for release.

The production process we have described in the preceding paragraphs can take months to complete. It is possible, of course, to rush the process. A simple commercial can be made in only a few days, but its cost will be greatly inflated by this accelerated schedule. Typical costs for the production of a commercial on 35mm color film in 1978 were reported to be just over $35,000. The following is a breakdown of costs for a commercial that was shot in a twelve-hour day with four on-camera actors at a location within the area of the studio:[2]

1. Production company, Net Bid . . . . . $20,458
2. Post production company, Net Bid . . . 3,393
3. Talent (On-camera talent included in #1)
4. VO/Announcer fee . . . . . . . . . . . . . . . . . 200
5. VO/Announcer recording . . . . . . . . . . . 200
6. Music (composition, arranging, recording) . . . . . . . . . . . . . . . . . . . . 3,500
7. Color-corrected packages . . . . . . . . . . . 800
8. 10% production reserve . . . . . . . . . . . 2,000
9. Agency commission . . . . . . . . . . . . . 4,582
   Total Cost of the Commercial . . . . . $35,133

## Filmed, videotaped, and live commercials

**Film** Film is the most widely used medium for television commercial production. Production

[2] "The Art of TV Commercial Production," *Advertising Age* (August 21, 1978), p. 40.

companies in every major city in the United States have elaborate facilities for photographing virtually any kind of commercial. The major film studios in California have giant sound stages available with an extensive variety of sets. Many studios also have facilities for animation, and there are excellent production houses in Europe where scenes requiring a foreign locale may be made at substantial savings. Paris and Rome are popular locations for perfume and fashion commercials.

In order to achieve the proper setting, certain scenes in a commercial or the entire commercial may have to be shot on location. This requires transporting the actors and the production crew to the desert or seashore location where the scenes will be photographed. To show an automobile driving down a deserted beach may require hiring a huge helicopter to transport the car to that location. Location shooting adds excitement and interest to a commercial, but it also adds considerably to its cost.

Few, if any, commercials today are filmed in black and white. The cost of crew and talent is the same whether black and white or color film is used, so black and white commercials offer little savings in production costs. For most national commercials, 35mm film is used. However, 16mm reduction prints are usually made from the 35mm film because some television stations require them. At the television station, the 35mm film is transferred to videotape, and the station holds the 16mm print in reserve for emergency use. Although the original print of a commercial can be shot with 16mm film, it does not offer the same variety of special effects that are possible with 35mm film. Also, when 35mm film is reduced to 16mm, the images remain sharp and clear; when 16mm is enlarged to 35mm, however, it tends to lose some clarity of detail.

All in all, film is exceptionally versatile. Many optical effects are possible: dissolves, wipes, split screens, cross-fades, and lap dissolves—the list is almost endless. (For definitions of the preceding terms, see the glossary on pp. 382–383.) One creative advantage of film is that the producer can have several takes made of each scene, shooting from several different angles, and then choose the best take later, in the editing room.

**Tape** Television stations use videotape extensively today to record sports events, news stories, and studio shows. Originally, almost all commercials were recorded on videotape because it was fast and

## HENRY WOLF

Henry Wolf is an advertising expert; he is a designer, a writer, and an artist. Above all, he is a photographer who brings a human touch to his art. His photographs do not happen by chance; he creates them to capture the facts, and, more importantly, the *feeling* about what is depicted.

During the past twenty-seven years, Henry Wolf has worked in many different areas of the advertising industry. He has been an art director for such publications as *Esquire* and *Harper's Bazaar;* an art director for the McCann-Erickson advertising agency; and executive vice-president/creative director of Trahey/Wolf Advertising. He has worked for such clients as Charles of the Ritz, Alka-Seltzer, Buick, Gillette, Coca-Cola, Philip Morris, Elizabeth Arden, Hamilton Watch, and Union Carbide. His work has received awards from the Society of Illustrators and from the Art Directors clubs of Los Angeles, Philadelphia, Chicago, and Washington, D.C. He has won six medals and thirty awards of distinctive merit from the Art Directors Club of New York, and, in 1976, he was awarded the gold medal of the American Institute of Graphic Arts "for work of elegance and strength."

When Saks Fifth Avenue, one of the most famous specialty stores in America, offered Henry Wolf the job of designing its mail-order catalogue, he applied an innovative concept to the task. Instead of merely illustrating the merchandise offered for sale, he integrated the illustrations, writing, and design of the catalogue as if it were a magazine. In addition to selling merchandise by mail, the catalogue conveyed the glamorous image of the store. The illustrations of the merchandise were color photographs taken abroad in interesting and exotic settings. The scenic backgrounds enhanced the customer's perception of the appeal by placing the models in a glamorous setting. A recent catalog contained photos taken in Dubrovnik, Yugoslavia.

*(For a brief biography of Jane Trahey, see Chapter 19.)*

inexpensive. Also, in the early days of television, when many commercials were live, broadcasters turned to videotape to eliminate such errors as an actor's fluffing a line, mispronouncing the name of a product, or being unable to open a package. Videotape was convenient and could be used over and over again. The main drawback to the use of videotape at that time was the huge size of the necessary cameras and recording equipment. Now, however, videotape recording equipment can be placed in mobile cruisers, and the new *mini-cams,* handheld video cameras with portable recorders, can be used by news teams everywhere.

Today, tape has several advantages over film. Film must be developed and printed before it can be edited, while tape can be played back immediately. A commercial can be taped in hours, and corrections and improvements to the original shooting can be made immediately. To correct or to add new scenes to a filmed commercial, the entire crew and talent must be reassembled several days after shooting the original film. Film, on the other hand, can be used in the production of any commercial; videotape cannot. The limitations of videotape—no reverse, no fast action, no slow motion, no animation—make it impossible to create many of the special effects used in film. Film can also be edited frame by frame—a procedure that is invaluable for commercials with children and animals, who may not always give us the performances we require.

**Live**    As we have said, live commercials were common in the early days of television. The problems that occurred—dogs that would not eat the advertiser's dog food or pantry doors that stuck—led to the use of film and videotape. Today, most live commercials are delivered by the hosts of personality shows on local and national television. The commercials are either read from prepared scripts or ad-libbed from product fact sheets. The scripts for these commercials must be kept simple and must not rely on any gimmicks or on product demonstrations.

## Restrictions

Television, considered a family medium, imposes a number of restrictions on advertisers. We may not show anyone drinking beer—pouring, yes; the empty glass, yes; but quaffing, no. Nor can we show undergarments on a live model. Undergarments, such as girdles and brassieres, may only be illustrated on a form or worn by the model over street clothes. We may not put white jackets on models and pretend they are doctors.

## Terms used in radio and television commercial production

*Ad-lib:* to extemporize lines that are not written into the script.

*Animatic:* a television commercial produced from semifinished art work, generally used only for test purposes.

*Announcer:* the member of the radio or television staff who delivers the commercial message live or the talent who delivers the commercial message either recorded (on a television commercial as a voice-over) or on camera.

*Back-to-back:* two commercials or programs that are shown directly after each other.

*BCU, TCU, ECU:* an extremely narrow angle picture: big close-up; tight close-up; extreme close-up.

*Beauty shot:* a close-up of a product advertised in a commercial.

*Bridge:* music or sound effect linking two scenes in a TV or radio program.

*Clambake:* a badly produced television or radio program.

*Close-up:* a shot of an individual with the camera moved in close so that only the head and shoulders fill the screen. An extreme close-up may include only the head or even just the eyes.

*Crawl:* graphics, usually mounted on a drum, that move slowly up the screen.

*Cross-fade:* in television, the fading out of one picture and the simultaneous fading in of another; in radio, the fading out of dialogue, sound, or music while simultaneously fading in other dialogue or music or sound effects.

*Cucalorus:* projecting a silhouette against a background by putting a shape before a strong light source.

*Cut-to:* a fast switch from the picture in one camera to the picture in another camera without a dissolve or a wipe.

*Dissolve (DS):* a combination of fade-in and fade-out. A new scene appears while the preceding scene vanishes. It is a transitional device used to indicate the lapse of time.

*Fade in:* to gradually increase the intensity of a video picture from dark to full brightness.

*Fade out:* to gradually decrease the intensity of a scene from full brightness to dark.

*Follow shot:* following an action with a stationary camera.

*Knee shot:* a shot of three-quarters of the actor's body. The bottom of the frame is just above the actor's knee.

*Lap dissolve:* cross-fading of one scene over another so that both pictures are momentarily visible.

*Live fade:* a diminution of transmitted sound created in the studio rather than in the control room.

*Live tag:* a short, live message added to a recorded announcement.

*MS:* medium shot, somewhere between a CU (close-up) and an LS (long shot).

*Pan:* to move the camera left or right without moving the base.

*Segue:* the musical transition that ties one theme to another.

*Sneak:* to bring in sound or music at low volume so as not to distract the listener.

*SFX:* sound effects.

*Split screen:* a special effect utilizing two or more cameras so that two or more scenes are visible simultaneously on separate parts of the screen. An example would be two people talking on the phone.

*Talent:* actors, announcers, musicians, or performers.

*Voice-over (VO):* the actor's or announcer's voice is heard but the person is not seen.

*Wipe:* an optical effect in which a line or an object appears to move across the screen revealing a new picture. The wipe may stop midway and become a split screen.

*Wipe-over:* optical effect in which one scene moves into another geometrically.

# Summary

Creating the art for advertising demands not only aesthetic sensibilities, but a knowledge of psychology in general and an understanding of consumer behavior in particular. The advertising designer must understand the purpose of the illustration or illustrations and the interests of the target market toward which the commercial message is aimed. The illustration often plays a major role in print advertising, and the designer must be aware that each market segment may have a different perception. Choosing the right illustration will enhance the impact of the ad. The layout itself, which is the arrangement of the elements, helps make the message easier to read and will often guide the eyes of the reader. The layout artist will begin by making several small sketches, called *thumbnails*, seeking to find the most effective arrangements for the elements.

Once the artist has settled upon the most effective arrangements, carefully detailed sketches, called *comprehensives*, are made to exact size. The idea is to make the layout resemble as closely as possible an actual ad in order to submit it for approval. The design itself will have the characteristics of any work of art: balance, unity, movement, and focus. However, advertising is not art for art's sake but a vehicle intended to convey a persuasive message. The ultimate objective of that message is to stimulate the reader to some form of action—to order the product, to visit a dealer, to send for more information, to accept an idea. As the artist works, there are choices to be made—of the typeface and the kind of illustration. Should the product be shown alone or in use? Should the illustration be a photograph or a drawing? Each method of representation adds a different effect. The choice of model, the background, can strengthen the message. Even the color used in an ad is an important element, communicating a mood or feeling. Good professional art—photography or illustration—is expensive. Some artists will try to use *stock art* where possible, buying photographs or drawings that are carried in stock by a number of firms. The cost of such stock art is far less than that of custom-prepared material.

The preparation of a television commercial is much more difficult and expensive than the preparation of a print ad. The designer works with sketches, called *storyboards*, which depict the sequence of scenes. Once the ideas and dialogue have been approved, the storyboard will be submitted to a *production house*—a firm that will produce the actual commercial. The production house, under the supervision of the agency, will arrange for the actors, the props, the music, and the filming. The entire process is complicated and expensive. The cost can be well over $1,000 a second for a thirty-second commercial. Today few commercials are presented live; most are prepared on movie film or videotape.

## QUESTIONS FOR DISCUSSION

**1.** Why is knowledge of the market essential to the visualization of an advertisement?

**2.** Why is it important for some advertisers to show their products in use? Why is it important for some advertisers to show their product's package?

**3.** Find examples of advertisements that demonstrate:
   a. gaze motion
   b. formal balance
   c. focus

**4.** Find several examples of advertisements that use the connotative value of color.

**5.** Describe two sets of circumstances in which an advertiser could justify the additional cost of color for an advertisement.

**6.** What are the advantages of photographs as illustrations in an advertisement? When would drawings be recommended?

**7.** What is the value of "white space" in an advertisement?

### Sources and suggestions for further reading

Book, Albert C., and Cary, Norman D. *The Radio and Television Commercial.* Chicago: Crain Books, 1978.

Littlefield, James E., and Kirkpatrick, C. A. *Advertising.* Boston: Houghton Mifflin, 1970.

Nelson, Roy Paul. *The Design of Advertising.* Dubuque, Iowa: Wm. C. Brown Co., Publishers, 1977.

Wainwright, Charles Anthony. *Television Commercials.* New York: Hastings House, Publishers, 1965.

Wales, Hugh G.; Gentry, Dwight L.; and Wales, Max. *Advertising Copy, Layout, and Typography.* New York: Ronald Press Company, 1958.

## REPRODUCTION PROCESSES

**Typography**

Measuring type
Typefaces
  Roman
  Sans serif
  Egyptian
  Miscellany
  Italics and bold type
Selecting the typeface
  Achieving emphasis
  Achieving readability
Specifying type
Typesetting methods
  Machine composition
  Monotype
  Photocomposition

**Printing processes**

Letterpress
Lithography
Gravure
Screen
Halftones
Plates, engravings, and duplicates
Color reproduction

**Paper**

## WORKING VOCABULARY

| | | | |
|---|---|---|---|
| points | spec | letterpress | screen |
| serif | repro proof | offset | cuts |
| italics | mechanical | gravure | electro |
| pica | slug | doctor blade | mat |
| flush | linotype process | screen printing | stereotype |
| justify | sheet-fed | squeegee | four-color process |
| leading | web-fed | halftone | coated stock |

# reproduction processes

*Advertisers make a mistake when they try to create distinction by using exotic type faces. The classic faces are always the best. And type size should be large enough for easy reading.*

HOWARD G. "SCOTTY" SAWYER
*Business-to-Business Advertising*

AFTER THE COPY HAS BEEN WRITTEN and the layout has been carefully worked out to everyone's satisfaction, the job is far from over. Once all the approvals have been secured for the copy, the illustration, and the layout, the material is returned to the art department of the agency or of the advertiser's own advertising department. There, the type for the headline and body copy must be specified by a member of the art staff who is a type specialist, familiar with the characteristics of the many typefaces available and with the purpose of the advertisement. Final art work for the illustration must also be prepared, together with instructions for its reproduction. The layout, illustration, and copy are then turned over to a commercial printer or to the printer for the medium in which the advertisement will appear. The printer, following the directions from the advertiser or the agency, will then set the type, prepare the art work for reproduction, and do the printing.

Advertisers should familiarize themselves with the mechanics of print production, since a poor-quality reproduction of an advertisement will blunt or destroy its effectiveness. Advertisers should consider the requirements, possibilities, and limitations of the preparation and printing processes right from the inception of their advertisements. They should know, for example, that small wash drawings or detailed photographs won't fare well on a newspaper's coarsely textured paper. Nor will

NOW!  CLEAN CLOTH INTERIORS
IN MINUTES
WITHOUT SOAP OR DETERGENTS

DON'T PAY FOR WATER
SAVE MONEY
Save shipping costs
Save drum deposits
Save pumps and pumping

THE EASY-WAY
CLEANING SYSTEM
IS CONCENTRATED
A little goes a long way
-- one ounce makes a gallon
of great cleaning solution.

MONEY-BACK
GUARANTEE
You must be satisfied . . . if not,
after 30 days trial, return the
unused portion and your money will
be refunded immediately.  The brush
and sponges are yours to keep.
RECON-KING PRODUCTS COMPANY
Automotive Chemical Division
P. O. Box 1066  Wilkes-Barre, Pa. 18703

SPECIAL OFFER  $39 95  POSTAGE PAID

Enough concentrate to equal
one 55 gallon drum of liquid
cleaner.  Included free a special
upholstery brush and 2 professional
sponges -- a $10 value.

Easy-Way cleans the entire car
seats in 10 minutes -- dries in
just 15 minutes . . . and it works
like crazy.  Car wash operators and
car dealers report that their men
like to work with Easy-Way
concentrate -- it's fast and easy.
Customers are delighted with the
results -- really clean upholstery.

Recon-King Products Company
Automotive Chemical Division
P. O. Box 1066, Wilkes-Barre, Pa.
18703

Yes, ship the Easy-Way concentrate.
( ) check for $39.95 enclosed
( ) ship C.O.D. I will pay $39.95
      plus shipping to carrier
Name
Company
Address
City               State      Zip

I wrote the copy for this business-paper ad and made the rough layout almost at the same time. The layout was not refined because it did not need to be shown to the advertiser. The photograph of the product had been supplied by the advertiser.

After the copy was set, I thought that a grey shape would help the guarantee copy stand out, so I had the engraver drop a benday tint over it in the shape of a modified arrow pointing to the coupon.

It was a very busy ad, but all the elements attempted to convince the operator of a car wash that the product would save money and speed the work. While the response to the first ad was excellent, I thought I could improve the ad by enlarging the coupon. I moved the guar-

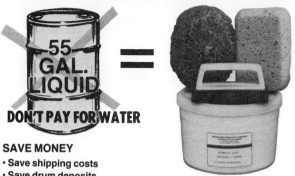

antee copy above the coupon, extended the coupon to the full width of the space, and inserted a prominent phone number to stimulate phone orders.

This was a full-page ad (7″ × 10″) in *American Clean Car*, a controlled circulation magazine addressed to the owners of car washes. The revised ad generated more inquiries and orders than the first ad. However, the additional response could be attributed to the repetitions of the message as much as to the improved appearance. The phone orders received were, of course, directly traceable to the revised version. The money-back guarantee was deemphasized because we learned that purchasers were not concerned. They would demand their money back if not satisfied even without a guarantee.

**TYPOGRAPHY**

delicate typefaces. It is appropriate, therefore, that we examine the characteristics of type and of the various printing processes.

# Typography

Typefaces differ in several ways—in style, in weight, in depth, and in width. We have to consider all the characteristics of the typeface or typefaces we use in our ad because these characteristics can make a contribution to (or detract from) the ad's effectiveness.

### Measuring type

Type is measured by the height, not of the letter itself, but of the body on which the individual letters sit. If you examine a printed line, you will notice how each letter varies—the *l* is tall; the *i* is short; the *p* extends below the *i*. But each of these letters sits on a body the same height. We specify type by a measurement called *points.* There are 72 points to the inch, but 72-point type is not one inch tall—the body is. That is to say, the body is uniform in size, but on that body each letter has its individual configuration.

Common type sizes are 6, 8, 10, 12, 14, 18, 24, 30, 36, 42, 48, 60, and 72 point. Not every face is available in the complete range of sizes. Some typefaces are only suitable for headlines and are, therefore, only available in the larger sizes. The text of an ad, called body copy, is usually set in 8-, 10-, or 12-point type, depending on the face. (For example, this book is set in 10-point Zapf Book Light, with 2 points lead; captions are set in 9-point Eras Medium, with 2 points lead.) Even in the same point size, some faces are larger than others—the space

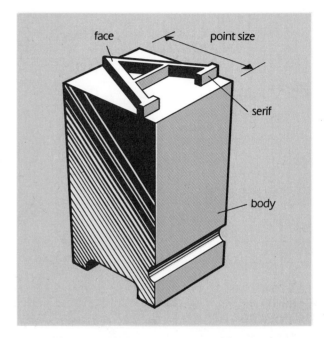

The point size is measured from one end of the body to the other. Some type faces may appear larger than others, although they are equal in point size. The reason this letter *A* does not occupy the total area available on the body is to permit room for the descenders. Thus, the lower case *p* on this body would need room below the feet of the capital *A*. A typeface with particularly long descenders has a lighter, more open look. A typeface with short descenders may require leading to achieve an open feeling and, sometimes, to improve legibility.

on the type body being occupied by long ascenders or long descenders. Newspapers are generally set in 8-point type. Headlines may be set in 18-point type and up, depending on the length of the headline, the space available, and the kind of effect we want the headline to make.

## Typefaces

**Roman** Typefaces fall into several families that bear a resemblance to each other, as families should. The most extensively used typeface is called *roman.* The family name derives from the inscriptions carved on ancient Roman monuments. The roman family is distinguished by two characteristics: (1) the letters are composed of thick and thin lines; and (2) they contain short bars, called *serifs,* at the ends of the main strokes of each letter. The main feature of this family is legibility. Newspapers, magazines, and books are usually printed in some variety of roman type. The legibility derives from the thick and thin strokes, the serifs, and the ascenders and descenders—the *d* that ascends above the *e*, and the *j* that descends below it. Our eyes can distinguish these letters fastest.

Since the days of ancient Rome, type designers have incorporated an endless variety of modifications into the roman family. The variations are still recognizable as members of the family, but they are more like cousins than brothers and sisters. For the most part, these modifications have affected the thick and thin parts of the letters. If the thick part is very thick as in *Ultra Bodoni,* it gives the face weight and a very contemporary look—strong, bold, modern. If there is little contrast, as in *Caledonia,* we get a clean look—modern, but not too modern. Compare these members of the roman family with *Goudy,* in which the thin line is much heavier than in Bodoni or Caledonia, and the face has an old-fashioned character about it.

**Sans serif** Designers interested in "modernizing" typefaces developed a range of faces that eliminated the serif as well as the thick and thin characteristics. The style is called *sans serif* or *gothic.* The

Although Giambattista Bodoni designed the original of these faces in the late 18th and early 19th centuries, they are classified as modern. They are characterized by strongly contrasting thick and thin strokes, as if designed with an engraver's stylus, and by flat, unbracketed serifs, which help to give the type a crisp, modern look. Shown here are Book, Regular, Bold, and Ultra.

A B C D E F G H I J K L M N
O P Q R S T U V W X Y Z
a b c d e f g h i j k l m n o p q r s
t u v w x y z fi ff fl ffi ffl . , ' - : ; ! ?
1 2 3 4 5 6 7 8 9 0 & $

A B C D E F G H I J K L M N
O P Q R S T U V W X Y Z
a b c d e f g h i j k l m n o p q r s t
u v w x y z fi ff fl ffi ffl . , - ' : ; ! ? "
1 2 3 4 5 6 7 8 9 0 & $

A B C D E F G H I J K L M N
O P Q R S T U V W X Y Z
a b c d e f g h i j k l m n o p q r s
t u v w x y z fi ff fl ffi ffl . , - : ; ! ?
1 2 3 4 5 6 7 8 9 0 & $

**A B C D E F G H I J K L M N
O P Q R S T U V W X Y Z
a b c d e f g h i j k l m n o p
q r s t u v w x y z . , - ' ; : ! ?
1 2 3 4 5 6 7 8 9 0 $ &**

Futura, a sans serif type designed by Paul Renner in the late 1920s, was inspired by Bauhaus functionalism. Shown here are several weights: Light, Medium, Demi Bold, and Bold. The italic of a sans serif is a slanted roman, and is technically an oblique.

A B C D E F G H I J K L M N
O P Q R S T U V W X Y Z
a b c d e f g h i j k l m n o p q r s
t u v w x y z fi ff fl . , ' - ; : ! ?
a b c d e f g h i j k l m n o p q r s

A B C D E F G H I J K L M N
O P Q R S T U V W X Y Z
a b c d e f g h i j k l m n o p q
r s t u v w x y z fi ff fl . , - ' : ; ! ?
a b c d e f g h i j k l m n o p q

A B C D E F G H I J K L M N
O P Q R S T U V W X Y Z
a b c d e f g h i j k l m n o p q r
s t u v w x y z fi ff fl . , - ' : ; ! ?
a b c d e f g h i j k l m n o p q

A B C D E F G H I J K L M N
O P Q R S T U V W X Y Z
a b c d e f g h i j k l m n o p q
r s t u v w x y z $ ff c . , - ' : ; ! ?
a b c d e f g h i j k l m n o p q

letters are mechanical in feeling, rather than hand formed as in most roman alphabets. They appear to have been designed by an engineer or an architect. The characters of the sans serif family are crisp, clean, geometric, and modern. Over the years, countless variations of this family have been created—some of the styles very tall and thin, such as *Alternate Gothic;* some delicate and graceful, such as *Vogue;* some bold and powerful, such as *Tempo Black.* Sans serif faces lend themselves well to headlines and subheads but, in blocks of body copy, they are more difficult to read. Such faces are rarely used for the editorial matter of any newspaper or magazine.

**Egyptian**   Striving for something different, type designers developed a family of hybrids known as *Egyptian,* perhaps because someone had seen a similarly styled inscription used on an ancient tomb. Be that as it may, the designer used the uniform thickness and geometric character of sans serif letters, and then added a square serif. The result is a series of typefaces called *Cairo, Memphis,* and *Karnak.* They, too, are more difficult to read than roman, but find application in circulars, brochures, and occasionally in ads.

**Miscellany**   Also available is an incredible assortment of typefaces that fall into none of the preceding categories. They range from *Old Gothic* to various kinds of simulated handwriting (such as *Commercial Script* or *Mistral*) to brush lettering styles (such as *Flash* or *Dom*), with dozens in between. Such faces can be used for particular effects or distinction.

**Italics and bold type**   *Italics* are *not* a separate type family but versions of regular faces that have been slanted to the right. We can use the slanted line formed by italics to add emphasis to a word or a phrase in the body copy, just as has been done throughout this textbook. In a headline, italics lend a feeling of motion or action to the word or words. Almost every typeface in the roman and sans serif families is available in italic.

In line with the same idea—to add variety, distinction, or emphasis—many typefaces are available in different weights; that is, the *thickness* of the characters can be increased. For example, *Bodoni* is available as *Bodoni Regular*, *Bodoni Bold*, and *Bodoni Italic*. *Futura* is also available as *Futura Light* and as *Futura Bold*. Naturally, the variety can be overdone, giving the body copy and the ad itself a cluttered, spotty look. When used sparingly, however, bold type can punch up a word or phrase.

### Selecting the typeface

As you may imagine, with such a wide range of type styles to choose from, a graphic designer could spend days deciding which faces to use for an ad. But, in actual practice, selection is very often influenced by a number of considerations, the most important of which are the nature of the product and the nature of the appeal. A cosmetic or fashion product would call for a typeface with a light, delicate, feminine style. A powerful detergent—although usually a product bought by women—would profit from a strong, masculine typeface to suggest the power and the utility of the product.

The medium, too, affects the choice of type style. The smooth surfaces of the slick paper used for magazines will hold the delicate serifs of slender faces. Not so with the rough texture of newsprint. The size of the ad and the amount of copy that must fit in that space will also influence the

ABCDEFGHIJKLMN
OPQRSTUVWXYZ
abcdefghijklmnopqrs
tuvwxyz fi ff fl ffi ffl . , - : ; ! ?
1 2 3 4 5 6 7 8 9 0 $ &

ABCDEFGHIJKLMN
OPQRSTUVWXYZ
abcdefghijklmnopqrs
tuvwxyz fi ff fl ffi ffl . , ' - : ; ! ?
1 2 3 4 5 6 7 8 9 0 $ &

ABCDEFGHIJKLMN
OPQRSTUVWXYZ
abcdefghijklmnopqrs
tuvwxyz fi ff fl . , ' - ; : ! ?
ABCDEFGHIJKLMN
abcdefghijklmnopq
1 2 3 4 5 6 7 8 9 0 $ &

choice of type style. If we want to print a lot of copy in a small space, we must specify a face that is tight, compact, and extremely readable even in a small size.

Fashion also influences the choice of typeface. Look through a current magazine and you will see that three or four styles of type are used for most of the ads. Compare those ads with ones that are ten or twenty years old, and you will immmediately see how the fashion has changed. Some type styles will look out of date—not old-fashioned, but simply out of date.

The characteristics that govern a choice of typeface are readability, appropriateness, and distinction, in that order. As was true of the layout, the reader should not be aware of the typeface as such.

**Achieving emphasis**   As we have already stated, most typefaces are available in various weights and most are available in italics. However, the techniques available are virtually endless when the artist wants to add emphasis: underlining, capitals, small capitals, boxes, reverse, even color can be used to snap out a word, phrase, or sentence. The purpose is to add interest, emphasis, and variety. But remember, although two or more typefaces may be used in the same ad, the faces must be compatible. One paragraph in roman and the next in sans serif may add variety but would be generally unattractive. To alternate a paragraph of light and bold in the *same face* would be more attractive, adding variety without calling attention to the type itself.

**Achieving readability**   Some typefaces are more legible than others. Obviously, the larger the typeface, the more legible it will be. We are constrained, however, by the size of the space available to us and

by the amount of copy that must be accommodated by that space. But readability is affected not only by the size and style of type but by the length of the line to which it is set. Most newspaper columns are less than 2 inches wide; most magazine columns are about 2 1/4 inches wide. For advertising copy, a line length of not more than 3 inches is most readable. Width of line is frequently stated in picas. A *pica* is 1/6 inch, so that a line length of 18 picas or less is recommended.

The lines of copy may be set to a uniform width, so that the text block is even on both the left and right edges, *flush left and right* as it is usually described; or the copy may be set *flush left, staggered right*, even on the left edge but not on the right; or *flush right*, even on the right edge but with an uneven left margin; or staggered left *and* right. Generally it is best to have long blocks of copy set flush left and right. When we wish to have all the lines of copy of equal length, we must *justify* them. The typographer *justifies* the lines by adding a little extra space between words (word-spacing) or by adding a bit of space between the individual letters of a word (letter-spacing). Look at the columns of type in any newspaper and notice how the lines were justified. This makes them neater and easier to read. Short blocks may be staggered on the right. Very short blocks may be staggered on both sides for a more informal effect.

Spacing is another technique used to improve readability. We can add openness to a block of text by increasing the amount of word spacing or even by increasing the amount of letter spacing. We may also add extra space *between* the lines of copy by increasing the amount of *leading*—a term derived from the former practice of using pieces of lead to separate lines of type. Typefaces with very long ascenders and descenders generally have an open, airy look and may require little or no leading. We can improve the readability of dense blocks of condensed or heavy type, however, by adding more substantial amounts of leading.

A block of copy in print carries a visual weight that is a product of the size of the block, the size of the type, and the openness of the type. If you squint your eyes when you look at a block of copy, you will see not the individual letters but a grey shape. The tone color of that grey area may range from light grey to dark grey, depending, as we said, on the face itself and its leading. Leading lightens the tone value. Compare two pages of typewritten material, for example, one single-spaced and the other double-spaced. The double-spaced page will have a lighter grey tone, although both pages were typed with the same black ribbon.

Reverse copy blocks (white type on a black or colored background) demand extra caution. The serifs of many roman faces tend to disappear when they are reversed, as do the thin strokes of the letters. In general, a large block of reverse type is difficult to read. Caution must also be exercised when the text is to be printed over a photograph, an illustration, or a patterned background. The light and dark areas of the background can seriously impair the legibility of the type.

## Specifying type

In ordering type, the instructions to the typographer specify the typeface, the size, and the width of the copy block or line. If a copy of the layout is included, the dimensions of the line or block may not be necessary. How can you tell if the typewritten copy will fit the ad space? The headline usually presents no problem. Examine any type specimen sheet or type "spec" book. A specimen sheet is a page, generally provided by a commercial typographer, which shows several lines of copy repeated in different sizes and styles of type. From such a page, the person who is to *spec* the type can judge how well the copy will fit when set in one of the various sizes shown. A specimen book is a compilation of type pages, usually provided by a commercial typographer. We can determine if the headline copy will fit by simply counting the letters in the headline and counting an equal number of the letters shown in the specimen.

Calculating the space required for the body copy often presents a problem, but there is a simple procedure to follow:

1. Determine the number of characters in the copy by counting the number of characters in the typewritten line and then multiplying that number by the number of lines. Each space counts as one character. Disregard any short lines that may appear at the end of a paragraph.

2. Measure (in picas) the width of the copy block in the layout. Use a pica rule or measure in inches and count six picas to the inch.

3. Select the typeface desired.

4. In the type specimen book usually provided by the typographer, find the number of characters per pica for every size (6-point, 8-point, 10-point, etc.) in the typeface you are considering.

5. Since the width of the copy block in picas is known, calculate the number of characters that will fit in the size you wish to specify. Simple multiplication will then determine

The type in this ad has been used not only to convey the message, but to be part of the visual impact. The sans serif italics—clean, slanted letters—suggest action and match the dynamic angle of the illustrations. The copy has been set flush on the left, staggered on the right, with a "run-around" the illustration. The reverse copy is somewhat difficult to read, but it is an acceptable trade-off for the visual impact the ad delivers.

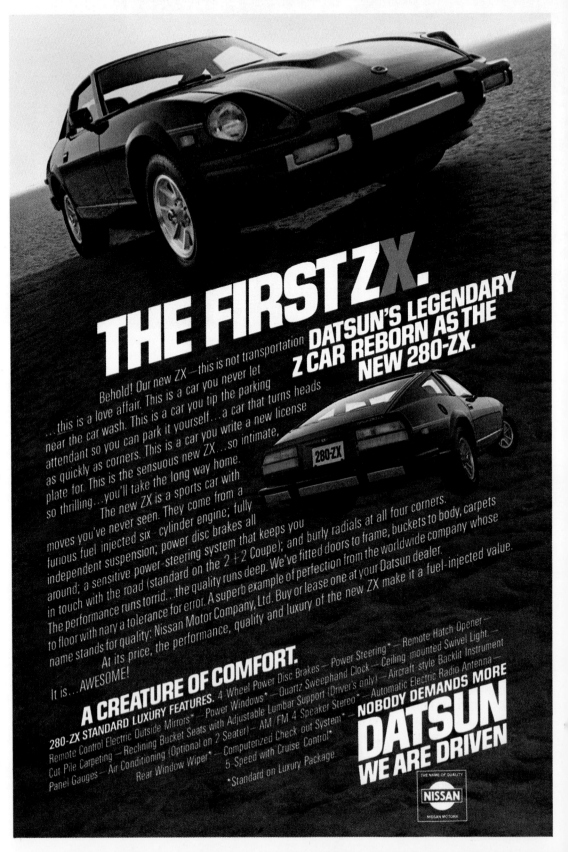

## THE FIRST ZX.

### DATSUN'S LEGENDARY Z CAR REBORN AS THE NEW 280-ZX.

Behold! Our new ZX—this is not transportation ... this is a love affair. This is a car you never let near the car wash. This is a car you tip the parking attendant so you can park it yourself...a car that turns heads as quickly as corners. This is a car you write a new license plate for. This is the sensuous new ZX...so intimate, so thrilling...you'll take the long way home.

The new ZX is a sports car with moves you've never seen. They come from a furious fuel injected six-cylinder engine; fully independent suspension; power disc brakes all around; a sensitive power-steering system that keeps you in touch with the road (standard on the 2+2 Coupe); and burly radials at all four corners. The performance runs torrid...the quality runs deep. We've fitted doors to frame, buckets to body, carpets to floor with nary a tolerance for error. A superb example of perfection from the worldwide company whose name stands for quality: Nissan Motor Company, Ltd. Buy or lease one at your Datsun dealer.

At its price, the performance, quality and luxury of the new ZX make it a fuel-injected value.

It is...AWESOME!

### A CREATURE OF COMFORT.

280-ZX STANDARD LUXURY FEATURES. 4 Wheel Power Disc Brakes — Power Steering* — Remote Hatch Opener — Remote Control Electric Outside Mirrors* — Power Windows* — Quartz Sweephand Clock — Ceiling mounted Swivel Light. Cut Pile Carpeting — Reclining Bucket Seats with Adjustable Lumbar Support (Driver's only) — Aircraft style Backlit Instrument Panel Gauges — Air Conditioning (Optional on 2 Seater) — AM/FM 4 Speaker Stereo* — Automatic Electric Radio Antenna — Rear Window Wiper* — Computerized Check out System* — 5-Speed with Cruise Control.

*Standard on Luxury Package.

### NOBODY DEMANDS MORE
### DATSUN
### WE ARE DRIVEN

THE NAME OF QUALITY
NISSAN
NISSAN MOTORS

Compare the style of this ad with that of the ad for the Datsun; the contrast is informative. The type face is our old, reliable Goudy—easy to read and made even more legible by splitting the text area into three blocks. Because there is not a large quantity of text, it is relatively easy to read in reverse. The type arrangement, like the illustration, is level; it is balanced to enhance the message. Taken together, all the elements of this ad give the reader the impression of stability, soundness, and reliability.

how many lines in the typeface will be needed. If the copy runs too long for the space allotted in the layout, it may be set in a smaller type size or in a more condensed typeface that will provide more characters per pica. If the copy runs too short, it may either be leaded to fill the depth or specified in the next larger size.

## Typesetting Methods

**Hand composition,** the oldest typesetting method, requires the typographer to assemble individual letters made of lead into words, letter by letter. Using a proof press, the typographer will then print three or four copies (called *repro proofs*) of the material on heavy glossy paper. An artist, following the layout as a guide, cuts these proofs and pastes the pieces into position on a board to create a *mechanical* of the ad. Hand composition, however, has for the most part been replaced by photocomposition.

**Machine composition** As you can imagine, setting a page of copy by hand is a slow and expensive process. These drawbacks spurred development of machines, operated with a keyboard resembling a typewriter's, that set type in lines of one piece called *slugs.* The process is ingenious. As the operator strikes the keys, a brass matrix falls into place, letter by letter, until the line is completed. It is spaced out to the width specified, whereupon molten type metal is automatically forced against the matrices and a line of type is cast. The slug falls into a tray and the brass matrices are automatically returned to a storage compartment called a magazine. The matrices are used over and over again. To change typeface or size, the typographer changes the magazine. This *linotype process* has been used

by newspapers for many years. It has also been used for setting advertising copy. When the printing is completed, the slugs are melted down and the metal is used again. Linotype, like hand composition, is being replaced by photocomposition methods.

**Monotype** is a typesetting process used primarily in book publishing. The typographer uses a keyboard that does not cast the letters but punches a roll of tape. The paper tape is then inserted into a casting machine that casts the individual letters out of molten metal, and the letters are then assembled into the words and sentences of the copy. There are three advantages to this process. (1) Revisions are easily made because a word or letter can be changed by pulling out the individual pieces of metal type. (2) If the type wears out after a long press run, it can be remelted and new type prepared by rerunning the tape. (3) If the publishers plan to reprint the book at a later date, they do not have to save the metal type, only the paper tape.

**Photocomposition** There are a number of systems on the market today that set type for advertisements in a form known as "cold type" to distinguish it from the "hot metal" of the linotype process. The basic element for most photocompositors is a revolving photo-matrix drum, which contains a collection of photographic negatives of every letter of the alphabet in a particular typeface, including upper- and lower-case letters and punctuation marks. In response to a command to set the letter *b*, for example, the matrix drum revolves until it reaches the negative image of that character. A strobe light flashes, projects the image of the letter through a photographic lens, and a print of the letter *b* is made on photosensitive paper. A turret

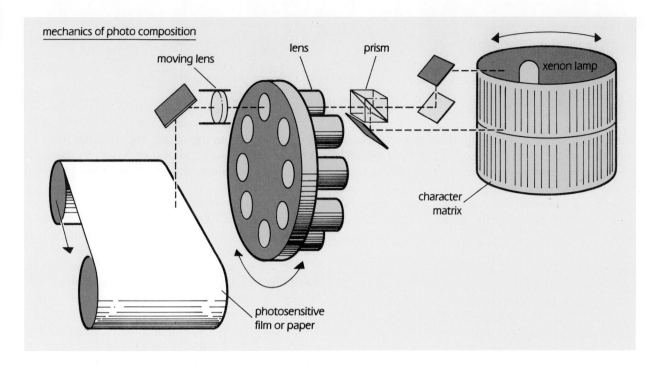

mechanics of photo composition

moving lens

lens

prism

xenon lamp

character matrix

photosensitive film or paper

on the lens assembly permits the typesetter to select one of several different lenses in order to obtain a predetermined size of type. Since a photo-matrix drum may hold a number of different typefaces, and since the turret on the lens assembly may hold a number of different lenses (usually eight), photocompositors are extremely versatile: the matrix can revolve from one typeface to another; the lens can be changed from one size of type to another.

Some photocompositors are exceptionally sophisticated and, with the assistance of a computer, can set the type for, and lay out, full pages of newspapers, books, or magazines. With the use of special transmission lines, copy can be sent from a photocompositor in one area of the country to a photocompositor in another area—an important feature for a newspaper, such as the *Wall Street Journal*, that is published daily in different cities around the country. Some systems can print copy at speeds of up to 500 characters per second. It is also possible to equip the machine with lenses that can slant, expand, contract, elongate, or otherwise change the shape of the letters. Some equipment

can provide negative as well as positive image prints, and some can set type of various sizes and styles within the same line of copy. The process is advantageous in book publishing because the composition may be stored on computer tapes.

## Printing processes

The printing process used for advertisements appearing in newspapers and magazines is specified by the individual publication. When preparing advertising material for other media, the advertiser chooses the printing process—a choice governed by considerations of cost, quality, speed, and the effect desired.

The job shop, as the small neighborhood printer is called, may use presses that range from small, slow presses into which the paper is fed by hand to large automatic presses into which the paper is fed automatically, the plate is inked automatically, and the printed sheets delivered automatically. When paper is fed to the press in cut sections, it is *sheet-fed*. When fed from a continuous roll, it is *web-fed*. Web-fed processes are so sophisticated today that the paper may be printed in four colors in sequence, different sections of the press applying a different color. At the delivery end, a knife automatically cuts the paper to the desired size.

## Letterpress

*Letterpress* is by far the oldest printing process. It is quite simple. The surface that prints is raised. A roller with ink is literally rolled over the surface, the ink coating only the raised areas. Paper is then pressed against the surface, and the matter to be printed is transferred to the paper. The process has long been used by artists for printing woodcuts. Gutenberg used a letterpress method to print his famous Bible. The process has, of course, been refined over the years. Newspapers, for example, are printed from curved printing *plates* onto continuous rolls of paper, but the letterpress principle still applies. The use of letterpress, however, has been declining in recent years as magazines and newspapers move more and more to lithography and gravure processes.

## Lithography

The lithographic process is a printing technique that has been used by artists for many years. The basic concept of the lithographic process is simple. The artist draws upon a soft, flat stone with a grease pencil. He or she then applies water to the surface of the stone with a roller. The water, which will not adhere to the drawing because the greasy lines reject it, is absorbed by the nonprinting areas of the stone. Then, with another roller, the artist applies greasy ink to the stone. The ink adheres only to the greasy design because the water in the nonprinting areas rejects the ink. Paper then picks up the image from the inked surface.

In adapting this simple process to commercial applications, the lithographer uses a grained plate made of aluminum or zinc. The image is applied to the plate photographically. Thereafter the process is the same as the one the artist uses: water dampens the areas that do not contain the photographic image; the greasy ink adheres only to the photo image areas; and the printing proceeds. The entire process is automatic, and is called direct lithography. The plate can be curved to accommodate web-fed paper. However, the process has advanced a step further, to offset lithography, usually simply called *offset*. The grained plate, instead of printing directly on the paper, prints on a rubber roller—the offset roller—which, in turn, prints on the paper. The advantage is that the rubber roller accommodates rough or textured paper. The result is a cleaner impression on a wider range of paper.

Today, small offset presses are widely used. They utilize very inexpensive plates made of aluminum or paper that are discarded after use. For large press work, the plates are cleaned and reused. Most of the magazines and about half of the newspapers presently published in the United States are printed by this offset process. It is by far the most widely used method for the preparation of brochures, circulars, and other direct advertising material.

## Gravure

*Gravure* is a printing process used primarily for magazines. This process reverses the letterpress technique: With gravure, the surface that prints is

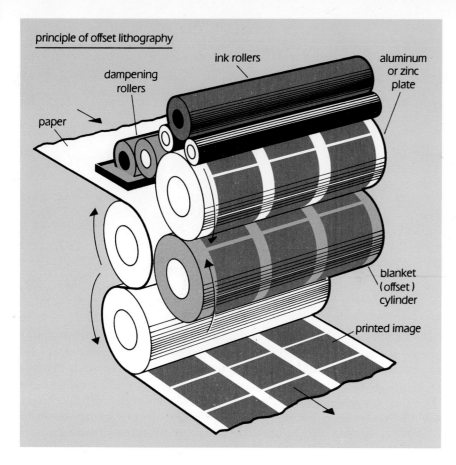

### principle of offset lithography

- ink rollers
- dampening rollers
- aluminum or zinc plate
- paper
- blanket (offset) cylinder
- printed image

The dampening rollers in a trough of water dampen the portions of the metal plate that are not to print. Using a greasy ink, the ink rollers apply the ink to the plate. The ink adheres only to the portions that are to print. From the plate, the image is transferred to the offset cylinder (blanket cylinder), which transfers it to the paper.

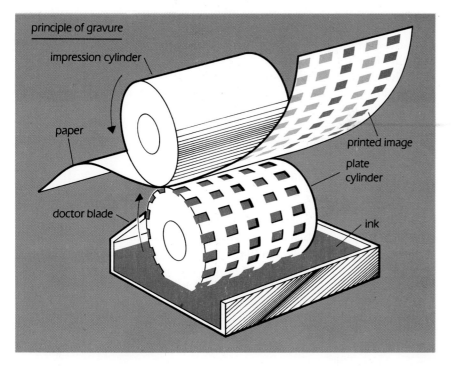

### principle of gravure

- impression cylinder
- paper
- doctor blade
- printed image
- plate cylinder
- ink

As the cylindrical plate rotates in its trough of ink, the surface is flooded with ink. A squeegee, called the doctor blade, automatically wipes the surface of the plate clean, leaving the ink only in the below-the-surface grooves. As the paper passes over the plate, the ink is drawn up by capillarity into the surface of the special gravure paper.

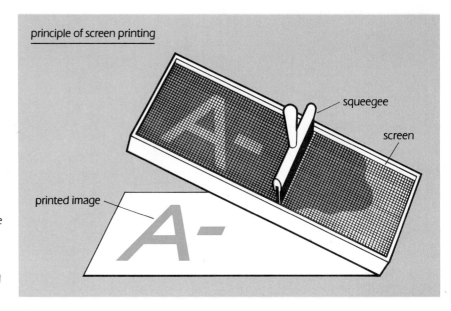

principle of screen printing

squeegee

screen

printed image

The plastic film that covers the screen prevents the ink from passing through the screen to the paper, except for those portions where the plastic has been cut away. A separate screen is necessary for each color, and the colors will be printed one by one. After the heavy deposit of ink has been laid down, the paper must be allowed to dry. Screen printing, because of its value in short runs, is the most common method for making street name signs and road signs on and over the highway.

*below* the level of the plate. The image of the material to be printed is transferred to a printing plate by a photographic process. This image is then etched into the plate with acid. The tiny grooves created by the etching are filled with ink that is deposited by a roller. The surface of the plate is then wiped clean by a *doctor blade*, leaving ink only in the tiny etched grooves. When the paper comes into contact with the plate it literally sucks up the ink in the grooves of the plate and thereby obtains the image of the copy. The greatest advantage of gravure is the superb reproduction quality it offers. The special gravure paper that absorbs the ink tends to give to the illustration a soft quality that most closely resembles the continuous tone of a photograph. Gravure is the process used to print the roto section of Sunday newspapers; it is also being used by growing numbers of magazines.

### Screen

Screen printing is used to reproduce advertising material needed only in limited quantities, such as car cards, posters, and point-of-purchase materials. The *screen process* is the simplest of all the printing techniques we have discussed. A screen, made of silk or other fine cloth or metal or some other porous material, is covered with a nonporous plastic

film. The plastic film is then cut away from the areas that are to be printed. Ink is then flooded onto the screen, penetrating the fabric only where the plastic film has been removed. The printer uses a *squeegee*, a tool with a rubber or sponge blade, to force the ink through the screen and onto the surface to be printed.

The principal advantages of this printing process are: its ability to print on a variety of materials, including glass, wood, plastic, and heavy cardboard; and the intense, brilliant colors that result from the very heavy deposit of ink, which resembles paint in density and consistency. Also, because the process is so simple, it can be used to print quantities of fifty or one hundred pieces, for which an offset run would be too costly. The process is coarse; it does not lend itself to delicate illustrations.

### Halftones

You will recall that the cost for placing an ad in a publication includes printing in black ink, and black ink only—not grey, or any other shade between black and white. But, when we examine a photograph or a wash drawing, we can see that its character is derived from the infinite variations in the middle tones—the areas that are neither solid black, nor white, but *halftones*. The printing pro-

402

cess requires the translation of those varieties of grey into black and white.

In order to reproduce all of the delicate tones that give an illustration its character, it is first necessary to make a film negative of it. The halftone art work is photographed with a *screen*, formed of fine black lines on a piece of glass or plastic, placed behind the lens of the camera and in front of the film. These lines are placed at right angles to each other, forming boxes, or dots, of clear space. When the illustration is photographed in this manner with a high-contrast film, the grey areas of the original are broken into black boxes or dots. The lines on the screen prevent the light from affecting the film, and each dot is separate and discrete. Areas of dark grey in the original art work will have a heavy concentration of dots, while the light grey areas will have fewer dots. The density of the dots in any area of the negative will vary with the tone quality of the corresponding area on the original photograph or drawing. We have literally broken up the illustration into black dots. If we could not do this photographically, we might still be using woodcuts to reproduce illustrations. Woodcuts utilize a similar process, except that the dots are cut by hand, as can be seen by examining the illustration on page 10 of this book.

Screens used for making halftone negatives may have from 65 to 150 lines to the inch, and the choice of which screen to use depends on the printing process. Because of the coarse quality of newsprint, newspapers generally require a 65 screen, that is, a screen with 65 lines per inch. Magazines that print by the letterpress process generally demand 110 or 120 screens. Magazines that use the offset process require 120 or 133 screens, depending on the kind of paper that they use. The smoother the paper, the finer the screen we can

65-line screen

85-line screen

110-line screen

133-line screen

The difference in the quality of detail obtained by the different halftone screens is made clear in these side by side examples. For letterpress printing on newspaper stock, a 65-line screen is needed. Any finer screen would fill in and look fuzzy on such coarse-textured paper. Notice how the details of the illustration become clearer as the screen becomes finer.

use. For publications that use the gravure process, we need provide only the art work, since they prepare their own printing materials.

## Plates, engravings, and duplicates

For magazines and newspapers that use the offset or gravure printing processes, the plates are prepared by the publications from material furnished by the advertiser. For letterpress work, the plates are usually provided by the advertiser; for offset, the advertiser provides the film negative. The publication specifies the screen to be used and any other pertinent technical details. If the publication uses letterpress, the advertiser must provide an engraving according to specifications supplied by the publisher. The engraving is ordered from any engraver. When, as is often the case, the same ad is inserted into several publications at the same time, it is necessary to provide duplicates to each publication. For publications that use offset, we can have the plate-maker prepare positive prints from the original negative. These are high-quality prints, ready to be photographed, which the publication will easily convert to its own use. We provide publications that use letterpress with *engravings,* commonly called *cuts.* If we need duplicates of the engraving, we order *electros* from an electrotyper. An *electro* (so called from the electrolytic process used in its manufacture) is an exact duplicate of the original, but costs much less.

For newspapers, an even less expensive method for providing duplicates involves the use of *mats.* A mat resembles a piece of stiff cardboard (actually it is made of asbestos fiber). The original engraving of the complete ad is pressed into the mat under heat and pressure to form a matrix of the original. Mats are used solely for newspaper reproduction, because they can only retain as much detail as is provided by a 65-line screen. The advertiser can then mail the mats to newspapers all over the country. They are lightweight and easy to handle. When the newspapers receive the mats, they pour molten type metal onto them (hence the asbestos content) and form a *stereotype,* which is a duplicate of the original engraving.

For duplicate insertions in roto publications, the advertiser must provide duplicate sets of film positives. Roto publications make their own film and plates.

## Color reproduction

To reproduce illustrations in full color, we use a technique called *four-color process.* To the three basic colors—red, yellow, and blue—black is added, and with these four colors, advertisers can reproduce all the mouth-watering realism of their food products or the scenic beauty of an outdoor background. Mixing red and yellow ink will give us orange. Red and blue provide purple, and blue and yellow provide green.

Printing a full-color advertisement is very different from printing a mere black-and-white ad. A separate screened negative is made for each color by using a filter that blocks out all the colors but the one we want to photograph. The screen for each color is also tilted 15° so that the individual dots or squares of color do not fall on top of each other when the ad is printed but print side by side, overlapping slightly. The reader's eyes blend the pattern of color dots into a uniform color. If the screen were not tilted for each separate plate, the black dot, which is printed last, would obliterate all the other dots. The colors are usually printed in the following sequence: yellow, red, blue, and black.

A four-color illustration, made from a color photograph. The wide range of colors—on the labels, the bottle caps, the cans, and the beverages themselves—is reproduced with just black, blue, red, and yellow.

**PRINTING PROCESSES**

Filters are needed to separate the original illustration or color photograph into its three primary color components. A green filter blocks out blue and yellow and creates the red portion of the plate. An orange filter blocks out all the red and yellow tones, permitting only the blue tones to come through. A purple filter is used for the yellow plate.

In printing a four-color illustration, the printers must make sure that each color falls precisely into its place in the order described above. A slight variation in paper or plate can spoil the effect. Color printing is far more costly than is black and white.

## Paper

A few words suffice to describe the advertiser's requirements for paper. Publications offer very little choice in paper: newsprint for newspapers, magazine finish for most magazines. The slick paper used for magazines has a clay coating that permits the use of fine screens with substantially better reproduction quality. Magazine covers are made of a heavier paper known as *coated stock*. Only with direct mail are our opportunities for using paper of different weights, colors, textures, and sizes virtually unlimited.

## Summary

Advertisers must be familiar with the various methods of reproducing print advertisements because even the best-written copy, the most effectively designed layout, and the most attractive illustration can be rendered ineffective through carelessness in the final assembly and printing of the ad. In preparing the final copy of an advertisement for publication, a typeface must be selected for the body copy and the headline and final prints of the illustrations must be obtained. The art department of the advertising agency or the printer will then assemble these elements, using the designer's comprehensive as a guide.

The typefaces that we chose for the body copy and the headline should enhance the total effect of our ad without being obtrusive. There are three major families of typefaces—Roman, Sans Serif, and Egyptian—as well as many different miscellaneous faces. Each of the available typefaces has a different degree of readability and weight, and each has different psychological connotations of masculinity, femininity, quality, or fashion attached to it. In selecting a typeface, the advertiser is constrained by limitations of available space, the process to be used in printing the ad, and the kind of paper that it is to be printed on.

An understanding of the major printing processes—letterpress, offset, rotogravure, and silk screen—will help advertisers arrange for the most effective reproduction of their ads. Illustrations that contain a wide range of tone values, for example, can be reproduced best by the rotogravure or offset process. Two other factors that affect the reproduction of an illustration are: the fineness of the screen used to make the halftone negative of the artwork and the finish of the paper on which the illustration will be printed. The finer the screen and the smoother the finish on the paper, the higher the quality of reproduction.

## QUESTIONS FOR DISCUSSION

**1.** What are some of the factors that help determine the choice of typeface?

**2.** What factors determine the legibility of type?

**3.** Explain the offset process. What is its major advantage?

**4.** Distinguish between agate line, point, and pica. How are they used?

**5.** Find an example of what you consider an appropriate type selection in an advertisement. Find another that you consider inappropriate. Justify your choices.

**6.** Find a sample of each of the three families of typefaces.

**7.** Find an example of a two-color ad and, then, of a four-color ad. What kind of illustration was used in each?

### Sources and suggestions for further reading

Bockus, H. William, Jr. *Advertising Graphics.* 2d ed. New York: Macmillan, 1974.

Brunner, Felix. *Handbook of Graphic Reproduction Processes.* New York: Hastings House, 1962.

Cardamone, Tom. *Advertising Agency & Studio Skills.* Rev. ed. New York: Watson-Guptill, 1970.

Croy, Peter. *Graphic Design and Reproduction Techniques.* Rev. ed. New York: Hastings House, 1972.

Gottschall, Edward M., and Hawkins, Arthur. *Advertising Directions.* New York: Art Directions Book Co., 1959.

Littlefield, James E., and Kirkpatrick, C. A. *Advertising.* 3d ed. Boston: Houghton Mifflin, 1970.

Nelson, Roy Paul. *The Design of Advertising.* 3d ed. Dubuque, Iowa: Wm. C. Brown, 1977.

Stanley, Thomas Blaine. *The Technique of Advertising Production.* 2d ed. Englewood Cliffs, N.J.: Prentice Hall, 1954.

● 月刊料理小冊子へキッコーマン・ホームクッキングをお送りします。8月の特集は、暑さを乗りきる四川風豚肉料理です。住所・氏名・年令を明記の上、年間購読料800円をそえて左記へお申し込みください。現金書留＝〒103東京都中央区日本橋茅場町1‐3‐キッコーマンCN係へ。郵便振替＝口座番号・東京5‐96667・キッコーマン東京支店へ。

キッコーマン醤油株式会社

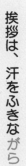

挨拶は、汗をふきながら

ガラスの鉢に青竹の箸

葉しょうがの緑さらさら

皿に美し、キッコーマン

# 5

# ADVERTISING WORLDS

**18**
The advertising campaign

**19**
Retail advertising

**20**
Industrial and trade advertising

**21**
Advertising and society

**22**
Advertising in the future

A full-page magazine advertisement from a long and continuing series showing
vegetables for the soy sauces made by Kikkoman Shoyu Co. Ltd., Japan.

# THE ADVERTISING CAMPAIGN

**Planning the campaign**

    Campaign objectives
    Tactical objectives
    The influence of the product life
        cycle
    Duration of the campaign
    The importance of repetition

**Types of campaigns**

    Regional
    Product promotion
    Corporate, or institutional,
        advertising
    Horizontal cooperative advertising

**Coordination with other
promotional efforts**

    Personal selling
    Sales promotion
    Publicity

**Media selection**

**Measuring results**

    Have consumers changed their
        behavior?
    Methods of evaluation
        Measuring individual ads
        Test marketing
        How to evaluate the overall
          campaign

## WORKING VOCABULARY

| | | |
|---|---|---|
| campaign | horizontal cooperative | loss leader |
| tactical objective | advertising | Starch rating |
| regional campaign | sales promotion | G-R rating |
| SMSA | forcing methods | split run |
| product promotion campaign | push strategy | test marketing |
| corporate advertising | pull strategy | trial purchase |

# the advertising campaign

*An advertising executive usually thinks of advertising in terms of an advertising campaign, a series of advertisements supporting a common objective and which may include such different media as television, radio, and magazines. This advertising campaign must be coordinated with other promotional and marketing efforts and will involve a host of decisions and decision makers.*

DAVID A. AAKER  and  JOHN G. MYERS
*Advertising Management*

As ADVERTISERS, we hope that our advertising investment will yield dividends in the form of brand-loyal customers. We want to create a continuing habit. One of the worst mistakes that advertisers make is spreading their advertising efforts thin. Most products have several good selling points, but it is very difficult to get the target market to grasp two or more equally valid facts simultaneously. If someone were to throw two or three balls to you at the same time, chances are you wouldn't catch any of them. But you could easily have caught one.

It is the advertiser's job, then, to make it easy for the target market to catch the ball—to understand one important point or benefit provided by the product. Therein lies the campaign concept: the choice of appeal, the selection of media, and the creation of the advertising layout must all be focused to achieve concentration and dominance.

Some chapters ago we talked about advertising as if it were a battle we were waging. The campaign concept perpetuates the analogy: we plan a strategy; we position our product; we concentrate our forces; we aim at a target market. Fortunately, that's as far as the analogy goes. In the advertising war, no one wins except the consumer. The battle for market share and for brand loyalty goes on and on. We *launch* a new product; *concentrate* our attack in certain markets; we *dominate* a field; we *capture* and *hold* a share of the market; we *defeat* competitive efforts. It really is a continuing battle.

## Planning the campaign

A *campaign* is an advertising effort that is planned for, and conducted over, a specific period of time. The time period may be as long as a year or as short as four weeks. A campaign to sell antifreeze may run its course in only a few weeks of intensive promotion—from the beginning of October to the end of November, depending on the area of the country. There are three criteria that distinguish a campaign from a mere series of unrelated advertisements:

1. Visual similarity
   In *print* the ads would have a similar format—the same kind of photo, the same type style, the same color arrangement. In *television* the commercials would involve the same kind of demonstration or the same actor, actress, or fictional character.

2. Verbal similarity
   The same words, the same slogan, the same jingle are used. *"Things go better with Coke."* On radio the listener would hear the same voice or voices and the same music.

3. Similarity of approach
   The use of a consistent approach to the market is difficult to describe, but is exemplified by General Motors' advertising for its

Chevrolet automobiles. For many years, GM's approach has been to portray the Chevrolet as the type of car all Americans want. Explicitly or implicitly, Chevrolet's advertising has told consumers: "Chevrolet is as American as apple pie."

In its broadest sense, the advertising campaign is the culmination, not only of our advertising program, but of all the components of our marketing program. Now, having defined our target market, set our advertising budget, agreed upon our appeal and creative strategy, packaged and branded our product, and analyzed the available media, we are faced with the difficult task of bringing all these elements together in a single campaign coordinated with all our other marketing efforts. The following is a brief summary of the factors that will influence an advertising campaign:

1. our company's financial resources

2. our company's position in the market

3. our product and its present stage in its life cycle

4. the extent to which our product can be differentiated from others of its type

5. the potential market in numbers and types of customers

6. seasonal variations in demand

7. media availability and costs

8. the channels of distribution and the extent of dealer cooperation possible

9. the competition—their number, strength, and apparent marketing strategies

# The Old Raisin Ploy, Part 4:

"My dad's real big.

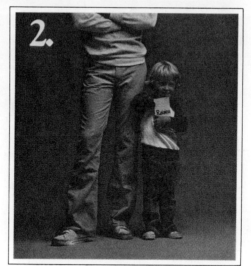

Mom says it's 'cause
he always ate raisins for snacks.

So I eat raisins, too.

...sure hope she's right."

This usually successful ploy is brought to you by
## Raisins from California. Nature's candy.

California Raisin Advisory Board

These ads (see also the next page) by the California Raisin Advisory Board were all part of a campaign to promote the consumption of raisins by children. The ads are not, of course, addressed to children, but to their parents. Notice the similarity of style, wording, and approach in both full-page and half-page ads. What is most likely to catch the attention of parents? Children in amusing situations.

# Raisin Ploy #5

"The kids didn't believe I got snacks
anytime I wanted. So I proved it."

"I invited them over and
we all had raisins."

This usually successful ploy
is brought to you by

## Raisins from California.
## Nature's candy.

California Raisin Advisory Board

# Raisin Ploy #6

"Cynthia is always pestering me for snacks,
so I give her raisins."

"And what Cynthia doesn't eat, I get."

This usually successful ploy
is brought to you by

## Raisins from California.
## Nature's candy.

California Raisin Advisory Board

## Campaign objectives

Important decisions that concern the duration of the campaign and the selection of media schedules are contingent upon the explicit purposes of our advertising effort. We must, therefore, very carefully define the objectives of our campaign. A careful statement of campaign objectives serves two purposes:

1. In choosing between two or more potential campaigns, we can turn to the objectives and use them as decision criteria, rather than relying on aesthetic judgment.

2. At the conclusion of the campaign, we can use our objectives to evaluate the effectiveness of our effort.

When asked to state the objective in any advertising program, an advertiser may be prompted to reply that it is to increase sales, or to maximize profits. Of course, we hope to maximize profits, but this objective does not satisfy our second criterion for a campaign objective. It would, however, be difficult to evaluate the results of an advertising campaign on this basis. Sometimes, in fact, the advertising effort may require the reduction of profits for the short term in order to develop an improved long-range position.

To increase sales is an enticing advertising objective, but such an objective is not always measurable. Advertising is only one of many factors affecting sales, and it is very difficult to isolate its contribution. A growing market may stimulate an increase in sales volume although the advertiser's share of the total market may be declining. Again, the contribution of advertising often only emerges over the long run. Since there is often a time lag before our advertising begins to work, the effect of an advertising campaign may not be evidenced until well after the campaign's end. It may require two years or more to change the attitudes of some prospects.

The ultimate objective of most advertising programs is usually the maximization of profits through sales. Such an objective may be very desirable, but it is not very operational. If, then, we cannot use immediate sales and profits to form the bases for evaluating the results of a campaign, what else can we use?

## Tactical objectives

Although we should never lose sight of our ultimate objective—profits through sales—we may have to set tactical objectives. *Tactical objectives* are short-range goals that will lead to our ultimate objective. Such tactical objectives may include:

1. to extend the selling season

2. to promote new uses for a product

3. to increase the unit of sale

4. to stimulate primary demand for a product type

5. to build a family concept for a group of products

6. to develop brand preference

7. to motivate dealers to stock or push a product

8. to develop a new image for the company

We may, for example, believe that our sales will be increased in the long run if consumers recog-

In this advertisement, the Ford Motor Company builds the image of one of its automobiles by informing us that people who can afford a Mercedes or two buy Ford Granadas for their second car. Notice that price is not mentioned. The emphasis here is on comfort and luxury. Notice, too, that there are no single men or women shown, only married couples, and that all the men are wearing jackets and ties. This enhances the general image of stability, responsibility, and affluence.

nize our company as one that produces only high-quality products. But their perception of the quality of our product must make them willing to buy it more readily; that is, we must be careful not to give them the impression that our product is too expensive for their budgets. Or, if our objective is to develop brand preference for our product, we may attempt to reposition it in the minds of consumers. Our creative strategy—positioning—is derived, then, from our objective. If we want to position the Ford Granada as an automobile superior to a comparable Chevrolet model, we can show the Granada in certain settings and with certain kinds of people that seem to put it in the same class as well-known luxury cars. By relating the Granada to a Mercedes, for example, we hope consumers will think of the Granada as being "as good as," or "almost as good as," a Mercedes. Look at the ad on page 421 and see that this is exactly what Ford did. Would such positioning help develop preference for the Granada? Ford thought so.

## The influence of the product life cycle

The duration and intensity of our campaign will be very markedly affected by our product's stage in its life cycle. A completely new product, for which no exact competitor exists, will require a different campaign from an old, well-established product that is fighting to retain its market share. In fact, every product has competition, even if it is only the old way of doing something. But, a new product demands a campaign that will inform and educate. An older product demands a retentive, or reminder, campaign. Campaigns for such established cigarette brands as Marlboro are good examples of reminder campaigns. With only the slogan "Come to Marlboro Country," the advertiser reminds

smokers—both present users and prospective switchers—of the Marlboro brand. We must, however, acknowledge that a product that has reached the mature, reminder stage of its life cycle did so through other types of campaigns. Again, we can turn to cigarette advertising to find good examples of introductory and competitive campaigns. Advertisements in the recent "tar derby," for instance, bombarded consumers with lengthy copy that was filled with information on the tar content or type of filter of each new brand or variant of an established brand.

## Duration of the campaign

A campaign for consumer products will usually last one year—the customary time period for setting advertising appropriations. The campaign may be of shorter duration, especially if it is based on the selling season of the product, the thirteen-week segments that are a feature of broadcast media schedules, or the frequency discounts offered by other media. Men's colognes, for example, have two short selling seasons—about two weeks before Father's Day and about four weeks preceding Christmas. This is not to say that such products are not bought all through the year, but their sales volume will peak during a short period and that's when their advertising will be most effective. We mentioned earlier that antifreeze has a short selling season. There is little point in advertising antifreeze after the first freeze of winter or during the summer. Certainly drivers do replace their antifreeze during other periods of the year, but the season for the vast majority of sales is very short.

Monthly publications, as we know, offer contracts based on a one-year period, with lower rates based on a specified number of insertions—three,

Do product sales vary with the season? They certainly do, and they vary from week to week *within* that peak season as well. Notice, for example, how barbecue sauce sales peak in June with the beginning of warm weather. Why do you think disposable lighters peak in late summer?

## SUMMER'S HOT PRODUCTS

Following are some supermarket products with above average sales during the coming summer months. Average = 100. This chart is compiled, with permission, from the SAMI (Selling Areas-Marketing Inc.) Seasonality Category Index for the full year 1978.

| | 1978 | | | |
|---|---|---|---|---|
| 4-week period ending: | June 2 | June 30 | July 28 | Aug. 25 |
| **FOOD** | | | | |
| Caramel corn | 125 | 113 | 90 | 109 |
| Barbecue sauce | 185 | 168 | 122 | 98 |
| Misc. bread products | 134 | 152 | 147 | 131 |
| Gelatin desserts | 100 | 127 | 94 | 88 |
| Dry topping mixes | 133 | 121 | 85 | 70 |
| Canned shrimp | 93 | 118 | 129 | 113 |
| Canned meat spreads | 106 | 120 | 105 | 107 |
| Pickles | 118 | 118 | 105 | 92 |
| Relishes | 190 | 162 | 122 | 98 |
| Pork & beans | 129 | 133 | 114 | 105 |
| Canned prepared salads | 146 | 148 | 136 | 123 |
| Fruit pectin | 142 | 340 | 261 | 160 |
| Soft drink mixes | 116 | 140 | 126 | 118 |
| Iced tea mix | 166 | 186 | 161 | 142 |
| Frozen ades | 170 | 223 | 202 | 172 |
| **NONFOOD** | | | | |
| Car wax & polish | 135 | 113 | 117 | 102 |
| Disposable lighters | 74 | 148 | 151 | 250 |
| Insect repellents | 167 | 256 | 253 | 174 |
| Charcoal | 198 | 227 | 171 | 146 |
| Insecticides | 156 | 143 | 131 | 122 |
| Paper & plastic plates | 147 | 139 | 111 | 106 |

six, or twelve—during the contract year. As the frequency goes up, the rate per ad goes down. Weekly magazines offer contracts for thirteen, twenty-six, and fifty-two insertions. Thus, the media lend themselves to schedules based on specific divisions of the year. It is possible for an advertiser to use two campaigns of six months each.

## The importance of repetition

By placing a single ad in one newspaper, a retail store might draw all the customers it wants for the particular product advertised. But, for that store to develop patronage—that is, a core of regular customers—it must place advertising over many months to build its reputation. In fact, the success of any single ad is more than likely the result of past advertising, perhaps placed over a period of several years, that has built the image of that store.

This same concept—the cumulative effect of advertising—also applies to national advertising. One or two ads are not ordinarily enough to do a selling job. We are not aiming for a single sale. We want our customers to repeat their purchase behavior. Otherwise, our advertising investment will never pay off. We know that our advertising is an interruption of the customers' other interests. We also know that they are being inundated with information on many other products. Repetition keeps our impression alive. The effect of repetition does not depend on the placement of large advertisements or color ads, or the use of dramatic copy or illustrations. It does require the steady investment of advertising dollars over a period of time.

Of course, the process of repetition cannot go on forever. After a while it is necessary to create a new impression. But a unified theme will provide psychological continuity for our advertising. We can make a fresh impact with a new illustration, a new appeal, or a new headline. We may even be able to obtain new impact from the same appeal or the same advertisement by placing it in a different context. For example, after consumers have passed the same transit poster twice a day for several weeks, it becomes part of the scenery. But by placing the same ad in a newspaper or magazine, we can make a fresh impression. We want to avoid *wear-out*. You may recall that one way to avoid it in outdoor advertising was to rotate billboards.

## Types of campaigns

Campaigns can be roughly divided into three basic categories, based on the advertiser's objectives. These categories are:

1. regional
2. product promotion
3. corporate, or institutional

A company planning to distribute its product nationwide may find it expedient to launch a regional campaign. The regional campaign, launched in a few neighboring states, will serve several purposes. First, it will save money. Although conserving money may not be the most important consideration for a large and prosperous company, it can be critical for a newly established one. By concentrating promotional efforts in a region close to its headquarters, a company can minimize its advertising costs and sales-force expenses. Management can also retain greater control over a localized promotional effort. Many large companies use a regional campaign to test the strength of their advertising appeal. They can get a feel for the market before investing the large sums of money that a national "roll-out" requires. You may recall that in the coffee-marketing case history in Chapter 2, Procter & Gamble moved from its strong position in the West to increase its share of Eastern markets, *area by area*. Sometimes, for inexplicable reasons, some brands remain strong only in certain areas. Special blends of coffees may hold their share in specific localized markets, despite the best efforts by the advertisers of nationally distributed brands to dislodge them.

### Regional

In discussing a regional campaign it is appropriate to examine a term that marketers use to describe different geographic areas. When marketers want to promote a product in a specific city, for example, they are aware that, for marketing considerations, they are concerned with areas *around* the city as well. We often use the terms *Greater New York*, which includes a portion of nearby New Jersey and Connecticut, and *Greater Chicago*, which includes Gary, Indiana. To help marketers define markets with a set of common terms, the United States Census Bureau developed the *SMSA*, the *Standard Met-*

This is an example of corporate advertising sponsored by Georgia-Pacific, a company that produces forest products, oil, natural gas, coal, and gypsum. Few of the company's products are bought directly by the general public. Why, then, would Georgia-Pacific want to advertise on television? The answer is that the objective of this commercial is to enhance the company's reputation with its publics—stockholders, consumers, government, and the company's own employees. The commercial achieves this objective very effectively by informing viewers of Georgia-Pacific's efforts to conserve natural resources.

*ropolitan Statistical Area.* Each SMSA contains at least:

1. One central city with a population of 50,000 or more

   or

2. A city with a population of at least 25,000 which, together with the population of adjoining areas, has a density of at least 1,000 persons per square mile, constituting for general economic and social purposes a single community with a combined population of at least 50,000. The county or counties in which such a city is located must have a total population of 75,000.

Thus, a marketer might start with the SMSA that encompassed its headquarters, and then move into SMSAs one by one. It's a convenient way to go national.

## Product promotion

We can also separate campaigns into those promoting a product and those that are institutional in nature. A *product promotion campaign* is intended to sell the product—to make it more desirable than competitive products. The campaign revolves around the benefits and satisfactions the purchasers will gain with the product; one of these will be the campaign theme. The theme becomes the point of each individual advertisement, provides the continuity that enables prospects to focus on the message, and thereby enhances the message's reception. For products that are totally new, the campaign has educational value. The advertising may have to change attitudes and habits of long standing. And that takes time. For a long-estab-

lished product, where differentiation is often trivial, the campaign may be based on something as minor as the product's package.

## Corporate, or institutional, advertising

Advertising that promotes the company rather than its products or services is called *institutional advertising,* or *corporate advertising.* The objective of an institutional campaign may be to influence favorably consumer attitudes by stressing company size, leadership, age, integrity, personnel, or facilities. At the same time, such advertising will influence members of the company's other publics—suppliers, stockholders, governments, and its own employees. The benefits expected from an institutional campaign (in addition to sales, of course) might be:

1. to promote more, or less, government regulation of an industry

2. to help open the door for company salespeople

3. to increase goodwill among suppliers

4. to enhance the reputation of all the company's products

5. to facilitate the recruitment of new personnel

6. to facilitate the sale of company securities

## Horizontal cooperative advertising

A group of competing companies will often sponsor a common advertising effort to promote the generic product—milk or fruits, for example. The cooperative group will attempt to stimulate *primary*

# Georgia-Pacific

## "LOG CABIN"-60 Sec.

When the early settlers came to America,

the first thing they did was clear the land . . .

and the timber they cut provided logs for their homes.

But today's forest has to provide more than shelter and warmth . . .

and at Georgia-Pacific, we've spent fifty years learning to make our forests yield more than they did before.

Today we breed trees that grow faster. And what used to be waste we convert into by-products for medicines, fertilizers, even cosmetics.

In fact, we've learned so much that the trees it took to build a one room log cabin

would build this 3,500 square foot home today . . . and provide tissue and paper products for an average family for a generation.

Georgia-Pacific . . . oil, gas, coal, gypsum, timber . . . and the skill to manage them.

*demand* for the products of the entire industry or to place a business or social problem before the public at large. In the first instance, the ad campaign will try to generate a widening interest in a *type of product*. In the second, the campaign will help the companies (generally combined as a trade association) influence the government's and the public's opinions on a current issue or a piece of impending legislation. The purposes of such a campaign are to educate, inform, describe, cajole, explain, or justify. Advertising by a trade association, usually referred to as *horizontal cooperative advertising*, is not meant to be a substitute for each company's own advertising program.

Typical objectives of horizontal cooperative advertising might include:

1. providing the public with a clearer picture of the products or services provided by the industry

2. explaining the position of the industry on a particular subject

3. influencing legislation and government regulation of the industry

4. promoting in a general way goodwill for the industry

## Coordination with other promotional efforts

### Personal selling

The advertising campaign must be coordinated with the efforts of the *field sales force*. Wholesalers and retailers must be persuaded to stock and push the product; otherwise, much of the advertising expenditure will be wasted. Distribution must be expanded. There is no sense in stimulating interest in and desire for a product among consumers if they are unable to find a dealer who stocks it. Trade advertising is usually needed to tell dealers about our upcoming campaigns. Such advertising helps establish a favorable climate even before our salespeople call. Our sales force must also know what appeal is featured in the advertising so that they do not in any way contradict that message.

### Sales promotion

The campaign must be coordinated with the company's sales promotion efforts. By *sales promotion* we mean the company's efforts to stimulate sales by methods other than media advertising or face-to-face selling. We are talking about *forcing methods* intended to get fast action at the retail level. A manufacturer's effort to stimulate sales through retailers is often described as a *push strategy*.

Manufacturers have no desire to reduce their prices. They do not wish to start price wars. They are also well aware that price is often considered an index of quality by consumers. A reduction in price might make consumers nervous about the quality of the product. Instead, the manufacturers will make special arrangements with retailers to promote a given product with coupons, cents-off specials, premiums, and deals. The retailers, because of the potential for extra profits or because of some other beneficial arrangement with the manufacturer, will feature the product (push). Coupons and cents-off specials are two ways of reducing the price to entice first-time triers. If brand-loyal users take advantage of coupons to save money, that is

# Myth:

Trains still go "clickety-clack."

# Fact:

## Modern, welded track is quiet and smooth.

There are those who like that rhythmic sound—but not most railroaders. That "clickety-clack" means wear at the places where rail is joined. That's why some 60,000 miles of today's railroad track are jointless welded rail—and more is being laid each year to provide a smoother and safer ride.

Last year, the railroads spent record amounts of money for capital improvements and maintenance—$9 billion for improvements to track, facilities and equipment—up 40 percent over 1975. Rail and tie installations are at the highest levels in 20 years.

The railroad industry is looking ahead to a growing freight load—especially coal. Railroads already are the nation's largest coal carriers and President Carter has called for a two-thirds increase in coal production by 1985. When it comes, the railroads can carry their share—and more, if needed.

Bigger cars, more powerful locomotives and modernized operations mean railroads are able to handle bigger loads with far fewer trains. And these improvements also mean there's a lot of additional capacity already available to handle the nation's future transportation needs.

In most cases, those needs will be met with much less fuel than is needed by other forms of transportation—an important consideration in this time of rising energy prices.

Association of American Railroads, American Railroads Building, Washington, D.C. 20036

# Surprise:

## We've been working on the railroad.

A perfect example of *horizontal cooperative advertising* by a trade association. The association has two purposes: (1) to stimulate greater use of railroad facilities for shipping; (2) to win support for the railroad industry from the public at large. The latter reason can be inferred from the fact that the ad appeared in *Time, U.S. News & World Report,* and other influential publications.

the price the manufacturer has to pay to win *new* prospects. A premium, as we discussed in Chapter 12, is a gift the consumer receives for making the purchase. It may, in fact, be self-liquidating, but it is nonetheless a promotion device.

In contrast to the push strategy, manufacturers may use a pull strategy. A *pull strategy* directs advertising to consumers, rather than to dealers, in order to attract (pull) customers into retail outlets. By stimulating demand for a product in this way, advertisers hope to convince retailers to stock it. Some manufacturers will emphasize push or pull strategies at different times for different objectives. Other manufacturers will launch a coordinated compaign, perhaps as the fastest way to get new products on the market or perhaps as a tactical maneuver to fight regional competitors.

Our advertising campaign must also be coordinated with any *point of purchase promotion efforts.* Where possible, a program to get preferential shelf space or to encourage the installation of POP displays must be timed so that the advertising enhances the display while the display reinforces the advertising message. Once more, trade advertising can play an important role in transmitting important information to the dealer network.

Deals are just what the word implies: they are an inducement for the dealer to stock the product. We may make a combination deal—for every two cartons of product X we will deliver one carton of product Y at half-price. Sometimes the deal may be the kind that dealers can't refuse—for instance, a reduced price that they may either pass along to consumers as a *loss leader* or retain for themselves as added profit. A loss leader is an item of merchandise that a retailer offers at a reduced price, often below cost (hence the term), in order to attract customers to the store. The idea is that customers,

coming in to buy the leader, will buy other items at regular prices. Supermarket "specials" are typical loss leaders. Whatever the deal, retailers are stimulated to buy and stock the product.

## Publicity

The final area that must be coordinated in the company's advertising campaign is public relations. *Public relations* is a communication technique and a component of the promotional mix. We distinguished between advertising and publicity in Chapter 1 of this book. Indeed, publicity and advertising may appear in the same media. Each has the same long-range goal. Our concern in this regard is to make sure that our publicity is consistent with our advertising message.

# Media selection

The campaign concept must also be applied to media selection. If our advertising objective is defined on the basis of a particular market segment, then our media planning must concentrate on reaching this target. Mass media are not capable of very sharp focus; it may, therefore, be of considerable value to us to concentrate our advertising in media that reach only certain demographic or psychographic segments of the public. In other words, the target market that we wish to reach will dictate our choice of media.

One issue that will arise during the planning of a campaign is scheduling—whether to use ten full-page insertions in one publication, for example, or five full-page insertions in each of two, or ten half-

Because of the growing numbers of smokers who have decided to abandon their high-tar, full-flavor brands, the fastest-growing segment of the cigarette market in the United States is now composed of low-tar cigarettes. In 1978, low-tar brands accounted for 35 percent of all cigarette sales, a percentage that is expected to increase in coming years. And the company that has managed to capture the second largest share (26 percent) of the low-tar market segment is Lorillard, the fifth-largest cigarette manufacturer with only a 9 percent share of the total market.

Until 1975, Lorillard had been actively seeking to develop a full-flavor, high-tar brand to compete with Marlboro. The company had invested $75 million in new plants and equipment; in addition it had introduced a new management system that made one manager responsible for the coordination of all advertising, market research, manufacturing, sales, promotion, and packaging for one brand, and had test marketed several new brands under the names Luke, Zack, and Maverick. Despite all these efforts, however, Lorillard was not able to obtain a significant share of the high-tar market. In fact, its overall share of the market began to decline. One reason that Lorillard's new brands were meeting resistance was that consumers were becoming aware of tar numbers. The low-tar race had already begun.

Early in 1975, Curtis Judge, president of Lorillard, held a three-day strategy session with members of his staff and representatives of Lorillard's four advertising agencies. In preparation for this meeting, each agency had had its marketing researchers draw up a study of the cigarette industry over the preceding ten years. All four studies agreed that low-tar cigarettes were going to be the fastest-growing brands of the future. It was determined that the low-tar market could be divided into three subsegments: (1) ultra low tar, with 0 to 5 milligrams of tar per cigarette; (2) very low tar, with 6 to 9 mg.; and (3) low tar, with 10 to 15 mg. Lorillard decided to market a brand to each subsegment. Its first new brand, with 9 mg. tar, would be aimed at the middle group.

The name chosen for the new brand was Kent Golden Lights, a name that is believed to have made an important contribution to the cigarette's eventual success. Curtis Judge felt that a name such as Kent Lights or Kent Milds would not have been as successful, because Kents were already perceived by smokers as being a light brand. It was John O'Toole, president of Foote, Cone & Belding, Lorillard's principal agency, who suggested that the word *golden* be used. This would position the brand as an alternative for Kent smokers who wanted to switch to a lower-tar cigarette and as an attractive new brand for non-Kent smokers who were ready to try something new.

Lorillard began test marketing Kent Golden Lights in Portland, Maine. If the test marketing proved successful, the company planned to launch the new brand first in the Northeast. But agency researchers had earlier predicted that Philip Morris would introduce a very low-tar brand before the year was out. And they were right. In December of
continued

Kent Golden Lights continued

1975, Philip Morris introduced Merit, a brand with 9 mg. tar, in a national roll-out without test marketing. Lorillard took several steps to meet this new competition. First, it reduced the tar level of Golden Lights to 8 mg., an important difference for tar-conscious smokers. Then, it decided to begin a national advertising campaign for the new brand without doing any further test marketing.

Kent Golden Lights blasted off with a high-powered campaign in April, 1976. Advertising emphasized the 8 mg. tar level by showing illustrations of a number of leading low-tar cigarettes with their tar rating printed in bold numbers over them. The copy emphasized both the new cigarette's low-tar rating and its rich flavor with the headline: "Taste it. You won't believe the numbers."

With Golden Lights making gains in its subsegment of the low-tar market, Lorillard introduced its contender for a share of the ultra-low-tar segment: True cigarettes. Originally introduced in 1966 as a low-tar brand with 11 mg. tar, True had been losing sales as new brands had entered the market with even lower tar levels. In repositioning True, Lorillard cut its tar level to 5 mg., below that of almost every other brand on the market. Little over a year later, True's sales had increased by 23 percent.

Finally, the company reformulated its Kent brand of cigarettes to appeal to smokers who wanted a brand with 10 to 15 mg. tar. Kent had originally been introduced in the early 1950s with a tar level of 16 mg. By reducing Kent's tar level to 12 mg. and reintroducing it in 1977 with a campaign that emphasized its low-tar characteristics, Lorillard hoped to capture new customers for the brand. Kent's sales, which had recently been declining, began to level off.

By covering all three segments of the low-tar market, Lorillard has provided a product for full-flavor brand smokers who want to switch to a low-tar brand that still has the rich taste they are used to. It also has products for low-tar brand smokers who are ready to switch to a brand that has even lower tar levels than the one they currently smoke. In this way, if the low-tar segment continues to grow at a much faster pace than the cigarette market as a whole, Lorillard's 9 percent share of total sales is bound to increase, drawing the present fifth-ranking company up to fourth place and perhaps even eventually boosting it into third.

Source: Peter J. Schuyten, "Lorillard Scores Big in the Low-Tar Derby," *Fortune*, August 14, 1978, pp. 124–130.

page insertions in each of two. Advertising readership is influenced by the size of the ad. According to a report by Cahners Research, the readership increases as the size of the advertisement increases. Cahners Research analyzed 2,353 business advertisements that were sorted by size and indexed against the overall average. A full-page ad had an index score of 124. A two-page ad had a score of 213. Half-page ads scored 91 and quarter-page ads scored 55.[1] Readership must be weighed against frequency as the advertiser decides whether a series of half-pages is better than a smaller number of full pages.

## Measuring results

In Chapter 14, we pointed out that a consumer's decision about whether or not to purchase a product is the result of a distinct learning process. During this process, the consumer becomes aware of a brand, develops an attitude toward it, and then decides to make a trial purchase. We also know that we cannot precisely measure which sales are the result of a particular advertising campaign, because it is impossible to separate these sales from those motivated by other factors in our marketing program. Unlike a change in the quantity of sales, however, a change in the number of people who are *aware* of a brand's existence can be attributed to advertising. Such a change in awareness will usually occur *immediately after exposure* to advertising, while trial purchases may take place at a much later date.

### Have consumers changed their behavior?

To measure the effect of our advertising, therefore, we have to consider the behavior that the advertising is expected to induce, influence, or reinforce. What behavioral action may be desired? We might want to encourage trial purchases by new customers, for example, or to reinforce brand loyalty among existing customers. We might want to increase the frequency of purchase or to encourage consumers to visit a retailer. Our problem is identifying methods to measure these actions.

When the objective is, for example, to encourage a new application of the product, we would find it impossible to measure the number of people who used the product in the new way as a result of advertising. But, if the task assigned to advertising is to communicate the idea of a new use, we could measure the extent of this *knowledge.*

It is difficult to determine to what extent brand loyalty is a result of our advertising effort. Brand purchases by loyal customers tend to be habitual and not likely to be influenced over the short term by advertising. A more appropriate analysis of what motivates brand loyalty might be obtained by measuring the consumer's *attitude* toward our product. In assessing the response of adult customers toward peanut butter, for example, we might find a mildly negative attitude. Perhaps adults consider peanut butter a food for children. From a position of zero, representing absolute neutrality, we might assign to peanut butter a *valence*, or measure of attractiveness, that could be quantified as minus one $(-1)$. Thus, the attitude being studied has both valence $(-)$ and strength $(1)$. If, after an advertising campaign that stressed the nutritional value of peanut butter, we measured consumer's attitudes again and discovered a value of plus one $(+1)$, we might conclude that advertising contributed to a change in attitude.

### Methods of evaluation

**Measuring individual ads**   What we learn from measuring the effectiveness of an advertising campaign can help make our next campaign better. Having

---

[1] *Cahners Advertising Research Report No. 110.1* (Boston: Cahners Publishing Co., no date).

spent large sums of money to launch the campaign, we want to know if the advertising did what it was supposed to do. As the campaign progresses, we have opportunities to evaluate individual ads. Starch Readership Reports, for example, is a syndicated research service that provides reports on the advertisements in about 100 business and consumer publications from *Air Transport World* to *Woman's Day*. The readers of a particular magazine are shown a copy of the issue being rated and are asked, page by page, about their reading of the ads. Advertisers or agencies interested either in a specific issue or in a publication not regularly scheduled, can have those publications "Starched" for a specified charge.

Starch tabulates the results for each issue and converts them into percentages of those who merely noted the ad, those who associated the product with the company, and those who actually read most of the ad. The individual components of the ad—the illustration, the headline, the copy, and the advertiser's logo—are also rated. The *Starch ratings* for each component are recorded on labels that are affixed to the advertisement.

Accompanying the labeled magazine are tables summarizing the readership response to each ad in terms of the Starch measurements and in comparison with other ads in a particular product category. Advertisers use Starch data to compare a current campaign against a previous one or to compare a single product's campaign against averages for specific product groups (cake mix X compared to cake mixes, detergent X against detergents). The cost for a report is approximately $165.

Gallup & Robinson (G-R) uses a different technique to probe the respondent's recall of sales messages in a particular issue of a magazine. Three levels of rating are provided: the PNR score, which gives the percentage of readers who proved they remembered the ad by describing it; a measure of the amount of the advertisement's sales message that readers can recall; and finally, the *Favorable Buying Attitude* score, which measures the message's persuasive power.

The Starch reports and the Gallup & Robinson reports are not custom services; they are syndicated. Advertisers receive the information by subscribing to the reports. Such data would be inordinately expensive to obtain independently.

Another simple method for determining the effect of individual ads or for comparing different appeals is the *split run*. Two different ads are inserted in the same issue of a publication so that some copies of the publication will contain the first ad while others will carry the second. The use of a coupon or of some other form of direct request will provide us with the data needed to judge the comparative effectiveness of the two ads. The split run merely eliminates the effect of other marketing variables when comparing two different appeals, two different headlines, or two different illustrations. However, the split-run evaluation procedure is more suitable for pretesting copy than for measuring the effectiveness of a campaign.

**Test marketing** Before launching a multimillion-dollar advertising program, the advertiser wants to be as sure as possible that the product is "right" and that the advertising approach is "right." One of the most common techniques is *test marketing*—advertising and selling the product on a geographically limited basis. If the city or cities for the test are properly chosen, the results of the test program should enable the advertiser to judge the reception of the product and the effectiveness of the advertising approach nationwide. A good test mar-

Illustration courtesy Road & Track magazine.

# We immodestly named it Great Little Car.

# Seems we were right.

Our new GLC is more than just a car. It's a reflection of the way we see the U.S. import car market.

Our analysis of that market tells us that it breaks cleanly into two segments: a market for high-quality economy cars, and a market for cars with some clearcut area of special appeal, such as high performance.

We've decided to move forward strongly in both segments, using our unique advantage as the only mass manufacturer of both rotary and piston vehicles. We are continuing to produce and develop rotary-engine models, including an exciting new sports car to be introduced next year. And we are producing the GLC, the latest in a 46-year history of piston-powered Mazdas.

We've designed the GLC to be more than just another economy car. From the very beginning, we wanted it to be versatile, handsome, easy to drive, long-lasting and offer excellent han-

dling. Our goal: a car with a lot of luxury features and creature comforts, at an economy price. How well have we succeeded? We'll let some of the world's foremost car experts answer for us:

"...a real charmer. It's roomy, the ride is comfortable and the car's behavior is so predictable you get the feeling you've driven it before...Mazda plans to bring the base GLC into the U.S. for less than $3,000. At that price, it really *is* a great little car."
*Car & Driver (U.S.) Feb. 1977*

"In the first trial runs with the new Mazda, test drivers clearly established that this Japanese

economy subcompact is roomy, comfortable and economical to operate."
*Die Welt am Sonntag (Germany) Feb. 20, 1977*

"A tight, sturdy little car... a lot of shoulder and leg room, especially when one co
the opposition..."
*Autocar (United Kingdom) Feb.*

"The GLC may end
one of the nicest small
packages sent to the U
*Road & Track (U.S.) Feb. 1977*

"...excellent handling, good high-speed stability and the ability to traverse abominable surface irregularities without undue disturbance."
*Motor Trader (United Kingdom) Feb. 9, 1977*

"Based solely upon the car's individual worth, any salesman who couldn't put a customer into a Deluxe GLC in half an hour should quit the business."
*Road Test (U.S.) March 1977*

So our new car looks like a winner. We wanted you to know. Because we're committed to growth in the U.S. And sound growth takes a lot of believers.

Mazda's rotary engine licensed by NSU-WANKEL.

## We want to make a believer out of you.

## GEORGE GALLUP

In the minds of most Americans, the name Gallup is usually associated with the word "poll." For many of us, the Gallup Poll has become virtually synonomous with opinion research, and Dr. George Gallup has provided information on our attitudes on various subjects of interest to political leaders and ordinary citizens alike. However, it was in the field of advertising research that Dr. Gallup first started nearly fifty years ago. And it is in that field that he and one of the organizations he founded, Gallup & Robinson, Inc., continue to make many important contributions that are used to guide advertisers and agencies in their search for the "right" appeal.

George Gallup's career in the research field began in 1922 when he took a summer job for the D'Arcy advertising agency as an interviewer. During that summer, he worked on a study to determine what articles and advertisements people read in the St. Louis newspapers. Believing that the methods used to conduct this survey could be greatly improved, he began to study research techniques when he returned to the University of Iowa in the fall, making them the subject of his Ph.D. thesis in 1928. In 1932, he was hired by Young & Rubicam advertising agency to help set up their copy-research department. The president of the agency, Raymond Rubicam, told Gallup that his only assignment would be to learn how Young & Rubicam could make the advertising it created more effective. George Gallup spent the next fifteen years learning how advertising does its work, and he has this to say about the importance of setting measurable goals for an advertising campaign:

> Almost every campaign, to begin with, has specific objectives. The whole process of advertising is designing a strategy that will create a sale. You can find out if the strategy is working. Are you changing people's minds about this particular fact about the product? You can measure that. Every advertiser, even if he spends only a few thousand dollars, should demand some kind of evidence of the effectiveness of his advertising.

In 1947, George Gallup moved into the field of public-opinion polling that has made him famous. But in the advertising field he is best known for the development of methods to measure readership interest in newspapers and magazines and for measuring the audiences of individual radio programs. He was elected to the Advertising Hall of Fame of the American Advertising Federation in 1978.

## PARATEST RECOMMENDED MARKETS

(Following is an example of a list of recommended test markets, as compiled by a market research company—Paratest Marketing, New York. The list includes 36 "B" county television metropolitan markets that would be used in controlled market studies. Lists of other markets—"larger" markets, "C" county micromarkets and markets that don't need to meet tv spillage requirements—are also available from the company.)

| | ADI % of U.S. | Metro Households (000) | | ADI % of U.S. | Metro Households (000) |
|---|---|---|---|---|---|
| **NORTHEAST** | | | **SOUTHEAST** | | |
| Albany, N.Y. | 0.68 | 245 | Birmingham, Ala. | 0.32 | 107 |
| Binghamton, N.Y. | 0.25 | 97 | Charleston, S.C. | 0.20 | 91 |
| Johnstown, Pa. | 0.47 | 200 | Charlotte, N.C. | 0.67 | 140 |
| Portland, Me. | 0.41 | 66 | Chattanooga, Tenn. | 0.32 | 107 |
| Rochester, N.Y. | 0.40 | 107 | Jacksonville, Fla. | 0.43 | 185 |
| Wilkes-Barre, Pa. | 0.47 | 200 | Savannah, Ga. | 0.16 | 61 |
| **EAST CENTRAL** | | | **SOUTHWEST** | | |
| Evansville, Ind. | 0.27 | 70 | Baton Rouge, La. | 0.21 | 89 |
| Ft. Wayne, Ind. | 0.29 | 94 | Beaumont, Tex. | 0.23 | 81 |
| Louisville, Ky. | 0.64 | 234 | Corpus Christi, Tex. | 0.19 | 89 |
| South Bend, Ind. | 0.26 | 136 | Lubbock, Tex. | 0.20 | 62 |
| Toledo, O. | 0.49 | 195 | Oklahoma City, Okla. | 0.62 | 246 |
| **WEST CENTRAL** | | | Tulsa, Okla. | 0.53 | 147 |
| Davenport, Ia. | 0.44 | 121 | **WEST** | | |
| Des Moines, Ia. | 0.44 | 124 | Bakersfield, Cal. | 0.14 | 97 |
| Duluth, Minn. | 0.26 | 88 | Eugene, Ore. | 0.18 | 78 |
| Madison, Wis. | 0.20 | 98 | Fresno, Cal. | 0.39 | 140 |
| Omaha, Neb. | 0.43 | 185 | Salt Lake City, Utah | 0.53 | 154 |
| Peoria, Ill. | 0.28 | 116 | Spokane, Wash. | 0.43 | 101 |
| Rockford, Ill. | 0.25 | 79 | Tucson, Ariz. | 0.21 | 143 |

ket will be (depending on the product) one that is demographically representative of the rest of the country. The degrees of media availability and of media isolation (will there be "spill-in" from media beyond the market being tested?), and the facilities for control and verification, also influence the choice of the test market. Every agency and every research organization has its preferred test-market cities.

Test marketing in different cities or regions of the country may provide an excellent measure of a product's potential, but such advertising does not provide enough information to evaluate a sustained effort. Intervening variables, such as weather, mar-

ket characteristics, position in the medium, and so on, may affect our results.

**How to evaluate the overall campaign** The effectiveness of entire ad campaigns can be judged according to the following criteria:

1. sales increases
2. trial purchases
3. awareness
4. attitude
5. knowledge

# Good Vibrations.

We have said that a unity of presentation is characteristic of a campaign. Here are some samples from a campaign created by Foote, Cone & Belding, Chicago, for Sunkist Growers, Inc. As the agency says in its strategy statement: "The Sunkist advertising program has been designed to generate widespread awareness and broadscale trial by building a distinctive and durable identity for the brand." Note the repeated use of the words "good vibrations," and illustrations of the same models to provide a relationship between all the elements of the campaign.

A car card for bus and rapid-transit rail lines (A).

A full-page, four-color ad that appeared in *TV Guide*. Note the strong product identification and the large cents-off coupon to induce trial by reducing risk (B).

A premium is used to stimulate sales with these in-store promotion ads—a "take-one" shelf display card and a hang-tag to fit over bottles (C, E).

A 30-second television commercial that identifies the largest market—young, active people (D).

436

C

**ANNCR:** A new soft drink has come to town

with a taste from Sunkist·

that'll turn you around.

**SINGERS:** I'm drinking up

good vibrations.

Sunkist orange taste sensations.

Good good good good vibrations.

Bubbly orange jubilation.

Sunkist is a taste sensation.

I'm giving out orange vibrations.

Bubbly Sunkist sensations.

Sunkist is giving out GOOD VIBRATIONS.

© 1978, Sunkist Growers Inc. Sunkist is a registered trademark of Sunkist Growers, Inc.

D

E

# NASHVILLE
## *"TEST MARKET, U.S.A."*

"Music City, U.S.A." may just become "Test Market, U.S.A." For in Nashville, lab conditions are ideal to test national products and campaigns.

Here's why...

**RIGHT SIZE.**
Nashville's 156,000 households and its SMSA's 260,900 are well within the limits required of good test markets.

**MARKET PROTECTION**
Nashville's media carries the message to its SMSA without outside media interference.

**REPRESENTATIVE POPULATION**
A healthy mix of blue collar, white collar and professional workers insure distortion-free test results.

**STABLE ECONOMY**
Nashville has been called a "recession-proof market" and its unemployment rates are always below the national average.

In '78, Dancer-Fitzgerald-Sample chose us as one of its 50 recommended test markets. We think D-F-S is only the beginning.

For more facts and figures, write or call:

NEWSPAPER PRINTING CORP., Agent
*Nashville Banner* • THE TENNESSEAN

1100 Broadway • Nashville, Tn. 37209 • (615) 255-1221
Joe Roper, Marketing and Promotion

---

In these advertisements, which appeared in a leading advertising trade publication, newspaper publishers in Albany, New York, and in Nashville, Tennessee, tell test marketers how the demographics of their cities match those of the nation as a whole. Albany, in particular, appears at the top of many lists of potential test cities.

## Albany, New York...

### As American as Apple Pie!

Want to know how America is going to respond to your new product? Test it in Albany, New York. Here's why:

|  | U.S.A. | Albany SMSA |
|---|---|---|
| Population age 18-24 | 12% | 13% |
| Population age 25-34 | 12% | 14% |
| Average Household Size | 2.9 | 2.8 |
| Average E.B.I. | $17.327 | $17,924 |
| Food Sales per Household | $2.114 | $2,099 |

Albany is a tasty test market that can give you highly reliable results, and it's an easy one to communicate with. Use the morning & Sunday **Times-Union**, and the afternoon **Knickerbocker News**. This three-way combination reaches 293,000 adults in the Albany SMSA a pretty big piece of the pie. For more information call Chris Cunningham, Jr at **(518) 454-5680** or your Hearst Advertising Representative.

Source: S&MM Survey of Buying Power, 1978.

**Capital Newspapers Group**
**Albany, New York 12201**

*Sales and trial purchases*   Coupon response and direct sales enable us to measure the effectiveness of an ad campaign. Count the coupons, add up the sales, and there are your results. Most consumer ads are not, however, intended to provoke direct response. The advertiser can often get clues on trial purchases from organizations that maintain consumer panels. A panel is actually a permanent sample, and the diaries of panel members provide valuable information about trial use. The question is: how many new trials do we require before we deem the campaign a success?

*Awareness, attitude, and knowledge*   Through the use of appropriate sampling procedures and questionnaires, the advertiser can question the target market to obtain some measure of their awareness of the product, their attitude toward it, and their knowledge of its use or purpose. Some of the recall (Gallup & Robinson) and recognition (Starch) tests used to evaluate individual ads may also provide a basis for judging a campaign. Recall tests tell us not only whether or not the respondent has seen or read the ads; they also measure the depth of the ads' impressions on the reader and, to some extent, the *meaning* the ads convey. The tests do not, however, indicate whether or not the respondent will buy the product; nor do they indicate whether or not the respondent believed the message even if he or she happened to remember it. If we are prepared to accept the limitations inherent in these recall and recognition evaluations, they can nevertheless be instructive. Provided with a measurement taken before the campaign and a measurement taken afterward, the advertiser can gauge the campaign's effectiveness either in reinforcing or producing *shifts* in consumer awareness, attitude, and knowledge or in maintaining existing attitudes.

## Summary

An advertising campaign is the culmination of our advertising effort. In a sense, it is a battle that the advertiser fights to capture the minds of a portion of the target market. The advertiser plans the campaign's advertising to provide a powerful selling message and then repeats that message in various forms that have visual or verbal similarity or a common approach.

In planning the campaign, an advertiser's most important task is setting measurable objectives. These objectives will help determine the creative strategy and will also be used at the end of the campaign as a means of evaluating its effectiveness. Advertisers must also take care to coordinate the campaign with the company's personal selling, sales promotion, and public relations efforts.

Advertising takes time to do its job because its function is to change or reinforce the buying behavior of the consumer. We are well aware of how difficult it is to break habits such as smoking or biting one's fingernails. Buying behavior, for the most part, is also a habit. Once consumers find a brand that satisfies most of their needs, they are not inclined to switch. Just as it takes time to build up a habit, time (and repeated advertising) is required to change that habit and substitute another for it.

Advertisers can rarely determine the effectiveness of a campaign by measuring the change in product sales that has occurred, because too many variables can affect this result. They must measure, instead, the prospect's awareness of, and attitude toward, the product. Any shift in awareness and attitude can be attributed to the advertising campaign. Syndicated research services such as Starch Readership Reports will measure the readership levels and persuasive power of individual ads. Advertisers may also use *test marketing* to help determine the effectiveness of a campaign. By testing a campaign only in certain regions or cities an advertiser can gather information that will improve it before it is rolled out nationwide. But the results of test marketing will also be influenced by variables beyond the advertiser's control, such as the weather. In order to obtain the most accurate evaluation of their campaigns, some advertisers measure sales increases and trial purchases, as well as awareness, attitude, and knowledge changes.

## QUESTIONS FOR DISCUSSION

1. What factors influence the length of an advertising campaign?

2. Why would an advertiser run more than one campaign at a time for the same product?

3. What are some measurable objectives an advertiser might set for an advertising campaign?

4. What are some objectives that an advertiser might set for an institutional campaign?

5. Why might advertising have an impact only a year or more after it has appeared?

6. What is the relationship between the product's life cycle and the kind of campaign planned?

7. If you were the advertising manager for a new toothpaste, what kind of advertising campaign would you recommend?

8. What is the role of trade advertising in implementing an advertising campaign?

9. What are the problems in attempting to use sales as a measure of the effectiveness of an advertising campaign?

## Sources and suggestions for further reading

Aaker, David A., and Myers, John G. *Advertising Management.* Englewood Cliffs, N.J.: Prentice-Hall, 1975.

Boyd, Harper W., Jr.; Westfall, Ralph; and Stasch, Stanley F. *Marketing Research.* 4th ed. Homewood, Ill.: Richard D. Irwin, 1977.

Day, G. S. *Buyer Attitudes and Brand Choice Behavior.* New York: Free Press, 1970.

Dirksen, Charles J.; Kroeger, Arthur; and Nicosia, Francesco M. *Advertising Principles, Problems, and Cases.* 5th ed. Homewood, Ill.: Richard D. Irwin, 1977.

Engel, J. F.; Kollat, D. T.; and Blackwell, R. D. *Consumer Behavior.* New York: Holt, Rinehart and Winston, 1968.

Holbert, Neil. *Advertising Research.* Monograph Series #1. Chicago, Ill.: American Marketing Association, 1975.

Hughes, G. D. *Attitude Measurement for Marketing Strategies.* Glenview, Ill.: Scott, Foresman and Co., 1971.

Roman, Kenneth, and Maas, Jane. *How to Advertise.* New York: St. Martin's Press, 1976.

Tull, Donald S., and Hawkins, Del I. *Marketing Research.* New York: Macmillan Publishing Co., 1976.

---

## RETAIL ADVERTISING

**Planning retail advertising**

Retail advertising objectives
What to advertise
Marketing information for retailers
What does the retailer want to
know?
Secondary data
Primary data
Budgeting methods
Percentage of sales
Task method

Advertising-to-sales ratio
Factors that influence the budget
decision

**Media for retailers**

Advertising schedules
Building the schedule
Retail copy
The retail advertising department
Vertical cooperative advertising

---

## WORKING VOCABULARY

scrambled merchandising

traffic

want slip

distress merchandise

big ticket items

omnibus ad

tonnage ad

vertical cooperative
advertising

slug in

canned advertising

Robinson-Patman Act

---

# 19

## retail advertising

*Retail advertising emphasizes immediacy. Individual items are placed on sale and advertised during specific, short time periods. Immediate purchases are sought.*

BARRY BERMAN and JOEL R. EVANS
*Retail Management: A Strategic Approach*

R ETAILING DESCRIBES THE PROCESS OF SELLING PRODUCTS OR SERVICES directly to consumers, usually through a physical establishment: a retail store. There are many different kinds of retail stores. Although a group of stores may join forces to form a national or regional chain with a common name and common brands of merchandise, their business is local, or retail, in nature. In general, we can separate retailers into three basic types:

**1.** The class store
This store stocks and sells the finest quality merchandise, appealing to upscale customers. The authority of the store in matters of style is very great, with prices to match this prestige. The store does some regular-price advertising and some institutional advertising. The percentage of its sales that this store devotes to advertising, however, is small.

**2.** The promotional store
The reputation of this store is built on aggressive promotion and reduced prices. Services are few and regular patronage is not considered important. Advertising is highly promotional—that is, the emphasis

Lord & Taylor is a leading fashion store that bases its appeal on updated classic fashion merchandise. Price does not dominate. The style of the ad, the focus on a single item, the use of wash drawings for illustration with the price simply mentioned in the copy—all combine to attract an affluent, fashion-conscious customer.

Alexander's is a *promotional store* for which price is the dominant advertising appeal. The use of photographs to strengthen the sense of real merchandise at a very boldly featured price is typical of a promotional store. The objective of such ads is to sell very specific merchandise.

J.C. Penny is an *in-between store* that often features nationally known brands. The emphasis is neither on high style nor on low price, but on reliable merchandise, a large selection, and good value.

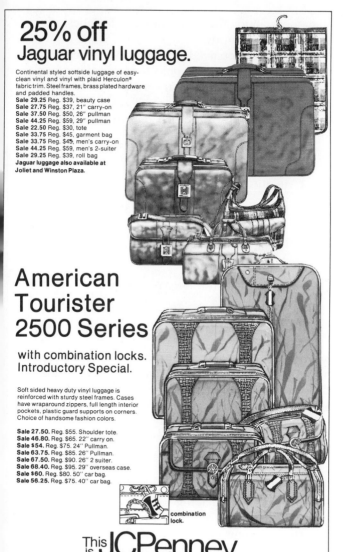

is on price or sales or special purchases. The percentage of its sales that this store devotes to advertising is large.

**3.** The in-between store
For the most part, this type of store does regular-price advertising, storewide promotions, and occasional clearances and special sales. It also does some institutional advertising. The percentage of its sales that this type of store devotes to advertising is moderate.

## Planning retail advertising

As we learned in Chapter 3, there are three distinguishing characteristics of retail advertising: (1) it is intended to reach only a limited area; (2) it emphasizes price; and (3) its appeal is for an immediate response. Retail managers are very much concerned with their stores' advertising for these very compelling reasons:

**1.** Advertising costs are probably the fourth largest retail cost after the cost of goods, salaries, and rent.

**2.** Advertising is a discretionary investment. It is the retailer's one cost that is most susceptible to change.

**3.** Advertising affects every other facet of store operations—buying, pricing, new store locations, personnel policies, and, most of all, sales activities.

**4.** There is increased competition between retailers as the result of scrambled merchandising and a population that is dispersed and mobile. *Scrambled merchandising* refers to the sale of products that are not traditionally found in a certain kind of retail outlet. Drugstores may, for example, stock hardware and garden supplies; ready-to-wear clothing stores may carry colognes or luggage.

5. We have increasingly become a service-oriented society. Buying decisions often hinge on intangibles—attitudes and images—which the store can project through advertising.

## Retail advertising objectives

Product promotion advertising is basically intended either to stimulate the immediate sale of merchandise at regular prices or to clear out certain merchandise at sharply reduced prices. In most cases, retailers want to create store *traffic*—that is, they want to get customers to visit their store to see and buy the advertised merchandise. The retailers assume that, once in the store, customers will see and buy other merchandise that was not advertised. Just as national advertisers hope to create brand-loyal customers, retailers want their customers to get into the habit of buying in their stores; they want their regular customers to buy more; and, at the same time, they want to acquire new customers. Retailers expect that the greater volume of sales thus generated will result in a greater profit.

A retailer can also use institutional advertising to build a store's prestige and enhance its reputation for merchandise. The object is to create a personality for the store. The retailer builds goodwill among prospects by telling regular and prospective customers about the store policies, facilities, services, and philosophy.

Just as national advertisers have advertising objectives, retailers have objectives for their own advertising. To be sure, retailers also use advertising to obtain more profit through sales, but let us briefly list some of the broad objectives a retailer might set and see if they are dissimilar to those of a national advertiser:

1. to attract new customers

2. to sell more merchandise to present customers

3. to sell specific kinds or brands of merchandise

4. to create a store image

5. to create store loyalty

To attract new customers, retailers might try to extend their stores' geographical trading area by introducing new departments and new merchandise. To sell more merchandise to present customers and to build store loyalty, they might want to inform those customers of new departments, new brands, new services, and new policies that will benefit them.

**What to advertise**  National manufacturers usually have no problem deciding what to advertise. They may make only one product, or they may want to advertise the one product most likely to produce profitable sales from their advertising investment. Retailers, however—particularly the large supermarket or department store—stock and sell hundreds of items. They have three options when considering what to advertise. They can:

1. Advertise the most popular products of the fastest-selling lines. These products would sell well even without advertising.

2. Advertise the seasonal specialties. They build traffic, and attract customers who will buy other, unadvertised, items. Supermarkets frequently advertise products as loss leaders to build traffic.

3. Advertise to clear out slow-moving merchandise or to clear out stock at the end of the season.

The choice must be made on a short-term basis, and most stores will plan for all three. Obviously, retailers hope that clearance advertising will not be necessary. Well-kept records on what products have sold well and when they were sold are the retailer's most valuable guide to advertising. Retailers can base their sales forecasts and budgets on the previous year's (or years') performance records and still remain flexible enough to capitalize on changing tastes or styles or on unexpected merchandise "buys." If all this sounds as if it requires careful planning, you are right. It does indeed.

## Marketing information for retailers

**What does the retailer want to know?** The retailer's need for information is much the same as the national advertiser's. Although small retailers are able to get to know many of their customers personally, they usually do not have the resources to conduct any additional market research. Large retailers, with more customers but also with more resources at their disposal, can conduct full-scale market research programs. What type of marketing intelligence would a retailer particularly want to have?

This *retail ad* is designed to accomplish two objectives: to create a store image and to draw new customers. The store builds its image by listing the names of the famous designer fashions it carries. The store hopes to attract new customers with clearance-price reductions. For prospective customers, the opportunity to save as much as 50 percent may be a sufficient inducement to visit the store for the first time.

DESIGNERS CLEARANCE SAVE 20% TO 50%

Enjoy Spring and Summer fashions from noted designers, now at generous reductions! You'll find:

● SPORTSWEAR: Anne Klein, Dalton, Givenchy

● EVENINGWEAR: Marita, Albert Nipon, Mollie Parnis

● DAY DRESSES: Baron Peters, Abe Schrader, Diane Von Furstenberg

● SUITS: Gamut, Baron Peters, Albert Capraro

Designers on 4, State Street; also our new Designers Shop in Water Tower Place on 6.

CHAS. A. STEVENS

STATE STREET ON FOUR AND WATER TOWER PLACE, SIXTH LEVEL. USE YOUR STEVENS CHARGE, FOR SHOPPING CONVENIENCE.

1. What are the attitudes of customers toward the store and toward its merchandise?

2. What local tastes and preferences are most significant?

3. Which family members shop at the store?

4. How many customers does the store lose and gain each year? What are the reasons for the turnover?

5. What are the demographics of the store's market?

6. What are the most important departments or product lines?

7. What are the most important selling days of the week?

8. Which media reach the largest possible number of the store's customers and prospects?

9. How large should the store's advertising allocation be?

**Secondary data**  Much of the information a retailer needs is available from secondary sources—that is, from data that was collected for some other purpose. For example, the store's own internal records are an excellent secondary source of information. Such records will show the retailer on what day, week, or month sales for various categories of merchandise peaked, and which colors, styles, and products sold best. From records of previous advertising programs, the retailer might learn which medium is the most effective for the advertising of certain merchandise. Charge account billings will provide records of where customers live, how often they shop, and what they buy. The store may also keep records of competitive advertising activities; if not, such information can be readily obtained from other sources.

Newspapers, radio and television stations, and transit media operators will provide retailers with demographic data on their medium's circulation and, often, with data on competitive advertising activities. The United States Department of Commerce is an excellent source of information. Trade publications, too, are a valuable source of sales data. *Women's Wear Daily* supplies information on women's and children's ready-to-wear clothes; *Drug Topics* supplies information on pharmaceutical store sales; *Sporting Goods Dealer* has information on sporting goods; and many other excellent retailing publications provide general as well as specific data that will be useful to a retailer in planning advertising. Two particularly good sources for retail advertising information deserve special mention. One is the *Newspaper Advertising Planbook*, which is issued to retailers by the Newspaper Advertising Bureau, Inc., and is a step-by-step guide for any retailer. The other is *Advertising Small Business*, which is published by the Bank of America and contains helpful information on all the media available to retailers.

Data on the percentage of sales allocated to advertising by various kinds of retail stores are available from many different sources. These figures are, of course, averages; some retailers will allocate a percentage of sales to advertising that may be higher or lower than the average, depending on their competitive situations and their stores' profit objectives.

**Primary data**  After the retailer has exhausted the available secondary data, there may remain questions that can only be answered by collecting primary data: customer attitudes, customer preferences, customer shopping habits. Such information is gathered by surveys, interviews, and observation. A mail, or a telephone, survey of a sample of customers or noncustomers may be made from time to time to determine how people perceive the store image. Personal interviews, although more expensive and time consuming, may be used to gather information to guide the retailer in its advertising, as well as its merchandising, operation. Skilled observers, sometimes with the aid of hidden cameras or one-way mirrors, can provide clues to shopping behavior. How do shoppers move through the store? How do they handle the merchandise? Or the retailer may want to conduct an experiment. Will toilet water sell in the lingerie department? Will barbecue-sauce sales increase if the display is next to the meat counter? Most retailers use *want slips* —forms used by store employees to record requested merchandise not in stock. An analysis of such requests may provide the retailer with clues to trends and changing tastes.

## Budgeting methods

The two methods that retailers most commonly use to determine their advertising budgets are the percentage-of-sales method and the task method. We examined both of these methods in Chapter 6.

**Percentage of sales**   This system is the method most widely used by retailers because it is based on past experience. This is not to say it is the preferred method, but it does work well. The percentage-of-sales method is particularly helpful when a store has to divide funds among departments. Store management has every opportunity to learn the percentages commonly used in their field of retail-

ing. Information for various retail categories is available in published reports. The percentages listed for advertising are averages, of course, and each store is expected to adjust that average as its marketing circumstances require. Among the different categories of retailers, variations in advertising budget are very wide. Low-budget retailers include bakeries, building-materials suppliers, food stores, service stations, taverns, children's-wear shops, and automobile dealers. Big spenders include department stores, movie theaters, sporting-goods stores, large dry cleaners, large floor-coverings dealers, florists, furniture stores, jewelers, toy dealers, and photography studios. But, as we pointed out in Chapter 6, the percentage-of-sales method has one important weakness: it is not based on present market conditions but on past performance. Times change, customers change, competitors change . . . entire markets change, and no retailer can afford to overlook today's opportunities.

**Task method**   This method for setting the retailer's advertising budget is based on a set of objectives. The retailer then allocates resources to attain those objectives. It is a forward-looking method that forces management to think carefully about what it wants its advertising to do. It is a method well suited to retailers, because retail management can determine very quickly the extent to which each objective is being attained: an ad in a Sunday paper will either achieve or fail to achieve its objectives within the next week. To be sure, a store will benefit in the long run from the cumulative effect of its advertising, but a retail ad for specific merchandise, unlike ads placed by national advertisers, demands direct action: *Visit the store. Order by phone. Do it today.*

**Advertising-to-sales ratio**  Large retailers may vary the amount of advertising devoted to different departments of the store because each department has different characteristics that affect the store's overall profitability. In this case, each department's advertising budget may be allocated on an advertising-to-sales ratio. Some merchandise classifications may be given as little as 1 percent of their projected sales volume, while others may receive as much as 5 percent. The furniture department of a large store, for example, produces many dollars of sales volume but very little traffic. Such a department may be profitable with a smaller advertising-to-sales ratio than the hosiery department, for instance, which produces a much smaller volume of sales dollars each month, but generates much more store traffic. Such a department may receive a higher advertising-to-sales ratio than its volume would justify because of the traffic it stimulates.

Large retailers segregate their advertising expenditures from their public relations and sales promotion expenditures. The legitimate expenses of advertising include the cost of media (space and time), advertising production costs, and the payroll of the advertising department. Small stores tend to lump everything together in one catchall account. There is always some confusion, too, about whether or not charitable donations (such as placing a message in a local high-school yearbook or in the program of a local garden club, or sponsoring a local Little League team) should be listed under the heading of advertising. Such expenditures properly belong in the public relations account.

## Factors that influence the budget decision

Regardless of which method is used to determine the budget, there are certain other considerations that strongly influence the retailer's advertising allocation.

1. The place of advertising in the store's basic promotion policy
   A center-city store that attracts pedestrian traffic must rely heavily on its window and in-store displays. Such a store might require less advertising to stimulate traffic. In a similar fashion, a store that is flanked by retailers that advertise heavily, as is often the case in shopping malls, will benefit from the traffic those stores draw.

2. The extent of manufacturer advertising
   If most of a retailer's merchandise is heavily advertised by the manufacturer, customers will come to the store presold. Retailers need only establish their stores as places to buy the branded, nationally advertised merchandise. The manufacturer carries the burden of advertising.

3. The nature of the market
   If the market is suburban and mobile, or if it is transient as in a resort area or a college town, retailers' advertising requirements are greater than usual because they are trying to attract new customers.

4. Available media
   The fewer the number of newspapers and broadcast media available in a retailer's trading area, the smaller the advertising investment that is required. When, as in large cities, there are two or three newspapers and fifteen radio and television stations to choose among, and none of them is dominant, the retailer must spend more to obtain effective market coverage.

**5.** The nature of the merchandise

Cantaloupes, fish, or fashion merchandise cannot be held over too long. To a certain extent, the perishability of the merchandise determines the need for advertising. Having a large quantity of high-fashion merchandise in stock at the end of the season is as serious as a power failure in the frozen-foods section of a supermarket. Advertising can be far less expensive than price reductions for *distress merchandise.* For example, at the end of the selling season for bathing suits, the retailer has several choices: hold the leftover merchandise until next season; drastically mark down the merchandise; or advertise a seasonal clearance sale. Styles may change. The colors may not be suitable. And the bathing suits held in stock tie up money. Instead, a modest markdown combined with clearance-sale ads helps move the distress merchandise and may attract new customers to the store.

**6.** The nature of the store

The age, the size, and the location of the store also affect the advertising allocation. A large and growing store with many departments has to reach a varied group of people in order to insure that all departments remain profitable. Advertising is needed to generate traffic, to bring in the crowds. For an established neighborhood delicatessen, advertising is of little benefit.

## Media for retailers

The greatest portion of retail advertising goes into *newspapers.* Retail advertising is concentrated in newspapers because they are geographically selective—they cover the retailers' trading areas. Newspapers are also a "now" medium: they evoke a quick response from shoppers who read the ads before they go shopping, and they offer high frequency. Unfortunately, small retailers cannot take advantage of newspapers in large cities unless they are offering a specialty—that is, some product or assortment that is not available everywhere and for which the customer will go out of his or her way. (Bridal apparel is a good example.)

For the most part, *magazines* are not a retailer's medium. Only chain stores, such as Sears, Montgomery Ward, or Woolworth's, can take advantage of advertising opportunities in consumer magazines. Even the demographic editions generally deliver circulation to an area far too wide for a local department store. A few consumer magazines do, however, offer metropolitan editions that are geographically very selective and are, therefore, of use to certain department and specialty stores.

*Broadcast media* have not been extensively used by retailers. Thirty seconds of radio or television commercial time are insufficient to present a wide variety of merchandise. And, because television is demographically not very selective, it is not very cost effective for retailers. Although highly segmented, radio offers retailers even less opportunity to supply consumers with the information they need to make a wise buying decision, and it provides no opportunity to display merchandise.

However, radio has proven to be an effective medium for some retailers who can take advantage of its selectivity and low cost. Discount electronics stores, discount furniture outlets, and auto dealers use radio extensively. Restaurants and theaters, too, have been able to use radio to reach very specific markets at relatively low cost.

This *institutional ad* appeared in *The New Yorker*. Notice that it does not even mention goods for sale. Why would a store in New York City advertise in this way in a national magazine? First, such advertising builds a national image for this famous store. Second, many of the readers of this magazine live and work within convenient traveling distance of the main store or its branches in the Greater New York area. Third, the date of the flower show mentioned in the ad is Easter week, when tourists from all over the United States visit New York City.

macy's 1979 flower show, april 8 to 14. **(Spring, we thought you'd never come)!**

See the beautiful Broadway Flower Windows on Herald Square through Easter Sunday, April 15.

macy's
New York

*Transit*, although offering some degree of geographic selectivity, does not offer adequate space for most retailers' messages. Its inflexibility effectively limits its value to institutional advertising. *Outdoor* is limited for the same reasons.

*Direct mail* is one of the most suitable forms of advertising for all retailers, small as well as large. Small retailers can control the circulation of their direct mailing, confining it to their specific trading area in order to reach only valid prospects. If a re-

## JANE TRAHEY

Jane Trahey is president of Trahey Advertising, Inc., a Chicago shop with a reputation for creativity. She is the author of nine books, two movies, one play, and dozens of magazine and newspaper articles. She has also been a guest on almost every major talk show in the country.

After undergraduate studies at Mundelein College and postgraduate studies at the University of Wisconsin, Jane Trahey went to work for the *Chicago Tribune*. Then, following a stint at Carson Pirie Scott, a Chicago department store, she moved to Dallas to take a job with Neiman-Marcus, where she worked for eight years, moving up to promotion director. She left Neiman-Marcus to become the advertising director of a New York manufacturing company, starting a house agency for the firm a few years later. After overseeing this house agency for two years, Jane Trahey decided to found her own advertising agency.

Jane Trahey has made a reputation in the fashion industry, where her clients have included Elizabeth Arden, Pauline Trigere, Adele Simpson, and Kaiser Hosiery. She created such advertising lines as "It's not fake anything. It's real Dynel" for Union Carbide; "What becomes a legend most?" for Blackglama (the acronym for the Great Lakes Mink Association); and "Danskins are not just for dancing" for Danskins. Other clients she has worked for include Charles of the Ritz, Borghese, Dorsay Perfumes, and Lanvin. She has also designed ad campaigns for B. Altman, New York; Bergdorf's, White Plains; Neiman-Marcus, Dallas; and Harzfeld's, Kansas.

Named Ad Woman of the Year and recipient of the Harper's Bazaar award as one of the 100 Most Accomplished Women, Jane Trahey is, as one writer has phrased it, "a sharp girl from Chicago with a mind like a burning glass and a restless imagination. Jane Trahey's talent and her independence are her trademark."

This commercial is an example of *direct response advertising;* it must actually sell a product much as a mail-order ad in a newspaper or magazine does. It differs from most retail advertising because no time is spent promoting or enhancing the image of a store—rather, the entire commercial promotes a single product. Direct response ads must generate immediate sales by creating a brand preference so strong consumers will place an order for the product by phone or mail. Total running time for this commercial is 120 seconds. Since prime time is rarely available in two-minute segments, commercials of this length are usually aired late in the afternoon and at other times when cost effectiveness and availability are greatest.

| PRODUCT: GINSU PRODUCTS INC. - KNIFE | DATE: May 31, 1978 | 4:38:00 PM |
| PROGRAM: "Movie" | STATION: WOR-TV | 120 Seconds |

ANNOUNCER: In Japan, the hand can be used like a knife...

(MAN MAKING SOUNDS IN BACKGROUND)

but this method doesn't work

with a tomato,

that's why we use the Ginsu.
It's a knife

that no kitchen should be without.

The Ginsu can cut a slice of bread so thin you can almost see through it.

It cuts meat better than an electric knife, and goes through frozen food as though it were melted butter.

The Ginsu is so sharp, it can cut through a tin can and still slice a tomato like this.

It can chop wood and still remain razor sharp.
What's more, it's a knife that will last forever.

How much would you pay for a knife like this? Before you answer, listen.

It even comes with a matching fork to make carving a pleasure. Wait! There's much, much more.

We also want you to have this six-in-one kitchen tool.
It peels and slivers carrots,

peels potatoes,

and slices paper thin potato chips,

this amazing little knife even grates carrots, grates cheese,

and makes beautiful decorative vegetables.

**LONGSTREET PHOTO REPORTS**
TV Monitoring Service          239-08 Linden Boulevard, Elmont, New York 11003   516 / 285-9540

PRODUCT: GINSU PRODUCTS INC. (P).2 DATE: 5/31/78
PROGRAM: STATION:

How much would you pay
for all these items?

Well, we'll even give
you this set of six
precision steak knives...

DISHWASHER SAFE

the handles even match
the Ginsu.  And to make
the offer completely
irresistible,

DISHWASHER SAFE

you'll get this unique
spiral slicer...

down and down, around
and around,

and you'll have a
beautiful garnish for
your dinner table.

Now how much would you
pay?
You get the Ginsu Knife,

the matching carving
board, the versatile
six-in-one kitchen
tool,

a set

of six steak knives

and the spiral slicer...

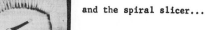

50 Year Guarantee

THE GINSU KNIFE SET IS
GUARANTEED FOR 50 YEARS
FROM DATE OF PURCHASE. IF
NOT COMPLETELY SATISFIED,
RETURN FOR REPLACEMENT
OR REFUND TO:

GINSU PRODUCTS, INC.
69 WEST SHORE ROAD
WARWICK, R.I. 02889

you get them all
guaranteed in writing
for 50 years, for only
$9.95.

It's the most
incredible knife offer
ever.
Here's how to order.

TO ORDER
1-800-228-2035
OR SEND $9.95 TO
KNIFE SET
P.O. BOX 833
RADIO CITY STATION
NEW YORK, NY 10019
MONEY BACK GUARANTEE
GINSU PRODUCTS INC.
69 W. Shore Rd, Warwick RI 02889

ANNOUNCER 2:  To order
call toll free 1-800-
228-2035...
save the COD charges,
send $9.95 to: Knife
Set, Box 833, Radio
City Station, New York,
N.Y. 10019.  You get
the Ginsu Knife, matching
carving fork, six-in-one
kitchen tool, six steak
knives and spiral slicer,
plus a 50 year guarantee.
So send $9.95 to:  Knife
Set, Box 833, Radio
City Station, New York.
Be sure to order yours
today.

TO ORDER CALL TOLL FREE
1-800-228-2035
OR SEND $9.95 TO
KNIFE SET
P.O. BOX 833
RADIO CITY STATION
NEW YORK, NY 10019
MONEY BACK GUARANTEE
GINSU PRODUCTS INC.
69 W. Shore Rd, Warwick RI 02889

TO ORDER CALL TOLL FREE
1-800-228-2035
OR SEND $9.95 TO
KNIFE SET
P.O. BOX 833
RADIO CITY STATION
NEW YORK, NY 10019
MONEY BACK GUARANTEE
GINSU PRODUCTS INC.
69 W. Shore Rd, Warwick RI 02889

**LONGSTREET PHOTO REPORTS**
TV Monitoring Service

239-08 Linden Boulevard, Elmont, New York 11003    516 / 285-9540

tailer maintains a mailing list of regular customers, direct-mail advertising can be the most effective way to reach prospects. Stores that maintain their own charge accounts have a ready-made mailing list, and the postage required to mail the customer's monthly statement can often serve to deliver an advertising message as well. Many manufacturers will supply statement stuffers without charge or at only a fraction of their actual cost.

## Advertising schedules

Unlike national advertisers, who have to choose between reach and frequency (or arrive at some compromise between the two), retailers can focus on frequency. Retailers do not schedule their ads in the context of a campaign. Flexibility is always the retailers' main consideration. They give most of their attention to deciding which seasons of the year to advertise which products and then, within the seasons, which day(s) of the week to run their advertisements. This is why newspapers are a prime medium for retailers because they permit a high level of frequency and flexibility. Retailers know from experience that Wednesdays, Thursdays, and Fridays are the best advertising days. Mondays, Tuesdays, and Saturdays are light. Of course, small retailers can purchase better positions for their ads by placing them on the light days.

Retailers must also anticipate peak seasons. Consumers start thinking about their needs days, often weeks, in advance of the actual time of purchase; this is particularly true for customers seeking high-fashion apparel. Naturally, retailers want every ad to draw customers for the advertised merchandise. At the same time, however, retailers must try to build a store image in the minds of cus-

tomers. The store must be seen by the public as a *source* for future purchases. A common fault of small retailers is their failure to build continuity, and only continuity builds an image.

## Building the schedule

A retailer's media schedule for the year ahead is usually based on the store's sales plan, that is, the sales projected by each department on a monthly basis. Each department breaks down its total allocation of advertising dollars into month-by-month appropriations, which are based on the department manager's or buyer's knowledge of consumer purchasing patterns.

Children's wear, for example, sells best in late August when parents make back-to-school purchases. There is, however, little value in promoting such merchandise in July. As a rule, retailers do not attempt to modify seasonal sales curves but are content to follow sales patterns of prior years. Even within the month and within the week there are better sale days and a retailer's ad schedule will go heavy on the better days and light on the off days.

*Big ticket items* (such as appliances and home furnishings) are usually featured on Sundays because they represent major buying decisions that require the deliberation of the entire family. Women's fashions are generally scheduled for Sundays, Mondays, or Fridays. Traffic-generating merchandise such as domestics (towels, sheets, tablecloths, etc.) and housewares are advertised on Wednesdays or Fridays. An *omnibus ad*—a storewide ad that features items from many different departments—produces traffic. A *tonnage* ad—an ad that features one item stocked in large quantities at a very special price—produces both sales volume and traffic. A store will usually develop some sched-

These ads are *image-builders* for their sponsors. Note the similarity of style among them—the generous use of white space, the minimal mention of price, the prominence given to the name of the store rather than to the merchandise itself. The objective of these ads is to remind prospective customers that each store is a *source* for selections of quality merchandise.

## LAURA ASHLEY

For cool cotton clothes in a myriad of prints and colors to match every mood. Sunsuit $32.00

714 Madison Ave., New York
85 Main St., Westport, Conn.

Boston, San Francisco, London, Paris

This is an *omnibus ad*, featuring merchandise from many different departments of one store. The ad has two objectives: to sell specific merchandise and to build store traffic. When customers visit the store to buy one of the advertised items, it is hoped that they will also be attracted to, and purchase, other merchandise.

*Wieboldt's* # buyers' sale

## SAVE $3
**men's sport and walk shorts**

regular $11    **7.99**

- polyester and cotton blends
- machine washable, too
- many solids and patterns
- perfect for summer strolls
- in waist sizes 30 to 40

WIEBOLDT'S—MEN'S SLACKS, ALL STORES

## SAVE $36
**classic vested suits for men**

regular $155    **$119**

- Wieboldt's own brand 3-piece suits, the Porcelli label
- polyester and wool blends
- choose from popular plaids, subtle stripes, classic solids

WIEBOLDT'S—MEN'S SUITS, ALL STORES EXCEPT LINCOLN VILLAGE

## SAVE 2⁴²
**durable denim jeans for men**

regular 11.99    **9.57**

- straight leg styling with tapered fit to hug body
- cotton Indigo denim fabric
- rugged and long-wearing
- buy in waist sizes 28 to 38

WIEBOLDT'S—MEN'S WORK CLOTHES, ALL STORES, BUDGET FLOOR AT STATE STREET

## 37% OFF
**light, plush fashion coats**

regular $80    **49.99**

- lightweight, yet warm
- with beautiful detailing
- choose soft grey or beige
- misses', petites', juniors' and junior petites' sizes

WIEBOLDT'S—FASHION COATS, ALL STORES

## 1/3 OFF
**brightly colored swimsuits**

examples of savings:
swimsuits, reg. $20   **12.99**
swimsuits, reg. $32   **20.99**

- variety of 1 and 2 pc. styles
- prints, florals, geometrics
- great for sunning, too
- of carefree polyester
- in misses' sizes 10 to 18

WIEBOLDT'S—SUBURBIA SHOP, ALL STORES

## 25% OFF
**men's cool and airy pajamas**

regular $12    **8.99**

- comfy polyester and cotton
- short sleeve, knee length
- full cut for total comfort
- in a choice of solids, fancies
- buy in sizes S-M-L-XL

WIEBOLDT'S—MEN'S FURNISHINGS, ALL STORES

## SAVE $5
**24-piece Set Ups glassware set**

regular $12    **6.99**

- lovely glassware is crystal clear
- perfect for casual or formal use
- 8 each: 8½ oz. Hi-ball, 9½ oz. on the rocks, 12 oz. beverage
- ideal for summer parties

WIEBOLDT'S—HOUSEWARES, ALL STORES EXCEPT LINCOLN VILLAGE

## 25% OFF
**fine imported European glass**

reg. $4 each    **2.99**

- a light blend of color and style
- with tulip bowls and taper stems
- softened by an iridescent finish
- in your choice of 5 popular sizes
- from Toscany Glass; call 263-7733

WIEBOLDT'S—CHINA AND GLASSWARE

## SAVE $1 to 1.50
**soft Dearfoam comfy slippers**

reg. $4 to 4.50    **2.99**

- terry ballerinas or rose scuffs
- wear inside or at the beach
- pamper your feet with comfort
- in blue, pink and white
- small, medium, large, x-large

WIEBOLDT'S—WOMEN'S HOSIERY, ALL STORES

## 28% to 38% OFF
**famous maker coordinates**

pants,
reg. $14 to $16    **9.99**

- comfortable, easy-fitting styles
- cool, carefree polyester
- variety of spring colors
- proportioned to fit petite or average sizes 8 to 18

**Coordinating print tops.**
S-M-L, regular $16 to $18 ... **10.99**

WIEBOLDT'S—MISSES' SPORTSWEAR, ALL STORES

# MONDAY—LAST DAY TO SAVE

uling expertise based on its own peculiar merchandise and determine a media mix that produces traffic, volume, and profits.

Finally, in addition to distributing their advertising allocation among departments and products, retailers must schedule extra advertising for special events, holidays, and seasonal promotions.

### Retail copy

Retailers know that they can catch the attention and interest of consumers more easily than national advertisers can because consumers often seek out retail advertising regularly and intentionally. These consumers may be interested in buying specific merchandise, they may be looking for a special sale, or they may merely want to keep informed on which new products are being offered. Therefore, retailers' advertising copy should stress news—new prices, new products, new assortments, new store hours.

Since selling peaks are brief, most retailers expect their ads to provoke customer response within a few days. It is not the job of retail ads to develop confidence in specific brands. National advertisers, on the other hand, must sell their brand, which, they hope, will satisfy the needs of consumers best. No other manufacturer can offer the same brand. But the retailer's assortment of goods is wider than that of most manufacturers, and many other retailers in the same area may offer consumers the same brands. This makes retail advertising copywriters' chore harder; they must generate interest not only in the products for sale but also in a particular retail store as *the* place to buy that product.

To do all this, retail-advertising copy usually promotes merchandise by stressing product fea-

tures. Good retail copy is informative and factual. Retailers must emphasize product features in order to stimulate interest in their products. And, because they do not have to strain to command attention and interest from consumers, retailers can devote more of their advertising time and space to describing a product's uses and features than national advertisers can.

Price is also a prominent feature in a retail ad. Although manufacturers avoid price comparisons, preferring to compete on the basis of product differentiation, retailers are not reluctant to emphasize price. When a number of retailers have similar merchandise assortments, locations, and services, price is the natural basis for comparison.

Most retailers cannot afford the luxury of institutional advertising. They prefer to let their regular product offerings demonstrate their values, variety, and pricing rather than devote dollars to building an image. Unlike the manufacturer, retailers do not produce merchandise; they merely sell it. There is, therefore, no reason to promote their plants, research, or industry reputation.

### The retail advertising department

A small store, as a rule, does not maintain an advertising department. Generally, small-store owners wear several hats, one of which is that of advertising manager. However, they can usually call upon local media for professional help. Radio or television stations will help prepare their commercials. Local newspapers will help retailers write, design, and produce their print ads.

Large stores, on the other hand, maintain an advertising department staffed with writers and artists and headed by an executive of the store who may also be responsible for supervising window

Many national advertisers offer retailers completely prepared advertisements for their merchandise. The ads, as you can see from this example, are ready for insertion in a local newspaper; the retailer need only add the store name and address in the space provided at the bottom of the ad. Quite often, the space charge for the ad will be paid for in part by the manufacturer as part of a *vertical cooperative advertising* effort.

and interior displays. Large stores will rarely make use of the artwork or mats supplied by manufacturers as part of cooperative programs. Nor do large stores require the assistance of media in preparing their ads.

As a general practice, retailers tend not to use advertising agencies for two reasons. First, the low retail advertising rate allowed by most media does not include a 15 percent agency commission. Any retailer using the services of an advertising agency would, therefore, be required to pay a fee over and above the space costs. The last-minute deadlines that frequently mark retail advertising are the second deterrent. When a stock of merchandise sells out, when merchandise has not arrived on time, or when a special purchase is suddenly available, a retail store's own advertising department and staff can be swiftly coordinated to take the necessary action. However, a larger retailer may employ an agency to create advertisements for media in which the store's own advertising department lacks expertise. In such circumstances, a retailer might use an agency for television or radio advertising, advertising in national magazines, or newspaper advertising of an institutional character.

## Vertical cooperative advertising

*Vertical cooperative advertising* is advertising for which the manufacturer and the retailer share the cost. The retailer places an ad in the local newspaper featuring one of the manufacturer's branded products over the signature of the store. The ad is usually prepared by the manufacturer and provided in the form of a repro proof or mat. Retailers who use these ads need only have their store logos *slugged in.* The procedure is most commonly used for ads featuring specialty goods, such as ready-to-

wear clothing, shoes, appliances, and cosmetics. It is also a common practice for advertising food products. Cooperative advertising is, on the other hand, rarely used for products that are distributed intensively through retailers of every type and size —products such as cigarettes, chewing gum, and soft drinks. *Co-op* is ideally suited for manufacturers who have given a few select retailers in each market the right to distribute their products.

There are advantages to co-op for both manufacturers and retailers. The manufacturers enjoy such benefits as:

1. Advertising that features their brands over the names of local retailers. Such advertising is a strong selling point when manufacturers want to add other retailers to their distribution networks.

2. The knowledge that retailers who take advantage of cooperative advertising programs will stock and display the merchandise that is being advertised.

3. The increased volume of advertising for a particular brand of merchandise. The very availability of cooperative dollars is a stimulus to retailers to do more advertising than they would normally do. In addition, co-op often stimulates other retailers to advertise the manufacturers' brands in order to meet competition.

4. An enhanced image for their products through association with prestigious retail stores.

5. The reduction of advertising costs, since co-op is placed at the retail advertising rate, which is not only lower than the national

# BETAMAX MAKES IT PRIME TIME ALL THE TIME.

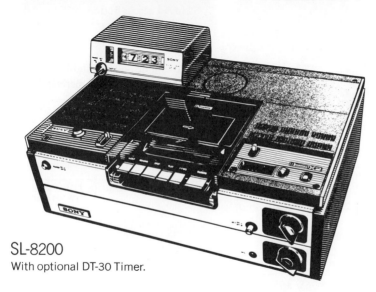

SL-8200
With optional DT-30 Timer.

The Sony Betamax lets you record your favorite TV shows, and watch them when you please. Record whatever you want—sports, specials, educational programs or news—any show up to 2 hours long. Record when you're not at home, then watch later…or record one show while you watch another. Come see Betamax now. The time is right!

## "IT'S A SONY®"

DEALER NAME

# The Washington Post

## DAILY & SUNDAY
## RETAIL DISPLAY ADVERTISING RATES

Open . . . . . . . . . Per Agate Line: Daily $2.30; Sunday $2.85

*The Following Bulk Space R.O.P. Rates*
*Apply to Yearly Contract Linage.*

Per Agate Line

| LINES | DAILY | SUNDAY | |
|---|---|---|---|
| 250 | . . . . . $2.03 | . . . . . $2.57 | |
| 500 | . . . . . 2.00 | . . . . . 2.54 | |
| 1,000 | . . . . . 1.96 | . . . . . 2.50 | |
| 5,000 | . . . . . 1.93 | . . . . . 2.47 | Required |
| 10,000 | . . . . . 1.92 | . . . . . 2.46 | Weekly |
| 30,000 | . . . . . 1.91 | . . . . . 2.45 | Column |
| 50,000 | . . . . . 1.90 | . . . . . 2.44 | Continuity (1) |
| 100,000 | . . . . . 1.88 | . . . . . 2.42 | . . . . . . . 5 |
| 250,000 | . . . . . 1.87 | . . . . . 2.41 | . . . . . . . 10 |
| 500,000 | . . . . . 1.85 | . . . . . 2.39 | . . . . . . . 18 |
| 750,000 | . . . . . 1.84 | . . . . . 2.38 | . . . . . . . 33 |
| 1,000,000 | . . . . . 1.82 | . . . . . 2.36 | . . . . . . . 48 |
| 1,500,000 | . . . . . 1.81 | . . . . . 2.35 | . . . . . . . 56 |
| 2,000,000 | . . . . . 1.79 | . . . . . 2.33 | . . . . . . . 56 |
| 2,500,000 | . . . . . 1.78 | . . . . . 2.32 | . . . . . . . 56 |
| 3,000,000 | . . . . . 1.76 | . . . . . 2.30 | . . . . . . . 56 |
| 3,500,000 | . . . . . 1.75 | . . . . . 2.29 | . . . . . . . 56 |
| 4,000,000 | . . . . . 1.73 | . . . . . 2.27 | . . . . . . . 56 |

### COMBINATION RATE DISCOUNT 40¢ PER LINE

*Discount applies to Bulk Space Rates on second insertion of an ad ordered to run Daily and Saturday, or Daily and Sunday, or Saturday and Sunday. First insertion may run on any day of the week, second insertion must repeat within 7 days with* <u>NO CHANGES</u>. *Minimum ad size 100 lines. Does not apply to amusement or entertainment advertising.*

---

ALL POSITIONS are at the publisher's option. In no event will adjustments, reinstatements or refunds be made because of the position and/or section in which an advertisement has been published. The Washington Post will seek to comply with position requests and other stipulations that appear on insertion orders, but cannot guarantee that they will be followed.

---

### (1) COLUMN CONTINUITY DISCOUNT

*A discount of four cents (4¢) per line on contracts of 100,000 lines or more may be earned by contracting for and meeting established minimum weekly space requirements as shown in the above schedule for a minimum of 44 weeks per contract year.*

---

### COLUMN REGULARITY DISCOUNT

*An additional discount of 1/10 of a cent a line will be allowed for each column up to 9 columns used 6 days a week in any calendar month.*

---

# The Washington Post

## DAILY & SUNDAY
## SPECIAL CLASSIFICATION RATES

Per Agate Line

| | DAILY | SUNDAY |
|---|---|---|
| Charity Rate . . . . . . . . . . . . . . . . . . . . | $1.74 | . . . . . . $2.28 |

(Available only to approved charities.)

| | | |
|---|---|---|
| Real Estate. . . . . . . . . . . . . . . . . . . . . . | 1.93 | . . . . . . 2.47 |

Strip Ad across bottom of financial page
9 col. by 14 lines (minimum) to
9 col. × 35 lines (maximum) only. . . . 2.13 . . . . . . 2.67

Shopping Center rate. . . . . . . . . . . . . . 1.90 . . . . . . 2.44

(Available only to established centers or organized merchant groups.)

Movie Directory . . . . . . . . . . . . . . . 1.58 . . . . . . 1.97

Box Number . . . . . . . . . . . . . . . . . . . . $9.00 Flat

Remnant Rate . . . . . . . . . . . . . . . . . . . . 1.38 . . . . . . 1.71

Remnant rate ads are inserted at the Publisher's option. Acceptable sizes are: 3 × 100, 3 × 150, 3 × 309; 6 × 150, 6 × 200, 6 × 309; 9 × 150 and 9 × 309. Information on request.

---

### CHARGES FOR PREMIUM POSITIONS
#### (When available)

Per Agate Line

| | |
|---|---|
| Pages A2 or 3 . . . . . . . . . . . . . . . . . . . . . . . . . . . . . . . . . . . . . . . | $1.75 |
| Pages A4 to 7 . . . . . . . . . . . . . . . . . . . . . . . . . . . . . . . . . . . . . . . . | 1.25 |
| Other specified pages. . . . . . . . . . . . . . . . . . . . . . . . . . . . . . . . . | 75c |
| Real Estate Section Front Page. . . . . . . . . . . . . . . . . . . . . . . . | 1.25 |
| Other specified pages in Real Estate Section. . . . . . . . . . . . . . . | 75c |
| Front Page of Sunday Food. One third page (9X100) unit, or combination thereof, at publishers option . . . . . . . . . . . . . . . . . . . | 75c |

---

### ZONE ADVERTISING

Published every Thursday in WEEKLY, a special local news section for Maryland, Virginia or the District of Columbia.

Per Agate Line

| | |
|---|---|
| Maryland Zone. . . . . . . . . . . . . . . . . . . . . . . . | 93c |
|     Montgomery County . . . . . . . . . . . | 53c |
|     Prince George's County . . . . . . . . | 48c |
| Virginia Zone . . . . . . . . . . . . . . . . . . . . . . . . . | 83c |
| District of Columbia. . . . . . . . . . . . . . . . . . . . | 60c |

Split Zone Tabloids available at Publisher's option. Information on request.

| Virginia: | North Zone . . . . . . . . . . . . . . . . . . . | 55c |
|---|---|---|
| | South Zone . . . . . . . . . . . . . . . . . . . . | 52c |

Only one zone available on any one date

Retail advertising information for the *Washington Post* is contained in a 20-page booklet, of which two pages are shown here. The rate differential between daily and Sunday is due to the difference in circulation—398,213 daily and 822,133 Sunday. Retailers are large advertisers. Notice that the paper offers contracts for linage as high as 4 million lines a year. There is a 57-cent per line drop from the $2.30 open rate to the lowest rate of $1.73. These are retail rates and apply only to retail businesses operating from a permanent store in the newspaper's trading area. The *Washington Post* also offers ROP color daily and Sunday, and on Sundays a magazine section, a television section, and a comics section.

rate but also enjoys the benefits of the retailer's volume-space contracts with local newspapers.

The retailer's benefits include:

1. A cost saving, since the manufacturer pays for a portion of the cooperative ad's space or time. The retailer is also spared the expense of copy preparation, since the manufacturer supplies top-quality advertising material.

2. An advertising link with an important nationally advertised brand that can enhance the image of a retail store.

The only drawback for retailers, and it is minor, is that manufacturers' ads tend to look *canned,* that is, they may look far too professional for small retailers in small towns.

Most cooperative dollars go into newspaper advertising, although cooperative advertising programs are also available for other media. The basis for sharing costs varies with the deal offered by the manufacturer. The manufacturer may pay from 25

to 100 percent of the costs, but the most common split is 50–50 with the manufacturer setting a limit on the total amount to be spent, based on the store's dollar volume of purchases. Thus, a manufacturer may agree to allow retailers up to 5 percent of their volume of purchases for cooperative advertising. A retailer who bought $10,000 worth of the manufacturer's goods, for example, would receive a $500 advertising allowance. The retailer would then have to spend $1,000 for advertising to be reimbursed $500 by the manufacturer. As a rule, the retailer is required to provide *tear sheets* as proof of insertion.

To facilitate the processing of tear sheets and notarized affidavits covering radio commercials, many manufacturers use the services of the Advertising Checking Bureau. As we learned in Chapter 8, the ACB, as it is designated, verifies rates, appearances, editions, and any improper use of brand names.

Whatever the arrangement, the manufacturer must be careful that there is no violation of the *Robinson-Patman Act,* which forbids discrimination among competing retailers. Any co-op advertising deal offered to one retailer must be available under the same terms to all retailers.

# Summary

Retailing describes the process of selling products or services directly to consumers, usually through a physical establishment. Although, in the case of national or regional chain organizations, a group of stores may be tied together by a common name or by common merchandise, retailing is local in nature. Retailers are major advertisers. The pages of our local newspapers are filled with advertising for department stores, home-furnishings stores, food stores, building-materials and automobile dealers, and movie theaters.

The retailer's need for marketing intelligence is similar to that of the national advertiser. As was true for the national advertiser, the retailer can draw on both secondary and primary sources for marketing data. Store records, charge-account billings, and trade publications are important sources for secondary data. Questionnaires, telephone surveys, personal interviews, and want slips can be used to gather primary data.

The retailer's methods of setting the advertising budget are also similar to those used by national advertisers. The percentage-of-sales method is perhaps the most widely used among retailers. Large retailers, however, may want to assign an advertising-to-sales ratio to each department of the store. A department that generates a high volume of store traffic but a low volume of sales can be assigned a higher advertising-to-sales ratio than a department that has a high volume of sales but draws little traffic.

Retail advertising is one segment of the advertising business in which an ad's effectiveness is often measured on the same day it is seen or heard by the public. The focus of retail advertising is on direct action, and most retailers maintain careful records of sales directly attributable to a given ad. Large retail organizations, such as department stores, discount stores, and chain stores, can afford to maintain complete advertising departments to produce all their advertising copy and artwork. Small retailers must depend on the creative abilities of the stores' owners or the advertising departments of the local media. The advertising department for a large retailer is usually part of the sales promotion division, which is also responsible for window displays and floor displays, market research, and public relations.

Vertical cooperative advertising, in which the manufacturer of a nationally advertised brand pays for a portion of the cost of the retailer's ad in a local medium, is an important component of many retail advertising programs, an arrangement advantageous to both retailer and manufacturer.

## QUESTIONS FOR DISCUSSION

1. How does retail advertising differ from national advertising?

2. What is the purpose and the nature of the advertising plan?

3. Why are newspapers the primary advertising medium for retailers?

4. What kind of market research could a retailer undertake to make its advertising more effective?

5. Find a national ad and a retail ad for the same brand. What differences do you note?

6. What are the benefits that the manufacturer derives from a vertical cooperative advertising program?

7. Explain the importance of price in retail advertising and its frequent absence from a manufacturer's national advertising.

8. Find some samples of "canned" cooperative ads in your local newspaper.

9. What differences do you see between the media scheduling of the retailer and the media scheduling of the national advertiser?

10. What are the media considerations that affect a retailer's advertising? What are the desirable characteristics of the various media from a retailer's point of view?

### Sources and suggestions for further reading

Berman, Barry, and Evans, Joel R. *Retail Management: A Strategic Approach.* New York: Macmillan, 1979.

Gentile, Richard J. *Retail Advertising.* New York: Chain Store Publishing Corp., 1976.

Haight, William. *Retail Advertising.* Morristown, N.J.: General Learning Press, 1976.

"Handling Co-op with Care." *Sales & Marketing Management* (November 1978).

Haugh, Louis G. "Retail Ads Inch Over $3 Billion." *Advertising Age* (November 13, 1978).

Littlefield, James E., and Kirkpatrick, C. A. *Advertising.* 3d ed. Boston: Houghton Mifflin, 1970.

# INDUSTRIAL AND TRADE ADVERTISING

## Industrial advertising

Classifications of industrial goods
Raw materials
Major equipment
Minor equipment
Component parts
Process materials
Operating supplies
The industrial-buying process
The importance of advertising

Setting advertising objectives
Industrial copy appeals
Schedules and campaigns

## Trade advertising

Why advertise to dealers?
Retailers buy for resale
What do retailers want to know?
Trade campaigns
One more look at co-op

## WORKING VOCABULARY

industrial advertising
trade advertising
raw materials
component parts

process materials
MRO
make or buy
new buy

short channel
cumulative recollection

# 20

## industrial and trade advertising

*Advertising is, actually, a simple phenomenon in terms of economics.* It is merely a substitute for a personal sales force—an extension, if you will, of the merchant who cries aloud his wares. It puts rapidly in print (or on radio and television) what would otherwise have to be handled by word of mouth.
It does this at lower cost.

ROSSER REEVES
*Reality in Advertising*

I N CHAPTER 9 we examined business publications as part of our general consideration of media. At that time we were concerned with the characteristics of the print media directed to men and women in business and with the decisions that face advertisers in evaluating these publications. Now, armed with far more knowledge about media, budgets, copy, art, and ad campaigns, we can take a closer look at business advertising and its place in our advertising program.

Business advertising is simply advertising that is addressed to people in their *business capacities.* Considered as a whole, a business is a consumer in

the truest sense of the word. A steel mill buys raw materials and consumes them in the production of steel. A retail store buys office supplies and packaging materials and consumes such supplies in the course of day-to-day business. And, much more importantly for national advertisers, a retail store buys manufacturers' products that it then resells to the general public. As you can see, businesses buy products and services for the purpose of doing business and rarely for the pleasure or satisfaction of an individual, and it is this distinction in purpose that differentiates business advertising from consumer advertising.

A typical ad for *raw materials.* Since there is little product differentiation among industrial goods of this type, The English Mica Company can only stress the wide variety of mica it can provide from warehouse stocks.

Our examples above of a steel mill and a retail store also illustrate the difference between the two major categories of business advertising: an advertisement aimed at selling goods or services to the steel mill to use in the production of steel would be an example of *industrial advertising;* an ad aimed at selling goods or services to retailers (or other dealers) for resale to consumers would be an example of *trade advertising.* But these two categories of business advertising are much more complex than this simple illustration suggests. Let us examine both in detail, beginning with industrial advertising.

## Industrial advertising

*Industrial advertising* is defined as the promotion of goods and services used in the manufacture and marketing of other products and services. Based on this definition, we can include farm advertising and professional advertising in this category. Farmers buy seed, fertilizer, and machinery used in the production of their goods. Doctors, lawyers, and other professionals buy equipment, services, and office supplies needed in the production of their services. Our definition would apply to both of these types of advertising.

Our purpose in this chapter, however, is to examine the advertising of machinery, chemicals, and components used by manufacturing and large service industries. It is on these products that most industrial advertising dollars are spent. There are six major categories of industrial goods: raw materials, major equipment, minor equipment, component parts, process materials, and operating supplies. Each category demands different advertising considerations.

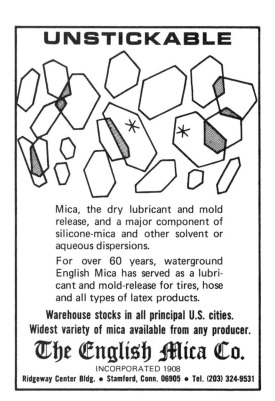

**UNSTICKABLE**

Mica, the dry lubricant and mold release, and a major component of silicone-mica and other solvent or aqueous dispersions.

For over 60 years, waterground English Mica has served as a lubricant and mold-release for tires, hose and all types of latex products.

**Warehouse stocks in all principal U.S. cities.**
**Widest variety of mica available from any producer.**

### The English Mica Co.
INCORPORATED 1908
Ridgeway Center Bldg. ● Stamford, Conn. 06905 ● Tel. (203) 324-9531

## Classifications of industrial goods

**Raw materials**   The designation *raw materials* describes basic commodities that have undergone no manufacture or only such processing as is necessary to store or transport them. Transactions for the purchase and sale of raw materials are generally conducted at high levels of company management. There is no product differentiation, most raw materials being marketed to recognized standards. The little advertising that is done for raw materials is institutional, or designed to stimulate primary demand.

**Major equipment**   Large machines that are charged to a capital account fall under the classification *major equipment.* The purchase decision is often extended over a long period of time, not because of price negotiation, but because of the many approvals needed for the expenditure of such large

# Get the efficiency of all-hydraulic for no more than you'd pay for an ordinary pneumatic drilling system.

Twice the energy efficiency and substantial increase in penetration rates. That's what you can expect with Gardner-Denver's all-hydraulic drilling package. But the real news—it costs no more than a comparable pneumatic percussion drilling system.

The system includes the Gardner-Denver HT3100 Hydra Trac™ percussion drilling unit with the HPR1 hydraulic drill and HCFM hydraulic feed, and the PHP1 Hydra Pac™ portable power unit. They're built the Gardner-Denver way—rugged—to keep downtime to an absolute minimum. Because the system is hydraulic, noise levels are way down, the entire operation is cleaner, and efficiency is high.

That translates to a better bottom line when you're working highway cuts, dam construction, quarries, general construction, or anywhere you need to drill 2½ to 3½ in. holes through medium to hard rock. Combine the efficiency and economy of all-hydraulic drilling with Gardner-Denver reliability and service, and you've got a good reason for talking with your Gardner-Denver representative. Or write Gardner-Denver Company, P.O. Box 1020, Denver, Colorado 80201.

No company decides to purchase *major equipment* of this kind without long and careful deliberation. Many of the company's executives would be involved in the purchase decision, from those responsible for the equipment's operation in the field to those responsible for making the financial arrangements. In most cases, the manufacturer's sales force cannot expect to see all the *hidden buying influences*—the executives who have a say in the purchase but do not make themselves available to the public.

GARDNER-DENVER

Since *minor equipment* is far less expensive and generally of more limited application than major equipment, its purchase requires fewer approvals or evaluations. This ad is for a table-top tester for milk products. Very often, minor equipment such as this is sold through equipment distributors.

amounts of money. The purchase decision for such equipment generally involves multiple influences, many of whom are unknown to the marketer. One of the most important objectives of industrial advertising is to reach all the decision makers who affect a major equipment transaction.

**Minor equipment** Purchases of small machines and pieces of equipment usually involve routine buying action and, therefore, require fewer approvals than do purchases of major equipment. In fact, manufacturers of minor equipment usually market their products through middlemen. Advertising plays an important communication role in the marketing of minor equipment.

**Component parts** Finished goods, usually made to custom specifications, are referred to as *component parts.* The purchaser is interested primarily in uniformity and reliability, and, for those reasons, will often use more than one source for component parts. The identity of the manufacturer of a component part may not only be visible in the finished product but may even be an important selling point for that product. Advertising can make a number of valuable contributions to the marketing of component parts. For example, component producers can advertise over the heads of the manufacturers who use their parts to emphasize their value to the ultimate user of the finished product.

**Process materials** Such materials are similar to component parts, except that such materials are purchased on standard specifications and, therefore, more emphasis is placed on price and service. Such *process materials* are not identified in the final product, so there is little value in advertising them directly to the ultimate customers.

The specification to which process materials, components, and raw materials are manufactured and sold are indicated by such abbreviations as NF, USP, ASME, and ASTM. The designations USP (United States Pharmacopeia) and NF (National Formulary), represent standards and specifications used to evaluate the quality of pharmaceutical ingredients. ASME designations, used to describe rated pressure capacities for boilers and other pressure vessels, have been set by the American Society of Mechanical Engineers. Particular specifications for construction components and materials are designated ASTM. For example, ASTM—A36 indicates structural steel with a specified yield point and tensile strength.

**Operating supplies** These goods are usually designated as *MRO,* which stands for maintenance, repair, and operating supplies. Although consumed during the manufacturing process, such supplies do not become part of the finished product. Of the six categories of industrial goods, operating supplies most closely resemble consumer goods. Companies buy MRO supplies in small quantities from middlemen and often buy several different brands of the same product.

## The industrial-buying process

Just as we have examined the purchasing behavior of the buyers of consumer goods, we must also examine the industrial-buying process; the differences are far deeper than mere terminology. In order to devise the most appropriate advertising strategy for our product, we must examine not merely the behavior of a single purchasing agent but the entire buying process within a company—which is influenced by many different people. The

Advertising for *component parts* is often similar to that for process materials. The advertiser must assure potential customers of reliable delivery of a quality product manufactured to specified standards. Unlike process materials, sources of supply for component parts may not be considered until after the product has already been designed. When this happens, the designer will have to face the possibility of increases in product assembly costs and sometimes is not able to take advantage of more modern components. In this ad, AMP suggests that by incorporating its component into the original design a company will be able to save material and labor costs.

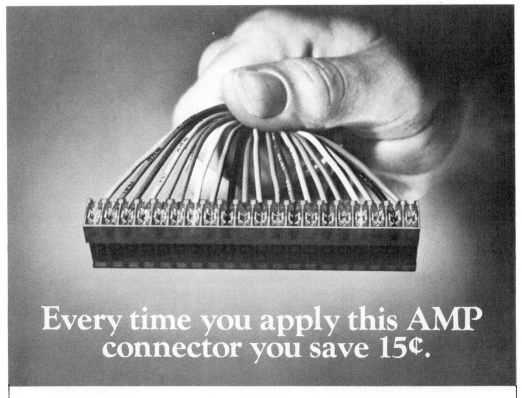

# Every time you apply this AMP connector you save 15¢.

**Many companies don't call AMP until they need electrical connectors or switches. But why wait till then? If you involve us early enough, we can help you save money. A lot of money.**

**Here's a recent example:**

Today, manufacturers are building more electronic and electrical sophistication into their products. And that makes life a lot tougher for the people who assemble them.

Each of the dozens of different wires has to be stripped and connected, one at a time, to form wiring harnesses.

Fortunately, AMP has found a better way.

We've invented a new way of connecting wire harnesses automatically. It's eight times faster than previous methods, virtually eliminates handling errors, and saves 15¢ per connector.

It's called Mass Termination Assembly System. And it's being used in stereos, washing machines, televisions and dozens of other applications requiring high technology electronics.

**Can we produce the same kind of savings for you?**

If your company manufactures electrical/electronic products, the answer is probably yes. But it's important for you to call us in early.

That's when our experience in developing connectors, switches and application equipment for hundreds of industries worldwide can help you the most.

**Early Involvement.**

At AMP, we call this approach to solving our customers' problems "Early Involvement." It's our better way. And it's what makes an AMP connector worth so much more than the 15¢ saving.

Ask for a copy of our brochure, "AMP Has A Better Way." Call (717) 564-0100, Ext. 8420.

Or write to AMP Incorporated, Harrisburg, PA 17105.

## AMP
**INCORPORATED**

**AMP has a better way.**

Barcelona • Brussels • Buenos Aires • Frankfurt • Harrisburg • Helsinki • s-Hertogenbosch • London • Luzern • Mexico City • Montreal
Paris • San Juan • Sao Paulo • Stockholm • Sydney • Turin • Toronto • Tokyo

# The preferred vulcanizing agent for chlorobutyl is in the best shape ever.

**Flakes.** Vultac® 7 offers all the benefits of Vultac 2, 3, 4 and 5. And it goes them one better.

It's convenient to use. It comes in flakes. Scoopable, weighable, easy-to-handle flakes.

Every drum is the same from top to bottom. There's no inert filler through which it can settle in storage. You get 100% active material.

Vultac 7 gives you the resistance to high-temperature aging that you need in chlorobutyl innerliners and provides improved adhesion to carcass stocks.

At normal storage temperatures (below 125°F), Vultac 7 will retain its free-flake form.

Vultac 7 can be substituted in your chlorobutyl recipe (in varying ratios) for Vultac 2, 3, 4 and 5. Find out more about these new Vultac flakes. Write Rubber Chemicals Department, Pennwalt Corporation, King of Prussia, Pa. 19406 and request Bulletin S-274.

In Europe:
Vondelingenplaat B.V., Rotterdam 3031 P.O.B. 7120—Telex 28919

## ⊳ PENNWALT
CHEMICALS ■ EQUIPMENT
HEALTH PRODUCTS

This ad for a *process material* stresses the convenient form in which the product is available, an appeal that is emphasized by the photograph of the scoop full of flakes. The details of the benefits provided by Vultac 7 are all spelled out in the copy. If this information were not available, the form of the material would be meaningless.

For a factory employing hundreds of workers, paper towels are important *operating supplies* needed for the maintenance of that factory. Purchasers of MRO supplies are concerned about two factors that household consumers usually do not consider: the number of dries per roll of towels and the frequency with which rolls must be changed.

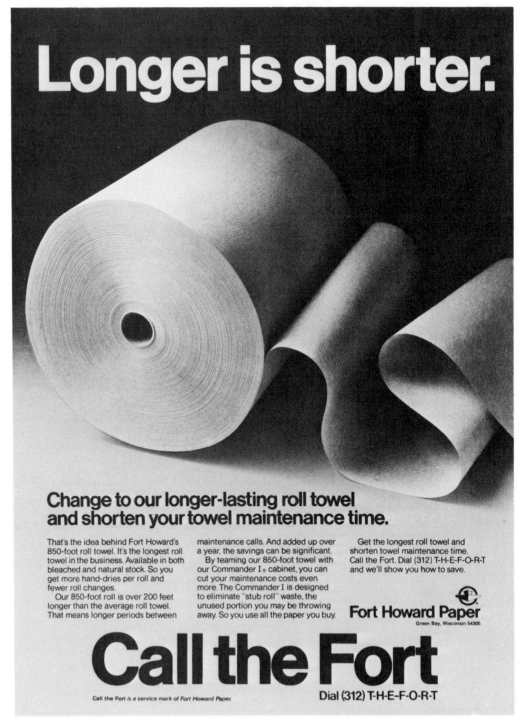

# Longer is shorter.

## Change to our longer-lasting roll towel and shorten your towel maintenance time.

That's the idea behind Fort Howard's 850-foot roll towel. It's the longest roll towel in the business. Available in both bleached and natural stock. So you get more hand-dries per roll and fewer roll changes.

Our 850-foot roll is over 200 feet longer than the average roll towel. That means longer periods between maintenance calls. And added up over a year, the savings can be significant.

By teaming our 850-foot towel with our Commander I® cabinet, you can cut your maintenance costs even more. The Commander I is designed to eliminate "stub roll" waste, the unused portion you may be throwing away. So you use all the paper you buy.

Get the longest roll towel and shorten towel maintenance time. Call the Fort. Dial (312) T-H-E-F-O-R-T and we'll show you how to save.

**Fort Howard Paper**
Green Bay, Wisconsin 54305

# Call the Fort

Call the Fort *is a service mark of Fort Howard Paper.*

Dial (312) T·H·E·F·O·R·T

buying process will vary—not only from organization to organization, but also within each organization from time to time—depending on the product and prevalent economic conditions. The following steps, however, are typical of the industrial-buying process:

1. A department discovers that it needs a product or service to overcome a problem.

2. The department head fills out a requisition form describing the specifications that the product or service should meet to solve the problem. The requisition is sent to the company's purchasing department.

3. The purchasing agent searches for qualified sources of supply.

4. The purchasing agent solicits offers from qualified suppliers. The offers are analyzed.

5. Comparisons are made between *make or buy*—that is, the company chooses whether to buy the components it needs from its suppliers or to produce them itself.

6. If the decision is made to buy, a source or sources are selected, and the order is placed.

7. After delivery and use, a follow-up is made with the department that originated the request in order to evaluate its level of satisfaction or dissatisfaction with the product or service.

Many variables will affect this process—variables that are entirely different from those that may affect a general consumer's purchasing behavior. For instance, there are considerations of make or buy for many industrial products, particularly component parts and process materials. Companies will always make the components they need if they can do so more cheaply than they can buy them from outside sources or if the component is so vital to their operations that they cannot allow another company to control production. In a *new buy*—a purchase from a supplier the company has never done business with before—the supplier's credentials may be more critical than the product or the price. Reciprocity, too, is an important variable in industrial buying. Paint company A buys fleet automobiles for its sales force from auto company B. Other things being equal, auto company B will reciprocate by ordering paint from paint company A. That's just good business.

## The importance of advertising

The place of promotion in the marketing mix of industrial products varies. Sometimes advertising serves little or no purpose, and a company may delegate all of its promotional effort to its sales force or, as is frequently the case, to agents or brokers. Our first category of industrial goods, raw materials —and other products with commoditylike characteristics—can rarely be differentiated. Their purchase is negotiated under long-term contracts by top levels of management. Obviously, if the product supplied by one company cannot be distinguished from that of any other company and if the market is limited to a relatively small number of customers, advertising can be of little use. But, for all the other industrial product categories, we set about formulating our advertising objectives and strategies in much the same manner as we do for consumer products.

Most people are familiar with the Exxon Corporation, but they may not recognize the names of some of its subsidiary companies. In this ad, Exxon seeks to build the reputations of four of these companies by pointing out that they are backed by "the resources of a large organization." The ad is given a light touch by using Exxon's well-known trade character to represent the fifth partner.

In 1977, the cost of the average industrial sales call was $96.79. This figure represents an increase of $25.52 since 1975; in the broader context of a 35-year period, the cost of a sales call rose from $9.02 in 1942 to the 1977 figure of nearly $100. Although advertising costs in industrial magazines rose steadily during the 1970s, the increase in advertising rates was far smaller than the increase in the cost of the personal sales call. Using an index of advertising costs (based on a black-and-white, twelve-time rate and CPM), the figures rose from 100 in 1967 to an index of 160 in 1977. Compare these figures with the index figures for the sales call, which rose from 100 in 1967 to 230 in 1977.[1]

The mandate for industrial advertising is very obvious:

1. Substitute advertising for as many sales calls as possible.

2. Use advertising to make the sales force's efforts more productive.

## Setting advertising objectives

If the marketers of industrial goods want to take advantage of advertising to increase their sales and profits, they must set specific objectives for their advertising programs. As we shall see, many of these objectives are similar to those of national advertisers of consumer products. Others, however, are vastly different, but are easily understandable when we reexamine the industrial-buying process. Consider these typical general objectives for the marketers of industrial goods:

[1] "The Cost of an Industrial Sales Call Climbs to $96.79," Laboratory of Advertising Performance, Bulletin no. 8013.4 (New York: McGraw-Hill, 1977).

1. Identifying the company that stands behind the product
   Once again we see the value of institutional advertising. If the reputation of a company is important in the marketing of a consumer product, it is doubly important for an industrial product. The reliability of a company is an essential consideration when an industrial buyer is looking for new sources of supply. As a matter of fact, reliability is more important than price.

2. Gaining the attention of the financial community
   This is rarely a primary objective, but it is certainly an important consideration for companies whose shares are traded on the open market.

3. Creating loyalty and demand
   Nothing new about these objectives except that, since industrial orders are large, every single customer becomes correspondingly more important. When a consumer is dissatisfied with a product and switches brands, one 59¢ brand wins a customer and a different brand loses one. But when a purchasing agent changes brands, the value of the sales lost may be many thousands of dollars.

4. Introducing a new product to buying influences
   Here's where advertising can perform a vital function. Industrial advertising may be the only way to reach busy, important executives who affect a company's buying decisions—executives our salespeople never see, can't find, or do not have the time to cover.

# You may not know our companies yet, but you know our partner.

These smiling faces hope you'll get to know their companies almost as well as you know the Tiger. They're the chief executives of four companies that are associated with Exxon Information Systems, Exxon's new business development activity in the information systems field.

Their companies have produced four of the brightest ideas we've seen in the information processing, communications, and storage fields.

Their relationship with Exxon Information Systems combines the resources of a large organization with their unique technological skills and entrepreneurial drive.

### Vydec
The Exxon Tiger and many others of the Fortune 500 already use the Vydec® Word Processing System to handle their growing paperwork needs.

Why? Vydec has a full-page 64-line visual display screen, not a "blind" magnetic card system. You proofread, rearrange and edit on the screen, then get perfectly typed copy the first time. Thus saving time, paper, money, and aggravation.

But Vydec doesn't stop

there. Recently, it introduced add-on options that let you turn Vydec-prepared text into camera-ready galleys, Telex® messages, and more. Vydec systems can even share memories with computers.

There's also a Text Reader that can bring regular typewriters up to word processing status. It scans typed text onto discs for editing and printing on the Vydec system.

The Vydec Word Processing System. It can triple office productivity, and more.

### Qyx
For individual secretaries' desks, consider Qyx®, The Intelligent Typewriter.™

Qyx has a quiet, high-speed interchangeable print wheel that floats along the carriage on a magnetic force field. It has automatic erase backspace, "white glove" changeable ribbons, and automatic recall of frequently used phrases and formats. All with far fewer moving parts than previously available.

And as office needs change, you can drop in an electronic module that gives Qyx a memory to store and edit text. Add another module, and you've got infinite storage on diskettes. Add a third, and you have a communicating typewriter.

There's even an optional mini-display for faster, error-free editing. Qyx, the typewriter that gets smarter without getting any bigger.

### Qwip
With a brilliantly simple machine called Qwip®, you can send words, pictures, and copies of just about anything on paper over your phone to another machine at any other phone in the nation. In just minutes. At surprisingly low cost.

Qwip has decisively beaten the high cost and technical bugs that plague other facsimile machines. It's so simple, you practically have to make an effort to make a mistake. But if anything should go wrong with your Qwip unit, it gets replaced immediately.

Amazingly, Qwip today rents for much less than competing machines. Which is one reason why, just four years after its introduction, Qwip is placing more facsimile machines than any other company.

### Zilog
Zilog designs and manufactures the most advanced, cost effective microcomputers available. The tiny circuits make possible the modules used, for example, in Qyx, The Intelligent Typewriter.

In 1947, the first electronic digital computer, ENIAC, was a thirty-ton monster consisting of 18,000 vacuum tubes and a spaghetti-festival of electronic wiring. Cost: $500,000. Today, a Zilog® microcomputer packs over twenty times ENIAC's computational power onto a less than quarter-inch-square silicon circuit. Cost: below $10.00 in quantities.

And Zilog doesn't just sell microcomputer components. It offers a complete line of microcomputer systems, software, hardware development systems, microcomputer board sets, and customer education, too. What's more, it's readying two more revolutionary "micros," including a state-of-the-art 16-bit processor on a chip.

By 1985 there may be upwards of 100 million microcomputers at work. With the Tiger's help, a lot of them should be from Zilog.

The Tiger would like you to know more about how his partners can help streamline information handling for your company. For a brochure that describes products and services in more detail, and information on where to contact our partners directly, call 800-223-2479 toll-free (in New York State, call 212-398-3141).

**EXXON** INFORMATION SYSTEMS

**5.** Securing sales leads

This is a new objective. Consumer advertising generally requires indirect action on the part of the target market—*visit your dealer.* Now we want our advertising to provide us with the names of potential customers so that *we* can arrange for *our* sales force to call on *them.* Remember, many industrial products are sold through a *short channel,* that is, they are sold directly by the manufacturer to the consumer.

**6.** Attracting good personnel

Many companies, particularly those in high-technology industries, must keep abreast of new developments in their fields in order to keep growing. To do this they rely on the knowledge and skills of highly trained personnel. Many companies are always wooing engineers and scientists away from competitors or from industries in other fields.

**7.** Maintaining an effective distribution network

Operating supplies, small equipment, and process materials are commonly sold through distributors. Advertising can play an important role in keeping distributors informed about, and sold on, the products and the company behind them.

These are by no means all the objectives that a company might set for its advertising effort. Every company will develop its own set of objectives based on its production capability, on the stage in its product's life cycle (yes, industrial products have a life cycle, too), and on the buying motives peculiar to that product or market. In any case, any general objective must be measurable and specifically related to the problems and opportunities of a particular product line and/or market segment. The strategy, the media mix, and the advertising appeal chosen are judgments dependent on the company's sales forecast, financial strength, and production capabilities. We have already mentioned the possibility of component manufacturers advertising over the heads of their industrial customers to reach those customers' customers. General business publications can often be used to reach both the hidden buying influences high up the corporate ladder *and* the financial community simultaneously. Direct mail can reach executives that we consider key buying influences but whom we do not know how to reach through other media.

## Industrial copy appeals

We mentioned at the beginning of this chapter that businesses buy products for the purpose of doing business. For this reason, we cannot resort to the psychic and emotional appeals that characterize some consumer advertising. The men and women in our target market are going to take a hard look at the cost and quality of our products. The future profitability of their businesses may be directly affected by their purchasing decisions. What do we tell business prospects about our product then? What do they want to know in order to reach a decision?

**1.** Will the product increase their company's production?

**2.** Will it decrease their manufacturing costs?

**3.** Will it improve the salability of their products?

# Gates abates fumes and saves $9,500 annually with a Du Pont Torvex® catalytic reactor and Harrison waste heat recuperator!

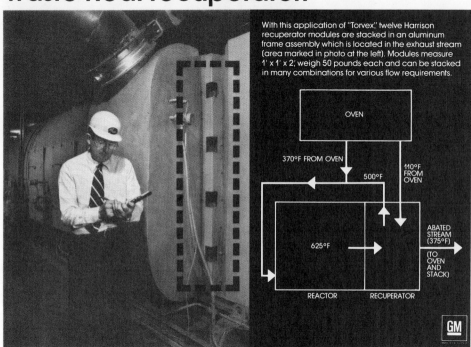

With this application of "Torvex," twelve Harrison recuperator modules are stacked in an aluminum frame assembly which is located in the exhaust stream (area marked in photo at the left). Modules measure 1' x 1' x 2', weigh 50 pounds each and can be stacked in many combinations for various flow requirements.

OVEN

370°F FROM OVEN

110°F FROM OVEN

500°F

625°F

ABATED STREAM (375°F)

(TO OVEN AND STACK)

REACTOR     RECUPERATOR

GM

This is a typical industrial ad, filled with hard facts about the benefits provided by the product. It is marked by an absence of rhetoric and the emotional words that distinguish consumer advertising. Notice the very restrained use of the GM symbol—this equipment must be sold on the results it achieves for the buyer, not the prestige of the seller.

**PROBLEM:** The challenge for Gates Rubber Company, Denver, Colorado, was to find a practical and effective method for controlling visible and odorous fumes from a cord-treating oven to meet emission standards.

**SOLUTION:** In July, 1976, Gates installed a Du Pont "Torvex" catalytic reactor. This reactor unit is equipped with a Harrison waste heat recuperator assembly to recover heat that normally would be exhausted into the atmosphere. Thus, the reactor not only abates the oven fumes, but also performs an energy-saving service!

**RESULT:** Gates is meeting emission standards and, at the same time, cutting oven gas consumption by 67%. According to Ernest Karger, Manager, Environmental Protection Engineering, shown with the unit, the oven is using only 700 cubic feet of gas an hour, as compared with 2,100 before installing the "Torvex" reactor. The saving is $9,500 a year. Gates Rubber recently started up a second "Torvex" unit and has installed a third!

## the energy savers

**HARRISON RADIATOR DIVISION**
**GENERAL MOTORS CORPORATION**
**LOCKPORT, NEW YORK 14094**

**FOR ADDITIONAL INFORMATION:** Call Harrison (716) 439-3220 today!

4. Will it help increase profits for their company?

5. Will it eliminate or minimize production bottlenecks?

6. Will it reduce downtime?

7. Will it minimize scrap or rejects?

8. Will it improve the durability of their product(s)?

9. Will it simplify maintenance and repair?

This list is far from all-inclusive, nor is it in order of importance. Of course, every industrial buyer wants to contribute to his or her company's profits; that's the role of the purchasing agent and all other personnel who influence the buying decisions. Although every one of these advertising appeals contributes to profit *indirectly*, increasing profits is listed as one appeal (no. 4) because in certain cases, the advertised product may contribute to profits *directly*.

Let us examine how the copy in some of the advertisements shown in this chapter appeals to the needs of business readers. In the first example (page 473), the copy addresses the question: Will the product decrease manufacturing costs?

> Harrison recuperators offer *to cut gas consumption by 67 percent.*

The second example (page 473) speaks directly to the business readers' desire to improve the durability of their company's products.

> Pennwalt's vulcanizing agent helps the user make a better product *with resistance to high-temperature aging.*

Our last example (page 469) promises increased production and decreased manufacturing costs.

> Gardner—Denver drilling equipment promises *twice the energy efficiency and substantial increase in penetration rates.*

To be effective, industrial copy should be as specific as possible. It should be related to the needs of the prospect, and, as far as possible, it should anticipate questions that industrial buyers will ask about the company and its product. This will make the sales force's job easier, freeing them to perform their main function—to sell the product.

## Schedules and campaigns

In the planning stage, an industrial advertising campaign is not very different from a consumer campaign. In fact, the industrial campaign is much easier to plan than a consumer campaign because our media choices are very restricted. We do not have to evaluate the effectiveness of broadcast as compared to print media. No weighting of GRPs. Comparisons are usually made between various industrial publications only, and once we have clearly stated our objectives, we can select among competing publications on the basis of CPM or whatever other media selection factors are important to us. From time to time, a business advertiser such as IBM or Xerox will place an ad in a consumer magazine or run a commercial on a television program directed to a nonbusiness audience. This advertising is almost always institutional. Many of the people watching a television program may work for companies that are considering purchasing Xerox copiers or IBM office equipment, but the main purpose of institutional advertising is to enhance the company's image, not to sell products.

Industrial advertisers do not have to make the critical media choice between reach and frequency. Frequency should be the rule. Since they do not know when a need will arise or how and when a purchasing decision will be made, they want to be certain that all the *buying influences*—all the people who can affect the decision to purchase their products—receive their messages. Months or even years of internal discussion and consideration may pass before a buying decision is finally made. A study by Cahners Publishing Co. revealed that 33.8 percent of industrial buyers see salespeople regularly, 42.8 percent see salespeople seldom, *and 23.4 percent never see salespeople at all.*[2] Obviously, two-thirds of the key decision makers in that industry (railroad equipment) rely on information sources other than salespeople. Do these decision makers read business magazines? The answer is an emphatic *yes.* To the question: "On the average, how much time do you spend weekly reading industrial and professional magazines?" the average recipient answered: "Two hours and 22 minutes a week."[3]

Seasonal influence on the sale of industrial products is moderate, not at all like the peaks and sharp dips that characterize the sales of consumer products. For this reason, much industrial advertising is spread out over the year. Unlike consumer advertising, industrial ads suffer less from wear-out. A successful, effective industrial ad can be repeated three or four times a year, or even more often, depending on the publication. Studies have been made that indicate that there is a minimum of *cumulative recollection.* When an industrial ad is repeated, it is usually seen and read by as many new readers as by readers who recall having seen it before. The McGraw-Hill Laboratory of Advertising Performance has documented a number of such cases.

Business publications, by virtue of the relatively lower cost of their ad space, also permit an aggressive advertiser to achieve a measure of dominance not possible in the consumer field. Multipage inserts are used much more frequently in business publications than in consumer publications. For example, Jones and Lamson Machine Co., a well-known machinery manufacturer, usually schedules six 12-page inserts a year in two business publications. Hilton Hotels used a forty-page insert in *Successful Meetings* magazine to tell business people about its worldwide meeting and convention facilities. The prize probably goes to Babcock & Wilcox, however, who used a seventy-five-page insert to celebrate their seventy-fifth anniversary.

## Trade advertising

To return to some of the military analogies we have used before—we are approaching the part of our campaign that deals with logistics. For the military, logistics is concerned with the problems of obtaining and transporting supplies and personnel to the front lines. In a similar fashion, advertisers are concerned with the problems of moving their products successfully through the various channels of distribution to the front line—the retail outlet. We have used media and creative strategies to guide us in

---

[2] *Cahners Advertising Research Report No. 2000.1* (Boston: Cahners Publishing Co., no date).
[3] *Cahners Advertising Research Report No. 420.1* (Boston: Cahners Publishing Co., no date).

# Introducing the IBM 8100 Information System

Today, nearly every organization has an urgent requirement to make information available to people who need it, wherever they are – plant or distribution center, headquarters or branch office.

Now IBM offers a comprehensive, cost-effective solution for your distributed processing plans: the new IBM 8100 Information System.

### Power. Choice. Versatility

The IBM 8100 is a versatile family of products. There's a choice of two processors, disk storage, multi-function display stations, a line printer, magnetic tape drive and two operating systems. And the 8100 is transaction based, which means you can keep up with things as they are happening – sales, orders, shipments – anywhere in your organization. That's because the 8100 is a distributed processing system that was designed from the start with communications in mind.

### A total systems approach

With the 8100, you build a total systems solution based on a cooperative sharing of data, resources and processing responsibilities between your central System/370 and your user locations.

You can begin your cooperative processing network at any operational level. You'll be working with a system with all the elements designed around a common communications plan, or architecture. That means you can manage, change or extend your distributed system without a major impact on your original investment.

### Match the system to your needs

The 8100 lets you gain the benefits of the two worlds of decentralized and centralized processing, while you retain control of what can be your organization's most vital asset: Information.

For example, you can have a cooperative processing network that links 8100's to your central System/370. Local offices can handle their own data processing needs and share information stored in the headquarters data base.

You can start by installing 8100's as standalone processors to satisfy local needs. Later on, you can link some or all of your 8100's to your central System/370. Or you can establish communications between your 8100's and close the link with headquarters at a later time.

IBM 8140 Processor    IBM 8101 Storage and Input/Output Unit    IBM 8809 Magnetic Tape Unit

And your basic investment gives you room for growth. You can attach a wide range of input/output and communications devices; in addition, the new system is compatible with the IBM 3790 Communications System.

### People can do what they do best

The 8100 was carefully designed to help make the best use of people's talents and training.

For example, your DP professionals at headquarters can write programs and distribute them to 8100 locations to provide greater productivity and consistency throughout your organization. Programs can also be prepared locally using high-level languages like COBOL, or with a special 8100 capability called Development Management System. This efficient approach enables users unfamiliar with programming to develop applications on the spot by simply filling in the blanks of easy-to-follow formats that appear on the terminal screen.

A big factor in the ease of operation is the new IBM 8775 Display Station. It offers such advanced functions as reverse

IBM 8775 Display Station    IBM 3289 Line Printer

video, blinking screen formats and variable screen sizes. And the screen can be divided, with data displayed for reference in one area, while the operator works in another.

On top of all this, program products available with the new system can give your headquarters DP staff a window to monitor what's happening at any 8100 location, right from the central site. They can help out if someone needs programming assistance, or if difficulties crop up. And remote program maintenance can be greatly simplified.

### Productivity...Plus

Like the System/370 and System/360, the IBM 8100 is remarkable in its own right. More than that, it can help you to capitalize on your investment in information, making it more useful to more people. Best of all, you don't have to choose between greater productivity today, or getting a head start on tomorrow's company-wide information network. With the 8100 and IBM's communications architecture, the choice isn't either-or. It's both.

Behind it all is the skilled assistance in application development, installation support, training, education and the quality service that we offer – and you've come to expect from IBM.

To learn all the details, call your local IBM Data Processing Division representative today. Or write, IBM Data Processing Division, Dept. 83-F, 1133 Westchester Avenue, White Plains, New York 10604.

Data Processing Division

**The way we put it all together is what sets us apart.**

---

our choices of a media mix and an appeal. If our powerful print ads, our dynamic, exciting television commercials, coupons, and samples have been successful, we will have brought our target market to the point of sale. Our concern now is what happens when the consumers go to buy the product at the retail outlet.

## Why advertise to dealers?

What happens if we don't reach the middlemen, the wholesalers and retailers, with our message? They stand between us and the customers we want. They are the people who can stock our product or run out of it. They are the people who can

These two ads for IBM computers are worlds apart in focus. In one ad (below), IBM is addressing top management, the ''hidden influences'' that its sales force may never get to see. In the other, IBM is addressing both top management *and* the operational executives one level below. These operational executives will be responsible for selecting the particular computer system that will meet the requirements specified by top management. One of the most important objectives of business advertising is reaching hidden buying influences.

No one can take the ultimate weight of decision-making off your shoulders. But the more you know about how things really are, the lighter the burden will be. **IBM**. Not just data, reality.

give it prominent shelf space or bury it behind other products. They are the people who can switch brands or push ours. Without the active co-operation of wholesalers and retailers, even the greatest consumer promotion can fall flat.

If the dealer doesn't have it, the consumer can't buy it. The consumer who asks for it in a store that doesn't carry it will most likely walk out with a substitute. It's a rare product that has no substitute. The trade must be told what the consumer is being told. Some advertisers believe that's what their sales force is supposed to do. And, it's true, the sales force should be able to do the best job of transmitting the product story to the trade. *If* they

Karl Malden has told us many times about the dangers of traveling without American Express Travelers Cheques. In this trade publication ad, which appeared in *Sporting Goods Dealer*, Mr. Malden tells retailers about the advantages of displaying the American Express decal in their windows. What is American Express ''selling''? They are selling an idea.

## "This sign is not just window dressing. It sells billions of dollars' worth of goods."

"People who carry travelers cheques do notice our sign. In fact, research proved that more than half of them prefer to shop where they see this sign.

"That means over 10 million shoppers looking for a place to spend billions of dollars. Displaying this decal will help keep them from taking their travelers cheques elsewhere.

"When they see the American Express decal they know their travelers cheques are welcome. In fact, some people think that stores that don't display our sign don't accept travelers cheques.

"Don't risk turning away valuable customers. Use this decal to help get a bigger share of a growing business. Order your decals now. Call us collect at 303-986-5523 or send in this coupon. And we'll put your decal in the mail right away."

### Send for the sign that sells billions

Send to: Mr. John E. Wason
Manager of Retail Relations
American Express Plaza
New York, New York 10004

Name_____
Address_____
City_____
State_____ Zip_____
How many decals do you need?_____

**American Express® Travelers Cheques. Don't do business without them.**

can get to all of the dealers in time. But no manufacturer has enough salespeople to call often enough on all the present and potential outlets.

Doesn't consumer advertising reach dealers too? Yes, it does, and very well, too. But, it reaches them as consumers, not as dealers. It reaches them when they are wearing their consumer hats, not their business hats. Consumer advertising tells them about the product while they are eating their dinners, watching a baseball game, or listening to music. Our consumer advertising wants to talk business when dealers are trying to forget business. How do we do it, then?

Trade advertising in business publications provides full coverage and frequency and does so very economically. Most successful manufacturers use business publications as their primary contact with the trade. The best part is that business readers do not find the ads an intrusion. Business magazines are their news sources. That's where they learn what's happening in their industry and about merchandising trends. The trade magazine is their marketplace.

## Retailers buy for resale

The difference between trade advertising and industrial advertising should now be patently clear. Retailers buy products for resale. Yes, we know they also buy equipment and operating supplies, and we can use the same trade media to sell them these industrial goods. But, our main goal in trade advertising is to sell dealers our product so that they will sell it to their customers.

**What do retailers want to know?**   What can we tell them in our trade advertising that will achieve our objectives and theirs?

1. Product description and consumer appeals
   In the area of product description, there is little difference between the advertisements aimed at dealers and the advertisements aimed at general consumers. Only the emphasis changes. Dealers want to know our product's major sales points, so we stress the product's uses, the colors and sizes available, the guarantee, the trade-in value, and the service.

2. The company behind the product
   If there is something about our company or the way the product is made or designed that could be vital to the sale, we have to tell our dealers about it. They would like to know about the manufacturer's design awards, research and development department, testing facilities, warehousing, and distribution systems. We cannot expect the sales force to pass on all of this information.

3. Proof of consumer acceptance
   Nothing succeeds like success. If our product is a winner, we want dealers to know that. If some dealers have had tremendous success with our product, the others will want to know how they did it. We can show them the window displays and the retail ads that our leading dealers have used. We can show them sales figures and offer them testimonials and data from market preference studies.

4. Pricing and financing
   Everyone is in this for the money, so we might as well tell retailers exactly how much they can expect to make. That's what the dealers most want to know. Markup,

# Fisher-Price Trucks are growing faster than all the rest put together.

## Can your truck department run full speed ahead without them?

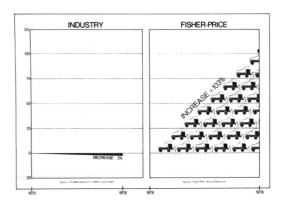

As you can see here, manufacturer shipment dollars for the entire truck category went down 2% since 1976, while Fisher-Price trucks have grown 103%. That's what we call a strong, hard-working line of trucks.

Fisher-Price Trucks have shown a surprising growth spurt since 1976. But *we're* not surprised.

*First,* because we consistently build sturdy, appealing trucks with lots of play value.

*Second,* because parents know and trust our name. They know when they buy a Fisher-Price truck it will be safe, long-lasting and fun for their children to play with.

*Third,* because more and more retailers have found it advantageous to display Fisher-Price trucks in their truck section, where parents are most likely to look for them.

In fact, there are many success stories in our files to prove that Fisher-Price products really move when displayed by category. Fisher-Price dolls have stronger sales in the doll section. So do Fisher-Price Adventure People when displayed in the action figure section. And of course, our trucks really take off in the truck section.

So it's not surprising either that we're the number one truck company in sales per SKU. We're also number one in plush. And Fisher-Price ranks in the top four for both dolls and action figures.

Which goes to show that when you put everything in its proper place, you can count on more profitable truck, doll, plush and action figure sections with Fisher-Price toys.

## Fisher-Price Toys.

© 1979 Fisher-Price Toys, East Aurora, New York 14052 Division of The Quaker Oats Company

---

This is a trade advertisement that appeared in *Toys, Hobbies & Crafts* —a publication aimed at the retailers of toys and games. The ad's objective is to convince retailers to stock their toy departments with Fisher-Price trucks. The ad points out that Fisher-Price trucks are well made and well accepted by parents who buy them. The company also mentions its doll line in the final paragraphs. Fisher-Price Toys is a division of the Quaker Oats Company.

# HARRISON KING McCANN

Harrison King McCann, who founded what was to become one of the world's largest agency networks, was born in 1880 in Westbrook, New Hampshire. He worked his way through Bowdoin College in Brunswick, Maine, as a bellboy, a hotel clerk, and a salesman for Poland Springs bottled water. After graduation he moved to New York City and joined the four-man Amsterdam Advertising Agency. There he was involved in every facet of the business from writing copy to keeping the books. He then accepted a job with the New York Telephone Company, where he spent eight years, rising to advertising manager.

In 1911, H. K. McCann was offered the position of advertising manager at the Standard Oil Company, only a few months before the famous antitrust decision forced the company to reorganize. H. K. McCann then proposed that he form an agency to handle advertising for the new Standard Oil Companies, and he incorporated the agency in the same year. In 1912, the H. K. McCann Company opened for business with a capital of slightly over $5,000. Its professional philosophy was expressed in a simple, three-word slogan: "Truth Well Told." The agency's first client (now Exxon/Esso) is still served by McCann-Erickson offices around the world.

In 1930, the H. K. McCann Company merged with the Erickson Company, a successful New York agency established by Alfred W. Erickson in 1902. The new McCann-Erickson then became the fifth largest agency in worldwide billings. In 1978, McCann-Erickson was the second-ranking U. S. agency in the world, serving such well-known clients as the American Express Company, the Coca-Cola Company, Del Monte, General Motors, Gillette, L'Oreal, and Nestle.

H. K. McCann served as president of the agency from 1930 to 1948, as chairman for the next ten years, and as honorary chairman of the board until his death in 1962. A man of great personal warmth and integrity, his success has been attributed to his foresight in business, combined with an understanding of advertising and, above all, to a particular gift for dealing with people.

In 1945, H. K. McCann, who had helped to launch the American Association of Advertising Agencies and the Audit Bureau of Circulation earlier in his career, was inducted into the Advertising Hall of Fame. He was a director of the National Outdoor Advertising Bureau and also devoted time and effort to many civic causes.

A trade paper ad for a pharmaceutical manufacturer that appeared just before the beginning of the hay fever season. Notice that the ad mentions that the manufacturer will run "the most advertising EVER for any allergy product." Often, trade paper ads of this kind will provide details on the consumer advertising for the product—the number of magazine insertions, the number of commercials scheduled—to convince retailers that consumers will soon be crowding their stores to buy the product.

# IN THE SPRING A.R.M.® RETAIL SALES DOUBLE!*

## Don't get caught short on the shelf!

Starting March 15 . . .
The most advertising
**EVER** for any allergy product!

Buy now . . .
The best A.R.M. Deal **EVER!**

Menley & James Laboratories, Philadelphia, Pa. 19101
a SmithKline company

*A.C. Nielsen

CASE HISTORY

**REACHING
HIDDEN
BUYING-
INFLUENCES
FOR
INDUSTRIAL
PACKAGING**

Early in this book, we noted that it is not enough for a company to make a good product; it must also be able to identify its product's prospective customers and to communicate knowledge of the product to these prospects. Identifying the market for an industrial product may be no more difficult than identifying the market for a consumer product, but it may be harder for industrial advertisers to reach all the hidden buying influences in their markets. This was the problem that faced Tri-Wall Containers, a small company that manufactures a triple-wall corrugated fiberboard. Under the name *Tri-Wall Pak*, the company's product was used in packaging metal fabrications such as automotive parts and in shipping dry chemicals such as powders and granules. For these industrial users, Tri-Wall packaging was an operating supply item, and its cost was a minor MRO expense compared with the value of the products it was used to protect.

When Tri-Wall Containers decided to launch its first advertising campaign, its principal objective was to obtain qualified leads for its sales force. The company was well-established in its field, and its salespeople may have called on prospects in the same sales territory for a number of years without being able to see all the important decision makers who influenced operating-supply purchasing decisions. It was hoped that advertising would be able to reach these buying influences with Tri-Wall's message: that its product would make an excellent substitute for other packaging material such as wooden crates.

To create the campaign, Tri-Wall retained the services of DDB Group Two, a division of the well-known advertising agency, Doyle Dane Bernbach. Using Standard Industrial Classification data and Tri-Wall's own sales records, DDB Group Two analyzed the market potential for the company's product and made a media recommendation. The proposed media schedule included the use of a horizontal industrial magazine, *Industry Week*, and also called for the insertion of ads in a group of vertical industrial publications that reach business people concerned with industrial packaging and material handling. This group of publications included *Distribution Worldwide, Handling & Shipping, Iron Age*, and *Packaging Digest*.

To maintain consistency among the various advertisements in the campaign, DDB Group Two used a series of ads that featured application case histories. These case histories told readers how Tri-Wall Pak had been used to solve special packaging problems and contained testimonials from satisfied users. To increase public awareness of the company behind the product, the agency also created a two-color graphic system and logotype for use on everything from the company's promotional material to its stationery and trucks.

What have been the results of this campaign? Since advertising is only one of the many factors that influence an industrial buying decision, sales increases will not furnish

continued

Tri-Wall continued

an accurate measurement of the campaign's success. One way of measuring the campaign's effect would be to determine whether or not awareness of company's name and product among its prospective customers had increased. But an immediate result can be seen in the attitudes of the company's own sales force. "We get good feedback from our sales force," Tri-Wall's marketing research manager reports.

Source: "Case Histories Used to Tell Tri-Wall Story," *Advertising Age*, June 25, 1979, p. S–20.

price maintenance, delivery, and inventory are all important considerations when the dealers come to the bottom line.

**5.** Consumer advertising strategies
Are we backing up the dealer with a well-planned campaign aimed at the consumer? Our consumer advertising, regional and national, literally pulls the product through the dealer. It can increase the amount of traffic in the dealer's store, too. We will want to tell our dealers as much as we can about our consumer advertising program: what the strategy behind it is and when and in what media the ads will run. We can show them how to tie in with the national campaign through our co-op program; we can mention all the advertising materials we supply, such as mats, logos, canned commercials, and radio scripts.

**6.** Point-of-purchase materials and sales aids
A good product demands good point-of-purchase displays and other sales-promotion materials. Good promotion materials boost sales, and if we want our dealers to promote our products, we have to *promote our promotional materials* to them. We should tell them about our training films,

contests, statement stuffers, display units, point-of-purchase merchandisers, give-aways, and premiums.

## Trade campaigns

There are trade magazines that reach every trade worth reaching. Most are national; a few are regional; all are highly selective with a minimum of waste. Schedules in trade publications usually run in advance of consumer advertising programs. This permits retailers to order and shelve the merchandise and to prepare their own tie-in advertising. Some trade advertising precedes consumer advertising by as much as six months. As for seasonal influences, trade advertising more closely resembles consumer advertising, with which it is closely tied. There are peaks and valleys representing the high seasons and the slack periods. Unlike industrial ads, trade ads are not often repeated. Trade advertising is generally news advertising. We cannot repeat the ad we used two months ago. By then the deal will have expired; the season may be finished.

## One more look at co-op

The dollars spent for cooperative advertising must be included in the manufacturer's advertising budget. As far as the media are concerned, the retailer is the advertiser. It is the retailer's contract with the newspaper that establishes the rate. The retailer bills the manufacturer according to the terms of the co-op contract. Co-op advertising may be an important consideration for many retailers. Our trade advertising should, therefore, point out to retailers the extent of our co-op effort.

This is intended as a reminder that we must budget co-op advertising because it is part of our total advertising appropriation. To establish some idea of costs, the manufacturer prepares a contract for co-op advertising. Some manufacturers offer a fixed allowance, a predetermined dollar amount to be used for a grand opening or for a designated seasonal promotion such as Mother's Day or Easter. Or, the allowance may be an open one, in which case the manufacturer will pay for half the cost of any and all advertising that the retailer employs as long as it is for the manufacturer's product. Some allowances are based on earnings accumulated by the dealer. The amount is proportional to the volume of business the retailer places with the manufacturer. The allowance will be a percentage of dollar purchases—5 percent is the most common figure. The percentage may be raised for brief periods to allow retailers to punch up their advertising to coincide with peak seasonal demand and with the manufacturer's own national advertising program. Under such terms, a retailer's $1,000 order generates a credit of $50 in a co-op account. The manufacturer then pays out this money to the retailer when the retailer advertises the manufacturer's product. Sometimes the credit is applied as a fixed amount per unit, such as 50¢ a carton or $50 a car, as is common in the automotive field.

## Summary

Business advertising is the promotion of products and services bought by business organizations for the purpose of doing business. In general, advertising appeals aimed at business people are rational, not emotional, and are related to saving or making money for their companies.

Advertising plays a very important role in industrial marketing; it can make the efforts of the manufacturer's sales force more productive. As the cost of an industrial sales call has risen, industrial advertising has become more valuable in stimulating sales leads, building brand loyalty, and developing a company image. The industrial buying process differs sharply from consumer buying behavior. A more careful search, more evaluation, and the required approval of more people distinguish industrial buying from consumer buying. The need to reach and convince more people, particularly hidden buying influences, becomes apparent as the price of the "buy" goes up. In industrial markets the loss of a customer can have grave financial repercussions.

Retailers and wholesalers are also business buyers, but unlike the industrial buyer they buy for resale. The manufacturer's consumer advertising campaign can be rendered ineffective without the active support of the dealers and distributors through whom the product is sold. Trade advertising is used to carry the message. Every trade has one or more magazines that reach dealers in that business with a minimum of cost and waste. Advertising to the trade keeps retailers informed about the manufacturer's product and sales policies, provides information on future consumer campaigns, and elicits the support and cooperation of dealers in co-op advertising, in the use of point-of-purchase displays, and in the assignment of shelf space. A trade advertising program is a vital component of the national advertiser's campaign to build profits through sales.

## QUESTIONS FOR DISCUSSION

1. What are some of the appeals the industrial advertiser might use?
2. What makes industrial advertising more difficult to prepare than consumer advertising?
3. How can industrial advertising substitute for a salesman?
4. How does advertising for major machinery differ from advertising for operating supplies?
5. Why would an industrial advertiser advertise in a consumer publication?
6. How does industrial buying behavior differ from the consumer's buying behavior?
7. What are some objectives we could set for our industrial advertising?
8. How does trade advertising differ from industrial advertising?
9. Name some appeals we could use in trade-paper advertising.
10. Why is trade advertising important?

## Sources and suggestions for further reading

Arthur D. Little, Inc. "An Evaluation of 1100 Research Studies on the Effectiveness of Industrial Advertising." New York: American Business Press, May 1971.

Haas, Robert W. *Industrial Marketing Management.* New York: Petrocelli/Charter, 1976.

"Industrial Advertising Effectively Reaches Buying Influences at Low Cost." Report by U.S. Steel. New York: American Business Press, 1969.

Littlefield, James E., and Kirkpatrick, C. A. *Advertising.* 3d ed. Boston: Houghton Mifflin, 1970.

Messner, Frederick R. *Industrial Advertising.* New York: McGraw-Hill, 1963.

"The Cost of an Industrial Sales Call Climbs to $96.79." Laboratory of Advertising Performance, Bulletin no. 8013.4. New York: McGraw-Hill, 1977.

*The Range and Depth of Buying Influences in a Typical Plant.* New York: American Business Press, 1975.

## ADVERTISING AND SOCIETY

**Criticisms of advertising**

Advertising adds to the cost of
   goods
    Economies of scale
    Advertising keeps the price
     of media low
    Advertising fosters diversity
Advertising makes people buy
   things they don't need
Advertising reduces competition
    Giants and giant killers
    Advertising inhibits price competition

Advertising is information
    Information encourages innovation
    Information satisfies wants
    Advertising is ideas

**Policing advertising**

The government regulates
   advertising
    The FTC
    Other regulatory agencies
Advertising polices itself
Policing by the media

## WORKING VOCABULARY

Federal Trade Commission
   (FTC)
Wheeler-Lea Act
cease-and-desist order

puffery
tombstone ad
bait-and-switch ad
corrective advertising

National Advertising Review
   Board (NARB)

# 21

# advertising and society

*The statement that "without advertising the U. S. economy would be better off" is widely rejected. Most people seem to feel that advertising is good for the economy.*

RENA BARTOS and THEODORE F. DUNN
*Advertising and Consumers New Perspectives*

As we learned in Chapter 1, throughout recorded history sellers have found it advantageous to send messages to prospective buyers and to send these messages in the most economical manner possible. History also shows that consumers search for information that can be acquired at the lowest possible cost to themselves. Supplying information to prospective buyers by means of mass media would appear to satisfy both buyers and sellers.

## Criticisms of advertising

Nevertheless, much criticism has been directed at the advertising business. Critics claim that advertising:

1. adds to the cost of products

2. causes people to buy products they do not need

3. reduces competition and thereby fosters monopolies

The purpose of this chapter is to examine these criticisms—social and economic—to see if they are valid.

### Advertising adds to the cost of goods

If advertising did add to the cost of the goods and services consumers buy, it would have no economic justification. From the standpoint of the manufacturer, advertising is used because it is considered to be the most *cost-effective* marketing technique. If manufacturers knew of a marketing tool that offered them lower costs or greater returns than advertising, it would be foolish for them to continue to invest heavily in advertising. In fact, manufacturers in many industries invest most of their promotional effort in their sales forces and do very little, if any, consumer or business advertising.

For the manufacturers of most mass-marketed goods, however, advertising is really only a substitute for salespeople who call in person on individual prospects. Advertising cannot completely replace a sales force; while an advertisement must be designed to communicate with large numbers of prospective customers, each member of a sales force can tailor his or her message to reach each prospect individually. Salespeople also receive instant feedback from the customers they call on—another advantage over advertising. Advertising, on the other hand, can greatly reduce the size (and cost) of the sales force required to promote a product by performing many tasks that would otherwise have to be performed by salespeople. Could a chewing gum company, for example, afford to employ salespeople to sell its product door to door the way the Fuller Brush Company does? Of course not; the gum company relies on advertising to perform this selling function, and advertising does so at a much lower cost. As we learned in Chapter 20, the average cost of a single sales call is $96.79, while the cost per thousand for an ad in *TV Guide* is only $1.19, or 0.119 cents per reader.

**Economies of scale**    Like everything that goes into the production, distribution, and sale of a product or service, advertising is a cost. There is no question that the consumer ultimately pays for it. But the reason for advertising's existence, as we have shown, is that it performs its essential selling function more efficiently and at a lower cost than any other method. If all manufacturers had to rely on salespeople to promote their products, the cost of retaining a large sales force would be passed on to consumers too. And these costs would be substantially higher than those of mass-media advertising. If manufacturers were not allowed to do any advertising at all (nor allowed to substitute another form of promotion for advertising), the cost of their goods might be reduced by a fraction of a cent, perhaps by even more for certain types of products. But the reduced number of sales brought about by this ban on advertising would force manufacturers to cut back on the amount of goods they produce. And the limited scale of production would, in turn, cause the price of these products to rise.

You can get some idea of the increased costs that would result from this turn of events if you compare the price of a custom-tailored garment with that of any nationally advertised brand. Can you believe that the national advertiser, buying thousands of yards of fabric, and employing high-speed cutting and sewing machines, cannot offer consumers lower prices than the custom tailor who buys fabric three yards at a time and cuts each piece by hand? And, in addition to lower prices, the national advertiser can offer consumers a much wider range of styles and colors than can the custom tailor.

In its role as a substitute for, and an aid to, a manufacturer's sales force, then, advertising helps develop the volume of sales that the manufacturer needs in order to take advantage of the economies of mass production. Thus, advertising helps make more goods and services available to more people.

# The Atomic Bond.

During these inflationary years when the price of everything seems to be going up, telephone service is a bargain. The Bell System has managed not only to hold down prices, but to offer more service for the money. We can dial directly to all parts of the United States and Canada, as well as to areas in Europe and Asia. In some areas of the country, a call from a phone booth is still only 10¢. How do they do it? In this ad, Western Electric, the manufacturing arm of the Bell System, tells us how.

Using tiny explosive charges, Western Electric engineers are bonding metals with the elemental "glue" of the Universe.

Here's how it works. The atoms of all metals have a natural attraction for one another. If it weren't for the ever-present film of impurities coating the surface—the oxides, nitrides, and absorbed gasses—all metal atoms would bond to each other when brought together.

### Exploding Things Together.

But the force of a high-intensity explosion on two adjacent metals will clean away the film of impurities. The explosion literally "blows" the impurities off the surfaces. So the atoms of the different metals can bond together.

The bond that results is stronger than both of the metals themselves.

As an industrial technique, explosive bonding has proved valuable in the manufacture of such heavyweight products as bi-metallic gun barrels.

### Pinpoint Explosions.

But how would explosives work in the delicate, intricate world of telephone circuitry?

Scientists at Western Electric's Engineering Research Center solved the problem by developing ways to miniaturize and control explosive bonding. Soon, they could splice the ends of two thin communications wires inside a miniature explosive-coated sleeve.

And they could repair tiny defective contacts on delicate circuit boards. These gold contacts (membrane-thin "fingers" 1/10 by 3/4 of an inch) are reclad by thin sheets of gold foil (.0005 inches thick), coated with explosives. The repairs are literally "blown" onto the contacts, without disturbing the delicate circuitry less than 1/10 of an inch away.

Miniaturized explosive bonding is only one way we're helping your Bell Telephone Company hold down the cost of your telephone service today. For the future, it promises the benefits of bonding widely disparate metals and all sorts of other materials.

### You Can Take It For Granted.

Most important, explosive bonds are contributing to the clarity of communications, the reliability of switching, the taken-for-granted assurance you have when you reach for your telephone.

The atomic bond—it's another innovation from Western Electric. *Keeping your communications system the best in the world.*

## Western Electric

Instead of raising the cost, advertising keeps it lower. Advertising raises our standard of living by keeping the wheels of industry turning.

**Advertising keeps the price of media low**    While on the subject of cost, critics of advertising might want to consider the fact that it is the advertising in our newspapers and magazines that makes it possible for readers to buy them at a price that is less than their cost of production. The entertainment enjoyed by millions of people on radio and television is delivered to them every day without charge. This is only possible because advertising revenues pay for the cost of producing and broadcasting television and radio programs. Even the programs on commercial-free public television are paid for in large part by grants from national advertisers. The most common reply made by critics of advertising to this point is a criticism of television. Terrible programs, they say; too much violence; too many commercials. However, advertisers are not ultimately responsible for deciding which types of programs will be broadcast and which will not. Advertisers (as sponsors of programs), networks (as producers of programs), and individual stations (as purveyors of programs) are extremely responsive to consumer tastes and desires. When consumers decide they do not like a program, that program goes off the air —and quickly. A program that is viewed by millions of households must be providing them with entertainment they enjoy. And it provides that entertainment for free. If millions of people want to watch situation comedies, advertisers will spend their money to sponsor comedy programs. If millions of people want to watch westerns, advertisers will sponsor westerns. If grand opera and Shakespearean plays were demanded by millions of viewers, advertisers would sponsor these programs.

**Advertising fosters diversity**    The argument that advertisers only sponsor programs demanded by millions of viewers is based on the assumption that the advertisers' only objective is to reach millions of people with their messages. As we have learned, however, advertisers would much rather have their commercials reach a small audience that contained a large number of prospective purchasers of their products than have them reach a large audience that contained relatively few prospects. For this reason, advertisers do indeed sponsor many programs that would not be seen on television if the size of the audience they attract were the sole criterion for media selection. Documentaries, travel narratives, special-events news programs, and new or classic films, plays, and operas are continually being sponsored by advertisers who are interested in reaching the specialized audiences that these programs attract. This is a trend that will become more and more important in the future as advertisers segment their target markets with greater precision. The broadcast media will take on more of the attributes of the print media, with programming that, like the wide array of consumer magazines, offers something for everyone.

## Advertising makes people buy things they don't need

The "things" that advertising is usually accused of "forcing" people to buy are either inferior products or products that people do not require or cannot afford. To the first part of this second charge, advertisers can reply that the ultimate test of the quality of any product takes place in the marketplace. While advertising may stimulate consumers to try a new product or a new brand, it cannot hypnotize them into continuing to buy a product that does

# COME AND SEE THE BURIED TREASURE.

An excellent example of a public service ad for a cultural exhibition. Note the manner in which the XEROX name has been placed at the bottom of this noncommercial message. The XEROX Corporation hopes that advertising of this kind, restrained and in good taste, will create a favorable image for the company and its products.

Nearly 2000 years ago, a prosperous, sophisticated city was buried under 12 feet of volcanic ash.

In less than two days, the homes and temples of 20,000 people literally disappeared. A civilization was frozen in time.

Now the glory that was Pompeii has come to New York. The stunning paintings, the gold and silver jewelry, the marble and bronze sculptures are alive again.

You can walk through an elegantly frescoed room, pause under a garden portico as if 20 centuries ago were yesterday.

Vesuvius destroyed Pompeii. And saved it at the same time.

For information, call (212) 999-7777. This exhibition is made possible by grants from the National Endowment for the Humanities and Xerox Corporation.

## POMPEII AD 79
American Museum of Natural History
April 22 through July 31

## XEROX

not satisfy. This is merely common sense: you would not continue to buy a soft drink that had an unpleasant metallic aftertaste, or a light bulb that burned out in a month, or a detergent that never seemed to get your clothes clean. And advertising is not only incapable of selling a poor product; it often cannot sell a good product that the public does not want. The marketing graveyard is filled with products no one bought despite the blandishments of powerful advertising. The Edsel and Corfam, a synthetic leather, spring to mind at once in this regard. Ford Motor Company and Du Pont, respectively, spent millions of dollars advertising these products, and yet they were failures in the marketplace.

To the second part of the above charge—that advertising makes people buy things that they don't really need or cannot afford—advertisers must again point out that advertising cannot hypnotize people into acting against their own best interests. The question of whether or not a consumer can afford to buy certain products is one that must be decided by each consumer individually. This is not to deny that advertising is a persuasive form of communication that may create wants, but wants are also created by people themselves, their aspirations, their friends, their families, and their educational and vocational backgrounds. As the economists have always told us, human wants are insatiable.

In general, when critics accuse advertisers of making people buy things that they don't need, much depends on how the word *need* is defined. All that people really require is enough to eat and drink, plain, serviceable clothing, and a place to sleep at the end of the day. They don't really *need* stereo components, washing machines, rock albums, paperback novels, motion pictures, toothpaste, deodorant, perfume, ballpoint pens, or jewelry. But all of these things make our lives easier or more pleasant to live.

## Advertising reduces competition

**Giants and giant killers**   Some critics of advertising contend that advertising fosters monopoly. In support of this claim they point to the rising costs of launching a national advertising campaign—costs that the critics claim are prohibitive to all but the established giants of each industry. In certain industries, such as soap, automobile, and cigarette manufacturing, it does indeed seem that advertising costs would tend to restrict the entry of new firms into these fields. In fact, however, the inroads made by foreign companies into several of these markets (most notably that for automobiles) speak well for the opportunities open to competing firms to wrest a market share from the well-entrenched giants. Similar opportunities exist for small domestic companies that can exploit a regional market and build a market share for themselves, even in the face of competition from larger, more established corporations. This has happened recently in the market for breakfast cereals, where manufacturers of "natural" whole-grain cereals have managed to achieve respectable market shares, and in the market for tea, where the manufacturers of herbal teas have managed to obtain market shares in spite of competition from such giants as Lipton. Such successes can be attributed in large part to the power of advertising.

In general, we can return to the point we made earlier: if manufacturers did not use advertising to promote their goods, they would have to depend on other, more expensive, methods of promotion. They would have to hire hundreds of additional salespeople to do the selling jobs now done by advertising. The cost of launching a nationwide advertising campaign may be formidable, but the cost of supporting larger, nationwide sales forces for mass-marketed goods would be greater still.

**Advertising inhibits price competition** Critics who claim that advertising fosters monopolistic practices also point to the tendency of advertisers in certain industries to promote their products on the basis of such attributes as package or brand name, rather than on the basis of price. This, they claim, enables these advertisers to keep their prices high while focusing consumer attention on trivial differences among the various brands. A number of studies have found, however, that although the manufacturers of certain brands choose not to compete on the basis of price, there is a considerable amount of price competition in the marketing of these products on the retail level. Discount drugstores, mass merchandisers, and chain supermarkets consistently offer consumers nationally advertised brands at prices lower than those maintained by traditional drugstores, grocery stores, and department stores. One reason for the rapid growth of these new discount retail outlets is the fact that, today, consumers are often equipped with extensive knowledge of product types and brand differences. Consumers have gained this knowledge from reading, watching, and listening to the advertising for these products. This, in turn, has made it possible for mass merchandisers to employ fewer salespeople to aid consumers in making purchase decisions. And this savings in labor costs is passed on to the consumer in the form of lower prices.

But, if manufacturers keep their prices high enough, won't consumers still be paying more than they ought to, even if they make their purchases at discount stores? No, not if the mass merchandisers offer a wide range of private brands to choose from. If the manufacturers of nationally advertised brands keep their prices too high, the makers of private-label goods will be able to make substantial profits even though they sell their products at greatly reduced prices.

If advertising does not do all the bad things its critics say it does, what *does* it do?

## Advertising is information

It has often been said that building a better mousetrap is not enough. We have to tell many people why it is better. Advertising teaches people about new products and, in doing so, hastens their adoption. Also, by describing new and different products, advertising broadens the range of choices available to the consumer. Advertisers who are interested in serving human wants, then, must have the opportunity to tell prospective customers news about what they are offering. Whether it is the choice of a tube of toothpaste or the choice of a president of the United States, the principle is the same. The freedom to choose depends on the freedom to provide information.

**Information encourages innovation** The competitive pressure of advertising has led to increasingly higher standards of quality that new products have had to meet in order to gain a share of the market.

The television set, now in over 94 percent of American homes, is an excellent example of the way technology combined with advertising has given the public more for its money. The original television sets, black and white only, featured a seven-inch or ten-inch screen that looks like a toy today. A giant color set today costs very little more than that black and white set did thirty years ago. Furthermore, in addition to receiving color transmission from more channels, we receive broadcasts from overseas via satellite, or we can connect to cable and receive first-run movies, major sporting events, and important documentary films. Many more programs are now available—in many cases, twenty-four hours a day.

By sustaining this pressure for better products and lower prices, advertising contributes directly to better values for the consuming public. When a company is confident of its ability to bring its product improvements quickly to the attention of the public, it is more willing to invest dollars in the research needed to bring that improvement from the laboratory to the marketplace.

## ADRIENNE HALL

Adrienne Hall is executive vice-president of Hall & Levine Advertising, Inc., an advertising agency that she founded with Joan Levine over seventeen years ago. Hall & Levine is headquartered in Los Angeles, and its client roster ranges from airline to automobile, fashion to packaged goods, cosmetics to travel industry accounts. Among this agency's well-known national accounts are nineteen divisions of Catalina, Inc., a manufacturer of men's and women's sportswear and swimwear; Neutrogena soap and skin-care products; and Redken Laboratories, a manufacturer of men's and women's hair and cosmetic products. The agency also creates advertising for the Singapore Tourist Board, the New Caledonia Tourist Board, and the Tahiti Tourist Board. Regional clients include Payless Drug Stores, Oakland, and Subaru of Southern California.

In the competitive, demanding business of advertising, Adrienne Hall has achieved many "firsts" in her career. She is the first member of the industry to head the three major advertising organizations in the western United States. She has been president of the Western States Advertising Agencies Association; president of the Los Angeles Advertising Club; and she is chairperson of the Board of Governors of the American Association of Advertising Agencies (AAAA), Southern California. She is also the only woman governor of the AAAA in the United States.

In 1976, Adrienne Hall was honored with the Leadership Award of the Year by the Western States Advertising Agencies Association, which chose her for her contributions to the industry and the community. In 1973, she was the American Advertising Federation's Woman of the Year, and in 1978, she received the Medal of Distinction from that organization.

**Information satisfies wants** Some critics say that advertising is not interested in providing information as much as in persuading customers to buy something. It is true that advertising is the art of *persuasive* communication; it is a business technique that has to pay its way. But note that we said it is communication—that is, an exchange of information. Manufacturers make products that people want. No manufacturer today can afford to make the product first and then hope that advertising will induce people to buy it. It simply does not work that way. Manufacturers cannot succeed with advertising unless they listen to consumers, understand their wants, and then attempt to satisfy them. If advertisers do not do this, consumers will not pay attention to the manufacturers' advertising or buy their products.

Once manufacturers have done everything they can, through market testing and research, to make their product a good one, then, as we learned in Chapter 14, one of the best ways to persuade consumers to try it is to describe what the product is and what it does. Print advertising is particularly suited to the dissemination of product information. A quick glance at any consumer magazine will reveal a number of ads that consist almost entirely of copy that describes the product—its uses and benefits—in detail.

A purist may claim that only price and ingredients should be classified as information. Consumers do not, of course, base their buying decisions, as industrial buyers do, on purely functional choice. There are psychic values in a product that provide satisfaction for the purchaser. Consumers want more than transportation in an automobile: they want style and status and pizzazz. Such psychic value carries no visible price tag. To separate the informational portion of advertising from the psychic portion is impossible because they are so much a part of each other.

**Advertising is ideas** Advertising also provides information in the world of ideas. Industry, consumer groups, and political parties advertise to encourage interest in current issues. Advertising is used to help build understanding among the various constituencies and ethnic groups around the country. Advertising is also a strong force for assimilation and democratization. It encourages freedom of choice. The Advertising Council, founded in 1942 to help support our war effort, places millions of dollars' worth of advertising every year to encourage charitable contributions, to promote traffic safety, to help stop forest fires, to find jobs for the unemployed, to win understanding for the handicapped, and to sell government bonds.

## Policing advertising

The efforts by the federal government to regulate advertising go back a hundred years to the passage of laws to combat postal fraud. Early demands for reform were stimulated by the blatant fakers who thrived in the patent medicine field in the late nineteenth century. Congress passed the first major federal law for the protection of consumers—the Pure Food and Drug Act—in 1906, and, at the same time, newspapers and magazines began to establish standards for the advertisements that they would accept. In 1910, the Curtis Publishing Company, which published the *Saturday Evening Post*, issued the Curtis Advertising Code in order to "protect both our advertisers and our readers from all copy that is fraudulent and deceptive." In 1911, the advertising industry itself was providing support for the adoption of state laws against deceptive advertising. Advertisers urged passage of a model statute, drawn up by the advertising magazine *Printer's Ink*, which made deceptive or misleading advertising a misdemeanor. In revised form, the model statute has been adopted by thirty-seven states. Thus, historically, policies governing the regulation of advertising have proceeded from three sources: the government, the media, and the advertising industry itself.

## The government regulates advertising

**The FTC**  The *Federal Trade Commission Act* of 1914 represented an entirely new approach to the government's regulation of business. The federal responsibility to guard against monopolistic practices was being extended (the Clayton Antitrust Act was passed in 1914, too) by making "unfair methods of competition" unlawful. It was hoped that the FTC would indentify unfair business practices and that the business community would avoid them. The FTC's authority over advertising was eventually derived from Section 5 of the original act which stated:

> The Commission is hereby empowered and directed to prevent persons, partnerships, or corporations, except banks and common carriers subject to the Acts to regulate commerce, from using unfair methods of competition in commerce.

In 1938, the Federal Trade Commission Act was amended by the *Wheeler-Lea Act*, which expanded the responsibility of the FTC to cover "unfair and deceptive acts in commerce." Under this provision, the FTC was given authority to act against a firm guilty of deceptive practices that might harm consumers, even though those practices might not have an effect on competition. Section 12 of the Wheeler-Lea Act then declared that "the dissemination or the causing to be disseminated of any false advertisement . . . shall be an unfair or deceptive act or practice in commerce with the meaning of Section 5." In addition, the FTC was given power to monitor deceptive business acts and practices related to contests, guarantees, and trade names.

Enforcement of the Federal Trade Commission Act and the provisions of the Wheeler-Lea Act is vested in five commissioners appointed by the President of the United States, with the advice and consent of the Senate, for seven-year terms. The president designates one of the commissioners as chairman. Not more than three commissioners may be members of the same political party. Their terms are staggered to assure continuity of experience, and, according to congressional intent, to keep the commission nonpartisan. The chairman has responsibility for the personnel aspects of the commission's operations. The full commission, however, must act on all matters involving development and implementation of FTC law enforcement policies.

The FTC has authority to stop business practices that restrict competition or that deceive or otherwise injure consumers, as long as these practices: (1) fall within the legal scope of the commission's statutes; (2) affect interstate commerce; and (3) involve a significant public interest. After an administrative hearing on a case, the FTC may issue a *cease-and-desist order*, which defines the offense and forbids such action in the future, or it may apply to the federal courts to issue an injunction against the offender.

In addition, the FTC defines practices that violate the law so that businessmen may know their legal obligations and consumers may recognize those practices against which legal recourse is possible. The commission does this through Trade Regulation Rules and Industry Guides issued periodically as "dos and don'ts" to business and industry, and through business advice—called Advisory Opinions—given to individuals and corporations requesting it.

The ever-present question concerning the enforcement of laws in the advertising business is: what is truth? Outright deceptions are usually easily recognized, but even well-intentioned advertisers will engage in puffery. *Puffery* is generally defined as exaggerated praise and is not actionable under common law. We often use puffery in our everyday speech. "That was a great movie," we might say. Do we mean to say that it was one of the best movies of all time or merely that we enjoyed the movie? In a similar vein an advertiser might say that a pen "writes smoother." Smoother than what? This is just puffery. Read any print ad; listen to any radio commercial; watch any television commercial; and you will find examples of puffery. It is often very difficult to draw a line between what is meant only as puffery and what is meant to be deceptive. In one area of advertising, however, the use of puffery is very strictly regulated. The Securities and Exchange Commission (SEC) has strict regulations against puffery in the advertising of securities. The *tombstone ads* in the financial sections of newspapers are closely watched by the SEC to insure that the ads confine themselves to basic statistical information about any forthcoming stock issue. No discussion of a stock's merits is permitted.

Years ago the priority of the FTC was action against fictitious price ads, misuse of words like "guarantee," and bait-and-switch ads. In a *bait-and-switch ad*, an advertiser would advertise one product at a very low price as bait to lure consumers to visit a certain store. When the consumers arrived at the store, however, they would be told that the advertised product had been sold out and store personnel would then attempt to convince them to switch to a more expensive product. Today, the FTC's objectives are much broader. Of particular interest is its "advertising substantiation" program. Under this program, many advertisers in widely varied fields have been required to prove the claims made in their advertising.

Recently, the FTC, when deciding its cases, has been attempting to restore conditions to what they were before the deceptive or misleading action took place. Some recent cease-and-desist orders included requirements for the offender to correct earlier misstatements.

A few examples of *corrective advertising* will serve to make the FTC's power in this area of advertising abundantly clear. In September 1978, an FTC administrative law judge ordered that $24 million in future Anacin ads state: "Anacin is not a tension reliever." Although American Home Products, the manufacturer, had stopped making the claim by December 1973, evidence showed that consumers believed tension relief to be an important attribute of Anacin. The judge said the image was likely to persist for "some time" in the absence of a corrective message. The $24 million represented the FTC's estimate of the average annual Anacin advertising budget from 1968 to 1973. The manufacturer was also barred from claiming in future ads that its Arthritis Pain Formula had "special" or "unusual" ingredients because such ingredients are also available in other products.

When you see a commercial for Listerine, you will also see the corrective disclaimer: "Listerine

Tombstone ads can be found in the financial section of a daily newspaper as well as in a number of general business publications. The format for these ads is fairly standard, and the disclaimer copy, "this announcement is neither an offer to sell nor a solicitation of an offer to buy," is mandated. The designation *tombstone* was probably suggested by an advertising designer who likened the ads to a tombstone that contains nothing more than the name of the person and the dates of birth and death.

## $200,000,000

# Mellon National Corporation

### Floating Rate Notes Due 1989

(Convertible by Holder Prior to June 15, 1988 Into 8½% Debentures Due 2009;
Convertible by Mellon National Corporation After June 15, 1980 and
Prior to June 15, 1988 Into Fixed Rate Debentures Due 2009)

Interest on the Notes for the period June 15, 1979 through December 14, 1979 will be at the rate of 11.50% per annum. The interest rate per annum for each semi-annual period thereafter will be .50% above the then current "interest yield equivalent" of the market discount rate for six-month U.S. Treasury bills, subject to a minimum per annum interest rate of 6%.

### Price 100%
plus accrued interest from June 15, 1979

*Upon request, a copy of the Prospectus describing these securities and the business of the Company may be obtained within any State from any Underwriter who may legally distribute it within such State. The securities are offered only by means of the Prospectus, and this announcement is neither an offer to sell nor a solicitation of any offer to buy.*

Goldman, Sachs & Co.

Blyth Eastman Dillon & Co.
Incorporated

The First Boston Corporation

| | | |
|---|---|---|
| Merrill Lynch White Weld Capital Markets Group<br>Merrill Lynch, Pierce, Fenner & Smith Incorporated | Salomon Brothers | Bache Halsey Stuart Shields<br>Incorporated |
| Bear, Stearns & Co.    Dillon, Read & Co. Inc. | Drexel Burnham Lambert<br>Incorporated | E. F. Hutton & Company Inc. |
| Keefe, Bruyette & Woods, Inc.    Kidder, Peabody & Co.<br>Incorporated | Lazard Frères & Co. | Lehman Brothers Kuhn Loeb<br>Incorporated |
| Loeb Rhoades, Hornblower & Co.    Paine, Webber, Jackson & Curtis<br>Incorporated | | L. F. Rothschild, Unterberg, Towbin |
| M. A. Schapiro & Co., Inc.    Shearson Hayden Stone Inc. | | Smith Barney, Harris Upham & Co.<br>Incorporated |
| Warburg Paribas Becker<br>A. G. Becker    Wertheim & Co., Inc. | | Dean Witter Reynolds Inc. |
| ABD Securities Corporation    Advest, Inc. | Arnold and S. Bleichroeder, Inc. | Atlantic Capital<br>Corporation |
| Basle Securities Corporation    Bateman Eichler, Hill Richards<br>Incorporated | William Blair & Company | Boettcher & Company |
| J. C. Bradford & Co.    Alex. Brown & Sons    Butcher & Singer Inc. | Dain, Kalman & Quail<br>Incorporated | F. Eberstadt & Co., Inc. |
| A. G. Edwards & Sons, Inc.    Elkins, Stroud, Suplee & Co. | EuroPartners Securities Corporation | Fahnestock & Co. |
| First Southwest Company    Robert Fleming<br>Incorporated | Janney Montgomery Scott Inc. | Kleinwort, Benson<br>Incorporated |
| Ladenburg, Thalmann & Co. Inc.    McDonald & Company | | Moseley, Hallgarten, Estabrook & Weeden Inc. |
| New Court Securities Corporation    The Ohio Company | Oppenheimer & Co., Inc. | Parker/Hunter<br>Incorporated |
| Piper, Jaffray & Hopwood<br>Incorporated    Wm. E. Pollock & Co., Inc. | Prescott, Ball & Turben | Rauscher Pierce Refsnes, Inc. |
| The Robinson-Humphrey Company, Inc.    Rotan Mosle Inc. | Stuart Brothers | Sutro & Co.<br>Incorporated |
| Thomson McKinnon Securities Inc.    Tucker, Anthony & R. L. Day, Inc. | | Wheat, First Securities, Inc. |

June 20, 1979 ·

will not help prevent colds or sore throats or lessen their severity." The colds/sore throat issue was the subject of years of litigation between the FTC and Warner-Lambert, the manufacturer. Warner-Lambert lost and was required to use that disclaimer in its next $10 million worth of advertising. What's more, the FTC contracted with a market research organization to do consumer surveys that would gauge the impact of the corrective ads on consumers.

Additional legislation has augmented the capacity and scope of the FTC in the years since the passage of the Wheeler-Lea Act. The Wool Products Labeling Act of 1939, administered and enforced by the FTC, was passed to protect manufacturers and consumers from the deliberate mislabeling of wool products. The Textile Fiber Products Identification Act, 1958, requires that clothing, rugs, and household textiles carry a generic or chemical description of the fiber content of these products. The Fair Packaging and Labeling Act, 1962, regulates packaging and labeling of the food, drug, and cosmetic products under the jurisdiction of the Department of Health, Education and Welfare and of all other consumer products under the authority of the FTC.

**Other regulatory agencies**   Paralleling the work of the FTC, the Food and Drug Administration polices the labeling of foods, drugs, and cosmetics. In 1938, the passage by Congress of the Federal Food, Drug, and Cosmetic Act divided regulation between the FTC and the FDA. The FTC is responsible for advertising in promotional media and the Food and Drug Administration has power over claims that appear on the label or package. Additional legislation in 1962 gave the FDA virtually unlimited authority over prescription drugs. While the FDA's jurisdiction is confined to the *label*, its role is broader than the word implies. If it finds that any claim in an ad is not supported by the information on the label, the FDA can proceed with a mislabeling action. The agency's interest in ads is deeper than it may seem from the enabling legislation. However, the FDA has not been merely a policeman. It has cooperated with the food industry in the development of standardized nutritional labeling systems for foods.

Closely allied to the FTC and FDA in much regulatory activity is the fraud staff of the U.S. Postal Service. Since 1872 post office fraud laws have provided criminal and civil remedies against the use of the mail to defraud. Because fraud, from a legal standpoint, involves "intent to deceive," postal service cases ordinarily involve misrepresentation that goes beyond the "false advertising" handled by the FTC. Most problems have been in the food and drug fields. The most serious cases of postal fraud are turned over to the Department of Justice, but the majority are handled administratively in civil procedure hearings similar to those of the FTC.

In the area of broadcasting, the Federal Communications Commission (FCC) enforces rules regarding the types of products that may be advertised on broadcast media, the number and frequency of commercials allowed within a certain period of time, and what broadcast programs and commercials may or may not state or show. Under the Communications Act of 1934, the FCC was empowered to operate our communications system in "the public interest, convenience, and necessity." Through its control over licensing, the commission wields indirect control over broadcast advertising. Specific problem areas with which the FCC has dealt include misleading demonstrations, physiological commercials considered in poor taste, and overlong commercials.

In addition to the FTC, FDA, the U.S. Postal Service, and the FCC, there are many other federal agencies with specialized roles related to advertising. Among these agencies are the following:

1. The Department of Agriculture, under the Packers and Stockyards Act, plays a role similar to that of the FDA in regulating the labeling of meat products.

2. The Environmental Protection Agency (EPA) does for pesticide labels what the FDA does for food labels.

3. The Consumer Product Safety Agency asks advertisers to avoid any themes that may promote unsafe use of products.

4. The Federal Deposit Insurance Corporation and the Federal Home Bank Board both exercise close supervision over the advertising practices of banks and of savings and loan associations.

5. Under the Truth in Lending Law, the Federal Reserve Board regulates installment credit ads by banks.

6. The Treasury Department's alcohol bureau enforces a rigid advertising code on the advertising of alcoholic beverages that precludes many of the advertising techniques used by other products. These regulations specifically ban any attempt to impute therapeutic benefits to alcoholic beverages. They also ban any brand names that might imply that a product was produced in another country. For example, American manufacturers of vodka may not name their products *St. Petersburg Vodka* or *Leningrad Vodka*. To avoid such problems, American vodka producers have been content to use Russian-sounding names with labels adorned with what may look like the imperial crest of the czars.

7. The Civil Aeronautics Board monitors the advertising of airlines and travel agents.

## Advertising polices itself

The degree of restraint and the quality of information in most advertising today reflects the integrity of advertisers themselves as much as the requirements of law. For the most part, the advertising industry polices itself. Advertising agencies and trade associations circulate standards set for advertising copy and appeals in order to alert their employees and members to bad advertising practices. In this way, much poor advertising is rejected or rewritten long before it might have been seen by the public at large. The Direct Mail/Marketing Association, for example, offers the following advice to advertising media to help them avoid inadvertently contributing to misleading or fraudulent mail-order advertising:

- If the offer is vague, do not approve it. If you have read the copy through twice and you still do not know what you are getting, ask the advertiser for clarification of the copy. Do not accept an offer unless it is clearly spelled out.
- Make yourself the surrogate viewer or reader or listener. Are the copy and/or pictures outlandish? Are the claims so strong as to be unbelievable? Be particularly wary of ads that claim to cure physical ills such as arthritis, psoriasis, or gout.[1]

[1] *1979 Fact Book* (New York: The Direct Mail/Marketing Association, Inc.), pp. 143–145.

As we have seen, the advertising industry began to formulate self-regulatory policy as early as 1911 by urging the adoption of the *Printer's Ink* model statute. Like the marketplace itself, self-regulation of advertising tends to be segmented, with different associations and agencies working to eliminate abuses in certain product categories or in certain media. With the creation of the *National Advertising Review Board* (NARB) in 1971, however, the entire advertising industry pledged to police deception and bad taste in advertising wherever it occurs. The NARB responds to complaints by the public and does its own monitoring as well.

The NARB consists of fifty members: forty advertising professionals and ten members of the public. Complaints about national advertising, whether from consumers, competitors, or from local Better Business Bureaus, are first referred to the National Advertising Division (NAD) of the Council of Better Business Bureaus. A staff of advertising professionals at NAD investigates the complaints and determines whether the offending advertising should be modified or discontinued. If the advertiser will not comply with the NAD's request to cease or modify advertising that is considered misleading or offensive, the matter is turned over to the NARB for review by a panel consisting of five members who act as judges in the case. This panel may then either find the advertising not misleading and dismiss the case, or it may accept the NAD recommendation that the advertising be discontinued or modified. If the advertiser refuses to comply with an NARB request to discontinue its advertising, the NARB may then turn the matter over to the appropriate government agency for further action.

The NARB—NAD procedure, which generally expedites complaint actions, alleviates the work-load of the FTC, while allowing advertisers to avoid the adverse publicity that usually comes from FTC action. In one month in 1978, for example, the NAD resolved twenty challenges to advertising, four of which were settled in favor of the advertisers; the remainder resulted in the discontinuation or modification of the questioned advertising.

## Policing by the media

While the NARB has been assuming a leadership role, broadcasting stations, newspapers, and magazines impose their own standards on top of the general ones. Self-regulation includes many problems of taste that are hard to define and for which legislation cannot be provided. These problem areas include, for instance: the portrayal of women in ads; the endorsement of certain products by athletes or other public figures; and the promotion of good ecological and safety habits. The demonstration of good ecological habits would include showing the proper disposal of empty containers, wrappers, bottles, jars, and packages (closed or capped). Homemakers are required to be shown neatly dressed in a costume appropriate to that activity. No one is supposed to be seen drinking beer or soda from the bottle. Athletes are not supposed to drink alcohol.[2]

The National Association of Broadcasters (NAB) requires the use of safety belts in commercials showing a moving auto. The NAB Code Authority offers free advice on Radio and Television

[2] An interesting case came up in April 1979 when the Bureau of Alcohol, Tobacco and Firearms (a division of the Treasury Department) objected to the appearance of the famous racing driver Mario Andreotti in a commercial for Schaefer beer. The BATF claimed Mr. Andreotti's appearance on the television commercial violated a 1954 ruling prohibiting the use of well-known active athletes in commercials for alcoholic beverages.

# The Television Code

National Association of Broadcasters
Twentieth Edition, June 1978

children. Exploitation of children should be avoided. Commercials directed to children should in no way mislead as to the product's performance and usefulness.

B. Commercials, whether live, film or tape, within programs initially designed primarily for children under 12 years of age shall be clearly separated from program material by an appropriate device.

C. Trade name identification or other merchandising practices involving the gratuitous naming of products is discouraged in programs designed primarily for children.

D. Appeals involving matters of health which should be determined by physicians should not be directed primarily to children.

E. No children's program personality or cartoon character shall be utilized to deliver commercial messages within or adjacent to the programs in which such a personality or cartoon character regularly appears. This provision shall also apply to lead-ins to commercials when such lead-ins contain sell copy or imply endorsement of the product by program personalities or cartoon characters.

#### Restricted or unacceptable categories

7. **Alcoholic beverages.**

A. The advertising of hard liquor (distilled spirits) is not acceptable.

B. The advertising of beer and wines is acceptable only when presented in the best of good taste and discretion, and is acceptable only subject to federal and local laws.

This requires that commercials involving beer and wine avoid any representation of on-camera drinking. *(Interpretation No. 4)*

8. **Vocational training.** Advertising by institutions or enterprises which in their offers of instruction imply promises of employment or make exaggerated claims for the opportunities awaiting those who enroll for courses is generally unacceptable.

9. **Ammunition; firearms; fireworks.** The advertising of firearms/ammunition is acceptable provided it promotes the product only as sporting equipment and conforms to recognized standards of safety as well as all applicable laws and regulations. Advertisements of fire-

13

rather than generalized statements or conclusions, unless such statements or conclusions are not derogatory in nature.

9. Advertising testimonials should be genuine, and reflect an honest appraisal of personal experience.

10. Advertising by institutions or enterprises offering instruction with exaggerated claims for opportunities awaiting those who enroll, is unacceptable.

11. The advertising of firearms/ammunition is acceptable provided it promotes the product only as sporting equipment and conforms to recognized standards of safety as well as all applicable laws and regulations. Advertisements of firearms/ammunition by mail order are unacceptable.

**D. Advertising of Medical Products**
*Because advertising for over-the-counter products involving health considerations is of intimate and far-reaching importance to the consumer, the following principles should apply to such advertising:*

1. When dramatized advertising material involves statements by doctors, dentists, nurses or other professional people, the material should be presented by members of such profession reciting actual experience, or it should be made apparent from the presentation itself that the portrayal is dramatized.

2. Because of the personal nature of the advertising of medical products, the indiscriminate use of such words as "safe," "without risk," "harmless," or other terms of similar meaning, either direct or implied, should not be expressed in the advertising of medical products.

3. Advertising material which offensively describes or dramatizes distress or morbid situations involving ailments is not acceptable.

**E. Time Standards for Advertising Copy**

1. As a general rule, up to 18 minutes of advertising time within any clock hour are acceptable. However, for good cause and when in the public interest, broadcasters may depart

16

cant lands, cooperative apartments and condominiums), and political advertising.

## The following describes some of the kinds of advertising which The Times will not accept:

### 1. Generally

• Advertisements which contain fraudulent, deceptive, or misleading statements or illustrations.
• Attacks of a personal character.
• Matrimonial offers.
• Unwarranted promises of employment in school advertising.
• Advertisements that are overly competitive or that refer abusively to the goods or services of others.

### 2. Investments

Advertisements holding out the prospect of large guaranteed dividends or excessive profits, or which solicit investments in nonproducing mining or oil property, oil royalties or pyramid sales operations.

### 3. Fortune Telling

Advertisements for fortune telling, dream interpretations and individual horoscopes.

4

### 4. Foreign Languages

Advertisements in a foreign language (unless an English translation is included) except in special circumstances and when a summary of the advertisement in English is included.

### 5. Salespersons

Advertisements for salespersons stating that specific sales volume or income will be achieved within a given period of time. Advertisements which do not include the type of compensation to be paid to salespersons such as salary, commission, etc., or which do not describe the articles and/ or services to be sold.

### 6. Discrimination

Advertisements which discriminate on grounds of race, religion, national origin, sex or age.

### 7. Offensive to Good Taste

Indecent, vulgar, suggestive or other advertising that, in the opinion of The Times, may be offensive to good taste.

This list is not intended to include all the types of advertisements unacceptable

5

Page from a pamphlet entitled "Standards of Advertising Acceptability,"
issued by *The New York Times*.

Code advertising standards, and pre-clearance of commercials in certain product classifications—children's toys and premiums, personal hygiene products and food products containing certain health-related claims. Each network has its own copy clearance staff who has the final say on what programs and commercials are acceptable for broadcast. The NAB has kept liquor advertising off television. The NAB has also eliminated the "man in white" commercials in which an actor who played the role of doctor "sold" health products.

Newspapers all have elaborate copy review systems. *The New York Times,* for example, maintains an advertising acceptability department that reads all advertising submitted for publication and screens out objectional ads. The *Chicago Tribune* distributes an "Advertising Acceptability Guide" through its space salespeople. Most major magazines have acceptance standards which, though differing in specifics, maintain an advertising environment consistent with their concepts of editorial quality. Products bearing the Good Housekeeping seal have actually been tested in laboratories operated by that magazine.

## Summary

No one will ever claim that advertising is above criticism. To be sure, some advertising is in questionable taste. On balance, however, advertising's social and economic contributions far outweigh its lapses. Most serious criticism of advertising centers on three claims: advertising increases the cost of products; advertising induces people to buy products they don't need; and advertising fosters monopolies.

To the first point, advertisers can reply that they, in fact, help to reduce manufacturing costs by making possible the large markets which permit the use of large-scale product facilities and techniques. Compared to other methods of promotion, such as personal selling, advertising actually reduces distribution costs and, therefore, the price of goods.

To the second point—the claim that advertising makes people buy products they don't need—advertisers can point to thousands of examples of high-quality, useful products that no amount of advertising was able to convince people to buy. Every year, in fact, many highly advertised products disappear from the marketplace because consumers simply do not want them.

Critics of advertising also claim that advertising fosters monopolistic business practices by inflating the cost of promoting products nationwide to levels beyond the means of most small companies, thus reducing price competition. Again, advertisers can point out that although the cost of launching a national advertising campaign is high, such campaigns are more cost effective than any other form of promotion now available. Advertising has also made possible the growth of mass-merchandising stores, which do their part in promoting price competition. Since consumers can make their buying decisions based on product information that they have obtained from advertising, these stores can reduce their costs by employing fewer salespeople.

Historically, advertising has been regulated by three sectors of society: government; the advertising industry itself; and the media. The federal government regulates advertising primarily through the offices of the Federal Trade Commission. Since 1971, the advertising industry has regulated itself through the National Advertising Review Board, while the various media have regulated the advertising that they carry by instituting media associations and individual advertising copy-review systems.

## QUESTIONS FOR DISCUSSION

1. From the point of view of the seller, advertising has two functions—to persuade and to inform. What is the distinction? Which is more important?

2. What would be the economic effect of banning all advertising?

3. What would the social effects be?

4. What is the difference between puffery and misleading advertising?

5. In what ways does advertising affect American tastes and culture?

6. What are the government agencies that watch over and regulate advertising?

7. Do you believe children should be permitted to view television commercials? Why or why not?

8. Do you believe that advertising for certain products should be banned? Why?

9. Which of the regulatory agencies should have the most influence over advertising? Why?

## Sources and suggestions for further reading

Aaker, David A., and Myers, John G. *Advertising Management.* Englewood Cliffs, N.J.: Prentice-Hall, 1975.

Backman, Jules. *Advertising and Competition.* New York: New York University Press, 1967.

Bernstein, Peter W. "Here Come the Super-Agencies." *Fortune* (August 27, 1979).

Chisholm, Roger, and McCarty, Marilu. *Principles of Economics.* Glenview, Ill.: Scott, Foresman and Co., 1978.

"Coca-Cola: A Spurt into Wine That Is Altering the Industry." *Business Week* (October 15, 1979).

Drucker, Peter F. *The Age of Discontinuity.* New York: Harper & Row, 1969.

Engel, James F.; Kollat, David T.; and Blackwell, Roger D. *Consumer Behavior.* New York: Holt, Rinehart & Winston, 1968.

Hanan, M. *Life-Styled Marketing.* New York: American Management Association, 1972.

"Jewel Cos.: Scoring in Mexico with U. S. Supermarket Techniques." *Business Week* (October 22, 1979).

Kent, Felix H. *Legal and Business Problems of the Advertising Industry, 1978.* New York: Practicing Law Institute, 1978.

McDaniel, Carl, Jr. *Marketing: An Integrated Approach.* New York: Harper & Row, 1979.

"Price Makes Perfection." *Forbes* (August 6, 1979).

Quirt, John. "Wickes Corp.'s Retailing Triumph in Europe." *Fortune* (August 13, 1979).

Robicheaux, Robert A., et al. *Marketing: Contemporary Dimensions.* Boston: Houghton Mifflin, 1976.

Schwartz, David J. *Marketing Today.* New York: Harcourt Brace Jovanovich, Inc., 1977.

Stanley, Richard E. *Promotion.* Englewood Cliffs, N.J.: Prentice-Hall, 1977.

Stanton, William J. *Fundamentals of Marketing.* 5th ed. New York: McGraw-Hill, 1978.

Toffler, Alvin. *Future Shock.* New York: Random House, 1970.

Ulanoff, Stanley M. *Advertising in America.* New York: Hastings House, 1977.

## ADVERTISING IN THE FUTURE

**International advertising**

The problems of advertising
overseas
The market structure
Cultural differences
The range of media available
The need for continuity
The advertising climate in other
lands
The challenge

**The service economy**

Characteristics of services
Services are intangible
Services are personal
Services are not standardized
Services are perishable
Advertising services
Government advertises services too

**Changing media**

## WORKING VOCABULARY

narrowcasting    microfiche    hotelvision

516

# 22

## advertising in the future

*For the society of the future will offer not a restricted stan-dardized flow of goods, but the greatest variety of unstan-darized goods and services any society has ever seen. We are moving not toward a further extension of material standard-ization, but toward its dialectical negation.*

ALVIN TOFFLER
*Future Shock*

DVERTISERS ARE CONCERNED WITH THE FUTURE: with changing consumer tastes and with shifting population groups. They spend large amounts of time and money in the analysis of current trends, trying to predict how consumers will behave a month, a year, or ten years from the present. But where does the future of advertising it-self lie? There appear to be two segments of today's advertising industry that offer the greatest promise of future growth: advertising to markets overseas, and the advertising of services.

## International advertising

Although exports account for less than 10 percent of America's gross national product, overseas earn-ings make very important contributions to the prof-its of many American firms. Coca-Cola earns 55 per-cent of its profits abroad, for example, while Gillette earns 51 percent and Revlon 36 percent—to name only a few.

The world market often offers growth oppor-tunities to American companies whose products have reached the mature stage of their life cycle or whose new products face strongly entrenched competition in the domestic market. Also, as foreign currencies have appreciated against the dollar in the late 1970s, American goods have become more attractive to foreign consumers. Thus, in recent years the volume of overseas advertising by American companies has been increasing. This fact is dramatically illustrated by the fact that the largest advertising agency in the United States, the J. Walter Thompson Company, received $113.3 million in gross income from its international operations in 1978, while it received almost $7 million less ($106.6 million) from its domestic operations.

## The problems of advertising overseas

American companies that market their products abroad, however, have discovered, sometimes to their great regret, that international advertising differs significantly from domestic advertising. Although consumers in foreign markets may purchase many products for the same reasons that Americans buy them, advertisers cannot merely translate their domestic advertising into the language of another country. Many factors prevent a successful American advertising campaign from enjoying an equivalent success in a foreign market. At one time, agency facilities were a problem, but during the past decade giant multinational agencies have come into being. Today, every major agency in the United States has overseas branch offices or affiliates that are able to serve the advertising needs of the international marketer. Many foreign-based agencies, too—such as Daiko Advertising, Eurocom, Publicis Conseil, and the largest advertising agency in the world, Dentsu Inc.—offer advertisers international facilities.

The major problem areas of international advertising now include:

1. differing market structures between countries
2. cultural differences
3. variations in the media available to advertisers

**The market structure** of each country is different. In the advanced industrialized nations of the world, these differences may not be extreme, but in less developed nations, channels of distribution may be highly fragmented or even nonexistent in some areas of a country. In general, small stores and businesses abound overseas, each serving a limited geographic area. In the United States, for example, the supermarket dominates the distribution of food products, while in France supermarkets are the channel for little more than 25 percent of all retail food volume.

**Cultural differences** in such areas as family structure, customs, and religious beliefs inevitably affect a company's advertising program. Advertisers in Japan, for example, find that they cannot make direct comparisons between products. Japanese consumers feel that even subtle comparisons run counter to their country's tradition of respect. Therefore, many advertisements in Japan use a light approach to deliver their messages. Cultural traditions and language differences may affect an advertiser's use of symbols and brand names. Although many symbols carry similar connotations throughout the world, advertisers should commission market studies to determine how their products' symbols will be perceived in each country. In

(All figures in millions)

Figures are based on total equity interest in foreign shops. AA must stress that this table represents only estimates due to reporting procedures of a few agencies that varied slightly from those requested.

| Rank | Agency | Gross income | Billings | Rank | Agency | Gross income | Billings |
|---|---|---|---|---|---|---|---|
| 1 | Dentsu Inc. | $321.4 | $2,210,0 | 26 | William Esty Co. | $41.2 | $275.0 |
| 2 | J. Walter Thompson | 221.5 | 1,462.9 | 27 | Eurocom | 41.0 | 278.5 |
| 3 | Young & Rubicam | 204.0 | 1,361.1 | 28 | Bozell & Jacobs Int'l. | 34.5 | 230.2 |
| 4 | McCann-Erickson* | 199.5 | 1,346.5 | 29 | Ketchum, MacLeod & Grove | 33.4 | 222.1 |
| 5 | Oglivy & Mather Intl. | 153.9 | 1,003.7 | 30 | Intermarco-Farner | 33.1 | 230.6 |
| 6 | BBDO International[1] | 132.4 | 888.9 | 31 | Tokyu Advertising | 31.9 | 207.3 |
| 7 | Ted Bates & Co.[2] | 130.9 | 890.0 | 32 | Dai-Ichi Kikaku | 29.6 | 201.2 |
| 8 | Leo Burnett | 129.5 | 874.0 | 33 | Cunningham & Walsh | 28.9 | 222.6 |
| 9 | SSC&B[3] | 127.8 | 842.0 | 34 | Publicis Conseil | 26.0 | 180.8 |
| 10 | Hakuhodo Inc. | 114.2 | 740.3 | 35 | Yomiko Advertising | 25.8 | 157.2 |
| 11 | Foote, Cone & Belding | 113.3 | 755.6 | 36 | Ross Roy | 25.0 | 167.0 |
| 12 | D'Arcy-MacManus & Masius | 104.7 | 698.8 | 37 | Asahi Kokoku-Sha | 23.4 | 159.4 |
| 13 | Grey Advertising | 92.9 | 606.6 | 38 | Campbell-Mithum | 21.1 | 141.0 |
| 14 | Doyle Dane Bernbach | 91.0 | 606.3 | 39 | Dai-Ichi Advertising | 20.5 | 147.9 |
| 15 | Dancer-Fitzgerald-Sample | 85.6 | 599.0 | 40 | Asahi Tsushin Advertising | 19.1 | 123.0 |
| 16 | Compton Advertising[4] | 82.7 | 557.4 | 41 | William Wilkens & Co.[7] | 17.9 | 77.1 |
| 17 | Benton & Bowles[5] | 76.6 | 548.8 | 42 | TBWA | 16.6 | 110.9 |
| 18 | Campbell-Ewald[6] | 70.1 | 467.1 | 43 | Orikomi Advertising | 15.9 | 125.2 |
| 19 | Daiko Advertising | 56.7 | 464.2 | 44 | Man-Nen-Sha | 14.9 | 130.0 |
| 20 | N W Ayer ABH Int'l. | 48.6 | 325.1 | 45 | Chuo Senko | 14.6 | 108.3 |
| 21 | Norman Craig & Kummel | 48.2 | 321.2 | 46 | Marschalk Co. | 14.3 | 95.7 |
| 22 | Wells, Rich, Greene | 45.4 | 293.8 | 47 | GGK | 14.0 | 93.3 |
| 23 | Needham, Harper & Steers | 45.0 | 299.4 | 48 | Keller-Crescent Co. | 13.9 | 80.3 |
| 24 | Marsteller Inc. | 43.3 | 285.4 | 49 | Leber Katz Partners | 13.7 | 97.8 |
| 25 | Kenyon & Eckhardt | 41.7 | 278.3 | 50 | Creamer Inc. | 13.1 | 87.3 |

* Figures include M-E's 51% equity in McCann-Erickson-Hakuhodo in gross income and billings though no gross income for minority-owned shops in Venezuela, Argentina, New Zealand and Iran.

[1] BBDO figures are estimates.

[2] Figures include 80.2% of gross income and billings of George Patterson in Australia, the only agency in the Bates network not 100% owned by Bates.

[3] Includes gross income and billings for SSC&B: Lintas, the overseas network 49% owned by SSC&B and 51% owned by Unilever in 1978. Interpublc is negotiating to buy SSC&B and its 49% network equity and plans to acquire the remaining 51% of the network from Unilever at a later date.

[4] Compton policy is only to report the "power" (note story at left) of an agency network. The figures shown here treat each of its network agencies as 100% owned by Compton, including Britain's 4th largest agency, Saatchi & Saatchi, Garland-Compton with gross income of $21,870,000 and billings of $131,000,000 in 1978. Compton owns about 23% of Saatchi & Saatchi, which is a publicly held company. Compton also owns a "token" share of Dai-Ichi Kikaku, but figures shown do not include any part of the Japanese agency.

[5] Benton & Bowles figures also include 20% ownership in Gestion et Recherche Publicitaire, a French agency group comprising B&B Publicite, Feldman, Calleux and Concurrence.

[6] Does not include Ervaco, the Scandinavian agency group (with $58,000,000 in estimated billings) which is part of Campbell-Ewald Int'l as a result of Interpublic's 21% ownership in Ervaco.

[7] William Wilkens & Co. figures include its percentage ownership in Wilkens & Lehmann wpt, Vienna, and Leuenberger & Aerni wpt, Zurich.

Reprinted with permission from the April 9, 1979 issue of *Advertising Age*. Copyright by Crain Communications, Inc.

Note that among the top fifty advertising agencies in the world, eleven are Japanese. The fabulous growth of Japanese exports is responsible for the importance of Japanese agencies in the international marketplace. Many of the leading American agencies have expanded their operations into other parts of the world in recent years—a process that will continue.

## (Man sieht es auf dem Foto nicht.
## Aber er verbraucht nur 10.9 l Normalbenzin auf 100 km.)

Der Buick Skylark Limited gehört zu einer völlig neuen Auto-
mobilgeneration: den Euro-Amerikanern von GM.
Besondere Kennzeichen: querliegender 2.8 l V6-Motor mit
85 kW (115 PS), extrem laufruhig und doch voller Temperament.
Erstaunlich: der geringe Normalbenzinverbrauch von nur 10.9 l
auf 100 km*. Frontantrieb, Servolenkung, Servobremssystem,
Automatic-Getriebe. Gewohnt amerikanisch: die komplette und
luxuriöse Ausstattung, vom Radio bis zum elektrisch verstell-
baren Sitz. Gewohnt europäisch: das kompakte Außenmaß
bei großzügig bemessenem Innenraum. Erstaunlich der Preis:
19800.– DM (unverbindliche Preisempfehlung inklusive
12% MwSt., zuzüglich Fracht ab Bremerhaven).
*Verbrauch Liter/100 km, nach DIN 700 30, Teil I Neufassung:
im Stadtverkehr: 13.8; bei 120 km/h: 10.87; bei 90 km/h: 8.74.

**Buick, Chevrolet, Oldsmobile, Pontiac. Die Euro-Amerikaner von GM.**

Can General Motors sell American cars in Europe? Of course. In Germany, an American car offers much the same status that a Mercedes or a BMW offers in this country. This ad reinforces the high-status image of the Buick Skylark—modest type for the headline; small, compact body copy; and a very simple illustration. All these elements suggest prestige.

many cases, it may be necessary to adapt or change a brand name that does not translate well into another language.

Cultural traditions and religious beliefs can also strongly influence foreign consumers' attitudes toward an entire product class. As Dr. Ernest Dichter has pointed out:

> In Puritanical cultures it is customary to think of cleanliness as being next to godliness. The body and its functions are covered up as much as possible.
>
> But, in Catholic and Latin countries, to fool too much with one's body, to overindulge in bathing or toiletries, has the opposite meaning. It is *that* type of behavior which is considered immoral and improper.[1]

**The range of media available** to advertisers in different countries is another complicating factor. Just as in the United States, the requirements of the marketing plan, the product, the cost, and other criteria influence media needs. In other countries, however, media planning is further complicated by the fact that the full range of media available in the United States either may not be available in a particular area of the world or may exist only in a greatly modified form.

*Broadcast* Commercial television is not available in some foreign countries. Television networks may be state-controlled and not available for use by advertisers. Even in those countries that do have commercial television, its programming may be extremely different from its counterpart in the United States. In some countries, for example, commercials are not run at intervals within individual tele-

vision programs, but are shown as a block at the beginning or end of each program. The single television network in Swaziland, in southern Africa, broadcasts only from 6:00 to 10:30 PM each day. In Japan, 70 percent of all television commercials are only 15 seconds long, making it impossible for advertisers to run heavy, fact-oriented messages.[2] Instead, most Japanese television commercials rely either on a humorous approach or on an image strategy. For instance, a typical commercial for Kleenex tissues in Japan shows a cherubic child pulling tissues from a box in slow motion and sending them airborne. The image conveyed to viewers is one of a delicate bird floating in a light breeze—suggesting the qualities of the product that Kleenex wants to promote.

Humor is an ingredient common to the television commercials of many countries. Here are a few examples:

1. A Frenchman, interrupted during the delivery of a commercial for fly spray when a fly lands on the demonstration table, smashes the fly with the butt of the spray can, saying, "It's not expensive and it works."

2. An Australian commercial for toilet paper opens with a wide angle view of a gingerbreadlike outhouse. The announcer informs the viewers that this particular toilet paper has played a trusted "roll" in Australian history.

In Western Europe, international commercial radio is important. Because radio stations there are allowed to have a transmitting power of up

---

[1] Ernest Dichter, "The World Customer," *Harvard Business Review* (July–August 1962), pp. 112–122.

[2] "Ad Week: An Ad in Any Other Land Is Not the Same," *Advertising Age* (September 4, 1978), p. 22.

# GEERSGROSS ADVERTISING LTD

7 SOHO STREET, SOHO SQUARE, LONDON W1V 6QU. TELEPHONE: 01-734 1655. TELEX: GG LDN (261878)

I'm a Gnu...

with a cuppa Ty·Phoo...

the most refreshing t'tea
that you can brew.

T'T'Ty·Phoo...

how do you do...

there's never been anything
quite as nice as you.

T'T'Ty·Phoo...

Oh! Tasty Ty·Phoo...

you really ought to be in
w' who's w' who.

Oh you're such a lovely cup

'cos you always pick me up.

Oh! T'too...t'too...t'too...
T'T'Ty·Phoo.

This is a storyboard for a tea commercial that was broadcast on English television. Would this kind of whimsical commercial appeal to American audiences? In America, tea is sold to compete with coffee as a "pick-me-up" beverage. Since most Englishmen prefer tea to coffee, it is not necessary to convince them to switch beverages; Ty-Phoo need only remind the audience of its brand name.

to 275,000 watts (the US limit is 50,000 watts), at least four radio stations in Europe reach audiences in several different nations. The leading station is Radio Luxembourg, which broadcasts in five languages. It counts over 40 million listeners throughout Western Europe—from England to southern France and into East and West Germany, Austria, and Switzerland. In Latin America, commercial radio is especially valuable in reaching illiterate audiences in remote areas.

*Print*    As is true in the United States, magazines in other countries provide advertisers with varying degrees of selectivity. In India, more than half of that country's total advertising volume is channeled through the print media; in Europe print is the dominant medium, with as much as 75 percent of total volume going into magazines. French advertisers rely heavily on two-page spreads with relatively little copy but striking illustrations. (Fashion advertisements in France are illustrated by famous photographers who sign their ads.) In Germany, the emphasis is 180 degrees in the opposite direction —advertisements contain loads of copy but fewer illustrations.

In addition to using local publications, international advertisers can use such American-based magazines as *Reader's Digest* and *Time*, both of which provide international editions. Newspapers are a universal medium and, like one or two American papers, some European newspapers have nationwide, rather than merely local, circulations. Nevertheless, in many other countries around the world, newspapers reach a much smaller proportion of the total population than they do in the United States. This circumstance is particularly prevalent in countries where literacy and income levels are low.

While the lack of a full range of media in many countries frequently limits the amount of advertising a firm can do, in countries where wages are lower than they are in the United States, marketers can compensate by hiring much larger sales forces. In Venezuela, for example, where advertising expenditures per capita are only $19.36 (compared to $156.69 in the United States), Philip Morris was able to employ 300 people in its sales department. Only 100 of these employees worked directly as sales representatives; however, the rest assisted with deliveries, displays, and other related tasks.[3]

## The need for continuity

We have pointed out that a specific campaign in one country will survive the move to another only if the advertisers are careful to adapt it to the characteristics of the available media and of the new target market. But advertisers have also found that it is important to establish a strong worldwide product identity. As far as possible, advertisers should have the same brand names and the same packages available in all countries, as well as a similar look to all their ads. The advantages of establishing a strong international product identity have been proven by the experiences of the European Economic Community. Many migrant laborers— Turks, Greeks, Italians, Spaniards, and North Africans—have moved to Germany, France, and other countries of northern Europe where jobs are plentiful and the pay better than in their native countries. Eventually, most of these migrant workers return to their homelands, bringing back with them new consumer habits. Smart advertisers make it

[3] Vern Terpstra, *International Marketing.* (New York: Holt, Rinehart and Winston, Inc., 1972), pp. 282–283.

Compare per capita expenditures for advertising among the various countries of the world. A portion of the difference in expenditures can be explained by lack of media availabilities, illiteracy, and by the fact that in many countries radio and television stations are noncommercial. In some areas television is nonexistent because of the lack of electric power. As for magazine availabilities, no country in the world publishes the variety of magazines that can be found in the United States.

## GLOBAL AD EXPENDITURE

| Country | Total* | Per Capita* | Country | Total* | Per Capita* |
|---|---|---|---|---|---|
| **WESTERN EUROPE** | | | **NORTH AMERICA** | | |
| Switzerland | 702 | 109.59 | United States | 33,720 | 156.69 |
| Denmark | 507 | 99.41 | Canada | 2,378 | 103.40 |
| Sweden | 753 | 91.81 | | | |
| Finland | 386 | 82.19 | **MIDDLE EAST** | | |
| Netherlands | 1,122 | 81.28 | Bahrain | 12 | 41.00 |
| Norway | 291 | 72.73 | Kuwait | 18 | 17.70 |
| Austria | 421 | 56.13 | Israel | 58 | 16.74 |
| West Germany | 2,986 | 48.56 | Lebanon | 35 | 11.63 |
| France | 2,502 | 47.31 | Saudi Arabia | 89 | 9.63 |
| United Kingdom | 2,250 | 40.25 | Syria | 21 | 2.72 |
| Spain | 1,322 | 36.73 | Jordan | — | 2.46 |
| Iceland | — | 35.50 | Iraq | — | 1.70 |
| Belgium | 294 | 29.73 | UAE | — | — |
| Luxembourg | 11 | 28.25 | | | |
| Ireland | 60 | 18.69 | **SOUTH ASIA** | | |
| Italy | 601 | 10.69 | Iran | 54 | 1.58 |
| Malta | 3 | 8.00 | Sri Lanka | 5 | 0.33 |
| Portugal | 69 | 7.24 | India | 138 | 0.23 |
| Greece | 62 | 6.70 | Pakistan | 15 | 0.20 |
| Turkey | 254 | 6.32 | Bangladesh | — | 0.13 |
| | | | Nepal | 1 | 0.05 |
| **AFRICA** | | | Afghanistan | — | — |
| South Africa | 342 | 13.11 | Bhutan | — | — |
| Libya | — | 4.36 | | | |
| Rhodesia | — | 2.79 | **SOUTHEAST ASIA** | | |
| Zambia | 11 | 2.24 | Singapore | 51 | 22.04 |
| Mauritius | 2 | 1.89 | Hong Kong | 88 | 20.00 |
| Egypt | 58 | 1.52 | Taiwan | 169 | 10.36 |
| Sudan | — | 0.95 | Malaysia | 42 | 3.42 |
| Kenya | 13 | 0.93 | Thailand | 131 | 3.04 |
| Nigeria | 53 | 0.82 | Philippines | 59 | 1.35 |
| Morocco | — | 0.71 | Indonesia | 64 | 0.45 |
| Liberia | 1 | 0.39 | | | |
| Ghana | 3 | 0.25 | **AUSTRALASIA** | | |
| Ethiopia | 1 | 0.03 | Australia | 1,116 | 82.06 |
| | | | New Zealand | 122 | 39.52 |

| SOUTH AMERICA | | | Jamaica | 36 | 17.24 |
|---|---|---|---|---|---|
| Venezuela | 240 | 19.36 | Costa Rica | 20 | 9.95 |
| Argentina | 432 | 16.80 | Trinidad & Tobago | 11 | 9.91 |
| Brazil | 1,260 | 11.54 | Mexico | 480 | 7.71 |
| Peru | 95 | 5.89 | Panama | 13 | 7.47 |
| Chile | 57 | 5.44 | Dominican Republic | 31 | 6.38 |
| Uruguay | — | 5.07 | Nicaragua | — | 2.50 |
| Ecuador | 35 | 4.78 | Guatemala | — | 1.95 |
| Colombia | 93 | 3.79 | El Salvador | — | 1.20 |
| Surinam | 2 | 3.75 | Honduras | — | 1.03 |
| Bolivia | — | 1.79 | **NORTHEAST ASIA** | | |
| Paraguay | — | 1.30 | Japan | 4,856 | 43.05 |
| **CENTRAL AMERICA** | | | Korea | 187 | 5.21 |
| Bermuda | 7 | 110.00 | | | |
| Puerto Rico | 96 | 30.09 | | | |

* In millions of U.S. dollars; per capita in U.S. dollars.

Source: International Advertising Assn. and Starch INRA Hooper for 1976.

Reprinted with permission from the April 9, 1979 issue of *Advertising Age.* Copyright by Crain Communications, Inc.

possible for such people to find their newly discovered brands in the retail stores of their native lands. In addition, the many millions of tourists visiting foreign countries are a market segment that makes the necessity for brand-name and packaging continuity all the more important.

Young people are another important market segment that has increased the need for advertising continuity. Throughout the world, young people tend to dress alike, eat similar foods, and enjoy similar diversions: dancing, music, books, and films. The youth market has spurred the spread of fast-food outlets all over Europe and Asia. There are about 100 McDonald's hamburger restaurants in Japan alone.

## The advertising climate in other lands

Following the pattern of the United States and Canada, the consumer movement in Europe has been gaining momentum. It has, however, made little headway in Latin America and Africa, where countries are preoccupied with laying the foundations for modern, technologically advanced societies. Paralleling consumer activities, government agencies have stepped in to regulate advertising practices in many countries. Taxes on advertising have already been passed in some countries and are under consideration in others. Government actions have also been taken against misleading advertising in the marketing of pharmaceuticals. Canada has

# Jeder Film, den Sie nicht machen, könnte Ihr schönster sein.

Zum Schmalfilmen gibt es viele Anlässe. Versäumen Sie keinen! So können Sie den Spaß an Ihrem Hobby verdoppeln. Der KODACHROME 40 super 8 Film zeichnet alles auf – in den schönsten Farben und scharf bis ins letzte Detail.

Zum Filmabend laden Sie dann alle ein, und wetten: es wird ein großer Erfolg.

Übrigens: den KODACHROME 40 gibt es auch als Tonfilm.

**Kodachrome 40
super 8 Film.
Die Farbe stimmt,
die Schärfe stimmt.**

Kodak film is sold the world over, using much the same advertising appeal in every country—beautiful action photographs. "No other film is as beautiful for color and detail." No modification of the Kodak name is necessary. This ad was prepared by Lintas, Hamburg, an agency that is partially owned by SSCB.

published "Truth in Advertising" guidelines which are used as models by other countries.

The major concern of most governments is cigarette advertising; it has been banned in many countries and in the coming years will be banned in still more. Canada, England, Ireland, Italy, Denmark, Norway, Sweden, Finland, and Switzerland have already banned cigarette advertising from all or some media. Another category of promotion that is receiving government attention in many countries is advertising directed to children.

Governments do not ignore the benefits of advertising, however; many governments use the advertising process to promote ideas and products deemed important to public health and safety. In Sweden and England, the transition from left to right side of the road driving was promoted through advertising. In France, the promotion of milk consumption and the conservation of energy were the subjects of concerted ad campaigns.

## The challenge

The challenge of world markets is certainly a provocative one for American companies. For one thing, American goods must often compete against foreign goods of a very high quality. The United States has not had a monopoly on product development. In the area of consumer products, for example, Europeans were first with a wide range of innovations—stainless-steel blades, enzyme detergents, cordless electric shavers, instant coffee, yogurt with fresh fruit, dried soups, soft margarine, throwaway ballpoint pens, and throwaway cigarette lighters. With the exception of automatic transmissions, most automotive innovations have come from Europe.

The weakening of the dollar, while making American goods less expensive in foreign markets, has made foreign companies more dependent than ever on their home markets because the value of the goods that they sell to the United States has declined. German and Japanese companies have been particularly hard hit by the devaluation of the dollar, and they have been scouring the world for new marketing opportunities. In many markets, then, American firms will face tough competition from large, foreign multinationals.

In general, for American companies to win a share of overseas markets, they must:

1. Adapt the product to the market.

2. Know the impact of cultural, social, and religious differences in each market.

3. Expand into new markets one at a time, rather than try to expand into several new markets at once.

4. Build a managerial staff composed of talented men and women native to each country.

5. Recognize that different levels of literacy among countries, as well as within a country, will affect media selection.

6. Develop a strong product identity through branding, packaging, and advertising, recognizing, however, that these promotional elements may have to be adapted to suit each individual country.

7. Recognize the differences between one nation's distribution practices and another's.

8. Recognize the differences between the range and impact of one nation's media and another's.

# Ningún desayuno es nutritivo hasta que alguien lo come.

Para que cada mañana su familia empiece bien el día, el desayuno tiene que ser lo más atractivo posible. Y ahí es cuando los Corn Flakes de Kellogg's caen de maravilla. Se sirven con leche y azúcar. Acompañados con jugo o fruta, pan y mermelada . . . proporcionan un delicioso desayuno para su familia.

Corn Flakes de Kellogg's. Un cereal sabroso que puede disfrutarse a cualquier hora del día.

## *Kellogg's*®
**Lo mejor para usted cada mañana.**

® KELLOGG COMPANY U S A
© 1977 1979 KELLOGG COMPANY

How are Kellogg's ready-to-eat cereals sold in Latin America? In much the same way they are sold in the United States: by telling parents that cereals—along with milk, juice, toast, and spread—are good for children. Notice the familiar Kellogg package and logo, and that the name of the product remains the same.

## The service economy

Out of every dollar that we as consumers spend, about 44 cents goes for services, and services provide about two-thirds of all private, non-governmental jobs. Furthermore, the forecast is that these figures will increase rather than decline.[4]

The long period of prosperity that the United States has enjoyed since the end of the Second World War has meant increased disposable income, increased leisure time, and a general rise in the standard of living for most American consumers. As the desire for goods becomes fulfilled and as many products lose their images as status symbols, consumers turn to services. Witness the growth in education, travel, and sporting events and such sporting activities as tennis and skiing.

The rate of growth has not been uniform, however. As personal disposable income has increased and as life-styles have changed, the demand for some services has grown faster than for others. There are services now that will walk your dog, drive your car to Florida or California, work out your loan payments, find you a job (or a husband or wife), rent you a garden tractor, clean your swimming pool, mow your lawn, and care for your house plants.

The attributes of services are entirely different from those of products—services are intangible, personal, unstandardized, and perishable. Consumers in the target market cannot see, hear, smell, taste, or touch a service *before* they buy it. This presents unique problems to the marketers of services.

A brief examination of some of the services available will provide clues to the nature of the advertising they require:

[4] William J. Stanton, *Fundamentals of Marketing*. 5th ed. (New York: McGraw-Hill, 1978), p. 482.

○ Housing—including hotels and motels

○ Household services—utilities, repairs, cleaning, landscaping

○ Recreation—entertainment and amusements, sporting events, the rental and repair of sports equipment

○ Travel

○ Personal care—laundry, dry cleaning, beauty care

○ Medical/health care—medical, dental, hospitalization, nursing

○ Education

○ Business services—legal, accounting, management consulting, and marketing consulting

○ Insurance and financial—investment counseling, credit and loan services, property and personal insurance

○ Transportation—airlines, bus companies, and automobile rental and repair companies

○ Communication—telephone and specialized communication services

### Characteristics of services

Consider the problems involved in advertising services.

**Services are intangible** In most cases it is impossible for the target prospect to try the service before buying it. There are no product ingredients or packages to describe or illustrate. The thrust of the advertising effort must be the benefit or satisfaction the user will derive from the service.

New York City is one of the most popular tourist attractions in the United States. To attract new visitors, the New York State Department of Commerce advertises special packages of theater tickets and hotel accommodations. The benefit of these special tours is made tangible by scenes from many of the plays and musicals running on Broadway. The advertising agency that created the commercial is Wells, Rich, Greene, Inc.

Wells, Rich, Greene, Inc. 767 Fifth Avenue New York, N.Y. 10022 Plaza 8-4300

# I LOVE NEW YORK
# BROADWAY SHOW TOURS

New York State Department of Commerce

60-seconds

(MUSIC IN)

(MUSIC IN)

(MUSIC UNDER) VO: There's only one Broadway . . . It's in New York . . .

(CAST OF "A CHORUS LINE" SINGING I LOVE N.Y.)

(CAST OF "THE WIZ" SINGING I LOVE N.Y.)

(CAST OF "GREASE" SINGING I LOVE N.Y.)

(CAST OF "THE KING AND I" SINGING I LOVE N.Y.)

(CAST OF "ANNIE" SINGING I LOVE N.Y.)

VO: Introducing "I Love New York"

Broadway Show Tours (CAST OF "CHAPTER TWO")

. . . 16 specially priced packages of shows and hotels.

For a free booklet, see your travel agent or (CAST OF "THE GIN GAME")

call toll free, 800 331-1000. (CAST OF "THE MAGIC SHOW")

DRACULA: I Love New York . . . especially in the evening.

(MUSIC OUT) (SUPER: I LOVE NEW YORK BROADWAY SHOW TOURS)

530

Hon, the mortgage payment's due. Did you deposit your check today?

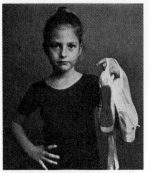

Mom, I need new ballet slippers.

# They need me.

When we got married, we said my income was for extras. We didn't want to be dependent on it when we had children. Well, we have a daughter now—and it's a *good* thing I went back to work when she went to school.

With the cost of day-to-day living, we couldn't possibly afford our house, let alone put money aside for her education on only one income. If anything happened to me, my family would have to make a lot of difficult adjustments—especially Jenny. That's why I have my *own* piece of the Rock—Prudential insurance—to help make sure they can live as comfortably as we do now. They need me.

### The more they need you, the more you need Prudential.

Life·Health·Auto·Home

Insurance is a service business, and, although the product is intangible, insurance companies must keep abreast of demographic changes just as the manufacturers of clothing, automobiles, and frozen foods must. In this ad, Prudential Insurance Company acknowledges the growing number of working women in the United States by suggesting insurance for mothers working outside the home.

**Services are personal**   For the most part, we cannot separate a service from the person who performs that service. The doctor's service is inseparable from the doctor. And the same is true of the barber, the dentist, and the manicurist. There is only one channel of distribution. What is the purpose of advertising if the number of customers is limited to what an individual can personally handle?

**Services are not standardized**   It is impossible to develop any uniformity among sellers of the same service; it is not even possible for a single seller to provide the same quality of service each time. The repair service performed by one mechanic is not always of comparable quality. The service at a hotel may vary with each visit. This week's concert given by a popular singer may be better (or worse) than last week's. Can we promise a benefit in advertising a service, if we are not sure we can deliver it?

**Services are perishable**   By *perishable* we mean that services cannot be stored or held in inventory. When a barber's chair is empty, it represents business that cannot be recovered. A ski resort without guests represents business that is lost forever. And this problem is exacerbated by widely fluctuating consumer demands. A haircutting salon may be overwhelmed with patrons on Friday and Saturday, but be empty on Monday and Tuesday. A movie theater that is empty Monday through Thursday may have to turn away customers on Friday and Saturday. Advertising can do much to help level demand; it can shift demand to slack periods or stimulate new demand for idle facilities. The telephone company, for example, has been using advertising for years to encourage people to make calls during off-peak hours and on weekends, when some telephone equipment is idle.

## Advertising services

We can see the difficulties inherent in creating meaningful advertising programs for services. In order to overcome these difficulties, our advertising will have to perform three critical tasks:

1. Portray clearly the benefits to be obtained from the service.

2. Differentiate as far as possible our service(s) from those of competitors.

3. Build an image for the provider of the service as a friendly, efficient, and courteous company.

Service firms have to segment their markets with more precision than do the advertisers of goods. They have to place greater emphasis on institutional advertising to develop their companies' "personalities," and they have to reconsider their advertising media. Some media do not provide an editorial climate suitable for the discussion of certain services. Since many services are local, the advertiser may be more concerned with newspapers or radio or spot television. Nor is the service organization as concerned with *reach* as is a company with a tangible product. They have to be more selective. They cannot afford to advertise in the hope that the necessary business will come to them at some future date. Services do not keep. Advertising can make abstract benefits concrete and appealing to consumers. The friendly image of a bank, for example, will tell consumers that it is receptive to inquiry for loans and that it avoids banker's jargon.

Advertising can raise the social and economic status of services and persuade customers that these services are, in fact, worth the money. A con-

CLIENT: The First National Bank of Chicago (CP78–460)
PRODUCT: Retail Savings (Calculator Premium)
FILM NO.: FN78T3
FILM TITLE: "Count On It"      FILM LENGTH: :30

DATE: February, 1978
PRODUCER: Sedelmaier Film Productions

1. (Music in and under) WOMAN #1: Who had the Asparagus Souffle?

2. WOMAN #2: Mother had the Shanghai Surprise.

3. WOMAN #1: Oh, Rose, now I lost count!

4. (Anncr VO) Chicago, when you need answers, we've got something you can count on--...

5. ...at The First National Bank of Chicago.

6. This ultra-thin pocket calculator from Sharp.

7. Put five hundred dollars in savings and it's yours for only $9.95. Put five thousand in and it's free.

8. So count on it! At Chicago's Bank.

9. WOMAN #2: Blanche,...

10. ...mother thinks she'd like some dessert!

11. (Singers VO) The First National Bank...

12. ...(Music)...

13. ...

14. ...

15. ...of Chicago.

Advertising an intangible product, such as a banking service, is very difficult because there is nothing to show, nothing to demonstrate. In this 30-second commercial, the agency—Foote, Cone & Belding—has developed a humorous skit that presents a premium offer in a tasteful, conservative manner. The audience smiles at the poor put-upon waiter serving four ladies. Notice that this commercial uses a number of different techniques—a skit with five actors, a close-up of the premium offer, an announcer, music, singing voices, and city views—to attract new savings-account depositors.

Doctors, dentists, and lawyers are now permitted to advertise, and some of them do. Advertising by professionals may serve the public by encouraging people to seek reasonably priced medical, legal, or accounting services. This advertisement is sponsored by a national professional organization, the American Medical Association.

# Exercise you can put your heart into
### ...your doctor wants you to keep up the good work

Today there are an estimated 10 million joggers, 15 million serious swimmers, 25 million regular cyclists and 29 million tennis players in the U. S. That's good.

A recent Gallup Poll found that the number of Americans who say they use some form of exercise *daily* has nearly doubled in the last sixteen years. From 24% to 47% today. That's even better. Because the evidence keeps piling up that regular physical activity may be of significant benefit in the prevention of coronary heart disease, America's #1 killer.

A case in point is the results from a recent study of San Francisco longshoremen. Those whose jobs required heavy physical activity had 46% fewer deaths due to coronary disease than longshoremen with less physically demanding jobs.

Now, just a word of caution from your doctor who is your partner in keeping you healthy. You are not a longshoreman, so don't overdo it. Your doctor can work out an exercise program with you, shaped to your capabilities and interests.

**American Medical Association, 535 North Dearborn Street, Chicago, Illinois 60610.**

## Your Doctor's Your Partner
Help your doctor help you

---

sumer will spend 50 cents for a cup of coffee and $6,000 for a new car, but may resent having to spend $40 to have a refrigerator repaired—even after the appliance has provided years of faithful service. With the help of advertising, service industries will expand and become more consumer-oriented. Advertising will then be able to do the job it does best—stimulate demand and motivate action.

Recently, restrictions against advertising by such professionals as dentists, doctors, and lawyers have been removed. These professionals may now advertise certain services and the fees they charge for these services. Because the market for the services of a particular doctor, lawyer, or dentist is a local one, advertising for such services appears predominantly in newspaper, transit, and radio media.

### Government advertises services too

Government advertising expenditures in 1977 amounted to $116.2 million—making the federal government the twenty-fourth largest advertiser in

## Which First Class Postage rate are you using?

In this example of advertising by the federal government, the United States Postal Service seeks to enlist the cooperation of the business community in its endeavors to provide the best service possible. This ad appeared, as might be expected, in *Business Week*, a broad business publication that reaches the target market with little, if any, waste.

Fifteen cents? Well, have you thought about presorting your mail by ZIP CODE? If you do the rate is thirteen cents (nine cents for postcards), in volume mailings of 500 pieces or more.

More than five thousand companies are now using PRESORT, and last year, overall, these companies saved more than $21 million.

You can join them and install PRESORT with just a few changes in your mailing system. All that is required is that you presort your First Class mail to 5- and 3-digit ZIP CODES and place it in special trays the Post Office supplies free. Then, just deliver the trays to the Post Office and save 2¢ on every piece, a penny on every postcard.

Not only do you save money, but presorted mail helps ensure consistent delivery since it requires less handling and can be forwarded almost as soon as you drop it off at a designated Postal unit.

If you'll mail in the coupon, we'll send you further information on how to save important money.

the country. In 1975, the government sector accounted for 23 percent of the gross national product, and we can expect government expenditures for social goods, such as environmental protection, health services, public housing, and transportation, to continue to increase. We can also expect increased government advertising as government agencies will use advertising techniques to market the social goods that they produce. The government already uses advertising to recruit for the Army and Navy and to "sell" Amtrak and the Postal Service. Other governmental advertising programs include efforts to promote safe driving, to counter alcoholism and drug abuse, and to stop pollution. The United States Travel Services advertises abroad to lure Europeans to visit America.

## Changing media

Advertising media will be affected by changes in consumer activities. We have already mentioned, for instance, that the increase in working women will mean that the audiences for daytime television programs will be smaller than in the past. But the media will be affected not only by demographic and social changes but by changes in technology.

It is difficult to believe that television became a *national* advertising medium little more than thirty years ago. And color television came to full flower only about fifteen years ago. Consider the new developments in communications that are awaiting their cue. We already have audio-visual cassettes, microfilm, satellites, and facsimile reproduction. Satellite technology will permit what E. B. Weiss

has called "narrowcasting."[5] The word *narrowcasting* refers to the manner in which radio is segmented into numerous groups of listeners, each with its favorite type of music and program format. E. B. Weiss recognizes that, in a much more limited manner, television is also moving in that direction. Audio-visual cassettes, cable tv, and satellite broadcasts have already given the public many more program choices than were available only a few years ago.

Newspapers of the future may be available on television—perhaps featuring editions broadcast from abroad and transmitted to your home via satellite. The age of the international newspaper may usher in a wave of international advertising and offer consumers throughout the world access to a truly global market. Or, imagine a newspaper delivered to your home as a sheet of microfilm about six inches long and four inches wide (called a *microfiche*), containing as many as 465 pages of printed material. This microfiche could be popped into a home reader for enlargement or examined on the way to work in a battery-powered portable reader. Even catalogue and direct-mail pieces could be sent out to consumers as microfiche.

What will happen to television advertising in the years to come? Recently, cable television has become more and more popular and, if it continues its growth, more people will be watching commercial-free television in the future. Video cassettes are also becoming popular. If a large market develops for rented video cassettes, then advertisers might place their commercials in these cassettes the way they now place ads in magazines. A soap-opera cassette might include commercials by food advertisers or by advertisers of household cleansers. A tennis cassette might include commercials for racquets, balls, warm-up suits, and resorts. The possi-

[5] E. B. Weiss, "Advertising Nears a Big Speed-Up in Communications Innovation," *Advertising Age* (March 19, 1979), pp. 51–52.

# HIDEHARU TAMARU

When Hideharu Tamaru was appointed president of Tokyo's giant Dentsu Incorporated (formerly Dentsu Advertising Ltd.) in June, 1977, one of his first official duties was presiding over the 76th celebration of the company's founding. That makes Dentsu not only one of the world's largest advertising agencies but one of the oldest. Despite the staid impression these facts may convey, under Hideharu Tamaru's guidance Dentsu is a progressive and forward-looking company. Of his role as president, he remarks: "I am confident that my function as president is to set up a bridge to the twenty-first century."

Hideharu Tamaru was not always so concerned with the future or with mass communications, however. Exhibiting a flair for literature and history, he entered the adult world as a high school teacher after graduating from Tokyo University in 1938. Ten years later, he was offered his first job in the field of advertising by the president of Dentsu himself, Hideo Yoshida, who also became Tamaru's self-appointed mentor. Yoshida repeatedly assigned Tamaru difficult tasks that a less determined man would have found impossible. Of those early years, Tamaru has this to say:

> For the first ten years at Dentsu, Yoshida kept me so busy I didn't have a minute to myself. I got to wondering why he always subjected me to those aggravating situations. But looking back on it all now I can see that he was whipping me into shape so I could get on an even footing with those Dentsu managers who had started with the company much earlier than I. Now I feel grateful for what he did.

Tamaru's perseverance paid off. During the ensuing years he worked in nearly every department, learning the business from the ground up. When it was announced that he would become the seventh president of Dentsu, however, the news came as a surprise to his many friends who know him by his affable and unpretentious manner. Indeed, Tamaru himself remembers the event as the shock of his life.

Reflecting his early life as a teacher, Tamaru's leadership of Dentsu proceeds with the well-ordered discipline of an academician. Tamaru is usually one of the first to arrive at the Dentsu building near Tokyo's Ginza district, and the last to leave. He exercises daily to keep fit and prepare himself for the arduous task of running the company. Reading is his favorite hobby, much of it centering on business and economics. Whenever possible though, he returns to the classics of Japanese literature and particularly the lyric "Manyo-shu" poetry that dates from the eighth century, a subject in which he is keenly interested and knowledgeable.

bilities are almost endless. Most hotels and motels today offer *hotelvision*, that is, a closed-circuit television system that transmits movies and other special programs only to the rooms of the lodging's guests. Hotelvision may provide advertisers of the future with a new medium. Local retailers and services in particular may welcome the opportunity to advertise to travelers.

## Summary

What does the future hold for advertising? We can expect to see emphasis in two areas and we can expect to see interesting changes in advertising media. One area that will grow in importance is international advertising. As American marketers seek to expand their sales around the world, they will use advertising and promotion techniques developed in the United States but modified to suit different cultures, distribution channels, and media.

Another area that will probably grow in the United States itself is the advertising of services. As we become increasingly service-oriented, the advertising and promotion of services—housing, repair, entertainment, travel, financial—will offer new challenges. The intangible, perishable, and unstandardized nature of services makes their presentation difficult. Difficult, but not impossible. And at the same time we shall see a more extensive use of advertising by every level of government. The federal government, already a major advertiser, will find more opportunities to use advertising techniques to "sell" the American public on ideas and attitudes deemed necessary to fight inflation, reduce unemployment, and save fuel.

As for media, the number of electronic miracles still possible is incalculable. Barely thirty years ago, television was in its infancy. And now we have everything from portable, battery-operated sets with seven-inch screens to color television sets with forty-five-inch screens, videocassette decks, and cable connections. Will changing electronic technology affect an advertiser's media mix? Indeed it will. And advertisers in future, as they do today, must keep a careful watch on the changing demographics of the marketplace.

## QUESTIONS FOR DISCUSSION

**1.** What are some of the problems that face international advertisers?

**2.** Why is export business important to American industry?

**3.** What are some of the problems inherent in advertising services? How can they be overcome?

**4.** What consumer services do you think will improve most from an increase in service advertising?

**5.** What will be the future impact of cable tv on advertising?

**6.** What future changes in print media advertising can you envision?

### Sources and suggestions for further reading

"Advertising 'Round the World: Variations on Similar Themes." *Advertising Age* (August 29, 1977).

"Ad Week: An Ad in Any Other Land Is Not the Same." *Advertising Age* (September 4, 1978).

Bogart, Leo. "As Media Change, How Will Advertising?" *Journal of Advertising Research* (October 1973).

Dichter, Ernest. "The World Customer." *Harvard Business Review* (July/August 1962).

Dillon, John, editor. *Handbook of International Direct Marketing.* London: McGraw-Hill, 1976.

Fox, Edward J., and Wheatley, Edward W. *Modern Marketing.* Glenview, Ill.: Scott, Foresman and Co., 1978.

Frey, Albert Wesley, and Halterman, Jean C. *Advertising,* 4th ed. New York: Ronald Press, 1970.

Mandell, Maurice I. *Advertising.* 2d ed. Englewood Cliffs, N.J.: Prentice-Hall, 1974.

"Overseas Shops' Income Hits $1.8 Billion." *Advertising Age* (April 17, 1978).

Stanton, William J. *Fundamentals of Marketing.* 5th ed. New York: McGraw-Hill, 1978.

Terpstra, Vern. *International Marketing.* New York: Holt, Rinehart and Winston, 1972.

Unwin, Steve. "Advertising of Services, Not Products, Will Be the Wave of the Future." *Advertising Age* (May 27, 1974).

"Watch That Foreign Market—Everything Changes." *Advertising Age* (April 29, 1974).

Weiss, E. B. "Advertising Nears a Big Speed-Up in Communications Innovation." *Advertising Age* (March 19, 1973).

"What Americans Can Learn from Europe—Market Segmentation." *Advertising Age* (February 16, 1976).

# glossary

**Account executive** A person in an advertising agency who works on a regular basis with one or more clients to provide continuous liaison between the various departments of the agency and the advertising manager of the client company.

**Adjacencies** Time periods preceding and following a regular network program that are available for local or spot advertising.

**Agate line** A unit of measurement, 1/14 of an inch deep and one column wide, used in selling newspaper advertising space.

**Agency network** A loose affiliation of small- and medium-sized agencies that exchange services and information.

**Agency of record** The agency designated to coordinate the media schedules of the various agencies employed by an advertiser to be certain that the advertiser is receiving the most advantageous rate.

**A la carte agency** Certain services provided by a full-service agency for which an advertiser may negotiate.

**Answer print** The final film of a television commercial, prepared for checking and approval before release.

**Appeal** Reasons an advertiser supplies to get consumers to act or to change an attitude.

**Artificially new** A term describing a product that appears to be new simply because of some cosmetic change, as designing a new package for an old product.

**Aspiration reference groups** Those groups to which a person does not in fact belong, but which he or she wants to join and uses as models for action.

**Bait and switch ad** An advertisement offering a product at a low price as bait to lure customers into a store where an attempt is then made to persuade them to switch to a more expensive product.

**Balance** The placement of elements in an advertisement so that they complement each other in terms of size and weight.

**Basic bus** In transit advertising, all the advertising space on the inside of a bus.

**Big ticket items** Merchandise, such as appliances and home furnishings, that represent major buying decisions requiring the deliberation of the entire family.

**Blind headline** One that does not tell the reader what type of product is being advertised or what its brand name is. The consumer must read the body copy in order to receive the sales message.

**Blitz schedule** An intensive campaign, particularly for the introduction of a new product, as, for example, when a media planner schedules two-page advertisements in three consecutive issues of a magazine.

**Boutique agency** A small agency that offers advertisers very creative, limited, and often expensive services.

**Brainstorming** A technique for prodding creativity in which ideas and suggestions are expressed by members of a group; no critical evaluation or negative responses are permitted. The prime consideration is generation of ideas, no matter how unusual or impractical they may seem at first.

**Brand name** The name used to identify a specific product. It is a variety of trademark.

541

**Break-out** Any of the various categories into which the names on a list can be separated by a computer.

**Budget** The dollar representation of planned activities over a specified period of time. A company's advertising budget is a plan that defines its proposed advertising activities in dollar amounts.

**Bulk mail** Third-class mail sent in quantity, for which the user pays an annual fee, exclusive of postage. The mailing must be printed, separately addressed, sorted, and bundled by ZIP code, and must include at least 200 pieces.

**Business advertising** Trade, industrial, or professional advertising directed to people in business who, in their operating capacity, buy and/or specify products or services.

**Buying power** The amount of money, or budget, that potential customers for a product have to spend on goods and services.

**Campaign** An advertising effort that is planned for, and conducted over, a specific period of time.

**Canned advertising** Advertising prepared by a manufacturer and distributed to retailers for publication in their local media.

**Certification mark** A mark used to certify a product's origin, mode of manufacture, quality, or accuracy. It may also indicate that the product was made by members of a particular organization or association.

**Channels of distribution** The distribution network chosen by the manufacturer through which a product will reach the ultimate purchaser.

**Car card** A standard-size piece of lightweight cardboard that is printed on one side and mounted in a retaining frame on the interior wall of a train or bus.

**Cease-and-desist order** An order issued by the Federal Trade Commission defining an unlawful business practice and forbidding such action in the future.

**Checking copy** A copy of the newspaper or magazine sent to an advertiser to verify the publication of an ad. It also provides an opportunity for examining the entire editorial and advertising content of the publication.

**Circulation** In radio and television, the number of homes within the area of a station's broadcast signal that actually tune in on a program. For newspapers and magazines, the number of copies that are actually sold (primary circulation). In outdoor advertising, circulation represents the gross potential audience and does not assume exposure.

**Clock spectacular** A large electric clock set in a display framework that may include a moving message.

**Closing date** Deadline by which a publication must receive advertising copy.

**Coated stock** Paper coated on the surface to produce a smooth surface.

**Collective mark** A trademark or service mark used by members of a cooperative, an association, or some other collective group.

**Combination rate** A special rate, paid by an advertiser buying space in two or more publications under the same ownership, that is usually far less than the total of the individual rates for each paper.

**Competitive strategy** An advertising plan that emphasizes the benefits of one brand over those of competing brands.

**Component parts** Finished goods, usually made to custom specifications.

**Comprehensive (COMP)** The advertising layout chosen to be presented to an advertiser for final approval and prepared to look as much like the finished ad as possible.

**Consumer advertising** Advertising directed to consumers of mass-marketed products.

**Consumer goods** Products that are bought for personal and family use. They include convenience goods, shopping goods, and specialty goods, as well as services and intangible products.

**Contract rate** A rate, lower than the open rate, charged for a single insertion offered an advertiser who plans to run a series of ads over a one-year period. It is based on either total linage used or frequency of insertion.

**Controlled circulation** The number of readers who receive free copies of a publication.

**Convenience goods** Consumer goods with low unit price, such as inexpensive candy, cigarettes, drug sundries, groceries, and hardware products, that are purchased, when needed, as rapidly and conveniently as possible.

**Copy block** The main body of words, or the textual matter, of an advertisement.

**Copy testing** Use of various methods to measure the effectiveness and appeal of an advertisement before it goes into a publication or on the air.

**Corporate advertising** Advertising that promotes the company rather than its products or services. Also called institutional advertising.

**Corrective advertising** Advertising sometimes required by the Federal Trade Commission to correct false or misleading claims made by a company in earlier advertisements.

**Cost effectiveness** The ability of a medium to deliver an advertising message to the largest number of prospective customers at the lowest possible price.

**Coverage** In broadcast media, the number of homes that can receive a radio or television station's transmission signals clearly. In outdoor advertising, the number and percent of people who pass and are exposed to a given showing of billboards during a 30-day period.

**Cost per thousand (CPM)** A ratio used to compare media charges in order to determine cost effectiveness. The form for determining CPM for print media is:

$$CPM = \frac{\text{cost of 1 black and white page} \times 1,000}{\text{circulation}}$$

For broadcast media, the formula is:

$$CPM = \frac{\text{cost of 1 unit of time} \times 1,000}{\text{number of homes reached by a given program or time}}$$

**Creative strategy** The words and images used to convey an advertiser's message or appeal to a target market. In general there are three basic strategies: (1) to emphasize product features and customer benefits, (2) to emphasize the product's or company's image, and (3) to attempt to position the product in the minds of the target market.

**Crop editions** Editions of a publication directed toward growers of a particular crop, who form a particular market segment for some herbicide or piece of machinery.

**Cume** The net cumulative audience: the number of different persons who are exposed to a single broadcast program or to an entire spot schedule over a four-week period.

**Cumulative audience** The number of people exposed to a medium over a given period of time.

**Cumulative recollection** After seeing an ad or commercial several times, the reader or viewer learns to recognize the ad or commercial.

**Cuts** Engravings of photographs or illustrations for use in letterpress printing.

**Dailies** In television or films, the takes or scenes shot on the previous day that have been developed and printed and are ready for approval.

**Demographics** Characteristics of a population, including sex, age, income level, marital status, geographic location, occupation, and other statistical classifications into which people can be separated and used for advertising purposes.

**Depth interview** Interview in which researchers encourage respondents to express their ideas freely on subjects that are important to the area being researched.

**Diffusion process** The process by which the acceptance of a new product, new service, or new idea spreads to the target market within a certain period of time.

**Direct advertising** A printed message that is delivered directly to prospective customers by the advertiser.

**Direct mail** Circulars, catalogues, brochures, leaflets, and other printed material sent through the postal service to prospects selected by the advertiser. It accounts for the third largest share (after newspapers and television) of advertising investment in the United States.

**Disassociative reference groups** Those groups to which a person does not belong and to which he or she does not want to belong.

**Distress merchandise** Items, such as perishable food or high-fashion merchandise, that have been held in stock too long.

**Doctor blade** In gravure printing, a knife that wipes the surface of the plate clean, leaving ink only in the tiny etched grooves.

**Double run** In transit advertising, the placement of two car cards in every vehicle.

**Drive times** The time periods from 6 to 10 in the morning and 4 to 7 in the evening, Monday through Friday, when radio stations reach their largest audiences.

**DS** Dissolve. In television, a combination of fade-in and fade-out. A new scene appears while the preceding one vanishes. It is a transitional device used to indicate the lapse of time.

**Duplication** The number of prospects who are reached by more than one of the media in a mix.

**Durability** The opportunity to deliver the same message more than once. Monthly magazines that a reader picks up and reads several times during the life of each issue offer the greatest durability and the broadcast media offer the least.

**Early adopters** Consumers who discover a product shortly after the first users, or innovators, and serve as role models for those who are slower to adopt it.

**Early majority** Consumers who are slow to adopt a new product, waiting for others to do so first.

**Electro** Short for electrotype, an exact but less costly duplicate of an original engraving, so called from the electrolytic process used in its manufacture.

**Embellishments** Extensions or cut-outs that protrude from the top or sides of a painted bulletin's frame.

**Empirical method** A method for determining an optimum advertising budget based on trial and error. By advertising at varying levels of expenditure, using the same medium in different test cities to see if sales vary with the level of advertising, a company can identify the most productive level of advertising expenditure.

**External house organ** A company magazine published on a regular basis that is distributed to customers, prospects, distributors, and dealers without charge to help build goodwill and to enhance the prestige of the company.

**Fact sheet** A rundown of information on a product. It is often provided to local radio announcers and disc jockeys as a guide in ad-libbing a commercial.

**Family name** The trade name used by a company producing an extensive line of products to help build strong identification among their entire family of products by grouping all products together under this single family name.

**Federal Trade Commission** A regulatory agency of the federal government established in 1914 by a law that extended the federal responsibility of guarding against monopolistic practices by making unfair methods of competition unlawful.

**Flexibility** The speed with which changes can be made in an advertising schedule for a particular medium.

**Flighting** A method of scheduling in which a period of advertising is followed by a blank period, which in turn is followed by a renewed period of advertising, and so on. The objective of this wave strategy is to give advertisers with a limited budget the means of adding greater impact to their messages by concentrating them within a short period of time.

**Flush** Type set to a uniform width so that the text block is even at both the left and right edges. Flush left means even on the left edge; flush right, even on the right edge.

**Focus group interview** Technique in which researchers work with a group of five or six consumers to speed the interviewing process and perhaps generate more information as a result of their interaction with each other.

**Forcing methods** Sales promotion efforts designed to stimulate fast action at the retail level.

**Four-color process** A technique to reproduce illustrations in full color, using red, yellow, blue, and black in combination to obtain a full range of colors.

**Frame of reference** The cultural and social forces that have acted, and are always acting, on an individual and that can affect the way a person interprets an advertising message.

**Frequency** The number of times a medium can be used to present a message to an audience within a fixed amount of time. Radio is a high-frequency medium that can repeat an advertisement several times an hour; newspapers and magazines have lower frequencies.

**Full run** In transit advertising, having one car card in every vehicle or every train car of the transit system.

**Full-service agency** Organization that provides complete service for advertisers, including copywriting, art, market research, media analysis and scheduling, and the services of creative people in producing print ads and radio and television commercials.

**Gaze motion**  The movement of a reader's eyes.

**Genuinely new**  Term describing a product entirely different from older products of the same type or from older ways of doing something.

**Gravure**  A printing technique in which the image is etched into the plate with acid. The grooves so made retain ink, which is then transferred to the paper.

**Gross audience**  The total number of people exposed to a medium without regard to repeated counting of individual members.

**Gross impressions**  The sum figure, used to describe the entire audience delivered by a media plan.

**Gross rating point (GRP)**  An index figure that represents 1 percent of the total audience of radio or television within a specified market or geographical area. Advertisers use it to measure the weight of an advertising campaign in specific markets.

**G-R rating**  Measurement by Gallup & Robinson of readers' recall of sales messages, using three levels of rating: (1) the PNR score, which gives the percentage of readers who proved they remembered the ad by describing it; (2) a measure of the amount of the advertisement's sales message that readers can recall; and (3) the Favorable Buying Attitude score, which measures the message's persuasive power.

**Half run**  In transit advertising, having one car card in half of a transit line's vehicles.

**Halftone screen**  A screen of glass or film with fine black lines crosshatched to form boxes or dots of clear space through which halftone art is photographed to produce the gradations of light and dark of the original photograph or wash drawing.

**Horizontal cooperative advertising**  A common advertising effort by a trade association or group of competing companies to stimulate primary demand for the products of the entire industry or to influence government and public opinion attitudes.

**Horizontal publications**  Industrial publications focusing on subjects of common interest to individuals in many different industries who hold similar job functions (Cf. *Vertical publications.*)

**Hotelvision**  A closed-circuit television system that transmits movies and other special programs to the rooms of guests.

**House agency**  The advertising unit of a company set up as a separate entity and granted recognition and the agency commission.

**Industrial advertising**  The promotion of goods and services used in the manufacture and marketing of other products and services.

**Innovators**  Those few consumers who are willing to take risks and try a new product as soon as it reaches the market.

**Insertion order**  Instruction issued by an agency specifying the particular date and space, or time and position, for each advertisement or commercial within the terms of a contract.

**Inserts**  Advertisements of one page or more that are prepared and printed by the advertiser or publisher and then bound into the magazine by the publisher.

**Institutional advertising**  Advertising intended to sell the consumer reasons for patronizing a firm other than for the products or services it sells.

**Island half**  An advertising space 2 columns wide by 7 1/2 inches deep. It may in some instances carry a slightly higher rate because it is usually surrounded by editorial material and therefore offers improved visibility.

**Italics**  Versions of regular type faces that have been slanted to the right.

**Junior panel**  A 6-sheet outdoor advertising poster used where space is not available for the full-size one.

**Justify**  In printing, to make lines of copy equal in length by adding extra space between words or letters.

**Laggards**  Consumers who are extremely conservative about adopting new products and who tend to remain rooted in past practice.

**Lanham Act**  The Federal Trade Mark Act of 1946, which defines and regulates trademarks and their registration and use.

**Late majority**  Consumers who need considerable peer pressure to stimulate them to adopt a new product.

**Layout**  The arrangements of elements in a printed advertisement—the headline, the illustration, the body copy, the subsidiary illustrations, the border, and the logotype.

**Leading**  Extra space added between lines of copy.

**Letterpress**  A printing process in which the raised surface of type is inked and paper pressed against the surface so that the matter to be printed is transferred to the paper.

**Life style**  A distinctive pattern of activities, interests, and opinions that often cannot be deduced from other demographic data.

**Line drawings**  Pen-and-ink drawings that show a product's features without tonal gradations.

**Linotype**  A keyboard-operated machine that sets solid lines or slugs of metal type.

**List broker**  A person who acts as rental agent for those who own lists of names.

**List house**  An organization that compiles lists of names (generally business lists) and sells them to advertisers.

**Logotype**  A representation of the brand name or trade name in an advertisement. Also used to designate the company name that appears at the bottom of its print advertisements. Often abbreviated to *logo.*

**Loose**  A term describing illustrations, such as those for high fashion, that are drawn in a somewhat imprecise way to give readers only a suggestion, not the details, of the product.

**Loss leader**  An item of merchandise that a retailer offers at a reduced price, often below cost (hence the term), in order to attract customers to the store, with the idea that customers coming in to buy the leader will buy other items at regular prices.

**Make-good**  A rerun of an advertisement, made in the first available issue by a publication that has made a mistake in an ad or inserted an incorrect ad.

**Make or buy**  The choice a company makes between whether to buy the components it needs from its suppliers or to produce them itself.

**Marginally new**  A term used to identify the degree of newness of a type of product that is changed merely by adding an ingredient or modifying a design.

**Market**  People with the desire for a product, the willingness to buy it, and the ability to pay for it. A market may be an industry, the government, schools, farmers, etc.

**Marketing concept**  The concept that every facet

of an organization selling goods and services should be dedicated to satisfying the wants of prospective customers.

**Marketing mix** The group of decisions on the product, the price, the channels of distribution, and promotional activities that are within the control of the producer.

**Marketing research** A systematic seeking out of facts related to a specific marketing problem. It is concerned with nonrecurring problems and is conducted on a project-by-project basis.

**Market potential** The ability of a market to absorb a specific volume of product sales.

**Market segment** Logical, identifiable, and reasonably homogeneous submarkets into which a target market is divided in order to direct the marketing effort most efficiently, with a minimum of wasted time, effort, and money.

**Mat** An inexpensive duplicate of an engraving made by pressing it into a mold resembling a piece of stiff cardboard. Newspapers that receive the mat can pour molten metal to form a stereotype.

**Matched color** A color that is not standard with a publication but is matched to the advertiser's specifications.

**Mechanical** A layout with all the parts carefully pasted into position and ready for reproduction.

**Media mix** The combination of media in which a company chooses to place its advertising message to achieve the best possible balance.

**Medium (plural, media)** A vehicle that conveys information or entertainment to the general public, such as a newspaper, a magazine, radio, or television. It may also be used for advertising.

**Membership reference groups** Groups, to which a person automatically belongs because of sex, race, income, age, and marital status, that can influence the way a person interprets an advertising message.

**Merchandiser** A point-of-purchase display that stores self-service goods.

**Microfiche** A sheet of microfilm, about six inches long and four inches wide, on which many pages of printed material appear in reduced form.

**Milline rate** An index developed by advertisers as a standard of comparison to help them make comparisons between newspapers with unequal circulations. The formula is:

$$\frac{\text{line rate} \times 1,000,000}{\text{actual circulation}}$$

**Mini-cams** Hand-held video cameras with portable recorders.

**Motivation research** The application of techniques of psychology, sociology, and anthropology by motivation researchers to attempt to explain what makes consumers react to various products and different appeals.

**MRO** Maintenance, repair, and operating supplies, which are consumed during the manufacturing process but do not become part of the finished product.

**Narrowcasting** The manner in which radio is segmented into numerous groups of listeners, each with its favorite types of music and program format.

**National advertising** Advertising placed and paid for by the manufacturer of the product advertised.

**National Advertising Review Board (NARB)** A board, of 50 members, established in 1971 by the advertising industry to police deception and bad taste in advertising.

**National brand**   A term generally used to refer to a manufacturer's brand.

**Network radio**   A group of radio stations permanently connected by telephone lines, making it possible for programming and advertising to be broadcast simultaneously over all the stations in the network.

**New buy**   A purchase from a supplier with whom the company has not previously done business.

**Objective, or task, method**   A method of determining the advertising budget by stating marketing objectives and determining how much must be spent to achieve these goals.

**Offset**   A printing process, also called offset lithography, in which a grained plate of aluminum or zinc prints on a rubber roller, which in turn prints on paper.

**Omnibus ad**   A storewide retail advertisement that features items from many different departments.

**100 showing**   A basic unit of sale often used in outdoor advertising. It indicates that a message will appear on as many panels as needed in a given market to provide a daily exposure equal to 100 percent of that market population.

**Open rate**   The highest newspaper rate quoted to an advertiser.

**Optical center**   A point, about three-fifths from the bottom of an advertisement, to which the eye seems naturally attracted and to which the designer tries to give a pivotal position.

**Package house**   An independent movie-producing company that creates and produces televi-

sion shows ranging from a single special to an entire series.

**Package inserts**   Advertising circular packed with a product.

**Package plan**   A plan broadcast stations offer advertisers that represents a number of spots broadcast within a seven-day period on a run-of-station schedule. The commercial may be scheduled at whatever time is most convenient for the station.

**Paid circulation**   The number of readers who buy subscriptions to a publication.

**Paint**   Walls or bulletin board structures on which advertising copy is reproduced by painting directly on the surface.

**Panel**   A group of people who represent cross sections of the entire population and provide a continuous source of information about consumer purchase behavior.

**Participations**   Commercial time on one program divided among a number of different advertisers in thirty- and sixty-second units. The announcements are made within the program instead of between programs at station-break time.

**Per-unit assessment**   Same as unit-of-sales method.

**Percentage-of-sales method**   A method of determining the advertising budget by taking a specific percentage of sales of a product and applying that sum to advertising.

**Photo offset**   See *Offset*.

**Pica**   A unit of measurement in printing, equal to 12 points or 1/6 inch.

**Plants**   Outdoor advertising companies that sell and install, or "post," the available locations.

**Plant operator**   A company that owns or leases the land or locations on which outdoor advertising structures are erected, builds and maintains the structures, and operates the trucks and other equipment necessary for mounting the posters, painting the displays, or installing the spectaculars.

**Point** Basic unit of measurement used to specify type. There are 72 points to the inch.

**POP** Point-of-purchase promotional material located in, at, or on retail stores and designed, produced, and supplied by national advertisers.

**Positioning** The place a product occupies in a prospect's mind in relation to the competition—its quality, value, shape, price, and function as compared to those of competing products.

**Poster** An advertising message that is posted on a structure built for that purpose. The original poster was one sheet of paper, 28 inches by 41 inches. Several "one-sheets" can be combined to make larger posters to fit different frames.

**Premiums** Merchandise that is offered in addition to, or in combination with, an advertiser's product for the purpose of attracting (and selling) people who do not usually buy the advertiser's product or who do not buy it very often.

**Pride foods** Cake mixes or similar foods that the homemaker prepares and that generate compliments.

**Primary data** Firsthand information, collected according to plan by a company, generally for its own private use, by observational or survey methods, such as personal interviews, mail surveys, diaries, telephone interviews, and panels.

**Primary demand** Demand for a type of product.

**Prime time** The most popular television-viewing time between the hours of 7:30 and 11 P.M., every day of the week.

**Principal register** The place where a trademark is registered under the provisions of the Lanham Act. Permanent legal right to a mark is acknowledged after it is in the register without challenge for five years.

**Private brand** A brand marketed by a wholesaler or retailer.

**Process materials** Raw materials used in manufacturing, specified by common standards.

**Product** A good or service that an individual or an organization buys in order to obtain a measure of satisfaction.

**Product life cycle** Stages in a product's life comparable to those people go through: introductory stage (infancy), a period of vigorous growth (youth), the maintenance of a relatively stable market (maturity), and a period when the market share of a product shows signs of decline (old age).

**Product promotion campaign** A campaign set up with the intention of selling the product to make it more desirable than competitive products.

**Production house** A company with elaborate facilities for preparing sets and costumes and photographing any kind of commercial.

**Professional advertising** Advertising directed to professionals, such as doctors, dentists, architects, lawyers, engineers, accountants, and teachers.

**Promotional mix** The combination of advertising, publicity, personal selling, and sales promotion that a company chooses for the purpose of increasing its sales and/or profits.

**Psychographics** The development of psychological profiles of several different types of "typical" consumers and their life styles to explain and predict consumer behavior when demographic and socioeconomic analyses are not sufficient.

**Public service advertising** Advertising intended to sell an idea about a social problem: for instance, to offer citizens free legal assistance, to remind them to "help prevent forest fires," or to ask them to conserve energy.

**Purchasing decision** The decision of a consumer to buy a brand and actually try it.

**Puff** Exaggerated commendation. The generous use of such words as *the finest, the best, the most popular*, to puff out an advertiser's claims.

**Puffery** Exaggerated praise in an advertisement.

**Pull strategy** The stimulation of demand for a product by directing advertising to consumers, rather than to dealers, in order to attract or pull customers into retail outlets.

**Push strategy** A manufacturer's effort to stimulate sales through retailers who, because of the potential for extra profits or because of some other beneficial arrangement with the manufacturer, will feature or push a product.

**Rate base** The circulation that is guaranteed by the publisher and on which the publisher's advertising rates are determined.

**Rate of adoption** A measurement of how long it takes for a new product to be adopted.

**Raw materials** Basic commodities that have undergone no manufacture, or only such processing as is necessary to store or transport them.

**Reach** The number of people who tuned in at least once during a specified period of time.

**Reader service card** A postage-paid postcard bound into a magazine. It is returned by readers, who circle numbers on the card corresponding to advertised products or services of interest to them. The publisher forwards the inquiries to the advertisers.

**Reassurance value** The postpurchase impact of advertising that provides the consumer with a reaffirmation of values that induced the purchase and reassures the consumer that the purchase was a wise one.

**Recognition** Agreement by the media to accept advertising placed by an agency.

**Reference group** A group of people to whom a person looks for establishing his or her own attitudes or behavior, as, for example, members of work groups, school groups, or social groups who appear to have a life style worth emulating.

**Regional campaign** A campaign launched in a specific geographic area, often used by companies to test the strength of their advertising appeal or to get a feel for the market before investing the large sums of money a national campaign requires.

**Remembrance advertising** A useful item advertisers give to remind the recipients of the advertiser's company and/or product every time they use it. Usually the advertiser's name, address, and telephone and perhaps a short sales message or slogan are imprinted on the item. See *Specialty advertising*.

**Repro proof** Short for reproduction proof—a type proof printed on heavy, glossy paper.

**Retail advertising** Advertising by an organization

selling goods and services at retail to consumers.

**Robinson-Patman Act** An act of Congress, passed in 1936, which forbids price discrimination among competing retailers.

**Rotary plan** In outdoor advertising, a procedure that involves moving the same poster panel to different locations over the course of a year, or rotating two posters in different locations.

**Rotosection** The magazine section of a Sunday paper.

**Roughs** Full-size, but unfinished, sketches of designs for an advertisement.

**Sales potential** The portion or share of the total market that a company can reasonably hope to persuade to try its product.

**Sales promotion** The company's efforts to stimulate sales by methods other than media advertising or face-to-face selling.

**Sample** A small, but representative, portion of the total population selected for study.

**Scrambled merchandising** The practice of selling products that are not traditionally found in a certain kind of retail outlet, as drugstores offering hardware and garden supplies.

**Scratchboard** A clay-coated cardboard covered with black India ink on which a drawing is scratched with a stylus or knife to produce a drawing of extremely fine lines and details in white on a black background.

**Screen printing (silk-screen printing)** A printing technique in which ink is forced through a fine cloth or metal screen or some other porous material to be deposited on the surface to be printed.

**Secondary circulation** Pass-along readership by persons who do not subscribe to a publication, but receive it from the original subscriber or purchaser, or who pick up and read copies in such public places as barber and beauty shops, offices, waiting rooms, and libraries.

**Secondary data** Information from records that have already been compiled and published by someone else, such as the government, publishers, trade associations, or syndicated services.

**Selective demand** A demand for one particular brand.

**Selectivity** The ability to aim an advertising appeal at a distinct demographic market segment.

**Self-mailer** A direct-mail advertisement that does not require an envelope, the address of the prospect being printed or typed directly on the piece itself.

**Semispectacular** A type of outdoor advertisement, smaller and less elaborate than a spectacular, that uses flashers and mechanical devices to draw the public's attention.

**Serif** Short bars at the ends of the main stroke of each letter in certain typefaces.

**Service mark** A symbol or name used in the sale and advertising of services or products that are not individually packaged.

**SFX** Sound effects.

**Share-of-the-market method** Establishing an advertising budget by taking the budget of a company that already has a share of the market and matching or exceeding those figures.

**Sheet** An outdoor advertising poster, originally one sheet of paper 28 inches by 41 inches. Several sheets are combined to make larger posters to fit different frames.

**Sheet fed** In printing, paper fed to a press in cut sections.

**Shopping goods** Goods, such as women's apparel, men's ready-to-wear clothing, home furnishings, jewelry, and fabrics, for which consumers are willing to shop around, visiting several stores in order to compare price, quality, and style.

**Short channel** The route by which goods are transferred from producer to consumer with few steps.

**Short rate** A charge amounting to the difference between the contract rate and the rate actually earned. It is paid to a medium by an advertiser who fails to fulfill a contracted schedule.

**Silk-screen printing** See *Screen printing.*

**Slogan** A carefully polished group of words intended to be repeated by consumers verbatim and to be remembered by them with a favorable reaction.

**Slug** A line of type cast in one piece as a metal bar.

**Slug in** In vertical cooperative advertising, the placement by retailers of their own store logo or name on an advertisement supplied by the manufacturer of the products featured in the ad.

**SMSA** Standard Metropolitan Statistical Area, developed by the United States Census Bureau to help marketers define markets with a set of common terms.

**Snipes** Strips imprinted with names and addresses of local dealers that national advertisers can add to the bottom of billboard posters in various geographic locations.

**Space position value (SPV)** An index of a poster panel's visibility, based on the length of the approach, the speed of travel, the angle of the panel to the traffic, and its space relationship to adjacent panels.

**Spec** In typesetting, to specify or determine from samples shown in a type specimen sheet or book the type faces and sizes to be used so that copy will fit in the space available.

**Specialty advertising** Items such as calendars, pencils, pens, key rings, shopping bags, and memo pads that an advertiser gives to target prospects without charge and that repeatedly expose the prospect to the advertiser's name and message. See *Remembrance advertising.*

**Specialty goods** Goods, such as expensive wearing apparel, gourmet food products, high-fidelity components, cameras, home appliances, and automobiles, that are distinguished by the customer's insistence on purchasing a particular brand and willingness to shop at some inconvenience for that brand.

**Spectacular** An outdoor advertising display designed for a particular advertiser on a long-term contract, with lights, flashers, or a combination of flashing or moving electrical devices.

**Split run** The placement of two different ads in the same issue of a publication; some copies contain the first ad, and others the second. The purpose is to compare the appeals of the ads.

**Spot radio** Advertising broadcast on local radio stations in a geographic area.

**Square third** A one-third page of advertising space measuring 2 columns wide by 4 7/8 inches deep.

**Squeegee** A rubber blade used in screen printing to force ink through the screen.

**Starch rating** A measurement of reader recognition of individual advertisements that includes the percentages of those who merely noted the ad, those who associated the product with the company, and those who actually read most of the ad. Individual components of the ad are also rated.

**Statement stuffer** An advertising leaflet that is mailed to charge-account customers along with their monthly statement.

**Station posters** Posters displayed in and on stations of subways, bus lines, and commuter railroads.

**Stereotype** A duplicate of an original engraving formed by pouring molten type metal on a mat.

**Stock art** Inexpensive, ready-to-use art obtained from a company that maintains files of photographs or drawings illustrating a variety of subjects.

**Storyboard** A set of shapes resembling a television screen on which artists sketch the number and content of scenes they envision to convey a sales message.

**Supplemental register** A register for certain marks not eligible for entry in the Principal Register under the Federal Trade Mark Act of 1946.

**Tactical objectives** Short-range goals that will lead to the ultimate objective of an advertising campaign—profit through sales.

**Taillight spectacular** A display, 21 inches by 72 inches, carried on the rear exterior of a bus.

**Take** In television or movies, the filming of an individual scene.

**Take-ones** Perforated postcards or leaflets attached to a pad and fastened to the bottom or corner of a car card, so they are easily detached by passengers, who are invited to send for information or to take the leaflet home and read it more carefully.

**Target market** The part of the total market comprising the most likely prospects for a particular product—those with a need for the product, a willingness to buy it, and the ability to pay for it.

**Tear sheet** A copy of the page, cut or torn from the particular edition in which an advertisement appeared, sent to an advertiser as verification.

**Tempera** Opaque watercolor drawings used when bright colors or heightened realism is the desired effect.

**Test marketing** A technique of advertising and selling a product on a geographically limited basis. It enables an advertiser to judge the potential reception of the product and the effectiveness of the advertising approach.

**30-sheet poster** An outdoor advertising poster, usually consisting of 14 printed sheets.

**Three-sheet posters** Outdoor advertising mounted on walls of buildings, particularly in shopping areas, where they remind pedestrians of a product as close as possible to the point of purchase.

**Thumbnails** The first tentative ad designs, usually very small, that include rough approximations of all the elements that must be incorporated into an advertisement.

**Tight** A term describing illustrations, for items like furniture and machinery, that are drawn with great precision and detail.

**Tissues** Full-size sketches of the best design for an advertisement drawn on textured white tracing paper.

**Tombstone ads** Advertisements in the financial sections of newspapers, confined by law to basic statistical information.

**Tonnage ad** A retail advertisement that features one item stocked in large quantities at a special price.

**Total bus** All the exterior advertising on a bus.

**Total total bus** Advertising using the basic bus and the total bus.

**Trade advertising** Advertising aimed at retailers and wholesalers who buy products or services for resale.

**Trade character** Real or fictional people or animals used to identify products or product families.

**Trademark** A pictorial device, number, letter, or other symbol used to identify a product or product family, usually registered and protected by law.

**Trade name** A commercial name adopted by a company (much as an actor or musician adopts a stage name) that is more easily remembered by the public.

**Trade show** An exhibition of the products and services of a particular market or industry, with attendance usually restricted to members of the "trade."

**Traffic** The number of customers who visit a store to see and buy advertised merchandise.

**Traffic audit bureau** An organization that audits traffic circulation figures supplied by outdoor advertising plants and also gathers circulation data on its own.

**Trial purchase** A product bought by a consumer to learn whether or not the buyer wishes to continue purchasing it for regular use.

**24-sheet poster** Traditionally the most popular size of outdoor poster. It once required 24 separate sheets, but with today's larger printing presses now requires only 10 sheets.

**Unit-of-sales method** A variation of the percentage-of-sales method in which a specific number of dollars or cents for each unit is allocated to the advertising budget.

**Vertical cooperative advertising** Advertising in a local medium for which the manufacturer of a nationally advertised brand and the retailer share the cost.

**Vertical publications** Publications reaching persons in all job functions and levels of a single industry.

**Visualization** The presentation of advertising messages in their visual form.

**VO (voice over)** In television, when an actor's or announcer's voice is heard but the person is not seen.

**Want slip** Form used by store employees to record requested merchandise not in stock.

**Wash** Drawings made from India ink or black water color and mixed with varying amounts of water to produce shades from intense black to pale grey.

**Web-fed** In printing, paper fed to a press from a continuous roll.

**Wheeler-Lea Act** An act of Congress, passed in 1938, amending the Federal Trade Commission Act and expanding the responsibilities of the FTC to cover unfair and deceptive acts in commerce.

**Work print** In a television commercial, the best take of each scene to which the sound track is synchronized and special effects, title, and dissolves are added.

# index

A & P Food Stores, 291
A la carte advertising agencies, 77
AAAA color, 184
Account executive, 69, 70
Ad-lib, 382
Adjacencies, 228
Adoption, rate of, 322
Advertisers, 63—66
    advertising department, 65—66, 154,
        459—460
    advertising managers, 63—65
    financial capabilities of, 48
    100 leading, 15, 124—125
Advertising:
    art, *see* Art
    budgeting, *see* Budgeting
    business, *see* Advertisers;
        Advertising agencies;
        Advertising media; Industrial
        advertising; Trade advertising
    campaigns, *see* Advertising
        campaigns
    categories of, 50—57, 59
    copy for, *see* Copy
    criticisms of, 495—503
    decision to use, 48—49
    decisions, *see* Advertising media;
        Budgeting; Marketing
        intelligence
    defined, 3—5, 50—57, 59
    in future, *see* International
        advertising; Service economy
    history of, *see* Advertising history
    marketing foundations of, *see*
        Marketing foundations
    nonmedia, *see* Nonmedia
        advertising
    objectives of, 49—50
    policing of, 503—513
    in promotional mix, *see*
        Promotional mix

    retail, *see* Retail advertising
    -sales relationship, 118—119, 120,
        450
*Advertising Age,* 12*n*, 15, 275, 306
Advertising agencies, 66—80
    compensation of, 77, 79
    functions of, 72
    historical development of, 10—12,
        66
    innovations in business of, 72, 77
    organization of, 66, 69—72
    recognition of, 79—80
    top 50 (world), 519
    top 25 (U.S.), 67
Advertising campaigns, 415—439
    during Civil War, 10
    coordination with other
        promotional efforts, 426, 428
    corporate, 424, 425
    duration of, 420, 422
    horizontal cooperative advertising,
        424, 426, 427
    industrial, 480—481
    institutional, 424
    measuring results, 431—439
    media selection, 428, 430—431
    objectives, 50, 419—420
    planning, 416—423
    product life cycle and, 420
    product promotion, 424
    regional, 423—424
    repetition in, 422—423
    trade, 489—490
    types of, 423—426
Advertising Checking Bureau, Inc.,
    166—167, 463
Advertising Council, 503
Advertising department, 65—66, 154
    retail, 459—460
Advertising history, 6—18
    advertising agencies, 10—12, 66

    ancient marketplace, 6
    Great Depression, 13
    magazines, 10—11
    modern age, dawn of, 11—12
    newspapers, 7—9
    printed word, 7
    radio, 12—14, 18, 216
    sandwich men, 9
    space brokers, 10
    trade and craft guilds, 6—7
    World War II, 13—14, 18
Advertising manager, 63—65
Advertising media, 135—157
    broadcast, *see* Radio; Television
    categories of, 136
    creative strategy and, 328, 330
    defined, 135—136
    future, 536, 538
    international, 521—523
    measuring audience of, 144—147
    media mix, 147—149
    media planner, 149—152, 154
    nonmedia, *see* Nonmedia
        advertising
    outdoor, *see* Outdoor advertising
    people in, 154
    print, *see* Business publications;
        Farm publications; Magazines
        (consumer); Newspapers
    scope of, 80
    selection factors, 136, 138—143
    self-regulation, 509
    strategy, 136, 137
    transit, *see* Transit advertising
Advertising schedules, 456—459
*Advertising Small Business,* 448
Advertising specialties, 274—276
Agate line, 170—171
Agency of record, 66
Agree-disagree scale, 108
Agriculture, Department of, 304, 508

AIDA (Attention, Interest, Desire, Action), 350
Albrecht de Menninger, 7
Alexander's, 44
Alternate Gothic typeface, 392
AM radio, 216—217, 221
American Association of Advertising Agencies, 13, 184
*American Bar Association Journal,* 201
American Broadcasting Company, 221, 228
*American Dry Cleaner,* 201
American Express Co., 484
American Federation of Television and Radio Artists (AFTRA), 376n
American Home Products Corp., 12, 505
*American Journal of Cardiology, The,* 204
*American Laundry Digest,* 207
American Marketing Association, 3
American Medical Association, 534
American Motors Corp., 126, 234, 397
American Newspaper Publishers Association, 11, 66
American Tourister Luggage, 350
AMP Inc., 472
Ancient marketplace, 6
Ancillary advertising services, 83
Answer print, 380
Apparel products, 120
Appeal, development of, *see* Creative strategy
Approach, similarity of, 416
Arbitron Co., 140, 229, 233, 235
*Architectural Digest,* 201
Area of Dominant Influence (ADI), 235—236
Art, 357—384
    attention, 363
    color, 366

constraints, 363
design principles, 359—363
drawings, 369, 371, 372, 373
illustration, 357—374
layout, 358—366
paintings, 369, 371
photography, 369
readability, 363, 366
small space ads, 366, 367
stock, 371, 374
television commercial, 371, 375—383
Art directors, 69, 72
Art studios, 83
Artificially new products, 320
Asahi Kokoku-Sha, 519
Asahi Tsushin Advertising, 519
Aspiration reference groups, 320, 321
Association of National Advertisers, 13
Attention:
    as advertising objective, 49
    layout and, 363
Attitude, 322—323, 439
Attitude change, as advertising objective, 50
Audience:
    business publications, 192, 194
    cumulative, 150, 223, 226
    gross, 149, 150
    measurement of, 144—147
    newspaper, 165
    outdoor advertising, 248
    radio, 221, 223
    television, 226—229, 233—236
Audience ratings (television), 233—236
Audio-visual cassettes, 536
Audit Bureau of Circulations (ABC), 10, 169, 194
Awareness, 439
Ayer, N. W., ABH International, 12, 66, 67, 519

Babcock & Wilcox, 481
Bait-and-switch ad, 505
Balance:
    layout, 359, 364
    media mix, 148
*Barron's,* 195
Bates, Ted, & Co., 67, 519
BBDO International, 12, 67, 519
BCU (big close-up), 382
Beck-Ross Group, 221
Belding, Don, 36
Believability:
    of copy, 340
    of illustration, 367
Bell System, 56, 497
Benton & Bowles, 67, 519
Berg, Thomas L., 30n
Bernbach, William, 128
*Better Homes & Gardens,* 176
Big ticket items, 456
Bill Communications, Inc., 174n
Billboards, 70, 242—243
"Bingo card," 204
Blackett, Sample, Hummert, 12
Blair, D. L., 76
Bleed page advertisement, 182
Blind headline, 341, 342
Blitz schedule, 152
Bodoni, Giambattista, 389
Bodoni typeface, 391, 393
Bold typeface, 391
*Bon Appetit,* 179
Book typeface, 391
*Boston Globe,* 167
*Boston Weekly News-Letter, The,* 9
Boutique agencies, 72, 77
Bozell & Jacobs International, 67, 519
Brainstorming, 330
Brand loyalty, 313, 441
Brand names, 22, 287—296
    attributes of, 294—295

choosing, 293—294
differentiation of, 48—49
family names, 295
legalities, 291
protection of, 295—296
vs. trademarks, 288, 291
Break-outs, 273
Bridge, 383
Bristol-Myers Co., 288
British-American Tobacco Co., Ltd., 241
Broadcast media, *see* Radio; Television
Budgeting, 115—132
advertising-sales relationship, 118—119, 120, 124—125
controllers and, 117, 118
costs included in, 130—131
decision to advertise and, 49
defined, 116
empirical method, 127—128
management philosophy and, 116—117
marketing executives and, 117—118
media mix and, 148
media selection and, 138
objective (or task) method, 121—122, 449
percentage of sales method, 122, 124—126, 128, 449
product, influence of, 119, 121
retail advertising, 449—451
share-of-the-market method, 122, 124
timing, 129—130
unit-of-sale method, 126—129
*Buffalo Evening News*, 140
Bulk mail, 274
Burke Marketing Research, Inc., 97
Burlington Industries, 34
Burnett, Ed, Consultants, Inc., 271

Burnett, Leo, Co., 67, 70, 186, 323, 519
Buros, O., 108*n*
Business advertising, 52, 467—492
*See also* Industrial advertising; Trade advertising
Business Publication Audit (BPA), 194
*Business Publication Rates and Data*, 191, 194, 205
Business publications, 80, 136, 140, 191—206, 212, 481
advertising volume of, 137
audience for, 192, 194
buying power, 192
buying space in, 204
general, 194—195
industrial, 196—201
institutional, 201
media decisions for advertisers, 204, 206
professional, 201, 203, 204
rates, 204, 205
trade, 201, 202
*Business Week*, 187, 194, 535
Busorama, 255
Buying influences, 481
Buying power, 192
Buying procedures, media, 152, 154, 155

Cable television, 225, 536
Cahners Publishing Co., 481
Cahners Research, 430
Cairo typeface, 392
Caledonia typeface, 391, 393
California Raisin Advisory Board, 417—418
Campbell-Ewald, 67, 519
Campbell-Mithum, 519
Campbell Soup Co., 53, 301

Canada, 527
Canada Dry Corp., 289
Caples, John, 280
Car cards, 254—255
Card rate, 184
Caxton, William, 7
Cease-and-desist order, 504
Celanese Corp., 57
Center spread, 182
Certification marks, 298
Channels of distribution, 26
Checking copies, 166—167
Chesebrough-Pond's Inc., 16—17
Chevrolet Motor Co., 12, 13
*Chicago Sun-Times*, 167
*Chicago Tribune*, 167, 170, 513
Chilton Research, 97
Chuo Senko, 519
Chrysler Corp., 126, 295
Circulars, 265—266
Circulation, 144, 147
business publications, 194
direct mail, 268, 270
magazines, 144, 180
newspapers, 144, 167
outdoor advertising, 248
radio, 221, 223
television, 226
Circulation department, 154
Civil Aeronautics Board, 508
Civil War, 10
Class magazines, 176
Class selectivity, 140
Class stores, 443
Clock spectaculars, 255, 258
Close-up, 383
Closing date, 165
*Club Management*, 201
Coach Leatherware, 319
Coca-Cola Co., 52, 300, 315, 517
Coded addresses, 50

Coined words, as brand names, 294
Cold type, 398
Colgate-Palmolive Co., 314
Collective marks, 297−298
Colonial advertising, 9
Color, emotions and, 366
Color reproduction, 404−410
    magazines, 184
    newspapers, 172−173
Columbia Broadcasting Co., 228
Columbia Broadcasting System, 216,
    221
Combination rates, 174
Combined Communications Corp.,
    253
Comic sections, 80
Commerce, Department of, 93, 94, 448
Commercial Script typeface, 392
Commission system, 77
Communications Act of 1934, 507
Company founder's name, as brand
    name, 293
Competition, 34−35, 37−39, 500−501
Competitive strategy, 315
Component parts, 471, 472
Comprehensive (comp), 359, 361
Compton Advertising, 67, 519
Computers:
    in direct-mail advertising, 272, 273
    in media selection, 152
Concentration, 148, 150−151
Cone, Fairfax M., 36, 58, 352
Conference Board, Inc., The, 21
Consumer advertising, 52
Consumer goods, 23−25
Consumer Magazine and Farm
    Publication Rates and Data, 168,
    206
Consumer magazines, see Magazines
    (consumer)
Consumer perceptions, 318−328

attitudes, customs, and habits,
    322−323
diffusion process, 320−322
positioning, 326−329
psychographics, 323, 326
reference groups, 318, 320, 324
Consumer Product Safety Agency, 508
Consumer Product Safety
    Commission (CPSC), 304
Consumer tastes, 30−31
Container Corp., 299
Contests, 13
Continuity, need for, 523, 525
Contract rates, 171
Controlled circulation, 194
Controllers, 117
Convenience goods, 23
Cooke, Jay, 10
Cooperative advertising, 165
    horizontal, 424, 426, 427
    trade, 490−491
    vertical, 460−463
Copy, 335−353
    direct mail, 350, 353
    fact finding, 336, 338
    function of, 336−340
    importance of, 335−336
    industrial, 478−480
    magazines, 340−344
    newspapers, 344−347
    outdoor advertising, 353
    radio, 347−348, 349
    retail, 459
    style, 338−340
    television, 348, 350, 351, 352
    writing rules, 340
    See also Art; Printing processes;
        Typography
Copy block, 363
Copy testing, 109
Corporate advertising, 424, 425

Corrective advertising, 505, 507
Cost, as media selection factor, 138,
    148
Cost effectiveness, 138
Cost of goods, advertising and,
    495−498
Cost per thousand (CPM), 138, 184,
    187
Council of Better Business Bureaus,
    509
Coupons, 50, 439
Coverage, 144−146
    outdoor advertising, 248, 249
    radio, 144, 146, 221
    television, 144, 145, 226
CPC Instrument, 232
CPM (cost per thousand), 138, 184,
    187
Craft guilds, 6−7
Crawl, 383
Creamer Inc., 519
Creative department, 69, 70, 72
Creative strategy, 311−331
    brainstorming, 330
    consumer attitudes, customs, and
        habits, 322−323
    consumer categories, 322
    consumer perceptions, 318−328
    diffusion process, 320, 322
    media considerations, 328, 330
    positioning, 326−329
    product features, 313−318
    psychographics, 105−106, 108, 323,
        326
    purchasing decision, 312−313
    reference groups, 318, 320, 324
Criers, 6, 7
Criticisms of advertising, 495−503
Cross-fade, 383
Cuisinarts, Inc., 30
Cultural differences, 518, 520

Cultural influences, 31
Cumulative audience, 150, 223, 226
Cunningham, John Philip, 141
Cunningham & Walsh, Inc., 141,
    377—379, 519
Curtis Advertising Code, 503
Curtis Publishing Co., 11, 503
Customs, consumer, 322
Cut-to, 383
Cuts, 404

Dai-Ichi Advertising, 519
Dai-Ichi Kikaku, 519
Daiko Advertising, 518, 519
Daily newspapers, 167, 168, 376—377
Dancer-Fitzgerald-Sample, 12, 67, 375,
    519
Dane, Maxwell, 128
D'Arcy-MacManus & Masius, 67,
    107—108, 519
Datsun, 396
Deadlines, 165
Deception, 505
Della Femina, Jerry, 327
Della Femina, Travisano and Partners,
    327
Demand:
    primary, 48, 57, 424, 426
    selective, 47
Demographic editions, 184
Demographics, 31—32, 33, 53, 91, 92,
    144, 178
Denby, Emanuel, 108n
*Dental Management*, 201
Dentsu Inc., 518, 519, 537
Depth interviewing, 105
Design principles, 359—363
*Detroit Free Press*, 167
*Detroit News*, 167
Dial Media, 232

Diary method of survey, 100
Dichter, Ernest, 106, 521
Dictionary words, as brand names,
    294
Die cuts, 273, 274
Diffusion process, 320—322
Digest-size magazines, 182
Diorama displays, 255, 258
Direct advertising, 265—276
    advertising specialties, 274—276
    direct mail, *see* Direct-mail
        advertising
    external house organs, 276
    premiums, 13, 276, 277, 428
Direct-mail advertising, 265—274
    advantages of, 266—268
    circulation, 268, 270
    copy, 350, 353
    forms of, 273—274
    limitations of, 268
    mailing lists, 270—273
    postal regulations and, 274
    retailer's use of, 453—454
    volume of, 137, 266
Direct Mail/Marketing Association,
    508
Direct-response advertising, 454—455
Directories, 255, 259, 260
Disassociative reference groups, 320
Displays, point-of-purchase (POP), 278
Dissolve (DS), 383
Distress merchandise, 451
Distribution channels, 26
Distributor brands, 291
Diversity, 498
Doctor blade, 402
Dom typeface, 392
Double run, 254
"Double-your-money-back" offers, 13
Dow Chemical U.S.A., 211
Doyle, Ned, 128

Doyle Dane Bernbach, Inc., 50, 67, 128,
    489—490, 519
Drawings, 369, 371, 372, 373
*Drug Topics*, 448
Drukker Newspapers, Inc., 175
Du Pont Corp., 296, 500
*Dun's Review*, 194
Duplicates, 404
Duplication, 149
Durability of message, 143
Dwiggins, W. A., 393

Early adopters, 322
Earned rates, 171
Eastman Kodak Co., 526
Economic conditions, 32
Economies of scale, 496, 498
ECU (extreme close-up), 382
Editorial department, 154
Editorial environment, media
    selection and, 143
Egyptian typeface, 392
*Electronic Business*, 196
*Electronic Component News*, 196
*Electronic Design*, 196
*Electronic News*, 196
*Electronics*, 196
Electros, 404
Eller, Karl, 253
Emphasis, typefaces and, 394
Empirical budgeting method,
    127—128
End cards, 257
*Engineering News-Record*, 201
England, 8, 9, 522, 527
English Mica Co., The, 468
Engravers, 83
Engravings, 404
Environmental Protection Agency
    (EPA), 304, 508

Equipment, major, 468, 469, 471
Erickson Co., 487
Esty, William, Co., 67, 519
Ethnic newspapers, 170
Eurocom, 518, 519
Evaluation of advertising, 431–439
*Executive Housekeeper*, 207
"Expense" school of thought, 116
Exterior bus displays, 255, 257
External house organs, 276
Exxon Corp., 15, 125, 477

Fact finding, 337, 338
Fade in, 383
Fade out, 383
Fair Packaging and Labeling Act of
    1962, 507
Family names, 295
*Family Weekly*, 170
Fantasy story commercials, 348
*Farm Journal*, 208, 210
Farm publications, 56, 80, 136, 140,
    206, 208–212
  advertising volume of, 137
  national, 208, 210
  regional, 210
  specialized, 210
  state, 210
*Fast Service*, 193
Federal Communications Commission
    (FCC), 216, 304, 369, 507
Federal Deposit Insurance
    Corporation, 508
Federal Home Bank Board, 508
Federal Reserve Board, 508
Federal Trade Commission, 37, 225,
    504–505, 507
Federal Trade Commission Act of
    1914, 504
Fee arrangements, 79

Fee system, 80
Ferriter, Roger, 306
Ferriter, Roger, Inc., 306
Fictitious names, as brand names, 294
Field sales force, 426
Filmed commercials, 380–381
Financial capabilities of advertiser, 48
First-class mail, 274
Fisher-Price Toys, 486
Flash typeface, 392
Flat rates, 171
Flexibility, media selection and, 143
Flighting, 152, 236
Floor displays, 255
Flush left and right, 394
FM radio, 217
Focus, layout, 363
Focus-group interviews, 105
Folger Coffee Co., 377–379
Food & Drug Administration (FDA),
    304
Foote, Cone & Belding, 36, 67, 352,
    436–437, 519
Foote, Emerson, 36
Forced-choice scale, 109
Forcing methods, 426, 428
Ford, Henry, 21
Ford Motor Co., 15, 21, 126, 295, 420,
    424, 500
Foreign-language papers, 167, 170
Foreign words, as brand names, 294
Formal balance, 364
*Fortune*, 194
Foss America Inc., 470
Four-color process, 404
Frames of reference, 318
France, 527
Fraud, 507
Frequency, 148
  media selection and, 143
  television, 236

Frequency contracts, 184
Frequency modulation, 217
Frequency rate, 9
Frey, Albert W., 298n
Full run, 254
Full-service agency, 72
Futura typeface, 392, 393

Gallup, George, 13, 14, 434
Gallup & Robinson (G-R), 432, 439
Garden Way, Inc., 346
Gardner-Denver Co., 469, 480
Gary Farn, Ltd., 346
Gaze motion, 363, 365
*Gazette*, 9n
Geersgross Advertising Ltd., 522
General business publications,
    194–195
General Foods Corp., 37, 288, 342
General Mills, 12
General Motors Corp., 107–108, 126,
    295, 479, 520
Genuinely new products, 320
Geographical selectivity, 140–142, 243
Georgia-Pacific, 425
GGK, 519
Gillette Co., 517
Ginsu Products Inc., 454–455
*Globe-Democrat*, 169
Godfrey, Arthur, 12, 14
*Good Housekeeping*, 49, 176, 336
Gothic typeface, 391–392
Goudy, F. W., 393
Goudy Old Style typeface, 393
Goudy typeface, 391, 397
*Gourmet*, 29
Government, *see* United States
    government
*Grange News, The*, 210

*Graphic Arts Monthly*, 196, 199, 200, 201
Gravure, 400, 402
Great Depression, 13
Grey Advertising, Inc., 67, 70*n*, 519
Groskin Group, 221
Gross audience, 149, 150
Gross impressions, 236
Gross rating points (GRPs):
    outdoor advertising, 248, 259
    radio, 223
    television, 226, 233
Ground waves, 216
Group W Radio, 222
GRT Corp., 232
Gunther, John, 36
Gutter bleed, 182

Habits, consumer, 322
Hakuhodo Inc., 519
Half run, 254
Halftones, 402−404
Hall, Adrienne, 502
Halterman, Jean, 298*n*
Hand composition, 398
Hattori, K., & Co. Ltd., 232
Headlines, 341−346, 390
Health, Education & Welfare (HEW),
    Department of, 304, 507
Heinz, H. J., Co., 48, 295
Hewett, Wendell C., 244*n*
HiFi, 172−173
Hilton Hotels, 481
Historical names, as brand names, 293
Hoffman-York, 68
*Holiday*, 108
Home Testing Institute, 103
*Hoosier Farmer*, 210
Hopkins, Claude C., 36

Horizontal cooperative advertising,
    424, 426, 427
Horizontal publications, 196
*Hospitals*, 201, 207−208
*Hotel & Motel Management*, 201
Hotelvision, 538
House agencies, 79−80
*House Beautiful*, 181
*Houston Magazine*, 142, 183
Hower, Ralph M., 66*n*

IDs, 225
Illuminated dioramas, 258
Illustration, 357−374
    drawings, 369, 371, 372, 373
    function of, 357−358
    in layout, 358−366
    paintings, 369, 371
    photography, 369
    stock art, 371, 374
    subjects for, 366−371
Image builders, 457
Impact, 243
"Impact" method, 13
In-between store, 445
Industrial advertising, 53−55,
    468−481
    campaigns, 480−481
    classifications of industrial goods,
        468−474
    copy, 478−480
    defined, 468
    importance of, 475−476
    industrial buying process, 471, 475
    objectives of, 476, 478
    schedules, 481
*Industrial Bulletin*, 196
Industrial goods, 23
    classifications of, 468−474

*Industrial Maintenance and Plant
    Operation*, 196
Industrial publications, 196−201
Industrial Revolution, 10
Informal balance, 364
Information, advertising as, 501−503
Initials, as brand names, 294
Innovation, 501−502
Innovators, 322
Insertion orders, 154, 155
Inserts:
    business publication, 204
    direct mail, 234, 269
    magazine, 184
Institutional advertising, 56−57, 59,
    424, 452
Institutional publications, 201
Institutions, as brand names, 294
Interest, as advertising objective, 49
Intermarco-Farner, 519
Intermountain Network, 221
Internal secondary data, 93
International advertising, 517−528
    advertising climate, 525−527
    challenge for, 527
    global expenditures, 524−525
    need for continuity, 523, 525
    problems of, 518, 520−523
    top 50 agencies, 519
International Business Machines
    Corp., 328, 480−481, 482
"Investment" school of thought,
    116−117
*Iowa Farm Bureau Spokesman*, 210
Island half, 182
Italics, 392−393

Japan, 518, 519, 521, 527
Job shop, 399
Jones and Lamson Machine Co., 481

Judgment sample, 104
Junior panel, 244
Justification of lines, 394

Kaley, P. Dudley, 192
*Kansas City Star/Times*, 167
*Kansas Farm Bureau News*, 210
Karnak typeface, 392
Keller-Crescent Co., 519
Kellogg Co., 528
Kennedy, John E., 36
Kenyon & Eckhardt, 67, 519
Kerlinger, Fred N., 108n
Ketchum, MacLeod & Grove, 67, 519
Kickbacks, 80
Kikkoman Shoyu Co. Ltd., 413
Kimberly-Clark Corp., 288
King-size display, 255
Knowledge, 439

Labeling, regulation of, 507
Laggards, 322
Lanham Act of 1946, 291
Lap dissolve, 383
Lasker, Albert D., 36, 58
Late majority, 322
Layout, 358—366
Leading, 394—395
Leber Katz Partners, 519
Legal climate, 32
Letterpress, 400
Letters, 273
Letters of the alphabet, as brand
    names, 294
Lever Bros., 295, 328
Life cycle of product, 45, 315, 420
Line drawings, 371
Linotype process, 398
Lintas, Hamburg, 526

Lippincott & Margulies, 307
List broker, 270
List houses, 270
Literature directory, 259
Lithography, 400, 401
Live commercials, 382
Logotypes, 298
Long copy, 344
Lord & Taylor, 444
Lorillard, 429—430
*Los Angeles Times*, 167, 170
Loss leader, 428
Lubalin, Herb, 306
Luck, David J., 103n

Maas, Jane, 330n
*McCall's*, 177
McCann, H. K., Co., 12, 487
McCann, Harrison King, 487
McCann-Erickson, 12, 67, 487, 519
McGarry, Edmund D., 89
McGraw-Hill Laboratory of Advertising
    Performance, 481
Macy's, 452
Magazines (business and farm), *see*
    Business publications; Farm
    publications
Magazines (consumer), 80, 136, 143,
    175—189
  advantages of, 176, 178, 180
  advertising volume of, 137
  buying space in, 152, 180
  characteristics of, 147
  circulations, 144, 180
  comparison of, 184, 187
  copy, 340—344
  demographic editions, 184
  in foreign countries, 523
  general interest, 138, 140
  historical development of

  advertising in, 10—11
  price to consumer, effect of
    advertising on, 498
  rates, 180, 182—184
  retail advertising in, 451
  seasonal concentration, 151
  special interest, 140
  types of, 176
Magic Mountain Tea Company, 153
Mail, *see* Direct-mail advertising
Mail survey, 99—100
Mailing lists, 270—273
Major equipment, 468, 469, 471
Make or buy, 475
Make-good ad, 166
Man-Nen-Sha, 519
Marcoa Direct Advertising, Inc.,
    74—75
Marconi, Guglielmo, 216
Marginally new products, 320
Margulies, Walter P., 304
Market potential, 49, 90
Market research organization, 83
Market structure, 518
Market testing, 218
Marketing, defined, 22
Marketing concept, 21
Marketing executives, 117—118
Marketing foundations, 21—39
  conditions affecting success,
    28—39
  marketing defined, 22
  marketing mix, 22—27
  markets defined, 27
  target markets, *see* Target markets
Marketing intelligence, 89—111
  copy testing, 109
  media research, 109—110
  motivation research, 104—106,
    108—110
  objectives for, 90

observational method, 96, 98
primary data, 96 – 104, 448 – 449
psychographics, 105 – 106, 108, 323, 326
role of, 90 – 92
sales potential, 90 – 92
sampling, 100 – 104
secondary data, 92 – 96, 448
survey method, 98 – 100
Marketing mix, 22 – 27
Marketing objectives, 44
Marketing plan, 44 – 48
Marketing research, 90
*Marketing Strategies* (Kaley), 192
Markets:
  defined, 27
  nature of, 45, 46
  target, *see* Target markets
Marschalk Co., 519
Marsteller, Inc., 67, 199
Marsteller, William A., 199
Mass circulation magazines, 176
Matched colors, 184
Matrix-type organization, 70 – 72
Mats, 404
Maximil index, 174
Mechanicals, 398
Media, *see* Advertising media
Media Basics, Inc., 77
Media-buying services, 77
Media department, 69, 70, 72
Media exposure diary, 100
Media mix, 147 – 149
Media planner, 149 – 152, 154
Media research, 109 – 110
*Medical Economics*, 201
Medium, 135 – 136
Memphis typeface, 392
Menzies, Hugh D., 37n
Mercedes-Benz, 345
*Miami Herald/News*, 167

Michigan Seamless Tube Company, 303 – 304
Microfiche, 536
Middle Ages, 6
Miles Laboratories, 261
Miller Brewing Co., 325
*Milwaukee Journal/Sentinel*, 167
Mini-cams, 382
Minimil index, 174
Minnesota Mining and Manufacturing, 288
Minor equipment, 470, 471
Mistral typeface, 392
Mobil Oil Corp., 4
Models, 369
*Modern Healthcare*, 201, 207
Monotype, 398
Montgomery Ward, 451
Motivation research, 104 – 106, 108 – 110
Movement, layout, 359, 363, 365
MRO, 471
MS (medium shot), 383
*Music Retailer*, 201
Mutual Broadcasting System, 221

Nabisco Inc., 290, 291
Narrowcasting, 536
National advertising, 50, 51
  farm publications, 208, 210
  newspapers, 166, 167, 172, 173, 174
  television, 232, 233
  transit, 254
National Advertising Division (NAD), 509
National Advertising Review Board, 509
National Association of Broadcasters (NAB), 509 – 510, 513

National brands, 291
National Broadcasting Co., 216, 221, 228
  Radio Network, 219
National Carbon Co., 12n
*National Geographic*, 270
National Outdoor Advertising Bureau (NOAB), 250
National rates, 51, 72
National Register Publishing Co., 11 – 12
Nature of the market, 45, 46
Nature of the product, 45, 48
Needham, Harper & Steers, 67, 519
Networks:
  agency, 77
  radio, 138, 140, 216, 221
  television, 138, 140, 151, 228
Neutrogena Corp., 343
New buy, 475
*New England Hardware*, 201
*New Equipment Digest*, 196
New ideas directory, 259
*New York Daily News*, 167, 170
*New York Post*, 167
*New York Times, The*, 167, 168, 512, 513
*New York Times Magazine*, 327
*New Yorker, The*, 452
Newspaper Advertising Bureau, Inc., 448
*Newspaper Advertising Planbook*, 448
*Newspaper Rates and Data*, 170
Newspapers, 80, 136, 140, 143, 163 – 175, 187 – 188
  advantages of, 163 – 165
  advertising volume in, 137, 163
  buying space in, 152, 170 – 171
  characteristics of, 147
  checking copies, 166 – 167
  circulation, 144, 167

color reproduction, 172 — 173

copy, 344 — 347

daily, 167, 168, 376 — 377

ethnic and foreign language, 167, 170

future, 536

historical development of advertising in, 7 — 9

limitations of, 165 — 166

national, 167

positions, 171 — 172

price to consumer, effect of advertising on, 498

rates, 171, 173 — 174

regulation of, 512, 513

retail advertising in, 451

seasonal concentration, 151

special, 174 — 175

Sunday, 167, 168

Sunday supplement, 167, 168, 170

tear sheets, 166, 463

weekly, 167, 168, 171

Nielsen, A. C., 13

Nielsen, A. C., Co., 13, 223, 234

Nielsen rating, 233, 234

NL Industries, Inc., 28

Nonmedia advertising, 136

direct advertising, *see* Direct advertising

point-of-purchase promotion, *see* Point-of-purchase promotion (POP)

trade shows, 281 — 282

Nonpreemptible time, 233

Norman, Craig & Kummel, 67, 519

*Northern Hardware Trade*, 201

Norton Simon, Inc., 289

Objective (task) budgeting method, 121 — 122, 449

Objective viewpoint of advertising agency, 72

Objectives of advertising, 49 — 50

Observational method, 96, 98

O'Connor, John J., 153

Offset lithography, 400

O'Gara, James V., 63

Ogilvy, David, 78, 330

Ogilvy & Mather International, 67, 78, 351, 519

OHMS (Out of Home Media Service), 250

Old Gothic typeface, 392

Omnibus ads, 456, 458

100 gross rating points daily, 248

100 showing, 248, 255

Open rates, 171

Operating supplies, 471, 474

Optical center, 359

Orikomi Advertising, 519

*Orlando Sentinel Star*, 164

O'Toole, John, 352

Outdoor advertising, 80, 136, 147, 154, 241 — 252

advantages of, 243

audience measurement, 248, 249

billboards, 80, 242 — 243

buying, 248, 250 — 252

compared with other media, 242

copy, 353

environmentalists and, 242

limitations of, 244 — 248

types of, 244 — 248

users of, 243

volume of, 137, 241

Outdoor Advertising Association of America, 242, 248

Out-of-pocket expenses, charges for, 77, 79

Over-door car cards, 254

Package house, 228

Package inserts, 234

Package plans, 225

Packaging, 22 — 23, 298 — 307

as advertising, 304 — 305

dealer requirements, 302 — 303

design essentials, 298 — 302

regulation of, 304

Paid circulation, 194

Paint, 245, 250

Painted bulletins, 244 — 247, 251

Paintings, 369, 371

Palmer, Volney B., 10

Pan, 383

Panels, 100

Paper, 244, 248, 250, 410

Paper Mill Study, The, 195

*Parade*, 170

Paratest Marketing, 435

Parker Pen Co., The, 362

Participations, 228

Penney, J. C., Co., Inc., 445

Pennsylvania Glass Sand Corp., 198

*Pennsylvania Packet and Daily Advertiser, The*, 9

Pennwalt, 473, 480

Pennysaver, 9n

*People*, 176

Per-unit assessment budgeting method, 126 — 129

Percentage-of-sales budgeting method, 122, 124 — 126, 128, 449

Perception Research Services, Inc., 98

Personal selling, 43

vs. advertising, 4

coordination of advertising campaigns with, 426

*See also* Promotional mix

*Personnel Administrator, The*, 203

*Philadelphia Bulletin*, 167

Philip Morris Inc., 241

Photocomposition, 398—399
Photography, 369
Photography studios, 83
Pica, 394
Piggybacking, 233
PKG/Cunningham & Walsh Inc., 73
Places, as brand names, 294
Planners, media, 149—152, 154
Planning campaigns, 416—423
*Plant Engineering*, 196
Plant operator, 244
Plants, 154, 244
Plates, 404
Plummer, Joseph, 323*n*
Point-of-purchase promotion (POP),
    276—281, 305
  attributes of, 278—279
  coordination of advertising
      campaigns with, 428
  distribution of, 279
  forms of, 278
  trade, 490
Points, 390
Policing of advertising, 503—515
Political candidates, 4—5
Political climate, 32
Pond's Cold Creams, 11, 16—17
Popups, 273—274
Positioning the product, 326—329
Postal regulations, 274
Postal Service, 505, 535
Posters, 11, 242, 244, 248, 250, 252, 255
*Poultry Tribune*, 210
Preemptible time, 233
Premium position, 172
Premiums, 13, 276, 277, 428
Pretesting, 109
Price, 25—26
Price competition, effect of advertising
    on, 501
Pride foods, 340

Primary data, 96—104, 448—449
Primary demand, 48, 57, 424, 426
Prime-time television, 226, 230
*Principal Register*, 292
Print media, 136, 154
  in foreign countries, 523
  *See also* Business publications;
      Farm publications; Magazines
      (consumer); Newspapers
Printers, 83
*Printer's Ink*, 504, 509
Printing, invention of, 7
Printing processes, 399—410
  color reproduction, 404—410
  duplicates, 404
  engravings, 404
  gravure, 400, 402
  halftones, 402—404
  letterpress, 400
  lithography, 400, 401
  paper for, 410
  plates, 404
  silk screen, 402
Private brands, 291
Prizes, 13
Probability sampling, 102—103
Problem-and-solution commercials,
    348
Process materials, 471, 473
Proctor & Gamble Co., 12, 37, 295, 423
Product, 22—23
  features of, 313—318
  influence on budget, 119, 121
  life cycle of, 45, 315, 420
  media selection and, 142
  nature of, 45, 48
  positioning, 326—329
  quality of, 49
  subjective appeal of, 315—318
Product identification:
  brand names, *see* Brand names

certification marks, 298
collective marks, 297—298
logotypes, 298
packaging, *see* Packaging
service marks, 298
slogans, 308
trade characters, 296—297
trade names, 288
trademarks, *see* Trademarks
Product promotion campaign, 424
Production houses, 376
Professional advertising, 55—56, 534
Professional publications, 201, 203, 204
Program objectives, media selection
    and, 143
*Progressive Farmer*, 208, 210
Projective techniques, 104—105
Promotional mix, 27, 43—60
  advertising as main trust, 48—59
  marketing plan, 44—48
Promotional store, 443—445
Proofs, 398
Prudential Insurance Co., 531
Psychographics, 105—106, 108, 323,
    326
Public-service advertising, 59
Publicis Conseil, 518, 519
Publicity, 43
  vs. advertising, 5
  coordination of advertising
      campaigns with, 428
  *See also* Promotional mix
Publisher's Information Bureau, 123
Puff, 340
Pull strategy, 428
Purchasing decision, 312—313
*Purchasing Magazine*, 196
*Purchasing World*, 196
Pure Food and Drug Act of 1906, 503
Pusey, Allen, 11
Push strategy, 426, 428

Quality-of-life ethic, 31
Quarter run, 254
Queen-size display, 255
Question headline, 344
Questionnaires, 99—100
Quota sampling, 103

Radio, 80, 136, 143, 147, 215—225, 237
  advertising volume on, 137,
    215—216
  AM, 216—217, 221
  audience, 221, 223
  buying time on, 223—225
  copy, 347—348, 349
  coverage, 144, 146, 221
  FM, 217
  gross rating points, 223
  historical development of
    advertising on, 12—14, 18, 216
  international, 521, 523
  network, 138, 140, 216, 221
  price to consumer, effect of
    advertising on, 498
  regulation of, 511
  retail advertising on, 451
  spot, 140, 218, 221
  statistics, 216
  terms used in commercial
    production, 382—383
Radio Advertising Bureau, Inc., 216n
Rand-order scale, 108
Ranking, 326
Rate base, 180
Rate Card, 224
Rates:
  business publications, 204, 205
  farm publications, 210
  magazines, 180, 182—184
  newspapers, 171, 173—174
  outdoor advertising, 248, 250

  radio, 223—225
  television, 230, 233
  transit advertising, 254—255
Rating services (television), 233
Raw materials, 468
RCA Corp., 328
Reach, 223, 228, 236, 328
Readability:
  of copy, 340, 366
  layout and, 363, 366
  typefaces and, 394—395
Reader service card, 204
Reader's Digest, 176, 182, 336
Reassurance value, 118—119
Rebates, 80
Recognition, agency, 79—80
Red Cross, 4
Reference groups, 30, 52, 318, 320, 324
Regional campaigns, 423—424
Regional farm publications, 210
Regular typeface, 391
Regulation, 503—513
Remembrance advertising, 274
Renner, Paul, 392
Rep, 154
Repetition, 422—423
Repro proofs, 398
Reproduction processes, 387—410
  See also Printing processes;
    Typography
Residuals, 376n
Resort Management, 201
Retail advertising, 50—51, 443—464
  advertising department, 459—460
  advertising schedules, 456—459
  budgeting, 449—451
  copy, 459
  marketing information, 447—449
  media, 451—463
  objectives, 446—447
  planning, 445—451

  vertical cooperative advertising,
    460—463
Retail impact, media selection and,
  143
Retail rates, 51, 72
Retirement Living, 176
Retouch, 369, 370
Revlon Inc., 517
Reyher, Paul, 11
Reynolds, R. J., Industries, Inc., 241
Rice Farming, 210
Robinson, Claude, 13
Rokeach, M., 108n
Rolling Stone, 182
Roman, Kenneth, 330n
Roman typeface, 388
Rome, ancient, 6
ROP (run of paper), 172—173
ROS (run of station), 225
Ross Roy, 519
Rotary plan, 250
Rotogravure, 173
Rotosection, 168
Roughs, 359, 360
Rubicam, Raymond, 14

Saks Fifth Avenue, 381
Sales-advertising relationship,
  118—119, 120
Sales & Marketing Management, 95,
  174
Sales potential, 90—92
Sales promotion, 43
  coordination of advertising
    campaign with, 426, 428
  See also Promotional mix
Sampling, 100—104
San Francisco Chronicle/Examiner,
  167
Sands, Saul S., 122n

Sandwich men, 9
Sans serif typeface, 391—392
Saxon Industries, Inc., 329
Scales, 108—109
Scheduling, 152
Schumer, Philippe, 9n
Schuyten, Peter J., 430
Schwartz, David J., 13n
Scott, Walter Dill, 11
Scrambled merchandising, 446
Scratchboard, 371
Screen Actors Guild (SAG), 376n
Sears, Roebuck & Co., 291, 451
Seasonal concentration, 150—151
Second-class mail, 274
Secondary circulation, 147
Secondary data, 92—96, 448
Secondary readership, 178, 180
Securities and Exchange Commission
    (SEC), 505
Segmentation, 27—28, 29
Segmentation analysis, 28
Segue, 383
Selective demand, 47
Selective perception, 105
Self-liquidating premium, 277
Self-mailer, 273
Serifs, 388
Service economy, 529—536
    advertising services, 532—536
    characteristics of services, 529—532
Service marks, 298
Seventeen, 176
SFX (sound effects), 383
Share-of-the-market budgeting
    method, 122, 124
Shattuck, L. F., 10
Sheet-fed processes, 400
Sheets, 242—243
Shopping goods, 23—24
Short channel, 478

Short copy, 344
Short-rate invoice, 171
Short rates, 171
Shorthorn World, 210
Showings, 255
Signs, 6—7, 80, 241—242
Silk screen, 402
Simmons, W. R., and Associates,
    140
Singing commercials, 348
Ski Area Management, 201
Skits, 347, 349
Sky waves, 216
Slice-of-life commercials, 348
Slogans, 308
Slugged in, 460
Slugs, 398
Small space ads, 366, 367
Snack Food, 201
Sneak, 383
Social influences, 31
Sony Corp., 46
Sound studios, 83
Southern Hardware, 201
Soybean Digest, 210
Space brokers, 10
Space position value (SPV), 252
Spacing, 394—395
Special newspapers, 174—175
Specialized farm publications, 210
Specialty goods, 25
SpectaColor, 172—173
Spectaculars, 246, 248
Speer Research, 97
Split run, 172, 432
Split screen, 383
Sporting Goods Dealer, 448
Sports Illustrated, 176, 178, 184, 185
Sports programming, 230
Spot radio, 140, 218, 221
Spot Radio Rates and Data, 225

Spot television, 140, 151, 228, 230, 231,
    232
Spot Television Rates and Data, 231
Spread, 182
Spudman, 210
Square-end car cards, 254
Square third, 182
SSC&B, 67, 519
Standard Gravure Corp., 172n
Standard Industrial Classification
    (SIC), 194
Standard Metropolitan Statistical Area
    (SMSA), 93, 423—424
Standard Rate & Data Service (SRDS)
    Inc., 168, 170, 191, 200, 205
    Business Publication Rates and Data,
        191, 194, 205
    Consumer Magazine and Farm
        Publication Rates and Data, 168,
        206
    Spot Radio Rates and Data, 225
    Spot Television Rates and Data, 231
"Standards of Advertising
    Acceptability," 512
Stanton, William J., 529n
Starch, Daniel, & Staff, 13
Starch INRA Hooper, Inc., 13
Starch ratings, 432, 439
Starch Readership Reports, 432, 433
State farm publications, 210
Statement stuffer, 270, 272
Station posters, 255
Stein, Herbert, 43
Stereotype, 104
Sterling Drug Inc., 12
Stevens, Chas. A., 447
Stock art, 371, 374
Store brands, 291
Story headlines, 342
Storyboards, 371, 375, 376
Streicker, Mitchell B., 261

Stuart Pharmaceuticals, 55
Style, copy, 338—340
*Successful Farming*, 208, 210
*Successful Meetings*, 481
*Sugarbeet Grower*, 210
Sunday newspapers, 167, 168
Sunday supplements, 167, 168, 170
*Sunflower, The*, 210
Sunkist Growers, Inc., 436—437
*Sunsweet Standard*, 210
*Super Marketing*, 201
*Supplemental Register*, 292
Survey method, 98—100
Sylvania Co., 51

Tabloid magazines, 182
Tabloid newspapers, 171
Taboos, 322—323
Tactical campaign objectives,
    419—420
Taillight spectaculars, 255
Take, 376
Take-ones, 254—255
Talent, 383
Tamaru, Hideharu, 537
Taped commercials, 381—382
Target Group Index, 228*n*
Target markets, 52, 54
    defined, 27
    matching media with, 138, 140
    segmentation of, 27—28, 29
Task budgeting method, 121—122, 449
Taylor, Donald A., 103*n*
TBWA, 519
*Tcha*, 9
TCU (tight close-up), 382
Tear sheets, 166, 463
Technological change, 32, 34
Telephone interview, 100
Television, 18, 136, 147, 225—236, 238

advertising-sales ratios for, 125
advertising volume on, 137, 225
audience, 226—229
audience ratings, 233—236
buying time on, 230, 233
cable, 225, 536
commercial production, 371,
    375—383
copy, 348, 350, 351, 352
coverage, 144, 145, 226
in foreign countries, 521
future, 536, 538
network, 138, 140, 151, 228
price to consumer, effect of
    advertising on, 498
regulation of, 382, 509—510, 513
retail advertising on, 451
seasonal concentration, 151
spot, 140, 151, 228, 230, 231, 232
UHF, 225
VHF, 225
Television Code, The, 510
*Television Households Book*, 229
Tempera, 369
Tempo Black typeface, 392
Test marketing, 432, 435
Testimonials, 11, 16, 348
Textile Fiber Products Identification
    Act of 1958, 507
Thematic Apperception Test (TAT),
    105
Third-class mail, 274
30-sheet poster, 244
*Thomas Register*, 255
Thompson, J. Walter, Co., 67, 70, 518,
    519
Thompson, James W., 10—11, 12
3-sheet posters, 244, 245
Thumbnails, 359
*Time*, 176, 178, 184, 347, 349
*Time B*, 178

Time signal announcements, 225
*Times, The* (London), 8, 9
Tipped in material, 184
Tissues, 359
Tokyu Advertising, 519
Tombstone ads, 505, 506
Tonnage ad, 456
Top-end car cards, 254
Top of the page paid, 172
Top-of-the-page position, 172
Total Bus, 255
Town criers, 7
Toyota Dealers Association of New
    York, 375
Toyota Industrial Trucks, U.S.A., Inc.,
    54
Townsend formula, 13
Trade advertising, 52—53, 468,
    481—482
    campaigns, 489—490
    cooperative, 490—491
    objectives of, 485, 486, 488, 490
    reasons for, 482—483, 485
Trade associations, 93
Trade characters, 296—297
Trade guilds, 6—7
Trade names, 288
Trade publications, 201, 202
Trade shows, 281—282
Trademarks, 287—296
    attributes of, 294—295
    vs. brand names, 288, 291
    choosing, 293—294
    legalities, 291—293
    objectives in, 293
    protection of, 295—296
Traffic Audit Bureau, Inc. (TAB), 248,
    252
Trahey, Jane, 453
Transit advertising, 252—255
    advantages of, 252

business of, 253–254
forms of, 254–258
limitations of, 252–253
media, 136, 147, 252
rates, 254–255
retailer's use of, 453
volume of, 254
Transit Advertising Association, Inc., 254n
Traveling bus displays, 255, 257
Treasury, Department of the, 304, 508, 509n
Trial purchases, 439
Tri-Wall Containers, 489–490
Truth in Lending Law, 508
TV Guide, 166, 176, 187, 268, 496
24-sheet poster, 244
Typography, 388–399
    measuring type, 390
    specifying type, 395, 398
    typeface families, 391–393
    typeface selection, 393–395
    typesetting methods, 398–399

UHF television, 225
Ultra Bodoni typeface, 391
Union Carbide Corp., 288
Unit-of-sale budgeting method, 126–129
United States Government
    as advertiser, 4, 15, 125, 534–536
    as intelligence source, 93

regulation by, 504–508
U.S. Industrial Directory, 259
Unity, layout, 363, 365
Urology, 204


Verbal similarity, 416
Verified Audit Circulation (VAC), 194
Vertical cooperative advertising, 460–463
Vertical programming, 218
Vertical publications, 196, 199
VHF television, 225
Vice-president for advertising, 65
Video cassettes, 536
Videotaped commercials, 381–382
Visual similarity, 416
Visualization, 357
Vogue typeface, 392
Voice-over (VO), 383
Volkswagen of America, 337, 353


Wales, Hugh G., 103n
Walker Research, Inc., 101
Wall Street Journal, 194–195, 399
War Advertising Council, 13–14
War bonds, 10
Warner-Lambert Co., 507
Wash drawing, 369, 371
Washington Post, 167
Wear-out, 423
Web-fed processes, 400

Weekly newspapers, 167, 168, 171
Weiss, E. B., 536
Wells, H. G., 3
Wells, Rich, Greene Inc., 67, 519, 530
Wells, William D., 108n
West Germany, 520, 526, 527
Western Electric Co., 497
Western Europe, 521, 523
Westgate Research, Inc., 110
Westinghouse Broadcasting Co., 216
WFTV Survey/Coverage Areas, 227
Wheeler-Lea Act of 1938, 504, 507
Wilkens, William, & Co., 519
WIND 56 (Chicago), 237
Wipe, 383
Wipe-over, 383
Wolf, Henry, 381
Woman's Day, 176
Women's Wear Daily, 448
Wool Products Labeling Act of 1939, 507
Woolworth, F. W., Co., 451
Work print, 380
World War II, 13–14, 18

Xerox Corp., 480–481, 499

Yellow Pages, 259, 260
Yomiko Advertising, 519
Young & Rubicam, 13, 67, 519

ZIP codes, 272–273

## EDITORIAL ACKNOWLEDGMENTS

**pp.** 3 H. G. Wells, *The Work, Wealth and Happiness of Mankind* (New York: Doubleday, Doran & Company, Inc., 1931), vol. I, p. 249. Reprinted by permission of A. P. Watts, Ltd.

21 *Some Guidelines for Advertising Budgeting* (New York: The Conference Board, Inc., Report No. 560, 1972), p. ii. Reprinted by permission of The Conference Board, Inc.

43 Herbert Stein, "Advertising Is Worth Advertising," in *Advertising Age*'s "The New World of Advertising" (November 21, 1973), pp. 4–5. Reprinted with permission from *Advertising Age*. Copyright, Crain Communications, Inc., 1973.

63 James V. O'Gara, "The Advertising Agency—What It Is and What It Does for Advertisers," in *Advertising Age*'s "The New World of Advertising" (November 21, 1973), pp. 34 ff. Reprinted with permission from *Advertising Age*. Copyright, Crain Communications, Inc., 1973.

89 Edmund D. McGarry, "The Propaganda Function in Marketing," *Journal of Marketing*, vol. 23, no. 2 (October 1958), pp. 56–58. Reprinted by permission of the American Marketing Association.

115 Rosser Reeves, *Reality in Advertising* (New York: Alfred A. Knopf, 1961), p. 11. Copyright 1961 by Alfred A. Knopf. Reprinted by permission of Alfred A. Knopf.

135 G. Allen Foster, *Advertising: Ancient Market Place to Television* (New York: Criterion Books, Inc., 1967), pp. 141–42. Reprinted by permission of Harper & Row, Publishers, Inc.

163 Jack Z. Sissors and E. Reynold Petray, *Advertising Media Planning* (Chicago: Crain Books, 1976), p. 187. Reprinted by permission of Crain Books.

191 Howard G. "Scotty" Sawyer, *Business-to-Business Advertising* (Chicago: Crain Books, 1978), p. 41. Reprinted by permission of Crain Books.

215 Sam J. Ervin, Jr., "Advertising: Stepchild of the First Amendment?" *Advertising Age* (July 17, 1972), p. 43. Reprinted with permission from *Advertising Age*. Copyright, Crain Communications, Inc., 1972.

241 Kenneth Roman and Jane Maas, *How to Advertise* (New York: St. Martin's Press, Inc., 1976), p. 56. Reprinted by permission of St. Martin's Press, Inc.

265 George L. Herpel and Richard A. Collins, *Specialty Advertising in Marketing* (Homewood, Ill.: Dow Jones–Irwin, Inc., 1972), p. 64. Reprinted by permission of Dow Jones–Irwin, Inc.

287 *The Nielsen Researcher*, no. 4 (1977), p. 2. Reprinted by permission of A. C. Nielsen Company.

311 S. I. Hayakawa, *Language in Action* (New York: Harcourt Brace Company, 1941), p. 29. Reprinted by permission of Harcourt Brace Jovanovich, Inc.

335 Aesop Glim, *How Advertising Is Written—And Why* (New York: Dover Publications, Inc., 1961), pp. 66–67. Reprinted by permission of Dover Publications, Inc.

352 "O'Toole of the Trade," *Advertising Age* (October 23, 1978). Originally from *The Wall Street Journal*. Reprinted by permission of Dow Jones & Company, Inc.

357 Pierre Martineau, *Motivation in Advertising* (New York: McGraw-Hill Book Company, 1957), p. 189. Copyright © 1957 McGraw-Hill Inc. Used with permission of McGraw-Hill Book Company.

387 Harold G. "Scotty" Sawyer, *Business-to-Business Advertising* (Chicago: Crain Books, 1978), p. 135. Reprinted by permission of Crain Books.

415 David A. Aaker and John G. Myers, *Advertising Management* (Englewood Cliffs, N.J.: Prentice-Hall, Inc., 1975), p. 23. Reprinted by permission of Prentice-Hall, Inc., Englewood Cliffs, New Jersey.

443 Barry Berman and Joel R. Evans, *Retail Management: A Strategic Approach* (New York: Macmillan Publishing Co., Inc., 1979), p. 430. Copyright © 1979 by Macmillan Publishing Co., Inc.

467 Rosser Reeves, *Reality in Advertising* (New York: Alfred A. Knopf, 1961), p. 145. Copyright 1961 by Alfred A. Knopf. Reprinted by permission of Alfred A. Knopf.

495 Rena Bartos and Theodore F. Dunn, *Advertising and Consumers New Perspectives* (New York: American Association of Advertising Agencies, no date), pp. 92–93. Reprinted by permission of American Association of Advertising Agencies.

517 Alvin Toffler, *Future Shock* (New York: Random House, 1970), pp. 234–35. Copyright 1970 by Random House. Reprinted by permission of Random House, Inc.

## ILLUSTRATION CREDITS

pp. i (top left): Prepared by Foote, Cone & Belding for Levi Strauss; (top right): Designed by Tadashi Ohashi for Kikkoman Shoyu Co., Ltd.; (bottom left): Courtesy, Institute of Outdoor Advertising. ii (top left): Courtesy, Anheuser-Busch, Inc.; (bottom right): This poster was designed by Ron Anderson of Bozell & Jacobs for Twin Cities Red Cross. xv (top left): Prepared by Foote, Cone & Belding for Hallmark Cards;

(top right): Prepared by Foote, Cone & Belding for C & H Sugars; (bottom left): Prepared by Foote, Cone & Belding for Clorox Soft Scrub; (bottom right): Prepared by Foote, Cone & Belding for Idaho Potatoes.

**Part 1**

p. xvi: Courtesy, Polaroid Corporation and the Museum of Fine Arts, Boston.

Chapter 1

pp. 4: © 1978 Mobil Corporation. 5: Derus Media Service, Inc. 6, 7 (left): From *London Tradesmen's Cards of the Eighteenth Century* by Ambrose Heal. Dover Publications, Inc., N.Y. 7 (right): New York Public Library Picture Collection. 8 (from the top): Radio Times Hulton Picture Library; Radio Times Hulton Picture Library; The New-York Historical Society; Courtesy, American Antiquarian Society. 12–13: Chevrolet Motor Division, General Motors Corporation. 14: Young & Rubicam, Inc. Photo by Dana Hyde. 16–17: Prepared by J. Walter Thompson for Chesebrough-Pond's Inc.

## Chapter 2

pp. 24: Copyright © 1979 Fisher Corporation. 25: Prepared by Marsteller Inc. for JVC High Fidelity Division, U.S. JVC Corporation. 28: Courtesy, NL Industries, Inc. 29: Prepared by Compton Advertising, Inc. for Cunard Lines Ltd. 30: Cuisinarts, Inc. 32: The Continental Quilt Shoppe, Inc. and Euroquilt, Inc. 34: Courtesy, Burlington Socks/Adler. 35: Prepared by Kelly Nason, Inc. for Church & Dwight. 36: UPI. 38: Courtesy Dannon Yogurt. Agency: Marsteller Inc.

## Chapter 3

pp. 46: © 1978 Sony Corporation of America. SONY and BETAMAX are registered trademarks of Sony Corporation. 47: Prepared by Foote, Cone & Belding for the California Raisin Advisory Board. 51: Prepared by Doyle Dane Bernbach Inc. for GTE Sylvania. 52: Reproduced with the authority of The Coca-Cola Company. 53: Campbell Soup Company. 54: Toyota Industrial Trucks, USA. 55: Reproduced with permission of Stuart Pharmaceuticals, Division of ICI Americas, Inc. 56: Bell System. 57: Celanese Fibers Marketing Co. 58: Courtesy, Foote, Cone & Belding. 59: The Advertising Council and The U.S. Forest Service.

## Chapter 4

pp. 68: Hoffman-York, Inc. 73: Courtesy, PKG/Cunningham & Walsh Inc. 74–75: Marcoa, Direct Advertising, Inc. 76: D. L. Blair Corporation. 77: Media Basics, Inc. 78: Ogilvy & Mather Inc. 81: WFTV/Channel Nine of Orlando. 82 (top): Astro Aerial Ads. (bottom left): Kraus and Sons, Inc. (bottom center): Nashville Sound Studios, Inc. (bottom right): Hamilton Productions Inc.

## Part 2

p. 86: New York Public Library Picture Collection.

## Chapter 5

pp. 94: U. S. Bureau of the Census, *Statistical Abstract of the United States: 1978* (99th edition) Washington, D.C., 1978, pp. 456–57. 97 (left): Chilton Research Services. (center): Speer Research. (right): Courtesy, Burke Marketing Research, Inc. 98: Perception Research Services, Inc. 99: American Association of Advertising Agencies. 101: Walker Research, Inc. 103: Home

Testing Institute. 105: Tyler Research Associates, Inc. 106: Reprinted from the *Journal of Advertising Research.* © 1977 by the Advertising Research Foundation. 110: Westgate Research, Inc.

## Chapter 6

pp. 123: © 1978 Publishers Information Bureau, Inc. 127: Courtesy, Doyle Dane Bernbach, Inc. 128–29: Photos by David Moskowitz.

## Chapter 7

pp. 139: Chart adapted from "Road Maps of Industry," no. 1797 (The Conference Board, December 1976), and *Advertising Age*, (January 9, 1979). Reprinted by permission of The Conference Board, Inc. 140: *Buffalo Evening News.* 141: Courtesy, Cunningham & Walsh Inc. 142: *Houston Magazine.* 146: WFTV/Channel Nine of Orlando. 150: Broadcast Advertisers Reports, Inc. 155: Courtesy, Cunningham & Walsh Inc.

## Part 3

p. 160: Courtesy, Anheuser-Busch, Inc.

## Chapter 8

pp. 164: *Orlando Sentinel Star.* 169: St. Louis *Globe-Democrat.* 172: Gordon's Dry Gin Company, Ltd. 173: © 1976 R. J. Reynolds Tobacco Co. 175: Drukker Newspapers, Inc. 177: Media Com. 178: Reprinted with permission of *Better Living* Magazine. 179: Copyright © 1978 by Bon Appétit Publishing Corp. Reprinted by permission. 181: Prepared by Staley, Fox Inc. for *House Beautiful* Magazine. 183: *Houston Magazine.* 186: Courtesy, Leo Burnett U.S.A. Advertising.

## Chapter 9

pp. 193: Prepared by Evans/Pacific, Inc. for Washington State Potato Commission © 1976. 195: Copyright Dow Jones & Company, Inc. 1978. 197: Grayhill, Inc. and *Electronic Products* Magazine. 198: Courtesy, Pennsylvania Glass Sand Corporation. 199: Courtesy, Marsteller Inc. 200: From SRDS *Business Publication Rates and Data*, March 24, 1979. 202: Courtesy, PQ Corporation. 203: Prepared by Burson-Marsteller for the American Dental Association. 205: From SRDS *Business Publication Rates and Data*, May 24, 1979. 209: Reprinted with permission from Merck & Co., Inc. 211: Dow Chemical U.S.A.

## Chapter 10

pp. 219: NBC Radio, a division of National Broadcasting, Inc. 220: From SRDS *Spot Radio Rates and Data*, February 1, 1979. 222: Westinghouse Broadcasting Com-

pany, Inc. 224: NBC Radio, a division of National Broadcasting, Inc. 227: WFTV/Channel Nine of Orlando. 229: The Arbitron Company. 231: From SRDS *Spot Television Rates and Data*, May 15, 1979. 234: From Nielsen Station Index Viewers In Profile Report for San Francisco–Oakland, California, October, 1978. 235: Courtesy, Wyse Advertising.

## Chapter 11

pp. 245: Courtesy, Institute of Outdoor Advertising. 246: Photo by David Moskowitz. 247 (top): Courtesy, Institute of Outdoor Advertising. 247 (bottom), 249, 251: Courtesy, Foster and Kleiser, a division of Metromedia. 253: Courtesy, Combined Communications Corporation, Phoenix, Arizona. 254–55: Courtesy, Chicago Transit Authority. 256–58: TDI/WINSTON NETWORK INC. Advertising in Mass Transit/Commuter Railroads/Airports. 260: Prepared by Cunningham & Walsh Inc. for Bell System. 261: Courtesy, Institute of Outdoor Advertising.

## Chapter 12

pp. 266: Reprinted with permission of Chesebrough-Pond's Inc. Owner of the Registered Q-Tips Trademark. 267: Courtesy, The Union Co., Columbus, Ohio. 269: John Blair Marketing, Inc. 271: Ed Burnett Consultants, Inc. 272–73: Courtesy, The Union Co., Columbus, Ohio. 275 (top left): David A. Bortner, Inc. (top right): Roach, Inc. (bottom left): Perrygraf, division of Nashua Corporation. (bottom center): Allyn Neckwear Inc. (bottom right): Courtesy, Robert Keith & Co., Inc. 277: Georgia-Pacific Corporation. 278: Point-Of-Purchase Advertising Institute, Inc. 280: Courtesy, Batten, Barton, Durstine & Osborn.

## Part 4

p. 284: Courtesy, Foster and Kleiser, a division of Metromedia.

## Chapter 13

pp. 288 (left): Courtesy, Ford Motor Company. (second from left): Courtesy, Eastman Kodak Company. (second from right): PEPSI-COLA is a Registered Trademark. Used with permission of PepsiCo, Inc., Purchase, New York, 10577. (right): Courtesy, Shell Oil Company. 289: Reproduced from the 1978 Annual Report of Norton Simon, Inc. with permission of Canada Dry Corporation. 290: © NABISCO INC. 292: Courtesy, Needham, Harper & Steers, Inc. 296: Courtesy, The F & M Schaefer Brewing Co. 297 (top): Courtesy, Green Giant Company. (bottom): Chiquita® is a registered trademark of United Brands Company. 298 (left): The Wool Bureau, Inc. (right): The

Travelers Insurance Company. 299: Container Corporation of America. 300: Reproduced with the authority of The Coca-Cola Company. 301: Campbell Soup Company. 302: Courtesy, Lippincott & Margulies, Inc. 305: Luther Ford & Co., Minneapolis, Minnesota. 306: Courtesy, Roger Ferriter. 307: Courtesy, Lippincott & Margulies, Inc.

### Chapter 14

pp. 314: © 1978 Colgate-Palmolive Company. 317: Courtesy, D'Arcy-MacManus & Masius, Inc. 319: Coach Leatherware, a division of Coach Products, Inc. 321: Courtesy, Epstein, Raboy Advertising, Inc. 324: American Motors Corporation. 325: Courtesy, McCann-Erickson World-Wide. 327: Della Femina, Travisano & Partners, Inc. 329: Saxon Business Products, Inc.

### Chapter 15

pp. 337: Prepared by Doyle Dane Bernbach Inc. for Volkswagen of America, Inc. 339: Courtesy, Heublein, Inc. 343: Neutrogena Corporation. 345: Mercedes-Benz of North America, Inc. 346 (left): Gary Farn Ltd., Stamford, Connecticut. (right): Garden Way, Inc. 349: Courtesy, Young & Rubicam Inc. 351: Courtesy, American Express Company. 352: Courtesy, Foote, Cone & Belding.

### Chapter 16

pp. 360–62: Courtesy, C. F. Hathaway and Ogilvy & Mather Inc. 364 (left): Burberrys International Ltd. (right): American Motors Corporation. 365 (right): Courtesy, Heublein, Inc. 367 (top): Henniker's, 779 Bush Street, Box 7584, San Francisco, CA 94120. (bottom): L. H. Selman, Ltd. 368: Courtesy Dannon Yogurt. Agency: Marsteller Inc. 370: Courtesy, C. F. Hathaway and Ogilvy & Mather Inc. 372: Patrick Shelter Group, San Diego, CA. 373: Lord & Taylor, New York. 374: Leo de Wys, Inc., New York. 375: Courtesy, Dancer-Fitzgerald-Sample, Inc. 377–79: Courtesy, Cunningham & Walsh Inc. 381: Henry Wolf Productions.

### Chapter 17

pp. 388–89: Courtesy, Recon-King Products Company, Automotive Chemical Division. 396: Prepared by William Esty Company, Inc. for Nissan Motors. 397: American Motors Corporation. 403: Detail of a photo of Abraham Lincoln by Alexander Hester, June 3, 1860. Courtesy, Chicago Historical Society. 405: Reproduced from the 1978 Annual Report of Norton Simon, Inc. with permission of Canada Dry Corporation.

### Part 5

p. 412: Designed by Tadashi Ohashi for Kikkoman Shoyu Co., Ltd.

### Chapter 18

pp. 417–18: Prepared by Foote, Cone & Belding for the California Raisin Advisory Board. 421: Ford Motor Company. 425: Prepared by McCann-Erickson Worldwide for Georgia-Pacific Corporation. 427: Courtesy, Association of American Railroads, Office of Information and Public Affairs, Washington, D.C. 433: Courtesy, Mazda Motors of America (Central), Inc. and Starch INRA Hooper, Inc. 434: Reprinted from the *Journal of Advertising Research.* © 1977 by the Advertising Research Foundation. 436–37: Prepared by Foote, Cone & Belding for Sunkist Growers, Inc. © 1978. Sunkist is a registered trademark of Sunkist Growers, Inc. 438 (left): Courtesy, Newspaper Printing Corporation. (right): Courtesy, Capital Newspapers Group.

### Chapter 19

pp. 444 (left): Lord & Taylor, New York. (right): Alexander's, Inc., New York. 445: J. C. Penney Company, Inc. 447: Chas. A. Stevens, Chicago, Illinois. 452: Macy's, New York. 453: Trahey Advertising, Inc. 454–55: Dial Media, Inc. 457 (top): Yves Saint Laurent, Inc. (bottom left): Laura Ashley. (bottom right): British American House, 488 Madison Ave., New York, 10022. Advertising Director: Herman Stolley. 458: Wieboldt Stores, Inc. 461: © 1978 Sony Corporation of America. SONY and BETAMAX are Registered Trademarks of Sony Corporation. 462: *The Washington Post.*

### Chapter 20

pp. 468: The English Mica Company, Inc. 469: Courtesy, Gardner-Denver Company. 470: Foss America Inc. 472: AMP Incorporated. 473: Courtesy, Organic Chemicals Division, Pennwalt Corporation. 474: Fort Howard Paper. 477: Prepared by McCaffrey and McCall, Inc. for Exxon Enterprises, Inc. 479: Prepared by Leo Burnett Company of Michigan, Inc. for Harrison Radiator Division, General Motors Corporation. 482: IBM Data Processing Division/Photo by Fred Schenk. 483: IBM Data Processing Division/Photo by Burt Glinn. 484: Courtesy, American Express Company. 486: Fisher-Price Toys, Division of the Quaker Oats Company. 487: Courtesy, McCann-Erickson Worldwide. 488: Courtesy, Menley & James Laboratories, Consumer Products Division.

### Chapter 21

pp. 497: Western Electric. 499: Courtesy, Needham, Harper & Steers, Inc. 502: Courtesy, Hall & Levine Advertising, Inc. 506: Mellon National Corporation. 510–11: The Code Authority, National Association of Broadcasters.

### Chapter 22

pp. 520: Prepared by McCann-Erickson, Inc. for General Motors Corporation. 522: Prepared by Manoff Geers Gross for Ty-Phoo Tea, London, England. 526: Prepared by SSC & B-Lintas International, for Eastman Kodak Company. 528: Reprinted with permission of Kellogg Company. 530: Prepared by Wells, Rich, Greene, Inc. for The State of New York. 531: Prudential Insurance Company. 533: Prepared by Foote, Cone & Belding for The First National Bank of Chicago. 534: American Medical Association. 535: U.S. Postal Service. 537: Courtesy, Dentsu Corporation of America.